PRAISE FOR THE PREVIOUS EDITION

"Sober and authoritative: This is gleaming, popular wartime history, John Hersey infused with Richard Preston and a fleck of Michael Crichton. . . . [Pellegrino] certainly studies every kind of fallout and does not neglect the spiritual variety. He writes about one doctor who recalled that, 'Those who survived the atomic bomb were, in general, the people who ignored others crying out in extremis or who stayed away from the flames, even when patients and colleagues shrieked from within them. . . . In short, those who survived the bomb were, if not merely lucky, in a greater or lesser degree selfish, self-centered—guided by instinct and not by civilization. And we know it, we who have survived.'"
—*New York Times*

"The tragedies and atrocities of World War II now belong to history, while Hiroshima is still part of our world, our continuing present, maybe our dreaded future. . . . Charles Pellegrino's account about what it was actually like to be on the ground in both Hiroshima and Nagasaki, culled from survivors' memories and his own work in forensic archaeology, is the most powerful and detailed I have ever read. It puts flesh on the skeletons. . . . This book offers more than just effective popular history. It is a kind of reminder. We have now lived long enough with the bomb to begin to take it for granted. [As] nations join an expanding nuclear 'club,' we are in danger, as MacArthur's committee was, of thinking of nuclear weapons as nothing but more sophisticated bows and arrows. [This book] gives us, instead, a glimpse of their horror. It makes us afraid again. As we should be."
—*Washington Post*

"A tragic cautionary tale as well as a celebration of human resilience.
—*People Magazine*

"Heart-stopping. Pellegrino dissects the complex political and military strategies that went into the atomic detonations and the untold suffering heaped upon countless Japanese civilians, weaving all of the book's many elements into a wise, informed protest against any further use of these terrible weapons."
—*Publishers Weekly* (Starred Review)

"Pellegrino here chronicles history's most destructive attack by human beings on others of their species. . . . The author includes stories of instant and total devastation—people vaporizing, buildings disappearing—and improbable survivals and bizarre effects: permanent human shadows cast onto walls; a teacher whose face bore the imprint of a student's writing she was examining when the flash came; a man whose eye problems were cured, another whose cancer went into remission. . . . Enormously painful to read, but absolutely essential to do so."
—*Kirkus* (Starred Review)

"The train of the title was bound for Nagasaki: thirty survivors of the Hiroshima bombing fled there, only to run straight into a second catastrophe. Pellegrino's account is full of such terrible ironies—which he describes with a lucid, almost lyrical precision."
—*Time Magazine* (Pick of the Week)

"A frightening, grim, yet fascinating examination of the nuclear attacks on Japan. . . . This is shocking, well-written, and will counter the oft-expressed opinion that [nuclear bombs] are 'just another weapon.'"
—*Booklist*

To Hell and Back

[Illustration: Patricia Wynne]

To Hell and Back

The Last Train from Hiroshima

Charles Pellegrino

ROWMAN & LITTLEFIELD
Lanham • Boulder • New York • London

Published by Rowman & Littlefield
A wholly owned subsidary of The Rowman & Littlefield Publishing Group, Inc.
4501 Forbes Boulevard, Suite 200, Lanham, Maryland 20706
www.rowman.com

Unit A, Whitacre Mews, 26-34 Stannary Street, London SE11 4AB

Distributed by NATIONAL BOOK NETWORK

British Library Cataloguing in Publication Information Available

Library of Congress Cataloging-in-Publication Data

Pellegrino, Charles R.
  [Last train from Hiroshima]
  To hell and back : the last train from Hiroshima / Charles Pellegrino.
      pages cm. — (Asia/Pacific/perspectives)
  Originally published under title: The last train from Hiroshima. New York : Henry
Holt and Co., 2010.
  Includes bibliographical references and index.
  ISBN 978-1-4422-5058-1 (cloth : alk. paper) — ISBN 978-1-4422-5059-8 (electronic)
  1. Hiroshima-shi (Japan)—History—Bombardment, 1945—Personal narratives, Japanese.
  2. Atomic bomb victims—Japan—Hiroshima-shi—Biography. 3. Hiroshima-shi
  (Japan)—Biography. 4. Atomic bomb—Social aspects—Japan—Hiroshima-shi—
  History—20th century. 5. World War, 1939-1945—Japan—Hiroshima-shi.
  6. Forensic archaeology—Japan—Hiroshima-shi. 7. Hiroshima-shi (Japan)—
  History—Bombardment, 1945. I. Title.
  D767.25.H6P45 2015
  940.54'2521954092—dc23

                                                                    2015014341

∞™ The paper used in this publication meets the minimum requirements of
American National Standard for Information Sciences—Permanence of Paper
for Printed Library Materials, ANSI/NISO Z39.48-1992.

Printed in the United States of America

To Tomorrow's Child

Contents

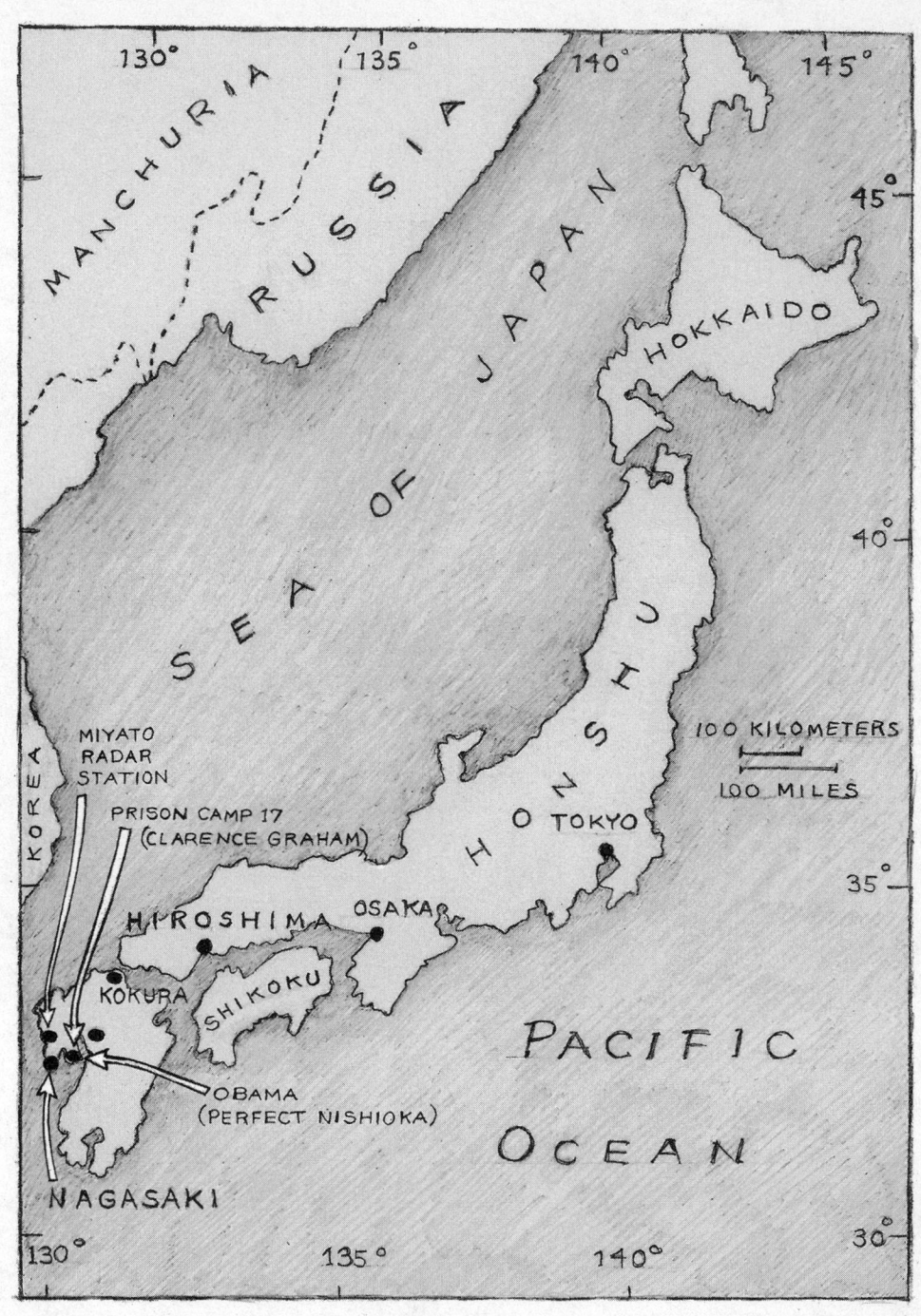

[Illustration: Patricia Wynne]

Preface

Mark Selden

Charles Pellegrino's riveting book chronicles the atomic bombing through the voices and lives of its survivors as it has never been told before. *To Hell and Back* captures the terror of the bombing from the perspective of the *hibakusha*, their torment suffered down to the present, and their continuing roles as emissaries for peace and reconciliation. Pellegrino combines cinematic eloquence and clarity with scientific rigor to reveal why some, even those close to the hypocenter, survived while others died instantly.

The author does not address the geostrategic issues of great power conflict and presidential decision-making that have been the staple of long-running debate among historians and remain contested today: the decision to unleash the bomb on Hiroshima and Nagasaki and the bombing of civilians; the number of lives lost (or saved); the role of the bombs in ending the Second World War; the legacy of that moment in subsequent Soviet-American and global conflict and contemporary threats of nuclear proliferation. Pellegrino never strays from his singular mission of chronicling the lives of ordinary and extraordinary people before and after the bomb, and the fates that sometimes intertwined their lives. His work invites comparison with the writings of Japanese poets, novelists, and ordinary citizens who recorded the bombing and whose words continue to inspire advocates of a peaceful future free from the threat of nuclear weapons. As primary school student Sakamoto Hatsumi wrote,

> When the atomic bomb drops
> day turns into night
> people turn into ghosts.

To Hell and Back implicitly encourages us to reflect anew on the ethics and horrifying outcome of World War II strategies of massive civilian bombing, whether by Germany, Japan, or England, or by American fire-bombing of German and Japanese cities and the atomic bombing of Hiroshima and Nagasaki, strategies that have continued with ever-greater technological sophistication during wars in Korea, Vietnam, Iraq, Afghanistan, and elsewhere to the present. And, though horrifying to recall, we know that today's hydrogen bombs have the capacity to destroy on a scale far greater than the Hiroshima and Nagasaki weapons that obliterated those cities in a flash.

Foreword

Steven Leeper

*I*n 1984, I moved to Hiroshima and have been involved with this city ever since. I translated for the Hiroshima Peace Memorial Museum for over twenty years, including countless accounts of the A-bomb tragedy. I suspect that no one alive has heard, translated, or interpreted the testimony of more A-bomb survivors than I have, with the likely exception of my wife. I know or knew personally many of the survivors Charles Pellegrino mentions in the book you are about to read. From April 2007 to 2013, I served as the first non-Japanese chairman of the Hiroshima Peace Culture Foundation, the organization that manages the Hiroshima Museum, and I now teach Hiroshima Studies at Hiroshima Jogakuin University.

I am not a scientist who can speak authoritatively about the inner workings of the bomb or its physical or medical effects. Nor am I a World War II historian who can say with scholarly assurance what led to the war or the bombings. But I have a comprehensive understanding of how the people of Hiroshima and Nagasaki experienced, remember, and talk or write about the atomic bombs.

I have attempted to establish my credentials as a person who knows Hiroshima—and above all the survivors and their stories—because I want it to mean something to you when I say that *To Hell and Back: The Last Train from Hiroshima* is by far the most insightful and powerful book I have ever read on the subject of the bombings. The horrors Pellegrino presents are accurate, based on eyewitness accounts supported by knowledgeable and reasonable guesses about the unknown (for example, what happened to people who vanished at the hypocenters). No book I know has articulated more fully, more accurately, and more effectively the essential nature of the atomic bombings, the experience of the people, and the endless aftermath. And, as all survivors will be quick to point out, the reality was vastly more horrific than even the talented Pellegrino can convey. With the world entering into a new era of nuclear weapons escalation, a book of this kind is needed now, more than ever.

As the filmmaker/engineer James Cameron has pointed out, "The bombings of Hiroshima and Nagasaki have always been controversial and are seen very differently through different cultural and national perspectives."* As an example of how perspective and even agenda can re-color history, in the first edition of *Last Train* (2010), Pellegrino was tricked by one informant. He believed an American veteran's well-documented, convincingly presented story that turned out to be false. When presented with new evidence, Pellegrino quickly admitted his mistake and corrected the book. Nevertheless, he and his book were attacked as if he had deliberately fabricated the evidence and, therefore, could never again be trusted. Obviously, the false Joseph Fuoco story (which added up to only five pages of the entire first edition) was not the cause of this rage. The fury became, Cameron concluded, "an example of how the strong emotions surrounding this subject are still coloring people's ability to see history clearly, when a relatively minor research error (a result of a fraudulent or self-deluded witness—and immediately corrected once exposed) could blaze up into a firestorm of controversy and invective almost seven decades after the event."

Last Train aroused such fury in 2010 because Pellegrino accurately depicted the cruelty of the weapon and, simultaneously, the humanity of those exposed to it. Hiroshima and Nagasaki, as they appeared in *Last Train*—and now in *To Hell and Back*—were cities full of people; real, admirable, often lovable human beings whose lives were destroyed or filled with suffering as a result of the atomic bombings. Thus, even though Pellegrino expressly refuses to address the issue of whether or not the bombs were justified, the sheer horror he describes makes the bombings and, by extension, the United States (and even humanity itself) look bad. This book elicits guilt, defensiveness, and rage because it transports readers, to the extent we are willing to go, into a world that is more frightening and painful than that of any "true story" we have ever been told. And it is a continuing story of survivor suffering seven decades later.

The Fuoco furor, the attendant ad hominem attacks against the author himself, and the kowtowing of an American publisher leading to the 2010 recall and pulping of the first *Last Train* drove Pellegrino to extend his research and write an even better book, more complete, more accurate, and more effective. In fact, history actually owes a debt to the more extremist critics. For example, their wild attacks led Kenshi Hirata to step forward from a half-century of trying to stay out of history's way and to tell, for

---

*James Cameron, July 2014, in support of a Japan young adult edition, *Ghosts of Hiroshima*, explaining his perspective on what had happened four years earlier in America.

the first time, the rest of his family's story. Having traveled aboard that "last train" from Hiroshima to Nagasaki and been exposed to both atomic bombs, he was among the dozens of survivors who came forth after 2010 to counter reports in the American press that asserted, "Hiroshima did not happen that way." Were it not for false claims that the survivors in the book should be regarded as possibly having never existed, Hirata would otherwise have taken his own story to the grave in 2013. Ironically, Fuoco's false story helped bring much truth to light.

At the deepest level, I suspect the main reason Pellegrino was attacked so intensely is that in 2010 *Last Train* was, and *To Hell and Back* is even more so now, a potential game changer in the struggle to eliminate nuclear weapons. Pellegrino worked with filmmaker James Cameron on *Titanic* and *Avatar*. He introduced Cameron to the late Tsutomu Yamaguchi, the most famous of the survivors of both the Hiroshima and Nagasaki bombs, and Yamaguchi secured from Cameron a promise to make a film about the bombings. If Cameron were to apply his full genius and arsenal of filmmaking skills to a film based on *To Hell and Back*, it would help make nuclear weapons public enemy number one and herald the end of the nuclear age. In the context of the current "humanitarian impact movement" (a movement led by Switzerland to reveal the true consequences of any use of nuclear weapons), such a film would forcefully bring to light the bizarre logic that continues to dominate strategic planning and make it impossible for any politician to both advocate for nuclear weapons and get elected.

With the revised and expanded second and third editions of *Last Train* published to acclaim in more than twenty countries, the languages of the world's two nuclear superpowers (English and Russian) are among the very few major ones in which this book has not been printed in the nearly five years since its first, briefly available English edition.

As Pellegrino has often said, the crucial meaning of the atomic bombings lies in the future, not the past. The future of our civilization hinges on what we decide to do now, based on what we know of the past. *To Hell and Back* is an astute, powerful, and positive contribution to that process.

Steven Leeper
International Studies Department
Hiroshima Jogakuin University

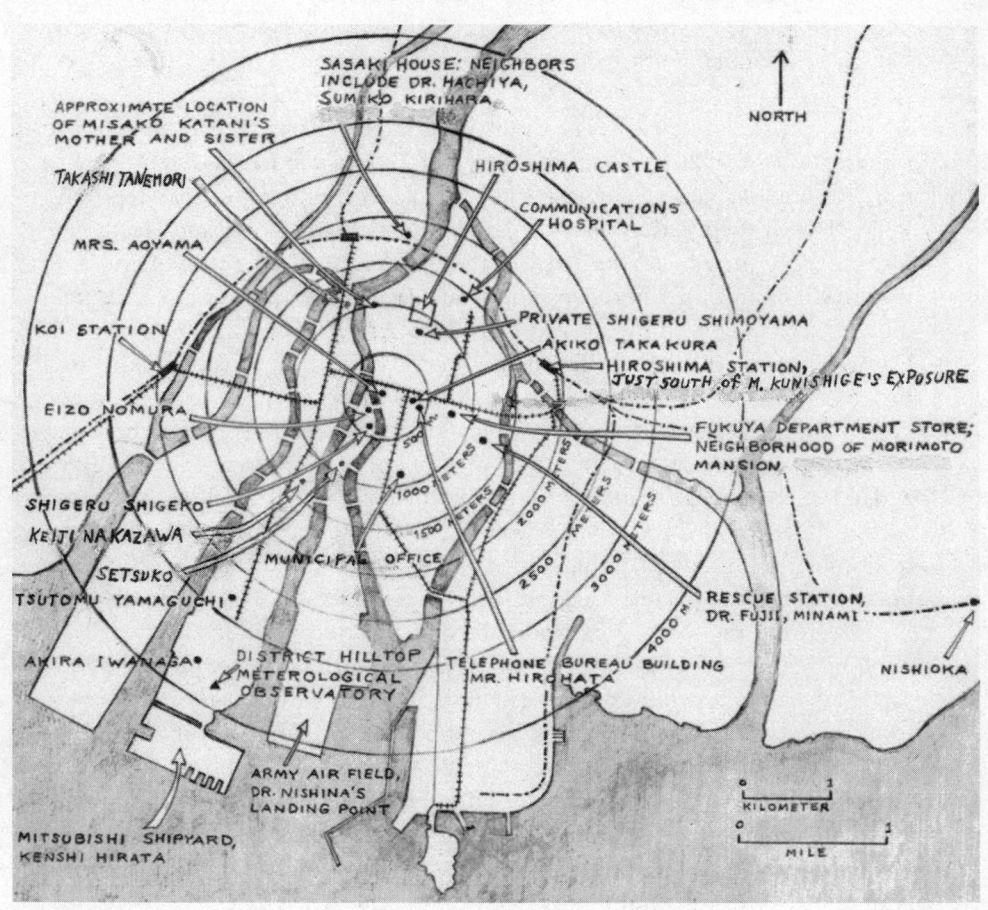

Hiroshima, August 6, 1945: Principal survivors and their locations at Moment Zero. [Illustration: Patricia Wynne, based on Pellegrino field notes with survivor annotations]

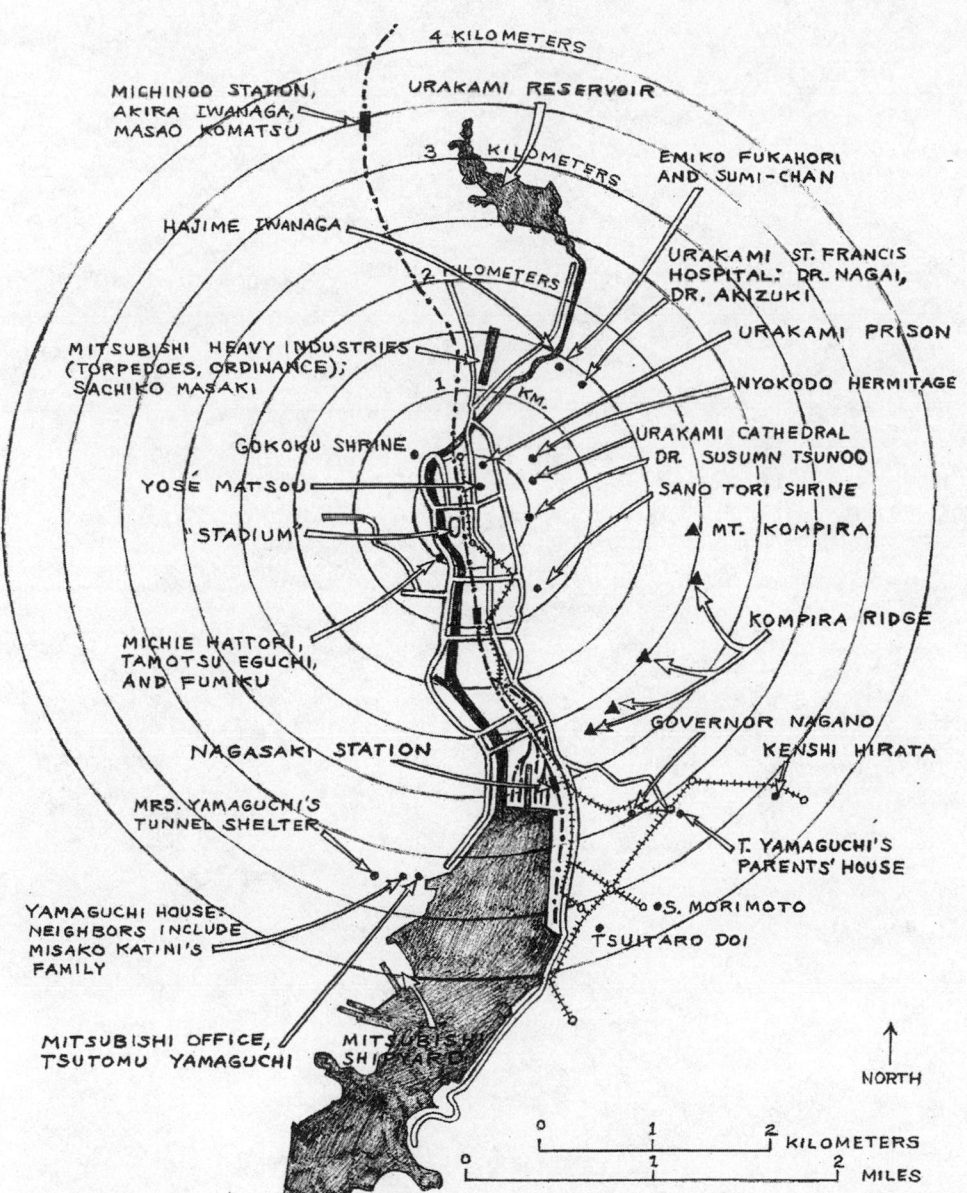

Nagasaki, August 9, 1945: Includes names of several "double hibakusha." [Illustration: Patricia Wynne, based on Pellegrino field notes with survivor annotations on U.S. Bombing Survey maps]

The Killing Star

$\mathcal{H}$ad Mary Shelley or Edgar Allan Poe been born into the mid-twentieth century, they would never have had to invent horror.

For the Japanese and American scientists who first ventured into the still-radioactive hypocenters of Hiroshima and Nagasaki trying to understand what had occurred, the most fearsome deaths were the quickest. On a bridge located in central Hiroshima, a man could still be seen leading a horse, though he had utterly ceased to exist. His footsteps, the horse's footsteps, and the last footsteps of the people who had been crossing the bridge with him toward the heart of the city were preserved on the instantly bleached road surface, as if by a new method of flash photography.

Only a little farther downriver, barely 140 steps from the exact center of the detonation, and still within this same sliver of a second in which images of people and horses were flash-burned onto a road, women who were sitting on the stone steps of the Sumitomo Bank's main entrance, evidently waiting for the doors to open, evaporated when the sky opened up instead. Those who did not survive the first half-second of human contact with a nuclear weapon were alive one moment: on the bank's steps or on the streets and the bridges hoping for Japan's victory or looking toward defeat, hoping for the return of loved ones taken away to war, or mourning loved ones already lost, thinking of increased food rations for their children, or concentrating on smaller dreams, or having no dreams at all. Then, facing the flash point, they were converted into gas and desiccated carbon and their minds and bodies dissolved, as if they had been merely the dream of something alien to human experience suddenly awakening. And yet the shadows of these people lingered behind their blast-dispersed charcoal, imprinted upon the blistered sidewalks, and upon the bank's granite steps—testament that they had once lived and breathed.

On that sixth day of August 1945, no one who conceived, designed, or assembled the Hiroshima bomb knew where uranium nuclei came from, or what science had actually achieved. Not Oppenheimer or Urey, Alvarez, or even Einstein would have known that they had resurrected something from the remote past, from a time and a place seldom encountered in human thought. Each of the uranium-235 atoms at the bomb's core had been forged more than 4.6 billion years earlier, in the hearts of supernovae. The core was assembled from the ash of stars that had lived and died long before the oldest mountains of the moon were born. Mined and refined to nearly 83 percent purity, and brought together in precisely the right geometry, the primordial remnant of Creation was coerced to echo, after ages of quiescence, the last shriek of an imploding star.[1] In all its barest quantum essentials, what happened above Hiroshima that morning—and three days later in Nagasaki, in a separate, plutonium cauldron filled with the by-products of a uranium reactor—signified the brief reincarnations of distant suns.[2]

None of the men who worked this strange alchemy understood yet that the carbon flowing within their veins was, like uranium, the dust of the stars. Nor did they know that the nuclei of carbon and uranium could possibly conceal anything much smaller than the diameter of a proton. Indeed, Einstein and Oppenheimer had difficulty acknowledging that such quantum worlds actually existed within the volume of each proton, each neutron. They therefore did not know what neutrons were made of or precisely how cracks in space-time—cracks in the universe itself—permitted matter to become energy. So primitive was their understanding on this point that it might have been compared to the thought processes of a Neanderthal discovering a cache of napalm. In like manner, the scientists never suspected that the forces they unleashed at that moment bridged their day with the origin of the universe and bridged mega-time with the travel time of light across the diameter of a proton. Though they knew next to nothing about how their briefly created echo from the past worked, next to nothing was enough.

Inevitably, someone was bound to be standing below Point Zero. This peculiar distinction fell to a thirty-five-year-old widow and a half-dozen monks. Mrs. Aoyama had sent her son Nenkai away to his school work-detail at least a half hour earlier than usual—which was why history was to claim the boy as the sole surviving resident of the neighborhood. The Aoyama home was attached on one side to a Buddhist temple with which the family shared and maintained a large vegetable garden. By 8:15, Mrs. Aoyama was probably working in the garden with her neighbors, just as she worked with them every

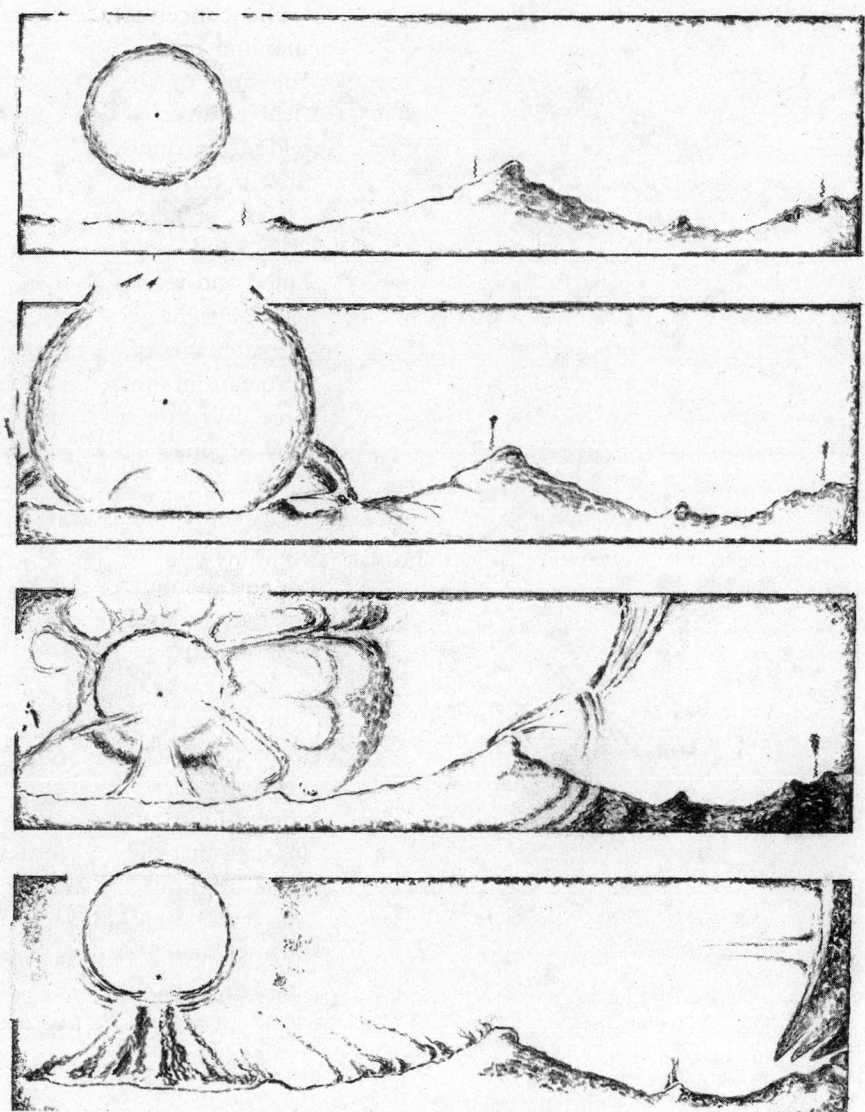

*Stages in development of the nuclear shock-bubble: (1) Sphere of plasma and com-
pressed air explodes away from bomb core; the ground is irradiated. (2) After 1/10th
second, lower hemisphere of bubble touches the earth; back-blast rebounds toward
bubble's point of origin; wedge-shaped compression wave races along ground. (3) After
2/10th second, start of shock-bubble collapse. (4) The bubble implodes and a fireball
begins to rise, vacuuming irradiated debris into the stem of a mushroom cloud, while the
leading edge of a blast-ring continues outward. [Illustration: CRP]*

Three stages of a split second: (1) During the first millionth of a second, not even light from the nuclear storm reaches the ground. (2) After 1/500th second, the surfaces of roof tiles, wood, and leaves have begun flashing to vapor. (3) At 1/10th second, the lower hemisphere of the shock-bubble passes the Hiroshima Dome—which, during a span of only 1/200th second, offers just enough resistance to cut through the descending bubble and shock-cocoon the walls below. [Illustration: CRP]

Nenkai Aoyama's mother was home, at Moment Zero, in a garden adjacent to the Hiroshima Dome. At far above five times the boiling point of water, iron separated from her blood and was compressed briefly into the soil, as a thin layer of carbon-steel. Nenkai never found any trace of her. [Illustration: Patricia Wynne.]

morning. If so, few if any other people were nearer the actual zero point, or more openly exposed, than she and the monks.

Overhead, the dome of Hiroshima's Industrial Sciences Building pointed almost straight up into the center of the detonation. The temple garden in which Mrs. Aoyama toiled was located immediately adjacent to what would become known to future generations as "the Peace Dome." During that final split second before Moment Zero, Mrs. Aoyama and the monks lived on the cusp of instantaneous nonexistence, on the verge of dying before it was possible to realize they were about to die. At the moment the bomb came to life, before a globe of plasma's lower hemisphere could burst down to ground level, the top millimeter of the Dome's metal cladding would catch the rays from the bomb and liquefy instantly, then flash to vapor. Bricks and concrete, too, were on the verge of developing a radiant, liquid skin, while the air above the cladding, and over the bricks and on the ground, soared into the thermal realm of steel emerging white from a furnace.

Unlike the man leading a horse across the nearby "T" Bridge, Mrs. Aoyama could not possibly leave a permanent shadow on the ground. From the moment the rays began to shine down through bones, and before the layer of super-heated air that enveloped her could move even an arm's length, her marrow would begin vibrating at more than five times the boiling point of water. The bones themselves would become instantly incandescent, with all of her flesh trying simultaneously to explode away from her skeleton while being forced straight down into the ground as a compressed gas. Within the first three-tenths of a second following the bomb's detonation, most of the iron was going to be separated from Mrs. Aoyama's blood, as if by an atomic refinery. The top few millimeters of soil, as they converted to molten glass, would be shot through with such high concentrations of iron that, had the greenish-brown layer of glass been permitted to slowly cool, it should have been hidden beneath a sheet of carbon steel; but a slow and stately cooling was not to be. By the time the sound of the explosion reached her son Nenkai two kilometers away, all the substance of Mrs. Aoyama, including blood-derived iron and calcium-enriched glass, would be ascending toward the stratosphere to become part of the strange radioactive thunderstorms that were to chase after Nenkai and the other survivors.[3]

On the south side of town, more than four city blocks beyond Nenkai's mother and the monks, Toshihiko Matsuda was about to leave his shadow on a wall in his family's garden. He appeared to be bending down to pick a piece of fruit or to pull out a weed. During the next few milliseconds, the wall behind Toshihiko would be flash-printed not only with his shadow, but also with the ghost images of the plants that surrounded him—and which were providing his skin with some small measure of flash protection from the searing white glare. On the wall print, at the moment of the bomb's awakening, could be seen the shadow of a leaf that had just detached from its vine and, though falling, would never reach the ground.[4]

From the Aoyama and Matsuda households to the shrimp boats in the harbor, human nervous systems were simply not fast enough to register how quickly the dawn of atomic death burst toward them on that August morning. In the beginning, it had all unfolded within the realm of nanoseconds. Within the core of the reaction zone, approximately 560 grams (or 1.2 pounds) of uranium-235 began to undergo fission before the compressive, shotgun-like forces designed to start the reaction, and to hold it briefly together, were overwhelmed by forces pushing it apart. While it held together, the business end of the bomb—the fraction of its uranium load that actually underwent fission—was astonishingly small. At the moment of compression, the most active ounces of the silvery, neutron-emitting metal occupied only one-third of a golf ball's volume. The total volume of reacting uranium measured slightly more than two level teaspoons. Within that 1.2 pound, two-teaspoon volume (enclosed, as within a clenched fist, by a larger uranium mantle barely wider than a peach), a sample of almost every element that had ever existed during the entire lifetime of the universe was instantly re-created, and many were just as quickly destroyed.

After only one-hundred-millionth of a second, the core began to expand and the fission reactions began to run down. During this ten-nanosecond interval, the first burst of light emerged with such intensity that even the violet and green portions of the spectrum (trailing slightly behind a huge burst of gamma rays) could be seen shining through the bomb's steel casing as if the casing itself were a bag of transparent cellophane. Five hundred and eighty meters (1,900 feet) below, no creatures on the ground could see this. During the first ten nanoseconds (equivalent to 1 second scaled against 3 years), light from the core traveled barely ten feet in all directions. Fission reactions occurred within time frames so narrow that they actually bracketed the speed of light. Thus, from the perspective of anyone located more than ten feet away, the bomb itself, though light was now blazing right through it, had not yet detonated and seemed to be perfectly intact. Directly below, Mrs. Aoyama was still alive and completely untouched by the flash.

One ten-millionth of a second later, a sphere of gamma rays, escaping the core at light speed, reached a radius of 108 feet, with a secondary spray of neutrons following not very far behind. Between the gamma bubble and the newly formed neutron bubble, electrons were stripped from every atom of air and accelerated toward the outer reaches of the gamma sphere. A plasma bubble began to form, producing a thermal shock that spiked hotter than the sun's core and glowed billions of times brighter than the surface of the sun.

Within this atomic flare, X-rays and gamma rays were repeatedly absorbed and scattered, polarized and reabsorbed, to such extent that the rays were as likely to reflect back toward the center of the storm as away from it. A result of this was that by the time the light reached the ground, the gamma and X-ray bursts would be accompanied by a randomly scattering "sky-shine" effect, by which a person shielded from the flash behind, for example, a solid brick wall, could still be pierced by rays emanating from all points of the compass.

During its first millionth of a second, the bubble of light grew to a radius of 300 meters—barely more than six city blocks wide. Though its own expanding dimensions had thinned and cooled the sphere's outer boundary to only a thousand times the boiling point of water, the temperature at the sphere's surface was more than three hundred times that necessary to convert a human body to carbonized mist and incandescent bones. During this same first millionth of a second, the light from the bomb still had not traveled far enough to reach the city. If either Toshihiko Matsuda or Mrs. Aoyama happened to be looking at the blast point at precisely this moment, and were their nervous systems equipped to register one-millionth of a second, the six-block-wide bubble would have appeared to them as an unexploded spear-point in the sky.

Above Matsuda and Aoyama—not merely unseen, but unseeable—the bomb's neutron surge, though traveling at a substantial fraction of light speed, lagged behind its flash and its gamma burst. From the place where the bomb had been—from its magnetic poles—nuclei of tungsten and iron shot ahead of the neutrons as a spreading shower effect, no longer behaving as if they had ever been part of the structure. Behind them, the outracing spray of neutrons (and to a lesser degree protons and short-lived anti-protons) now became a significant secondary source of prompt, and deadly, radiation.

After one ten-thousandth of a second, the air began absorbing the burst and responding to it. The surrounding atmosphere developed into an expanding gulf of near-perfect vacuum, snapping away from the place where the bomb had been, forming a cave of plasma. Along the cavern's walls, the neutron spray generated a second great burst of gamma rays. By now the initial flash had traveled beyond the cave, out to a radius of 30 kilometers (approximately 18 miles), and the light was just beginning to be registered by the rapidly firing nervous systems of mantis shrimps on the bottom of Hiroshima Harbor. Under the hypocenter, the blood in Mrs. Aoyama's brain was already beginning to vibrate, on the verge of flashing to vapor. What she experienced was one of the fastest deaths in human history. Before a single nerve could begin to sense pain, she and her nerves ceased to be. Several city blocks away, Toshihiko Matsuda, and the plants that surrounded him, would live a while longer. At a radius of ten city blocks, koi and turtles swimming just below the surface of Hiroshima Castle's ponds would still be alive the next day, though before they could even begin to flinch or seek deeper water, they were going blind, with the scales and shells on their backs already searing.

Reaction rates were slowing down now—shifting from quantum time frames into the realm of biological time. During the next three milliseconds, a span in which a housefly could execute a single wing flap and start to alter course, the fireball began to form. Initially, it expanded at a hundred times the speed of sound, but by the time its lower surface neared the Hiroshima Dome and the roof of the Matsuda house, 97 milliseconds and 31 wing flaps later, it was down to only a fiftieth of its initial velocity. Near the periphery of the fireball, new fission-generated atoms with very short half-lives were undergoing rapid decay, sending forth a third gamma-ray burst. For all its capacity to cause harm, this third death ray was dwarfed by the heat ray that preceded it and by the gathering storm of a shockwave laced with lightning.

Throughout Hiroshima, one-tenth of a second after detonation, telephone wires and clothing had begun to send forth vertical columns of black vapor, yet all the buildings of the city still stood (during these first hundred milliseconds). Compared to its beginnings, the shockwave was now sluggish. This slowest of the three major atomic bubbles touched the earth at only twice the speed of sound, scarcely faster than human reflexes.

People require a full thirtieth of a second to register motion; a tenth of a second to flinch. The neural pathways of flies fire and reset, scan and respond, almost fifty times faster than a human brain. From the fly's perspective, humans all but stand still, living in a universe of slowed time, much as humans view the time frames of garden-variety slugs and snails.

For miles in every direction, flies registered the initial pulse of light less than five milliseconds after it reached the ground, and they were capable of changing course and seeking shade a hundred milliseconds later, during the next thirty wing flaps, or within the average blink or flinch interval of human time.

After 300 milliseconds (or three-tenths of a second), the fireball had reached its maximum potential for inflicting flash burns at a distance; but by then most of Hiroshima's flies were already sheltering in the shadows of the nearest walls, or under the nearest leaves, or behind the nearest people. The gamma ray sky-shine effect scarcely mattered to them, because a fly's DNA repair systems were nearly two hundred times more efficient than a man's.

At three-tenths of a second, the bomb itself was long gone. Everything that followed, as events shifted from bullet-time and fly-time into the time frames humans knew best, signified nothing more than aftershocks.[5]

Akiko Takakura and her friend Asami—though nearer to the bomb than Toshihiko Matsuda and his shadow garden—were located deep within the granite and concrete shell of the Geibi Bank when the gamma and infrared bursts started. Except for random shafts of sky shine that came in through windows in the building's sides, the two women were more or less cocooned against the death rays.

Akiko would always remember how the clock in the main gallery stopped at a quarter past eight, the same time that the big clock atop the Hiroshima University tower had stopped three days earlier. Because the war effort had drained almost all manpower and all spare metal parts, the resources to repair the city's main timepiece were lacking. During the past three days, Akiko and Asami had joked about how the broken clock tower, frozen seemingly forever at 8:15, underscored the futility of everything. For decades to come, their joke would be clothed in the mantle of prophecy, for in the end repairing the clock or leaving it unrepaired would have made no difference at all. It would only have stopped again at a quarter past eight—like every other clock in central Hiroshima.

Akiko and Asami were located only 250 meters (820 feet) from a hypocenter that originated more than twice as high—which placed the shock bubble's angle of approach, more or less, right above their heads. Women sitting on the steps outside the bank were simultaneously igniting and carbonizing when, about one-tenth of a second before their nerves began to transmit pain, the blast wave intervened. Because the shock-front came down from overhead, telephone poles and trees, and the vertical supports of the bank were able to resist and were largely bypassed by the forces of compression. Trees and poles and up-thrusting steel beams behaved much like the noses and fins of rocket-bombs cutting through supersonic air. Akiko and her friend were spared much by an effect that needed to work only during the first two or three milliseconds of the shock-front's passage, in order to shield them through the entire five-second bypass of blast and turbulence that followed. The building had literally punched a hole through the advancing wave front, forming a shock cocoon for the two friends (and for a bank manager located in the basement) as the hammerhead of air rebounded outside, spreading away from them.

Akiko felt as if her lungs were being crushed by a surge of dense air. Asami was buffeted and tossed, struck in the back by decorative cladding from a wall that compressed like accordion skin and then erupted as granite shrapnel; but the two friends had been shielded within one of nature's strangest quirks. The shock-cocoon effect accompanied all major explosive events and tended not to occur where anyone acting on common sense alone would expect survival to be even remotely possible. Sometimes, the safest place to be was nearest the very heart of the explosion.[6]

Like Akiko and Asami, Shigeyoshi Morimoto received a quick and intensive education in the physics of shock cocoons. Morimoto was one of Japan's four champion kite-makers, which was why he and three of his colleagues had been drafted and transported to Hiroshima, to design high-altitude observation kites for ship convoys. At a quarter past eight on the morning of August 6, Morimoto was not much farther from the bomb than Akiko Takakura. Like Akiko, he recalled no sound accompanying the flash. The multi-tiered, heavily tiled mansion shook and compressed around Mr. Morimoto and the two cousins he had been visiting; but the combination of ceramic roof tiles and three layers of thick wooden beams overhead attenuated the gamma bursts by a factor of about seven, and possibly as high as ten. Rooms filled floor-to-ceiling with shelves of books further attenuated the rays, along with the compression waves that quickly followed. In a sense, the three cousins were being safeguarded by culture. The compression of the upper three floors occurred as if the building had been designed with lifesaving crumple zones of wood and shelves (or shells) of thick paper in mind, cocooning the Morimoto family so gently that they survived in the center of Hiroshima with only a few minor bruises.[7]

At up to twice the Akiko and Morimoto radius, nearly six city blocks north of the hypocenter, Private Shigeru Shimoyama had just stepped into a concrete-reinforced warehouse—where, as he would recall later for historians, he was "shaded from the flash, but not from the bang." The hand of the vengeful giant seemed to have flung him toward the back wall, while in this same instant the roof was pushed down and the floor was pulled up. The walls, too, were yanked inward, toward the center of the room, and the rear wall stopped the flying private like a catcher's mitt. Outside, all of Shigeru's fellow draftees died instantly. When he discovered that the reason he appeared to be suspended almost a meter above the floor was that his shoulders were nailed to a wooden crossbeam, and when a never-ending silence made him feel as if he were the only living person in Hiroshima, he began to suspect that everyone else might have gotten away with a better deal.[8]

Just beyond Private Shimoyama's radius, at the edge of the army burial grounds, the sisters of a local girls' school were extracting oil from camphor trees when the sky ignited. The trees flew apart into thousands of flaming shreds. The granite tombstones nearby glowed cherry red, as if to herald the resurrection of the soldiers buried beneath, before the shockwave hurled them end over end off the top of Kyobashi Hill. Days later, former Pearl Harbor squadron commander Mitsuo Fuchida (saved by a new assignment that had called him away from Hiroshima, hours ahead of the flash) would arrive in the city center, searching for the nuns and their students. Finding the granite stones, and discovering that their outermost layers had boiled and turned to sand, he would understand that there was no point in looking for his friends. The stones would tell him everything he needed to know.[9]

In the neighborhood of the Misasa Bridge, almost two kilometers upriver of the hypocenter, Sumiko Kirihara's family had been gathering for a portrait when the flash came. Sumiko was fourteen years old; she had seen the war pull teenage relatives to diverse places, including islands at which they would forever be remembered among the ranks of the missing. Now her sixteen-year-old brother was being drafted to arsenal work, so the family came together from distant towns for what they believed might be a final reunion. Drawn now into the death zone, they had scheduled a photographer to arrive by eight, to pose them in a sunny, open-air garden; but for one reason or another he was delayed. And so, in a region where anyone standing outdoors and exposed to the flash from the bomb was likely to receive lethal burns from the light alone, an unexpected change of schedule placed a family within the protective shadows of a tea room's wood and terra-cotta roof. When the heat ray flashed out from the direction of the Dome and the Geibi Bank, the Kiriharas were safely indoors, reminiscing and playing music, and sipping cups of wartime tea so diluted that it might have been described as warm water sprinkled lightly with flakes of reused dried leaves.

Outside, the garden vanished in a searing glare. Sumiko perceived the flash as a pale blue radiance that came from everywhere and seemed very hot, even indoors. At the same instant, she heard an electronic crackling, so loud that she feared it might split her eardrums. Her parents' two-story wooden house—along with the house of a neighbor—rode through the shockwaves almost completely undamaged, in a neighborhood where the only other buildings left standing were a steel and concrete hospital and, along the southern horizon, office buildings and a department store in flames.[10] Mrs. Sasaki stepped away from her similarly shock-cocooned house with two-year old Sadako in her arms. Though one wall had blown out and the house was leaning, most of the Sasaki family, like the Kirihara family, appeared to have survived the *pika-don*—or "flash-bang"—completely unharmed, physically. Years later, little Sadako would insist that, though she was only age two at the time, she could still recall the radiance of a thousand suns bursting through the windows and a heat that pricked her eyes like needles. The false sunrise became her earliest memory.[11]

The uranium fist was capricious, killing some and sparing others, even when people were within direct sight of one another. Mrs. Teruko Kono had kept her little boy from school that day, and when the fist struck, she had just seen him at play on his raft, from the second-story window of her riverside home. Located within the same zone as the Sasaki and Kirihara families, less than two kilometers from the hypocenter, Mrs. Kono was shielded from the heat ray but her boy was fully exposed. He flashed out pallid white and sent up a column of black smoke before her home was pitched on its side, hoisted into the air, then dropped into the river practically on top of her son.[12]

On the bank of this same river, at this same radius and within sight of the Hiroshima Dome, Nobuo Tetsutani had been enjoying a peaceful respite at 8:14, a minute that would be burned into his memory by the strange circumstance of everything he loved being here one moment, gone the next.

The air was beautiful, filled with the sounds of cicadas and crickets rubbing their legs together, filled with the buzz of flower flies and the laughter of three-year-old Shin and his friend Kimi from next door, as they rode together on what Nobuo believed to be the last tricycle in Hiroshima to escape being melted down for the construction of steel hulls or artillery casings. Nobuo let out a laugh, and in the next 300 milliseconds he was spared by a wall's shadow-shield effect, while the children were taken.

The tricycle's dark red paint caught the bright rays and held them, causing the outermost layers of steel on one side to flake apart, mixing explosively with the paint and igniting like iron filings on a birthday sparkler. The children's black hair caught the rays with equal efficiency, during the half-second before their world started to become deep rubble and glowing red coals. In a city fated to be rebuilt upon the ashes of "the disappeared," forty years would pass before Shin and Kimi were finally unearthed for a traditional funeral ceremony. Their little white bones would be found hand in hand, near a blistered brown pipe that turned out to be the handlebar of Shin's tricycle.[13]

Some parents recalled premonitions, that morning, from children who only appeared to be trying to get out of school-based work details.

Etsuko Kuramoto (Fujikawa) was a fifth grader who had already stayed home three days before with a recurrent stomachache. She did not want to go to school again—insisting that something was about to happen and she did not wish her mother to be lonely.

"Well then," Etsuko's mother said, "we'll die together when we die." She was laughing as she said this. And when she laid down the law that Etsuko would go to school even in a universal deluge, the child insisted that she be allowed to wear her best outfit that morning. The last time Sumie Kuramoto saw Etsuko, her adored child was walking toward the National Elementary School in the direction of the hypocenter, wearing "her Sunday best" and crying.[14]

Another fifth grader was more direct about his fears.

"Hiroshima will be totally destroyed today," Hiroshi Mori told his mother.

Yoshiko could not imagine where the child had heard such a horror. She warned him not to utter such words again, then ordered him away to school. But before he went away to a building whose steel beams were soon afterward stripped of their concrete shells and bent like blades of grass caught in a strong wind, the boy told his mother to take care of herself, and asked her not to pack any food into his canvas backpack, because he would not be needing lunch that day.

In another neighborhood school, at a radius of two kilometers, a teacher named Arai received an unforgettable lesson in the differential effects of black and white surfaces in absorbing light. When the flash came, she happened to be standing alone in her schoolroom, having decided to give the children a few minutes extra playtime outdoors. Arai was hanging the best examples of her students' script in a window facing the hypocenter. One little girl, working her delicate calligraphy in India ink, had brushed her teacher's name onto white rice paper. The flash was so bright that Arai thought a thousand-pound bomb must have fallen right outside the window. In accordance with her air-raid training, she ducked instantly for cover, expecting nothing except "quick oblivion" from a bomb full of dynamite and phosphorus charges dropping so near. She was puzzled, therefore, when the light faded and the anticipated blast failed to come for what seemed many long seconds. She was on the verge of lifting her head for a peek outside when the window burst indoors and a thousand slivers of glass flew harmlessly over her back.

When Arai stood again, she beheld a giant volcanic cloud full of fireflies, shifting from gold to violet to a brilliant shade of green more dazzling than any emerald she could imagine. After the false fireflies had risen out of sight and after a real fly alighted on a cut in her forearm, she became aware of two new realities: the children outside were missing, as if something had spirited them silently away, leaving smoldering piles of rags in their place. Arai's second realization was that her arms, her face, and anything else that had not been shadow-shielded behind the papers on the window felt badly sunburned.

In her hand, Arai still clutched the sheet of rice paper; but it had changed dramatically. The black Japanese characters had absorbed the light and flash-burned out of existence, whereas the surrounding white paper threw the light back at the source of the flash and survived more or less intact. By the time the heat ray burned through the brushstrokes, the power of the bomb was all but fractionally spent and beginning to fade. A thin sheet of rice paper had shielded the teacher's eyes, sparing her from blindness, but even a dwindling fraction of the bomb's unspent fury was significant. Its light blazed through the missing letters like paint sprayed through a stencil. It struck Arai's face with the equivalent force of four or five full days under the August sun, stenciling the tender script of a child who was lost, permanently on her skin.[15] All of this happened before she could even begin to duck—all of this within four-tenths of a second.[16]

Perception of the "flash-bang" seemed to change depending where one happened to be located. Akiko Takakura recalled that, within a shock cocoon beneath the bomb, it had all begun for her with a white flash, in utter silence.[17] At one kilometer, Hiroshi Mori's mother saw a blue flash, accompanied almost instantly by a loud clattering noise.[18] At almost two kilometers, Sadako Sasaki's mother remembered the flash as yellow[19] while her neighbor Sumiko was certain that the bomb had flashed blue.[20] At this same distance, a shock-cocooned postal worker named Hiroko Fukada clearly recalled that it was yellow.[21] Yosaku Mikami, one of only a handful of firefighters who survived within the perimeter of Ground Zero, saw the sky flash blue at a distance of 1.9 kilometers (1.2 miles).[22] At 4.1 kilometers (2.1 miles) a physician named

Sawachika saw his world turn suddenly bright red.[23] 2.4 kilometers farther out, at a radius of 4.1 miles and in the bottom of a protected valley, photographer Seiso Yamada witnessed the whole spectrum of colors—"like rainbows and magnesium flashing overheard. Like ripples from a stone thrown into a pond, the rainbows came in waves"—and afterward he was shaken to the ground by the sound of a tremendous explosion.[24]

Those witnesses nearest the hypocenter seemed never to have heard the blast. With increasing distance, the noise grew perceptible, then bone-rattling. At 1.8 to 1.9 kilometers, in the home where her family was kept safely indoors by the lateness of a photographer, young Sumiko Kirihara heard a loud electronic buzz and crackle;[25] but other survivors at this same radius, including the Sasakis, heard nothing.[26] At almost three kilometers, ship designer Tsutomu Yamaguchi had been walking along the edge of a potato field, and was approaching a woman dressed in a black mompe, when something like a photographer's magnesium flashbulb blazed before his eyes. Responding instantly with his navy air-raid training, he dove to the ground and rolled into the nearest irrigation ditch, simultaneously flinging his hands to his head, locking fingers over his eyes, and jamming a thumb protectively into each ear. Even with his ears plugged by his thumbs, the sound that came to Yamaguchi was ear-shattering. What he remembered most about the seconds preceding the flash and the shockwave were beads of morning dew glistening on the potato leaves, the distant drone of a B-29, the woman looking up into the cloudless sky and seeming confused—and two parachutes opening, causing the woman to run. Now, even with fingers locked over his eyes, Yamaguchi could see and feel the glare of the fireball. It seemed to him that the sun had fallen to Earth, and that even the mountains let out a scream.

The ground roared and quivered, snapped and leaped, tossing Yamaguchi out of the ditch and nearly a meter into the air. As he fell, the fireball imploded over the city and began to rise at stupendous speed, creating a vacuum effect that for a second or two threatened to draw the engineer upward from the face of the earth and toward the center of the city; but instead it merely whirled him about for what seemed an impossibly long time on a cushion of air and rushing dust. In later years, Yamaguchi would guess that at no point was he ever more than two meters above the potato field. He felt as if the tumult in which he was caught had levitated him atop a river of rapids made out of thick dust—rapids through which random openings of clear air allowed him glimpses of distant houses warping out of shape and flying toward him in pieces. Completely disoriented, the engineer fell into one of the muddy furrows from which the implosion had drawn him.

When Yamaguchi regained his composure and peeked out of the ditch, a blizzard of burning paper and shreds of smoldering clothing were falling out of the sky, flickering like thousands of tiny lanterns and incense burners in the trees and on the leaves of the potato plants. It appeared to him that the contents of an entire office building had been hoisted into the heavens, then ripped up, blown apart, scorched, and strewn about. He could not find the sun. The blue sky had been erased and darkness prevailed, making Yamaguchi feel as if he were in the depths of the ocean. Pieces of buildings were still in flight. "I could hear the sound of flying roof tiles shattering in the air," he would write later—"objects falling, and the noise of all manner of destruction. It was impossible to identify each noise or its cause."

Sitting in a mud pool, Yamaguchi became suddenly aware that one whole side of his body was intensely hot. The exposed skin on his left arm had been literally roasted brownish-black, like the skin of an overcooked chicken. Even then, before he knew anything about atomic bombs, the engineer began to suspect a heat ray of some sort; and he realized that his white shirt and his light-colored pants had spared him much. The woman in the black mompe had run toward the center of the field, where, standing upright, she exposed her entire body to the full fury of the flash, while clothed in the all-absorbing equivalent of India ink. She was nowhere in sight.

When the noise subsided and the ground-hugging swirls of dust began pulling apart into long streamers, Yamaguchi looked up and saw a pillar of fire and ash reaching toward the stratosphere. It looked like a giant tornado enclosed within a volcanic plume; but its long, tree-trunk base moved hardly at all. Only the top of the monster seemed active, growing higher and wider. *When this cloud falls to the earth,* Yamaguchi told himself, *every living thing will die.* He realized that even if he survived the cloud—which soon splashed him with a brief oily rain, the B-29s might return. And all the burning of his body went away, to be replaced at once by the image of his wife and child alone at home. He contrived a plan, then, to find a train or an automobile that was still working, or a horse that was still alive and, by any means necessary, go home to Nagasaki.[27]

Isao Kita was on a mountainside when the sky caught fire. He was the chief military weather forecaster for the District Bureau, and he remained at his post, recording and observing even after an unexplainable sense of dehydration and nausea took hold of him. The closer people were to the center of the storm, the less they could see of what actually happened around them. At a distance of three kilometers, Mr. Yamaguchi had understood almost at once that he was witness to a high-energy device whose primary effect was a concussion of searing light. Nearer the hypocenter, all Shin's and Sadako's families could see were ruins, sheets of wind-driven dust, and rising seas of flame.

From the weather station, poised high above Hiroshima, a kilometer beyond Mr. Yamaguchi and just outside the bomb's radius of first degree flash burns, Mr. Kita had a grandstand view. He was looking north across the city and the winds had been following their normal course for this time of the year—approaching from behind him. In the river basins below, the flash was partly obscured by brilliant white clouds that formed instantly around the hypocenter; they resembled the plain of Saturn's rings, viewed from a vantage point only slightly lower than edge-on, yet *this* cloudy layer of rings was in motion, rippling across the blue sky. Kita would always remember it as an amazingly colorful sight: "It was as if blue morning glories had bloomed in the sky." Then the air around him began to crackle and expand. Kita and the entire mountainside seemed to plunge suddenly into a hot oven. Like Yamaguchi, he realized immediately that something unusual had exploded over the city, and it appeared likely that a shockwave was already racing toward him.

Quickly estimating the seconds that had passed since the flash, Kita dove for cover and began to count. Two seconds later, a groaning sound reached him, building quickly to a rumbling roar that caused the observation deck to buck and kick. In one moment he was looking directly at the ground, believing he had successfully aimed his hands and feet protectively in the right direction. In the next instant, he glanced up in the direction where the sun and the fiery clouds should have been; but the heavens rushed down and struck him in the jaw. It seemed as unfair as it was disorienting that the sky should be paved with concrete instead of clouds; but Kita recovered quickly, and realized that the shock must have flipped him like a coin, two meters up into the air, then dropped him with tooth-cracking force onto the weather station's deck.

Pulling a piece of paper from his pocket, Kita jotted down the number five, representing the number of seconds between the flash and the bang. The distance from the center of the flash, near the "T" Bridge and the Dome, told him the speed of the shockwave: about 700 meters per second. Kita recorded that it must have been traveling at twice the speed of sound.

When the young scientist stood up and looked down upon the damage, only the word *unearthly* began ("and *only* began") to describe what happened.

Hiroshima no longer belonged in Kita's world. After the first five seconds, the whole city was converted to a lake of yellowish boiling dust, left behind by a billowing red cloud that rose at impossible speed. By the time Kita jotted the number 5, the cloud had already climbed more than five kilometers—maybe ten, maybe higher.

About five minutes later, the yellow lake of dust became stained with columns of inky black smoke; and two minutes after that, the layer of air above the dust was full of worms. After a while, Kita realized that the worms were whirling spouts of smoke and fire—sometimes moving off along separate paths and dying out, other times coalescing into actual tornados of flame orbited by uprooted masses of sheet metal and unrecognizable debris.

The wind at Kita's back seemed to be pushing all of the worms and the towers of smoke northwest toward Hiroshima Station and the Misasa Bridge, dividing the city into day and night. On Kita's side of the divide, the boiling dust layer settled or moved off and the ruins below were revealed as fields of broken wood and sparkles of glass, upon which the sun was still shining brightly, during an otherwise normal summer morning. Everything in the south and east appeared to have turned into yellow desert sand. In the north, and upriver, the world was a darkness that even at a distance could be felt, broken only by lightning, and by glowing whirlwinds that sometimes towered five and ten stories tall. There were strange updrafts and downdrafts within the smoke; and through binoculars Kita was able to discern great sheets of black hail or snow, swooping down from on high.

"Noooo . . .," he said. "Oh, no."

He could see that there were still people moving on the plain below. Thousands of people in open view, and probably thousands more trapped behind the black curtain.[28]

• 2 •

Gojira's Egg

For Nenkai Aoyama's mother and the man leading a horse across Hiroshima's "T" Bridge, life ceased so abruptly that it was as if nothing happened. Nothing at all.

Only beyond the zone of instant vaporization, or within the shock-cocooned gallery of the Geibi Bank, could people begin to wonder what had just occurred. Akiko Takakura, who would make her mark on history as the long-term survivor who had been nearest to the bomb, faded in and out of consciousness during the first three minutes. Her lungs ached from the sudden burst of compressed air, and from the equally fierce decompression that immediately followed.[1] Several blocks north of Akiko's position, Private Shimoyama contrived a plan to protect his lungs from a rising flood of soot and hot smoke by urinating into his shirt and using it as a filter, but the plan fell apart because it appeared to him that someone had nailed both arms and his right hand to a board while he lay unconscious.[2] Only slightly nearer the hypocenter, kite-maker Shigeyoshi Morimoto noticed that all of his books had been knocked from the shelves, and the ceiling was lower by more than a meter—which led him to conclude that he and his cousins must have survived a very close shave from a one-ton bomb landing on the front lawn. He could not imagine that most of the district that surrounded the mansion had disappeared.[3] Ship designer Tsutomu Yamaguchi climbed out of the irrigation ditch into which he had been dumped, and tried to understand a world that seemed to be turning darker than a total eclipse of the sun. One side of Mr. Yamaguchi's face felt as if a thousand white-hot needles had pierced his skin, and he tried to soothe the heat with mud from the ditch.[4] Five kilometers away on the far side of Ground Zero, Sumiko Kirihara, the young girl whose family was saved by the lateness of a photographer, was coughing up yellow dust.[5]

Before and after views of the area around the Hiroshima Dome and the T-Bridge, based on U.S. Bombing Survey photos. [Illustration: Patricia Wynne]

Scattered in random fashion throughout a city of a quarter-million people—a city in which survival appeared to be governed by sheer chance—any two random survivors were all but guaranteed to be strangers. Despite an arithmetic that should have rendered the survivors strangers, their lives tended to defy probability, becoming oddly connected.

The Sasaki and Ito families were examples of this. Although Masahiro Sasaki lived on the opposite side of the Misasa Bridge and more than ten kilometers away from ten-year-old Tsugio Ito, the two boys had already crossed paths at the State Middle School and College Complex's swimming pool—which, during this particularly hot Hiroshima summer, had become a widely used cooling off center, frequented by families living in the area, along with students from the local school/factory. Two members of the Ito and Sasaki families seemed fated to eventually forge a lifelong friendship. Neither knew as yet that Tsugio's older brother Hiroshi and Masahiro's little sister Sadako were already drawing their families into a convergent path through history.

Only a few months before, Tsugio's brother Hiroshi had been accepted into one of Japan's most prestigious and competitive schools, from which the government typically recruited its top engineering students. Lately, twelve-year-old Hiroshi Ito's school had been converted from classrooms into makeshift factories supplying armaments for the soldiers of Hiroshima Castle. The older engineering students were being assigned to figure out how to manufacture triggers and other traditionally metal gun parts from more readily available hardwood—recovered from neighborhoods selected by the government to be flattened into firebreaks. In Hiroshi's classroom, brass shell casings were being substituted with a newer, clearly inferior alloy made available mostly by demolishing tin roofing and siding. Bullets were being carved from mahogany—"for fighting at close range," a teacher had explained. Two-shot wooden handguns were being manufactured for distribution to children and their mothers. Everyone knew that the little guns would not be particularly effective if the Americans swarmed into the city, but the men who planned the final battle had decided that one or two shots from every citizen might work just long enough to slow the enemy down, perhaps even force Americans to rethink the idea of a building-by-building fight. In another classroom, the students were sharpening bamboo spears. *This is what happens to a nation that loses a war,* a local physician named Hachiya observed in his diary. *Wooden bullets and bamboo spears.*[6]

Five minutes after Moment Zero, Hiroshi Ito climbed out through the roof of his seventh-grade classroom, now reduced from a two-story building to less than a half-story. The Ito boy emerged completely unharmed into a mist of black water droplets whipped into motion by a combination of erupting fires and downpours of freezing black rain. The rain stung Hiroshi's skin and sent him running with thirty or forty other students into the swimming pool, crying for help. All of the other boys appeared to have been severely burned, and in every direction, Hiroshi's world continued deteriorating into confusion. At the water's edge, schoolgirls, lying in rows, were dying one after another before his eyes. They had been wearing white blouses and black work pants. Most of them still wore only their white shirts, their dark pants having flashed into flame and ashes, removing all of the skin from the girls' legs. When Hiroshi looked in the opposite direction, toward the Misasa Bridge, a navy boat or a fuel tank disappeared in a huge explosion, from which something black and cylindrical rocketed up on streamers of flame. If it were possible, the sky became even darker after that, like a demonic pall drawn over the school and the river—a malediction.

At this moment, Hiroshi's mother, Hanako, was running toward him from ten kilometers away in the eastern hill country. She knew that somewhere up ahead her son must be struggling for survival under the stem of the mushroom cloud. The initial flash had given one side of her face a slight but nonetheless noticeable "sunburn," even at a distance of nearly seven miles; and she could not venture a guess at what the monstrosity might really be. Near the base of the same Ground Zero mushroom stem, ship designer Tsutomu Yamaguchi was still trying to plan a way home to Nagasaki. He and Hanako Ito were also following convergent pathways. Both of their families would be touched by Ground Zero a second time.[7]

South of the stem, Yamaguchi's plan was almost thwarted by a whirlwind of brownish-yellow mist that descended suddenly from a great height and enveloped him.[8] The mist was surprisingly cold, like frost, but it radiated an imperceptible heat, born of leaking neutrons and other exotic particles.[9]

North of Yamaguchi, the Ito boy also felt the bite of freezing mist, from the moment he climbed out of the pool. By now Hiroshi Ito knew that he and only one other boy (a senior named Ryuzo) had survived the destruction of their school without melted skin and crushed limbs. Their injured class-mates moved in unearthly silence. There was no point in asking any of them for some clue or opinion about what had caused the blast and the burns. The others seemed to have given up on everything; and so the two survivors set off to explore on their own, seeking answers.

Realizing that even their clothes were completely intact, the boys felt like intruders in a strange land where everyone else's eyes and lips had be-come blisters caked in black ash. Only a few minutes earlier, no one from this school had ever witnessed such injuries. Now, everyone else except Hiroshi and Ryuzo displayed the unusual wounds, as if what was normal became the rarity and what was abnormal switched places with normal and became the prevailing condition. The reversal reminded them of stories their grandparents had told, about the prophesied breaking of the world.

"My God, my God," Ryuzo said. "What just happened?"[10]

Across the river, on the other side of the Misasa Bridge, Masahiro's and Sumiko's families were shadow-shielded and shock-cocooned—just like Hi-roshi Ito and Ryuzo. And, just like the two boys, they were initially unsuc-cessful at finding clues to the cause of the trouble. All they knew was that the phenomenon that converted idyllic backyard gardens glistening with morning dew into yellow dust and swirling black mist had manifested like an instant dream. Mercifully, Masahiro's little sister Sadako would remember only the flash. Their mother wished never to add to those memories. Especially, she would never tell the girl about the tap dancer they saw.

Once the two families were safely outside of their weakened and sud-denly crumbling homes, they discovered that all the people had gone away—except for a strange man who burrowed his way out of a wrecked house and began to run past them toward a curtain of whirling hot sparks. He flapped his arms like a bird's wings as he ran, and neither cried for help nor gave his onlookers any notice at all. The only sound he made was a rhythmic clicking on the road surface, as if he were dancing down the street with metal taps on his shoes. But he wore no shoes. In fact, his feet were gone and the bony stilts of two tibiae—chipping and fracturing with each step against the pavement—were the source of the tapping. No one saw what eventually happened to him. The tap dance in Dante's Hell was first muffled, then completely cut off by thick drifts of oily smoke—which enveloped both families in a gloomy quiet.

Beyond a radius of six or seven steps, their world became a silent and shadowy motion picture. After the tap dancer had passed, all that could be heard were the steady nearby pings of pebbles and grit from the sky, raining down upon sheets of corrugated zinc that had been blown into the neighborhood from somewhere far away. Sumiko Kirihara wondered if the instantaneous change in her world might actually have no connection at all to the war, and might instead be connected to the final shattering of the Earth itself, as people had been warned against, by many religions, for thousands of years. She began to believe this was the end of Hiroshima, of Japan, of humankind.[11]

In a hospital near Ground Zero, a military physician had been recently reassigned, in preparation for the anticipated American assault on the mainland. His orders, issued to him at gunpoint, included the teaching of new soldiers—some as young as fourteen and fifteen—how to follow the latest procedures for strapping bombs to their bodies and throwing themselves under vehicles. The doctor now stood every bit as mystified as Sumiko by the silence of his surroundings. Decades would pass before anyone realized that he belonged to a very small coterie of shock-cocoon survivors. The riverside hospital in which he had been standing disappeared up to about the height of his waist. Everything was lifted away in a puff of dust, leaving him the only survivor, standing on the ground floor with not a single scratch. All the bomb had done to the doctor was snap the eyeglasses off his face. Looking down, he saw a little music box, also standing undamaged in this sudden purgatory of smoke and rising dust. The music box still played *Let Me Call You Sweetheart*. Beyond that old Western tune everything else was silence, and everyone else seemed to have vanished.

The mystery deepened when, through occasional clearings in the dust, the physician began to see the true extent of the damage. And then he found his glasses, and discovered that he could no longer see clearly when he put them on . . . then he discovered that everything came into sharp focus again when he took them off . . . became blurry again when he put them on. Some sort of pressure wave, he theorized, must have changed the shape of his eyeballs.

"But of course," he told a science student years later, in a tone of genuine understatement, "I would not recommend nuclear detonations as a means of corrective eye surgery."[12]

Elsewhere along Ground Zero's fringe, one of Mrs. Ito's conscripted co-workers had an equally remarkable story of survival to tell—owing to a precise combination of distance and obstacles, angles and forces, and luck. At Moment Zero, Mrs. Sumako Matsuyanagi's dark pants had ignited in the searing blue glare, but her long-sleeved white shirt protected the upper part of her body and the airburst instantly extinguished the flames of her pants before they could do any real harm. The hammerhead of air also scooped Mrs. Matsuyanagi off the sidewalk and flung her more than fifty meters—about halfway down a city block. She was much farther away from the airburst than Akiko Takakura and the Geibi Bank, so the lower edge of the shock bubble did not bypass her. Instead it struck out laterally, and its bowl-shaped undersurface, spreading out along the flat anvil of the earth, compressed a precursor wave ahead of the outracing shock front—which was both a good thing and a bad thing, in terms of survival. The precursor wave had shot several dozen meters ahead of Mrs. Matsuyanagi, gathering strength as it went. In this manner, the air, caught between shock front and anvil, became like a semi-fluid watermelon seed squirted between thumb and forefinger, with Mrs. Matsuyanagi cushioned in the center of the seed. Thus did the precursor wave, while propelling her at deadly speed, simultaneously perform the lifesaving service of clearing all the large windows of a house from Mrs. Matsuyanagi's flight path—which landed her in someone's sitting room, along with much of the room's ceiling.

Years later, Mrs. Matsuyanagi would recall, in a style of understatement exceeded only by the doctor whose vision was corrected by the bomb, that the people inside "were very surprised to see me."

"Where did you come from?" said an elderly woman.

"Are you hurt?" a kindly old man asked.

Mrs. Matsuyanagi looked around the demolished room in silence, not knowing what to say. The white-haired man pulled a broken chair out of the wreckage and asked her to rest. When she sat, her clothing began to crumble like brittle rice paper.

"What's causing *that*?" the man asked.

Mrs. Mastuyanagi answered absently, "Something seems to have happened." Her thoughts were only with her two boys, now. She thanked the couple and told them she had to go outside and find the school. *Had* to.[13]

Thirteen-year-old Yoshitaka also survived the blast. He was attending one of the city's smaller schools, and the entire building seemed to have collapsed around him; yet some quirk of nature had sheltered him in an air pocket, from which he was able to push his way to the surface, quickly enough to witness the still-radiant cloud growing in the sky, almost directly overhead. The plasma within was still shockingly bright; Yoshitaka could feel its heat radiating against his face. It seemed to be catching the rays of the sun and throwing back every color of the rainbow—"And God forgive me," he would say later, "I could say that it was beautiful."

All around him, in the bricks and the rubble, other children were half buried and dying. Hands grabbed at Yoshi's feet and shins. He was horrified at the thought of so many hands trying to grab at him—the seemingly dead and the still-moving dead, trying to pull him down through the rubble—and all he could think of was to get away from them. So he kicked at the hands and ran away, continuing to look up at the beautiful apparition—to look anywhere but at the ground.

Had Yoshi stayed buried under even an ankle-deep layer of bricks for just a few seconds more, the rays might never have fallen upon him. The beauty he beheld in the cloud arose largely from the creation of secondary fission products, most of them with half-lives ranging from milliseconds to as long as three minutes. The decay of those isotopes, as pieces of matter began to disappear from the universe, leaving bursts of energy in their place, had fueled the third gamma ray surge—which diminished by more than 90 percent during the first ten seconds and continued to radiate the majority of its remaining power for a half-minute more.[14]

When Mrs. Matsuyanagi found her two sons running aimlessly near the wreck of the school, they appeared to have survived the flying glass and the collapsing walls without injury, but each had absorbed body-piercing gamma rays. Both were granted only the briefest respite in which to presume they escaped unharmed, before succumbing by individual degrees to an epidemic no one had seen before. One boy had been shielded for only a few seconds inside a collapsing building, while his younger brother was shaded from the heat ray under a large tree whose thick trunk protected him from the lateral slam of the shockwave. The blast forces must have diverged around the boy, but the bomb had unleashed an eerie menagerie of high-energy particles, some of them even deadlier than heat rays and blast waves. Among them were nuclei of iron and tungsten—shot-gunned from the bomb's interior along magnetic field lines, at up to 90 percent the speed of light. If a single uranium nucleus, chipped by a neutron bullet, releases enough power to make a grain of sand jump, an entire nucleus of iron shotgunned through a human body at relativistic velocity can deliver the force of a baseball squeezed through that same path at nearly 170 kilometers per hour. Along a path no wider than a human hair, flesh turns to ash, water explodes, and protein synthesis in the surrounding tissues is stopped dead. On that day, there existed rare, narrow kill zones where the bomb's magnetic field lines could guide *thousands* of such particles through a single body with an effect that was, in essence, nuclear machine-gun fire.

Both of Mrs. Matsuyanagi's children, as they wandered about the rubble pile that had been their school, were already feeling ill. One would overcome the bomb's effects; the other would be taken. The younger boy had gone to school hungry, but in the aftermath of the rays and the particle beams he lost all desire to eat. By the time his mother found him, he was overcome by dry heaves and seizures. Within minutes, the child's arms turned black-and-blue and he began to bleed despite the apparent lack of injuries. Hemorrhaging under the skin developed with such astonishing rapidity that scientists would one day wonder if a heavy ion stream had somehow been magnetically lensed upon a specific child under a specific tree; or whether he was abnormally sensitive to doses of gamma radiation that would have taken hours or days to sicken others; or whether Mrs. Matsuyanagi's memory of her child bleeding through the pores of his skin and dying only hours later, "like smoke fading away," was in reality a misremembered timing of events. A relativistic shotgun effect seemed just as likely, but no one would ever know for sure. On that day, Mrs. Matsuyanagi could not make even a bad guess at what had hurled her down a street and caused her clothes to fall apart like ancient parchment, or what manner of illness had pounced upon her two boys.

Before he left the house for the last time, the younger child cried because there had been no white rice available for many weeks, and he was allowed only a small portion of soybean mash for breakfast—which was anything but filling. Worse yet, in the near total absence of fresh fish or dried meat or other flavorings, the mash left an aftertaste like wet sawdust. For decades to come, Mrs. Matsuyanagi would pray for her child to visit with her in a dream, where she would take him in her arms and give him all the white rice and meat he could eat.[15]

Mrs. Matsuyanagi's prayer reflected the emotions of many parents who remembered the ungranted wishes of their children in an era of wartime famine. In the Peace Park that would one day occupy Ground Zero, one mother eventually left a poem to the child who had asked for a tomato from the garden before he went to school. The boy's mother had told him that there was only one tomato left, and that it would stave off his usual bedtime hunger if he waited to eat it until he returned home. The poem spoke of the little shrine that would be constructed for him, on which she would leave a paper box covered with white cloth—and on top of the cloth, every day, she would place a tomato.[16]

Like everyone else in the city, Akiko Takakura, the shock-cocooned Geibi Bank clerk, did not know about gamma rays, neutron spray, or relativistic heavy ions. She could not define what was happening to her body, but what she wished she did not know now was a thirst she had never known before. She and her friend Asami had filled air-raid helmets with water from a ruptured pipe, but still their thirst intensified.

They were the only two souls inside the building's main gallery when the flash came, because by convention the cleaning chores were assigned exclusively to the female bank clerks and they were obligated to arrive a half-hour ahead of the managers and the customers. At 8:15, almost everyone else had been outside.

During the first minute after the flash, the air inside the bank had become unbearably hot. Akiko decided that it would be dangerous to stay indoors and any other location, in any direction, must be safer. As it turned out, Asami's back was more badly injured than either of them had initially supposed; so it was not until 8:25—ten minutes past Moment Zero—that they were able to emerge into open air and see what happened. Then, of course, they wished they couldn't see at all.

The sun was gone. In the red glare of a fire whirlpool that appeared to be dancing itself out over the graves of buildings already reduced to flaming

During the first minute after Moment Zero, on ground that had been heated instantly to several times the boiling point of water, fire worms began rising like summoned spirits, from the graves of buildings already destroyed by the bomb. Here, at Hiroshima's Water Works, 550 meters (nearly 6 blocks) from the hypocenter, the steel-frame building was kicked sideways and instantly stripped of its cladding. There were no survivors. [Illustration: CRP]

rubble, Akiko could see that the street was full of people turned to charcoal and piles of burning wax. At first glance the street had simply looked empty, but when she looked again it was easy to see how people who had been walking toward the bank were doubled up dead over one another, as far as she could peer through the smoke and the flames. Several of the bodies seemed to have flaked apart, like sacks of burned leaves spilled onto the ground. The red tornadoes—or fire worms—scattered the black leaf piles impartially, and the words "city of death" came quickly to mind.[17]

Akiko was among the first survivors to conclude that everything she saw had been wrought by a single, overpowering explosion. One of the people who had been sitting on the steps of the bank was still sitting there, converted mostly to carbonized flesh yet, like Akiko, this person was somehow untouched by the blast. Not very far away, the body of a man still standing appeared to have been flash-fossilized while pulling a large, two-wheel cart in which two charcoal-crusted children sat, holding their knees. Stunned, and trying to comprehend, Akiko crouched near something that had remained soft and fleshy. Its fingers were burning. Some sort of oil was being brought to the fingertips from the tissues below, and the five fingers burned like candles.[18] She found it difficult to believe that fingers could burn like this—fingers that must once have held babies or turned pages. Akiko burst into tears, and then it began to rain.[19]

For several minutes the two friends had forgotten about their thirst and were able to keep it at bay, but now the strange fever had returned and seemed to be calling back payment of their borrowed time with interest—which was why they began to drink the rain.

Some of the raindrops were as large as grapes—so large and falling with such force that they stung when they pounded down on Akiko's face. But she and Asami turned their faces toward the sky and drank the rain anyway, opening their mouths as wide as possible.

When she looked down at her arms, Akiko realized that the water was staining her skin black. The rain was as dark and repulsive as crude oil, but the two young women's thirst was so great that they continued to drink.

The bomb had vaporized river water and pond water all across Hiroshima. Out to a radius of two kilometers, every leaf gave up a substantial portion of its moisture—as did every bird and cricket caught out in the open, every blade of grass, every soldier, and every child. All the accumulated vapors of the city were hoisted up through the basement layers of the stratosphere, where they cooled and condensed, and began to fall.

The rain was black because it had coalesced around the stratospheric soot of Hiroshima and around the fission products of the cloud itself. Even with half-lives that lasted only a few minutes, any mouthfuls of black rain ingested between 8:30 and 8:45 that morning were capable of delivering, during the next seven hours, at least half the DNA-scattering dose necessary to kill.

Akiko's body was evidently more resilient than her friend's. Asami succumbed quickly, but in 2005, Akiko tried to keep a faith with the dead by keeping her friend's memory alive.

"She was a year younger than me," Akiko said. "I am nearly eighty years old now. She was only eighteen. Whenever I think of her, she is still eighteen years old. She was a very pretty, very gentle person."[20]

Like Akiko, most people believed that anyplace except where they happened to be when the sky opened up had to be safer. From his post atop the weather station, Isao Kita arrived at the same conclusion as Akiko Takakura: a single stupendous explosive was the only explanation that made sense. Unlike Akiko, or anyone else below, Kita had a clear overview of what was happening on the ground. He was able to observe through binoculars how thousands of survivors on his side of the smoke and black rain, though reasonably safe, had begun a disorderly migration in random directions. Only gradually did they start to form strange, ant-like caravans zigzagging away from the fires and the darkness in the north.[21]

Two of the wanderers, walking within Mr. Kita's ant trails, were a watchmaker and a surviving physician named Michihiko Hachiya. The watchmaker had merged, machine-like, into the first trail of survivors who seemed to him to be showing any signs of organization. They were moving in one direction over a mound of yellow dust and broken roof tiles, so the watchmaker was taken more or less automatically into the movement and went along with them. The phrase he would use later was *muga-muchu*, which translated literally to "without self, like being in a dream." He felt that he could no longer make a decision on his own, so he followed the other people, losing himself in a hive mentality and being carried away by it.[22]

Dr. Hachiya was completely naked when he fell in line. His clothes had been blown off before he entered the same dream-like shock-state as the watchmaker and the rest of the ant-walkers, and he only half-realized that there was something remotely disturbing about the sudden desertion of his usual sense of modesty. Later, he would explain, "Those who were able walked silently toward the hills, their sprits broken their initiative gone. When asked where they had come from, they pointed to the city and said 'That way.' And when asked where they were going, pointed away from the city and said, 'This way.' They were so broken and confused that they—[we]—moved and behaved like automatons. Our reactions [would] astonish outsiders who reported with amazement the spectacle of long files of people holding stolidly to a narrow, rough path [over hills of jagged debris] when close by there was a smooth, easy road [to travel], going in the same direction. The outsiders could not grasp the fact that they were witnessing the exodus of a people who walked in the realm of dreams."[23]

In this strange shock realm some of the survivors traded panic for an illusion of control by latching onto what became known (to those who studied survivors of the *Titanic*, the *Yorktown*, and other disasters) as the Edith Russell Response: the tendency to focus on absurd details in the midst of horror or grave danger. One of the city's youngest military officers, who was normally stationed deep within Ground Zero, had been sent away on the morning of August 6 to a small town ten kilometers outside of Hiroshima. After receiving confirmation that all radio and telephone contact with Hiroshima had ceased, he packed his gear and headed back in the direction of the city.

The first flash-burn victim he encountered did not seem to be human. There was no face, only a swollen mass of charcoal above his shoulders that displayed an alligator-skin pattern reminiscent of burned wood. As he moved closer to the city, the young officer encountered more creatures with the same burned-wood faces.

After more than an hour, he stopped, not knowing which road to take. The fire and the smoke and the charcoal people brought him to the point of bolting randomly in any direction, but a sudden thought about the military code book stopped his panic dead, and brought the young man back to self-control. He assigned himself the task of finding and securing the code book. As he walked, he firmed his resolve to recover the book and keep it away from the enemy even if nothing remained of it except flakes of blackened paper.

The officer walked past many ant trails along the outer-blast perimeter. Though his canteen was full, he ignored the ant people's pleas for water. He had to find the code book. Nothing else mattered. He quickened his pace as best he could, increasingly worried that when he finally arrived at the army camp, he would be severely reprimanded by his senior officers for having taken so long to return. When he arrived at his camp, however, there was no one left alive. Tents and buildings had either disappeared or been hammered flatly into the earth. Only the sturdier supply warehouses were recognizable.

A rectilinear depression in the ground led him to a flattened cabinet and, ultimately, to the ashes of the code book. The officer wrapped the book covers and the burned pages in a length of cloth he had torn and folded specifically for the recovery of documents. He then jogged away from the city, heading several kilometers upriver to military headquarters where, to his utter surprise, a senior officer reprimanded him for having obsessed on such an irrelevant detail as the disintegrated code book.[24]

Meanwhile, inside one of the supply warehouses the obsessed officer had passed, Private Shigeru Shimoyama finally managed to pry himself free from the five protruding nails that held his arms to a thick crossbeam. Somehow, through the explosion and through a process of de-crucifixion that had spattered blood in his eyes, Shigeru's glasses remained intact on his face. When he stepped out into daylight and thick swirling clouds of dust, the private realized that the glasses were not needed. In the manner of the physician who saw a music box on the ground and his glasses lying nearby, and who was unable to see as clearly after he picked up his glasses and put them on, Shigeru's vision had improved enormously. Whatever force descended upon the city had simultaneously corrected his eyesight.

Across an artificial lake, Private Shimoyama observed, between gusts of smoke, that only a short distance away, near the outer fringe of the central "flat zone," Hiroshima Castle had burst apart. From that direction, a bureaucrat named Yasuda and four other men from the General Affairs Office were struggling toward him between burning piles of debris, holding high over their heads a life-size portrait of the Emperor. A second commotion drew Shigeru's attention to the river, where a naval boat was plying its way upstream through a field of shattered houses and floating bodies. The private watched, spellbound, as the boat slowed to a complete stop so that the crew could salute the Emperor's portrait. At the sight of this, even some of the burned and bleeding ant people seemed to become suddenly aware, and to stop following the people walking ahead of them. They saluted and bowed, and clasped their hands in prayer and wept. Dozens broke from their lines and joined the effort to rescue the painting, as smoldering telephone poles on either side of them ignited at random intervals into torches. The Edith Russell response and culture lag—these were powerful distractions.

By now, Shigeru had seen enough. He was in possession of better information than the Sasakis and the Itos, than Akiko Takakura, Isao Kita, and the ant people.

Someone has been smashing atoms today, he concluded.

Shigeru's brother-in-law had informed him as early as 1943 that such bombs could be built, at least in theory. According to "the Professor," Yoshio Nishina, there was no reason to fear an actual race with the Americans or the British in developing a nuclear weapon because the electrical output of an entire country might not even be enough to refine the necessary few kilograms of rare neutron-emitting metals. Nishina and other Tokyo scientists believed that an atomic bomb could be built if only Japan could obtain a pomegranate's volume of 90 percent pure uranium-235; but because they also believed that refining such material was technologically premature by about fifty years, they saw no point to investing everything they had in a race toward development of the bomb.

All well and good, thought Shigeru, *so long as Nishina's fifty-year figure was not off by a multiple of ten, and so long as the Americans had not bolted out of the starting gate five years ago.*

Only one grim chain of certainties obsessed private Shigeru: *We were in a race all along and didn't know it. And we lost—which means that there can be many more of these things waiting to be dropped and I must get out of Hiroshima and return home to see my daughter one last time.*[25]

Two others who thought of departing for another city were teenager Misako Katani and her father. After the blast, strange whirlwinds of fire had come from the direction of the Geibi and Sumitomo Banks and now stood between them and the wreckage of their house. As they watched, the flames spread like a tsunami over an area that surely included home, then spilled across a firebreak and overflowed the army stables.

"They're not home," Mr. Katani said. There was no emotion in his voice, no life. "They're gone." He was talking about Misako's mother and little sister, but all the younger Katani could think about were the screams of the horses as they broke free of the stables and ran toward her with flames leaping from their backs. They did not run very far; they fell and died and sent forth a strange-colored smoke.

Katini's father grabbed her by the hand and seemed to be running in no particular direction, except away from the flames.

"Where are we going?" Misako asked.

"Away from here," he said flatly. "I have relatives in a town three hundred K from here. Anyplace far away must be safer than Hiroshima. We must go to Nagasaki."[26]

Within the first twenty minutes, over vast areas of Hiroshima, the fire worms had begun merging into actual tornadoes that sent decks of corrugated metal cards flying with decapitating force and tore burning trolley cars from their track beds—while, behind them, nests of newborn fire worms rose from the ruins, like summoned spirits. Near the Misasa Bridge, the sky was a black firmament, illuminated only by the worms. Fire now raged everywhere, sending Sumiko Kirihara's and little Sadako Sasaki's families fleeing toward the river.

Two of the fire worms actually followed them down to the river's edge, their approaching glare so intense that Sumiko's family had no choice but to run into the water. The surface was glutted with drifting wreckage. Entire neighborhoods of houses appeared to have been charred and mauled, then scattered in pieces over the river. On both banks, fire worms, rearing up and swirling more than five stories tall, seemed to take deliberate pause, as if surveying the scene, before deciding what action to take. Then one of the burning whirlwinds struck the water, converting at once from a column of fire to a column of foam and rushing droplets—dashing a naval boat about and pausing threateningly near the place where Sumiko was wading.

Next, from the opposite bank, one fire worm followed another into the river, one after another turning into a waterspout before crossing over and drawing up new fire from the ruins. Nearby, eighteen-year-old Hiroko Fukada tried to out-swim one of the spouts but she was overrun by it and battered by drifts of wood, and spun about. Then, as the waterspout passed, huge chunks of black hail began to fall with bone-chipping force and Hiroko ducked beneath the water for shelter.

Surrounded by whirlwinds of fire and water—and by falling black ice—Sumiko Kirihara wiggled free from her mother's grasp, ran out of the river, dug a shallow hole in the mud, and tried to crawl into it. At least two waterspouts followed her out of the river, raising clouds of gritty matter that tore her shirt and pelted her back like a volley of little needles fired from a cannon. Finally, her mother grabbed her arm and she fled with the rest of the family to a ridge overlooking the river.

Everyone around them appeared to have been terribly burned. Sumiko would later recall feeling embarrassed about having survived the *pika-don* without injury, but she could easily see that her troubles were far from over. The heat from the landward side was becoming so great that she and her family were forced to reenter the river, where they were obliged to push corpses aside and drink blackened water to quench a scorching thirst that seemed only to intensify with each passing minute.[27]

The waterspouts and the whirlwinds of fire cost Hiroshi Ito—the boy who had climbed out of his wrecked engineering school completely unharmed—the last of his courage. Looking around in panic and trying to find a way out, he lost sight of his classmate Ryuzo. Along the opposite shore, people fleeing from the direction of the Sasaki house were falling into the river like swarms of insects. Riverside houses were also tumbling in—smashed in half with their rooms exposed and most of their furnishings curiously still in place, though in flames. Soon, the people in the water were pursued and overtaken by burning sticks and logs; and as a new picket of fire worms glared down at him, the Ito boy bolted in any random direction, then in another. A waterspout followed, eventually collapsing and blasting something slippery and sandy into his mouth. He spat it into his palm but could not see what he had almost swallowed because another gust of icy black rain overtook him and chased him slipping and stumbling over a pair of railroad tracks, which finally decided his direction.

He believed it likely that his mother might now be walking toward the city, searching for him; but against the black sky, the flames seemed to be strengthening everywhere, and especially in the direction of the school. Hiro-shi Ito knew that his mother was smart enough not to come striding suicidally into this place. As he shook the rainwater from his hair and began following the tracks out of town, black hailstones started to fall, and the Ito boy found it impossible to believe that, less than twenty-five minutes before, the sky had been blue and clear.[28]

Ship designer Tsutomu Yamaguchi, who was somehow spared while a woman in a black mompe disappeared nearby, realized, as the usual sensations of shock passed, that he was in severe pain. Ahead of him, the river offered the coppery scent of recent slaughter, but when Yamaguchi arrived at the river's edge, he filled his canteen and drank the water anyway. He had no choice. The flash burns on his arms and neck had brought dehydration and thirst.

The engineer did not have to look far to understand that he was luckier than most. There were people floating down from the direction of the hypo-center, whose up-raised arms looked twice as long as a normal human being's because the flesh of the shoulders and arms had literally melted and peeled away from the bones and now floated on the surface of the river like broken cobwebs, still connected to people by the tips of their fingers. And there was the discovery of the pierced boys. At first it had seemed to Yamaguchi that their burned and lacerated backs had grown strange mutant hair. Then he real-ized that the great wind had driven sharp blades of glass into their flesh, like nails. He helped them for a while; but all he could advise them to do was to pull out the blades one by one from each other's backs. This turned out to be easier advised than accomplished, because they appeared to be weakening and dying before his eyes. Their thirst, like Yamaguchi's, was more overwhelming than their pain. Even hunger seemed not to matter anymore. The boys simply wandered away, one leading the others—apparently nowhere.

Yamaguchi had no intention of joining the ant-walkers. More sober concerns were driving him. He needed to get home to his wife and child, and home was a long way off. Ordinarily, as a precaution against the unexpected, and especially against the possibility of having to travel far without food or water, he carried a canteen and an emergency ration of two small biscuits. Today, however, ordinary precautions did not seem to matter. After swallowing a bite from one biscuit, the engineer immediately vomited. From then on, he decided, he would only drink water. He did not yet suspect that he might have absorbed radiation.

The bomb had created more abstract injuries than radiation sickness and the pierced boys. "De-gloving" would become a polite, antiseptic term used by physicians to describe what happened when skin, whether or not it had been burned, was exposed to the ring of compressed supersonic air that radiated out from the central shock-cocoon zone of the Geibi Bank through the zone of glass nails. The skin was often pulled off by the wind—pulled off as if it had been bound to the body with all the adhesive quality of a leather glove, and could be stripped away just as easily.[29]

Private Shigeru Shimoyama, having survived the peculiar horror of being nailed to a wooden beam by the bomb, now found a pinkish-white horse standing alone in his path. All of its skin and fur were gone. The sight fascinated more than horrified him, and it horrified him quite a lot. The animal did not appear to be in pain at all, and in fact it tried to follow the soldier as he moved on.

Every time the soldier looked back, the horse—its flesh de-gloved all the way down to layers of pale pink musculature—stared at him pleadingly and made faltering steps in his direction. Like Sumiko Kirihara and the Ito boy, Shigeru began to wonder if the end of the world might look something look this.

Shigeru had been studying to become a Christian, and when he dreamed of the pink horse—as during many a night for the rest of his life he would—he recalled a passage from the Revelation of John:

> *And I heard the voice of the fourth beast say, "Come and see."*
> *And I looked.*
> *And I beheld a pale horse.*
> *And his name that sat upon him was Death.*
> *And hell followed with him.*[30]

· 3 ·

Setsuko

$\mathscr{B}$y comparison with Hiroshima, the explosive detonations of Vesuvius or Krakatau were relatively gentle upheavals, long and drawn out, releasing their energy over many, many seconds. Because the core of the atomic bomb was much more compact, its energy was released in one small part of a lightning bolt's life span, within a cauldron measured in cubic centimeters of metal, instead of across several dozen cubic kilometers of explosive, gas-saturated magma.

And yet, for all its fury, the Hiroshima bomb had not lived up to its designers' specifications. Though the Truman Administration and the media would officially list it together with the first atomic test in the New Mexico desert, and with the Nagasaki bomb, in the 20–30 kiloton range, it was in fact a 10–12.5 kiloton "disappointment." The design would never be used again. Some engineers and scientists would even go so far as to call it a "dud," but humanity would be forever haunted by the power of a bomb that merely "fizzled," like a damp firecracker.[1]

At a quarter-past eight, near the center of a pomegranate's volume of compressing uranium, the vast majority of the bomb's energy had radiated from a spark scarcely wider than the tip of young Setsuko Hirata's index finger. By the time the golden white plasma sphere had spread eighty meters wide—still within only one small part of a lightning bolt's life span—the spark had generated a short-lived but very intense magnetic field. Where the bomb had been, the metal rod and tamper system that ran down its center from nose to fin produced a cluster of dense metallic nuclei—stripped of their electrons, positively charged, and magnetically confined within forces that were trying to blow them apart at nearly the speed of light. The minds that conceived the bomb had accidentally created, for an instant, a predecessor to Brookhaven

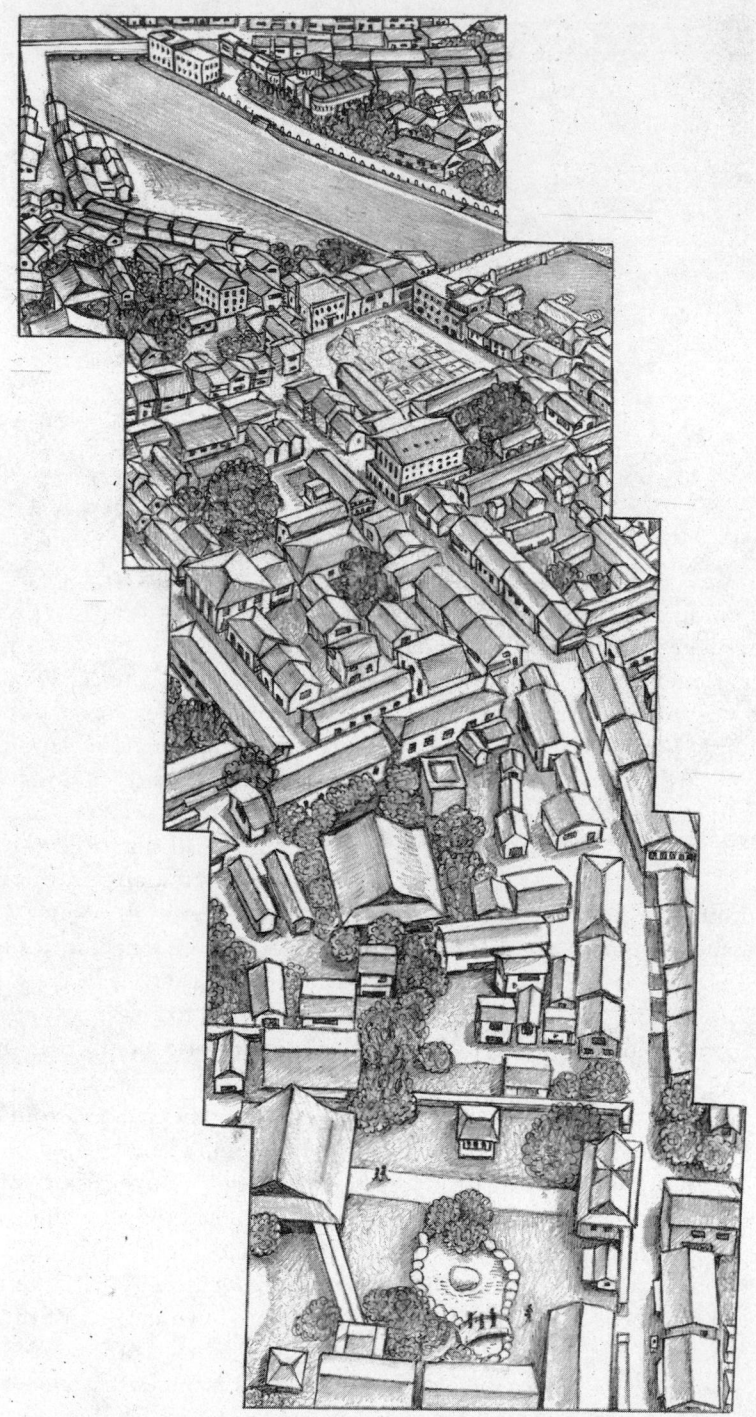

Before and after *views of Hiroshima [this page and facing page], looking from a circular fishpond (approximately 500 meters from the hypocenter), toward the T-Bridge and the Dome. Setsuko Hirata was located in a house in the vicinity of the pond. [Illustrations: Patricia Wynne]*

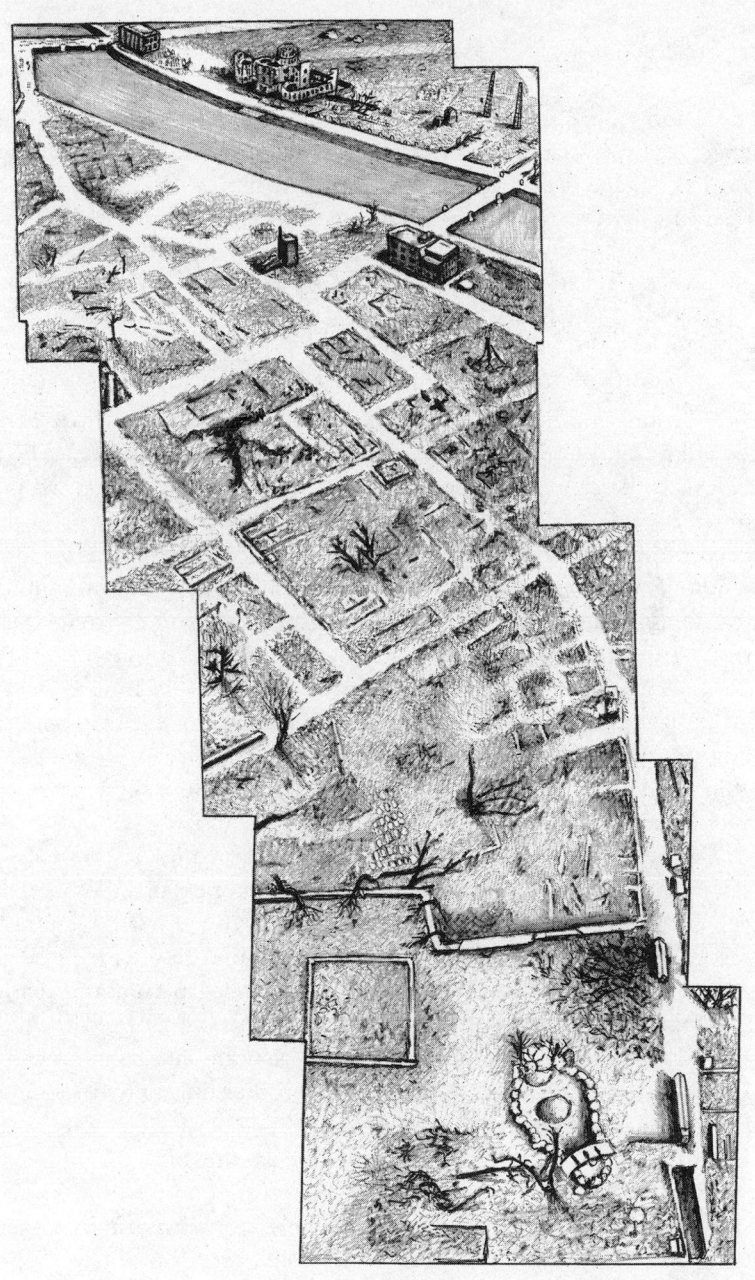

National Laboratory's relativistic heavy-ion collider. The bomb was an atomic accelerator whose magnetic shotgun barrels were aimed straight up and straight down. One stream of iron and tungsten nuclei went to the stars at up to 90 percent light speed, passing the orbit of the moon about a second and a half later. The other stream followed magnetic field lines to the ground. Both streams produced "strays" that arched along field lines almost twelve miles away, brushing through the planes that had delivered the bomb.

Setsuko Hirata was seated in her living room, slightly to the south and almost directly beneath the magnetic shotgun. Fast neutrons and heavy ions came down through tiles and roof beams and either stopped inside her body or kept going until stopped by the first hundred meters of sand and bedrock. Neutrinos also descended through the roof. Born of the so-called weak force, their interactions with the world were so weak as to be utterly ghostly. Almost every one of them that encountered Setsuko continued through the floor without noticing her, then traveled with the same quantum indifference through the Earth itself. The very same neutrinos that passed through Setsuko, drawing a straight line between her and the bomb, and through nearly 5,000 miles of rock, emerged through the floor of the southern Indian Ocean and sprayed up toward interstellar space. Setsuko's neutrino stream would still be traveling beyond the stars of Centaurus, beyond the far rim of the galaxy itself—still telling her story (as it were), long after the tallest skyscrapers and the Pyramids had turned to lime.

When Setsuko's neutrino spray erupted unseen, near the French islands of Amsterdam and St. Paul, not quite 22 milliseconds after detonation, she was still alive. Ceramic roof tiles, three meters above her head, were just then beginning to catch the infra-red maximum from the flash—which peaked 150 milliseconds after the first atoms of uranium-235 began to come apart. The tiles threw a small fraction of the rays back into the sky, but in the end, they provided Setsuko with barely more protection than the silk nightgown her beloved Kenshi had bought her only a few days earlier during their honeymoon at the Gardens of Miyajima.

Overhead, along the lower hemisphere of the blue-to-gold to blue-again globe that expanded from the place where the bomb had been, droplets of moisture had dissolved into a scatter of electron-stripped hydrogen and oxygen nuclei. A very small number of those hydrogen nuclei were smashed together and fused, and collectively an amount of mass not quite equal to a fleck of the finest-grained beach sand disappeared from the universe, adding a little kick of fusion to the fission power that burst down toward Setsuko. The instantaneous transformation of matter into energy produced a light so intense that if Setsuko were looking straight up she would have seen the hemisphere shining through the single layer of roof tiles and wooden planks as if it were an electric torch shining through the bones of her fingers in a darkened room. And within those first two-tenths of a second, she might have had time enough to become aware of an electronic buzzing in her ears, and a tingling sensation throughout her bones, and a feeling that she was being lifted out of her chair, or pressed into it more firmly, or both at the same instant—and the growing sphere in the sky . . . she might even have had time enough to perceive, if not actually watch, its expanding dimensions.

Setsuko's husband, Kenshi, had been working as an accountant at the Mitsubishi Weapons Plant, slightly more than four kilometers away, when through a window came the most beautiful golden lightning flash he had ever seen, or imagined he would ever see. Simultaneously there was a strange buzzing in his ears, a sizzling sound, and a woman's voice crying out in his brain. He would suppose years later that maybe it was his grandmother's spirit—or more likely Setsuko's. The voice cried, "Get under cover!"

With all the speed of instinctive reflex, he dropped the papers he was carrying, dove to the floor, and buried his face in his arms. But three long seconds later when the expected shockwave had not arrived, he was left in adrenalized overdrive—with time to pray.

Outside his Mitsubishi office, in utter silence, a giant red flower billowed over the city, rising on a stem of yellow-white dust.

Kenshi's prayers seemed to have been answered—yet again. He had walked away from the fire-bombing of Kobe without a single blister or bruise, initially thinking himself a bit unlucky because he should never have been there in the first place; and Kenshi *would* never have been there, had he not finished his work in Osaka a day early and departed for Kobe ahead of schedule. Two nights after surviving Kobe, he learned that Osaka, too, had been heavily bombed. Indeed the very same hotel in which he should have been sleeping took a direct hit, with no survivors. At Hiroshima, Kenshi owed his survival to an instinct to obey an inner voice, and to the fact that the bomb had disappointed its creators, yielding a blast wave that was all but fractionally spent by the time it reached him. Kenshi's next instinct did not serve him so well as his obedience to the voice. When he dropped to the floor, his initial impression was that a number of huge incendiary bombs were exploding right on top of the building and that he would be cremated even before he could finish the first lines of a prayer. But nearly five full seconds followed the flash, and the light itself began to fade without a hint of concussion—*The bombs have not struck the building*—

The multiple bombing-raid escapee raised his head to see what was happening around him. A young woman nearby had crept to a window and peeked outside. Whatever she saw in the direction of the city, Kenshi would never know. She stood up, uttered something guttural and incomprehensible, and then the blast wave—lagging far behind the bomb's light waves—caught up with her. By the time the windowpanes traveled a half-meter, they had separated completely from their protective cross-hatched net of air-raid tape, emerging as thousands of tiny shards. Like the individual pellets of a shotgun blast, each shard had been accelerated to more than half the speed of sound. The girl at the window took at least a quarter-kilogram of glass in her face and her chest before the wind jetted her toward the far wall.

Kenshi did not see where she eventually landed. Simultaneous with the window blast, the very floor of the building had come off its foundation and bucked him more than a half-meter into the air. He landed on his back, and when he stood up he discovered to his relief that he was completely unharmed, then discovered, to his horror, that he was the only one so spared. All of his fellow workers—all of them—looked as if they had crawled out of a blood pool.

We must have taken a direct hit after all, Kenshi guessed. He did not realize the full magnitude of the attack until he stepped outside. In the distance, toward home, the head of the flower was no longer silent. It had been rumbling up there in the heavens for more than a minute, at least seven or ten kilometers high now, and it had dulled from brilliant red to dirty brown, almost to black. As he watched, the flower broke free from its stem and a smaller black bud bloomed in its place. It was, a fellow survivor would recall, like a decapitated dragon growing a new head.

A whisper escaped Kenshi's lips: "Setsuko . . ."[2]

Being immersed in death, Father M. ("Mattias") would recall, could be as bad as being counted among the dead. At the presbytery of the only Catholic church in the city, 1.3 kilometers east of the hypocenter, he, Father Hubert Cieslik, and Father Lassalle had heard two planes moving overhead, revving their engines to full throttle and diving, as if trying to escape something. Overlooking a garden patio, the young Novitist who would become Fr. Mattias saw two parachutes drifting overhead and the otherwise empty sky suddenly strobed blue, then yellow—and then the ceiling dropped.

Mattias did not know what happened after that. His memory seemed to be recording only disjointed pieces. His first clear recollection was of walking toward the river; but time was playing tricks on him. All the usual reference points—the church and every other landmark—were lost to him. Some time ago—

A minute? An hour?—he had joined hundreds of other dazed, half-naked people and become one of the ant-walkers. The skin of the man in front of him flapped loosely from his back, like pieces of a tattered shirt; and all of the flesh on his forearm had been pulled off. The priest related twenty-nine years later how he followed the walking corpse aimlessly until it—and the scarecrow in front of it—bumped headlong into the frame of a charred and smoldering streetcar. When Mattias peered inside, he saw that the passengers' clothing and skin had been stripped off. Only one of them stirred: an unborn baby still struggling inside its dead mother.

He stumbled away, leaving the man who had led him to the streetcar gaping and swallowing on the ground, like a fish on dry land. Mattias did not know where he was going, but more than a dozen people fell in line behind him anyway, and began to follow.[3]

Another who walked in a state of shock was, compared to the rest of the population, only mildly burned. He was a fourteen-year-old named Akihiro Takahashi. The boy followed streetcar tracks past wrecked, corpse-filled trolleys, until he heard a friend calling his name. Then he veered off in the direction of his friend, and a new ant trail began to form behind them.

The friend whose call the boy had followed was already so severely penetrated by radiation that his teeth would soon be falling out. Akihiro would hear later that, "Before he died, his belly turned purple and he vomited up a continuous stream of some blue-gray substance." The fourteen-year-old encountered a woman with an eyeball dangling on her cheek, and a horse with its skin blasted away to expose raw, blood-drenched muscle, lying dead with its head in a concrete, water-filled cistern.

Coming out of his daze, the boy became increasingly aware of people following him; but most of them did not look like people anymore and they were pressing uncomfortably close. *How is this possible on Earth?* he thought, quickening his pace toward the nearest river, trying to leave the ant-walkers behind. Ahead, the smoke and the dust parted, as if to taunt him with the realization that there was no escaping what he had walked away from at the blackened trolley cars. Next to a mother whose body had been completely de-gloved lay a screaming infant, its entire skin surface either converted to or covered by a thin veneer of charcoal. This was not the last or even the worst horror Akihiro passed in his search for home. There were others for which descriptive words had not yet been invented. Only an hour earlier, it seemed, Akihiro had been standing in a sunny schoolyard watching a B-29 making a strange acrobatic swerve miles overhead, as if it were about to crash. And then, at a radius of 1.4 kilometers from the target area, blistering heat consumed the school and a crypt-like darkness descended. For the fourteen-year-old, the margin between life and death was determined by a shadow-casting tree that had allowed an arm to be seared and air-blasted but had otherwise shielded his body from the flash.

More than twenty-five years later, the boy would be seated at a bus station in Washington, D.C., with an American chaperone and Paul Tibbets, the pilot of the plane that dropped the bomb; and Akihiro would listen to another survivor telling Tibbets how from the presbytery he had heard the plane's engines straining to get away from the bomb on this sunny August morning. Akihiro sat in silence for a very long time, knowing about Tibbets's reputation—about a willingness to reenact the bombing at air shows, and even to joke about his role in history by eating from birthday cakes shaped like mushroom clouds. Nervously, Akihiro told Tibbets that though it was amazing to wonder how a man could be close enough to have heard *Enola Gay*'s engines and to have survived, he had actually *spotted* Tibbets's airplane. And Tibbets remarked, "Yes, I could see all of Hiroshima below me."

Akihiro pushed his badly healed and partly de-gloved hand toward Tibbets, and the pilot asked, "Is this the effect of the A-bomb?"

"Yes," Akihiro replied, and it seemed to him that Tibbets looked surprised and shocked, but he gently took hold of Akihiro's hand, and the survivor said, "We must overcome the pain, sorrow, and hatred of the past—and [we must] work together to make sure that people never experience this again."

"I understand," Tibbets said, adding the inevitable *but*: "I would have to do the same thing, under the same circumstances; because once war breaks out, soldiers can do nothing but follow orders." He closed both of his hands around Akihiro's scars and said, unexpectedly and with clear sincerity, "We should never let war happen again."

Akihiro said later to one of the other survivors that he believed Tibbets felt some pain and remorse in his heart. But the friend replied, "I doubt it."

Whether his perception of Tibbets was real or not, Akihiro came away from the meeting with a sense of inner peace. Later, he wrote, "Among humankind's abilities, it is said imagination is the weakest and forgetfulness the strongest. We cannot by any means, however, forget Hiroshima, and we cannot lose the ability to abolish war. Hiroshima is not just a historical fact. It is a warning and a lesson for the future."

For Akihiro Takahashi, there was resolution and a hope for the future. For the priest who had followed the same sets of tracks past incinerated rail cars, there was neither resolution nor hope, forever. Till his last breath, he would remain a man trapped by his past, in August 1945.[4]

Far beyond the streetcar and Akihiro's ant trail, the corner wall of what appeared to have been a brick apartment house—all that remained of the building—had towered three stories above Father Mattias's head. Three children clung to the top of the tower, screaming. They were naked, and it registered somewhere in the back of the young man's mind that one of them seemed to be bleeding from his entire body.

At first grateful that he had been spared, once the unreality of the walking numb-state succumbed to clarities born of atrocity, he began slowly, surely to blame himself for having survived. As he reached the river and the first rescue boats began plucking corpses out of the water and as he waded into the water himself and watched a woman carrying her child toward him—pleading with the infant to open his eyes—barely noticing that as she stepped into the water her own skin and musculature began to fall away from the bones, the merciful numb-state began to crack. And he was touched by merciless guilt.

That's when he began thinking, truly thinking for the first time, about the three children he had seen at the brick tower. There were no familiar landmarks pointing the way back, and the fire worms had begun gathering themselves together into roving walls of flame. And he would wonder, every day for the rest of his life, whatever happened to the children at the tower. Each night, they would become the very last thing he thought about before he fell asleep. And he would dream about them. And they would be the first image that came to mind when he awoke.[5]

As Kenshi made his way toward the center of the city in search of his wife, the streets and fields sprouted what seemed to be thousands of tiny flickering lamps. He could not determine what the lamps might actually be. Neither could any of the scientists who would hear of this later. Each jet of flame was about the size and shape of a doughnut. Kenshi knew that he could easily have extinguished any "ground candles" in his path merely by stepping on them; but he was "spooked" by an instinctive sense that it might somehow be dangerous to touch the fiery doughnuts, so he stepped around them instead.[6] He thought of Setsuko. He passed men and women whose backs had been seared by the flash, but it was not the flash-burns that caught his attention and stuck in his memory. The people appeared to be growing strange vegetation out of their roasted flesh. It occurred to Kenshi only much later that thousands of glass slivers must have been pulled from the windows of every building and driven through the air like spear points. He thought of Setsuko. Limping, the young accountant circumnavigated a giant column of flame in which steel beams could be seen melting. He thought of Setsuko. Nearer the hypocenter, not very far from the city's Municipal Office, he passed over a warm road surface upon which a great fire must have risen, then inexplicably died. All of the people simply disappeared here, and all of the wooden houses, on either side of the road, were reduced to grayish-white ash. He thought of Setsuko. The main street leading toward home and the famous "T"-shaped bridge seemed more like a field than a road. In the middle of the field, he found two blackened streetcars. Their ceilings and windows had vanished, and they were filled with lumps of charcoal that turned out to be passengers carbonized in their seats. The trolleys had apparently stopped on either side of the street to pick up more passengers, and two people were about to ascend the steps of one vehicle when the heat descended, and caught them, and converted them into bales of coal with shirt buttons and teeth. In every direction, Kenshi saw pieces of people, and horses, and oxen, looking like charcoal. He thought of Setsuko, now blaming himself for their ill-omened honeymoon excursion, nearly two weeks earlier, to the Shrine Island of Miyajima.

There was a strange taboo in connection with the Miyajima Shrine. It had been dedicated to a goddess who was believed by the older generations to become jealous if a newly married husband and wife climbed the sacred steps together. If the taboo was violated, the old people said, the wife would shortly die. But Kenshi's friend, a local innkeeper who had arranged honeymoon lodgings for them near the island's gardens, had scoffed at this and said it was pure superstition. Since they had come all the way to Miyajima together, he advised, surely they should go at once to the famous shrine. So they did. And now, during the journey from his office into the heart of Ground Zero, Kenshi repented of it many times.[7]

Yosaku Mikami had missed his streetcar by only a few seconds, so he had to wait for another one, and he was therefore running nearly a quarter-hour behind his normal schedule when the next streetcar carried him by chance under the protection of a shadow-shielding effect from the train office and other structures near the Miyuki Bridge, rendering him one of the few surviving firefighters in all of Hiroshima.

Many of the buildings around Yosaku were made primarily out of wood. At a radius of 1.9 kilometers, the shockwaves pulled them apart; but they held together just long enough to keep the streetcar hidden in their shadows, as if within the protection of a valley or tunnel, through the duration of what Yosaku recalled as a blue flash. As the flash began to fade, and as the buildings flew apart, a blast of black smoke filled the rail car, carrying with it an odor that instantly pervaded the city, across a diameter of nearly three miles and on all sides of the hypocenter. It was partly the scent of flash-burned wood and leaves, partly an acrid metallic smell, and partly a dreadful stench already familiar to most firefighters. Yosaku and the minority of firemen near central

Hiroshima who were still able to move and breathe after the first five seconds understood at once exactly what they were inhaling. The odor that human flesh emitted when it was burned happened to be quite similar to the smell of squid when it was grilled over hot coals—and so, as Yosaku ran toward the place where his fire house had been, he was breathing in the smoke of people, tens of thousands of people.

During what seemed to be several minutes after the blue flash (though in an adrenalized state of mind it became difficult to determine spans of time), Yosaku saw a fire truck maneuvering around piles of rubble toward one of the main roads. Uninjured, he jumped aboard and joined colleagues who drove him to a main fire station where, in a manner consistent with the tradition of firemen spontaneously migrating from outlying regions into a destroyed region, they found a half dozen other firefighters already gathered. There did not seem to be much that they could accomplish, with only one truck known to be operating and all of the city's water pressure knocked out. They were located near the two-kilometer radius, and anything much nearer the center of the city appeared to be enveloped in a constantly expanding maelstrom of smoke and chaos. There was no point in moving nearer the center. More lives could be saved by finding survivors who were still able to walk and to lead them farther away.

In a house at Yosaku's radius from the hypocenter, the piano that seventeen-year-old Misako's father bought for her in 1932 would ultimately be saved for future generations by the child of another Hiroshima firefighter, named Mitsunori. Young Misako's piano had been shrapnel-studded along one side by more than a hundred pieces of speed-slung glass. And yet what historians would later call "the *hibakusha* piano" was, except for the embedded glass, safely cocooned in an air pocket, while the rest of the house imploded. Misako, who had played the instrument from the age of four, survived by having been sent away from central Hiroshima, to a munitions factory work detail. She never did play the instrument again, after that day. For a long time, a part of her believed that no one should ever play it again.

Throughout the coming decades, the black stand-up piano would set out on a convergent course with the family of a Hiroshima fireman who had been located within less than half of Firefighter Yosaku's radius.

Much like the piano, Firefighter Mitsunori was shock-cocooned, while most of the building in which he had been standing disappeared around him. In years to come, Mitsunori would tell his story of the shock-cocoon and fire worms to his yet-to-be-born son, Yagawa—who did not arrive until seven years after the war.

Yagawa would always remember the expressions of bitterness and pain—and even remorse that creased his father's face when he spoke of having emerged from a steel and concrete stairwell into a fire station that no longer existed, and how he beheld an instantly changed landscape whose sky was becoming full of worms. The story seemed unreal and even irrelevant to the boy, like something that must have occurred in a distant country, and long ago. After he came of age during Japan's economic surge of the 1960s, Mitsunori's son would look back from the second decade of the next century and say, "My youth, compared to my father's, was extremely fortunate. That's why I did not understand. I realized later that I took peace for granted—just like the inexhaustible supply of electricity, and water, and never having experienced anything like the war-time rationing of food."

The younger Mitsunori grew up to become a musician and restorer of old instruments; but the son of a shock-cocooned fireman came to his own sense of understanding and remorse after Misako, who had followed through with her vow never to hear the piano played again after Hiroshima, contacted him in her seventy-eighth year, pleading with him to take care of her shock-cocooned relic.

"I wonder what will happen to my piano when something happens to me," she said, hoping that the memory of its place in history would not die with her. "That has been my concern," she emphasized, before passing the instrument down to the fireman's son. "I fear that it could be thrown away as just another old piano."

As he repaired two deteriorating strings and re-tuned them, Yagawa Mitsunori came to wish that he had listened more closely to his father's story, had tried to understand while he was still alive.

During his long and careful repair, Yagawa was surprised to discover that the piano, well-kept in a ventilated room but silenced by its owner since 1945, could produce so deep and powerful a sound. "A miracle piano," he called it. "Listening to its sound, I thought it was a piano that was inevitably left for a purpose."

In 2010, he would bring the piano to Lower Manhattan, partly to honor the 343 firefighters who had died nearby (in the World Trade Center), and partly to provide background music for a floating lantern ceremony. Trains of flickering paper lanterns on the Hudson, most of them inscribed with personal messages to the future, were part of a Buddhist tradition imported to New York by a handful of monks on September 11, 2002. By 2010, the 9/11 floating lantern ceremony was attended by uncounted hundreds of people. On a small plywood outdoor stage, the *hibakusha* piano's tones became the backdrop against which a rabbi, an imam, and a Catholic priest spoke together about hope, while the Sikhs brought food for everyone in attendance.

"Before I worked on this piano," Yagawa would tell one of the first 9/11 families to attend the lantern ceremony, "I had no interest in peace movements. I did not think I would change this much. Music has nothing to do with religion, ideology, or national borders. I hope that through this piano, many people will begin to think." Yagawa really did not hold onto any great hope that music from a glass-scarred, slightly radioactive Hiroshima piano would bring enough people to believe that the concept of "limited nuclear war" could only lead to the full-scale death of civilization and must be put aside; but impossible hurdles would not discourage him from trying.

While repairing the piano, Firefighter Mitsunori's son thought often about him. The musician could not help feeling that the instrument had come to his studio with a piece of his father's soul in its deep tones, along with a piece of the old woman's soul.

On that sunny 1945 morning transformed into a sky full of worms, Firefighter Mitsunori climbed out of a stairwell only 800 meters from the hypocenter. Although a thick shell of steel and concrete had shadow-shielded him from the flash, had absorbed most of the outdoor gamma-shine and neutron spray that reached twice the usual lethal human dose, and had shock-cocooned him from the blast, the firefighter was all but instantly buried alive. He was obliged to worm his way up through brick and concrete rubble, slicked with his own blood and trying his best not to further damage an arm he already knew to be fractured.

What no one understood in 1945 was how poorly evolved human minds were for coping with a catastrophe that manifested in a split second over multiple square miles.

For Dr. Hachiya, for the schoolboy who ran away from the hands clutching at his feet, for the priest-in-training who walked in a daze past three children trapped and bleeding, and for Firefighter Mitsunori, the conscious part of human thought had retreated in a manner only rarely seen during the gradually unfolding approach of a typhoon, or during a fire that begins in one home and spreads over the course of several minutes to its neighbors. Mitsunori's catastrophe was born of micro-time frames that belonged to the cosmos. By the fireman's own account, the conscious part of "self" had moved from the driver's seat to the passenger seat of his brain, ceding control to subconscious, instinctive thought—which acted by snatching up and analyzing every sight and sound, operating so frantically in its search for a means of self-preservation that the reduced-to-observer-status forebrain usually later recalled time itself seeming to have been distorted, along with a sense of somehow standing partly outside of the event, watching it happen to someone else.

Mitsunori could vaguely recall for his son how he became trapped beneath the rubble—and how, if not for at least two men who heard his calls and dug him out of the stairwell, and pulled him to the surface, he probably would not have survived at all. His rescuers could not have known that, having been exposed to the bomb only 800 meters from its hypocenter, and outside of Mitsunori's steel and concrete shell, they probably had only two or three days left to live. The firefighter also recalled, with deep remorse, having clasped his hands together as if in prayer and bowed like an automaton before walking away, still machine-like, from the brick pile of the fire station. Behind Mitsunori were the men who had rescued him, and beneath them were people—some of them undoubtedly fellow firefighters—crying out from under the bricks.

No one else was ever known to have survived in a fire station at the Mitsunori radius. Only photographs of the aftermath would live on. At 800 meters, one photographic set (which was eventually widely published) showed fire trucks half buried in broken concrete and bricks. The positions of the trucks indicated where the station's engine bay had been, though so little else remained that the elder Mitsunori could never be sure that it was the firehouse from which he had escaped. Only the trucks and the building's foundation lines were recognizable, after the firestorm swept through. The foundation lines were no longer straight. Before the storm carbonized him, one firefighter had either been scorched to death by the flash or shot through by flying debris, behind the wheel of the most intact of the station's trucks. The man looked as if he must have been standing near the truck when the flash came, and had jumped into the cab and was about to start the engine so he could fight a fire—but then, of course, he could not.[8]

The streets of Hiroshima were full of intriguing, seemingly impossible juxtapositions between the utterly destroyed and the miraculously unharmed. The roof tiles of Kenshi's home had boiled on one side and were cracked into thousands of tiny chips, and evidently the entire structure was simultaneously roasted and pounded nearly a half-meter into the earth. A few doors away, evidence of a gigantic shock bubble, in which the very atmosphere had recoiled at supersonic speed from the center of the explosion, could be seen in the evidence of the bubble's immediate aftereffect—the "vacuum effect" that had developed behind an outracing shockwave, pulling everything back again toward the center, toward the actual formation point of the mushroom cloud, almost directly overhead. The force of the imploding shock bubble had also pulled air-filled storm sewers up through the pavement. These manifestations only hinted at the forces unleashed when the low-density bubble, its walls shining with the power of plasma and super-compressed air, had spread and cooled to a point at which the press inward by the surrounding atmosphere started to become stronger than the heat and shock pushing away from the uranium storm. At this point, the shock bubble was only about 250 milliseconds old—just a quarter-second past Moment Zero and 400 meters in radius. When the bubble collapsed, less than two-tenths of a second later and nearly twenty blocks wide, the updraft experienced directly below, in Kenshi's neighborhood, was amplified by the almost simultaneous rise of the retreating plasma, which behaved somewhat like a superheated hot-air balloon. As it rose and lost power, it had cooled from a fireball to an ominous black flower head, and had begun to shed debris the way a flower sheds pollen. Bicycles, bits of sidewalk, planks of wood, even half of a grand piano, fell out of the cloud, more than 800 meters away from the hypocenter.

And yet, amid all this havoc, pieces of bone china and jars of jellied fruit lay unbroken upon the ground. Kenshi discovered that trees, although dry roasted and stripped of their leaves, were still standing upright and unbroken in a 30-meter-wide area just outside of his immediate neighborhood. A three-story house, too, appeared to have survived among the stands of upright trees, suffering only a severe shaking and some compression, and a bit of searing. The owners were not there anymore, of course, but not for the reasons Kenshi would have expected.[9]

Morimoto, the master kite-maker who happened to be visiting with two wealthy cousins in that house at Moment Zero, had walked away with only the most minor scrapes and bruises. The triple-tiered roof and the thick expensive wood, combined with the capricious nature of the bomb effects, rendered the house just strong enough to shield three men as they sipped tea on the ground floor. Morimoto and his cousins had simply walked away from the very eye of a nuclear detonation, and walked into the record books as charter members in one of history's most exclusive survivor minorities. The large house, with its broad beams and layers of thick tiles, must have absorbed just enough of the gamma rays, X-rays, and neutron spray to spare their lives—and the near light-speed blasts of heavy nuclei evidently missed the Morimoto house entirely.

Still, as he climbed out of the steaming wood-and-clay pile in which the fire had been miraculously blown out, Morimoto walked into a dusty wilderness with an awareness that he was suddenly very thirsty, and his skin felt as if every square centimeter had just become sunburned. His stomach and his intestines also ached, as if his insides, too, had been sunburned. He felt disoriented and confused, and by now Morimoto was beginning to suspect that even his brain must have been slightly sunburned. And after he stood atop a ridge of wreckage, and looked through breaks in the smoke, his disorientation multiplied. Normally, he would not have been able to see the mountains or the weather station's transmission tower from this location because there were tall buildings in the way. But the obstructions were all gone, now. The city was . . . *flat*. The whole thing. Amid sheets of shifting dust, he could recognize only burning sewing machines, concrete cisterns, blackened bicycles and streetcars, and piles of reddish-black flesh everywhere, a few vaguely in the shapes of human figures, or occasionally in the shapes of horses.

The thirst and the burning sensations intensified quickly, and Morimoto began to vomit—the first signs of gamma ray and neutron dosing, which blended undetectably with a shock state in which an unknowable interval of time had passed before the kite-maker realized that he had wandered off alone and could no longer see his cousins.

More than almost anyone else in the city this day, Morimoto would be able to tell future historians that his troubles were only beginning. He knew that Hiroshima, though overflown by bomber groups on their way to Osaka and other city targets, had been left unharmed. He heard many rumors about why—including the ever popular, "Hiroshima has too many gardens and shrines and is too beautiful to be bombed." But now Morimoto was among the first to conclude correctly that the Americans must have spared Hiroshima for something special—for how else could the designers of a new weapon hope to understand the damage wrought if the city were already carpeted with craters or eradicated by fire-bombs? If there were more of these special bombs to come, then they too would come to those cities intentionally left in pristine condition.

Most of Morimoto's family lived in one such city, Nagasaki—so it was from logic, and not from a superstitious dread, that he had come to understand with a heartfelt certainty that his wife and children would be next, that the bomb was about to follow him home. But being followed did not matter to Morimoto.

If I am to die, he decided, *let me die with my family. So let me go back to Nagasaki.*[10] And from such logic, history was destined to receive two impossible shock-cocoon perspectives from the same person: Ten to twelve kilotons at such close range—within a radius of 0.8 kilometers—as to seem almost directly overhead, and nearly thirty kilotons at 2.4 kilometers (a mile-and-a-half) away.[11]

Assembly Prefect Takejiro Nishioka had been completely shadow-shielded behind a tall ridge as his train approached Kaidaichi Station in the hilly suburbs of Hiroshima. The prefect had observed a glowing, reddish-yellow ring in the sky—huge and rocketing up from behind the hills in the direction of the city. As it faded into a cauliflower billow of multicolored vapor, soldiers on the train announced that an ammunition stockpile must have exploded. Nishioka knew better.

No ammunition explosion had ever behaved like the cloud over Hiroshima. From almost this same distance, Dr. Hachiya's friend Hashimoto watched as, on either side of the rising column, "beautiful" smaller clouds spread out like a golden screen. "I have never seen anything so magnificent in my life," Hashimoto would explain. "[The cloud] was as clear-cut as if a straight line had been made in the clear blue sky. Other straight lines spread out one after the other."

Dr. Michihiko Hachiya survived under the same coal-dark cloud that enveloped the Ito boy and the Sasaki family. "I tried to picture in my mind, the beautiful sky with the golden screen [Hashimoto] had described," Dr. Hachiya would write later. "While he was admiring the sky, we were trying to escape our ruined homes and were wandering through a darkened town. There was a vast difference between what those inside and outside the town had to say."[12]

Prefect Nishioka did not have time to admire the fire in the sky. He had sensed, even behind the shadow of a mountain, that the *pika* (the flash) radiated from a single, point-source explosion. He knew this, and he knew more. He knew of whisperings about new weapons; and he knew, worst of all, that the war was drawing very near the end. He had been returning south from Tokyo with instructions to withdraw publishing facilities, administrative barracks, and whatever great works from antiquity might be saved into mountainside vaults.

During the past week, while Nishioka planned for the end and while vast portions of Tokyo lay under the black shroud of a fire-bomb raid, Professor Yoshio Nishina and his student Eizo Tajima expressed bitter regrets that the late Third Reich never shared the fruits of its uranium-refining facilities. The scientists estimated that given current production rates, working twenty-four hours a day, seven days a week, the country's two cyclotron accelerators might produce enough fissile material to assemble a single atomic bomb in about the year 2020. The plans for a heavy-ion relativistic shotgun weapon did not appear to be progressing much faster. Using power from the large dynamos at the Sakidaira plant, they had managed to prove that nuclei of gold were less easily scattered and more easily focused than iron nuclei—and in theory it was but a simple matter to aim particle beam weapons at B-29 bombers. But in practice, they would need a giant, ring-shaped accelerator nearly two kilometers in diameter, and the magnetic cannons would have to remain stationary, essentially anchored to the giant ring. The machines were therefore vulnerable to being neutralized even if the enemy chose not to attack the dynamos. All that the Americans, the British—and soon the Russians—needed to do was choose not to fly within range.[13]

Dr. Nishina had asked if he should continue with his plans for the accelerator ring. The Emperor's representative did not answer.[14]

And so it came to pass that Nishioka, unlike the officers on his train, understood at once what had probably happened to Hiroshima. The soldiers needed a little more time to grasp the magnitude of the problem. As a precaution, they ordered the train to stop at Kaidaichi Station and to remain there until they made contact with the city. They shortly discovered that the phone lines were all dead, and even the usual daytime radio broadcasts had ceased. Then, from the direction of Hiroshima Station, came a train. All of the coaches had lost their windows, and apparently most of their passengers as well—save for a few stunned souls, looking out with blank expressions on their faces. The cars were all smoldering. At least two were actually afire. The train did not stop. The engineer, looking more like a scarecrow than a man, leaned out the portside window and vomited foaming streamers of bile, and he either did not care or derived a perverse delight from the fact that he was picking up speed and fanning the flames as he passed.[15]

The soldiers on Nishioka's side of the tracks immediately ordered the passenger coaches unhooked from their train. They took command of the locomotive and decided to proceed at once toward the stricken city. Nishioka, shaking the image of the scarecrow engineer out of his mind, ran after the crew, flashed his credentials, and ordered them to take him along in the cab of the engine. He did not know it yet, but he had just embarked upon one of history's most incredible journeys.

Within minutes of turning the curve of Kaidaichi Hill, Nishioka and the soldiers began to be confronted by lines of the walking wounded, following the railroad tracks away from the city. Pressing slowly and cautiously ahead—blowing the whistle to signal *Make way! Make way!*—they noticed that the burns on the refugees became progressively worse, and increasing numbers of the wounded were murmuring in low voices, "Water . . . Water . . ."

As they drew closer to the Cyclopean curtains of black smoke, the railroad tracks began shifting out of line and the locomotive was forced to stop.

The prefect decided to continue on foot toward the appointment he had arranged two days earlier at the home of Field Marshall Hata. Nishioka had a reputation for punctuality, and neither tsunami warning nor typhoon had ever made him late before. He was not about to let an atomic bomb break his spotless record.

Even after Nishioka discovered that the ground between the trapped train and the field marshal's house was sprouting little flickering jets of strange fire, preserving his reputation obsessed him—no matter how disturbing those flames appeared to be. They emerged like miniature volcanic plumes, as if from burning bits of sulfur. They could have been extinguished easily by stepping on them as he passed, but he did not want to do that, believing later that merely by walking among the little jets he had exposed himself to radiation that caused his feet and shins to bleed beneath the skin.

For all of this, he was on time. The field marshal was late, despite the fact that his house had been shaded by a hill from the full effect of the *pika-don* (what people were already calling the *flash-bang*). Nishioka expected that Hata would still have been inside at such an early hour, but he was met by an elderly officer whose face had first- and second-degree burns on one side and whose uniform had been torn apart. He asked for Hata, and the officer replied that he believed the field marshal to be dead.

The officer added, "I believe Hiroshima has been hit by an atomic bomb."

"I believe so, too," Nishioka said, and then decided to follow the tracks a little closer and see for himself.

A bridge stopped him. Its steel was sagging grotesquely and the wooden railway ties were on fire. No more survivors were crossing over from the city, but some of their cats had made it across. Six of them, their hair only slightly singed, were licking a ropy tangle of intestines hanging from a wounded horse that seemed not to notice.

Nishioka did not particularly like cats. About the time Kenshi Hirata reached Ground Zero, the prefect was deciding he hated them. He also decided that there was nothing more he could accomplish in Hiroshima, and that he could better serve the empire by returning to his own regional headquarters at once with news of what he had seen.

Following the tracks away from the sea of smoke, he met a schoolboy who had been drafted into factory work by his teachers. The contours of the land—and especially Hiroshima Castle's moats and deflecting stone ramparts nearby—had somehow compressed the shockwave and focused it like a cannon shot through his school-turned-factory. The boy explained over and over again that he appeared to be the sole survivor. He was headed away from a zone, Nishioka later learned, that was most heavily exposed to radioactive fallout (near the Misasa Bridge). The boy reportedly walked directly through the black rain zone, following a set of railroad tracks past Hiroshima's Communications Hospital and toward one of the suburban railroad stations—toward a place his family had arranged as a gathering point in the event of a severe air raid.

As they parted paths, the prefect gave the boy most of the provision of rice and water he had been carrying, and also a card with his name and the address of his headquarters, offering help and asking that his family contact him later. But he never did hear from the boy again, and he would wonder if this was because he and his family were to be counted among the dead or because they had counted him among the dead. The latter seemed just as likely as the former, because the address on Prefect Nishioka's card was the hypocenter of Nagasaki.

Historians would never be able to pin down the identity of the boy with any degree of certainty. And yet Hiroshima's Ito family would bear the distinction of a survivor's account that contained familiar congruences—which resounded hauntingly like the other side of Nishioka's story. Tsugio Ito's older brother Hiroshi was a schoolboy who emerged as virtually the sole survivor from the Central School and who followed a set of railroad tracks eastward out of town, toward a pre-arranged family gathering place near the prefect's position. During a time in which food had become so scarce that few if any people ever gave rice away to strangers, the Ito boy reported to his family that a tall, authoritative stranger had given him food and offered him help.

During the hours that followed the encounter, nausea and weakness attacked Hiroshi, went away, then came after him more fiercely, causing him to vomit up the rice he had been given. Whether or not Hiroshi Ito was the same boy the prefect encountered, history dealt the Ito and Nishioka families each an improbable hand, from the bottom of the deck. Heading off in opposite directions, it mattered little whether the schoolboy and the prefect eventually went to Nagasaki or to the Hiroshima suburbs. Nishioka would later record that the demon of atomic death seemed determined to stalk after them—for it was already deep within their flesh, sharpening its claws and waiting to pounce.[16]

Kenshi Hirata would probably have escaped with no radiation injury at all had he not gone into the center of the blast area searching for Setsuko. Once he breathed the dry dust, then cleared the dust from his throat by drinking brownish-black water from a broken pipe, his cells were absorbing strange new variations on some very common elements. These new incarnations, or isotopes, tended to be so unstable that by the time he awoke in the morning most of them would no longer exist. Like little energized batteries, they were giving up their power. Unfortunately, they were discharging that power directly into Kenshi's skin and stomach, into his lungs and blood. The quirk that spared him a lethal dose was the initial collapse of the shock bubble and the rise of the hot cloud. A substantial volume of pulverized and irradiated debris had been hoisted up into the cloud, and most of the poisons had already fallen kilometers away as black rain. Even in terms of radiation effects, in its own, paradoxical way, the central region of Ground Zero was sometimes the safest place to be.[17] It was all relative, naturally: Mr. Hirata's neighborhood was still hot with radioactivity; but places farther away were even hotter.[18]

By nightfall of that first day, Kenshi had positively identified a particular depression in the ground as his home. Only a day before, the house and garden were surrounded by a beautiful tiled wall—and now, chips of those distinctive tiles were strewn through the embers. The large iron stove that had heated bathwater for Kenshi and his bride seemed to have been hammered into the ground, but it still appeared to be located in the right part of the house. Only a few steps away, he unearthed kitchen utensils, which though deformed by heat and blast looked all too painfully familiar. They were gifts from Setsuko's parents.

Kenshi had an odd instinctive feeling that the ground itself might be dangerous, and that he should leave the city immediately. The thought that stopped him was Setsuko: *If she is dead, her spirit may feel lonely under the ashes, in the dark, all by herself. So I will sleep with her overnight, in our home.*

Around midnight, he was awakened by enemy planes sweeping low, surveying the damage. The sky, in a wide, horizon-spanning arc from north to east, glowed crimson—reflecting the fires on the ground. Though there was little left to burn in what American fliers were already calling Ground Zero, flames grew all around the fringes of the bomb zone, creeping outward and outward.

The planes circled and left. Kenshi put his head down again, upon the ashes of his home, and lay in the otherworldly desolation of the city center. The silence of Hiroshima was broken intermittently by more planes and by explosions near the horizon in the direction of the waterfront and the Synfuel gas works. As the ring of fire expanded to the gas tanks, there were no working fire hydrants or fleets of fire trucks, and only a handful of firefighters were left alive to prevent the tanks from igniting. Kenshi heard huge metal hulls rocketing into the air on jets of flame, crashing back to earth one by one, and shooting up again. But Ground Zero itself was deceptively peaceful, and the noises that reached Kenshi from the outside did not trouble him. He was too exhausted and too filled with worry about Setsuko's fate. If anything, the distant crackle of flames—even the occasional pops and bangs—lulled him into a deep slumber.[19]

Sumiko Kirihara's and Sadako Sasaki's families tried desperately to get out of the city, but by midnight many of the people Prefect Nishioka had seen staggering away from Hiroshima were finding the roads blockaded by residents of the outlying villages. In the countryside, during the space of only a few hours, the survivors had been transformed into fugitives, as localized councils made crystal clear through megaphones. By argument and by the occasional drawing of weapons, local authorities directed the walking wounded back toward the pyres and the places where black rain had fallen—and, though they did not know as yet that such poisons existed, toward the radioactivity.[20]

Even before the bomb fell, city dwellers had found themselves unwelcome. After Osaka was cluster-bombed with incendiary weapons, no one wanted to live in any city. Children were sent off to relatives if they happened to have kin in the countryside. Satoko Matsumoto, another woman whose family had fled to the river with the Kirihara and Sasaki families, had hoped they could all cross together over a railroad bridge to the other side of a mountain, where some of her father's personal property had been sent a month earlier for storage. Then she remembered what her father had said at the time: that the townspeople were willing to accept luggage for safekeeping, but all refugees would be turned away. There were already food shortages in farming communities overtaxed by the military. Extra mouths to feed from the city, they had said, would push whole families over the edge from severe rationing and hunger to starvation.

Around the hour Kenshi Hirata laid his head down near his wife's grave, the first refugees returned to Hiroshima bearing unbelievable news of the "outlanders" turning them back with threats and even with lethal violence. So the three families decided to find an open space where they could spend the night.

Satoko Matsumoto's father would be stricken by "atomic bomb disease" in only a week. Developing huge purple bruises under his skin, losing his hair in large clumps, and bleeding cupfuls of blood through his nose, Mr. Matsumoto would stand up one evening, gaze at the setting sun, and without any warning or fuss, fall dead.

That first night, Satoko lay on her back and watched towers of smoke drifting up against the stars and blotting them out. Only at their bases did the towers dance with reflected light from the flames. Higher up they ceased to reflect anything at all; rather, they absorbed the light as if someone had spilled ink across the heavens. Like her father, she had suffered no visible injuries; still, she found it painful to spend the interminable night lying on her back under that oppressive fried squid smell, listening to the fires consuming what was left of the city. Occasionally, the black shadows of American reconnaissance planes passed overhead. And when the smoke finally shifted to reveal more than half the sky, Satoko beheld more shooting stars than she had ever seen before.[21]

Something managed to send a chill up her spine—during a night that had already been so full of fearful moments that just one more seemed bound to pass without her notice—and yet Satoko was chilled to the bone when a woman mentioned that the unusual number of falling stars must mean that more people than they had already seen die had only now joined the dead, or were about to die.[22]

The first soldiers to reach the hypocenter came only an hour ahead of sunrise. The War Ministry had sent them in with stretchers—for what purpose, they could not understand. "There was not a living thing in sight," one of them would later recall. "It was as if the people who lived in this uncanny city had been reduced to ashes with their houses."

And yet there was a statue, standing undamaged in a place where not a single brick lay upon another brick. The statue was in fact a naked man standing with arms and legs spread apart—standing there, where everything else had been thrown down. The man had become charcoal—a pillar of charcoal so light and brittle that whole sections of him crumbled at the slightest touch. He must have climbed out of a shelter about a minute after the blast, chased perhaps by choking hot fumes from an underground broiler into the heart of hell. The fires killed him and carbonized him where he stood.[23]

The soldiers found an even more disturbing statue, covered in gray ashes. It appeared to have spent the last moment of its life trying to curl up into a fetal position. One of them probed it with a rod, expecting it to crumble apart. Instead, it opened its eyes.

The soldier flinched and asked, "How do you feel?" There seemed to be nothing else to say.

Instead of saying what he felt like saying—*How do you think I feel, you moron?*—the man replied that he was uninjured and explained, "When I came home from my job, I found that everything was gone, as you see here now." The man insisted he needed no aid in leaving, nor did he wish to leave.

"This is the site of my house," he said. "My name is Kenshi."[24]

During that first night, Akira Iwanaga had taken shelter in a tunnel near the ruins of his boarding house. He marveled at the power of the air-burst, nearly two miles from the hypocenter. "All the glass that had been in one side of the house was embedded deeply, in spears, in the opposite wall," he would report to his managers at Mitsubishi headquarters. On that first day and night of the bomb and the fire worms, he had crossed paths twice with his roommate and fellow ship-design engineer Tsutomo Yamaguchi, but neither man saw the other.

Akira had been standing outside Hiroshima's newest Mitsubishi plant when the *pika-don* was born. He was shielded from its full force by a low hill, at a distance of 3.7 kilometers. Even at a radius of slightly more than two miles, and behind a hill, Akira had felt a strong wave of heat in the air, followed quickly by a high wind and whirling dust. Overhead, the mushroom cloud's cap had seemed to glitter with flashes of bright golden lightning. And then had come black rain and a darkness that swallowed all the sounds of the world, and which seemed to know no end.

Sunrise now brought only the briefest respite. The winds—which had been drawn into the pyre like warm air drawn into the eye of a typhoon—were finally stalling and abating. The fire worms were dying. By now the arc of flame beyond the hypocenter burned with a steady, crackling roar, and Akira could begin to see clearly in the strengthening daybreak.

The river was still glutted with bodies and debris, just as he had seen it at sunset. In the outside world of countryside villages, the water-bloated bodies and the tide of ravenous black flies that seemed to be rising everywhere would have been shocking. But Akira now believed he was beyond the point at which he could be shocked. And then daylight continued to strengthen, revealing a young and hauntingly petite woman carrying a dead child on her back. She was insane, screaming a scream that only grew louder with time. There was a second girl whose mind had just as clearly been wiped away. Only twenty-four hours before, her smile must have been absolutely beautiful. Even now there was something mournfully beautiful about her. She had apparently escaped without any flash burns and seemed completely uninjured . . . except for the huge slash across her abdomen. Having propped her back firmly against a wall, she seemed to have spent much of the night carefully rearranging her intestines and trying to push them back inside, but the baby—which appeared to be only halfway to term—had come out with her insides and died and she did not seem to know quite what to do with it . . . whether to leave it outside her body or to continue pushing. She gave a hideous grimace that became a smile, then flopped over to one side, dead—while the screaming woman with the broiled and bloated child on her back showed no signs of growing hoarse.

Akira bolted, slipped on a loose brick pile, fell hard on a splintery shard of scorched wood, and let out a scream of his own. He stood up and began running again, slipped on something soft, recovered his pace this time without falling, and continued running as fast and as far as he could, putting as much distance as possible between himself and those horrible beautiful girls.[25]

Dozing nearby in a half-sunk fishing boat, Akira's roommate, Tsutomu Yamaguchi, dismissed the screams in the Hiroshima wilderness as merely another pair of anonymous minds that had snapped. He had not eaten for nearly twenty-four hours but had managed to keep dehydration in check by forcing himself to drink dirty water from broken pipes. The shipbuilder still carried most of his ration of two biscuits, but was having trouble keeping down even a few sips of water. Appetite had failed him hours earlier.

During the night, a soldier told Yamaguchi that the local Mitsubishi plants appeared to be permanently out of action, and that any surviving engineering personnel should return to headquarters in Nagasaki. Yamaguchi had assumed that the rail services were every bit as dead as the Mitsubishi shipyard, but the soldier informed him that there were plans to send a train out of Koi Station to Nagasaki in the late afternoon.

After only two hours of rest in the ruins of the boat, Yamaguchi felt well enough to set out for Koi. Normally, he could make the trip in forty-five minutes. But now? Who knew if he would ever reach the station, much less Nagasaki?

The soldier had assured Yamaguchi that as a high-ranking naval engineer, a priority seat would be available. The shipbuilder no longer cared very much about military priorities or the war effort. All he wanted was to get home to his wife and his infant son.

With nothing else in mind, he was able (with varying degrees of success) to harden his heart against all that the grim sunrise revealed: a mother singing a lullaby to her dead child, a horse's head burning like an oil lamp with an eerie, bluish-green flame. Yamaguchi came across a body that at first appeared to have been completely shielded from the searing rays, and then he realized that the shielding had only protected the man from his midsection down to his feet. The upper third of him was a carbonized corpse whose features had been eroded by the wind. The musculature and even the ribs were being carried away as soot on the morning breeze, revealing a blackened heart. Yamaguchi noted for future reference that whatever had shielded the man's lower body and turned his head and chest into loosely packed soot could easily have been worse the other way around—leaving the heart and eyes and brain intact while allowing the victim to see his bared pelvis and femurs before he died.

The engineer had to cross two rivers on his way to the station. The narrower of them no longer had a bridge, but in the shallows bodies were piled up like a natural dam that could also be crossed like a bridge. Even when he tried to keep his mind focused on nothing except the recollected faces of his wife and child, crossing that bridge pained him severely.

At the broader of the two crossings, he encountered an even more challenging bridge: a high railroad trestle whose iron frame was sagging omi-

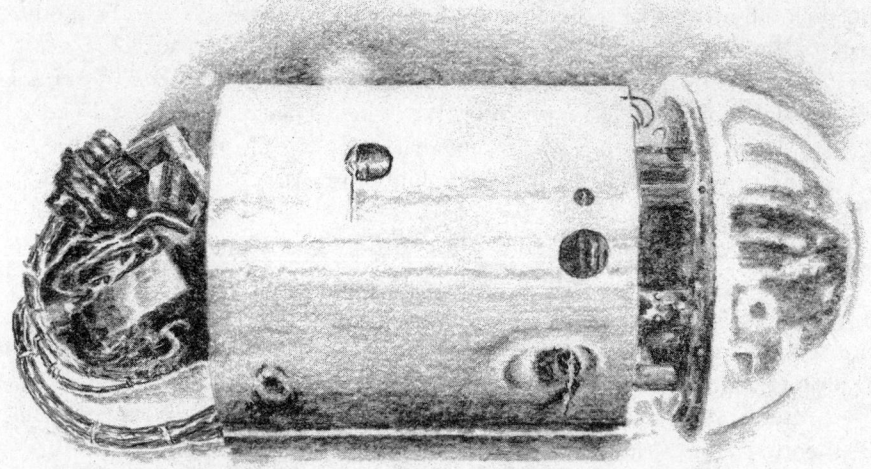

One of the three scientific instrument packages dropped by Charles Sweeney and Luis Alvarez from the Great Artiste, *August 6, 1945. Alvarez had tucked a letter inside each cylinder, addressed to former colleagues in Japan. Suspecting that his old friend Yoshio Nishina had been leading Japan's race toward development of nuclear weapons, he hoped Nishina would convince the warlords that in addition to the experimental fire-bombs then being dropped across the homeland, atomic bombs had just been added to the B-29 fleet's tool box. [Illustration: CRP]*

nously, as if on the verge of collapse. Almost all of its wooden ties had been burned, so he was obliged to belly-crawl and straddle and pull his way along a narrow steel track rail, as if he were a trainee in a high-wire act.

En route to the train station, the engineer and Prefect Nishioka passed near several military officers gathered around a large aluminum cylinder. The object was flash-burned on one side and appeared to have come crashing to earth like a meteorite. Yamaguchi had actually seen the cylinder, and other cylinders like it, being dropped over the city on parachutes, only seconds ahead of the flash. Inside the canister, the officers found a radio transmitter attached to atmospheric and scientific monitoring devices.[26]

What they did not tell the engineer or anyone else passing by—what only the officers and one or two key officials knew at this stage—was that they had discovered an envelope among the pressure wave, gamma ray, and neutron sensors. The envelope contained an appeal addressed to Professors Ryokichi Sagane, Nishina, Tajima, and the rest of Japan's leading physicists. The appeal came from atomic bomb scientist Luis Alvarez, who four decades later would leave his mark on the history of nuclear arms reduction with the discovery of the "nuclear winter" effect.

"You have known for several years that an atomic bomb could be built," the letter began, "if a nation were willing to pay the enormous cost in preparing the necessary material." Alvarez continued, "Now that you have seen that we have constructed the production plants, there can be no doubt in your mind that all the output of these factories, working 24 hours a day, will be exploded in your homeland. . . . As scientists, we deplore the use to which a beautiful discovery has been put, but we can assure you that unless Japan surrenders at once, this rain of atomic bombs will increase many-fold in fury."

Alvarez was not telling the whole truth, of course. The end of World War II was more a game of poker than chess, and like any good poker player, the American did not hint at the cards he really held. The fact was that the factories alluded to could produce barely more than two troy ounces per day of the necessary material. The production facilities were only now beginning to successfully expand, now that it had been demonstrated that the machine would actually work. Once the next bomb was dropped, another would not be available until September or October; but the gradually accelerating production of fissionable metals was presently moving into a trajectory that seemed fated to become unstoppable, even if the war could be ended in just a few short weeks. No one seemed capable of predicting what would happen next, not Luis Alvarez, not any of the soldiers who flew the atomic mission with him, not even the president of the United States—truly no one.

Whatever happened tomorrow or the day after really had very little to do with American behavior or with Japanese behavior. What it all came down to was that most of human history was fated to be forged by primal instincts, and not by civilized thought. The dawn of atomic death was a distinctly human story, told by tigers with uranium-and-plutonium-tipped claws.

Once upon a time there existed only three atomic bombs in all the world. The tigers tested one in the New Mexico desert, to be certain that the machine would work. Three weeks later the other two were dropped.[27]

Even when Kenshi realized that the cloud had risen directly over his home, he prayed and held out hope that Setsuko might have somehow escaped harm. When he left the dockyard, he had packed a few extra biscuits for her. Now, a day later, he dug on all fours into the compressed ashes of his kitchen, descending nearly a half-meter—almost knee-deep. Whenever he paused to eat a biscuit or to sip water from a broken pipe, he sprinkled a share of the food and water ceremonially onto the ground—an offering to his bride of ten days.

As the August sun climbed higher and a snowfall of gray ashes blew through, the pipe stopped dripping. Kenshi was soon out of water as well as running low on biscuits, but he continued digging, hoping against knowledge that his failure to find any bones meant that Setsuko might not have been home when the flash came. For a while, believing he might have dug

deeply enough to have found Setsuko if she had died at home, Kenshi left to
search the nearest riverbank, wishing he might find her miraculously among
the living. But hope died the moment he understood the condition of the
few who were still moving among the bodies. Kenshi would never be able to
forget their desperate faces, calling for "Water . . . water . . . water," while
he cried out for Setsuko. Finally taking some small measure of relief from the
realization that Setsuko was not among this suffering multitude, Kenshi Hirata
walked back toward the center of Ground Zero, and continued his excavation
of the kitchen.

As exhaustion, thirst—and now hunger—began to compete with the first
mild signs of radiation sickness, three women from his neighborhood returned
to the ruins. Like Kenshi, they had been away, sheltered from the *pika-don*.
The oldest of them, the head of their neighborhood association, had rediscovered the place where emergency rations were buried and had directed the
excavation of three large sealed cans of dry rice. Seeing Kenshi, and hearing his
pleas for anyone who might have encountered Setsuko, she went straight off
to a nearby pit in the ground that was filled with glowing red coals of wood.
She mixed some of her own water ration with rice and cooked a bowl of
mildly radioactive gruel for Kenshi. He would recall later that he was moved
to tears by the kindness of this woman. He never saw her again.

After he ate the bowl of rice soup, he felt reenergized despite slight waves
of nausea and resumed his search for Setsuko.

He excavated the entire kitchen, knowing that his wife loved cooking
more than almost anything in the world, and that she fancied herself a top chef
who could turn even the most meager rations into the most subtle flavors by
coaxing spices and herbs from what most people called termites and weeds and
citrus ants. The kitchen, he decided, was where he would most likely have
found her at 8:15 a.m.—planning how to bulk up a cup of stale soybeans and
turn it into what she had promised to be "a taste like walking on a cloud."

When the dust of the kitchen had produced not the slightest trace of her,
Kenshi began to grasp again, ever so slightly, at hope. He was soon joined by
ten men who worked in the city's sawmill. They knew the couple well and
had heard of Kenshi's distress.

They moved from the kitchen to the living room, excavating almost
knee deep, and not a single trace of bone was found.

"She is not here," Kenshi said. "She is still alive somewhere."

"In order to make sure, we must dig a little deeper," one of his friends said.

Minutes later, hope died again. His friend unearthed what seemed to
Kenshi to be only a bit of a seashell.

"We both love conches and giant clam shells," Kenshi insisted. "Setsuko
uses them as table decorations!"

But already he knew in his heart that it was a fragment of human skull. The men quietly stepped back. Suppressing an uneasy feeling, Kenshi excavated gently with his fingertips, slowly widening and then deepening the area from which the "shell" had come. He touched little white scraps of spine, and found in them a pattern that indicated to him her final moment. She had been sitting when . . . it happened.

From the kitchen he excavated a metal bowl, singed but otherwise completely undamaged. Kenshi recognized it as the very same bowl he and Setsuko had brought with them from her parents' home on the train to Hiroshima, only ten days before.

Ten days, he lamented, *and this poor girl's bones are to be put in this basin that she had brought with her from her native place.*

He was thirsty under the broiling sun of midsummer. Sweat had formed long streamers down his back and his trousers were soaked. He felt faint. His friend from the sawmill offered him water and he drank, then sprinkled some of the water over the basin—in the sense of giving his wife the last water to the end of her short life.

"The lumber mill is gone and there is no guessing what will become of us now," his friend said, then announced that he and his wife had been hoarding a small ration of fine white rice and dried fish, just in case the gradually worsening conditions came down to what westerners called "a rainy day."

"Well, it's been raining fire and black ice and horse guts," the mill owner said. "So, this must be the day."

He invited Kenshi home for a late but hardy lunch, and offered a place to stay until he decided where to go next.

Kenshi had already decided. As a surviving member of Mitsubishi management, he would be able to get priority seating on any trains still running. "If I can get to Koi or even all the way out to Kaidaichi Station," he said, cradling the bowl of bones close to his chest, "then I will be able to find a way to bring Setsuko home to her parents."

"Then all the more reason for you to have a good meal before you leave," his friend insisted.

On the outskirts of the city, the mill owner's house had survived behind a hill with only a few roof tiles dislodged. Nausea came and went, which made it easier for Kenshi to eat slowly and to keep his portions small. He did not want to take too much of the last good meal in town for himself, and away from his friends. All the while, the bowl from his own kitchen lay at his side. From the bones of his wife, isotopes of potassium and iodine were being liberated. They settled on Kenshi's trousers, and on his skin, and in his lungs.

While they ate, a young soldier came to the door with news that Hiroshima Station might never run again, and all of the high-priority seats at

Koi Station were already taken for the afternoon of August 7. No trains were running out of Kaitaichi, owing to what the sixteen-year-old message-runner called "the most amazing train wreck ever!"

He explained excitedly how a train leaving Hiroshima during the flash had been fried so severely that even its deadman switches must have failed: "The thing shot right through Kaitaichi and just kept on flying. They say it was doing at least a hundred-and-fifty K when it finally hit a truck in a crossing and went off the rails!"

Kenshi merely thanked the boy for his report and asked him if any trains would be leaving Koi tomorrow.

"Yes," he said. "There's one leaving at 3 p.m., and you have provisional seating—which means you're on it, as long as you can get there."

Kenshi decided to make an early start. Many roads and bridges had ceased to exist, and how long the walk to Koi would take was anybody's guess. He filled his canteen and put two biscuits and a few grains of rice into his pants pocket, then cut some strings and wrapped a cloth tightly over the top of the basin so that Setsuko's bones would not spill if he tripped on the debris that filled the streets.

Before he left, Kenshi asked his friend for permission to pick a flower from his garden. Then, saying his thank-yous and good-byes, he went down to the river, where he threw offerings of a flower and rice grains into the water and bowed three times, in accordance with a Buddhist tradition that acknowledges a place of the dead.

Bodies were now being pulled from both sides of the river, and on the road ahead, mass cremations had already begun.

How, Kenshi wondered, was he going to tell Setsuko's parents what happened to her? He could think of nothing else. He did not know yet that he would soon have much else to think about. It might even be said that his rendezvous with history these past two days had been merely the twilight before the dawn. Kenshi Hirata would reach Koi Station with time to spare; and at three o'clock on the afternoon of August 8, he would set out to bring Setsuko's bones home to her parents, aboard the last Nagasaki-bound train to depart Hiroshima.[28]

And the Rest Were Neutrinos

On August 6, 1945, after President Truman announced the ongoing development of bombs even more powerful than the one dropped on Hiroshima, few outside of the Kremlin or Japan's Imperial Palace would have imagined that only one more nuclear weapon existed in the arsenal. Nor would any among the millions of people gathered around radios in the living rooms of the world have doubted Truman's statement that the Hiroshima bomb "had more power than 20,000 tons of TNT." Officially, it would be listed in the history books as yielding 22 kilotons; yet subsequent scientific evaluations would run considerably lower. Even the 509th Composite Group's Timeline of *Operation Centerboard* (the Hiroshima Mission) eventually listed the final yield at only 12.5 kilotons. Compared to the bomb that would soon ignite over Nagasaki, the Hiroshima weapon was weaker, by at least half. The leaves on the Hiroshima-facing sides of trees were flash-dried out to a radius of almost seven miles. The flash from the Nagasaki bomb would extend this same effect nearly eight times as far.[1]

Before he climbed aboard the scientific observation plane *Great Artiste,* physicist Luis Alvarez had assured pilot Charles Sweeney that he expected the bomb to detonate; but not necessarily up to its maximum intended strength. Sweeney did not know very much about the interior of the "Little Boy" device. Alvarez knew the beast inside and out, the power and the geometric precision of every uranium ring, every beryllium-polonium plug. He knew this, and much more. He understood that while it took the efforts of an entire government industry to tease naturally occurring atoms of uranium-235 out of the rocks, and to slowly enrich the neutron-emitting metal to higher and higher levels of purity, putting uranium together into a bomb design that would work was a fairly straightforward engineering problem.

Given the right purity, in the right amounts, an explosive result could be achieved simply by dropping one mass of U-235 down a long drainpipe, on top of another, with one of several initiator/enhancer elements smashed in between. The challenge lay in obtaining the right materials, at which point even an amateur (albeit a sharp-witted amateur) could improve the efficiency of the drainpipe model to a yield of about 5 kilotons. Professionals like Alvarez spoke in terms of 20 kilotons, and believed they could enhance a uranium weapon up to 50 kilotons with reasonable ease.

Somewhere in the sequence of production and delivery of the weapon, a design flaw, a misunderstanding, or a miscalculation had crept into the "Little Boy" device and diminished its yield. Probably, no one would ever know the cause. The weapon took all evidence with it the moment it came apart into electron-stripped nuclei.

Of all the design challenges, the greatest of them lay not in getting uranium to undergo fission but in coaxing it to fission efficiently and preventing it from detonating prematurely.

Few besides Luis Alvarez and pilots Paul Tibbets and Charles Sweeney knew the true extent of worry and debate that had existed, over how ready for detonation "the gadget's" internal geometry really needed to be at the moment of takeoff. If already primed in *Enola Gay*'s bomb bay, the carefully divided uranium masses in the aft end of the bomb could all come into contact with the cone-shaped needle in the bomb's nose and undergo partial fission if the plane crashed or even if it hit a very hard bump along the runway. The outcome of this scenario—which Dr. Alvarez called "an unscheduled energetic disassembly"—had five possible endings. None were good. The least of five worries would shoot tiny beads of molten uranium hundreds of feet in every direction, exhausting the greater portion of America's (bomb grade) uranium supply and becoming a threat to the health of anyone who happened to be within breathing distance. At the high end of Alvarez's five-point "Sphincter Scale," a runway crash involving fire could easily trigger the bomb's detonators, destroying the entire Tinian Island air base.[2]

The debate over how and precisely when to arm the device had been settled on the morning of August 5 by the crash of a B-29 on one of the runways. Up to that moment, the debate appeared finally to have been pointing toward a plan for taking off with the bomb fully primed and ready. Navy Captain William Parsons, a weaponeer from Los Alamos Labs, interpreted the August 5 crash as a final warning, and reversed the plan. He spent the afternoon practicing the arming and disarming of the bomb's triggers until the skin on his fingertips began to wear thin from abrasion. Parsons refused to handle the explosive charges and the hatches with protective gloves. He insisted on learning the feel of every charge, plug, and screw thread during what promised to be a difficult procedure on a vibrating and rocking bomb-mount while *Enola Gay* and its two scientific escort planes flew toward their target.

Shortly before midnight on August 5, Parsons briefed the crews of the three planes that would actually fly the mission, stating for the first time that they would be carrying only a single bomb.[3] No mention of atomic power was ever made. Indeed, Parsons' navigator, Theodore van Kirk, knew nothing more beyond his own suspicion that a new kind of fire-bomb had been developed by the chemists.[4]

Russell Gackensbach, the navigator assigned to the photographic plane *Necessary Evil,* had made similar guesses about what they might be carrying; but even at this late stage, no one had told him, and he was under instructions not to ask. Gackensbach's path to the Isle of Tinian and *Necessary Evil* had been long and strange—from Allentown High School to factory work as a bomb casing inspector whose obsession with aviation eventually placed him aboard B-17 Flying Fortress missions, operating the new navigation and radar devices—until, during the summer of 1944, transfer orders came seemingly out of nowhere, to a new base on the edge of Utah's Great Salt Lake desert.

The base scarcely began to define the word "remote"—and that was the whole point of it, Gackensbach realized. The new commanding officer, Colonel Paul Tibbets, told his team only that the mission for which they were being trained would be something completely different, adding, "What you do here, what you see here, when you leave here, let it stay here." All the way up to the night of August 5, Russell Gackensbach would recall, "They only told us what we needed to know to do our job, and we didn't even know what our job was."

From the start, even before the new B-29s left Utah, Tibbets had assured that nothing would be normal about their mission profile. He kept true to that promise. Through June 1945 they made training runs to target areas all around America, dropping bombs of various sizes and often bizarre shapes, including a large "pumpkin" with fins. As training progressed, the planes were streamlined and modified to fly higher, faster, farther—and with bigger loads. The "improvements" included stripping off all of the exterior guns, except for a single tail gun.[5]

"A few bursts and we'll be toothless," pilot Charles Sweeney observed; but he was not particularly worried. If the enemy sent up a picket of fighter planes, the maximum velocity of a Japanese Zero was only 350 mph. The B-29s flew at up to 450 mph. They could never be chased down, and if a Zero dove at them from directly ahead, it would only be capable of a single pass.

During the months that had elapsed since the February capture of Tinian Island from Japan, the island became a maze of runways, and the Emperor's homeland was brought within range of massive B-29 raids. Ahead of Hiroshima, more than sixty cities already lay under black shrouds of smoke and ashes. In swarms sometimes three hundred planes strong, every sort of experimental incendiary chemical, from phosphorous to napalm, began to fall night, after night, after night.[6]

In Hiroshima, a fourteen-year-old schoolgirl named Hiroko Nakamoto had noticed that since at least February, schoolwork was moving steadily away from mathematics and calligraphy and increasingly toward assignments to help manufacture machine parts in the army buildings. She heard stories about other cities being bombed; but all of the radio broadcasters denied this, dismissing the tales as "exaggerations" about only minor damage. The radio told only of glorious victories against American ships by Japan's elite pilots, and about successfully repelled American invasions of Saipan, Okinawa, and other outlying islands.

About the time Russell Gackensbach made his last training run before moving to Tinian, an older girl on Hiroko's work detail had said, "I don't believe we are being told the truth. I don't think the war is going well for Japan."

Hiroko hated the girl and called her a liar, wondering if the upstart might be pro-American and should be reported. But by then the air raid sirens were whooping and wailing at random hours, day and night. Above Hiroshima, the strange new, silvery planes called B-sans seemed only to be passing by at very high altitude, never dropping any bombs, as if little groups of two or three of them occasionally became lost, or as if they were by now becoming so confident in their command of Japanese airspace that they could afford to go sight-seeing.

During the course of only a few months, Hiroko and her classmates had witnessed their entire world falling into decay and despair. All the fuel and food supplies were beginning to run out; and the rate of decline seemed to be accelerating.

Photographs brought back to Tinian by Hiroko's "lost" or "sight-seeing" B-29s were showing gunboats and fishing boats evidently out of fuel and anchored in the same places around Hiroshima, day after day, week after week. Except for trolley cars and the occasional military vehicle, all traffic on the streets of the city had been reduced to people on horseback or on foot or on bicycles.

On the day William Parsons nearly wore his fingers out perfecting his arming procedure for the Hiroshima bomb, there was little left to eat in Hiroko's home except government rations of a reddish-brown grain called Korian—which in prior years was given only to horses. Families were also given a ration of something called "weed cake," a food made literally from weeds. It tasted so nauseatingly awful that Hiroko had learned to burn the

weed cakes until they turned into something very much like charcoal—
"because," she would record later, "the taste of the ashes was better than
the taste of the weeds."

Despite the food shortages, one of Hiroko Nakamoto's greatest concerns was for the two albino mice given to her as pets by a local medical
officer. Even the mice refused to eat the weeds and the Korian. For a while,
Hiroko had been able to keep them alive with the shreds of radish leaves
stolen from a farm. Briefly, her pets gained enough energy to use the little
swing set she had made for them. "They played happily and I never tired of
watching them," Hiroko would recall; but by the time Russell Gackensbach
was assigned as navigator aboard a plane named *Necessary Evil,* Hiroko's
supply of radish leaves had run out and her mice were dead from starvation.
They were among the lucky ones.[7]

In another part of the city, a child named Keiji Nakazawa would live to
tell how only now were the wealthy citizens who had wanted the war and
who had called for "a fight to the death"—though often it was the sons of
their neighbors who went off to war and died—only now, during the last days
leading up to Moment Zero, were they beginning to feel the war's burdens,
including personal poverty and dwindling food supplies.[8]

On Tinian, Paul Tibbets had selected the aiming point for the bomb as
the Aioi Bridge, the "T" Bridge that crossed Hiroshima's Ota River, because
it was a distinctive feature that could be immediately recognized by the bombardier, even at an altitude of nine kilometers (or 30,000 feet). The precise
aiming point, like the very nature of the bomb itself, remained hidden from
navigator Gackensbach and his flight engineer, James R. Corliss, as they gathered their gear and were escorted at 2:00, on the morning of August 6, to
one of three planes—*three planes,* constituting less than one-fiftieth the normal
contingent sent out on a fire-bombing.[9] An inordinate number of the crew
appeared to be civilian scientists, who had been appearing on Tinian in greater
numbers lately, and who kept completely to themselves, speaking only when
absolutely necessary.[10]

Everything about the August 6 launch had a surreal aspect. Chaplain
Downey stepped forward and beseeched God to bring an end to war. Flashbulbs popped in the chaplain's face as he spoke. Nearby, Paul Tibbets withdrew a box and spoke with his crew. He explained that the flight surgeon had
provided pills—one for each man—in case the planes went down in enemy
territory. The surgeon knew some of the methods of torture that could be
expected; and he knew that most people talked under torture.

"I'll give them to any one of you if you want the pill," Tibbets explained.
"Six minutes and you're gone," the flight surgeon had assured. "You won't
know anything."

The men simply stared at the box—silently, except for Captain Parsons. "I'd like to have one," the man from Los Alamos said. Tibbets understood Parsons's position. Next to Luis Alvarez, Parsons knew more technical details about how "the gadget" worked than anyone on the runway.[11]

Russell Gackensbach did not take Tibbets's offer. If Luis Alvarez carried one of the deadly pills with him aboard the *Great Artiste,* no one noticed and he decided never to speak of it. Gackensbach and Corliss had been kept in the dark about what their team was carrying; so, probably, there was no need to offer them pills—only dark goggles, with instructions to put them on when their captain gave the order, about three minutes out from the target.[12] They were not to look at the source of light.[13]

Parsons, who had been present at the Alamogordo test of a tower-mounted plutonium version of the weapon they were about to deliver, had told them that this new species of fire bomb was "the brightest and hottest thing on this Earth since creation." He warned that a soldier standing more than five miles away from the test firing was temporarily blinded by the flash. Parsons never mentioned atoms or kilotons, though he knew Alamogordo's artificial sun had unleashed almost 22 kilotons of energy—exceeding *Enola Gay*'s device by about 10 to 12 kilotons.

Some of the crew relied on earlier assumptions that what they were about to deliver was a new nightmare dreamed up by the chemists. A few suspected a physicist's nightmare. Fewer knew for sure.

Gackensbach's and Corliss's plane was number 91, flown by Captain George Marquardt. The plane had all of Runway C to herself. Runway B held Captain Sweeney's still uninscribed *Great Artiste.* The next runway over, "A," was the center of some sort of commotion. Flashbulbs were igniting again—all around Paul Tibbets and *Enola Gay*. His was the only plane in the trio with a name painted behind its nose. Tibbets had named her after his mother. All any of the photographers knew about the plane was that Tibbets would be carrying "something special." If he came back, they would know the rest later.

After George Marquardt and the ground crew finished their walk-around of Number 91—*Necessary Evil*—searching for minute stress fractures or signs of leaking hydraulics, James Corliss followed Marquardt up through the hatch of 91's nose wheel well, and took his position in the flight engineer's seat, located behind the co-pilot on the plane's starboard side, and above the bombardier. Russell Gackensbach took the navigator's position on the port side. The B-29, though spacious by comparison to Gackensbach's previous experience on the B-17s, was still a cramped ship. If he wanted to, he could easily have reached across from port to starboard and shaken hands with Corliss.

On Runway A, Paul Tibbets started the atomic strike plane *Enola Gay*'s run at 2:45 a.m. Three minutes later, Charles Sweeney flew Alvarez's scientific escort plane *Great Artiste* off Runway B; and three minutes after that, George Marquardt followed in the photographic escort plane, *Necessary Evil*. The three planes remained staggered at sixteen kilometer intervals throughout their three-hour flight to their first rendezvous point.[14] Thirteen minutes out from Tinian, while flying only at 4,600 feet, Parsons descended into *Enola Gay*'s unpressurized bomb bay and began inserting the cordite charges into the bomb, following the detailed checklist he had written during his practice sessions, and keeping Tibbets informed through an intercom link of his progress on the arming procedure.[15] Aboard the other two planes, members of the scientific team closed their eyes and attempted to take naps, reserving their energy for the business end of the mission.[16]

At 5:45 a.m., Gackensbach and Corliss became aware of a familiar banking motion, indicating that the time of rendezvous had arrived. From the starboard side, Corliss could see the red hull of the sun emerging on the horizon. Directly below, the captured runways of Iwo Jima spread out before Mount Suribachi—already sanctuary for hundreds of B-29 crews returning from firebombings with half-crippled aircraft. Sweeney and Marquardt drew in behind each of Tibbets's wings, circled Iwo with him, and set course for Japan.

Two hours later, Claude Eartherly's advance scout plane, *Straight Flush*, triggered a brief air raid alert throughout Hiroshima while conducting weather reconnaissance. Because radar and ground observers judged the plane, correctly, to be just another flyover by a lone observer—just like dozens of previous photo-recon flights—the alert was called off with an all-clear siren. The city's defenses quickly returned to their usual stand-by status—just as Luis Alvarez and Paul Tibbets had planned. The scout crews did not know as yet that one function of their previous Hiroshima flybys was to lull the target into a sense that flyovers by one or two B-29 "strays" without fighter escort were commonplace and, presumably, mostly harmless.

The tactic was cold and mathematical, cheerless and logical. Because "the gadget's" interior geometry needed to be machined so precisely that a single whack with a large hammer could knock the pieces out of line and degrade or disarm it, the idea of lulling ground-based flak gunners and fuel-poor fighter pilots into complacency was judged to be a "best defense." As Sweeney saw it, induced complacency reduced the probability that a bullet or a piece of shrapnel would pierce the plane's hull and "pooch" the bomb's delicate geometry. To Charles Sweeney, every one of the "harmless" flybys leading up to this day had been directed by the mathematics of probability theory mated to psychology. *Cold*, he acknowledged to himself. *But somewhere along the line, cold math became our new co-pilot. Logically, it had to.*

About 7:30 a.m., *Straight Flush* sent out a coded message: "C-1"— which translated as, "*Clear* weather, *primary target*." At that moment, Tibbets's three planes were crossing over from the ocean to the mainland of Japan, while ascending to their bombing altitude of nine kilometers. Parsons was out of the freezing bomb bay, with the pressurized hatch sealed behind him and the device below now fully operational. Everything was proceeding as Tibbets had promised: The mission for which they had been training was going to be completely different. Fire-bombers usually cruised at only one-fifth this altitude.

Three minutes from the Aioi Bridge, Captain Marquardt ordered his crew to put on the goggles. Before their world went dark, Gackensbach's and Corliss's instrument readings were nominal; and according to the view through *Necessary Evil*'s forward dome, no one was sending up flak bursts. Nor, it seemed, were enemy planes being scrambled to intercept Tibbets's three "strays." As a handicap, the darkness of the goggles did not particularly worry the navigator or the flight engineer. Whatever the purpose of this strange mission, it appeared that no one and nothing was going to interfere.[17]

According to plan, Marquardt's plane banked to one side and fell two miles behind *Enola Gay* and the *Great Artiste*.[18] In the tail section, Professor Bernard Waldman prepared to fire the trigger on his high-speed camera, designed to capture the first fifteen seconds of the detonation in ultra-slow motion.[19]

Ahead of *Necessary Evil*, aboard the *Great Artiste*, Kermit Beahan and Luis Alvarez waited for their signal to open the bomb bay doors and release the three parachute-equipped scientific instrument cylinders. The mission profile called for *Enola Gay* and the *Great Artiste* to drop their packages at precisely the same second. The bomb would free-fall to an altitude of just under 579 meters (1,900 feet) before detonating, with the instruments deploying their chutes about twenty seconds earlier and 12,000 feet higher. The mirror-like canister surfaces and pure white chutes would, it was hoped, resist the flash effects and give the transmitters a second or two more of life before they were overcome by plasma and blast.

The two leading planes would not be much farther away than the canisters. They were moving into a realm of total uncertainty. No one had ever tried flying away from a nuclear blast before, yet if unprecedented risk was the price of throwing open the doors to a nuclear frontier, then the planes and their crews would be expendable.

Planning for the worst, and hoping for the best, Beahan's and Alvarez's captain was placing his bets on what he would later call "The Tibbets maneuver," and what one critic, on first hearing of it, had already labeled "The Bonehead Maneuver." It required a reversal of course and a crash-dive acceleration—at one point straight toward the ground—during a time frame in which the bomb itself was also falling earthward.

The genesis of the maneuver was a question of simple spatial geometry. During the forty-three seconds between release of the bomb and detonation, how much space could a B-29 put between itself and the bomb so that the B-29 would still be flying in one piece?

Tibbets's maneuver was a variation on an ancient geometric formula he had learned in junior high school—"A gift from the Babylonians and Egyptians," he said, "with which we can calculate the distance from a point on a tangent to a semicircle." If the plane were traveling at a ground speed of 450 miles per hour (or 727 km/hr) at an altitude of 30,000 feet, then on release the bomb would start out with the same forward momentum as the plane, falling on trajectory toward its target. The last thing in the world any pilot still taking in air and in his right mind wanted to do was what bomber pilots had been trained to do; stay in a tight formation into and away from the target—which amounted to flying in formation with their bombs.

Under the old rules, the Hiroshima formation would have traveled almost 5.5 miles by the time the bomb detonated below them, and barely more than a mile behind. Tibbets saw immediately that if the planes simply shot off perpendicular to the line of trajectory, the bomb's forward momentum would carry it roughly four miles down-range during the critical forty-three seconds; and if instead of fleeing sideways at a mere 90-degree angle, he dove at the ground for a few seconds and used gravity to accelerate a little bit beyond his fastest cruising speed, while turning in a direction exactly opposite the bomb's trajectory, he would take the plane more than nine slant miles away from the blast.

The tactic was totally unheard of by pilots Sweeney and Marquardt, and totally brilliant. Aboard *Necessary Evil,* navigator Russell Gackensbach's first clue that his world was about to change forever came after *Enola Gay* radioed a high-pitched warning signal to its companions. Thirty seconds later, at precisely 8:15:15, the signal stopped and four objects dropped simultaneously—one from *Enola Gay*, and three from *Great Artiste.*

Gackensbach did not see this; neither did George Marquardt. Before the thirty-second warning, Marquardt had glanced over his shoulder and observed Hiroshima lying peacefully within the braided outlines of its seven rivers, during what would be burned into his memory as one of the most beautiful, clear, and sunny mornings he had ever seen, mingled with the realization that it could not last.

Somewhere within *Necessary Evil*'s radius from the target point, Luis Alvarez was presently being squeezed into his seat by Sweeney's execution of the Tibbets maneuver. Sweeney discovered, to his growing discomfort, that the dark goggles made it impossible to read his instruments, or even to properly gauge how close his escape dive was bringing him to the ground. All that mattered now was being able to see clearly, so he shoved the goggles up to the top of his forehead, regarding any impending flash-damage to his eyesight of only secondary concern. More than two miles beyond Sweeney and Alvarez, Gackensbach and Corliss were being pressed into their seats by an only marginally less extreme version of the same peel-away and run maneuver.

The bomb erupted almost nine miles behind Sweeney and Alvarez in the *Great Artiste;* but to Sweeney, without his goggles it seemed that a thousand suns were bleaching the sky white, directly ahead. The pilot reflexively squeezed his eyes shut, but the light filled his head with pain, while someone in the tail section began yelling gibberish over the intercom.

At a distance almost three miles past Sweeney's blast radius, Captain Marquardt heard similar inarticulate calls from physicist Bernard Waldman. The men at the tail gunner positions of both the *Great Artiste* and *Necessary Evil* were trying to describe phenomena no one had seen before.[20]

Waldman had aimed *Necessary Evil*'s high-speed movie camera in the general direction of what would become known to future generations as the Hiroshima Peace Dome. Surrounded by high-strength Plexiglas, the tail gunner's seat provided an incomparable, 180-degree wrap-around view. Waldman saw exactly how it all began, near the Aioi Bridge. The initial pinpoint of light was so intense that even in full obedience to Alvarez's warning to cover his eyes, even with both hands cupped tightly over his black goggles during the first three seconds, the light filled his head with a dazzling red glare, as if shining directly through his skull and reaching into his retinas—which, in fact, it was.

When Waldman uncupped his hands, the fireball was already ascending at tremendous speed, dragging behind itself a stem of roiling black dust wrapped in flames. During those first few seconds, Waldman had missed his opportunity to press the trigger at the assigned moment, to make sure the movie camera was aimed in precisely the right direction, and to set the right filters into motion in their proper sequence. The film was off target, mistimed, and irretrievably damaged.

In the navigator's seat, Russell Gackensbach aimed his Agfa 620 camera through his window and snapped two photos of the rising plume about a minute after the detonation, as *Necessary Evil* circled to within twelve miles of Ground Zero. His film had also recorded scores of little white flare spots, the apparent result of exotic particles traveling at a substantial fraction of light-speed, somewhat like cosmic rays—except that in this case, they emanated from below, and not from the sky. Eleven miles nearer than *Necessary Evil*, about a mile southeast of the hypocenter, X-ray film plates that had survived in a hospital without their protective casings being broken, were nonetheless thoroughly overexposed by the surge of gamma rays, neutron spray, and particles.[21]

To Gackensbach's right, flight engineer James Corliss looked on in stunned silence; but he would later write about the mushroom cloud: "All the time it was churning all around, sometimes inside out, with red, yellow, purple, and brown colors." He knew that down there in the city, or in what remained of it, the vortex must be hoisting cars, buildings, bodies, and dirt into the sky. The initial flash was describable only in the language of silent disbelief. Even behind the protection of dark goggles, Corliss had been forced to squint. The light filled the entire interior of the cabin, like a huge magnesium flash bulb indoors and directly in Corliss's and Gackensbach's faces.[22] They experienced a slight sunburning of facial skin not covered by the goggles.[23]

Forward of them, in the cockpit, George Marquardt was now partly blinded by a bright green afterimage, floating in the center of his field of vision. Unlike Sweeney, who was nearer the detonation point and who had removed his goggles but who could now see clearly, vision was returning much more slowly to *Necessary Evil*'s pilot. The difference lay in the fact that Sweeney had been looking straight ahead along his escape path and almost 160 degrees away from the explosion, while Marquardt had glanced back upon the doomed city during that first split second. Even through the obscuring effects of his dark goggles, Marquardt was able to discern the thick film of black smoke that rose instantly from every tree, rooftop, and wood-framed wall touched by the flash. That quickly, the black fog had covered more than half the city. "Smoke boiled around the flash as it rose," he would record later. "It seemed as if the Sun had come out of the Earth and exploded."

Paul Tibbets, Jacob Beser, and other crew aboard two of the Hiroshima mission's B-29s, reported a taste like molten metal emerging from fillings in their teeth. Examination of plexiglass and the crew's flash-protective goggle-plates revealed microscopic melt-trails consistent with the cores of metallic atoms passing through the planes at between 30% and 90% light-speed. Under the short-lived magnetic fields of the detonation, certain planes and certain city locations were randomly targeted by something very next-of-kin to Brookhaven National Laboratory's (modern) Heavy Ion Collider. [Illustration: CRP]

Marquardt and other members of his *Necessary Evil* crew became aware of a taste like lead in their mouths. More than camera film had been damaged by the particles and the rays. Something from the bomb itself had evidently passed through their teeth and interacted with their fillings. Marquardt began to wonder about the other planes.[24] He knew they must have been at least two miles nearer, at Moment Zero.[25]

At the helm of *Enola Gay*, Paul Tibbets also became aware of a strange taste. As the flash blazed forth, he heard and felt a crackling in his jaw, and simultaneously came the unpleasant taste, "like an out-flowing of lead." Pieces of the bomb (quantum artifacts) had embedded in his fillings and passed through his flesh. The pilot would recall later that the light from the bomb seemed to have substance—a light that could be felt, and even tasted.

During that first chip of time, the most destructive particles were fortunately among the rarest. A heavy, positively charged nucleus of iron, tungsten, or uranium from the bomb's interior, traveling at a substantial fraction of light-speed and following the bomb's short-lived but extremely powerful magnetic field lines, could pass through Plexiglas and through people, shedding energy as it passed. The heaviest and fastest nuclei could disperse an amount of energy equivalent to the force of a baseball pitch, along a line of destruction only slightly wider than a few red corpuscles lined up side-by-side. Whenever and if ever any of the crew were penetrated by heavy ion collisions, the impactors did more than merely vibrate fillings in teeth. They formed flesh-melting lines of cauterization narrower than a human hair, but reaching all or most of the way through a human body. For several seconds afterward, veins and arteries in the line of fire would have been shooting micro-clots of seared blood in random directions. With all else that was happening in and around the planes, the occasional pin-prick or stinging sensation might not have been noticed at all.[26]

In the co-pilot's seat of *Enola Gay*, as he and Tibbets circled around for a closer look, Captain Robert Lewis noticed that, unlike the successful completion of a standard fire-bombing mission, there were no signs of relief, no cheering.

After an initial moment of amazement that the gadget had worked—"My God, look at that son-of-a-bitch go!" Lewis shouted into radar operator Jacob Beser's headphones, a moment of disbelief followed, and he whispered, "*My God . . .*" Beser removed his headphones, climbed aft, and looked down. He could not see the city at all. Something shadowy and strange was moving across the surface of the Earth; it reminded him of what sand at the beach looked like if he stood in two feet of water and stirred up the sand as vigorously as he could until it billowed. He quickly came to terms with the taste of molten metal leaking out through his teeth, but the image of roiling sand in water—with new fires breaking out every second along the periphery of the swirls, was harder to shake off. Beser loved the sea, and though nothing would ever keep him away from sailing on deep water, he could never again go to the beach and wade into the surf, after Hiroshima. Tibbets seemed mesmerized by the view. What had once been distinctive rows of houses looked to him now like fields of boiling black tar.[27] He would report later that once Iwo Jima and Okinawa and the kamikaze attacks had prepared his mind for reception of the idea that the entire population of Japan would fight to the death till the very end, the ground-hugging dust and the sparkling debris fields meant to him only that, if this bomb did not end the war, there would at least be fewer of the enemy to contend with during the final invasion of the mainland.[28] Presently, he kept the thought to himself, and prepared to cede control of the cockpit to co-pilot Robert Lewis.[29] He wanted to go to the back of the plane, where he planned to catch about three hours of sleep during the return to Tinian.[30]

Miles away, surveying the damage from the navigator's seat of *Necessary Evil*, Russell Gackensbach shared the same thought as Tibbets—*there are fewer of them now*—while Tibbets's co-pilot came to an altogether different thought, and wrote in his log: "*My God, what have we done?*"[31]

One day, relating what he witnessed to his son and grandson, Jacob Beser would refer to Hiroshima and Nagasaki as, "the most bizarre and spectacular two events in the history of man's inhumanity to man." Presently, however, he was content to look down and to know, "There are fewer of them."[32]

Down there in the swirls of fire and debris, Hiroko Nakamoto was aware of a smell she had never known before—which turned out to be her own flash-burned skin. In the direction she was walking, all the houses seemed to have vanished and the tallest structures were streetcars, filled with bodies. Some of the people were burned so black that it was impossible to tell whether they were lying face-down or on their backs. Indeed, it was difficult to believe they were human beings. Hiroko felt as if the side of her face that was exposed to the flash was now somehow detached, and no longer belonged to her. A woman approaching out of the smoke stared at Hiroko, then turned away with a gasp of horror. Hiroko wondered why.[33]

In the cockpit of *Great Artiste*, Charles Sweeney had a less close-up and personal view. After he leveled out from the shockwave, and began circling back, Hiroshima lay to the west, on his starboard side. He looked down and saw a dirty brown stain on the Earth, boiling over the city—spreading out horizontally and without detail. Out of it had emerged a vertical plume that contained every color imaginable, along with colors he had never imagined. Sweeney swore that, impossible as he knew this to be, he was seeing colors that simply did not exist in the electromagnetic spectrum—new colors, never before seen by human eyes. He circled once, so that the scientists could film the cloud, but much of the camera equipment and the film inside had been damaged. The plume towered more than three miles overhead and was still growing when the B-29s turned back toward Tinian Island. They were nearly a half hour and 200 miles away from Hiroshima before the tail gunners began losing sight of the mushroom cloud.[34]

Far behind the Tibbets planes, in Tokyo, Dr. Yoshio Nishina and Eizo Tajima were already trying to convince War Minister Anami that the sudden, simultaneous cessation of all radio and telephone communication from Hiroshima was consistent with an atomic bomb. Even after Prefect Nishioka managed to patch a line through from the suburbs, and to confirm Dr. Nishina's assessment with his own eyewitness account, Anami would not believe it. Even after the American president broke the secret to the whole world many hours later— *"The world will note that the first atomic bomb was dropped on Hiroshima, a military base"*—the war minister refused to accept it.

Just the same, he decided that it would only be sound logic to discover what captive American airmen knew about their country's atomic bomb program. Anami was working under the dual certainty that everyone talked under torture and that the American program was as open a secret as Dr. Nishina's program. The second "fact" was a myth. However, Tibbets and Parsons had been aware from the start that the first fact was true, and for this reason they carried already loaded sidearms during their mission—not for self-defense in the event of imminent capture but for self-silencing, just in case the cyanide failed.[35]

The first pilots questioned by the Japan War Ministry died without revealing anything. Anami was beginning to suspect that perhaps they really did know nothing at all—which enabled him to latch on to hope that the atomic bomb might not exist—until, after nearly twenty-four hours, the interrogators brought in Lieutenant Marcus McDilda, a fighter pilot who had been downed near Osaka. Marcus knew nothing about uranium or initiators, but as near as he could tell, his interrogators seemed to have uranium on the brain, and they were telling him much more than he knew. Being a pilot, what he already did know, very well, were the mathematics of spatial geometry. Meanwhile, his interrogators already possessed one of the uranium bomb's biggest secrets: the business end of the bomb was all about spatial geometry—and childishly simple. Given enough of the highly refined neutron-emitting metal, there were many ways of skinning this particular mathematical cat; the truly difficult part was designing a bomb that would not surge when you did not want it to surge.

After a general pierced Marcus's lower lip with a sword and displayed for him the severed head of an airman who had "pretended" to know nothing about uranium, the pilot began designing a totally imaginary atomic bomb on short notice—having no real idea what he was doing but, rather, making it all up as he went along. Marcus described two uranium spheres separated at opposite ends of a lead shield, inside a bomb-shaped box small enough to fit inside a single B-29's fuselage. When the bomb was dropped from the plane, the shield was removed and two steel pedestals slammed the uranium spheres implosively together.

The general stood back, awestruck. What the airman described was consistent with an early version of the Nishina-Sagane design.

Marcus sensed that something unprecedented had just occurred. He had never heard of a prisoner striking fear into a Japanese interrogator.

"What is the next target?" the general demanded.

Marcus grinned and spat blood. "Right here!" he said. "Tokyo will be bombed in the next few days.[36] We're bringing it right down your throats!"[37]

On the evening of August 7, as the interrogations began, as Hiroko Nakamoto found safety among relatives in the suburbs, and as Kenshi Hirata tossed a flower into a Hiroshima river and prepared to carry his wife's bones to Nagasaki, War Minister Anami assigned a pair of planes to Dr. Nishina and Lieutenant-General Seizo Arisue, with instructions to land in Hiroshima the next day and determine whether or not the bomb was indeed atomic.[38]

Ahead of them, dozens of American planes had already returned from Tinian for the first photographic reconnaissance of the ruins. The scouting sorties reported that over most of the city, only the physical geography remained recognizable—appearing much as it would have seemed ten thousand years ago, before city builders came to the river's edge. A few of the bridges were still there; but they were broken and "bleached out;" and during those first days the shadow people on the Aioi "T" Bridge were much more distinct than they would appear to latecomers, two or three months after the first strong rains. In the middle of the "Flatland" known to the scientists as Ground Zero, the Dome and some of the municipal buildings and the telephone poles that surrounded them were still standing—and, farther off, reconnaissance experts were shocked to see the partly intact frame of a church.

Far beyond the church, amid a stand of mauled and dislodged buildings, Tsutomu Yamaguchi boarded the second-to-last train to Nagasaki. He had developed a high fever and was suffering continually from dry heaves. There was no longer anything left in him to be vomiting up. By now he had discovered to his growing horror that he could not even keep down small sips of water, and thirst was tearing at his throat.

Prefect Takejiro Nishioka was aboard the same train, his only symptoms of radiation sickness a stinging and itching sensation in his legs, which he attributed to the strange "candle garden" through which he now wished he had never walked.[39]

Engineer Akira Iwanaga was also aboard—thirsty and fending off mild bouts of nausea.[40]

All three men were destined to become double atomic bomb survivors.[41] A fourth passenger, Dr. Susumu Tsunoo, dean of the Nagasaki Medical College, would meet a somewhat different destiny. He had escaped from the first bomb with scarcely a scratch, and was showing no symptoms at all of radiation sickness—yet, in less than forty-eight hours, he would be running an errand to a district about to disappear from history.[42]

On Tinian, now that his own eyes and President Truman's announcement had rendered the weapon no longer a secret, Russell Gackensbach and virtually every other serviceman began keeping, as souvenirs, samples from the many thousands of leaflets that had been dropped over Japan by the recon planes, urging evacuation and "an honorable surrender" and warning about the accuracy of President Truman's statement—that the power now existed to completely destroy Japan's power to make a war.

On one side of each bill-sized leaflet was printed a perfect counterfeit of Japanese currency; on the reverse, the message. Aware that civilians picking up and reading the leaflets might be punished by military police, they were disguised as currency to make concealment and private reading easier. It seemed inexplicable to pilot Charles Sweeney that in response to the bomb and to the president's message, and to the leaflets, there came only a desert of silence from Tokyo.

As the sun set on Hiroshima and Tinian, Curtis LeMay ordered 152 B-29s aloft, to inflict conventional fire-bombings upon Japan.

The night of August 7 came and went, and still no response came from Tokyo.

As the dawn of August 8 approached Tinian, Charles Sweeney was called to the Intelligence hut. According to reconnaissance photographs, Hiroshima's activities as an industrial base had ceased. Preliminary casualty estimates were approaching 100,000 people.

Sweeney walked over to the air-conditioned compartment, called "the shed," and put his hands upon the hull of the plutonium bomb. Several of his fellow officers had already signed their names on its yellow-painted surface. Sweeney knew that plutonium emitted constant streams of alpha particles. The bomb's casing was warm to the touch—"as if it were a living thing," he would tell future historians.

The shape of things to come, Sweeney told himself. Luis Alvarez had just explained to him that this bomb was only a firecracker, compared to what would soon be on the drawing boards. Dr. Alvarez enthusiastically quoted a friend named Harold Urey, who had declared, "When humanity sees what science has done, they will see immediately that here is the end of war."

Sweeney did not believe that scientists understood humanity very well. "Still no word from Japan, I presume?" he asked.

"No," said the scientist. "It looks like we're going to have to do this again."

"Understood," Sweeney said, and walked out of the shed without saying anything more. He borrowed a Jeep and drove away from his own bombardment wing, the 509th, and toward the 313th. Captain Downey, the chaplain who had given the three Hiroshima crews a blessing on the morning of August 6, was a Lutheran. A priest, Father Zabelka, had also attended the blessing. Sweeney was a Catholic. He needed to find the priest.[43]

• 5 •

The Crazy Iris

*F*rom Hiroshima to Fukuyama is 160 kilometers, and there, at a distance of nearly one hundred miles, the blast could be heard. Masuji Ibuse believed that had it not been for the surrounding walls of hills, he would certainly have seen and perhaps even felt the effects of the bomb.

He was thankful for the hills. In Mihara, a town only 49 kilometers nearer to Hiroshima and located on a hillside that gave everyone a grandstand view. The hills themselves tended to give the shockwave a little boost of compression and reflection. Witnesses at the Etajima Academy were knocked off balance by the concussion, and every window facing the city cracked.

Masuji was a writer and a poet who happened to be staying at a friend's house on the outskirts of Fukuyama, and who believed that the bomb had in some way been responsible for the beautiful purple iris he saw flowering suddenly and out of season. When he first noticed the iris from a window, he was not at all sure it could be a flower and must instead be a piece of colored paper floating near the edge of his friend's pond.

On the morning of August 8, only the suburbs of Fukuyama had been left standing. It seemed conceivable to the poet, when he wrote of it later, that a piece of paper was carried aloft with the ashes of the city. During the night, incendiary bombers had flown over the valley like swarms of giant locusts. Just before daybreak, through a rift between the hills, Masuji could see a pillar of fire rising above the place where an ancient castle tower had stood. The pillar burned so brightly that, even in the strengthening daylight, a huge pinnacle of limestone nearby was bathed in the glow of the dying tower. The "paper," Masuji believed, had merely fallen out from the soot and the smoke of Fukuyama's dying.

He did not know, on August 8, that death had come much nearer than Fukuyama. A body lay beneath his friend's pond, seeming to have been hidden there with eerie gentleness and still several days short of bloating with methane and breaking the surface. Looking back on the event years later, and infusing it with his own sense of imagery and poetry, the story began and ended for Masuji with the twisted purple shape at the water's edge.

Now, what is it really? Masuji wondered. The unexpected splash of color in a world that was becoming increasingly covered with ashes obsessed the poet. And when finally he uncovered the source of the mystery—and what lay beneath it—Masuji, who had always prided himself on remaining stoic and analytical in even the most distressing situations, drew his breath in horror and let out an involuntary wail.

The lady beneath the pond was wearing a beautiful nightgown tied with a red sash. The image that would forever haunt Masuji's imagination was a girl's nightgown with its long sleeves hovering near the surface like the fins of a large goldfish. She was lying on her back—and the purple object: it really was an iris bloom after all. The flower stalk had bent down along one side, toward the water's surface—as if, Masuji thought, the iris was trying to touch the girl's cheek.

Masuji Ibuse learned later that the woman was only twenty years old. Drafted into "volunteer service" by the Fukuyama Council, she had been sent to a munitions factory in Hiroshima; and except for a minor burn on one cheek, she had survived with no visible injuries, as she navigated a sea of dead and the still-moving dead on her way to Koi Station and the last train home to Fukuyama. The fire-bombing followed her arrival by a margin barely measurable in hours—and this, too, she appeared to have escaped without physical harm.

The police officer who came to examine the body found her sandals near the water's edge. She seemed to have run headlong from the burning town and, without any signs of struggle or hesitation, lay down and submerged herself by exhaling all of the air out of her lungs and then taking a deep, deliberate breath of water.

Even as the officer explained his theory of a young woman frightened into madness, the iris with the strangely twisted stem and the belated blossoming buds held Masuji spellbound.

"Do you think the iris was frightened into bloom?" the poet asked.

"It's extraordinary," came the reply. "I've never heard of an iris flowering this late. It must have gone crazy."

An apt analysis, Masuji told himself, and wrote, later: "The iris blooming in this pond is truly crazy, and belongs to a crazy age."[1]

"This cannot be," General Seizo Arisue told his pilot. The Chief of Intelligence's plane flew over the ruins ahead of Dr. Nishina—and even after he had circled twice, nothing below except the geography of the rivers seemed to make any sense.

General Arisue had seen Osaka, Kobe, and vast regions of Tokyo after carpet bombings with incendiaries, and in all three cases emergency shelters and kitchens were sprouting amid the ruins within forty-eight hours. Yet, below, little more than a grayish-yellow desert stretched across the missing military barracks, onward through the place where the castle and the Communications Center had been; and the ashes spread for kilometers beyond, with no signs at all of human activity.

"No, this cannot be," the general said again. "Where is Hiroshima?"

"Sir," the pilot said, "this is supposed to be Hiroshima."

The Dome and the "T" Bridge were down there in the center, somehow standing defiantly. All around the Dome, the trunks of trees—though stripped of their branches—were also standing defiantly, while across square kilometers in every direction whole rows of trees appeared to be leaning away from the Dome. The general was reminded of the pictures he had seen of the forested area around Tunguska, Siberia. On June 30, 1908, a piece of solar driftwood had struck the atmosphere at more than 30 kilometers per second, burning high above Tunguska as a dazzling white fireball, sending forth a series of concussions heard as far away as Kiev and London. When an expedition arrived at the point of impact more than a decade later, they found the trees standing vertically in the middle, while all the trees for kilometers and kilometers around had been plowed down, facing away from the hypocenter. To the general, the Hiroshima explosion looked strangely like Tunguska.

When he touched down on a grassy field near the harbor, the similarity became undeniable. Individual blades of grass were apparently flash-grilled on one side until they turned the color of terra-cotta clay; and every blade was leaning—along with the trees of Hiroshima and just like the trees of Tunguska—away from the center of the explosion, as if pressed by a giant hot iron. Arisue and the pilot were met by a lieutenant colonel whose face, just like the grass, appeared to have been burned on one side.

"What happened to you?" Arisue asked.

"*Pika-don*," the young officer replied, and began to describe the flash and the blast that followed. The general interrupted him, wanting to know specifically whether the unharmed side of his face had been shaded from the *pika*, and whether his blistered flesh had been facing the center of the city when the flash occurred.

The officer confirmed Arisue's suspicions that the destruction of Hiroshima must indeed have begun with a single explosion, centered high above the Dome and the little cluster of trees standing near it.

The first thing Dr. Nishina did after he landed behind Arisue's plane was to examine the pressed and burned grass. He then set his own very brisk pace in the direction indicated by the grass, filling vials with dirt samples as he went and seeming not to care whether the general or anyone else followed.[2] At the "T" Bridge, several trolley cars appeared to have been tossed into a pile-up, as if by a tsunami. Although the sheet metal roofs must have provided some measure of protective shading from the flash, it was clear that none of the passengers had survived the first three seconds.[3] Some of the trams had all but completely disappeared, except for iron wheels and little strewn-fields of human bones.[4] Passing through the ruins of the Geibi Bank and tracing the hypocenter toward the Dome and the charcoal-encrusted tree trunks, Nishina discovered that even the thick bones of people's skulls and femurs had been converted into something like burned leaves and dust, if they happened to be caught unsheltered outdoors. Teeth were more resilient than bones, and at one intersection, where more than sixty individuals must have been standing fully exposed beneath the flash, the only evidence of their existence was a sidewalk strewn with teeth.

When Dr. Nishina brought a handful of blackened molars and canines close to his Geiger counter, the distinctive clicks told him beyond all serious dispute exactly what had happened.

"Human remains do not normally emit radiation," the physicist told Arisue.

"So, that's it?" the general said. "Just those few clicks tell it all?"

"That's it," Dr. Nishina said. "Just these little clicks, and it's over. We must make War Minister Anami understand: If the Americans have many more of these weapons, then take my word for it, General—there is no defense against this kind of power."[5]

In Moscow, Stalin was not nearly so skeptical as Tokyo's war minister. Not very long after Yoshio Nishina began filling evidence vials with isotope-infused soil and radioactive teeth, Japan's ambassador to Russia was called to the Kremlin. There, he received an official declaration of war, to become effective at midnight—ostensibly in honor of a pledge to England and the United States that the Soviet Union would enter the Pacific War three months after the defeat of Germany.

Already, two Soviet armies were poised at the border of Japanese-occupied territory in Manchuria, and advance forces had begun to cross. After Ambassador Naotake Sato was escorted out of the Kremlin, the American ambassador, Averell Harriman, was escorted in for several toasts of vodka. Harriman found Stalin in an unusually jovial and talkative mood. On the surface, the most feared man in Russia congratulated the U.S. ambassador on his country's scientific triumph, and expressed gratitude to whatever gods may be that the universe had put him on the side of the people who discovered the atomic bomb.

Privately, the dictator had known about the American discovery months ahead of the Hiroshima event, and he had already put Lavrenti Beria, Commissioner of State Security, in charge of concentrating Russia's leading physicists and engineers in one laboratory and jump-starting the long-dormant nuclear program. Stalin told Beria that his program would have two great advantages over America's Manhattan Project.

First: Russia had captured nearly half of Germany's rocket scientists, and Stalin was confident in Beria's skills at persuading them to work toward building a missile able to drop an atomic bomb from orbit. The difficulty of refining fissionable metals and fashioning them into efficient bombs would be further simplified if Russian forces could penetrate quickly into the Japanese mainland and capture Drs. Sagane, Tajima, and Nishina.

A second and even more important advantage was that, when the Americans started out, no one knew that the problem could actually be solved. "Now," Stalin told Beria, "the world knows that it can be done. That's the hardest part of the problem. Far, far more important than knowing *how* it can be done, is knowing that it *can* be done."[6]

In Tokyo, the coded radio message from Dr. Nishina was answered with defiance. Eizo Tajima confirmed for War Minister Anami that radioactive human remains and soil from the center of Hiroshima meant that atomic bombs must in fact exist. His confirmation changed nothing.

Dr. Ryokichi Sagane supported Nishina's findings, but he and a handful of colleagues underscored their report to Anami with an observation that if an ordinary American fighter pilot like Marcus McDilda was allowed to have even a crude understanding of how the uranium bomb functioned, then the Americans, for some reason, had *wanted* their "secret" to be known. The public broadcast from the president of the United States about "the first atomic" bomb seemed to confirm this.

Sagane believed he had figured out the reason. He calculated that all of the American refining facilities and power plants that could be devoted exclusively to yielding fissionable materials—if allowed to operate twenty-four hours a day, seven days a week, for three years—might be able to produce two or three atomic bombs. He reasoned that the enemy would have tested one bomb, to make sure it would work; and he concluded that after Hiroshima, if they were not already out of atomic bombs, they only had one more left in the arsenal.

This was exactly what Anami wanted to hear. Sagane's calculation was based on sound reasoning and was only slightly off target. Nevertheless, he had not factored in the expanding nuclear industry already being devoted to plutonium production, or the booster shot given slightly more than two months earlier, by a ship arriving in New York Harbor with more than three hundred troy ounces of captured German uranium, refined to nearly 10 percent purity of U-235. Nor had Sagane accounted for the inevitable FUBAR factor—which more or less balanced itself against plutonium and uranium gains. The latest ground-based plutonium trigger tests had misfired in lopsided fashion—instead of in accordance with their near-impossibly precise spherical implosion design—and they had fired prematurely, meaning that, if provided with a real plutonium core and dropped from a B-29, the triggers would have wrecked both the bomb and the plane. The latest uranium bomb casing and tamper fared no better. It met with misfortune when it (minus its priceless uranium) was dropped by mistake near a Chicago runway, and now a replacement would have to be built from square one.

A fourth atomic bomb core would not be ready until mid-September, and perhaps not until October. Reality told it so. And the Sagane equation also told it so in spite of its defects: One bomb had been tested. Another bomb had been dropped. Only the third bomb remained.

War Minister Anami saw the proof of Sagane's math in the multiple fire-bombings of the previous night. "We only have President Truman's word for it that enough atomic bombs exist to strike down every one of our cities and ports," Anami told the rest of the warlords.[7] "Certainly, if they possessed more of these weapons, they would not be wasting their time dropping ordinary incendiaries on our cities."[8]

The war minister remained insistent on "staying the course," despite Foreign Minister Shigenori Togo's counterargument that the Americans were running out of Japanese target cities and ships, and there was precious little fuel left for what remained of Anami's navy and air force.[9]

"Presently," Togo explained, "the Americans *own* the sea and the air. Even if Dr. Sagane's theory turns out to be correct and the enemy is running out of atomic bombs, the fire-bombings alone will destroy us all."

General Yoshijiro Umezu was every bit as insistent as War Minister Anami. Even with the navy now rendered impotent and even with cities aflame, he believed fanatically in making a last stand in which the people of mainland Japan would either inflict unacceptable losses on the invading ground forces and repel them; or they would die in defeat and take the Americans down to hell with them.

Foreign Minister Togo realized that trying to guide these men toward the reality of the situation was like trying to guide a typhoon away from land. The Russian invasion of Manchuria had raised more concern in them than the bombing of Hiroshima, and if anything could be stated as a certainty in these times, it was that the Russian wound, if not Hiroshima's, had made Anami and Umezu more dangerous than ever. Only a joker or a fool would think of fighting against the Americans under these conditions; only the heir to the throne of the king of jokers and fools would consider fighting against the Americans *and* the Russians, *and* the Chinese.

Sooner or later—and sooner rather than later, the foreign minister decided, *we must forget about bravado and ask the Emperor to consider surrender, while there still exists a Japanese people to be saved.*

Shigenori Togo was now acutely aware that he and Dr. Nishina were trying to tread softly in a burning house—a task rendered all the more dangerous when the house was filled with wounded animals.[10]

On Tinian Island, news of the Russian invasion was received with consternation.

In the shed, Luis Alvarez was visited by an admiral who wanted to discuss concern about Russia's wholesale land-grab of formerly German-occupied Eastern Europe, including the annexation of East Berlin. During recent weeks, Wernher von Braun and his rocket team faced a choice between capture by the Russians and capture by the Americans, and most of the engineers had made a desperate and near-fatal mad dash toward the advancing Americans. Scientists from the German atomic bomb program faced the same choice and generally fled west, knowing that their countrymen had killed far fewer Americans than Russians, and hoping, therefore, that imprisonment across the Atlantic, in the States, would be better than in Siberia.

Not all of them reached the Americans, the admiral explained. The Russians had managed to capture about half of Germany's top scientists. More so than silver and gold, and priceless works of art, they were considered by the survivors of Leningrad, Stalingrad, and the Cherkassy Pocket as valued war-won assets.

The admiral was concerned about a coming nuclear arms race, but Alvarez started naming German scientists and asking which of them had made it to Eisenhower's and Patton's side, and which were trapped in the east and presumably now owned by the Russians. About two-thirds of the way through the list, the physicist put up a hand and said, "Don't worry. Our Germans are better than their Germans."

"And what do you think it will mean for us if the Russians or the Chinese take Japan before we do?"

"Then we must not let that happen," the physicist said. "By now, I hope Sagane and Nishina have received our message. If so, they're smart enough to know what a delayed surrender must mean for Japan. If not, then letting them fall into any other nation's hands is simply not an option. We must get in there quickly, and pull those scientists out, dead or alive."

At the time, only Alvarez and a select handful of physicists and military commanders, along with President Truman, knew that just one atomic bomb remained in the U.S. arsenal and that nearly two months might be required to build more.

Outside the shed, almost all of the other B-29 crew members believed, as the Truman announcement had led them to believe, that at least a dozen of the devices must already exist and only awaited delivery.

In the mess hall, an atmosphere of dismay and fear predominated whenever the rapidly expanding Russian front—from Eastern Europe into Manchuria, and toward Japan—was discussed. Only six months earlier, the final agreement between Churchill, Roosevelt, and Stalin had specified reconstruction of vanquished nations, including a policy of returning ownership of all countries to their own people. By now, however, it was becoming clear that in Manchuria, as in Eastern Europe, the Russians intended to take, and to keep, all the land over which they passed. A solution most frequently voiced involved finishing off Japan as quickly as possible with nuclear force, and then moving on to Russia with the same force.[11]

The second atomic bomb had not yet blazed over Nagasaki, and yet newly minted veterans of the first atomic mission were already witness to friends who cast their gaze beyond Japan toward Russia, and let loose with the very first use of the phrase, "Nuke them." Paul Tibbets's navigator, "Dutch" van Kirk, shook his head in disbelief. Nearly sixty years later, he would still be shaking his head. "You always have these oddballs who say, 'Oh, we ought to drop a nuke over in Iraq,'" he would tell a filmmaker. "The stupid jerk doesn't even know what a nuke is.[12] If he knew, he wouldn't say that."[13]

No one in America or Russia or on Tinian knew, on August 8, 1945, what "nuke them" really meant. Even the men who flew the Hiroshima mission and who watched a city splash apart could furnish barely more than criteria for detailed understanding. Only on the ground, in Hiroshima itself, did anyone truly understand.[14]

When he grew up, Keiji Nakazawa would tell the world—beginning with a Manga crime novella titled *Pelted by Black Rain* and a Manga autobiography titled *I Saw It*—that everyone must begin to listen and to understand, while there was still time.

What he remembered most vividly was running through the smoke and the embers, trying in vain to outpace twin streamers of fire that snaked through the wooden structures on either side of him, along the road leading toward home. The road itself suddenly began functioning as a chimney, drawing the two fiery serpents head-to-head before the six-year-old Nakazawa. Blocking the way home, the serpents spiraled overhead into a unified column of flame, terrifying and strange to behold, fed by strengthening gusts of hot wind. On the other side of the column, all alone and beyond Keiji Nakazawa's view, his mother Kimiyo tried to claw a path down through planks and beams to his already dead sister, his dying father, and his trapped little brother, Susumu. The unearthly tumult of a gathering flame-tide cut off from being heard by the boy, almost mercifully, the way his father's pleas for Kimiyo to "do something" shifted to cries against any further digging and clawing; the terrestrial din shielded the boy from his mother's screams of despair when finally, a fire that seemed to emerge from within the ruin itself lashed out at her fingers, and a neighbor rushed up from behind and dragged her away.

Thirteen years later, Kimiyo Nakazawa would still be struggling awake from recurrent nightmares of little Susumu pinned by a support beam under the flattened and burning house, screaming, "*Mother! It's hot! So hot!*" On the second day after the bomb, Keiji discovered that flies were among the only things surviving in central Hiroshima, circling over the dead. Soon, they were hatching and maturing with such frightful rapidity that when he and his mother trekked nearer the T-Bridge, looking for a missing aunt, young Keiji Nakazawa suddenly felt as if tremendous volleys of pebbles were pelting his body. At first, he thought of black, wind-driven hail; but there was no wind, only soft rain. The volley forced Keiji's eyes shut, and when he squinted them open, he saw that his skin and every shred of clothing had become as black as the charcoal people near the Geibi Bank.

"What's this? What's *this*?" he asked, and realized that a dark, living mass of insects was wiggling all over him.

"It was a godforsaken place, covered with death," he would record for future generations. "Round fat flies had leapt onto our bodies, stuck there, and our bodies had turned black all over. At first (surrounded by such manifestations of death), you feel completely overwhelmed. Then you become numb and you can't feel anything."

Born of the atomic light, and the blast, was an extraordinary witness and chronicler. In time, the Nakazawa boy would create for himself the name and embodiment of "Barefoot Gen," whose little brother's spirit, in its own turn and on Keiji's own terms, came to embody the form of at least one among the many orphans Keiji would soon encounter in the ruins, alternately befriending them and fighting with them as they struggled to survive in the nuclear wilderness. His chronicles of Gen would breathe in—sometimes in contradictory or even composite fashion—the stories of Keiji Nakazawa and his mother, and every other survivor who touched their lives. He needed to tell it. He needed to tell it all and he needed to tell it long—through multiple volumes, articles, paintings, and interviews—as if by taking into himself every poisonous memory of Hiroshima, he could exhale a breath of hope into the world.

Keiji Nakazawa's great outpouring of Hiroshima memories would eventually come to resemble a Buddhist meditation technique, called giving and taking. He could take in and receive the fires, the carrion-feeders, the suffering of orphans, and the cruelty of people who would dream of bringing a thousand more atom bombs into the world. Then, as he let it out through his artwork and his writing, he prayed that only the lesson of hope, human resilience, and an aversion to war would linger in the air. As one Buddhist sage would describe the method, "I take inside my body all these bad things. Then I replace poisons with fresh air. Giving and taking."

"I was six years old," the boy who would write of himself as "Barefoot Gen" said sixty years later. "I remember every detail. If I had to create it as a movie set, I could." And so, he told the world how a concrete wall at one end of a schoolyard had shadow-shielded him from the flash, and how a question from a classmate's mother at just the right moment made all the difference between life and death.

"Will today's classes be moved away from the school?" the woman asked, expressing concern about an air raid alert that had sounded just under an hour before, at 7: a.m.

"We won't know until we ask the teacher," he said, and looking up, saw a vapor trail.

"A B-29," the classmate's mother said. "Strange that the air raid alert hasn't sounded again."

Every clock, and virtually every watch in the city was about to stop at the precise moment the dead Hiroshima University clock had been pointing to all along—8:15. Years later, Nakazawa's examination of documents that survived intact within the city's main communications bunker would reveal the hand of a broadcaster logging an air raid call at 8:15 a.m. The alert was evidently being broadcast, with the sirens either just beginning to wail or on the verge of doing so, as the bomb itself silenced the warning.[15]

During his interrupted conversation, Keiji Nakazawa had moved nearer the wall. His backpack was practically against the concrete shield; his classmate's mother stood several steps in front of him, gazing up at the suddenly gyrating path of the vapor trail and facing the Hiroshima Dome, when the entire upper portion of her body was bathed in searing rays from the weapon. Nakazawa was close enough never to hear the explosion, only to *see* what happened. At a radius of 1.3 kilometers (almost 13 city blocks) the bomb's light lanced down across the schoolyard at an angle of about 23 degrees. The combined dose of gamma rays and neutron spray at this radius was a sickening 90r; but the nearly one-foot-thick wall that stood between the boy and the bomb intercepted almost ninety percent of this radiation.[16] Still, the wall could not protect him from the sky-shine effect, or from the microwave burst, or from the fallout that was soon to follow.[17]

At age six, and with the heat ray angling across the ground at 23 degrees, Nakazawa was just short enough to be almost completely shadow-shielded behind the wall, except for two small spots where the heat ray touched him: on the back of his head and along the top of his neck, at angles suggesting that he had been briefly looking down at something on the ground, just before the ray struck. The woman with whom he had been talking stood significantly taller than a six-year-old, and on the wrong side of the 23 degree angle. She caught the full force of the ray and the blast. During the first second or two, even though Nakazawa was shaded from the flash, the bomb's light blotted out everything, and his whole neighborhood seemed simply to have disappeared. A second later, as the flash weakened from blinding blue to a pallid white glare (framed red around the edges), and as details, though misty and vague, began returning to his world, the shockwave took the wall apart and snatched away consciousness so quickly that awakening gave the illusion of momentarily vanishing from Hiroshima to a safe and featureless place filled with white light, only to be suddenly transported back again to a changed and changing Earth. The woman's face and arms had dissolved at the touch of the rays, while a column of dense smoke darted from her head. If she screamed, it was a silent scream. The blast wave was also eerily silent.

When Keiji Nakazawa regained his bearings and looked around, the classmate's mother and the school were gone, along with most of Hiroshima. In a world transformed from clear blue skies to midnight in a moment—a man-made night pierced only by emerging fires—he saw that the woman had not disappeared after all but, rather, was hoisted into the air and dropped across the street. Her white eyes seemed to glare at him from a corpse that, except for those eyes, was converted to the color and apparent texture of a roasted chicken covered in soot. Beyond the body, looking southward toward Isao Kita's weather station and across a landscape becoming more and more densely populated by serpents of fire, the boy saw that houses had collapsed in undulating rows all the way out to the horizon, resembling a set of waves on a stormy sea, somehow frozen in motion.

The burn on the back of Nakazawa's head was small, but severe. The contrast between a lifesaving shadow and death-dealing heat had been knife-edge sharp, marking a portion of Keiji Nakazawa's body not shielded by the wall. His hair had vaporized along the line of exposure, and the skin beneath was seared all the way down to the surface layer of his skull—as though by a clean slash from a blade of light.

Now, on the second day after his race against two serpents of flame, the wound was festering and the Nakazawa boy had been vomiting yellow fluid since the first day. He tried to hold back the vomit when he was around his mother. Already, people who survived with what appeared to be relatively minor injuries had begun vomiting and dying. The boy knew that letting signs of illness show would only add to his mother's burden of worries. It was a miracle to him that she was alive in the first place. At the moment of the flash, she had just finished hanging clothes on the second-floor laundry porch and was on the verge of entering the house again. The clothing and the porch's single layer of wooden boards had shadow-shielded her from the heat ray (but provided much less radiation shielding than Keiji Nakazawa's concrete wall). Had she stepped inside the house by the time the blast wave struck, Kimiyo Nakazawa would probably never have survived even the first six seconds.

The blast collapsed the ground floor like a balloon bursting, and drove everything on the second floor down into the wreck—everything except the porch, which Keiji's mother felt separating from the house and floating up as the largest shock bubble ever created above human heads imploded and objects initially blasted toward the ground sometimes reversed course and were suctioned toward the ascending fireball. At just the right instant to make survival possible, the porch broke away from the vacuum effect and began dropping down through gusts of ascending air, seeming to fall no faster than a leaf dropping from a tree, despite the weight of a woman whose belly was swollen from nearly nine full months of pregnancy. The porch landed in an alley behind the house, like an airplane skidding onto a runway.

The house was only a block away from the school, but the firestorm eventually chased Keiji Nakazawa's mother south toward the farmhouses and potato fields at the end of the local trolley line. "And in the carnage of atomic hell," Keiji would one day record, "she had given birth on the pavement to a baby girl."

Keiji Nakazawa's oldest brother, Koji, found them on the street. Like Kenshi Hirata, Koji had been shadow-shielded and shock-cocooned at the local navy yard, but there was little sense of rejoicing over improbable survival. The first two days under the bomb had so many horrifying events crowded into them that they felt like two months, or two years. Kimiyo Nakazawa was torturing herself endlessly with thoughts of being unable to save Dad, Eiko, or Susumu. To help her, Keiji and his brother decided that they must soon return to the center of the city and retrieve the family bones. The boys found the road home flanked by flattened and burned ruins, with charred hands and feet poking through the debris piles—"quite like the flowers in an artistic floral arrangement."

The smell was both metallic and fleshy—and somehow alien to human experience. The bodies strewn nearest the road were being hauled to cremation piles by soldiers, who hooked them in their necks and waists and dragged them away on ropes. Occasionally, the brothers saw a blackened corpse suddenly gasping like a fish after it had been hooked, but the hooks had done their work, speeding these souls toward death perhaps an hour or two early. Keiji Nakazawa understood, now, that he must not let his sickness cause him to fall near the corpses, or a soldier might mistake him for one of them.

The combination of the August sun, the effects of gamma shine, black rain, and an overabundance of corpses made missteps inevitable. Time and again, the boy who would embody Barefoot Gen of Hiroshima slipped on something foul and black. It felt to him like slipping on banana peels, except that the peels were really the burned skin of other people clinging to the soles of his feet. He scraped the skin off on the road. The realities of what science had taken from the cosmos and could not give back continued to project themselves toward Keiji Nakazawa. He would recall passing a woman who seemed to have bluish leaves growing out of her flesh. She must have been standing near a stained glass window when the sky opened up, and the strange plants were in fact leaves of glass deeply rooted in one whole side of her body. She walked by without uttering a word or a sound, like a ghost; but with each step, the leaves chimed with what seemed, to a boy of six, like a strange jingle-jangle tune.

The brothers paused at the fallen wall that had shielded Keiji at the school. The younger Nakazawa began to understand that had he been two or three steps further away from the wall, the upper part of his body would have been exposed fully to the flash and he should have died just like his classmate's mother. He also realized that if not for the perfect combination of air currents that had landed his own mother gently on the ground, he'd have become an orphan in a society hostile toward children growing up without the guidance of their parents. Keiji Nakazawa concluded that he had been spared by a double miracle.

When the Nakazawa boys reached the mound of ashes that had been "home," Koji excavated their father's skull from the foundation level near the front entrance. Something appeared to have erupted through the empty eye sockets. Brain matter had boiled, expanded, and oozed as the house burned. It seemed to Keiji that his father's skull was weeping.[18]

Takashi Tanemori had embarked along a path on which he would be misrecorded in documentaries and then very nearly by history itself, as simply the schoolboy who was playing hide-and-seek with his friends when the flash from the bomb illuminated the entire interior of his skull and permanently damaged his eyes.

About fifteen minutes before the clocks stopped, he had raced to school with his friends. As they had done every morning, no matter how fast they ran or who won the race, they stopped at the entrance and bowed deeply to the statue of Emperor Hirohito before dashing onto the school grounds, usually for a quick game of hide-and-seek.

At 8:15 a.m., Tanemori had been "it." Shielded inside the building, he stood in view of a window with his hands cupped over his eyes, while periodically peeking between his fingers, trying to pinpoint some of his friends' hiding places outside. The game, and Tanemori's "cheat," were interrupted by the purest white he ever saw, or ever would see. The second-grader snapped his eyes completely shut and bunched his fingers together over his closed eyelids.

"And do you know what I saw?" he would ask future generations, sixty-five years later. "I saw the bones of my fingers, just like an X-ray photograph. I cannot tell you how I saw this, but the memory is so deep that when I am washing my face with my hands, there are times when my fingers on my face bring me back to the moment of that flash. It returns so painfully, even when I am washing my face."

The three-story schoolhouse was compressed into a rubble pile not even one story high, within which Tanemori was simultaneously cocooned and trapped by an air pocket. He heard the voices of children crying out for their parents from other pockets nearby, as searing heat began spreading into the underground chambers, silencing the occupants of the cocoons one by one, before finally moving toward Tanemori and dripping something molten near his face.

A soldier saved him, drawn by cries so piercing that Tanemori himself had difficulty believing in later years that his own vocal cords were capable of creating and sustaining such a sound. The soldier moved burning debris with his bare hands to excavate Tanemori, and to pull him out alive into his arms.

"And so began my long journey," Tanemori would recall—at a starting point just over eleven city blocks (1,160 meters) from the hypocenter. The children who had been hiding from Tanemori, outside, were charred and lifeless. He never did learn the name of his rescuer. The soldier simply ran from the scene with the second grade's sole survivor clutched in his arms, weaving a path through streets that were becoming a maze of erupting fires. A woman was running along with them between the flames, calling out the names of her missing children.

Tanemori noticed a baby in a padded carrier, strapped to the woman's back. Half of the baby was missing. As he watched, the mother suddenly stopped calling out to her lost children and uttered the words, "Oh! My poor, poor baby. I forgot to feed you."

"And she unlatched her straps, and brought the baby to her face," Tanemori reported, more than six decades later. "Even to this day, I don't want to *think* of that moment, because I see the mother's face, when she realized what happened to her baby."

"You are the savior of my son!" Takashi Tanemori's father cried out to the soldier, when, "as a miracle," they met at the river. The soldier handed the boy over and turned back toward the fires, never to be seen again.

The boy and his father were among the very few people who seemed to have survived near the bomb's half-mile radius without having their skin flash-seared or blast-shredded until it hung from their bodies like long strips of cloth. There was little time to wonder how they had escaped such injuries, or what had struck the city, before the sky opened up again—this time with thunder and torrents of black rain. A ripple ran through the crowds of charred, blast-shredded humanity. Like a herd, the people at the river's edge pushed and shoved and stampeded into the water, and Takashi Tanemori's father barely managed to avoid being dragged along with the herd as the suddenly swollen river rose up with frightful power, here and there generating foaming black rapids that swept people toward the sea and piled them against the foundations of shattered bridges—thousands and thousands of people.

On the day Keiji Nakazawa and his mother were pelted by black flies, Takashi Tanemori and his father crossed the river at a place where the surge had piled the dead, creating an unearthly bridge of human flesh. The bridge was so strong that the Tanemori child believed a tank could have driven over it without sinking. Father and son crossed homeward over the backs of the dead.

"My mother and my fourteen-month-old sister were never found," Tanemori would tell history. "I want you to know that Hiroshima, and Nagasaki likewise—although both cities were rebuilt and ended up thriving in the twenty-first century—do you know what those cities are built upon? Those

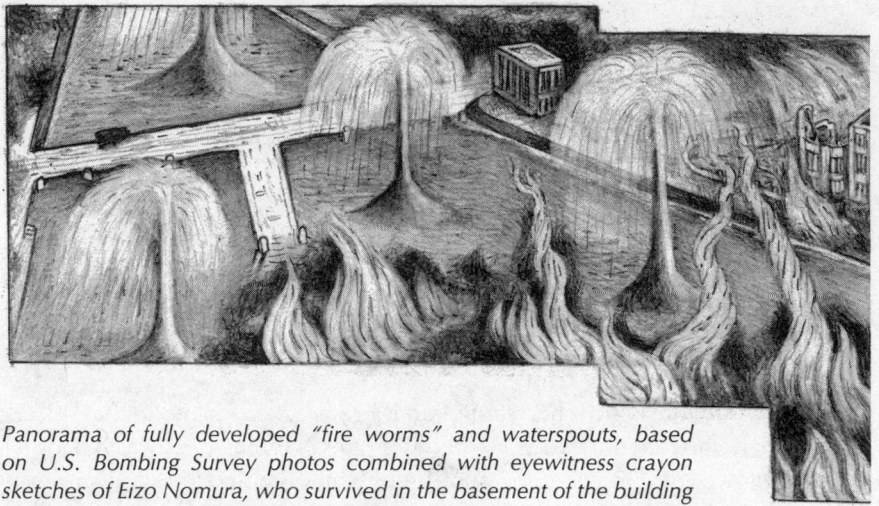

Panorama of fully developed "fire worms" and waterspouts, based on U.S. Bombing Survey photos combined with eyewitness crayon sketches of Eizo Nomura, who survived in the basement of the building in the lower right, and who escaped the fire worms by diving into the river. [Illustration: Patricia Wynne]

skeletons remain buried (and they are occasionally accidentally unearthed). They made a foundation so strong—which includes my baby sister."[19]

By the time Keiji Nakazawa found the crying skull and Takashi Tanemori crossed the bridge, a man who would enter history as the survivor nearest the hypocenter arrived at Hiroshima's Communications Hospital with the same symptoms the Nakazawa boy had decided he must now keep his mother from noticing. When the sky first opened up, Eizo Nomura was located literally within shouting distance of the Hiroshima Dome, in the basement of the city's Rationing Union Hall. Even underground, he became aware of the flash— and the whole room simultaneously thumped.

Mr. Nomura clawed his way out of the cave-in, emerging from a shock-cocoon onto ground that was barely more than 100 meters (328 feet, or one city block) from the absolute hypocenter. He stood on pavement hot enough to burn through the soles of his shoes, feeling as if the earth had disappeared and he had been placed in a strange new land. His guess was only half wrong. Nomura's little corner of planet Earth had in fact disappeared, and much of it was placed in the stratosphere. And so it came to pass that one small patch of Hiroshima real estate was transformed into something so strange and unprecedented that in the future the foundations and the impossibly intact frame of the Rationing Union Hall would become the site of a tourist "rest house," near the center of the city's Peace Memorial Park. Few visitors would guess that its walls were still standing against the sky after the blast, or that someone had survived behind those walls, in a region where every living thing on the

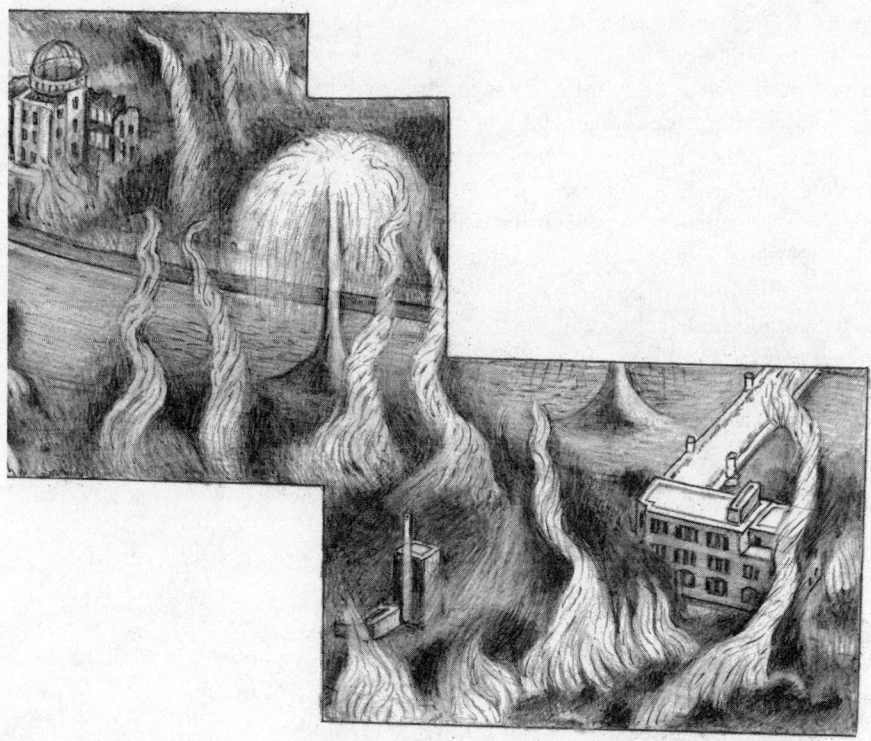

sidewalks and on the streets had been converted to charcoal and vapor, or blown apart, or both.

When Nomura dusted himself off and looked up, the sky was black with smoke, and sparks seemed to be raining down from everywhere. On his side of the Motoyasu Bridge, he had found no one and nothing still alive, unless waterspouts and the serpent-like motions of the fire worms could be considered the actions of something brought to life. To Mr. Nomura, they moved and behaved like sentient creatures, advancing with giant slithering strides from the opposite riverbank and chasing him away from the bridge and under the water, where he held his breath until he was in agony. When finally he surfaced and cleared his lungs, and flung the hair and water from his eyes, the worms were moving away and he felt a measure of triumph at having survived; but he was also beginning to feel the first effects of radiation sickness, creeping up inside of him and starting to gnaw, like bites from a thousand little rats' teeth.[20]

After two days, there were few doctors and nurses well enough to help Mr. Nomura, or anyone else. All of the medicines were gone, and there were no working microscopes with which the medics could begin to make even a crude diagnostic guess at the nature of the disease that had sickened Eizo No-mura, Keiji Nakazawa, and almost everyone else who entered the hot zone.

The building Nomura eventually came to was located only 1,500 meters from the hypocenter. Most of its second floor had splashed away and burned. The lower floor was still marginally intact, having been, to one degree or another, shock-cocooned behind Hiroshima Castle and the steel and concrete Communications Bureau Building. One of the directors, Dr. Michihiko Hachiya, was now a patient in his own hospital.

Dr. Hachiya had been in amongst the streams of ant-walkers Isao Kita observed from the weather station. On the first day, he wandered burned and battered and naked through updrafts and downdrafts so violent that sheets of metal roofing hummed and twirled above his head, and pieces of flaming trees whirled out of the sky like fiery swallows. The doctor vaguely remembered seeing birds dying on the ground at his bare feet, with their wings and feathers scorched. And he vividly recalled following a row of people who, like him, were naked—and he had wondered absently what force of nature had deprived them of their clothes.

The physician remembered little else about the past forty-eight hours. For most of his missing time, he had been drifting in and out of fever and sleep. On the afternoon of August 8, he wanted nothing more in the world than to get off the floor and start helping the other patients, but the chief of surgery, Dr. Katsube, said, "You are too impatient. You should be thankful that you are going to live."

It had not occurred to him that he might have come close to death.

"Was I that bad off?" Hachiya asked.

"We were all worried about you," Katsube replied, and explained that he had lost a lot of blood and suffered forty wounds. Mr. Iguchi, the ambulance driver, had rigged a makeshift operating room by scavenging unbroken lights and connecting them to one of several still-functioning truck batteries. In this manner, Dr. Hachiya and as many as sixty other patients—including the "miracle survivor" Eizo Nomura—had been and would continue to be treated, until the last battery was drained. As Katsube brought Hachiya up to date on events of the past two days, the doctor-turned-patient noticed that the surgeon's hands were badly burned.

A noise outside the window drew their attention to a patient Dr. Katsube had neglected to mention.

From time to time during his long and fitful sleep, Hachiya remembered hearing him stumbling about the garden. Hachiya looked out through a shattered window whose steel frame appeared to have been uprooted from its bed. The patient bumped his nose against the broken frame.

"Has he been fed?" Hachiya asked.

"Don't worry, Doctor," came the reply. "There are plenty of potato leaves in the garden, so I don't think he'll be hungry."

The patient happened to be a horse, who was burned along one whole side of his body, and who seemed to have been simultaneously blinded by the *pika* (the flash). He had come staggering to the front gate about the same time as Dr. Hachiya, and Dr. Katsube explained that he did not have the heart to turn the poor creature away, so he was sheltered in the garden, outside the doctor's window.

For Hachiya, the horse was not only a distantly remembered companion but a constant one as well. Companionship had meant a lot to him whenever he awoke in the night, recalled what he saw along the ant trail, and fell into despair. At first, he felt lonely. He would write later that "it was an animal loneliness. I became part of the darkness of the night. There were no radios, no electric lights, not even a candle in the room. The only light that came to me was reflected in the flickering shadows made by the burning city. The only sounds were the groans and sobs of the burn victims."

In the midst of such loneliness, Hachiya always heard the blind horse bumping against a wall and pawing at leaves.

By now the patient had already eaten most of the doctor's potato leaves. The garden was once a tennis court, but the war effort had required every available piece of land to be converted into a so-called victory garden. Hachiya became infamous throughout the hospital for breeding strawberries and potato plants that produced huge, lush leaves, but yielded dwarf, peanut-size strawberries and strawberry-size potatoes.

Dr. Hachiya lifted his head and asked, "Don't you think we should dig up the potatoes? They must be quite big by now."

Dr. Katsube and his nurse Kado laughed, and for a moment (albeit only for a moment), misery was forgotten.

When Dr. Katsube began to explain how patients were succumbing to vomiting and diarrhea, and how not even plumbing was available and the battery-powered operating room was just about finished—and how the army was bringing no food to the hospital—a new reality began to bite down. It bit down with all the force of sudden realization and mortality: Dr. Hachiya's constant companion had become the only source of protein any of the patients would be able to count on, for many days to come.[21]

Hanako Ito and her husband, Akio, had waited for the firestorm to weaken before venturing into central Hiroshima, where their son Hiroshi had attended the highest-ranked school in the province. They did not know, when they

At a radius of nearly 1,500 meters (up to 17 city blocks) from the hypocenter, on the other side of a window frame that had been pulled into crazy angles by the bomb, Dr. Hachiya's constant companion, though blinded by the flash, seemed to be keeping watch over the wounded physician. [Illustration: Patricia Wynne]

found the school converted to a desert of ashes and cracked bricks, that Hiroshi had escaped uninjured, and followed the railroad tracks homeward. The school's only recognizable landmark was an Olympic-size swimming pool, into which more than two hundred people had fled, seeking shelter from the flames. Their bodies were boiled and bloated. Their faces appeared to have been roasted before the boiling began.

By the time Charles Sweeney learned he was going to have to do this again, and drove into the night searching for a priest, Mr. and Mrs. Ito had seen enough. Corpses—none of them identifiable—were being dragged from the pool and stacked for pyres by soldiers who moved to and fro in stunned silence. Of all the students, not a single child was known to have been found alive. Clinging to her husband's hand, Hanako followed a set of trolley tracks toward home, her only light the growing numbers of mass-grave funeral pyres on either side of the road. Firelight guided her, and something the color of moonlight.

"Between the pyres, we could see trails of silvery phosphorous weaving all about," wrote one witness. "They looked for all the world like the spirits of the dead in the old storybooks."

Hanako believed that the "blue fireflies" might be the ghosts of Hiroshima searching for their loved ones, and she wondered if little Hiroshi might come looking for her in this way. When she arrived in the eastern hill country, however, she found her son alive, though quite exhausted from the ordeal.

"I was chased by the fire," he explained, "and I had to cover my ears because I could hear people crying for help behind me." As he told the story of the fire worms and the black rain, Hiroshi was stricken by chills and vomiting. A doctor was called to the house, but he could not diagnose any known disease, and it did not seem to matter because by midnight the boy's appetite began to return and by the morning of August 8 he was feeling well enough to assist his brother Tsugio's fifth-grade class in a new assignment from the Association of Homeland Security.

The Itos' town was among the few that did not turn all the nonresident survivors back toward Hiroshima. Instead, trucks and horse-drawn carts were being sent westward beyond the Kaidaichi train wreck to bring Hiroshima's injured to the local school. Though the Truman announcement that the weapon used in Hiroshima was atomic was kept secret from the town, Tsugio Ito knew from the appalling size of the August 6 cloud, and from the blast that broke windows nearly thirteen kilometers away, that he and his brother Hiroshi were witness to an unusual bomb. The flash burns and the de-gloving injuries of the people arriving in the trucks confirmed its uniqueness beyond dispute.

By the afternoon of the second day after the bomb, 360 survivors lay on straw mats, filling all of the tiny classrooms. Homeland Security assigned children to heal the injured, but provided no ointments or medication. A local farmer offered thinly sliced cucumbers and advised the children to apply them to burns—*cucumber Band-Aids for* pika-don *wounds,* Tsugio thought bitterly. It seemed a completely hopeless assignment. Some of the people were hemorrhaging and losing their hair and were certainly dying; and Tsugio felt a jolt of fright when Hiroshi removed his work hat and most of his hair came away clinging to the straw weave.

But it *can't be THAT bad,* Tsugio told himself. His brother had suffered none of the burns that appeared to be killing the other survivors; and after all, when the day's work at the school finished, Hiroshi felt well enough to play ball; and he was not vomiting like the others; and his appetite was holding up well. And he would be dead by the second week of September.[22]

"You must remember," Dean Susumu Tsunoo told Professor Koyano and the students of Nagasaki Medical College, "you must never forget that the atomic bomb gives you very little time to get under cover." Connecting together everything he had seen and heard in Hiroshima, he emphasized, "If you see the flash, you'll have maybe three seconds to duck and roll and seek cover before the blast wave strikes."

The dean of the Nagasaki College Hospital had run straight to the school from the Hiroshima train on a self-assigned mission of warning and preparation. What seemed to horrify him above all else were the intense heat waves—which, even if the bomb did allow three seconds to duck and cover, tended to burn anyone standing under the flash.

"Whatever you do," Tsunoo warned, "you must not just stand still, looking around. The burns of those who immediately dove facedown to the ground, and into shade behind walls or in ditches, were comparatively mild."

Tsunoo went on to describe, in a lesson his listeners were sure to remember and heed, how a man who had been sitting at a trolley stop, reading a newspaper, survived with a pattern of burns indicating that white paper reflected the glare of the *pika* and protected his face and the upper part of his body—and also protected his thumbs—though his other fingers, curling around the front of the paper, were seared and fused together. The man happened to be wearing black suit pants, and they absorbed the light, with the dye heating up and burning the fibers deep into his groin and his legs.

Dr. Tsunoo reported numerous instances of women and children wearing patterned clothing, sometimes displaying decorative flowers on white cloth. The dark flowers were now branded permanently onto their skin.

As a precaution, he advised the students to wear white clothing and white, wide-rimmed hats, and to hang white sheets in all of the hospital's windows. The dean was describing how ordinary sheets of calligraphy paper, being hung in a window by a teacher, were substantial enough to protect the teacher's face from the flash. As his lesson neared its end, wrapped up as a warning, a student who would later be described by a doctor named Akizuki as "young Mr. Fujii from the theological school," became sick with worry.

"Given what I have seen of this new bomb," Tsunoo concluded, "I feel sure it won't be enough as an air-raid precaution for you to simply be on alert when you hear enemy planes approaching. You must all—and you students in particular—be more on your guard than ever before and prepare for the worst."

As Dr. Tsunoo spoke, his own agitation increased, and seemed to become contagious. "What had been a city," he said, "is now a prairie, baked reddish-yellow." His voice cracked when he related the story of a little girl who had tried to help a man calling out to her for water. Sitting against a wooden column, the man begged her to help him stand up and walk down to the river. The entire side of his body facing her had been flash-burned black. The wood behind him was also burned black, and when she grabbed the man's hand and helped him to stand up, she saw that his perfectly clean shadow was etched behind him on the wood, like a pale image on a photographic negative.

"This was only a little less than two kilometers away from the center of the flash," Dean Tsunoo explained, adding that he would not have believed the tale the girl had told, had he not seen such horrors with his own eyes.

At almost this same radius from the *pika*, a castor bush's leaves and branches had completely disintegrated near the ruins of the Meiji Bridge. The telephone pole behind the bush had been flash-burned from light-brown to charcoal black—and yet every point and crevice of the vanished leaves lived on as a light-brown shadow against the black. The trunk of the castor plant still existed, albeit as a blackened nub of blown-apart wood. Nearer to Hiroshima Castle—which was "simply gone"—Dr. Tsunoo crossed the Misasa Bridge, and there he saw a bicycle leaning against the bridge railing, with its smoldering, partly skeletonized rider still upon it. Trying to make sense of the inexplicable, Tsunoo said he had searched for the man's flash-shadow, but could not find it.

At this point, Mr. Fujii, the theology student, ran out of the room—ran nearly a kilometer uphill to his friend, Dr. Akizuki. The student's girlfriend lived in Hiroshima. Rage and fear were taking control of him. A small tabloid that according to Akizuki hardly deserved the title of "newspaper" would turn out to have made the right call—"New kind of bomb dropped on Hiroshima,

Throughout Hiroshima, walls and other still-standing structures preserved the shadows of objects, each pointing toward the origin of the flash. 1,300 meters (or about 15 city blocks) from the hypocenter, a telephone pole recorded the shape of a castor bush, during the instant before the plant shriveled and flew apart. American scientists discovered the bush a month later, sending up new shoots. [Illustration: Patricia Wynne]

much damage done"—while, outside the tabloid, and outside of Dr. Tsunoo's lecture hall, the governor's office and the local military authorities were trying to hide the facts, all the way down to pronouncements of only "slight damage to Hiroshima."

"*Slight damage?*" the student cried out to Dr. Akizuki. "According to what we have just heard, at least fifteen kilometers square have been burned to the ground!"

Dr. Akizuki understood at once what the student was planning. "No," he said. "You must stay away from that place."

"As long as the trains are still running in that direction, I've got to try. Until this moment all we really knew was that no news was coming out of that area. I've got to find out what's happened to her."

Akizuki tried to dissuade him, warning that several cities along the rail lines had been fire-bombed only the night before, and that he could be killed along the route north if the fire-bombings continued tonight. But the young man set off toward the rail station with a rucksack on his back, and Dr. Akizuki would record later, "No one knew how fortune smiled on him that afternoon, as he left Nagasaki to go to Hiroshima."

He would also record that, as one of the few doctors who was to survive in the Nagasaki region, his first tasks were fated to involve triage, which amounted essentially to mercy killing. The Urakami medical complex was located barely more than 1,600 meters from the hypocenter of a detonation at least two times more powerful than the previous atomic bomb. Here and there, random shock-cocoon effects were going to diverge around hills, leaving perimeter concrete walls and multiple floors of the medical buildings mysteriously intact. Just the same, 42 professional physicians, 206 office workers, 109 nurses, and 535 students were about to be lost.

Dr. Akizuki would always attribute his own survival, and the survival of many others, to the warnings from Dean Tsunoo. The dean, he learned later, became a Hiroshima witness who did not survive his second atomic bomb. At Moment Zero, he would be located in a wood-framed medical center, almost 1,000 meters nearer the hypocenter. In fewer than twenty-four hours, Dean Tsunoo was fated to survive in a second shock cocoon, but he would have little more than wood to shield him against a deep-penetrating gamma shine nearly three times more powerful than the one that had blazed forth over Hiroshima. Impossibly, while Tsunoo was given a few more days in which to live, people fifteen meters from him (barely more than 49 feet away), throughout the outer rooms of the very same wooden building, were fated to be literally vaporized, becoming part of the radioactive fallout that Akizuki and the other survivors would inhale.[23]

Prefect Takejiro Nishioka wanted, for himself, nothing more than to be with his family, before Nagasaki suffered the same destruction he had seen in Hiroshima. Yet in spite of his desire to see his wife and child, a sense of duty sent him directly from the Nagasaki train station to the office of Governor Nagano.

Up to that point in time, on the afternoon of August 8, the governor had been told only that a new bomb had been involved in the loss of contact with Hiroshima, which was due largely to some disruptive pulse effect on radios and transmission lines. The bomb was said to have killed several hundred people and damaged some buildings as well as the power grid. The American president's threats of massive destruction, according to Governor Nagano's top military advisors, had been grossly exaggerated. And then Prefect Nishioka came rushing into the office, describing tornadoes of fire rising from a horizon-spanning sea of flames . . . and large trees felled by the blast at a radius of several kilometers . . . steel-reinforced buildings and bridges uprooted and flattened.

The governor asked him if he was describing something he actually saw, or rumors told to him.

"I saw it," Nishioka said. "Everybody on the train with me saw it, and they're telling everybody about it."

The governor seemed more concerned, in that moment, with the spread of the story than with the actual facts behind it; and when Nishioka recognized this, he begged Nagano's word that he would not be quoted. Spreading "bad stories" and "rumors of defeat" were treasonable offenses that threatened not only the prefect with military retribution but his entire family as well.

Nagano gave Nishioka his oath that he would not tell, and proved himself a liar the moment the prefect stepped out the door. He immediately assembled the police and the government executives and related what the prefect revealed to him. Each of them took the cue from the tone of Governor Nagano's voice and from the expression on his face, and responded with a sense of fear and a need for preparation, rather than an old indoctrinated reflex to retaliate against the messenger.

In years to come, the prefect would regret that death-dealing censorship protocols had forced him to confine his report to the governor's ear alone. Nishioka would grow prematurely old, knowing that had he been allowed to publish what he and Dean Tsunoo already knew, in the newspaper that he owned, uncounted thousands of lives might have been saved.

From the governor's office, Prefect Nishioka went directly to the site he had selected to shelter the largest generators and printing presses and the greatest national treasures. With him were the executives and the Prefectural Police and the chief of the *Tokko*, Japan's special plainclothes military and "thought criminal" police. Temporarily, vital equipment and treasures would be stored at the governor's private shelter. This was to be the final, virtually impregnable Crisis Command Center. A broad tunnel was to be dug, allowing heavy equipment to be trucked into a cavern beneath the hill of the Gokoku Shrine. The site was located away from central Nagasaki, "far enough" from likely primary aiming points. Yet, as history and chance would have it, the site was being built barely outside the coming hypocenter, in a region where rebounding compression waves were going to converge and echo with such force that not a single foundation stone would remain in place to suggest where the shrine had been; even the original geography of the hill would be rendered unfamiliar.

Nishioka arranged to meet again at the shrine with equipment ready—promptly at eleven o'clock on the following morning, August 9.

Radiation sickness soon intervened, and kept the prefect from his appointment with destiny. All his life, he had been healthy. Now, out of nowhere—out of the deep, impersonal nowhere—nausea and debilitating fatigue, and a feeling that he was being flayed from the inside, seized total control over him. He remembered the miniature volcanic plumes that had sprouted near Field Marshal Hata's house, and how he understood even then that he should have given the plumes a wide berth, but he had walked through them anyway.

Sitting down on the ground now and rolling up his pants, he cursed himself. Just beneath the skin, Nishioka's legs had sprouted dark blue, star-like spots, tinged with yellow on the edges—as if he had suddenly developed something next of kin to hemophilia.

That quickly, his only directive became to simply head home and get his family away from this place. He did not think he could travel very far, but he did not have far to go. *Home* was within walking distance of the Gokoku Shrine, near the Roman Catholic Cathedral of Maria.

"God! Where were you?" Mrs. Nishioka asked, when she saw how ashen and sickly—even how filthy—her husband had become.

"I've been in the city of corpses," he answered. "Now, don't ask anything more. Just follow my instructions if you want to live."

The prefect ordered his wife to leave at once with their child to the village of Unzen, about two hours away by car. He filled the car's tank with the last of the family's gasoline (which he had been hoarding for more than three months), and he refused to let her pack any belongings. Unzen was less than a town—nothing more than a hamlet and shrine in the middle of a national park, and this suited the prefect just fine. There was only enough gasoline for a one-way trip, and this too was satisfactory. No one would target a national park, and two hours by car, one way, had to be far enough from Nagasaki.

"Go. Go now and don't look back!" he commanded. The prefect's wife had never seen him so close to losing his composure. Mrs. Nishioka, who had grown up in the Far East's largest Christian town, was reminded suddenly of Lot's instructions to his own wife.[24]

Akira Iwanaga, one of the surviving ship designers from Hiroshima, had disembarked the prefect's train at a town called Isahaya, some 29 kilometers northeast of Nagasaki. Akira's parents lived in Isahaya, and as the train came near, he was feeling too ill to travel on to the Mitsubishi shipyards. He decided to spend the remainder of the day and perhaps the coming night at his parents' house, hoping that after a little rest, he would awake feeling better. Besides, he had urgent information to relate about how he had survived what he witnessed in Hiroshima. He was insistent that his parents and his friends understand the danger of glass daggers created by the blast wave. To judge by what he saw when he explored the ruins of his own dormitory, everyone indoors had been pierced by glass; but all of the blades appeared to have followed straight-line trajectories.

"This meant," Akira explained, "that people were spared if they had ducked when they first saw the flash, and if they were below the window-line when the blast came. So, I want you to tell everyone to open their windows as high as they will go."

A friend explained that he intended to take the advice a bit further than lifting the windows; he hurried away to remove all the glass from his house, based on Akira's warning.

As the afternoon wore on, Akira discovered that the idea of recovering his strength and being able to complete his journey to the shipyard was a vain hope. The pains in his abdomen were growing worse, and while it became possible to believe he might pass out from the sheer intensity of the pain and attain something *like* sleep, he realized that refreshing sleep was simply out of the question.[25]

Tsutomu Yamaguchi was feeling no better than Akira or the prefect. His burned arm and face were swelling, stinging, and itching mercilessly when he reached Nagasaki Station. About the time Prefect Nishioka discovered the bleeding under his skin, Yamaguchi stumbled into the Mitsubishi Company's hospital, seeking treatment. He had arrived during an air-raid alert that had sent the medical staff fleeing into underground shelters. Yamaguchi was feeling too weak to join them, so he wandered through a hospital turned suddenly into a ghost town. His left arm was feeling so swollen with accumulating fluid that he believed the skin would pop like a balloon at the slightest touch. The flesh on the left side of his face was stretched too tight to let him call out for help—not without extreme pain. Through what he would later regard as providence, one doctor had disobeyed the air-raid alarm and stayed above on the ground floor. He was an eye doctor named Sato, a former school friend of Tsutomu Yamaguchi.

The engineer's old friend was clearly curious about a survivor of the weapon, but it bothered Yamaguchi that Sato did not recognize his face until he identified himself. The survivor suddenly realized that his wounds must look even worse than they felt.

Sato took Yamaguchi straightaway to an office where he began practicing burn treatment in the Ophthalmology Department. When Dr. Sato cut away a thin sheet of dead skin from his arm, the basin Yamaguchi held for him filled with a watery substance and overflowed onto the floor. The doctor was honest with him, describing the flesh below the "dead layer" as "bright, raw, red—like whale meat." He applied oils to the wounds and bandaged them. There was only ophthalmic medicine available, and the only treatment Dr.

Sato could provide for his friend's facial and scalp wounds was to cut away the outer layers of dead skin and singed hair, sterilize the area, and cover him with bandages. Neither man quite understood at the time that Sato had just stepped into history, as the first doctor to treat an atomic bomb survivor in Nagasaki.

When Yamaguchi walked outside, the afternoon sun, though it had begun to climb down in the sky, burned his skin wherever it was exposed. Fortunately, the doctor had left his face well covered with sun-blocking bandages—which explained in part why his mother let out a shriek after he entered the house, and called him "Ghost!"

While he was being treated by Sato, stories from the Hiroshima train had spread quickly through the Nagasaki region, and Yamaguchi's parents began to prepare their minds for reception of the news that he was among the missing. And then, while his family hid in a shelter during yet another air raid alert, he entered his parents' house, lit candles at the family altar, and prayed quietly. "I did not believe in a particular god," he would recall, "yet I could not help but thank someone for my safe return from hell." And in this state—with his face covered in white bandages and sitting cross-legged before the altar with his feet hidden from view—his family found him when the all-clear sounded.

In Japanese mythology, ghosts did not have feet.

"Have you got feet?" his mother asked timidly.

Yamaguchi showed her his feet, and reassured her that he did indeed have feet and was not the ghost of her son. His wife, Hisako, came running into the house and took him by his one good hand, and kissed him as if nothing at all had happened to his face.

Yamaguchi forgot his pain and tried to reassure her that he was fine in spite of all the bandages. Seeing that his son was peacefully asleep in the sling on Hisako's back, "I just stroked his head gently," Yamaguchi would write later, "for I did not want to surprise him with my bandaged appearance."

Hisako announced that they now had a new house of their own, which she had bought with some of their savings and which he had not yet seen. The little frame house was more than a half-hour's walk from his parents' home, but he was sustained by the thought that once the three of them were home alone, they would be able to rest quietly. He made the forty-five-minute trek falteringly but happily.

The place was small, but beautifully crafted from hardwood. There was even a balcony built for two, from which Yamaguchi and his wife could look across the river in the direction of the Maria Cathedral and the Urakami hills. However, the peaceful family time Yamaguchi had been hoping for was not to be. As with most Mitsubishi families, they had been required to choose living quarters located almost adjacent to the shipyard and its offices. Everyone knew that this put them at an increased risk of being killed, if the B-29s came.

Only a week earlier, a study of maps by several priests had revealed that almost every city of any importance had been all but erased, one after another by nightly fire-bomb raids. There had remained only the quadrant of Tokyo in which the Imperial Palace stood, the Kokura industrial center, Kyoto, Nagasaki, and Hiroshima. Now there were only Kokura, Kyoto, Nagasaki, and a wide perimeter around the Palace grounds. Those who were aware of the situation—including the Yamaguchis and their neighbors—expected that the B-29 raiders would leave the Palace and its Emperor unharmed because therein lay the only hope of extracting a surrender from Japan. This meant a one-in-three chance that Nagasaki would be next.

Almost from the moment Tsutomu Yamaguchi and Hisako arrived home with their child, neighbors started arriving at the door, wanting to know what Mr. Yamaguchi had seen in Hiroshima. He was nauseous and fatigued and his fever felt as if it were still climbing; but he decided to answer every question, and offer advice: "Wear white clothes—which will reflect the heat rays. Black clothes tend to catch fire easily. Keep all of the windows open, because if glass shards are stuck in the body, treatment is very difficult. And if you see the *pika*, you must at that very moment hide yourself behind a sturdy object."

He hoped that his advice to his neighbors was unnecessary. He prayed that the white flash and the black cloud would not follow him to Nagasaki. He hoped so, but he really did not believe so.[26]

After sending his wife and child away to the Unzen forest, Prefect Nishioka gathered as many critical papers as he could carry from his office, asked his men to pour some gasoline into a small army truck, and set off for Unzen. About 33 kilometers out, both the gas supply and his health gave out. Throwing open the driver's side door, he fell to his knees and began vomiting thick bile flecked with hundreds of little black blood clots. The prefect pulled himself to his feet and, through faltering painful strides, walked the remaining kilometer to an old-style bed-and-breakfast house overlooking the sea.

I'm dying, he thought. And then he pushed the thought away. Nishioka would not let himself die until he saw his wife and child again. He hoped Unzen was far enough away for them, but he was unsure. His own condition was proof enough that one did not have to be so near an atomic bomb as to be directly injured by it, to be poisoned by it. The only certainty in his mind was that Hiroshima was not the end, and that Nagasaki would be next.[27]

On Tinian, Charles Sweeney learned at an afternoon briefing that the Kokura Army Arsenal would be the next target. Kokura was surrounded by antiaircraft batteries, and was one of the few sites remaining where command of the air was not guaranteed. A hornet's nest of airstrips and intercept fighters still existed there.

In the unlikely event, given current weather conditions, that excessive cloud cover obscured Kokura, then Nagasaki would become the secondary target.

Sweeney hoped the conditions would be right for him to hit the primary target, Kokura. After more than a week of intensive study, he knew the streets and buildings of his secondary target as well as he knew the layout of his own hometown. Nagasaki and its neighboring suburb of Urakami lay in the middle of a steep valley. According to Alvarez's analysis and Tibbets's orders for a Nagasaki-run, maximum blast and rebound effects in the target region could be achieved only by detonation high above the flat landscape downriver of the Mitsubishi torpedo factories and submarine support facilities. The commercial and residential districts of downtown Nagasaki were also located in this same maximum effect zone; and by everything Sweeney knew, the civilian casualties would be even higher in Nagasaki than in Hiroshima.

And so Sweeney firmed a resolve to give it everything he could, to drop his package on the almost purely military target of Kokura. He had doubts, however, that the bomb would get that far. Sweeney was familiar with the fusing malfunctions that, had they occurred in a live plutonium-supplied bomb, would have unleashed the fury of a thousand suns right below the belly of a B-29. He hoped that Alvarez's team had finally solved the problem.

The plutonium bomb was so many orders of magnitude more complicated than Hiroshima's uranium device that it could not be armed in flight and had to be made live before it was hoisted up through the bomb-bay doors.

Four kinds of detonators had already been installed—with two fuses of each kind, leaving nothing to chance. The two air-pressure sensors were set to trigger their fuses at 1,890 feet. The two time-bomb fuses would fire forty-three seconds after the bomb was released, at which point it would have dropped from 30,000 feet to about 1,890 feet. The two radar fuses would be attached to a device that pinged the ground with radio waves and timed the echoes, down to an altitude of 1,890 feet. If the first three pairs of detonators failed and the bomb continued to fall below 1,890 feet, the last two detonators, located in the nose of the machine, would implode the plutonium core and set the chain reaction in motion within one-hundred-millionth of a second, before the impact itself could damage the bomb.

The two final, last-resort triggers were what worried Charles Sweeney. A single hard bump on a runway could incinerate the entire island.

He was considering this, underneath the bomb itself, when Admiral William Purnell stepped up behind him and asked, "Son, do you know how much that bomb cost?"

"No, sir," Sweeney replied.

"Two billion dollars," Purnell stated.

"Well," Sweeney said, and let out a slight whistle, "that's a lot of money, Admiral."

"And do you know how much your airplane costs?"

"Slightly more than half a million dollars, sir."

The admiral nodded sternly, and said, "I'd suggest you keep those relative values in mind for this mission."[28]

The last train to reach Nagasaki was now departing Hiroshima Station. Master kite-maker Morimoto and three of his helpers—Doi, Shinji, and Masao—were traveling together in the same car. All four of them had survived Hiroshima without any visible injuries, but Morimoto was trying to fend off a persistent nausea and Doi was drenched in perspiration—yet at the same time he complained about intermittent chills.

In another part of the train, a survivor named Kuniyoshi Sato was sitting across from a pale figure who, much like Doi, was sweating profusely. Kuniyoshi would record more than two decades later that the anonymous fellow traveler was holding a cloth-covered bowl on his lap, and this he jealously guarded, as if it were filled with gold.

"What are you holding, there?" Kuniyoshi asked.

"I married just last month," the stranger replied. "But my wife died. I want to take her home to her parents." And then, after a pause, the man lifted the cover from his bowl.

"See? Do you want to look inside?" He spoke these words in a tone that also said, *See? This is what you get for sticking your nose into other people's lives.*

The bowl was filled with scraps of human bone. And, though the train was very crowded and it seemed very unlikely that Kuniyoshi would be able to find another seat, he stood and hurried away. Kuniyoshi never did learn the name of the man with the bowl of bones, but there would be little doubt among future historians that this was Kenshi Hirata.

Far behind Kuniyoshi, beyond the kite-makers, and the others who were fated to experience the atomic bomb a second time (only a small percentage of whom would survive), rescue crews were now moving from the countryside into Hiroshima, more and more of them each passing hour.

At the Communications Hospital, a doctor named Minoru Fujii passed through with a team he had assembled in the suburbs. En route to another field hospital, Dr. Fujii left behind a crate of ointments and bandages and enough food for two days. Any other Wednesday, two days' supplies would not mean very much, but today they were everything. Given the increasing incidence of what appeared to be flu-like symptoms and contagious anorexia, Dr. Hachiya believed the food supply might last four or five days. It seemed to him that the horse in the garden (the hospital's nutritional safety net) now had a reprieve, if only a fleeting one. The Communications Hospital, like the Hiroshima Dome and the multistoried Fukuya Department Store, stood apart from the landscape, crying out for attention. For acres and acres in every direction, this region of the city was a prairie that sprouted no grass and whose rocks were wind-scoured bricks and roof tiles. In the midst of this, the hospital was like a lone outcrop of bedrock, and also like a magnet. And so, all but inevitably, the building drew a gang of soldiers to its entrance. Guns out and displayed, they demanded bandages and food for the Second General Army. Four days later, when he felt well enough to write, Dr. Hachiya would record in his diary that the thugs had left behind essentially nothing for the treatment and feeding of more than eighty patients.

Dr. Hachiya, though he seemed to be the only member of his staff still possessing a healthy appetite and feeling as if he were getting stronger, was not yet well enough to get out of bed and to be walking around visiting patients. In fact, the other doctors loudly forbade the former ant-walker from trying to move. So he took reports instead, serendipitously recording history.

None of the patients had any appetite. One by one they had developed symptoms ranging from migraine headaches and chills to profuse sweating, bleeding under the skin, and bouts of severe vomiting.

By now, most of the vomiting had turned into dry heaves, and many of the patients were reporting shooting pains in their lower spines. Often the pains spread to the area of the kidneys.

What alarmed Hachiya most was that many of these patients—with the whites of their eyes now turning bright red from subsurface bleeding and with the skin on their faces displaying brilliant star-like speckles of red—had not been battered or burned at all by the *pika-don*. Several of the apparently uninjured did not seem to know any longer exactly where they were.

Hachiya's friend Koyama cursed the soldiers who had looted the last of the hospital's medicines, but Dr. Hachiya was beginning to suspect that conventional drugs would have no effect on the illness. The symptoms were consistent with severe hemorrhaging throughout the body. There were diseases known from Africa and New Guinea that caused people to bleed out, and which were immune to sulfa drugs and even to powerful new antibiotics. Hachiya began to worry that the Americans had followed the *pika-don* with disease warfare, and the thought of this filled him with dread.

As reports of the air raid's secondary effects progressed from sickness to sudden death among the afflicted, a doctor who had been treating blast victims brought Hachiya the gift of a brief distraction from worries about bio-weapons.

"Doctor, do you think a girl could still see if the blast pulled out her eye from its socket?" He asked this in a completely matter-of-fact way; and in years to come, Dr. Hachiya would marvel at how quickly human minds adapted, rendering even the unbelievable commonplace.

In the same, matter-of-fact fashion, Hachiya asked, "Was the optic nerve still attached?"

"I think so," the physician said. "She held the palm of her hand against her cheek and the eye was resting in her palm and she insisted she could see me—and I can swear to you that her pupil was staring right at me."

On an ordinary day, in an ordinary place, Hachiya would have been chilled to the bone. But today his mind shifted easily into speculation about how the girl's brain might have tried to deal with the problem of constructing a three-dimensional picture from such a distorted binocular view.

This train of thought was interrupted by more horrifying concerns. Drs. Koyama and Hanaoka reported that the patients were becoming too weak to walk away from their floor mats and leave the building to relieve themselves of urine and feces. More than half of them were now lying in pools of watery, bloodstained feces—which explained, Dr. Hachiya thought, why the building was beginning to smell like a charnel house filling slowly with sewage.

The most alarming part of the report involved two male patients who had shown some improvement in the morning but who over the course of only a single hour had become dramatically worse. The red spots under their skin expanded to massive bruises, turning their faces purple. And then, long after the previous day's vomiting had emptied their stomachs down to the level of ineffective dry heaves, their mouths began bringing up fresh arterial blood. Dr. Hachiya guessed that something was breaking down their capillaries and blood vessels while something else drastically reduced the blood's ability to clot, as if the bone marrow had begun to die. By the time the men vomited their first mouthfuls of blood, their kidneys and vast regions of their spines and brains must have begun bleeding from the inside and shutting down, following the bone marrow into death.

As Dr. Koyama told it, one of them rolled onto his side and vomited more than two liters of blood; and then the other produced a sound like a long, long sheet of silk ripping—the sound of his dead, oxygen-starved intestinal lining pulling away and being extruded onto the floor through his bowels—or rather, what was left of his bowels.

"Neither of these men had been injured at all by the *pika-don*," Dr. Koyama said, over and over. "Not at all!"

Dr. Hachiya was convinced now that he was dealing with a contagious and possibly weaponized disease, in which case there was no choice but to make sure his people cremated the dead quickly, and isolated the infected. Dr. Koyama, as the new provisional deputy director, was assigned the task of setting up the isolation ward. With the help of suburban rescue and recovery workers who were drawn to the only standing shelter in the neighborhood, he was able to construct what amounted to a crude, open-air, and partly tented-over pavilion beyond the south side of the hospital. What they were doing probably was not worth very much, Dr. Hachiya would record later, but it helped his morale to think they were doing *something*.

The next step was to get all of the still-uninfected patients and staff into fresh air and away from the contamination hazard of bloody diarrhea in the ground-floor corridors. The upper floor had splashed and burned during the attack and no longer had a roof, but it seemed a far better option than remaining below.

Dr. Hachiya was carried on a stretcher to a new second-floor home, where almost all of the walls had disappeared, but where rows of twisted and charred bedframes still stood mysteriously in place.

One might complain about the soot and ashes, Hachiya observed, but he had probably never lived in a hospital ward so nearly free of bacteria as this one, sterilized by flash, blast, and flame.[29]

Thirteen-year-old Setsuko Thurlow had been instantly buried by a blast-generated blanket of rubble—which she would describe many years later as a lifesaving blanket. Unlike Mrs. Matsuyanagi's two sons, she did not witness the atomic cloud while it was still burning brightly overhead. During those first critical seconds, she was shadow-shielded from flash burns behind a wall, then cocooned in a pocket of cool air beneath a thick, gamma-and-neutron-attenuating shell of bricks. When at last the Thurlow girl broke through to the surface, the army headquarters building to which she had been recruited for a student work detail was gone and the entire world had become dark as a mineshaft. Through occasional clearings in the dust, she saw that all of the military drill ground buildings nearby—and, just beyond them, Hiroshima Castle—seemed to have disappeared along with Army Headquarters. There was little time to question how. Fires began to pierce the dust with an orange glare that came from near and far, and apparently from every direction. In the strengthening glow, she had begun to discern blackened objects, filing by like ghosts. Thurlow moved closer, unable to quite believe what she was seeing.

Some terrible force appeared to have reached behind people's faces and drawn the eyes out through the sockets of their skulls—no matter how tightly their eyelids must have been slammed shut against the flash. Many were trying desperately to cup their hands close to their faces, cradling their eyes. Almost everyone on the trail was so badly burned that the eyeballs—still attached by string-like optic nerves—were usually the only major clue Setsuko Thurlow had for distinguishing the front of an ant-walker's head from the back. In the region whence they came, the people had been burned on all sides of their bodies, by flash-heated air as well as by the flash itself. They were too weak and shocked to scream out for help. When she walked up to them, they simply murmured for water. The young survivor ran away to the river, past the place of Private Shimoyama's strange crucifixion. She snatched up rags of clothing that seemed to be lying everywhere, soaked them in river water, then ran back to the ant-walkers, trying to help them in the only way she knew, by answering their murmurs with sips of water from rags.

Setsuko Thurlow wished she could forget about the ant-walkers; and for years to come, keeping silent about them would help, at least until she received a scholarship to study in America. There, she would begin to speak about surviving the atomic bomb—which resulted in a newspaper article that brought a steady stream of hate mail. Thurlow's classmates advised her that she should go back again to being quiet about it and trying to forget; but she firmed a resolve to do neither.[30]

Another student, Shigeko Sasamori, had walked away from Ground Zero with a retrograde amnesia. She remembered being with her school's work crew, assigned to create a firebreak between two parts of the neighborhood by tearing down homes marked for destruction by the military. She was the only one in her class who survived the heat ray. Every one of them were fully exposed—outdoors. A wooden pole or a wall had shadow-shielded seventy-five percent of Shigeko's body, except for her face and her hands. The last thing she remembered, before awakening to her own ant-walk in Dante's hell, was calling out to her friends and pointing up to a beautiful silver plane glittering against the blue sky, laying behind itself a long white thread of cloud. Then something seemed to have gone wrong with the plane, and a parachute suddenly bloomed above. Shigeko remembered thinking that whoever dove out of the plane must have been a very brave man, to be parachuting into the middle of a Japanese city.

Shigeko's next memory was a world so black and so silenced by the muffling effects of the dust that until the fires began to create light and until the dust cloud had shifted and thinned enough to let a baby's cries reach her, she believed she might have gone deaf and blind. In the strengthening glare of roving fire worms, Shigeko realized that there were things—*just gray things*—moving ahead of her through the orange light. She was one of them. Their clothes and their skin were falling off in shreds, as they shuffled single-file toward the river, whispering and murmuring for water. One by one, as the ant-walkers strode into the river, they died and were carried away by the current. Coming more and more into conscious thought, Shigeko decided to turn in another direction, and joined another ant trail, walking north and away from the city.

By the second day after the bomb, Shigeko's parents had found her and taken her to the home of relatives in the countryside. Not until December would the schoolgirl's weakened immune system be able to overcome the burns and the secondary infections to a point at which she felt well enough to venture outside. She barely noticed that her mother and her aunts removed or hid every mirror in the house, their only explanation being that her face was healing and she did not need to see it yet.

"You'll get better," her mother assured.

Shigeko would hold onto her mother's words as a truth—until the day she found a broken piece of mirror in the garden: "A shock like someone dropping a pail of icy water down my back," she would tell future generations. The first look in the mirror was "like a thousand icy knives digging in all at the same time; but my family kept telling me—gently, kindly—that I was still in the process of healing and that if I gave myself up to despair, I would also be giving up the day when everything would be all right."

Healing would eventually pick up speed, with help from what in August 1945 seemed the most unlikely of sources in the world. The American journalist Norman Cousins, aided by plastic surgeons volunteering their services—and by donations that included a check from *Enola Gay*'s co-pilot Robert Lewis—brought Shigeko and several other *pika*-scarred survivors to America, for surgeries aimed at allowing "Hiroshima maidens" to come out of hiding, and to live more normal lives.

Then, for the first time, Shigeko Sasamori would begin to tell the world what she remembered.[31]

The first thing Takehisa Yamamoto's mother remembered seeing, after she entered Hiroshima in search of her husband, was a woman who must have given birth on that first day, or whose baby had been pulled out through her abdominal muscles by the forces of blast and implosion. It was difficult for Takehisa's mother to figure out one way or the other what had happened to the young woman—for Mrs. Yamamoto had followed the riverbank into the city two days after the bomb, and most of the bodies were bloating like balloons in the August sun. Many were actually bursting like balloons, expelling their insides along with the accumulated gases of putrefaction.

Takehisa Yamamoto was too young to remember any of this. He was only sixteen months old when his mother carried him into the wasteland on her back. She eventually found his father—injured by neutron spray and black rain but still alive. He had been teaching one of the few classes not to be canceled during preparation for "the final battle." Something in the school's structure, possibly nothing more substantial than a single support beam angled in just the right direction, had allowed the force of the blast to diverge around it—and around Mr. Yamamoto's body—shock-cocooning him only one kilometer from the hypocenter, while the building itself shadow-shielded him from the heat ray, and to a lesser degree from the gamma rays. Every student in front of Yamamoto died instantly.

Mr. Yamamoto was suffering from radiation sickness when his wife found him; but around the time Shigeko Sasamori discovered the broken mirror, he would begin to recover.

Every year thereafter, Takehisa Yamamoto's mother would call August 6 a day of remembrance, insisting that family members tell—and commit to memory—the stories of what the atomic bomb had done, in the hope that by passing on this oral history, the survivors might prevent another city in another time from becoming another Hiroshima.

Takehisa did not want to hear it. Especially he did not want his mother ever again to describe to him the blackened balloon girl and her ghastly balloon baby. As he grew older, Takehisa would run away from his mother as August 6 approached.

He did not want to commit any of it to memory; and he would manage to make a nearly successful effort at forgetting his family's history, until he grew up, married, and knew the indescribable heartbreak of losing his son to leukemia, pornographically young. During the years after the bomb, leukemia would grow to such epidemic proportions in Hiroshima that it was to become known as "atomic bomb disease."

"From one generation to the next after an exposure," Takehisa would tell a gathering of American students nearly seven decades later, as another day of remembrance approached, "this is how radiation affects people."[32]

Nancy Cantwell had already undergone the first of several name changes. She was born Namsun Koh, and as a young Korean nurse inducted into a Japanese military hospital, she had suffered less than most under the prevailing racial arrogance of the times; yet she had suffered. The conquered Koreans

Nurse Minami (Nancy) Cantwell in 2008 and 1945. Like Tsutomu Yamaguchi, her life was ultimately touched by two Ground Zeros. [Illustration: CRP]

were generally regarded as an inferior slave caste. The work details assigned to Namsun were exceedingly strenuous, but she had impressed a head nurse with her commitment to working even harder, saying, "Because I certainly won't die of the work."

The head nurse transferred Namsun to a new hospital in the suburbs of Hiroshima, and gave her the protection of a new, Japanese-sounding name: Minami.

The hospital was surrounded by tall hills, and by parkland that had been converted to farmland. During the months leading up to the bombing, all food shipments were suspended and an order came down from the military, dictating that the hospital would have to "live off the land." Minami and the rest of the medical staff doubled up their workload, and became farmers and caregivers for wounded and tuberculosis-infected soldiers. Most of their patients were the latter. It seemed strange to Minami that fewer and fewer military personnel appeared to be coming home with wounds. The majority of the beds were occupied by elderly veterans who had become ill. It occurred to her that perhaps the war was becoming more deadly to young soldiers than anyone admitted.

The problem with trying to grow food at a hospital during the approach of war's end was that seed was becoming scarce. Corn and tomatoes had been off the menu for months. Fortunately, potatoes could be made to bud and multiply easily enough, and for all of her hard work Minami was occasionally given two potatoes from her crop. She was learning now that constant hunger could make even the small and the ordinary seem huge. Minami would recall more than sixty years later that few things could ever taste so wonderful as a simple potato, before or since.

Up till the first week of August 1945, the patients had been steadily weakening and dying even without the added hazard of black rain and radioactive fallout. Dr. Minoru Fujii, who by now had become Minami's mentor, explained that the three key elements in the treatment of tuberculosis were rest, fresh air, and good nutrition. Of these three, nutrition was the cornerstone. In desperation, during the final weeks leading up to August 6, Dr. Fujii contrived a plan to drain a pond in the park adjacent to the hospital. The blueprints for his trenching operation were simple but exhausting, though they had the benefit of having worked. Hundreds of carp and catfish were trapped, dying and baking in the mud. Cleaned, salted, and sun-dried, they supplied the necessary nutrients during the last week of July and into the first week of August—with a little left over for the rescue mission to Hiroshima. Up to the time of "the great fish kill," the patients who were strong enough to leave their beds sneaked away into the countryside at night to dig up radish leaves and soft plant roots, which they cooked in salted water with a small amount of potato-and-rice porridge. One patient claimed credit for a recipe that included soup nutrients derived from the hospital's "mouser." He had strained juice from hairballs vomited by the cat.

Having already known such hunger, and despite knowing that it would likely return again, the staff and the patients decided to pack nearly half of their remaining fish and potato reserve (which did not amount to very much), and let Dr. Fujii bring it with him to the stricken city. The army's theft, from the Communications Hospital, of even a small donation of food was therefore a far greater loss than even Dr. Hachiya could have guessed.

On the evening of August 8, Dr. Fujii brought Minami and the rest of his team to the ruins of the Motokawa Elementary School, where a new makeshift hospital had been set up in a now roofless gymnasium. They found hundreds of burned, bleeding, and mostly naked survivors crowded all the way out to the school's gates. Conditions at the new hospital were much worse than at the Communications Hospital. Volunteer groups from the suburban towns were overwhelmed by what they saw and smelled, and they had begun to wander around like ant-walkers, not knowing what to do.

Dr. Fujii supposed that the words to describe what he found must exist somewhere, in some dictionary, in some language, but he would never be able to find them. When he saw the wounds for the first time, he thought he might lose his bearings completely. *This will help no one*, he warned himself, and he made a decision to harden his heart. Fujii allowed himself precisely five minutes to stand in the midst of it, and to be utterly horrified by it; and then, when his watch ticked off the three-hundredth second, he was able to numb his sensibilities, and take command, and call the rest of his medics to work.

Minami seemed as stunned as anyone else, but Dr. Fujii saw that she was coming out of it faster than the rest. He went to her directly, and propped her up with an old proverb: "They say that a hunter does not see the mountain."

Dr. Fujii did not know exactly what the words meant and he was glad that Minami never asked him. All he knew for sure was that the proverb seemed somehow appropriate and it worked.

His first action was to circulate instructions for triage by which only those patients most likely to be helped by whatever medical aid was available would be treated. This meant that those who seemed likely to die within forty-eight hours would be left alone. The vast majority fell into the most likely to die category.

Even those patients who seemed to have a chance at survival could be given little more medical care than bowls of rice and water. The only medicines available for the treatment of burns and gashes were a few stitching kits, and Mercurochrome for sterilization. A mixture of zinc-oxide powder and oil could be applied to burns. Any thoughts of surgery were simply not in the equation.

Minami was not sure she could tell who would survive and who would not. She simply moved from patient to patient, following a Buddhist philosophy of trying to shine a little light wherever she could. She rubbed the zinc-and-oil mixture onto the faces of flash-burned victims whose features were so swollen that there was no way to tell male from female just by looking at them.

As sunset approached, vast quantities of food were brought into the gymnasium. The sudden contrast between the makeshift hospital and the Communications Hospital just a few hundred meters away became extreme.

No one could understand at first where all the white rice, fresh vegetables, peaches, and boxes of fish and chicken were coming from. "Important people" came with them, and then medics realized that a wealthy family from outside the city had discovered relatives alive in the gymnasium. They were literally trucking in supplies. For a while, Minami was angered that veterans in a town just over the hills had been trying to squeeze nutrition from cat vomit while such reserves of high-quality food existed nearby. She wasn't the type, however, to let her anger seethe for very long. Nor was she the type to, as she believed the Americans phrased it, "look a gift toss in the mouth." So she helped herself to some rice and meat and walked out to the front gate.

Her appetite did not last very long. There were still a few ant people wandering about; although by now there were not enough of them to form long lines, so most wandered aimlessly in twos or threes, or alone. The last of the ant-walkers displayed open sores on whatever side of their bodies had been exposed to the flash, where the skin had been almost instantly roasted and then blasted away. Often the skin was so completely flayed that the musculature of the arms and legs became exposed. They were bleeding a watery substance from the muscles themselves, dripping trails of it as they walked.

Dr. Fujii explained that the higher functioning of the outer regions of the walkers' brains must already have died, erasing *who* they had been and leaving behind only an animal-like core instinct to continue walking blindly ahead. He advised Minami to stop looking at them and return to the gym, but she stayed outside a little while longer anyway, until she observed enough to know that they could no longer be conscious of pain and that the watery substance flowing so freely out of their bodies eventually stopped them dead in their tracks with dehydration.

The sights inside the gym were scarcely less distressing.

Dr. Fujii showed Minami a technique—newly invented—for washing hundreds of maggots from a wound by squirting saline solution under peeled-back and dying skin. Fujii and the other physicians expressed great fear of the maggot infestations and instructed everyone to either flush them away or remove them one by one with tweezers. Minami was mortified to find the very air filling with swarms of flies. She discovered that each patient had grown a kilogram or more of maggots. Many of these creatures were direct descendants of parents who had dodged the flash effects during those first few milliseconds of the *pika*. Minami found it impossible to believe that writhing carpets of fly larvae could come to life under the skin of human beings. The sudden abundance of human protein in Hiroshima, she judged, was causing the white worms to grow rapidly.

Minami wanted to cry and vomit; but she remembered Dr. Fujii's advice, hardened her heart, and removed the maggots, cleansed the burns, applied disinfectant, and painted the skin and any exposed muscle with the zinc-oil mixture.

What Minami and Dr. Fujii could not know—what few people in all the world would understand until America's Food and Drug Administration formally classified fly larvae as "medical devices" in 2007—was that Hiroshima's plague of maggots probably delivered more healing than harm. Although the city's adult flies often carried bacterial infection as they flitted from decaying bodies to patients whose immune systems were already weakened by radiation, the eggs they laid on and in the wounds were unleashing one of nature's most efficient cleanup crews. The white worms were, like all carrion feeders, very fussy eaters. They shunned living flesh, liquefying and digesting only dead and bacteria-permeated tissue. Already, American military surgeons were noticing that Okinawa survivors with maggot-infested wounds were faring better than similarly wounded soldiers without the infestation. They learned also that it was almost impossible to wash out all of the maggots, for each creature removed seemed to be replaced within hours by ten more from newly hatched eggs. And then the surgeons discovered that infested limbs scheduled for amputation no longer stank of putrefactive bacteria and gangrene and had begun to heal.

About three hours after sunset, Minami left the lair of the white worm to stretch her muscles, straighten her spine, and take a breath of reasonably fresh air.

From the front gate, she could see that some of the distant buildings were still burning, and that mass grave funeral pyres were being lit near and far. A light, misty rain began to fall, and with it came the blue fireflies. Before sunrise on August 9, hundreds of other rescuers and survivors would witness the same "firefly" phenomenon. The worst of the radiation had already passed; and so, even in the context of twenty-first-century physics, no known effect of the bomb would be able to adequately account for the brilliant blue fireballs darting like phosphorous through the air.

"They simply appeared here and there in the dark," Minami would recall. "They were not solid; they were more like fire moving through the air, disappearing and reappearing. They were neither exactly flame-like nor wisp-like. They were more like points of light, like fireflies—only bigger. One would dart away and another would reappear in another place; or perhaps it was the same one darting away and reappearing. There was no way to be sure. What I *was* sure about is simply this; they were not appearing where the fires were burning. These were something else. They appeared everywhere and shot away to nowhere."

Appearing everywhere made sense to Minami. The blue sparks were moving busily to and fro over the ruins of the entire city, and Minami knew by now that people died and were still dying everywhere. Even the ant-walking water

On August 8, 1945, Minami Cantwell stepped out of Dr. Fujii's Hiroshima rescue center into "the night of the blue fireflies," a phenomenon apparently similar to St. Elmo's Fire—which Minami believed represented the ghosts of Hiroshima. [Illustration: Patricia Wynne]

bleeders had not filled her with a fright such as she knew the night of August 8, while standing all alone in the dark, in what used to be the city center of Hiroshima. Minami let out a groan, held her head low, and sat down hard on the damp earth, drawing her knees in tight against her chest and shivering. She had never been so frightened before, and even though she would be shot in Korea and would live to see American Airlines Flight 11 pass over her head in Hell's Kitchen, on its way to the killing of a favorite student on September 11, 2001— even these events would be incapable of putting such fright into her ever again.

Hiroshima was a city of ghosts. That was how Minami would remember this night. She had stepped from the lair of the white worm into the domain of the blue fireflies.[33]

Kenshi Hirata almost dozed off, but a sudden bump in the train tracks and a bright flash outside his window snapped him to full alertness. Off to one side, an orange glow began blooming against the sky, spreading there, brightening. The city of Yahata was dying under what he guessed to be at least a fifty-strong B-29 raid.

He thought of Setsuko.

Kenshi's intestines still did not feel quite right, and he noticed bleeding under the skin of his fingers—and though he felt weak and achy, he was afraid that if he started to doze off again, he would drop the bowl of precious bones lying on his lap.

Two additional swarms of night-raiders helped him to keep sleep at bay. En route to Nagasaki, he witnessed the fire-bombings of two more towns: Tobata and Yawata. It was difficult for him to believe the situation had deteriorated to such an extent that B-29s were being sent far afield of the cities, to target even the small towns. The bombing of Yawata introduced a new FUBAR factor into the equation, guaranteeing that tomorrow, Kenshi Hirata's and Charles Sweeney's paths would converge a second time.[34]

For years to come, Dr. Hachiya would be awakened about 2:00 a.m. by the same recurring nightmare. He found himself in a great city—larger than Tokyo—a city where buildings stood a half-kilometer high. At daybreak, towers of all shapes and sizes gleamed like mica, and by noon they were only ashes and smoke, and twisted steel. All around him, the city was heaped with decomposing bodies, all of whom were looking at Hachiya pleadingly. He saw an eye sitting in the palm of a girl's hand—and high above another city whose towers dwarfed the tallest skyscrapers of his day, the eye blinked, then opened again as a huge fireball.

About two o'clock in the morning, on August 9, the physician awoke to the odor of burning sardines. For a moment he wondered what could cause such a smell, and then he remembered where he was. Looking down from the splashed and charred second floor of his hospital, he could discern several fires scattered about the ruins, all the way to the most distant hills. In the beginning, the fires were mostly burning rubble, but not anymore. Toward Nigitsu, an especially large blaze rivaled the fire worms of August 6. There, the dead were being burned by the hundreds. To suddenly realize that Hiroshima had become a city of funeral pyres made Hachiya shudder.

Near the center of the city, the Dome and one or two of its concrete neighbors—having somehow been left standing by the *pika-don*—were still afire on the inside. In a city that no longer had street lighting, they made eerie silhouettes against the night sky. These glowing ruins and the blazing pyres—and the occasional flashes of blue phosphorescence—set Dr. Michihiko Hachiya to wondering if Pompeii had looked like this on that last night. And it occurred to him that there were not nearly as many dead in Pompeii, as in Hiroshima tonight.[35]

· 6 ·

Kaiten and the Faithful Elephants

$\mathcal{N}$ow that President Truman had announced the atomic bomb's existence to the world, the veil of secrecy began to disintegrate. Along with the scientists assigned to Charles Sweeney's plane was Bill Lawrence, a talented engineer/science-writer who was allowed, now, to prepare a dispatch for the *New York Times*; but because he was not familiar with the squadron's never-ending variation on the theme of musical chairs, for decades to come, history books would mistakenly record the plane that dropped the bomb on Nagasaki as *Great Artiste*.

The plane that actually dropped the bomb was typically under the command of Fred Bock, and he had named her *BocksCar*, after himself. Both *Great Artiste* and *BocksCar* were, on the morning of August 9, identified only by their numbers without the usual names and artwork painted on their noses. Each had been modified in specific ways; one to monitor the world's largest bomb, the other to drop it. Logically, no one was going to switch tons of specialized equipment from one plane to another when pilots Charles Sweeney and Fred Bock switched planes. No one told Lawrence about the switch; so when he was assigned to climb into a plane filled with scientists under the command of Fred Bock, he concluded, quite naturally, that the scientific instrument plane was Bock's own *BocksCar* and that the bomb-carrier was Sweeney's plane, the one called *Great Artiste*.

At 2:00 a.m., Charles Sweeney strapped himself into the cockpit of *BocksCar*, and began running through his preflight systems check with co-pilot Don Albury and flight engineer John Kuharek. Sweeney was about to start the engines when his flight engineer leaned forward and said, "We have a problem. The fuel in our reserve tank in the rear bomb-bay bladder isn't pumping. We've got six hundred gallons of fuel trapped back there."

131

"Any idea what the problem *is*?" Sweeney asked. "Could it be instruments?" he suggested hopefully.

The engineer replied that checking and double-checking had proved his gauges to be giving accurate readings—which meant that the only means of correcting the problem involved replacing a pump.

Sweeney ran some quick calculations through his head. George Marquardt had already taken a weather plane to the primary target of Kokura. The forecast called for clear skies, but not for very long. A band of rain and mist was expected to move in from the Pacific and might linger for several days. Indeed, most of Japan's large southern island might become clouded over for a week or more—and then the cyclone season would be coming along in full swing.

Sweeney called an "All Stop," unlatched his shoulder straps, and climbed down the nosewheel ladder. Paul Tibbets was already waiting under the wing when Sweeney emerged. Their discussion was all about mathematics, crisp and unsympathetic.

Fully fueled, *BocksCar* carried 7,000 gallons, including 1,000 gallons in two reserve bladders—600 gallons of which were now trapped. If their primary target became clouded over and they had to fly extra miles from Kokura to Nagasaki—or if anything else caused them to consume extra fuel—the plane would not be coming home. Replacing the pump would take hours and might scrub the mission for days if clouds began moving over the targets—and then again, the cyclone season was looming straight ahead. Transferring the bomb to another plane would be even more time-consuming and was out of the question because its contact fuses were live.

If he left now, Sweeney would probably beat the weather window, but he would still have to fly at 17,000 feet to stay above the turbulence of a Pacific storm front, which would consume more fuel than if he flew at the optimal altitude of 8,000 feet. Due to a design plan that had never considered this situation, the 600 gallons of trapped fuel could not be drained without fixing the faulty pump. So *BocksCar* would be obliged to lift and carry—in addition to a plutonium bomb far heavier than the Hiroshima device—600 gallons of extra mass, causing the plane to consume more fuel just to carry the "dead" fuel.

"It's your call," Sweeney's commander said.

The math told Sweeney that he could certainly fly 2,000 miles (or 3,200 kilometers) to the target and return to Tinian, so long as none of the snafus that tended to intervene in even the best of plans caused target changes or other delays.

"To hell with it, boss," Sweeney said. "We're going." And so Charles Sweeney strapped himself into his leather seat for a second time this night. Less than ten minutes later, and only slightly behind schedule, he lifted off from Runway A. The clock ticked forward to 2:56 a.m., Tinian time; 1:56 a.m., Kokura and Nagasaki time.[1]

Dr. Paul Nagai, like Dr. Hachiya, was now a patient in his own hospital, but for a very different reason. The cancer diagnosed only several months before had begun to spread from his bone marrow throughout his body; and as his closest colleagues put it when they tried to assess how long he had to live, "Sometimes people at this stage can remain reasonably active for six months. Sometimes they can survive for up to three years. And sometimes they fool us all."

"I hope to fool you," Paul said. He hoped so, but he really did not believe it likely. Tonight he did not even have the strength to walk down the hill to his home and be with his wife. He simply crashed at his job on a spare hospital bed. To judge from a daily assessment of his own strength, the deterioration was progressing steadily and even seemed to be gaining speed. The physician supposed that he would come through the remainder of the summer and through autumn as well, into what was promising to be a short winter.

About 3:00 a.m., Dr. Nagai awoke from uneasy dreams and found that he could not go back to sleep—which was unusual, since the advancing cancer tended to leave him wanting to do almost nothing except sleep.

He went to a window and looked down upon the town of Urakami, from the hill of Nagasaki Medical Complex. The wartime blackouts now hid a river valley of more than 200,000 people from view, but in the glow of the stars alone, with his eyes properly night-adapted, he was able to locate his house, where his wife, Midori, was doubtless sleeping peacefully and above the covers.

Three a.m. became four and four became five, and still Dr. Nagai could not sleep. Lying in bed and watching the first hints of daylight gathering in the eastern sky, he thought about the number of patients he would have to visit today; and the more he thought about lost sleep and the job to be done, the more impossible sleep became.

Nor was it possible to escape the nightmare that had snapped him awake in the first place. An eye opened up, somewhere in the jungles of the night, and it was searching for him. The doctor-turned-patient tried to dismiss the horror as a fever dream brought about by a natural and instinctive fear of the cancer that was growing inside of him. There was a rational explanation, therefore, for what gave the illusion of being a deep interior alarm bell, warning that a horror worse than cancer was coming this way.[2]

At 6:00 A.M., Nagasaki time, *BocksCar's* master alarm warning lights began signaling that the fail-safes, designed to prevent the bomb from detonating inside the plane, were neither safe nor unfailing. Apparently, plutonium was very unfriendly to electrical systems.

Lieutenant Philip Barnes looked up from his black box (the fuse-monitoring device connected to the bomb) and called out to Sweeney, "We have a master alarm."

"Repeat that," Sweeney called back, wanting to make sure he had heard correctly.

Commander Fred Ashworth confirmed Barnes's observation that the red warning light on the fuse monitor had started flashing. If this warning, like the fuel warning, was accurate, then a multi-kiloton nuclear weapon's firing circuits were closing and one or more detonation fuses were about to pull the trigger. In all of three seconds, Sweeney ran the fusing checklist through his mind. If either of the two contact fuses in the bomb's nose were self-activating, he and his crew would already be a false sunrise over the Pacific, about to register on Japan's seismographs. If the barometric or radar fuses were involved, they would be fine unless *BocksCar* fell below 1,890 feet . . . and unless the altimeters were giving the fuses faulty readings. Again, he'd already be ions and gamma rays if the latter case were true. This left the timing fuse— in which case Barnes and Ashworth had less than forty seconds remaining to solve the problem.

Oh, sweet suffering Lord on ice skates . . .

During the next two seconds, with his mind racing at maximum over-drive, Sweeney considered the two available options: jettison the bomb and hope to escape the blast, or pray that it was not the timing fuse and hope that even if it was, his weaponeers could find the problem and fix it in a half-minute. He had no intention of jettisoning the weapon. The admiral's lesson about the relative values of the bomb and the plane now seemed sickeningly prophetic. If worse ever came to absolute worst and the plane became flacked full of holes and was bleeding fuel from dead engines, Sweeney had already resolved himself to bail his crew out while he and Kermit Beahan drove *Bocks-Car* as far as they could into Japan, aiming for a fuel depot or, if no other target existed, a cow in a rice paddy.

Sweeney doubted it would ever come down to that. He had faith in his men, his plane, and himself. Behind him, Phil Barnes already had the bomb's hatch open and was giving the maze of wires, circuits, and switches one of history's most rapid inspections. With more than seven seconds to spare (as the timing fuse measured time), Barnes determined that the timer was not involved. A few moments later, he traced the source of the problem to a false-positive warning and corrected it.

"False alarm," Barnes called forward. "None of the firing circuits were closed."

Good. I'm breathing again, Sweeney thought. His voiced reply was a whispered, "Oh, Lord."[3]

Fourteen-year-old Hajime Iwanaga had been awakened with a stomachache about 3:00 a.m. and never did get back to sleep again. Now his work at the school was sure to suffer, although school was not really a place of learning anymore. The school was in fact now attached to the Mitsubishi Torpedo Works, and instead of calligraphy and mathematics, students were being recruited to the factory's tool-and-die presses.

During the past few weeks, Hajime and two of his friends—who, like him, were of small stature for their age—were offered the honor of someday actually working the torpedoes themselves. The "work" involved manual controls for the torpedo guidance system, with the worker lying prone and sealed inside. Adolescent boys were preferred guidance systems, because the torpedoes—which were actually mini-subs modified into guided bombs—allowed for a maximum shoulder width of only 55 centimeters (about 22 inches).

These days, the veteran submarine *I-58* was typically equipped with four of the special *Kaiten* torpedoes, each of them resembling a cross between a midget submarine and a long bomb. The *Kaiten* represented the undersea equivalent of the "divine wind" or kamikaze raiders.

At 11:40 on the night of July 29 (with its Kaiten arsenal mostly depleted) an array of conventional torpedoes launched from the *I-58* tore open all the watertight compartments of the American heavy cruiser *Indianapolis*, three days after it delivered the core components of the Hiroshima bomb. "*Indie*" became historic for two other reasons: for history's worst-known feeding frenzy of sharks upon humans, and for being the last American capital–named ship sunk during the Second World War.[4] Presently, the *I-58* was returning to port, with a request for four new *Kaiten*.[5]

Hajime, like the rest of the students, had grown up knowing nothing except indoctrination to all-out war. Though not yet old enough to truly understand the meaning of death, he was nonetheless prepared to die for his Emperor. He was taught to be a proud and daring soldier in a holy war that would attain a sure peace. The Americans, the British, and the Chinese were lower than animals—a nameless, faceless "them," barely suitable as slaves. Only Japan's late-great German and Italian allies could be considered human.

The Japanese were the chosen children of the gods. So the *Kaiten* volunteers were taught, and so they believed.*

Like other children of his age, and in this time and this place, Hajime trusted what the officers who came to the armaments factory told him—never doubting their instructions, even when told that the special mission for which he would be training was to be kept secret from his mother, his sister, and his teacher. He had been chosen by the Emperor himself, he was told.

When the chosen showed signs of fear, they were reminded of all that the zookeepers in Tokyo had been willing to suffer, to prove their love and dedication to the Emperor. The tale of the faithful elephants was already legend—at once horrible and wonderfully patriotic. To a later generation it would become a legend about the cruelty and foolishness of war, but presently it was taught as an example of war's glory. To the would-be *Kaiten* children, and those headed for other front lines, the recent and unprecedented agony of the zookeepers, demonstrated by great action and not just by empty words, was testament to the lesson that one must be ready to suffer whatever was necessary for the greater good of Japan.

The testament had its beginning in wartime food shortages. During the summer of 1943, scarcely more than a year in advance of November 1944's first nightly fire-bombings of refineries, depots, and transportation centers (which brought severe rationing to the entire country), the army had put To-kyo's Ueno Zoo at the bottom of the food and fuel priority list, cutting off all supplies for the animals, instantly. Somewhere along the chain of command, someone remembered that body parts from some of the animals themselves—and especially from bears, tigers, and cobras—were highly sought as medicinal folk remedies, sometimes worth their weight in gold. By command of the army, the animals' caregivers were forced to put almost all except the zoo's three performing elephants to death, sometimes with gunshots, sword thrusts, or lethal doses of sedatives; other times (as in the case of the zoo's doves) by military-ordered starvation. Those carcasses judged to be valuable were carted away by the army and harvested for their remedies and meat. The rest were dragged to the city dump.

Military planners had a special, propagandistic fate in mind for the zoo-keepers and their elephants. The field marshal understood that elephants, being among the most intelligent of animals, developed strong bonds with

---

*The young age of some *Kaiten* workers was not, at this point in history, unique to Japan. One of the last German submarines sunk during the war (off the south shore of Long Island, New York), turned out, when it was explored during the 1980s, to contain the skulls of crewmembers as young as 14. In Philadelphia, Italian immigrant boys were permitted to enlist for combat positions at 17, and a few entered the service as young as 16. On British ships, the legal age of entry into military service during World War II was 15, and occasionally as young as 14. Throughout most of the 20th century, adolescence was rarely recognized as a distinct age group, separate from adulthood.

their trainers and caregivers. Soldiers had observed firsthand that the bond was mutual and ran deep.

The zookeepers were denied guns and swords and every other relatively humane means of euthanizing their elephants. Next, they were ordered to live in the zoo with their animals, and watch them starve to death.

The smallest of the elephants, who had been named John, died after seventeen days. As the starving began, the zookeepers were allowed to grow potatoes for their own nourishment, and from day to day they offered the two surviving elephants, Tonky and Wanly, portions of their own meager rations—although an occasional sweet potato was to an elephant as a raindrop is to the sea. At best, their mercy only prolonged the agony. And the field marshal saw, and understood. The trainers and the caregivers were told that their sacrifice was small compared to what soldiers on the outer islands had recently suffered: "For this is what it means to be a true son of the Emperor."

By callous mathematical certainty, the rule of three held sway: Men and elephants could live for three minutes without air, up to three days without water, three weeks without food.

As the third week came and went, Tonky's and Wanly's ears began to appear too large for their bodies—and, as one of the zookeepers would later describe it, whenever he approached the cage with water, his two friends would stand on their hind legs with their trunks held high, their still-loving eyes seeming to beg, "Please give us something to eat."

By then, the zookeepers were themselves succumbing to grave hunger. And still, when they believed the soldiers were not watching, they gave freely of their own rations, until their ribs began to show and their clothes became too large for their bodies.

The elephants' primary trainer, it was said, loved them as if they were his own children. More than two weeks after John died, the trainer found Tonky and Wanly dead in their cage, with their trunks stretched high against a horizontal cross bar, seeming to have died trying to perform their famous, crowd-pleasing bonsai trick. "Faithful for all eternity," as the *Kaiten* officers told it: "Faithful to the friend who might reward them again with food, as he used to reward them every day, before the enemy invaded Guadal [Canal] and the [Solomon] Islands."

The trainer sat down on the concrete floor and lovingly caressed the dead elephants' trunks and legs. He had no more tears left in him, but a later generation would relate how this did not matter, because in the Ueno Zoo, it was believed that even the rocks shed tears that day.

The moral of the story, as told to Hajime, was that he must be ready to sacrifice anything to help bring the war to an end. Throughout Japan, such lessons were preached, over and over, to a generation that was beginning to resemble, more and more, a Children's Crusade. North in Hiroshima, sixteen-year-old Keijiro Matsushima, whose brother was a Zero pilot, took every story of sacrifice into his heart and waited with agitated impatience for the day he would join the kamikaze force. But now he had seen the city burning like phosphorous on both sides of the river, from which he concluded that the Americans must have invented "a really tough weapon," rendering the war almost impossible to win. "At the time, I never believed in surrender," Keijiro would record, on the sixtieth anniversary of the bombs. "We were ready for suicide attacks." A generation later, he and the other children of the bombs would tell an altogether different tale than the one they had been given about honor and ultimate sacrifice—a tale of how they trusted without question what adults said, what the government said, and what the men in uniform told them the highest levels of government had meant to say.

"But what's most important," Keijiro, Hajime, and their fellow students would endeavor to teach, "is that we must question as well as trust."[6]

Allied Prison Camp Number 17 was located 63 kilometers northeast of Nagasaki, on the opposite side of Ariake Bay. On August 6, Corporal Dale Frantz had observed a strange cloud penetrating the stratosphere in the direction opposite Nagasaki—237 kilometers away, 145 miles northeast, in the direction of Hiroshima. The cloud must already have risen more than 10 kilometers when he first noticed it, and the strange shape continued to build high and fast. Fellow prisoner Earl Bryant also saw the cloud. He watched its cap turn pallid white, tinged with a pinkish glow. A narrow column followed the mushroom cap into the heavens, but the column was black and appeared to be made of smoke and lightning.

On the morning of August 9, about the time Lieutenant Barnes was clearing master alarm warnings aboard *BocksCar*, the prisoners of Camp 17 were already working 439 meters underground in Omuta district's condemned Fukuoka coal mine. Bryant and Frantz had been working the mine for almost two years, but they were by no means holders of the endurance record. Clarence Graham, now twenty-five years old, displayed a strange mixture of strong muscles and emaciation, and appeared to be at least twice his actual age. He was captured on the island of Corregidor in May 1942, and had been surviving as a slave miner a year longer than anyone else.

Nearly a half-kilometer down, the atmosphere was filled with dust from the unusually soft coal. The pumps brought down only enough fresh air to minimally sustain life, so the cave atmosphere was stagnant and hot. Water pumps barely kept pace with underground seepage. The streams of ankle-deep and knee-deep water provided Clarence Graham and the other miners with their only source of refreshment. They could splash the sweat and dust from their brows, and drinking the black seepage washed the coal from their throats, held dehydration at bay, and even allowed them to stave off some small measure of hunger by filling their stomachs with water. Clarence had survived longer than anyone else on account of not yet having been crushed during a cave-in and by keeping his wits about him. If a man developed a reputation for staying quiet, never looking his captors in the eye, and working hard, he was usually permitted to live long enough to be worked to death on a near-starvation diet. Clarence's main task involved engineering huge piles of slate into pyramid-like pillars that held up the ceilings of the caves wherever they began to weaken—which was pretty much everywhere. On twelve-hour rock-moving shifts, he lived on three bowls of rice per day, sometimes coughing up so much black phlegm that the pain in his lungs never abated and he had to take off his loincloth and dip it into the stream and wrap it around his face so he could breathe.

Clarence knew he had to keep his mind focused on seeing his family again, lest he raise a shovel, curse a guard to his face, and go after him, as others had done: suicide by armed guard. From the world above, only the Japanese equivalent of buck privates were actually sent into the caves with the prisoners. The officers knew that death underground reached out from many directions, so they stayed above, while their underling Morlock caste took its fear and frustration out on the prey. *Shit rolls downhill*, Clarence reminded himself, *and we're at the bottom of that hill.*

Whenever a new shift of workers shambled into the tunnels, the old shift would ask, "What's new topside?" For two years, the answer had been either "Nothing" or made-up rumors about the approach of war's end. Today, the answer was, "Nothing. Same old bullshit—*except* that something's got them stirred up like hornets, and they've decided to stop feeding us."

On August 9, Clarence Graham's crew emerged into daylight about an hour-and-a-half after the replacement shift began work. He and the other arrivals from the night shift were ordered to line up and stand at attention under the rising sun. They were given no food, and an officer announced that they would be given no water, either. Anyone who spoke, or who fell, or who made any sound at all, would have his head cut off immediately.

"Because of Hiroshima," an officer shouted, "the Emperor has commanded that you shall work without food until he decides that you do not have to work anymore."

The prisoners knew the meaning of the words: They would all be dead in only a few days. Clarence was hot, but he supposed that the sun would not burn him too badly today. A bank of clouds was drifting in from the east, promising shade. Some twenty or thirty miles away in the direction of Kokura, a silvery glint caught his eye. *One of ours*, he guessed, *mapping and gathering weather reports.* As a distant siren whooped and hooted, and the power plant shut down the mine's water pumps, Clarence wondered, *Why don't the planes stop joyriding and just come here and do something?*

Clarence did not own a wristwatch, but he guessed from the angle of the sun that it was almost eight o'clock.[7]

At 7:45 a.m., the next weather plane reached Kokura and *BocksCar* reached its rendezvous point, 30,000 feet above the island of Yakushima. *Great Artiste* appeared on Charles Sweeney's starboard wing, but the photographic plane, *Big Stink*, was nowhere to be seen. Fifteen minutes and 125 gallons of fuel later, the third plane still appeared to be lost. By coded signal, two distant weather planes called out "C-1" and "C-2/10-2." Though morning haze had been anticipated at both targets, Kokura was clear, and only about two-tenths cloud cover could be expected at the secondary target.

This was the first snippet of good news Sweeney had received through the entire mission, and it soon began to look as if it would be his last.

At 8:30, after thirty minutes more of circling for rendezvous—and after another precious 250 gallons of fuel were consumed—Sweeney scanned the empty sky one last time, then told his co-pilot and bombardier, "That's it. We can't wait any longer." Maintaining radio silence, he wiggled *BocksCar*'s wings, signaling to *Great Artiste* that they were to depart the rendezvous point and proceed to the primary target.

The missing photographic plane was circling almost two miles too high, and over the wrong point on the Earth's surface. At nine o'clock, *Big Stink* broke radio silence and called out to Tinian Base: "Has Sweeney aborted?" The pilot's voice was sharp and stressed, and the message came through as, "Sweeney aborted."

On Tinian, the against-protocol breach of radio silence, followed by no further transmissions, could be interpreted only as a sign that something had gone very wrong with Sweeney's plane. The most likely scenario was that *BocksCar* had been shot down, or was just barely limping along somewhere between Yakushima and Kokura. Those who knew Sweeney understood that in a crisis, rather than bring home a wounded plane on the verge of crashing with an atomic bomb's impact fuses armed, he would ditch the weapon over the nearest military target he could find, on a return path that would take him over Yakushima toward an emergency landing on Iwo Jima. All of Tinian's air-sea search-and-rescue resources were therefore realigned along Sweeney's newer, more apparent return route—which, by a life-and-death margin of hundreds of miles, was now more apparent than real.

If *BocksCar* ran out of fuel and actually did have to ditch in the ocean, all the rescue ships and planes were presently being sent in the wrong direction.[8]

In Nagasaki, Governor Nagano was still skeptical about Prefect Nishioka's descriptions of Hiroshima. What stopped him from dismissing the report as a gross exaggeration was that he knew the prefect to be unflappable almost to a fault. In the end, he weighed logic against incredulity. If the prefect's description was indeed accurate and he took no extra precautions to protect his family and his staff, the result could be catastrophic. If he took action and nothing happened, then no real harm was done and he could punish the prefect later for spreading false rumors.

On a hill overlooking Nagasaki Harbor on one side, and the suburb of Urakami on the other, a multi-chambered tunnel wide enough to accommodate two trucks side by side had been excavated with great haste during the previous two months. Power generators and air-filtration systems equipped with the newest lithium-hydroxide-based carbon dioxide scrubbers had already been in place for more than two weeks. An outer blast door of steel-reinforced concrete and asbestos rendered the tunnel system so airtight that it might just as well have been a submarine, sealed inside a mountain and resistant even against a hurricane of fire.

Ancient works of art were now sheltered deep within. All that remained to be installed were beds, food supplies, and the rest of Prefect Nishioka's printing presses.

While *BocksCar* and *Great Artiste* closed the distance between Yakushima and Kokura, Nagano brought his family into the shelter with everything they could carry. Then he called in his administrators and officers from the Regional Air Defense Ministry to assess the situation and to plan the day's work details accordingly. The official word from Tokyo was to expect nothing serious but to remain on guard. Officially, everything was under control.

Governor Nagano was not so sure. If the prefect's description was even half accurate, very little was under control.

The governor called a special meeting to order and had just begun to describe what he was told about Hiroshima when the mayor of a town called Sasebo came running into the shelter, stammering about urgent news.

"Is this how you present yourself to your governor?" Nagano shouted. And then, after a pause, he noticed that the man's clothes were soggy with sweat, and realized that there must be a good reason why he looked like a vagrant.

Nagano walked up to the mayor, and asked him gently, "Where were you?"

The mayor stared fiercely into his eyes and replied, "I am in hell."

"I am about to start a meeting, but I can listen if you keep it brief."

"Hiroshima is gone!"

"Wait a minute—who told you this?" Nagano demanded. "We are having a meeting about that very problem right now. But *who* told you?"

"You don't understand," Mayor Koura said, believing that Nagasaki would be next. "Hiroshima is devastated! We are *all* in hell."[9]

More than two kilometers upriver, Dr. Tatsuichiro Akizuki had just begun his examination of several outpatients, including Dr. Paul Nagai. Despite a fitful, almost entirely sleepless night, Dr. Nagai insisted he was feeling well enough to carry on with his duties. Akizuki approved. Both men shared a belief that the best defense against sitting down in a worry chair and letting an affliction dominate one's life was to have a job that kept the afflicted engaged in thoughts about everyone except himself.

Akizuki left Nagai with the outpatients and was walking toward a second ward when another B-29 weather plane approached, breaking over the airwaves with a call of "C-2/10-4," which meant: "Four-tenths cloud cover, secondary target." Simultaneously, a siren let out a long, continuous wail signaling "Yellow Alert," which meant: "The enemy planes are on their way. Prepare to take cover."

Dr. Akizuki hurried from room to room, warning patients to stay away from the windows. Under Yellow Alert, all doctors were to drop whatever they were doing and proceed immediately to basement shelters. Akizuki went to a window instead, looking for B-29s. There were none to be seen; and the siren stopped, then blasted out the signal for all clear, Status Green. This was the second false alarm in as many hours. The sky appeared to be clouding over a little, which would have made the planes difficult to see; but other than that, there seemed to be no cause for concern. Indeed, a buildup of clouds was cause for the opposite of concern. Formations of B-29s did not like to drop bombs, day or night, when targets were clouded over. Rainy days were always known to be the safest.

It was hot outside and the humidity was steadily rising. *It looks like rain,* Dr. Akizuki told himself; so he was humming cheerfully as he walked downstairs to the consulting room. When he entered, he found Dr. Yoshioka performing an emergency pneumo-thorax operation on a patient. She was about ten minutes into the procedure.

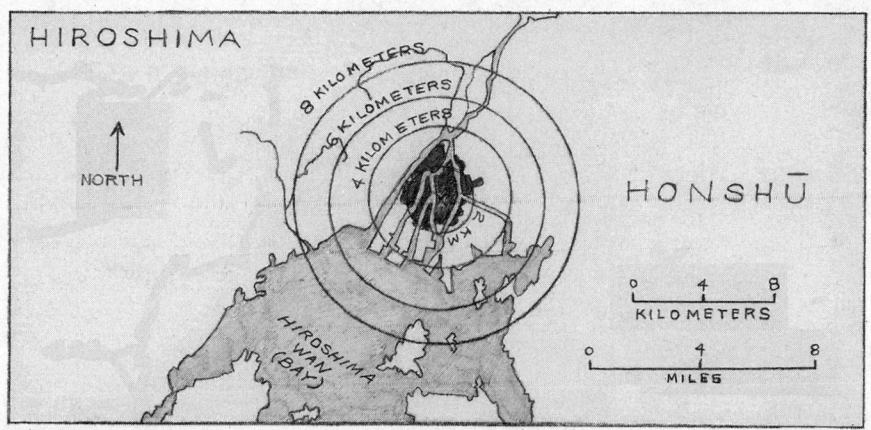

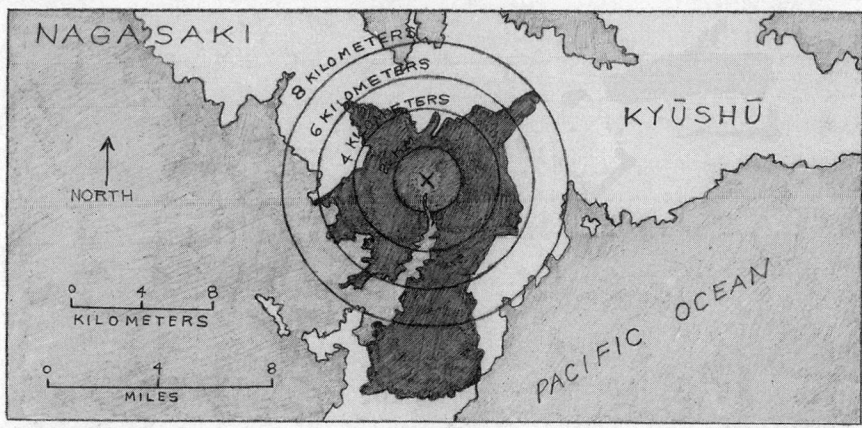

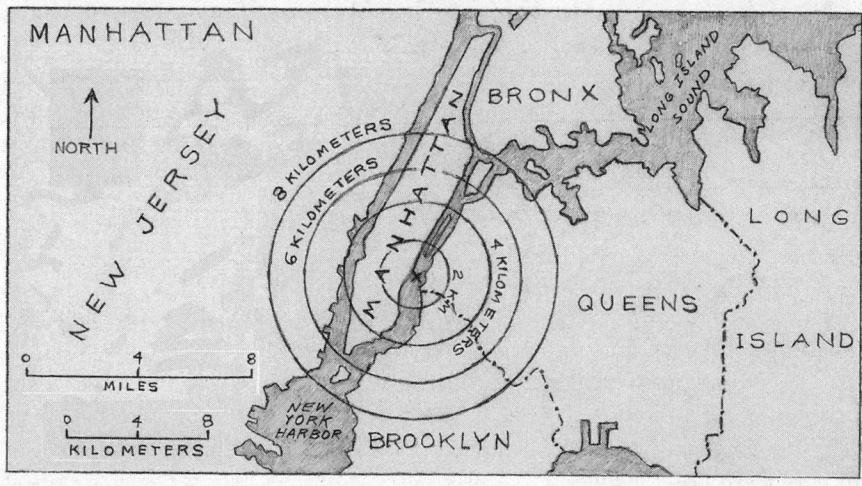

The chief difference between the scale of Ground Zero and the flash-effect firestorms in the two cities (represented by darkened areas) lay in the substantially greater power of the Nagasaki bomb: 22–27 kilotons (Nagasaki), as opposed to 10–12.5 kilotons (Hiroshima). [Illustration: Patricia Wynne]

"You ought to stop working when the air-raid warning goes off," Akizuki said, trying to sound stern.

"Thank you," she replied, "but there were so many patients waiting."

Dr. Akizuki did not believe it was possible, but Dr. Yoshioka looked even more tired than Dr. Nagai. Lately, even the streetcar service seemed to be running out of power, so she had begun walking the more than five kilometers across Nagasaki, starting out every day just after dawn, toward a shift that would not end for at least twelve hours.

"Have you eaten today?" Akizuki asked.

"Later," she replied.

"No, *now*," Akizuki insisted. "Doctor's orders. I'll help you finish up here; and then I want you to go upstairs and take a rest. I'll carry on for a while in your place."

"Well . . . thank you," she said, and smiled. "But how long is a while?"

"As long as you need," said Akizuki. "I guess we'll just have to see."[10]

At 9:45 a.m., Kokura lay directly ahead. Charles Sweeney set course for the final bomb run and was about to hand the controls over to bombardier Kermit Beahan when Beahan yelled, "I can't see it! I can't see it! There's smoke obscuring the target."

Between the time that George Marquardt had radioed his last "C-1" weather report and the moment of final approach, the wind had shifted. Below, and now directly upwind of the Kokura arsenal, the town of Yawata was still in the same condition Kenshi Hirata had observed from his train the night before—burning out of control. The arsenal was completely hidden beneath a sheet of thick, oily smoke.

Sweeney yelled into the intercom, "No drop. Repeat, no drop."

A single pass-and-drop would have left Sweeney with just enough fuel to make a try for landing at home, on Tinian. If he had to circle thirty miles out for a second pass and then divert to his secondary target, even the nearest base at Okinawa might soon be out of reach.

Sweeney banked sharply to port and began a long, southward arc to a return approach, with *Great Artiste* following close behind. That's when the first flak shells began bursting on all sides. Tail gunner Pappy DeHart reported that the detonations were targeting wide; but the gunners on the ground were setting their altitude fuses perfectly—"almost to the inch."

"Roger that, Pappy," Sweeney replied. Through trial-and-error settings, gunners were now "crawling" the flak toward him, slowly zeroing in on the target. Throughout the month of July, and leading up to the August 6 bombing, the ruse Alvarez and Tibbets had been part of worked out quite well. Most of the enemy observers and gunners were eased into a false sense of security about two or three B-29s traveling together and dropping no bombs, as if they had strayed off course from their main squadrons or were just taking weather and reconnaissance reports. Clearly, a deception that had worked one time for Hiroshima was not going to work a second time for Kokura.

Charles Sweeney would recall later that he was now doing something a bomber pilot in a pressurized aircraft at 30,000 feet—vulnerable to being popped by flak bombs like a rubber balloon—rarely, if ever did: he was making a second run on a hotly defended target. Second runs gave antiaircraft gunners second chances. Sweeney knew that if *BocksCar* popped, the contact fuses would surely detonate the bomb during that first, all-important hundred-millionth of a second. He was not certain that a twenty- or thirty-kiloton explosion at 30,000 feet could reach all the way to the ground and take out the arsenal. *But even if it doesn't kill them down there*, he mused, *it will sure as hell give them something to think about.*[11]

Sweeney resolved to give Kokura a second try. It wasn't only the added fuel consumption of a Nagasaki detour that firmed his resolve. His secondary target was much wider than the Kokura arsenal, with a significantly larger population. Between Nagasaki and the suburb of Urakami lay nearly a quarter-million civilian souls.[12] So he climbed *BocksCar* up another quarter-mile, hoping to ride above the gunner's latest altitude settings, but Pappy called excitedly from the tail: "Damned flak is right on our ass and getting closer!"[13]

"Forget it, Pappy," Sweeney said evenly. "We're on a bomb run." But the second approach revealed more smoke blowing over the target than during the first approach. This time, the flak bursts were close enough to make the floor jump. Sweeney decided to take her up another fifth of a mile to throw the gunners off track again, even though the thinner air would put a higher tax on dwindling fuel reserves. He wheeled around into another very long arc and began plotting a third approach from a different angle, gambling on the slim hope that from a new angle they might find a hole in the smoke screen. But the third run was no more successful than the first two, and the flak was beginning to home in even nearer. This time, there were actual clanging sounds as well as floor jolts, and Pappy began to wonder, *How the hell did I get into this fine mess?*

"You can relax, guys," Sweeney announced. "It's time to leave all of this behind. We're going to the secondary."

Sweeney wagged his wings for *Great Artiste* and led the way south. A minute later, flight engineer Kuharek leaned forward and said, "I'm afraid our fuel situation has reached critical."

"Define critical."

"We have enough to reach Nagasaki and make just a single run. But we won't make it to Okinawa. We're going to fall short by at least fifty miles."

"Do you have any more good news of that sort?" Sweeney asked, and his radar operator replied over the intercom:

"Fighters below and coming up to meet us!"

It sounded to Sweeney like the old sick joke about the doctor who says, "Bad news and good news. I'm sorry to report we amputated the wrong leg. But don't worry, the other one is getting better."

Sweeney's sharp turn southward had caught Fred Bock by surprise. He was flying *Great Artiste* through flak, starboard and only slightly aft of *Bocks-Car* when the turn occurred. *Great Artiste* was now on the portside wing and a little farther behind. Looking to starboard and not seeing Bock's plane where he expected it to be, Sweeney called out to the gunner's positions, "Where's Bock?"

The FUBAR factor intervened—again. An elbow or a clipboard had struck the selector button. Instead of speaking to his crew over the intercom, "Where's Bock?" was broadcast for hundreds of miles in every direction.

Immediately, a return call came from the long-lost pilot of *Big Stink*— "Chuck? Is that you, Chuck? Where the hell are you?"

At the moment, Sweeney did not know who he wanted to kick harder—himself for hitting the wrong switch, or the captain of *Big Stink*, who evidently expected him to broadcast who he was and exactly where he was to the whole empire.

He made sure the selector button was set for intercom, bit hard into his lower lip, and directed his navigator to plot a "straight-line" course from Kokura to Nagasaki.

During the flak runs, Navigator Jim Van Pelt had completed the calculations and was ready with a precise compass heading. "But of course," he added quickly, "this route will take us right over the Kyushu fighter fields."

As Sweeney saw it, he had no other choice. If he swung more than fifty miles westward over the sea, and then added another sixty miles by swinging southeast toward Nagasaki, the fuel situation would become doubly critical. A direct, southeast line of flight was the sole option. Jim was right about the hazards of the overland route. Even though *BocksCar* and *Great Artiste* were now beyond the range of Kokura flak and had quickly left the fighters behind, the enemy was, if anything, smart. For anyone watching from the ground, the planes' contrails pointed like twin compass needles toward their destination. Sweeney tried to comfort himself with the calculations of experts—who had assured each crew that, given the greater speed of the B-29s, the best that a Japanese Zero could hope for was a single pass and less than one second of actual firing time. *But no,* he reminded himself, *how often have we seen those experts actually flying inside the planes they claim to have designed so well that we need no guns to defend ourselves?*

"We can't avoid Kyushu, Jim," Sweeney said, and chose the direct route. He was short 600 gallons from the moment of takeoff; and now, the hour-and-a-half of extra flight time over Yakushima Island and Kokura had put him another 750 gallons behind. At Nagasaki he would have enough fuel for no more than a single flyby if he hoped to ditch anywhere near the American-controlled waters of Okinawa. Considering all the other little gremlins that had been sticking hands into this mission, Sweeney supposed that even with less than a second's firing time, perhaps this would be some Zero's lucky day.

He almost asked the forbidden question—and caught himself, holding the question back. Then, looking more than a hundred miles ahead, he observed a silvery-white sea of cumulus clouds marching toward the target area. That's when Sweeney finally lost his grip on the question's reins. He turned to his co-pilot, and unleashed what was never to be uttered by submariners or airmen: "Can any other goddamned thing go wrong?"[14]

Kenshi Hirata reached his parents' home, on what was to become the shadow side of a tall hill, about the same time Charles Sweeney asked the wrong question. Seconds later, flight engineers aboard *BocksCar* and *Great Artiste* reported that a ground station in the direction of Nagasaki had begun pinging the planes with radar. Less than an hour now separated them from Moment Zero, and barely more than 3.3 kilometers separated Kenshi from the next hypocenter.

As he approached the steps, Kenshi's parents came running through the door with tears in their eyes. At that same moment, an air-raid siren began to signal what was likely just another in a seemingly endless series of false alarms. False or not, he was not taking any chances. Mindful that a second flash might appear, he told his parents to come inside with him quickly and to stay away from the windows.

Kenshi's father was shocked at the sight of him—pale, with shaking hands, and with perspiration running down his cheeks, his chest, and his legs. He looked like a man half starved to death.

"Have you eaten?" his mother asked.

"Not hungry," he said. "I can't seem to keep anything down." He cradled the wedding bowl to his chest and rocked it gently, and his father bowed his head.

"I knew you were alive," Mrs. Hirata said. "Even when no more word was coming out of Hiroshima, I knew you were still in this world."

"And Setsuko?" his father asked, almost at a whisper.

Kenshi lifted the bowl and bent his head toward its rim, and kissed it. "This is all that's left of her," he replied.

"We already knew this," his mother said.

"How can that be?"

"Because early this morning," she explained, "Setsuko's mother arrived at our door with the news. She knew her daughter was dead in Hiroshima because Setsuko has been visiting her in dreams."

His mother's words brought no comfort, only more agitation. He remembered how, when the *pika-don* came to Hiroshima, a woman's voice had cried out in his brain and had made him stay under cover while everyone else stood up and was either grievously injured or killed. At first, he had thought it might have been his grandmother's spirit—then he thought, later, that it must have been Setsuko, urging him to live. Now he knew it was her. *Knew* it.

Kenshi held back his tears, stood, and said to his father, "We must go at once to Setsuko's parents, with this bowl, and bring her home."

When they stepped outside, though only a few minutes had passed, the day had become noticeably drearier. Thick clouds now covered more than half the sky.

The air-raid siren wound down and blasted the all-clear signal. *Another false alarm*, Kenshi reassured himself. The Hiroshima blast had come out of a perfectly blue and clear sky. Dreary days were good news, in these times. The Americans never dropped bombs if they could not see the ground. Everyone knew this, and took it for a fact.

Passing a row of houses and a Buddhist shrine, Kenshi and his father heard a radio playing loudly. For some reason, everyone who possessed a functioning radio these days delighted in cranking up the decibels for the whole neighborhood to hear. Someone only a little farther down the road was also booming out the same station. Presently, an announcer broke into the music to tell his listeners that several B-29s had been deterred from their attempt on Kokura and were presumed either shot down or headed out to sea. Consequently, the air-raid warnings for Kokura and the Saga Prefecture in the north and the Yellow Alert for Nagasaki were being lifted.

As Kenshi walked, the cloud cover thickened quickly, and his stomach spasms abated ever so slightly. He believed that he might even be able to drink a little water now, and to keep it down. All he needed was a little breathing space. All he needed was for Nagasaki to be safe today.[15]

Ship designer Akira Iwanaga had arrived from Hiroshima at his parents' house on August 8. They lived a safe distance from Nagasaki, more than twenty kilometers north, in Isahaya.

Sickness had continued to keep Akira safe in bed through the night, but in the morning he awoke feeling a little better and had even regained some of his appetite. So he boarded a train at the local station and caught the last connecting segment between Hiroshima and Nagasaki. In a different compartment on the very same train, one of Morimoto's military kite-makers, Masao Komatsu, was also returning from Hiroshima to Nagasaki. On August 6, while Morimoto and two cousins were about to be cocooned inside a book-filled mansion, Masao had gone to a warehouse to collect supplies for the day's work and was drawn outside by a roar that sounded like a B-29 on the verge of crashing straight down on top of him. At a distance of three kilometers from the hypocenter, Masao was shadow-shielded from the flash and completely cocooned from the blast. The warehouse splashed completely apart on one side, and although his skin was struck by what felt like a wave of very hot air, he did not burn. He did not even become sick.

About the time Kenshi arrived home, Masao and Akira were approaching Nagasaki's outer suburbs. Masao was feeling well enough to finish the last of his biscuits. Akira, though he had awakened at his parents' home feeling a little refreshed, quickly lost his appetite again, and his strength, too. Deep in Akira's tissues, the rays and the black rain continued to do their work. He had slumped down in his seat and fallen into a deep but dreamless sleep.[16]

Akira's fellow ship designer and friend, Yamaguchi, was already at work. Although still feeling pain from his burns and barely able to drag himself out of bed even with his wife's help, he remained obedient to an order to present a full report about Hiroshima at the headquarters of the Mitsubishi Industrial Combine.

"Orders are orders," he told his wife Hisako. "That's the beginning and the end of it."

At the conference room, still bandaged and bleeding, he told the executives and engineers about the woman in the black mompe—and how anyone wearing dark clothing near the flash zone had been simultaneously grilled and flayed. He told them how even a harmless twig could be propelled with bone-piercing force.

"This piercing hazard goes doubly for flying glass," Yamaguchi warned. "If a similar device should explode here, at the instant you see the flash, you must seek any shelter available, even if all you can do is duck behind a desk or a chair." He then ordered his colleagues to open every window in the room.

"This is beyond common sense," a section chief interrupted. "The damage to Hiroshima is nothing like this hoax you are trying to weave. How can one bomb turn out such energy to destroy an entire city? You are an engineer. Calculate it!"

"I already have," Yamaguchi said flatly, motioning with his one good hand toward his left arm and the left side of his face, covered with bandages.

"Exactly," the section chief said. "You were injured, Yamaguchi. Your brain was not working properly."

Outside the windows, a siren came suddenly to life again.[17]

Prefect Nishioka still had only one goal: to join his wife and child in the imagined safety of the Unzen national park. He was able to reserve a special services taxi at a station near the town of Isahaya. The driver's original routing plan would have returned him with the prefect directly to Nagasaki, but Nishioka saved the driver's life with the words, "New plan."

"You mean, we're not going to Nagasaki?" the driver asked.

"We're going to Unzen," the prefect said.

"But that's—that's way off in the opposite direction."

"I understand," he explained, and directed the driver on a detour to Unzen.

Once again, Nishioka did not get very far. Sickness stopped him outside of Akira's neighborhood, in the hot spring resort town of Obama, overlooking Ariake Bay. As he stood beside the car, wiping vomit from his lips and trying to recover his strength, a wide break in the clouds revealed a contrail very high up, reaching eleven kilometers or more. He saw twin glints of silver at the head of the contrail—meaning not one, but two B-29s, scratching a vapor trail across the heavens, traveling wing to wing. They were pointed like an arrowhead toward Nagasaki, only thirty-three kilometers away.[18]

Almost as if nothing at all out of the ordinary were happening, the officer whom Ichiro Miyato was assigned to relieve stood away from the radar screen, rubbed his eyes, and offered Miyato the chair. Normally, the two "techies" liked to talk shop or about girls between shifts, but not this morning. Both of them had been worn down by a very difficult seventy-two hours of doubled-up schedules. Whenever relieved from their ten-hour screen watches, they were trucking new equipment to bomb-resistant tunnels—which, when completed, would provide retractable and more powerful radar installations that in theory could detect the invading American ships and planes at distances out to 1,000 kilometers.

Miyato could easily see that all his friend wanted to do was get out of the room and go to sleep. Looking at a blip coming down from the direction of Kokura, he made a try at conversation anyway.

"What have you got?" Miyato asked.

"Only another false alarm," came the reply. He scarcely bothered to look back, as he put on a hat and left the South Kyushu compound. Miyato supposed that the intensifying schedule and the atmosphere of defeat were enough to fray the nerves of anyone, but he had expected better. At the end of the previous shift, his friend looked so exhausted that this time Miyato decided to relieve him at 10:40 a.m., even though his tour was scheduled to begin at eleven.

Miyato took his seat and watched the blip notch down from the northeast with the next two sweeps of the radar beam. This was nothing new to him. Surveillance planes were now joyriding all over the region, triggering at least three false alerts this very morning and generating an increasingly deadly complacency about air-raid sirens. Miyato did not want to be responsible for calling in another false Yellow Alert, so he made a note in the logbook, recorded the time as 10:45, and adjusted the scanning frequencies. On the next sweep, the object looked vaguely like an echo from two separate blips, but on a subsequent sweep he could not be sure. The intruder was now putting out interference—pinging back at Miyato with its own radar.

He picked up the phone to Command Headquarters.

"What do you see?" a voice on the other end said.

"Looks like a lone B-San running radar," Miyato replied. "My guess is that it's mapping. Altitude above 10,000 meters—probably above fighter range."

"Thank you," the voice said, and hung up. Like most conversations these days, the person at the other end spoke with a curious mixture of politeness, boredom, and resignation.

Several sweeps later, Miyato noticed that the object appeared to be holding to a straight-line path. He plotted the vector and lifted the phone again.

"What do you see?" the same voice said.

"If they stay on present heading, their course will take them straight to you. It should pass directly over Nagasaki in about ten minutes. You may want to take countermeasures."

Putting the phone on speaker mode to free his hands, Miyato adjusted the scan and tried to resolve the blip more clearly; but it was interfering again, using its own radar. He poured himself a cup of tea and waited for a response. Six sweeps, two sips, and it was still following a straight-line heading toward Nagasaki. Miyato was expecting another polite "Thank you" and hang-up. He knew almost to a certainty that no interceptors would be sent. The Boeing B-29 was too high, and there simply wasn't enough reserve fuel to waste in a futile attempt to bring down a lone "stray;" and there did not even appear to be enough time. What he did not know was that Command was now acutely aware of Hiroshima having been bombed by two or three planes flying together, as opposed to a lone "weather plane" or the more than fifty-strong B-29 fire-bomb raid.

The response Miyato received was not what he had anticipated. Two or three clearly agitated men were speaking in the background, and the polite voice asked, "Are you certain that you are tracking only a single plane? Is there any possibility that they are really two or three, flying in a very close formation?"

"I *did* note an anomaly about ten minutes ago. For a moment, it looked as if I might have been tracking two planes."

"Hold on!" the voice said, and cupped a hand over the phone so Miyato could not hear anything of what was being said. The blip remained on its beeline to Nagasaki. The city was only 25 kilometers from Miyato. Thirty seconds more passed, and the object inched closer to Command Headquarters.

The voice came back, more with sad resignation this time than with detached politeness: "Any change?"

"Negative. It's still on a firm heading for Nagasaki. I'm going to scan the frequencies again and see if I can get a clearer resolution of—"

"No! Keep this line open!"

"I've got you on speaker!" Miyato said, a little more sternly than was necessary. And then, more politely, he added, "I just need to keep both hands free for the radar."

"Understood," the resigned voice said, and then began to say something else but cut his words short, as if to leave unsaid, *You really don't understand.* In later years, it would occur to Miyato that what the anonymous voice actually wanted to say was, *Please stay with me. Please.*[19]

Fifteen-year-old Michie was about to be saved by a refusal to think like everyone else in her class and to join them in dismissing the latest air-raid alert, like the ones that preceded it, as just another false alarm.

At 10:55 a.m., Michie Hattori was located only 600 meters (or six blocks) from the hypocenter of a detonation that would be at least two times more powerful than Hiroshima. When the school day's second preliminary condition Yellow Alert sounded, her teacher ordered all of the students out of the classroom and into the tunnels that Governor Nagano's people had dug into the side of a hill, behind the playing fields and bamboo gardens of the schoolyard.

Michie's teacher never underestimated the seriousness of an alert. She hollered for the girls to *run* for the shelter, following slowly to make sure no child was left behind. Like the captain of a foundering ship, the teacher was unwilling to seek escape for herself until everyone else was safely away ahead of her. But most of Michie's friends shuffled along through the field, talking quietly among themselves and even stopping to look around, as they marched a city block closer to the approaching hypocenter.

Only Michie and a half-dozen others actually ran to the tunnel. As usual, she entered ahead of the rest of her class.[20]

Seven-year-old Emiko Fukahori would be saved by the same reflex. She was playing with her best friend, Sumi-Chan, in a bamboo grove nearby. The grove was a favorite neighborhood gathering place for families. Sumi-Chan's mother had spread a straw mat on the ground and commenced with her usual restful routine of needlework while the children played tag among the tall reeds.

Emiko was totally absorbed in a hide-and-seek chase with Sumi-Chan and three other children when the siren began to howl. She stopped and scanned the skies, and through a clearing in the north she observed a distant glittering speck.

"Enemy plane!" Emiko shouted.

"It can't be an attack," Sumi-Chan's mother called back, "because it's only a *preliminary* air-raid warning."

"No!" Emiko screamed. "Bad plane! *Bad Plane!*" and she broke into a sprint toward one of the tunnels.

"I'll race you!" Sumi-Chan shouted, and immediately outpaced her. Another child followed; then five others, shrieking and laughing. Sumi-Chan's mother put down her knitting and also began to follow. After all, what point was there in setting a bad example during an alert? If a week or a month from now, something genuinely bad approached, then demonstrating that it was okay to sit outside the shelter—should children copy such behavior—could mean all the difference in the world to them. The line between the slow and the saved, the quick and the dead, was a cheerless bisector. Razor sharp, it divided sister from friend and mother from daughter with reptilian indifference.[21]

Barely more than a kilometer from the school and the bamboo grove, Hajime Iwanaga, the boy who would be a *Kaiten* driver, was swimming with classmates in the Urakami River. Being a *Kaiten* trainee had its privileges. The volunteers ate better food than the other children; and they were encouraged to take exercise breaks from work in the Mitsubishi torpedo factory. Typically, these breaks involved water sports, including contests to see which child would be first to succeed in holding his breath for more than two and a half minutes underwater.

The two boys were about a half hour into their morning break when the siren announced the approach of the *Kaiten* program's end. Looking around, they observed through an opening in the clouds what Hajime's friend believed to be "a very brave plane, flying alone over enemy territory."

Hajime did not agree. "No," he called out, "friendly plane," then dove under water, grabbed onto some eelgrass anchored to the bottom, and began to hold his breath for as long as he could.[22]

Even as the planes approached, the only sound grade-schooler Yukiko Kobayashi could hear was the soothing buzz of cicadas. An illness in the family had kept Yukiko and his older, fourth-grade brother home with their younger brother, and away from student work details nearer the hypocenter.

Yukiko, his older brother Takashi, and six other children were playing marbles together on a neighbor's veranda. During the past winter, the boys had used hard stones to grind pieces of broken cups and terra-cotta bowls into marbles—which had become their treasures.

Yukiko's younger brother, who always called him "Yukko," usually joined the boys in games of marbles; but today he had been unable to find them and had gone searching first at the wrong house. During the final critical minute, the child had zeroed in on the right house and was approaching the safety of the veranda and a tall stand of trees, but he stopped abruptly in an open space between the house and the trees, distracted by a silvery object in the sky.[23]

At first, Charles Sweeney did not want to believe what his eyes were seeing. Were he a more superstitious man, he would have blamed this latest serving of bad luck on having asked the forbidden question. Nagasaki was now obscured by more than 80 percent cloud cover.

On the heels of this unhappy realization, flight engineer Kuharek reconfirmed for Sweeney that *BocksCar* would be down to flying on vapors in little more than a half hour. Despite the fact that the engineer was finally able to coax the faulty pump into drawing small amounts of fuel from the dead bladder, only 300 gallons remained accessible to the engines. This meant only enough flight time for a through-and-through, single-bomb run, followed by a short dash to a ditching in friendly waters. Sweeney called Navy Commander Fred Ashworth forward. He was the weapons expert, officially in charge of the bomb itself. Officially, Sweeney was only in charge of the plane.

"Here's the story, Commander," Sweeney began, summing it up as fast as he could. "If we can't drop on the first run and if we have to circle back for a second try, we might be forced to crash-land on the ground in Japan. The rulebook calls for getting a visual fix on the target or we can't drop. If we don't get a visual on the first run and then depart, our best scenario is probably losing the bomb and the plane and the crew when we crash in the ocean—unless we try to dump the bomb at sea."

"That's if we go by the book," Ashworth said.

"By the book," Sweeney acknowledged. "So let's say *to hell with the book*, and with its 'no-win' scenario, and let's put a little faith in the new imaging radar. I'll personally guarantee we come within . . . well—within a few hundred feet of the target."

"You mean, maybe within a half-mile?"

"Let's be a little real here, okay? With this thing, a miss is as good as a mile."

"I don't know, Chuck," Ashworth said.

"It's better than losing it in the ocean, isn't it?"

Ashworth nodded, and asked cautiously, "Are you sure of the accuracy?"

"I'll take full responsibility for this," Sweeney said.

"Okay, then. Let's go for it."

There was no time for discussion with the navigator or the bombardier. Sweeney had confidence that they knew exactly what to do. Jim Van Pelt checked his navigational figures and Ed Buckley monitored the outlines of the city on his imaging radarscope, inviting verification from Van Pelt. Buckley then called out the headings and precise closure rates to bombardier Kermit Beahan, who fed the data into the world's first portable computer—which weighed almost as much as a Jeep and was connected directly to the bombsight.

The outlines of the city were fuzzy at the edges, but the river and the rail lines were reasonably easy to see, and all three men were confident that the machines would work. Just the same, Beahan continued searching for a break in the cloud cover.

"You own it," Sweeney announced, and turned command of the plane and its payload over to his bombardier.

"I've got it! I've got it!" Beahan suddenly shouted. He wasn't acknowledging control of the plane, but rather a hole in the cloud cover that was yawning open directly ahead, near the Mitsubishi armament factories in the industrial valley. The hole was more than two kilometers upriver of the assigned aiming point—almost into the wrong district, almost into the wrong town, with much of Nagasaki now shielded behind low hills. Through the opening, the oval-shaped Urakami Stadium was easy to see—as distinct a landmark as Hiroshima's "T" Bridge. It looked to Sweeney as if the suburb of Urakami, and not Nagasaki proper, was going to be Ground Zero. The off-center aiming point was (and always would be) perfectly fine with Sweeney. A blast along the river valley would not kill as many people as a central Nagasaki strike; but every major military target on Sweeney's map was located along the valley, and he was certain that this bomb would erase all of them. Beahan locked onto the oval outline of the Urakami racetrack as a reference point and fed whatever last-minute course adjustments could be made into Sweeney's indicator panel. Thirty seconds from release, the tone signal was activated, the bomb-bay doors snapped open, and *Great Artiste*, flying nearby and ready to drop its three monitoring cylinders, simultaneously opened its own bomb-bay doors.

The tone fell silent and *Bocks Car* lurched upward, suddenly five tons lighter.

"Bombs away," Beahan announced, and then quickly corrected himself: "*Bomb* away."[24]

· 7 ·

A Vapor in the Heavens

*T*hree hundred kilometers away in Hiroshima, Dr. Hachiya lay on his back on a charred bed frame, looking up into a cloudy sky and wondering what alarm had shaken him awake. Something deep-rooted and instinctive crept out of Hachiya's subconscious, filling him with a strange belief that thousands of voices had just cried out. Before he awoke, others had seen something flashing in the southern half of the sky, like a lighthouse search beam aimed briefly into the heavens, brighter than day.

Glancing down at the Hiroshima wilderness and trying to determine the direction of the sun, the doctor guessed that it was about 11:00 a.m. No one was calling out from the prairie in alarm, or making any other noises. Central Hiroshima was as silent as a tomb—which, essentially, it was.

The night before, once Hachiya had come to accept the city as another Pompeii, he became ever so slightly less restless, and was able to snatch little intervals of sleep lasting up to two or three hours, interspersed by an hour or two of intense wakefulness. Shortly before sunrise, he dozed off, and slept until awakened about nine o'clock by visitors, among them an old friend and current supervisor, Mr. Okamoto of the Communications Ministry. Three days earlier, Okamoto almost became part of the ash and debris in Hiroshima Castle's foundations—and it should have ended for him that way, if not for a near-fatal reaction to a bee sting 40 kilometers away, in the town of Kure.

"That bee saved your life," Hachiya had said; and as the two men laughed about a strange swerve of fate, the doctor realized he could sit up without pain.

After his friend left, he waited until none of the other medical staff were watching and tried to stand, but the stitches began to pull at his shoulders and hips, and he was obliged to lie down again, crestfallen and exhausted. He had slept from then until now.

Why, he wondered, did he feel as if a spectral hand had suddenly reached out and shaken him awake? Dr. Hachiya did not believe in the motility of consciousness—or in anything like the meaning nurse Minami and the rest of Dr. Fujii's crew had taken from the blue fireflies—and yet, for an instant, a bone-chilling sense of dread stole into him, and seemed intent on staying.

The same hand that shook Hachiya awake grabbed all four legs of his bed and shook again, and the doctor began to laugh at himself, and to calm down. When all was said and done, it registered as a most gentle shaking: *A baby sine wave quivering through soft earth,* Hachiya told himself. *Richter 2; Richter 3 or 4, at most.*

The shaking continued for several seconds more, dislodging little drifts of soot that had been lying for days on a blackened pipe overhead.

Richter 3 or 4, he told himself again. *It's just an earthquake, nothing more.* Then, from the general direction of Nagasaki, some 183 miles away in the south-west, a low rumbling roar reverberated through the heavens, building to a loud crack that definitely was not the sound of an earthquake.

Hachiya drew a deep breath, held it wistfully, and expelled it in a sigh.[1]

Ichio Miyato's radar station was located almost halfway between Clarence Graham's prison camp and Ground Zero. At 11:02 a.m., Miyato had just told the anonymous controlled voice at Command Headquarters, "The object should be over Nagasaki now—" when his radar screen overloaded and went completely blank. Simultaneously, the wires inside the speakerphone were seared. During a chip of time in which the telephone at the other end of the line began to vaporize, the many kilometers of intervening wire swept up some small measure of the *pika*'s electromagnetic pulse, and conveyed the surge toward Miyato at light speed. Had he been holding the telephone receiver to his ear, both he and the officer at the other end of the line would probably have died at precisely the same second, though they were more than 25 kilometers apart.[2]

At a radius of 63 kilometers, Clarence Graham could not tell where the flash came from. It arrived as an all-encompassing brightness, filling the whole sky and then only slowly beginning to fade. The energy released by the Hiroshima bomb was barely if at all above the equivalent of 10 or 11 kilotons of TNT. The Nagasaki bomb blazed forth at greater than 22 kilotons, and nearer to 28–30 kilotons; so even at Clarence Graham's distance of 38 miles, it loomed large—first with stinging bright light; then, many seconds later, with a great tremor in the ground. The airburst arrived almost a half-minute after the tremor—manifesting as a strong wind that came from the direction of

Nagasaki. And, following the first wind, there came a second hot, hot wind—
"terribly hot," Graham would recall, "hotter than direct sun on your face."
And next came a brief lull, as if a typhoon had now passed overhead and the
prisoners were standing in the calm of its eye—and, just like the rapid passing of a typhoon's eye wall, a strong blast struck suddenly from the opposite
direction, rushing backward toward Nagasaki. The third wind was so strong
that it toppled some of the weaker prisoners.

Clarence remained standing—perplexed; but he observed that one of the
prison guards seemed to know what was happening, and more, to *understand*
it. The huge dome of a rising sun appeared over the hills in the southwest;
and this single guard glared as if analyzing the fireball, as it turned white and
ascended on a column of smoke.

All of the guards except this one stood in awed and confused silence. The
one who understood—the one Clarence had listed among the most sadistic in
the camp—offered a prisoner water and a ration of food, and said, "You and
I are now friends."

You've got to be fucking kidding, Clarence told himself. And he wondered
what the guard really understood about the fire in the sky.[3]

Thirty kilometers nearer the hypocenter, at a radius of nearly twenty miles,
Prefect Nishioka covered his face from the flash—and still, when he opened
his eyes several seconds later, the golden-white ball rising above the city was
so brilliant he was forced to close his eyes again.

"Don't look at it!" he shouted to his driver, and to anyone else who
would listen. "Get under shelter—right away!"

Glancing back, the prefect saw, on the surface of the water, a spreading
white arc racing toward him from across the bay. Behind the expanding arc,
the entire surface was turning white. Nishioka estimated that the people of
Obama had about fifteen seconds.

"Hurry!" he yelled one last time. Shockwaves traveled much faster
through rock than through air, so he did not have to shout his orders a third
time. The ground itself was already booming, frightening everyone into immediate action. A half-dozen men ran ahead of the prefect and dove into a
well-protected space behind a bus. Nishioka's driver fell in on top of him—
followed by a hammerhead of compressed air that smashed windows and almost tipped the bus on its side. Nishioka kept his head down through the lull
and the back-blast, which pulled the bus in the opposite direction and nearly
toppled a house. When he looked again, most of the cumulus clouds that had
been there a minute before were gone, and the atomic cloud was now tower-

ing more than sixteen kilometers over the city—the color of a muddy white cloth mixed with splashes of fresh blood.

He did not believe that anything could grow so tall, in only a few seconds.

"Shall we continue to Unzen?" the driver asked.

"No," the prefect replied, suddenly no longer aware of how sick he had been feeling. "We must go back to Nagasaki."[4]

"Oh, no—not again," Kenshi cried out to his father.

This time, he actually heard one of the planes straining to turn around and fly away from the bomb, sounding at one point as if it were flying straight at him. Once again, he was slightly more than three kilometers away from the center of the explosion, owing to the fact that the home of Setsuko's parents—located dead center between several key military targets and therefore near the original aiming point of Sweeney's bomb—had been obscured by clouds during the critical three minutes of *BocksCar*'s final targeting maneuver.

At the moment of the bomb's release, the puffy white clouds that covered most of the river valley were pulling apart on the opposite side of Kompira Hill, above Urakami Stadium. Instead of Kenshi witnessing his second nuclear explosion from beneath the actual aiming point, the target had been shifted abruptly, almost two miles upriver, away from Kompira's southern ridge and central Nagasaki.

The first time, distance combined with a voice in his head and an instinct to stay away from the windows until the blast wave passed had kept Kenshi alive. This time—in the presence of a bomb up to three times worse—what saved Kenshi was not so much a matter of distance and response as the shielding provided by Kompira Hill. Despite the greater fury of the plutonium device, Kenshi found the blast and roar "not so terrible as Hiroshima." He would not be aware for some time to come how a small mountain (standing only 366 meters high) had shadow-shielded him from the heat rays and shock-cocooned him from the blast. Not very far from where Kenshi and his father stood, at the same radius from the hypocenter—and all within those same few seconds—people down in the shipyard were simultaneously flash-grilled, uplifted, shotgunned by flying glass, and hurled through walls. Only a short distance away, on the other side of Kompira Hill, almost everyone who witnessed the *pika* was either grievously grilled or dead. Only two miles further north, the people on the streets were now steam and phosphorus, ashes and radioactive fallout.

Walking through a neighborhood that if not for a cloud bank would have been located deep within the circle of Ground Zero, Kenshi was buffeted by a harsh wind and saw only a few roof tiles loosened. And after the wind had passed, dragonflies still flitted about, seemingly unshaken. *But the bones*—Setsuko's bones, to which he had made offerings of flowers and rice and which he had held close to his chest for most of two days—the bomb had ripped the cover from Kenshi's wedding bowl and flung the bones out of his hands.

"All this way," Kenshi said to his father, weeping. "All this way, and her bones are scattered who knows where—and to what purpose?"

There *was* no purpose. No dignity in it, either, Kenshi told himself. No purpose. No dignity. No purpose.

Except, Setsuko might have said, *to bear witness.*[5]

West of Kompira Hill, Kuniyoshi Sato had been waiting with a crowd of people on the Oohato Pier when, like Kenshi Hirata, he survived his second encounter with the atomic bomb. He knew, even before the planes began counting down the last five miles to the new hypocenter, that he would forever be haunted by a single image of atomic death: the man on the train, transporting a bowlful of his bride's skull fragments to her parents in Nagasaki.

During the minutes before the bowl of bones was knocked out of Kenshi's hands, Kuniyoshi Sato prepared to board a ferry that would bring him to the main office of Mitsubishi Heavy Industries, on the west bank. He had no way of knowing that across the river, at his destination, fellow engineer and double-survivor Tsutomu Yamaguchi had just been reprimanded for losing contact with him in Hiroshima, and failing to convey him safely to the office. What Sato did know, to a certainty, was that Hiroshima had been destroyed by a single bomb.

"We have heard rumors of this," a shipyard worker said. "The whole city? One bomb?"

"I saw it," Sato affirmed. He began to describe the kaleidoscope of strange colors in the pillar of fire, and the city stamped flat, when a B-29's engines let out "a high-pitched squeezing noise," somewhere over Urakami Cathedral, nearly 3.5 kilometers upriver. Instinct moved Sato; and before anyone else on the dock could respond, he dove into the water, and stayed under. The sky caught fire. The blast wave pounded down and passed in less than a half second, taking with it almost everyone who had been standing on the pier above. The water thoroughly shielded the young engineer, though he did not yet fully comprehend how, or from what.[6]

Only once before had more than a hundred thousand voices cried out together in startled surprise, all within the same second. Half of them yelled again. The other half ceased to be.

The bombing survey photographs—and hence the history books—would record much of the Nagasaki shoreline's architecture standing intact, and this would help to create for many the false impression that the Nagasaki bomb was not so bad as the Hiroshima bomb. The most enduring photographs of Ground Zero, including those showing a Catholic church, the Josei Girls' School, and the Mitsubishi Steelworks—all reduced to protruding nubs of structural bone on an otherwise featureless plain—would memorialize what happened in Urakami, not Nagasaki.

Despite Charles Sweeney's guarantee to Commander Ashworth, the bomb missed central Nagasaki and obliterated the suburb next door. It erupted in the hot, overcast sky above Matsuyama, the riverfront section of Urakami. The blast rebounded against the valley walls on either side of the Urakami River the way a shotgun blast is focused down the barrel of a gun. Ground Zero, the zone where everything was essentially leveled, ran 3.2 kilometers upriver and an equal two miles south; and it spread just over a half kilometer (or just over six city blocks) east and west of either bank. On the other side of a valley wall, not very far from Kenshi Hirata's neighborhood, Dr. Paul Nagai's four-year-old daughter Kayano was playing in the village of Koba. She survived in a shadow-shielded eddy, behind a small mountain called Kawabira, which completely blocked the flash and the wind radiating out of Urakami.

Kayano's older brother Makoto had offered to take her downhill to a local stream for a swim with a cousin and some of the neighborhood children; but she decided to play near the family cottage instead. As if by a miracle, both children were shadow-shielded. After the *pika* (the flash) and the *don* (the blast), the grass on Kayano's side of the valley, in the shadow of the mountain, remained green and virtually unruffled. Viewed from high above, Kayano's cocoon survived as one of several islands of green in a sea of desiccated brown leaves and gray ash. Yet very soon, her cocoon was to experience a strange rain of yellow oil, and the stream would not run clear again for a very long time.

The *pika*, when it blazed forth, was completely silhouetted by the mountain, making the peak look black against streamers of bright red. Then, on the heels of the red, came a flash of blue. "The red was bright enough to stun a person," Kayano's cousin Fujie would recall—but once the heat ray and the compression waves had squeezed the nearest clouds out of existence, the blue was no longer filtered out and blazed bright enough to cause a slight sunburn, even behind the mountain's shadow.

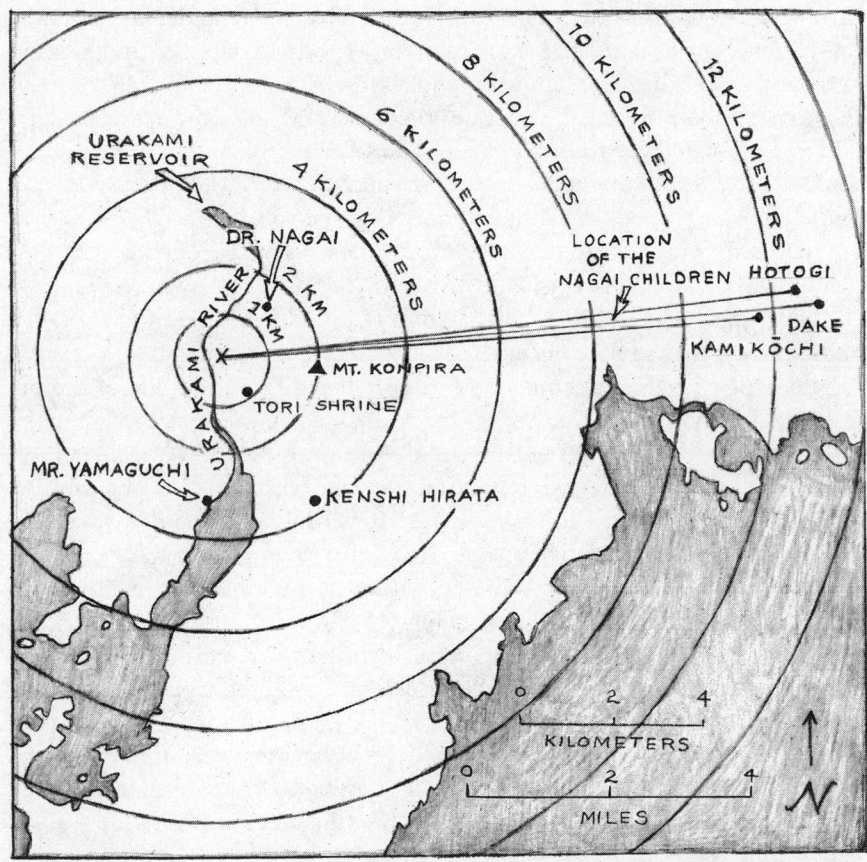

The Nagai family carried a lingering guilt, based on Dr. Paul (Takashi) Nagai having brought his two children to his Ground Zero research center in 1946. In 2008, Dr. Nagai's grandson was correspondingly insistent that there was no connection between the children's subsequent cancers and radiation from the bomb. This was an undeserved guilt. At the Nyokodo research outpost, the September 1945 typhoon had washed fallout deep into the ground and out to sea. The main exposure (according to U.S. Bombing Survey data) came during that first day of the bomb, when the fallout was fresh and "hot" and while prevailing winds carried the highest concentration of radioactive dust—within minutes—directly across the valley in which the children had been shielded from the flash and blast effects. The fallout path continued eastward toward the Hayasaki farm. [Illustration: Patricia Wynne]

Both flashes—the red and the blue—came within the first half-second. During that same fraction of a second, directly opposite the sheltered side of the stream—outside the shadow of Mount Kawabira and directly in the glow of the bomb—rooftops and chickens and clothing sent up vertical columns of smoke. People on the stream's far side, just like people caught outdoors throughout

Hiroshima and in downtown Urakami, became like ants smoldering under the focused sunbeam of some diabolical schoolboy's magnifying glass. As the glare faded, the grayish-black columns of smoke rose three meters or more, over the monk's robes, the child's mompe, the gardener's hat, the refugee's rags. Chickens running away from the gardens and lawns sent up more erratic columns—until, after another three or four seconds, the shockwave crested the hill, overflew Kayano's head, and slammed down on the far side.

The little stream in the center of the ravine seemed to divide Kayano's world in two: one side normal and alive and still inhabited by butterflies, the other side strange and terrible, populated only by dead or unconscious people and blackened, twitching chickens.

Looking directly overhead, Kayano saw "from the other side of the big green mountain, a giant tree rising into the sky." A tree made of fire, she recalled. "First it was all red but then it began to be different colors—oh, so bright! The tree made my eyes hurt. And just then, my brother came running up from [the protected side of] the stream. He was all excited and he said, 'My goodness! What was that? That plane must have crashed into the sun!' Sure enough, the sun was no longer shining. I looked up at it through that awful cloud and it was the color of a dead thing."

And then the ravine became suddenly dark, and cold. Astonishingly cold, and as black as night. Things began falling out of the cloud—impossible things: flurries of burning paper . . . a door frame . . . a singed cat that hissed, and ran away . . . the hood of a fire truck . . . and farther afield the head of a woman who seemed still alive. There wasn't a single sign of bleeding. A gold tooth gleamed in her wide-open mouth. Then the raindrops came, as wide as pearls, and greasy.

Kayano's brother took her by the hand and led her behind a sasanqua tree. "There were pumpkins—and lots of pretty strawberries all around," she would write years later. But Kayano did not feel like eating strawberries. Ever again. Not after the head and the cat and the oily, yellowish-black rain.[7]

At approximately this same radius, Dr. Nagai's friend Takami-san was one of the people Kayano saw on the "wrong side" of the stream. Outside the mountain's shadow-shield, he left a shadow of his own, as a patch of unburned grass.

Even at a distance of nearly 9 kilometers (almost 4.5 miles), one whole side of Takami-san's body was severely "sunburned" by the *pika*. He lived for barely a week, but it was not the heat ray that killed him. Before the boy died, Dr. Nagai recorded that he was succumbing to an unknown source of intense radiation. Nagai believed that either some metallic object had been simultaneously irradiated and hurled into the sky or something from the bomb itself had rained down upon the young man; for he had lived long enough to describe strange fireballs rocketing down at him from the direction of the *pika*. Takami-san was returning to the neighborhood stream with his cow when the flash came. The cow saw it, too, and lifted her head. Takami-san felt nothing at first and happened to be facing away from the light. He saw the cow burst into flames, and then realized that silent white balls of fire seemed to be raining down upon both of them. Two or three had struck the cow, killing her instantly. One struck Takami-san's foot, all but burning it off.

Dr. Nagai noted in his medical log that it did not seem to matter that the boy was located at a reasonably safe distance from the *pika-don* when the strange balls of light came after him. There were several such cases, and Nagai recorded that even if the fireballs grazed only the extremities of the hands and feet, everyone touched by them succumbed quickly to symptoms of radiation poisoning.[8]

Barely more than two kilometers closer to the hypocenter, the train carrying Masao the kite-maker and Akira the shipbuilder had just passed Urakami's Michinoo Station when Masao heard the familiar strains of a propeller-driven B-29 trying so hard to get away from something that it dove perilously close to splattering in pieces through the sound barrier.

"Get down!" he shouted to the other passengers, rolling to the floor and saving the lives of many who followed his example.

During the next twenty or thirty seconds, the plane slowly faded into the distance. A man laughed nervously and stood up. Then another stood. And another.

"Stay down," Masao warned. "It's a new kind of bomb. When the flash comes, you need to—"

The entire car was bathed in a stark, silent white light. Masao's hands were covering his eyes and ears, but he felt the hair on an exposed eyebrow sizzle and curl up. By now, almost everyone was heeding his warnings, but some who were still standing, and who had not covered their eyes, fell victim to an involuntary reflex to look in the direction of the flash. Their retinas began to scorch even before a secondary reflex—shortcutting through a nerve arc faster than the actual pain of the scorch—tried to stop them from looking.

The cries of pain from those still standing—and shadow-shielding him—shocked Akira out of his radiation-induced sleep. Because he had seen this awful thing before, he was hiding under his seat long ahead of the airburst. He and Masao counted five seconds or more, between the searing *pika* and the *don*. Those passengers who had not responded to Masao's warning, and who stood with their eyes burned, were shotgunned from waist to head by fragmenting windows traveling at more than half the speed of sound.

The train's conductor was one of those who had looked directly at the *pika*, and who was now completely blind. If there was any saving grace at all, to keep Masao and Akira's train from reenacting Hiroshima's occurrence at Kaitaichi Ridge, it was that this time the dead-man's switch remained operational, and brought the train to a stop as soon as the conductor removed his hands from the controls.

A conductor's assistant came stumbling through Akira's car, urging passengers to evacuate the train and take shelter in the woods nearby. The man's face was a scarlet stew.[9]

A half kilometer nearer the hypocenter, but shadowed behind (and inside) a hill, Governor Nagano and his entourage survived without even being scratched. The mayor of Sasebo was summarizing what the commander of Hiroshima's Naval Station had reported when the shelter's electric lights failed. Nagano was ready to order start-up of the emergency generators when it seemed to him that the doors to the shelter were suddenly pulled open and far more light than he was about to call for came streaming in, accompanied by what sounded like either several large planes or a multi-ton bomb crashing very nearby.

When Nagano stepped outside, he saw the shelter's construction workers gathered on a steep hill and looking toward Urakami. The hill's contours and its position had placed the workers and everything in their vicinity off to one side of a shotgun's barrel, instead of positioning them like fleas inside the barrel. A tremendous pall of smoke was rising over the valley walls from the direction of Urakami, but as the governor climbed toward the workers, the hill allowed a view only of lower Nagasaki—which appeared to be standing unharmed. Glancing back, Nagano was surprised to see that his house had suffered no damage at all. Not a single window appeared to have been cracked, and all the flowerpots on either side of the front steps were still in place.

The *pika-don* effect had been bright and noisy, and what Nagano saw and heard in the shelter seemed consistent with what Prefect Nishioka had described about a new weapon used against Hiroshima. Yet Nishioka's conviction that Nagasaki would be the next city destroyed by an atomic bomb seemed both anticlimactic and puzzling when the governor looked around and saw his administration headquarters and the region he administered surviving essentially unchanged.

Nagano was beginning to suspect that the prefect's story about square kilometer after square kilometer of buildings blown down had been exaggerated. And then he reached the workers on the crest of the ridge, and saw much of Urakami transformed into a giant crematorium, where a mountain of flame appeared to be growing out of the earth. The mountain was slowly rotating, creating a vortex of fresh, in-rushing air to supply itself with oxygen. As the flames rose, convection effects drew gales in from both ends of the valley—force-feeding the firestorm.

By some accounts the fire mountain, acting more like an actual hurricane of flame than a mere column or pyre, was unable to draw in enough oxygen to sustain runaway growth. At times, it seemed to stall and even flare out, sending forth great waves of black suffocating fumes.

On a side of the storm opposite Governor Nagano's hilltop vantage point, only 850 meters (or almost 10 blocks) from the center of the blast and not very far from the tunnels in which Michie, Emiko, and other young girls had taken shelter, junior high school student Tamotsu Eguchi had just crawled out from an air pocket deep, deep within the debris of his school. Looking up, he beheld the outer skirt of a cyclone whose flames and smoke surged almost to the altitude of a small seaplane that had apparently strayed *way* in the wrong direction, and seemed on the verge of falling like a dead bird.

What most mystified Tamotsu was the realization that, given his close proximity to whatever had flattened his school and created the wall of flame, and given that the school building was mostly wood, the wood itself had never caught fire. He appeared to have been near the center of a great wind that had blown out all of the fires nearby. On opposite sides of the blown-down school—upriver and downriver—at least two giant cyclones of fire were trying to be born. One had begun to suffocate and was collapsing into a sea of smoke. But near the outer wall of the larger, still-living storm, burning objects several meters across were being uprooted and carried skyward. When the skirt of the monster stalled and its flames appeared occasionally to be snuffed out, Tamotsu was able to catch clear glimpses of the wreckage as it fell to the earth: the upper portion of a trolley car . . . the roof of a house . . . the tail end of a small boat, shooting out its own flames as it tumbled end over end.[10]

Yukiko Kobayashi's little brother, the boy who paused between two houses on his way to a game of marbles, was fully exposed to the flash within two kilometers of the hypocenter. During the moments before the blast struck, the five-year-old cried out, "It's hot! *Hot!*" and Yukiko's oldest brother, Takashi, saw the child's linen shirt burst into flame and smoke. At Moment Zero, the older brother was also standing outside the shadow-shield of the veranda, under which the game had been in progress. Still, he was located in the relative safety of a persimmon tree's shadow, and the only part of the flash that reached him was a single beam, lancing down through a space between the leaves. It pierced his earlobe with a pea-sized burn.

Then, everything around the boys came apart in a symphony of devastation that, according to Yukiko, no photograph could fully convey. His little brother's last words, spoken through seared lips, were, "Come on, Yukko, let's play marbles."[11]

At Moment Zero, seven-year-old Emiko had been only the second child out of the bamboo garden and into the shelter. Located a little nearer than the Kobayashi boys, at the 1,600-meter mark, where the light from the bomb lanced the earth at an angle of approximately 20 degrees, she raced inside just a few steps behind her friend Sumi-Chan. A third child—laughing loudly and almost close enough to tag Emiko on the back—was caught in the glare and all but ceased to exist. Glancing over her shoulder, Sumi-Chan thought the third child looked like a beautiful sculpture in her final instant, outlined by a blue atomic aurora. Emiko also flashed with the radiance of a solar corona. She felt an intense heat touching her shoulders and her neck, even though she and Sumi-Chan were deep in the shadows of the tunnel.

When Emiko and Sumi-Chan stepped outside again, they found their friends seared and literally stamped into the ground. Some were still breathing, but they quickly died one after another. Emiko forgot that her home should have been visible across the now missing bamboo grove. Sumi-Chan was just beginning to register—though not with complete understanding—the fact that her mother had disappeared. Neither child had begun to surmise the possibility that she was now orphaned.

Only Emiko's older brother had survived long enough to come looking for them. Shadow-shielded outdoors from both the flash and the blast, the sky-shine effect had pierced him with gamma rays. Soon, he would start suffering nosebleeds. Believing himself lucky to have escaped the bomb without any serious burns, he was fated to vomit up disintegrating chunks of his own tongue, along with the lining of his stomach. The final bleeding out would be so extreme that it was to be recalled a generation later that the boy's corpse contained no blood at all.

Emiko's mother had been running an errand more than two kilometers beyond the hypocenter when the storm began. Her sister and younger brother were with their mother in the end; and Emiko would soon learn from a kindly, radiation-doomed uncle that her last two siblings died weeping over their mother's body.

On August 9, 1945, the difference between life and death was often determined by actions taken during the last few seconds before the 11:02 a.m. detonation. Within that margin of seconds, fifteen-year-old Michie Hattori, located 600 meters (6–8 blocks) from the hypocenter, and seven-year-old Emiko Fukahori (at a radius of 1,400 meters) survived by being among the first children inside the bomb-shelter tunnels, dug into hills behind the city's schools. Their friends, lagging behind or sitting on benches outside, disappeared with the rest of Nagasaki's Urakami district. [Illustration: Patricia Wynne]

Emiko and her friend looked up at a fire-cyclone. Vast, radiant, and indifferent, it swelled and stalled, and tried to rear up again. For all the storm's fury, the children's world seemed eerily silent. Thinking of her whole world, and not just of her family or herself, Emiko began to believe that she and Sumi-Chan were the only ones left alive.

A kilometer nearer the hypocenter, having safely emerged from another tunnel, Michie Hattori was coming to a similar belief. She had been standing deep inside the shelter, calling for the other fifteen-year-olds to hurry and join her when the brightest light she had ever seen blazed through the Urakami cloud-cover and into the cave, flashing down violet and then bleaching even the back of the cave a brilliant, brilliant white. Though she was safely inside, the light itself, reflecting off ground and atmosphere, blasted Michie with a great heat. In the next second, the *pika* seemed to flash more dimly, shifting canary yellow and sapphire pink, and through that crevice in time, Michie thought she saw her classmates "skeletonizing" inside the cave entrance, as if the rays were so bright that one could actually see them shining through clothing and flesh, and silhouetting bones. The girls' clothing and skin had begun bursting into flames when the air-blast reached down and scattered them like bowling pins. Michie believed she saw nothing for a while after that. The same powerful wind that beat down upon her friends shotgunned her toward the rear of the tunnel; then in an instant, just before she would otherwise have been smashed against the back wall, the wind reversed direction and drew her out through the tunnel's mouth.

Though shielded from direct exposure to the flash, the heated air had singed Michie's hands and face before it pulled her out of the shelter-tunnel and rose to join the fireball. Once she looked around, she realized that most of her classmates were barely more than shivering corpses. The skeletons she had seen silhouetted through the light were still clothed in flesh, though there was very little life left in any of them. The hill outside the tunnel, the tall stands of bamboo and sunflowers all around had absorbed much of the bomb's glare and gone a long way toward shadow-shielding Michie's friends—but not far enough.

The strange horrors Dean Tsunoo witnessed in Hiroshima were now manifest for the children of the shelter. Michie found one of the older girls still sitting outside the cave. The girl pleaded, "Come, help me to get away from here." Unable to think of anything else to do, Michie reached down and pulled her up by one hand; but the girl seemed to lose her grip and she fell slowly to the ground. Michie was still holding her classmate's hand—or what appeared to be all the skin of her hand and arm, down to the elbow. Like a long glove, the charred and blast-loosened skin had pulled away. Michie could see a girl's shadow imprinted where she supposed her friend must have been sitting and talking with someone when the *pika* came. Either a strange eddy in the blast wave had left the girl near her own shadow, or it was the shadow of another on the ground. In any case, Michie henceforth believed it to be the imprint of her friend.

About the time the shadow girl died, the only other classmate to run far enough into the tunnel before the heat ray struck, walked up behind Michie and suggested, "I think we should go back to the school."

Her name was Fumiko, and she seemed transfixed by the roiling black clouds overhead and the bright flames off to one side. The clouds were so dark that they blocked out the sun like a total eclipse, rendering the wall of flame the only real source of illumination. "Jigoku," Fumiko called it, meaning hell. She could not take her eyes away from the objects falling out of the sky and whirling aloft into the cyclone of fire. Exploded houses and all of their contents had gone spiraling up. A whole library of burning books came flapping down across the hundred-meter desert that now separated the shelter from the school. The bow section of a fishing boat came crashing down amid the books and was quickly followed by what Michie at first believed to be several sets of bars from the Urakami prison.

Fumiko corrected her: "They must be animal cages from the zoo."

Bars from hell, Michie thought. This was the closest she ever wanted to come to Jigoku.

Save for the strange meteors, the route to the school was flat and empty. Michie began to accept the idea that sunflower gardens could be ironed into the ground and turned black in an instant, and that buildings could disappear. "Weren't there houses here when we went to the shelter?"

Fumiko did not answer. She ran about thirty meters ahead into the smoke and gloom, and began calling excitedly for Michie to follow. She was pointing toward a large black reptile that appeared to be waddling toward them on its belly from the direction of another fallen cage.

"See!" Fumiko said. "I told you they were cages from a zoo. The alligator has escaped."

This did not make sense to Michie. All the zoos had been closed and there were no longer any animals in them. The alligator did not seem to know this and lay in their path to the school anyway. Fumiko hefted a broken piece of concrete in one hand and approached with caution, raising the rock above her head and ready to throw it at the animal's head if it did not allow them to peacefully pass it by.

Fumiko's footsteps stopped abruptly, and she started screaming. The face looking up at her from the alligator's body was human. No clothes or hair were visible—nothing except large, scale-like burns that resembled the alligator-skin pattern on burned wood. Fumiko's screams prevented Michie from hearing what the face was trying to say. She could only see that it appeared to be begging for something—probably water, Michie guessed later.

The head fell forward, face down in the dirt and the piles of smoldering books. The alligator man did not move again. One minute later Fumiko dropped the rock and fell to her knees, still shrieking. Michie knelt down beside her.[12]

Where Yose Matsuo survived, not even alligator people still stirred. At eleven o'clock, she had been part of a bucket brigade assigned to remove water from a newly dug air-raid tunnel located only 185 meters (or approximately two city blocks) from the hypocenter, on land that was eventually to be named Nagasaki Peace Park.

Survival in a basement beneath the bomb or in a steel-reinforced building, or in a multistoried house, was just barely possible near the Hiroshima hypocenter. In Urakami, a great deal more shielding was required. At the instant of the *pika-don*, Yose was working deeper inside the tunnel than the other fifty-two women in her brigade. Six meters of overlying dirt, combined with fifty meters of tunnel, protected her from more than 98 percent of the prompt radiation effects. Along the tunnel's length, the intervening water, carbon, and iron in the bodies of the other women blocked off and attenuated the rest. In addition to becoming radiation shielding, those women nearest the tunnel entrance became natural dampers against much of the heat that was trying to reach in toward Yose.

Death came to them within one two-hundredth of a second, and two-tenths of a second after that, all the soft tissues in their bodies became incandescent gas and soot. Vaporizing brain matter and blood tried to escape through the eyeless sockets of a woman's skull as jets of black steam, but the sudden rise of pressure was so great that the skull exploded from the inside.

What happened during the next tenth of a second probably saved Yose's life—by a very slim margin, if the large oak tree standing near a tennis court overhead served history correctly. During the same few milliseconds in which a combination of steam pressure from the tunnel entrance and the first impact of the lower hemisphere of the bomb's shock bubble sent a wave of dense air shooting toward the back of the tunnel, the blast rippled down the tree trunk's sides from directly above. The trunk, though stripped of its branches and seared instantly to a depth of several centimeters, remained sufficiently intact to indicate that once the deadly precursor waves began bunching together and surging outward in every direction, the very center of the impacting hemisphere was back-blasted skyward. Still within a time frame of milliseconds (bracketed within one-tenth of a second), the shock bubble began to deform and implode; the back-blast from the ground began to form the stem of the fireball and the tree's shredded branch stumps were raked upward as the forces that initially shot down against the trunk and the hypocenter suddenly reversed direction.

Inside the tunnel, the steam jets and the rapid rise in air pressure instantly killed twenty or thirty more of the women standing between Yose and the

Urakami Cathedral (center) and the hospital complex of St. Francis (1/2 mile uphill and to the left of the cathedral's two spires)—before and after the bomb, viewed from the east entrance of the Urakami stadium. [Illustration: Patricia Wynne]

entrance; and if not for the almost simultaneous vacuum effect outside, the rear wall of the tunnel would have become, for Yose, an insider's view of a pipe bomb. And yet, though the jets of steam were drawn out of the cave almost the moment they burst toward her, Yose suffered blistering burns and was knocked instantly unconscious. She would remain asleep in the back of the tunnel for three days, until a rescuer found her still breathing, and carried her on his back to one of Urakami's temporary first-aid shelters.

Yose's husband had been on the surface at 11:02 a.m., assigned by the military to work in the open air of Ground Zero. He had surely died nearby. In and around the building to which he had been sent, all of the walls disappeared. Not a single stone still lay upon another stone that was not thrown down or hoisted into the sky.

Yose had married a stone mason–carpenter named Zenkichi Kawaguchi, one of the hardest workers she would ever know. He had also been exceptionally kind and considerate to her; so as soon as she was well, she would make a Hirata-like journey to the hypocenter, searching for any trace of him. When none was found, she would place a sample of soil from the hill above her shelter in a small container, and she would convince two Buddhist monks to hold a funeral service without a body. Then, until her death in 1975, Yose would keep Zenkichi's picture with her always, along with a vial of Urakami dust laced with constantly half-lifing isotopes.[13]

Cadet Komatsu was stationed ten minutes' flying time from Urakami when the naval air base at Sasebo was rocked by shockwaves. A false sunrise in the direction of Nagasaki meant only one thing to him: the Truman announcement was not an exaggeration, and this was another Hiroshima.

Komatsu and two of his friends boarded a seaplane and flew toward the target for a close-up view of the cloud. The flight was unauthorized and in direct disobedience of orders, but as almost anyone who could fly a plane was being "volunteered" to kamikaze duty, Komatsu asked his friends, "What can they do? Kill us?" He would tell future historians that he, fellow Cadet Tomimura, and Chief Petty Officer Umeda suspected that the war might soon be over, and this could be their last chance to "sky surf" an atomic cloud.

Komatsu's friends laughed at his joke about their "last chance," and the story they lived to tell arose from a remarkable combination of initiative and luck, mixed with mid-morning alcohol and the Japanese equivalent of the words, "I double-dog dare you."

By 11:35 a.m., their plane emerged through clouds on one side of the Urakami Valley, and Komatsu saw a broad pillar of black smoke looming straight ahead. He was flying at a height of three kilometers—and from this 10,000-foot vantage point, the top of the "mushroom" already towered more than nine kilometers overhead. The cap was a massive storm on a stem—swelling up and fading slowly from an orange-red ring to a ball of white vapor.

Komatsu banked hard to port and began to circle the mushroom's stem, little bothered by large objects falling out of the cloud—a whole section of roof sweeping by like a giant fly swatter, a crate trailing what looked for all the world like a swarm of tennis rackets, the saucer-shaped lid of a water tower, and endless streamers of burning paper.

The earth below was boiling soot. The men's moods alternated abruptly between wonder and horror, laughter and tears. They could see nothing of Urakami or upper Nagasaki through the waves of black fog. At about twenty-of-twelve, Komatsu announced, "We've circled long enough," and decided to ride into the cloud. Adding spice to the danger of his adventure, Komatsu slid the cockpit window open and extended his gloved hand outside. Dust burned through the leather like a blast of live steam, and within two seconds he had pulled his hand in and sealed the window again, but it was too late.

The world outside had gone completely dark and the cabin was now filled with yellowish-brown mist; and Komatsu's glove was covered with sticky black matter. In the co-pilot's seat, Tomimura's eyes were suddenly burning and he could barely see the control panel. No more than five seconds after Komatsu burned his hand, the engine overheated and began to sputter. The air intakes were sucking in tremendous quantities of dust, along with something like burned twig fragments mixed with a hot, gluey liquid. By the time the plane burst into daylight again several seconds later, Umeda was already vomiting. Tomimura opened his window and cleared the heat and dust out of the cabin, fighting off his own sudden surge of nausea.

By now the engine was beginning to make noises like a vacuum cleaner sucking up chunks of taffy-coated glass, and Komatsu felt the plane dying in his hands. Fortunately, he was flying a seaplane—easy to control even in a glide with a dying engine.

Fighting off his own onset of nausea and weakness, Komatsu descended around one side of the mushroom stem in a long arc. Taking advantage of a fire-induced updraft, the young pilot was able to gain enough altitude to aim the plane toward a landing in the bay before his engine "gave up the ghost." He had hoped to stay aloft long enough to take photographs, but the heat of the Urakami updraft forced him to veer off and set down as quickly as possible.

As soon as the pontoons touched water and the plane came to a stop, they dove in and washed the gluey, stinging dust off their bodies. As if to prove that human bodies were not machines, each responded differently to whatever poisonous isotopes had entered the plane, exposing them each to approximately equal amounts of radiation. Umeda seemed to recover after vomiting blood and descending into a short-lived delirium. He would die of leukemia two years later. Tomimura would die of leukemia in 1964. Cadet Komatsu would survive into the 1970s, with a burn on one hand that never quite healed.[14]

∼

BocksCar was long gone by the time Komatsu rode into the cloud at 11:40 a.m.

At 11:01, the bomb-bay doors had snapped shut, and Sweeney took the B-29 into a steep 155-degree turn to port, diving along a northeasterly Tibbets trajectory. By now Sweeney had become somewhat addicted to the time-dilation illusion that accompanied high-adrenaline situations. He never ceased to be fascinated by the sense of a single second stretching out to whole minutes—or to occasionally be tricked by the effect. The expected detonation seemed never to come; and Sweeney was beginning to wonder if he had dropped a dud when, 42 seconds after the bomb-bay began to snap shut, the entire horizon was bathed from behind in a super-brilliant burst of light, far more intense than the Hiroshima flash. Then, even in a state of suspended time, the shock of heated air recoiling from the *pika* seemed to come very quickly, striking with unexpected force. At Hiroshima, Sweeney had experienced four distinct shockwaves of rapidly diminishing fury, while George Marquardt, though evidently just under three miles further from the bomb in *Necessary Evil*, had noticed only one shock, like a slap to the plane's side. But here, each shock was like a flak bomb bursting right outside the windows—and at least five of them came one after another, with equal force. Each one felt as if it might burst the hull.

After Charles Sweeney completed his turn and the last of the shockwaves died away, he looked back. The top of the plume was rising much faster than at Hiroshima—alive with those strange purple and orange hues, colors whose brilliance he had seen only once before and hoped he would never see again. The cloud continued to accelerate upward after it passed above Sweeney at the bombing altitude of 30,000 feet, and it continued shooting up to at least 45,000 feet, almost to the edge of space. The Nagasaki cloud seemed more intense, more angry.

Sweeney's flight engineer reported that *BocksCar* had just under 300 gallons of fuel remaining and was 350 miles away from Okinawa, the nearest gas station and landing field in the neighborhood. The math was depressingly simple: using approximately one gallon per mile, they would fall fifty miles short of Okinawa, splashing down on water about the same time as Komatsu's plane.

Despite the fuel shortage, Sweeney continued to bank to one side, to allow his bombardier to begin writing an assessment of the strike.

Sweeney, who knew every street and railway yard of the valley, made his own quick assessment. The center of the mushroom's stalk was rising over the Urakami district, with a terrific firestorm breaking out on one side. The high slopes along one whole face of the valley appeared to be aflame, while the center of downtown Nagasaki, sheltered behind a ridge of hills separating the Urakami Valley from the coastal plain, looked as if it might have survived. This outcome was fine with Sweeney. The focus of the impact, though considerably northward of the original aiming point, was still concentrated near enough to the Morimachi industrial plants, the Mitsubishi steelworks, the Mitsubishi shipworks, and the Mitsubishi torpedo factory. There was no doubt in the pilot's mind that, in a single stroke, the name Mitsubishi had been stricken down forever.[15]

"Friendly plane!" Hajime had called out as *BocksCar* approached. Then he dove under the water in a contest with another *Kaiten* boy to see who could hold his breath longer. At Moment Zero, they happened to be swimming near the Mitsubishi torpedo factory. Conserving energy by holding onto river-bottom eel grass instead of kicking with his arms and legs to stay down and fight the currents, Hajime found the first forty seconds quite easy, and believed he might hold out for a minute and a half longer, when the *pika* erupted.

Even under more than two meters of muddy water, with his eyelids instantly snapping shut, the flash was dazzlingly bright. Because water was not packed with large heavy nuclei that could be chipped and accelerated—and even the occasionally accelerated oxygen ion could not travel very far through the liquid shield—a couple meters of water provided better protection against gamma rays and neutrons than sheets of lead or steel. If one had to be caught near the hypocenter of a nuclear explosion, then underwater was definitely the right place to be. The boy's only injury—caused by the apparent lensing effect of a ripple on the river's surface—had focused a narrow shaft of light onto his left shoulder, leaving a permanent brand on his skin.

His ears ringing, Hajime surfaced into a world very different from the one he had left only a minute or two earlier. His friend was nowhere to be seen—and it would occur to him later that if the other boy had surfaced ahead of the *pika*, then he was simply gone.

The shore was covered with smoke, obscuring the schoolhouse and the Mitsubishi building, both of which had been simultaneously stamped flat along one side and ballooned grotesquely out of shape on the other side. The sky above was absolutely black, and from the center of the river two spheres of greenish-black flame were suddenly streaking directly at Hajime over the water's surface. Each was about the size of a baseball. On their way to the shore, the fireballs parted on either side of him and disappeared.

He did not need to see much more to send him splashing and then wading toward the riverbank. As he reached knee-deep water, a shower of huge

Hajime Iwanaga, the boy who would be Kaiten, became one of the atomic bomb's most unusual survivors—shielded beneath at least 2–3 meters of water while everything above him essentially disappeared. His only injury came from a lensing effect shaped at the water's surface—which focused a single beam onto his shoulder. [Illustration: Patricia Wynne] oily raindrops came and went. More dark green, incandescent spheres also came and went. One of them struck a dead animal or a bundle of rags, set it afire, and disintegrated.

When the oily rain and the green fire passed, a rank smell came to Hajime and did not go away—a smell like squid and sweet pork, coming from near and far. Hajime realized it must have been the people who were making that smell—the alligator-skinned people who were running toward the water and toward him—the dozens of them coming out of that same dark hell in which the green fire must have been born. He did not want to look, and yet he could not take his eyes away from them. They were at once utterly obscene and utterly fantastic, terrifying and yet at the same time spellbinding.

Hajime's journey along the riverbank—whether deeper into Ground Zero or farther out, he could not tell—should have been totally unforgettable. Yet four weeks later it would come to him only in flashes of memory. Some of the alligator men, as they staggered knee-deep into the water, literally fell apart—disintegrating before young Hajime's eyes. One man who did not make it to the river lay on his back, puffing up as if he were being inflated, or steamed, from the inside. His stomach burst open and instead of blood, black fire came out of him.

Hajime could not guess what the black fire might actually be, and years later, none of the scientists he spoke with could tell him what he saw. One would suggest that perhaps events were misremembered in both sequence and detail, and that a body bloating in the heat days later (and not right after the *pika-don*, as Hajime seemed to remember it) sent forth a swarm of black flies and not tongues of black fire. Among themselves, a few scientists would give the Hajime phenomena at least some probability of being vivid hallucinations brought about by concussion. That a multi-kiloton shockwave traveling underwater along a radius of not quite one kilometer could provide a sufficiently powerful blow to the head seemed beyond serious dispute. And yet, strange balls of light had been witnessed by nurse Minami and more than a dozen others who were with her in Hiroshima. Dr. Nagai's friend and his cow were fatally wounded by miniature fireballs more than eight kilometers from the bomb, and Prefect Nishioka had been sickened by ominous flaming "candles" that fell out of the Hiroshima cloud. The large raindrops, the shadow people, and the disintegrating alligator people had been witnessed by multiple survivors in both cities, along with many other strange and inexplicable events.[16]

Inside the Mitsubishi torpedo factory, Sachiko Masaki was shock-cocooned. Hajime's age, she had been assigned to precision finishing work on the smallest parts of the torpedoes, including the *Kaiten* controls. Under a childhood of indoctrination, Sachiko's highest goal was to die a hero for her Emperor—and her greatest regret was that girls were allowed to build and test equipment for the *Kaiten* torpedoes, but never to steer the controls and become *Kaiten* themselves.

The Mitsubishi factory stretched nearly a half-kilometer—more than four city blocks—along the Urakami riverbank. Sachiko and her teacher Komaichi were located approximately three city blocks farther from the hypocenter than Hajime, in a section of the building that ballooned out and burst like a ripe grape, while the sections nearest to Hajime were squashed. Sachiko and Komaichi perceived two distinct flashes, the second one blazing much brighter than the first, accompanied by enveloping waves of heat and ear-popping pressure. The steel and concrete sub-ceiling did not live up to its bomb-resistant label, but as the walls burst outward and flew away and as the ceiling frame came down almost to floor level, it performed a serendipitous function of all but stopping the heat ray, and absorbing much of the gamma-ray surge. Turbines and torpedo stands kept the ceiling from falling to the level of Sachiko's head, while intercepting a substantial portion of the rays and neutrons. During that critical, three- or four-second period, she felt wind roaring in her ears and had a strange sensation of floating gently in midair.

When Sachiko regained her bearings, her teacher Komaichi appeared to be in a daze. Everyone else was gone—with the rest of the factory. It was beyond Sachiko's ability to take in the disappearance.

"We should go to the protection of the tunnel factory," Komaichi said, and Sachiko agreed. As it turned out, the imagined safety of the tunnels was precisely that—imagined. With the electric pumps immobilized, they were filling quickly with ground water. And the enemy was coming out of them. American, Australian, and Javanese prisoners had been assigned to dig the tunnels—and they, too, appeared to have been safely cocooned against the *pika-don*.

"There are more of them than there are of us," Komaichi observed.

"I think I should go home now," Sachiko said, and Komaichi nodded agreement and ran away.

When her older brother came searching for her, he found Sachiko smeared with oil from the factory and with the blood of the disappeared, but she had escaped with only a few minor bruises and with none of the characteristic nausea of Ground Zero survivors. This was her brother's second experience of the atomic bomb. Three days earlier, the elder Masaki was stationed at Etajima Island's Naval Academy when, before his eyes, all of Hiroshima "went into the sky like the smoke of a furnace." He returned to Nagasaki on Kenshi Hirata's train, with friends whose entire families were lost in the firestorms of August 6. One had identified the foundations of his mother's house and his mother's half-melted wristwatch, and nothing else. All of them had been ill since August 7. Sachiko's brother appeared to be dying from a scratch on his hand that would not stop bleeding.

After the two Masaki siblings, Hajime, and another fourteen-year-old named Inosuke abandoned the Mitsubishi buildings, only the prisoners still stirred within. Beyond the tunnel they had been excavating, and outside of a few smaller, radiation-blocking shock cocoons here and there, everyone else was dead. The POWs decided to hunker down among the wrecked torpedoes and turbines of Ground Zero, hoping that the local military commanders, if any of them remained alive, now had much more important matters on their minds than hunting down escaped prisoners.[17]

A half hour after the explosion, Michie Hattori was still in Jigoku. It would seem to her later an absurd thing to have done in the aftermath of a nuclear attack, but she separated from her friend Fumiko and went into the battered remnants of her school, searching for her books. All Michie could think about was how her parents had spent every spare coin they could scrape together to pay for those books. In a building that had been half squashed, half splashed apart, she found her schoolbooks intact. Looking around the rest of the neighborhood, it occurred to her that the central supports of the school were the only landmark structures that might be called, even by exaggeration, "somewhat intact." That books could survive—somehow still stacked in the same order in which she had left them—seemed all the more mysterious.

Strapping her schoolbooks on her back, Michie set out in the direction she believed to be home. She rubbed her eyes repeatedly, not only because of the hot smoke, but because the landscape through which she walked defied imagination. Electric poles and wires had become a crazy network of cobwebs, spun over collapsed houses that, along block after block, appeared to have been squashed and kicked about by stampeding giants. Along one side of a ridge, a huge flowing debris field had been deposited by a wave of dust and compressed air that crested like water, crashed, then abruptly retreated. At the top of the heap, leaking something thick and foul-smelling, a train of tanker cars lay sprawled, wheels pointed up at the sky, like a dead worm bleeding poison.

Farther uphill, about an hour's walk beyond the place where the air seemed to have flowed liquid, a second ridge of land was more natural appearing and familiar. Standing some thirty meters high and forming a natural wall that paralleled the Urakami River, the ridge had acted as a flash shield and blast barrier between the flattened school and the little valley containing Michie's neighborhood. Buildings nearly a kilometer-and-a-half farther downriver no longer existed, yet when Michie climbed a saddleback atop the ridge and looked down, a perfectly cocooned world met her eyes.

In the glen below, all the grass had remained green. Clothing still hung unburned and undisturbed from undamaged laundry lines, and not a single door or roof tile appeared to have been dislodged. People were riding bicycles along the main street. Among them, a lone truck moved along at a leisurely pace as if nothing at all out of the ordinary had occurred. Michie walked back to look down the other side of the ridge, needing to convince herself that her journey through the wasteland had not been a dream.

Following a path that led down to her neighborhood, Michie asked people she met on the street if they knew what had happened. Most did not want to walk to the top of the ridge and see it for themselves. Hearing was enough. Others, like Michie, had come down the path and told them about the column of fire and the disappearance of almost everything between the ridge and Urakami. They did not know what had happened, only that it was something terrible. Michie told them about the flattened school and the alligator man, then hurried home.

At 11:02 a.m., Michie's parents had been at work in a small neighborhood factory, assembling munitions for fighter planes. They saw a flash through the windows and they felt the room shake, but the glass in the windows remained unbroken, so everyone shrugged off the event as an earthquake and continued working. Eventually, the factory manager returned with news that only the factory and their own town in the bottom of the glen still existed—everything outside had been destroyed.

The manager released Michie's mother and father to go over the ridge in search of their daughter. There were no landmarks leading to the school, and the cyclone of flames was throwing off so much whirling debris and black smoke that they could not continue into Urakami. Slicked with soot and sweat, they turned back, and arrived home only a few minutes before Michie.

"Do you have feet?" her joyful father asked, as he caught sight of Michie. It was the first time she ever saw him cry. Long before she reached the ridge and saw the town, Michie had counted her parents among the lost. And from the moment her parents crossed the ridge and looked down in the direction of the school, they had counted her among the ghosts of Urakami.[18]

On the other side of Michie Hattori's ridge, in the bottom of the Urakami Valley, fourteen-year-old Inosuke Hayasaki had been completely shadow-shielded and shock-cocooned, deep within the Mitsubishi Steel and Arms Works building, only 1.1 kilometers north of the hypocenter.

Presently he was pinching his own arm, not quite convinced that the rapidly developing series of events unfolding around him were not a dream or the result of his having died and arrived in hell without ever realizing that he had been about to die. During the minute before a blueish-white flash transformed his world, Inosuke's supervisors were about to crane-lift parts into place for a submarine engine. One of the engineers ordered the boy to run over to the machine room and file down a steel pin, and in that manner, he came to be located in just the right corner, beneath the shield of a multi-ton motor, in the shade of a steel-reinforced support column wider than the spread of his arms, and just a few steps from a thickly insulated refrigeration room that suddenly no longer had a door. Within that small part of a second in which the door failed, the air pressure inside the refrigerator room, relative to the atomic shock bubble bursting down through the rest of the factory, became a vacuum, sucking him instantly inside. The suction tore off the boy's shoes and shredded away his clothes, drawing him in so fast that if not for a thick padding of insulation along the compartment walls, the impact would have been lethal. During that same part of a second, all of his supervisors, all of his co-workers around the engine, died.

Inosuke was among the few Ground Zero survivors in either city who actually heard the sound of the bomb: "The light brought the roar of a hundred blasts, almost as if it was a hundred blasts of thunder." He had emerged from the refrigerator room into a fog of black dust and ash that seemed to have risen everywhere, accompanied by the distant and growing roar of a firestorm—which pierced the dust and the missing factory roof with its light, giving the upwelling streamers of smoke a strange, tiger stripe appearance. "And the smoke gave off a stench," he would recall—"a smell that cannot be explained in words."

During the first minutes after the flash, he discovered that the great, multi-ton machine—which had been overhead at the time of "the hundred blasts of thunder"—had vanished with most of the building. He walked outdoors without even noticing that he had crossed a border where steel-reinforced concrete walls once stood. The people outside were mostly charcoal, some streaked with scarlet against Bible-black, indicating where flesh had survived unburned, or where blood had seeped out, or both. They were pressed down onto the ground, some in parallel, like rows of logs. Once he stepped out of the refrigerator room, no one and nothing in his area seemed to be alive: "Everything above the river's shore was completely burned away."

Every green plant was black carbon. The factory was a steel skeleton, twisted and kicked apart, and the firestorm in the south gave off a sound Inosuke had never heard before. It sent him scurrying north along the railroad tracks, in the direction of the Michinoo Station and Akira's wrecked train.

The wooden cross ties crackled underfoot, and smoke rose up from them. Huge pine trees had been blown down like the people outside the factory, plowed down from the south toward the north, with not a single pine needle seeming to have remained on them. A stiff wind came down from the direction the trees were pointing, following the contours of the valley floor toward the fire in the south. The boy could not know it at the time, but the wind brought with it fresh oxygenated air, and carried away from him, toward the south, most if not all of the localized fallout particles that would become known to others, during the weeks that followed, as "death sand."

About the time Michie Hattori reached the crest of a ridge and saw her entire village shock-cocooned, the young factory recruit was still in doubt that this could all be a real experience. At a railroad crossing, he saw a horse, its driver, and the wreck of a horse-drawn lunch wagon where people had been preparing food outside the dormitories at 11:02 a.m. Their bodies, along with the wagon, had been thrown into a nearby field of blackened rice plants. On either side of the tracks, buildings were smoldering, crackling, and bursting suddenly into flame. Dormitories that housed thousands of young people, plowed down now into strewn-fields of wood, added something new to the unreality of Inosuke's world—"A really bizarre, screeching voice that did not belong to a human or even an animal." The voice was coming from beneath the fires. As he walked onward, the flames from the dormitories merged into cyclones, and the sight of the whirlwinds chased him more quickly along the tracks, toward Michinoo Station. The voice, too, chased him, once he realized that it was the collective yell of people trapped beneath the woodpiles. He would forever recall how the voice began gradually to die, until it ceased to be even a murmur.

Not very long after Michie was reunited with her parents, Inosuke passed the ruins of Masao and Akira's train. At last he encountered people who were still alive; but most of them could scarcely move. Those who *could* move had already fled into the eastern hill country.

The injured lay on the ground together, near the railroad tracks. They all spoke essentially the same words to him, in weak, whispery pleas: "Can you please give me water? Water, please."

Their hair was burned off and their skin, what remained of it, was a purplish color. One of them stood on shaky legs and announced to the others, "If you drink the water, you're going to die."

But it seemed to young Inosuke that none of these people were any longer of his world. Torn between what the man had warned, and a sense that the flash-burned people had perhaps only hours left to live, he decided to give them water. Seeking and finding rags of cotton, he ran to the nearest rice paddy and soaked the cloth, wringing the water out from the rags into the mouths of the people near the tracks. The boy had never seen such thirst. As they drank, it was as if even muddy water from the fields was something that had never tasted so good to them before. He continued down the line of people alongside the tracks, giving everyone he encountered a drink of water. After the twenty-fifth person, he needed to break away and re-soak the rags. On the way back to the rice paddy, he stopped to visit the first boy to whom he had given water. Inosuke asked him to sit up, but he did not utter a sound. Touching the child's chest, to see if he was still breathing, Inosuke discovered to his horror that not only was the child dead, but that the skin peeled away from the ribs and clung to his hand.

Years later, he would record: "I looked back to the people I had given water to, after [the boy], and I saw that all of them were now dead. What a horrible crime I had committed. Those who were still alive—those I had *not* tried to help—sent up a continuous moan, a wail: *Please give me water*. And I started running. I started fretting on the fact that I had become a murderer. And I began to cry."[19]

Governor Nagano's sense of anticlimax and well-being did not last any longer than it took him to climb up from his shock-cocooned mansion and crest the hill that had sheltered him. He understood now that Prefect Nishioka had not exaggerated Hiroshima. Not by a gnat's breath. Just as he had warned, Urakami was transformed into a manifestation of hell on Earth. Impenetrable black dust hugged the ground—and, off to one side, the rotating mass of fire and smoke reared up higher than the Pyramids. Somewhere near the heart of the storm, one of the army's major communications hubs must by now have become clouds of ash.

From the far side of the cyclone, the head of the Urakami Council called in a report to the governor through one of the few still-functioning police radios. The flames seemed to be throwing up a wall of static, but with many repeats, the full picture was coming in. Hundreds—perhaps thousands of people burned by the flash—were fleeing into the mountains behind the medical complex, and the stream of the wounded was becoming a flood of the dying.

"They have been coming in droves," a stenographer recorded. "They are all begging for help and water when they arrive. They grab on to your legs and they can't walk. Is the Prefectural Office aware of this situation?"

Another report described the scattered dead and the dying in an area between the firestorm and a town that stood apart from the rest of the landscape—like an oasis in a desert.

"In the desert," the caller said, "there was a young woman, about twenty years old, lying face down and calling for water—just, 'Water . . . water . . . water' in a voice so small it was like a mosquito humming."[20]

"How many fatalities are you estimating?" Nagano demanded.

"In the hills below the medical [buildings] . . . I believe we're looking at fifty thousand dead in Urakami alone."

Nagano had already prepared a telegram to Tokyo reporting his own estimated total of 20,000—and it would be sent before Nagano could correct his estimate. In time, the initial estimate would be used to corroborate an official low-mortality statistic favored by General MacArthur's investigators.

But Urakami was not a statistic.

"*Fifty thousand?*" Governor Nagano was practically wailing over the airwaves. "What are the police doing? Where are the fire brigades?"

"Most—" and the caller broke off in a wash of static.

"Repeat?" the governor called. He just did not seem to understand. "Why haven't the police and the local administrators been sent to see what's going on?"

"Most of them are dead," came the reply. "And those who are still alive can't go into the middle of a fire."

"Who's in charge over there?" the governor asked.

The obvious reply was "Aren't you?" but the caller kept the snipe to himself and said, "We've got turmoil erupting—with everyone looking for doctors, nurses, and police. The hospitals on this side are burning and the doctors are evacuating the patients. Forget about fighting the fires or policing the area. We're going to need doctors, nurses, and medicine."

The initial shock-state appeared to be passing, and the governor seemed to regain control of himself. "The situation is understood," Nagano assured the caller. "I've decided to order the head of the health department to mobilize all doctors and nurses on this side into a medical team that will head into your area."

At approximately the time that would normally have marked the governor's late lunch schedule, an assistant informed him that the local health minister appeared to be missing in action.

"Then, has anyone seen Prefect Nishioka?" Nagano asked. It seemed incomprehensible to him that the prefect would not have come to the mansion and taken his assigned post in the shelter by now. As far as Nagano could tell, Prefect Nishioka had never in his life been late for anything.[20]

In the hilly suburb of Isahaya, Nishioka and his driver encountered the first refugees streaming away from the city. Ant-walking alligators. At first they took his thoughts back to Hiroshima, and then he realized that he was fully ten kilometers from the center of the storm. He was almost as far away from the hypocenter in Urakami as Harlem and the Bronx are from the lower tip of Manhattan. This *pika-don* appeared to be worse than the one in Hiroshima. The alligator people said so, without saying a word. The prefect knew that they could not have walked very far from the places in which they had been injured. Many were now eyeless and faceless—with their heads transformed into blackened alligator hides displaying red holes, indicating mouths.

The alligator people did not scream. Their mouths could not form the sounds. The noise they made was worse than screaming. They uttered a continuous murmur—like locusts on a midsummer night. One man, staggering on charred stumps of legs, was carrying a dead baby upside down. Its diapers and legs were burned even blacker than the clouds from Urakami.

Millions of tons of dust and vapor had been hoisted into the crown of the mushroom, and ashes were spreading across the heavens like ink poured into water. Objects still dropped out of the cloud—little black flecks of wood, concrete grit pinging against the windshield, a pebble, a wisdom tooth.

"What is this?" the driver asked.

"Fallout," the prefect said. *Atomic fallout*, he emphasized for himself, and left unsaid.[21]

Elsewhere, almost everything Nishioka had said the day before was saving lives. His observation that people in Hiroshima who were even minimally sheltered had a good chance of surviving the *pika-don* had been passed on by the governor to the district police chief, who passed this advice on to his thirteen-year-old son as a stern instruction.

At 11:02 a.m., the chief's son had been standing outside his middle school with three friends, near a street called Daikoku-Machi, on the fringe of Ground Zero. On this particular morning, his father sent him to school wearing a white, wide-rimmed hat. He feared his father's displeasure more than embarrassment, so without any fuss he wore the embarrassing hat and the long white pants. When the flash cut across the sky, the boy responded instinctively to a duck-and-cover maneuver, practiced before breakfast—over and over, until he performed it perfectly for his father, in under a half-second. Just as quickly, he ducked and rolled into a gully-like "shrapnel shelter," cut into the pavement. He shouted as he ducked, calling for his friends to dive in with him. Only one obeyed, rolling in practically on top of the boy. The other two stood, watching the *pika* grow into a shock bubble.[22] They were never seen again.[23]

Another saved by a witness to Hiroshima was Dr. Tatsuichiro Akizuki. Dean Tsunoo had described a monstrous flash-and-bang, brought about by a single plane that dove earthward before the flash. This warning sign was very different from the steady drone produced by an approaching fleet of fire-bombers—which allowed up to two or three minutes to take cover. Tsunoo advised that the sound of a single plane's engines straining would provide only a few seconds' advance warning.

At 11:01 a.m., Dr. Akizuki had just struck a pneumo-thorax needle into the side of a tuberculosis patient, when he became aware of an extremely sharp low sound, like a B-29 diving toward Earth.

"What's that?" Akizuki said to an assistant. "The all-clear has sounded, hasn't it?"

The sound of the diving B-29 intensified, leaving little doubt about what was happening.

"Get down!" he yelled, withdrawing the needle and dropping to the floor. Seconds later, the hypocenter was created, almost 1.4 kilometers away. Urakami's Medical College Hospital and St. Francis Hospital were located high on a hill that became, after a fashion, the barrel of the valley's shotgun effect. The building's roof and many of the outer walls were stripped away and not a single window survived, but this was a shock-cocoon effect, compared to the seething hell below in the river valley. After the flash, the ceiling crashed down like a tidal wave. Akizuki and his assistant stood amazed at having survived the concrete and plaster tsunami without wounds. The patient had not been so lucky. He took a direct shot in the head from a spray of glass and concrete.

The rest of the patients did not come toward Akizuki and the nurse. Instead they ran away, fleeing the hospital as if chased by demons, covering their bloodstained faces with their hands as they ran for the imagined safety of the highest hill.

Most of them were looking back as they ran; and when finally Akizuki looked toward what they appeared to be fleeing, he saw the southwestern sky turned every bit as dark as coal; and below the black veil, over the surface of the earth, hung a strange fog that—as the dust cleared little by little—rooted him to the spot with horror.

The fog was fire.

Dr. Akizuki was among the few who lived to see, and to tell, how the great Urakami cyclone formed: "To say that everything burned is not enough. It seemed as if Earth itself emitted fire and smoke, flames that writhed up and erupted from underground. The sky was dark, the ground was scarlet."

And then, as he watched, a crimson-and-yellow-flecked figure rose up from the ocean of flame and tried to become a mountain. It seemed to Akizuki, and to many others who saw it that morning, that the whole world was dying and they with it.

When Dr. Paul Nagai looked down from the hospital and saw the cyclone, he, too, thought about the end of the world. Yet, as a man who had taken a Christian name when he was baptized and confirmed, it became an end foretold for thousands of years, from the time of Daniel. To Nagai, the dizzying display in the valley was the brink of the beginning, and a warning—not of things that had to be, but he hoped only an antidote against what might be. He did not want to believe that he was witnessing the world to come. A Jesuit teacher had said as much after Osaka burned. He told the little-known story of Jesus and James, in which James learned that even when a fate was foretold by prophecy, there really was no fate except that which people made. The Jesuit had explained Jesus' lesson in a more modern vernacular: "And the Lord said, 'Children, do you remember that part about *love one another*? Don't make me have to come down there and smack you—because it will be pale horses and pale riders, and it will be really bad.'"

Dr. Nagai did not believe it was merely a coincidence that the hospital and Urakami Cathedral overlooked the place where Saint Paul Miki—the samurai who became a Jesuit—was crucified with twenty-five of his followers in 1597, on Tau-shaped crosses. Dr. Nagai wondered if what might seem to most people to be a mere accident of history—the convergence of hypocenter and crucifixion—was a reminder to all humanity that though everything about man except man's way of thinking had changed, if man's way of thinking did not change, then indeed all of this was prologue to the way the world ends.[24]

On the front lawn of the hospital, Dr. Akizuki was discovering that the ground must have been briefly heated to at least the boiling point of water. The grasses—and the leaves of all the vegetables—were flattened, scorched, and smoldering. Most of the people who were working in the garden had their backs turned toward the *pika* when it flashed red, and they must have involuntarily turned their heads in time to behold the full fury of the blue flash—before they had time to realize they must not turn around and look. The gardeners' backs were scorched raw by the heat rays. Their faces were burned within those same first three seconds. And they were blind.

At first, Dr. Akizuki wanted to run away, but when he looked up, he saw fires beginning to spread little by little through the ruins of the hospital's uppermost floor. For a moment, he thought it a bit odd that the pulled-apart roof was the first portion of the building to catch fire. And then, in the next moment, he thought of Dr. Yoshioka. She was up there somewhere. And he had *sent* her there.

When he ran inside and climbed the stairs, Akizuki found several Jesuit brothers from the local chapel already assisting in the evacuation. During the next ten minutes, the brothers and the staff, along with several of the uninjured patients, helped Akizuki to evacuate everyone from the building.

As the empty hospital burned, taking almost all of the medicine and equipment with it, someone called out Akizuki's name, shouting over the roar of flames, "Please come quickly, sir!"

He followed the man to a hill behind the hospital, where one of the brothers had carried Dr. Yoshioka on his back.

"She is about to die from loss of blood," said Nurse Tsuyako, quietly reproaching Dr. Akizuki for being so long in coming.

A gauze cloth had been wrapped so many times around Yoshioka's head that only one eye peered out at Akizuki as he took her pulse and checked the bandages.

"I don't think you're in any danger," Akizuki said, not sure he was telling the truth. "Your pulse is strong, you're not too pale—and the bandages have stopped the bleeding."

"Have you found out anything about your mother?" Dr. Yoshioka asked.

"No," he said, with polite resignation. "She's probably been burned." Looking toward the cyclone of flames, he could not make a good guess at the precise location of his mother's house. As he watched, people began moving up the hill toward him, groaning and murmuring for help. The ant-walkers' faces were like masks, and the physician felt as if he were watching a procession of ghosts—as in a dream he recalled from childhood. But this was worse. With the hospital now sending up flurries of sparks, there was no medicine except what the staff had grabbed on the way out. There was not even a roof under which to shelter the wounded. Akizuki felt that he could be of no help without medical supplies, and he really did want to run away, but he decided that even if it became impossible to provide much actual treatment, sometimes the comfort of a medic's presence or just a caring human hand could be enough to keep a patient's will to live alight. Once he heard the people's pleas for help, he could not leave them.

As the stream of survivors from the valley increased in number, the groans and murmurs grew in strength, sounding to Dr. Akizuki like a prophecy from the Buddhist scriptures: "re-echoing everywhere, as if Earth itself were in pain."[25]

Ship designer Yamaguchi's section chief had still been trying to explain how he did not believe an atomic bomb could possibly work, when the second *pika* concluded the argument in Yamaguchi's favor. Barely more than three kilometers downriver of the hypocenter, the heat that burst into the room was so great that, this time, Yamaguchi believed he was gone.

4.4 kilometers from the Urakami hypocenter—at a radius of nearly 3 miles and just beyond Tsutomu Yamaguchi's location—black tar paper covering a wall absorbed the flash and instantly evaporated, leaving shadows behind. During a pulse that lasted about a half-second, the shadow of a man standing near a ladder was sharply imprinted, except for a blurring of the head—which was evidently turning, perhaps reflexively in the direction of the flash, or toward a sudden commotion nearby. The blurry shape at the base of the ladder is consistent with a second person, trying to duck and cover during that same part of a second. [Illustration: CRP]

Once more, he was standing on the edge of Ground Zero. All around him, all wooden structures and almost all light steel-frame buildings were flattened by the blast. Within this zone, even exposed concrete could be briefly ignited to produce a secondary flash of limelight. Here and there, aluminum burned like rocket fuel. Anyone standing outdoors unshielded at Yamaguchi's radius was safely beyond the range of lethal gamma-ray dosing (with the air itself, at 2mi, equally 2 meters of water shielding)—but this condition was rendered irrelevant by the instant lethality of the blast wave and the heat ray.

During the critical first three seconds, Yamaguchi's arguments were instantly recalled, and his listeners dove under tables and behind doorframes. In the end, Yamaguchi's section chief did exactly what Yamaguchi had said he should do if he saw the bright flash, and he survived with almost no injuries—in a room that, unlike the rest of the building, appeared to have been cocooned between diverging shock waves. Somehow, in a hilly region where during a period of about six seconds shock fronts were actively rebounding and converging with bone-granulating force, a wave bearing down upon Yamaguchi's location parted harmlessly around an adjacent steel-and-concrete stairwell, like water shunted to either side of a boat's prow. The wave appeared to have carried away everything and everyone except Yamaguchi's conference room, and the people there with him. Even the superheated air seemed to have eddied around the outside of the office, before retreating backward toward Urakami and following the fireball into the sky. Before they collapsed into smoke and dust, multiple floors of concrete and steel had provided their own added layer of protection by absorbing the heat and most of the gamma rays that were still trying to get through, but Yamaguchi still felt a renewed sensation of heat throughout his body—followed by a chill and nausea.

He ran down through a broken stairwell that no longer had walls, through a once familiar hallway with no ceiling into a neighboring building that was now a field. The only familiar structure was an old steel-and-concrete watchtower that used to be a lighthouse.

Like Yamaguchi and his colleagues, the tower appeared to have been inexplicably spared, though its steel door was almost hot enough to burn his fingers when he pulled it open. For the first time he became aware that his burns from Hiroshima were now fully exposed to the increasingly powerful gusts of smoke and wind. Though the precursor wave had bounced and diverged as it burst through the Mitsubishi office building, the gale that came with it had blown off all of his bandages and even de-gloved some of the skin beneath.

The tower's lookout was still at his post. Evidently, he had been watching the B-29 through powerful binoculars. In the end, he was perhaps watching the bomb itself, as it fell. His face was a mask of blackened alligator skin, but his brain took the brunt of it. The binoculars had focused the heat ray into twin beams that must have burned through both eyes and almost to the far side of the man's skull—all within one small part of a millisecond. The engineer merely shrugged at another new horror and looked out from the top of the lighthouse, trying to find home.

In home's direction, everything had been kicked sideways and seared—then something apparently came through and snuffed out the fires that should now have been there. The ground appeared to have been scratched and raked, as if by the devil's talons. Fighting off nausea, chills, and new wounds, the engineer climbed down and began to walk.

Tsutomu Yamaguchi discovered that one side of his house was a curiously intact box, filled with raked table and chair parts, and balcony splinters—all of it sheathed in a veneer of black carbon. The rest was ruin. As Kenshi had done in Hiroshima, Yamaguchi now searched the area, and dug frantically for his family—and eventually he came upon a tiny bone fragment, clearly belonging to a baby. But the bomb's effects seemed to go hand in hand with the random deviations of human routines. Sometimes Yamaguchi attributed the fortune and misfortune in his life to a path planted for him by one god or another. Other times he believed that what appeared to be destiny only appeared so, and really happened "just because."

Yamaguchi soon found Hisako and little Katsutoshi alive. After he left for work on the morning of the second bomb, a cousin's wife came to visit Hisako, bringing along her own baby. Hisako had offered tea and stepped out earlier than usual for what was only to have been a brief errand prior to her afternoon-through-evening shift, directing the expansion of a Mitsubishi tunnel. Her husband's injuries from Hiroshima sent Hisako along a path she would not otherwise have taken. She would normally have been at home, preparing lunch for relatives before setting off for work. As the critical split second approached, Mrs. Yamaguchi walked away to visit a local medicine dealer who knew something about treating burns. Like most young mothers, endearingly overcautious Hisako tended to take Katsutoshi everywhere with her—even when relatives were at home willing to look after her child. When the final air-raid alert sounded, Hisako's mission to find a remedy for her husband's burns had altered her normal routine and brought her to the Mitsubishi shelter ahead of schedule. Hisako sought out the coolest, deepest part of the tunnel in which to preserve the white skin cream she had bought for her husband. And this was how she and Katsutoshi, and a teenage baby-sitter, came to be sheltered when the fires came—and fortunately, the fires themselves ignited far away.

Sometimes it worked out. "Sometimes by God's will," Tsutomu Yamaguchi liked to believe, "and maybe sometimes, just because."[26]

Kenshi Hirata had escaped the fire-bombings of Kobe, Osaka, and now, after only three days, his second atomic bomb. It must have seemed to Kenshi that the American B-29 crews were seeking him out personally.

At Nagasaki, he had been completely shielded behind one of his neighborhood's many hills. The neighborhood itself was mysteriously cocooned against harm. The grasses remained green and the cicadas, though silent, were still alive. The blast wave had done little more than loosen roof tiles, yet it kicked the wedding bowl out of Kenshi's hands, in which he had carried fragments of his wife's bones all the way from Hiroshima. Kenshi and his father spent the first few minutes after the blast searching for the metal bowl and tracking down every piece of bone they could find, all but oblivious to the cloud rising overhead, and the strange objects falling out of it.

When they reached the house, Setsuko's five-year-old brother appeared at the door, and saw the bowl of bones. The child called out for his parents, noticing that his brother-in-law seemed to be very ill, and scarcely noticing the blizzard of charred paper and clothing that was falling along the street.

The parents gazed with amazement, at Kenshi and the bones.

"Oh, you had a hard time," Setsuko's father said, in a calm and uniquely Japanese manner by which multiple feelings and complex messages could be represented by only a few words.

"You had a hard time," Setsuko's mother repeated, and Kenshi understood, immediately, the real meaning of this: *We are not blaming you. We sympathize.*

Then, in one of history's quintessential examples of how, in Japan, what was said directly and on the surface often conveyed an ocean of meaning, Setsuko's father said, "You were not registered yet with the city, as a couple. Please don't worry."

The words shocked Kenshi. Setsuko's parents were using a legal technicality as a tool for releasing him from what happened to their daughter and from any obligation to her—past, present, or future. They wished him to move forward with his life and, without looking back, to find love again one day, and to raise a family.

Kenshi did not say anything. He simply left the porch; and even in this silent response, an ocean of emotions was communicated. He was very thankful to the parents for not reproaching him with blame, for instead understanding his situation, understanding his love, his sympathy for Setsuko. And at the same time, their words meant that this was the moment in which their relationship with him was to be terminated. Unspoken, yet said: *Because your marriage was not officially registered, we can restart everything. You have your life. We can continue to live together as neighbors, and we will never talk about the contract of marriage.*

According to the traditions of Kenshi Hirata's generation, the wife's family was permanently bound with the husband's family because, by tradition, the parents of the wife either encouraged or discouraged the marriage. *We don't blame you, Kenshi,* Setsuko's father had tried to say. *Blame the parents for the hastened marriage, and for this sadness. We release you.*

"*Please don't worry.*" In that simple phrase was hidden a lifetime of meaning.

"The true sadness of the moment was unfathomable to most people," Kenshi would tell history, as the sixty-fifth anniversary of Setsuko's death approached. "I felt very sorry for the parents, because they had to say, 'Please don't worry.' I felt so sorry for Setsuko."

The words, "Please don't worry" signified, as a rule, the end of all communication between the two families. And yet, after Kenshi Hirata eventually remarried, and after a newspaper report mentioned that his children were fathered by a man exposed twice to radiation, Setsuko's parents would help him to protect his children from a widespread prejudice that began rising against atomic survivors and their offspring. They helped the Hirata family to disappear, and to stay out of history's way.

Even during the 1970s, when an American who studied the physical effects of the atomic bombs applied all of his skills as an FBI agent to finding where Kenshi Hirata had fled with his family, he failed to turn up a clue, and eventually died without knowing that Kenshi had disappeared in open view. Setsuko's family, and Kenshi's parents, and all of their neighbors, would protect his identity and the identities of his children so well that he never had to move from the neighborhood.

In the end, the same man who slept on the ground where his wife had been vaporized in Hiroshima, desiring only that her spirit would not feel abandoned, never lived more than half of a city block from the stone pinnacle where Setsuko's parents had buried her bones. Even after sixty-five years passed, Kenshi continued to make offerings of water at the shrine, keeping his own private promise that Setsuko would never be left behind, or forgotten.[27]

Kenshi Hirata [Illustration: CRP]

Dr. Nagai's first thought, after the blast wave had passed through the hospital, was gratitude to still be taking in air and able to think clearly, and to walk. His next thought was of his position as an officer of the Rescue Committee. Looking downhill, toward central Urakami, he knew that his wife lay somewhere under the flames. He would learn much later that a sister who last saw her had urged Midori Nagai to spend the rest of the day in what was to become the shadow-shielded cottage, near the stream where little Kayano and Makoto were playing at 11:02 a.m. His wife had declined, explaining that the cancer was making Paul sicker than usual lately; so she wanted to make a nutritious lunch for him and bring it to the hospital. Paul Nagai would eventually discover that she must in fact have died in the midst of preparing something for him. Mixed in with her bones were cooking utensils—mashed flat, then melted.

Dr. Paul Nagai had begun the morning with about six months of life left to him, but four years later, haunted by survivor's guilt, he would write (in one of history's most starkly introspective memoirs) that in choosing to stay near the hospital after the *pika-don* instead of trying to return home to his wife, he had discharged his responsibility. "What will be my reward," he wondered, "in the eyes of Makoto and Kayano when they are grown?"

Believing that he would soon die from his cancer, Dr. Nagai's initial guiding instinct was to be remembered as a hero. Distraught over the disappearance of Urakami and his wife, he forced himself to control his emotions and direct the evacuation of patients from his end of the hospital complex. He was fully conscious of seeking posthumous praise, of wanting to be recognized as someone who rescued people from a burning building without showing any private feelings.

From Paul Nagai's perspective, the students, the nurses, and the Jesuit brothers were not driven by such vanity. They kept going back into the danger zone under Nagai's sometimes draconian supervision, while he later received the praise: "The dying doctor who thought only of others."

On the fifth anniversary of the bombing, he would recall a young nurse who appeared to have received no cuts or bruises from the *pika-don* but who collapsed three times in a state of utter exhaustion, pleading for him to bear her along part of the way. Instead, he reprimanded her for showing such weakness and commanded her to stiffen her spine, and continue the work of rescue. Two days later, she was vomiting blood. On the morning of the bomb, Nagai noticed that several of the other nurses were also weakening and stumbling.

"I allowed them no help," Nagai lamented, when he understood the truth. "These girls were all far sicker than they looked—some were actually in the death agony—and, not knowing it, I made them all stand up and walk without help. I often wonder what their families would think of me now."

Those nurses and brothers who (though shaded from the heat ray) had been outdoors when the gamma rays burst toward them, or who were near the hospital's outer lobby, were irradiated with approximately one-third of a lethal dose. Even within the building's shell of steel and red brick, Nagai's location exposed him to almost one-fifth of a lethal dose from prompt radiation, and at least twice as much from the subsequent fallout—a total dosage that killed approximately half the people it impacted. The reason radiation struck hardest at the lining of the intestinal tract and at the bone marrow was that its disruptive effects were most pronounced against rapidly dividing cells. Cancer cells fell into this category. As the nurses sickened before Dr. Nagai's eyes, the bomb—while still causing nausea and making his skin brittle—was killing Nagai's healthy blood-producing cells and cancer cells with equal ease. Almost from the start of the first gamma-ray surge, his cancer was being driven toward remission.

Unlike Kenshi Hirata and Tsutomu Yamaguchi, Nagai did not believe God or fate had spared him merely to bear witness. He believed there was a penance to be paid as well, as if life on Earth was just some other planet's purgatory.

If not for the fact that it would have left her orphaned, Dr. Nagai would rather have died than lived to hear what happened when an aunt told his little girl that her mother was dead. Kayano was only four. She did not know what it meant. She did not cry; she simply smiled and asked, "When is Mommy coming home?"

That night, Kayano's cousin Ritsuko developed diarrhea. Cousin Takeo developed the same symptom, along with an upset stomach.

On the unburned side of the ravine, where the grass still remained green in spite of a strange rain of what looked and felt like "dead jellyfish goo"—in spite of the smoldering paper and the other objects that seemed to have no business falling out of the sky—fireflies had lived through the blast. The children saw them flying around with their reflections in the stream. Auntie Urata would recall that the fireflies, along with the scent of live grass, gave a wonderful sense of life to the air—which made it all the more impossible to believe the tragedies that were yet to unfold.

On the fifth anniversary, though only a child, it would be clear that Kayano Nagai was being compelled to acquire wisdom beyond her years. "Cousin Ritsuko died," she would record for a memorial memoir. "Before she died, she coughed up a lot of blood. (Her sweat was blood.) Cousin Takeo also coughed up a lot of blood and he died, too."

It would never escape Kayano's notice that the war had begun on the Feast of the Immaculate Conception, December 8 (the day of the Pearl Harbor bombing on Japan's side of the International Date Line).

It ended the day Ritsuko died, August 15. *How many cruel swords must have pierced the Holy mother's heart all this time*, Kayano wondered.

"I can remember when I was little, but mostly bad things," nine-year-old Kayano would tell history. "The year I was born, the war began. The whole time I was little there were air raids all the time. It was awful but anyhow I had my mommy there, so it was nice; I was so happy. I saw the atomic bomb. I was four then. The atomic bomb was the last thing that happened during the war and no more bad things have happened since then; but I don't have my mommy anymore. So even if it isn't bad anymore, I'm not happy."[28]

Resident populations of Hiroshima and central Nagasaki before the bombings, according to records of rice ration registrations:

	Survey Date	Population
Hiroshima	June 1945	245,423
Nagasaki	May 1945	206,996

· 8 ·

Threads

About the same time Cadet Komatsu flew into the cloud's radioactive stem and Michie Hattori made her acquaintance with the alligator man, Charles Sweeney was coming to terms with the depressing mathematics of his situation, and with another of Paul Tibbets's "bonehead" maneuvers.

From Nagasaki to Okinawa was 350 miles. After the bombing run, *BocksCar* and *Great Artiste* had risen from 20,000 to 30,000 feet for a quick high-altitude reconnaissance to confirm that the target was indeed destroyed, and also to stay above and ahead of ascending fighters. At this starting point for the voyage home, Sweeney's engines were burning approximately one gallon of fuel per mile. He was starting out with a total of only 300 gallons, including a small volume that the flight engineer was able to siphon from the dead bladder. To conserve fuel, he needed to reduce altitude and get down to more richly oxygenated air. In addition, he could throttle the propellers back from the by-the-book speed of 2,000 rpm to 1,800 rpm. This would save a little more fuel but not a significantly large amount, by Sweeney's math. So he decided to throttle back to 1,600 rpm, which would unfortunately reduce the necessary inflow of lubrication and the levels of cooling needed to keep the engines in good condition. This decision was all but guaranteed to damage all four engines, but the machinery would be much more thoroughly ruined by a crash on salt water and could therefore be considered a burnable resource.

The throttle-down reduced *BocksCar*'s speed by a hundred miles per hour. Sweeney was now consuming 300 instead of 500 gallons per hour, but he would still drop into the sea fifteen minutes and several miles short of his destination.

Sweeney hoped that Tibbets's boneheaded theory might just make up the difference. Tibbets's name for the theory was "flying the staircase." Accordingly, with velocity and power settings being equal, a gradual step-down-and-level-out, step-down-again-and-level-out-again descent would give the aircraft a brief, temporary acceleration with each down-step, without using any extra fuel. Theoretically, Sweeney would be able to milk a few extra miles out of the remaining fuel reserve. *And in practice?* The pilot wondered. Starting out from 30,000 feet, Sweeney believed he had plenty of time to find out; so he began his climb down the stairs, trusting the mathematics of Paul Tibbets and Isaac Newton to do most of the driving.

Fifteen minutes out from Okinawa and over the original estimated crash point, the fuel supply, though down to barely more than a dozen gallons, was still providing food for the engines. Sweeney gave thanks to Tibbets, Newton, and the Lord when finally the island came into view. Unfortunately, America's closest airfield to Japan was also its busiest. Even ten minutes out, Sweeney could see signs of air traffic over every runway.

"Yontan. Yontan tower!" Sweeney called out to a receiver who seemed too busy to answer. "This is Dimples 77. Mayday! Mayday! Over."

"All gauges now reading empty," Kuharek called forward, and immediately after he said this, Number 4—the starboard outboard engine—shut down.

"Increase power to Number Three," Sweeney called back.

The revving up of Number 3 steadied *BocksCar*'s starboard wing, but if by now any outcome was at all certain, it was that the only way to land was along a straight-in glide path. Being waved off by a flight controller to a "circle-round-and-try-again" landing was not an option.

Sweeney told Van Pelt to fire the red and green emergency flares, signaling *Aircraft out of fuel*. He backed this up with another call of, "Mayday! Mayday! Dimples 77." Streamers of red and green were now trailing behind *BocksCar*, and Sweeney could hear the control towers talking to other planes as if nothing unusual was happening on the horizon.

"Are they blind as well as deaf?" Sweeney shouted to his crew—and then, into the mike, "Mayday! Mayday! I'm calling any god-damned tower in Okinawa!"

Not even static came back. Sweeney put down the landing gear and yelled back to Van Pelt, "Fire off every damned flare we have on board!"

"All of them?"

"*All* of them! Do it now!"

Seconds later, the flares were bursting on all sides—reds, blues, and greens; purple and sparkling white stars. Van Pelt was signaling, *Aircraft out of fuel! Aircraft crashed on water, over here! Prepare for incoming crash! Aircraft on fire! Dead and wounded aboard!*

Sweeney imagined that *BocksCar* must now look like the Fourth of July, barreling in fast.

"Who *is* that jackass?" called a weary air traffic controller.

At least now I have their attention, Sweeney thought, as planes began swerving out of his path, allowing him to pound down onto the nearest runway with only two of the four engines still sucking in air and providing thrust.

Barely more than ten seconds after Sweeney came to a stop, emergency vehicles were at *BocksCar*'s side. One of them began spraying down the engines, though clearly nothing appeared to be burning. A medic poked his head up through the nosewheel door and asked, "Where are the dead and wounded?"

Sweeney flipped a thumb over his shoulder, indicating the direction of Japan. "Back there," he said, and said nothing more on the subject. He was a long way from the Tinian Air Base, and even if President Truman had already spilled the beans and announced the bomb's existence, the pilot understood without being told, that he was to say nothing to any under-officer on the base about where he had been, where he was going, or what he had done.

As an order came in from Admiral Purnell on Tinian for the ground crew on Okinawa to give Sweeney everything he needed for the next leg of his journey, and as the hours ticked by, the response from Tokyo continued to be a desert of silence.

Could their actual response to two atomic bombs be contemptuous indifference? Sweeney wondered. *Could that possibly be true?*

It certainly appeared so. Instead of news about a Japanese surrender, the headline story on Armed Forces Radio was all about the pending Russian invasion of Japanese-occupied China, followed in second place by the discovery of "lost" archival recordings of the late Glenn Miller's "Caribbean Clipper" and "Little Brown Jug," followed not very far behind by future Rock and Roll Hall-of-Famer, Count Basie.

Sweeney was the only member of his crew who knew that the plutonium cores of the next two atomic bombs would not exist for another month or more. He would record in his memoirs that this thought left him colder than any other. The gap between bombs might convince overlords in the Imperial Palace that if the country could absorb two atomic blasts and regroup, then this new horror—just like the "conventional" fire-bombings—could be fought through and survived.

Jesus, Sweeney said to himself. *If only we had another bomb that could be dropped tomorrow or the day after, then Tokyo would believe we were able to load them one after another like shotgun shells. And then they'd surely surrender and stop the madness. But this? This?*

The delay of a whole month would communicate only one lesson: Truman was playing poker and the vast nuclear arsenal did not really exist. And the tragic irony of it was that when the next bombs became available in a few weeks, Sweeney would have to fly more of these missions. At least three more of them, he guessed.

Just what the hell must they be thinking back there in the Emperor's Palace?[1]

As his contemporaries told it, "Nero fiddled while Rome burned."

During the passage of nearly two thousand years, those words had rarely been more apt. Field Marshal Shunroku Hata, who had missed his meeting with Prefect Nishioka but had survived the fires of Hiroshima and arrived in Tokyo with barely more than a "sunburn" on one side of his face, insisted with Dr. Sagane that the Americans possessed only enough nuclear material for the delivery of two atomic bombs.

"They appear now to have used both of them," Hata said. "They have now done the worst that they can do."

Foreign Minister Shigenori Togo, with the evidence from physicist Yoshio Nishina weighing heavily upon him, had been pressing, as politely as he could, for a unified plea to the Emperor for a decision.

War Minister Korechika Anami seemed to have stopped worrying altogether and was actually learning to embrace the bomb. Having heard descriptions of the atomic cloud booming into the stratosphere like a radiant flower, he waxed poetic and said, "Would it not be wondrous for this whole nation to be destroyed like a beautiful flower?"

The self-styled warrior poet's lesson to young kamikaze and *Kaiten* pilots had been much the same. He taught them that their destiny was war—"to fall for the Emperor like petals from a flower." In several days, following revelations that he knew of and was now considering fellowship in a military coup against the Emperor, aimed at eliminating all possibility of surrender, Anami would commit ritual suicide after treating his friends to sake, showing them two of his "death poems," and lamenting both his great crime against the Emperor and the great poet that the world was losing.

At this moment, Anami was refusing to tolerate the foreign minister's phrase, "The war situation grows more unfavorable for us every hour." Togo was forced to rephrase his words, "The war situation has developed not necessarily to Japan's advantage."

General Yoshijiro Umezu assured Anami that antiaircraft countermeasures concentrated against two or three planes traveling alone should be able to repel an atomic attack.

"And what if they should have another atomic bomb already in waiting on one of the islands?" Foreign Minister Togo broke in. "And what if they know we have learned by now to beware especially of only two or three planes? Do you not believe they are smart enough to hide one bomb among a fleet of fifty B–29 raiders? Or a hundred? And how are we to shoot them all down?"

For a moment, it seemed to Togo that War Minister Anami had no answer; but with cheeks flushing red and glistening with tears, he said, "I am quite sure we can inflict great casualties on the enemy; and even if we fail in the attempt, our hundred million people are ready to die for honor, glorifying the deeds of the Japanese in recorded history."

General Umezu agreed, and announced, "We must fight on with courage and find life in death. It is the only way we can honor so many brave men who have already died for the Emperor."

And for what? Dr. Nishina thought, upon hearing of such words. *We honor our war dead by piling more corpses on top of them?* But after Admiral Ugaki began singing the praises of a suicide rocket-plane squadron, Nishina kept his thoughts to himself, for he could see all too clearly that standing rationally and tall at this time was a quick way to be made short—by having one's head cut off. So the physicist listened to news of the events, as they were related to him, and held his tongue while the war minister and the foreign minister argued in political double-speak about whether the war was turning truly "unfavorable" or just "not necessarily desirable," while the people of Hiroshima succumbed to a disease no human population had seen before, while Urakami and the Nagasaki shipyards burned.[2]

Far to the south of Tokyo, in the smoldering prairies of Hiroshima, Keiji Nakazawa, the boy who was saved behind a schoolyard wall by a margin of only two or three steps, was still trying to conceal from his mother the continual waves of nausea, the pain from an unhealing burn at the center of an expanding bald spot, and other telltale signs of "Disease X."

Since the second day, people who seemed to have been uninjured but who remained in Hiroshima were losing their hair, vomiting, developing uncontrollable diarrhea, and dying. Keiji knew that trying to conceal his sickness was a futile effort; his mother was sure to notice. So he began sneaking away from the small shelter he had helped her to erect near the trolley tracks, setting off in search of food. He was worried about his newborn sister, who only rarely cried, and who seemed to be sleeping throughout the day.

Between the foundations of Hiroshima Castle and the Communications Hospital, soldiers unearthed bales of carbonized rice still standing in orderly stacks, even though the army warehouse in which they had been stacked appeared to have been lifted off the ground and carried away. A handful of army personnel who had survived the blast and the fires resolved to organize something at least resembling a rescue operation despite their own steadily deteriorating health. They burrowed into the bags of black-powder rice, trying to find something edible. Sacks of sugar—once reserved for officers and for families of the politically well-connected—had become a brownish, amber-like resin, preserving grains of blackened rice alongside some of Hiroshima's tiniest casualties: thick clusters of ants that in their final seconds of life must have raced one after another into the sweet molten lava.

In his chronicles of *Gen*, Keiji Nakazawa would record a scene such as this. During the last minutes before the *pika-don*, in diverse places throughout the city, people had observed ants filing out of vegetable gardens and into their homes, by the hundreds, if not by the thousands.

The fossilized ants in the army warehouse neither concerned nor satiated the soldiers, or the children they handed the "bug candy" off to as "gifts." Nor could the sweets have enticed many children, even without the ants. It was the clouds of flies and the stench that came with the clouds, and the unexplained spasms of vomiting that repulsed children like Keiji, despite not having tasted anything so sweet as rock candy for a very long time.

Somewhere below the layer of fried ants and rock candy, the soldiers discovered rice that had been insulated from carbonization. In the lower strata, the rice appeared to have been darkened only by black rain seepage and the first growths of black mold. The deeper layers also contained pockets of rice that were merely dampened by seepage and only slightly boiled by the heat—and there, the rice seemed quite edible.

The soldiers grilled the soggy rice and pressed it into piles of rice balls large enough to fill the back of a truck. North of the Hiroshima "Dome," the majority of the people wandering and falling between the city's exploded castle and the riverbank seemed beyond saving. As one of the truck drivers described it, "We could do nothing to help. A lady who said thank you when I put [rice] porridge in her mouth with a spoon was soon dead. There was a mother and a nursing baby. The mother's breasts were gone. The baby was crying. There was no milk. By dawn, both [would surely] be cold bodies."

The truck teams decided to drive south toward one of the main trolley paths, where people had built scores of makeshift shelters along the sidewalks. Here, the survivors seemed to be in relatively good health and therefore more likely to thrive if provided with food.

When Keiji Nakazawa found a truck with its mountain of rice balls on the flatbed, he grabbed a steel helmet and secured a place for himself in line, behind dozens of other survivors, none of whom seemed to have any appetite left for the white rice they had craved for so long.

A soldier shoveled the rice balls into Keiji's helmet until it was heaped almost to overflowing. Normally, the Nakazawa boy would have gulped a rice ball down in a matter of seconds; but most of the time he felt like vomiting. Keiji noticed that much of the rice seemed to have been crisp-burned, and he guessed that this was because the soldiers believed that balls of burned rice would take longer to spoil. He also noticed that his mother had difficulty eating, but she forced the rice into her mouth anyway, saying, "For the baby. I've got to produce milk."

The waves of nausea continued to come and go. During another hunting mission for food, Nakazawa entered fields of sweet squash and cucumbers, not very far from the field where Tsutomu Yamaguchi had survived. There, the black rain had fallen only briefly, but it was enough. As he collected the vegetables, most of which had been flash-broiled on one side, his sickness went into one of its curious states of remission, in which both strength and hunger returned. He ate until he felt full, and carried a basketful of vegetables home.

During his repeated journeys through the wastelands, in search of whatever sustenance he could find, Keiji Nakazawa saw piles of bones already stacked two meters high around the army's funeral pyres. Such scenes no longer disturbed the boy. In only three days he had become accustomed to bones and corpses. As he chewed a morsel of sweet squash, the first-grader learned, with a sense of grim fascination, that human bodies burned like overdone seafood. When the flames reached the dead, it seemed to him that they reared up and sort of sat up—"just like squid on a grill."

The army's pyres would continue to burn for nearly a month.

The rice and vegetables Keiji Nakazawa brought home had been penetrated by the same black rain that, on the first day, seemed to him to have gleamed with an eerie, inner heat as it pattered on the pavement. Though most of the radioactive elements had been so short-lived that they faded and dissipated within hours, isotopes of iodine decayed with a half-life of eight days, and strontium-90 would still retain half of its original potency after thirty years. The much rarer and less active plutonium generated by uranium fission irradiated flesh more slowly and a little less severely than iodine-131 and strontium-90, but it had a half-life decay rate of 24,000 years.

Keiji Nakazawa had no way of knowing at the time that the food he carried home to his mother was crawling with slow death.

Not even Drs. Alvarez and Urey understood yet that radioactive fallout released into a city or a stream did not merely dilute with each passing rainfall like ink spilled into water. It had a sneaky habit of concentrating inside biological systems. Keiji's situation could thus be described by a frighteningly simple biological arithmetic: If three micrograms of iodine-131 were dissolved and mixed with three liters of water, it could indeed be said that three micrograms of the isotope (in liquid form) had been diluted evenly through the water. However, if those same three liters of fallout-laced water were poured into a pond and passed through the living tissues of a fish, then a person monitoring the water excreted by the fish might be led to conclude that because the water coming out was less radioactive than the water that went in, a pond polluted with radioactive iodine was growing cleaner all by itself. In reality, almost all of the critical three micrograms of radioactive iodine would have been absorbed by the fish, and a person eating three fish from three ponds exposed to this same condition (of three micrograms each) would likely absorb up to nine micrograms—concentrating most of it, like any other form of iodine, in the thyroid gland.

The same principle of absorption and concentration applied to the fallout-tainted rice and sugar the soldiers had mined out of the ruins and the vegetables Keiji had picked for his mother. Plutonium, like iodine, tended to get caught up in living systems; it concentrated in the lungs, liver, and bones, exposing surrounding cells to long-term radiation. Though the element did not even exist on Earth until humans created it, the body's chemical machinery was easily fooled into grabbing plutonium—often confusing it with calcium, iron, and other metallic vitamins and thus allowing it to migrate into the glands that produced mother's milk. Similarly, human metabolisms confused strontium-90 with calcium, and sent it to the bones and the milk glands—giving priority to the milk glands if a mother happened to be lactating.

Keiji Nakazawa's little sister Tomoko was only three days old. A scarcity of food could easily make her mother's milk run dry; and Keiji's most immediate concern had become providing good nutrition for his mother, so she could produce milk for little Tomoko.

The rice and the vegetables worked, after a fashion, but Keiji Nakazawa's baby sister, who entered a state of "crying her life out," he would recount later, eventually "died like a candle consuming itself." The child was doomed by the air she had already breathed, doomed by the milk she was about to drink.[3]

Takashi (Thomas) Tanemori, the second-grader who had crossed a bridge of corpses with his father, found his older sister alive on the far side of the river but never saw his mother again.

The girl was ill, so they had decided to rest for a while at the river's edge, hoping to recover their strength.

When Tanemori looked back, he saw a glassy-eyed parade of ant-walkers advancing toward him, one following another across the same gruesome bridge. Some lost their balance, collapsed, and contributed their own bodies to the putrefying structure, while the parade, scarcely interrupted, marched over the fallen. In such manner, the bridge continued to grow until a tidal surge from the Pacific overpowered both the river and the bridge, and pulled the mass of flesh and bone apart into a flotilla of roving islands, tossed amid clouds of flies.

Only a few days before, while the city still stood, Takashi Tanemori and his father had been located in a small, outlying suburb that was shielded from the horrors of central Hiroshima, behind a tall, forested hill. One night, the boy had dreamed of riding on the back of a white crane, larger and mightier than a thousand of the great birds. The crane carried him above the braided river branches, and the concrete bridges, and the seven hills that surrounded the city. Then, "A vacuum of silence consumed the air. The sky spawned a rushing, white and unforgiving flash." In Tanemori's dream, the heavens were suddenly filled with uncountable thousands of white butterflies, scattering above him like startled spirits, sometimes fanning his face with the beat of their wings. And all of them, it seemed, were born of the nova above Hiroshima.

As the butterflies left him, Tanemori felt his father's hand shaking him awake. "Takashi, we can go home now."

The latest air raid alert was over and the clock had just touched 2:20, on the morning of August 6. On a day that was of even greater significance to futurity itself than to recorded history, Takashi Tanemori and his father had begun walking toward a hypocenter yet to be born.[4]

At war's end, it really did come down to the brutality of a children's crusade. Kiwamu Ariga, his friend Maeda, and 130 other conscripted schoolchildren had been excavating and hauling rocks out of a mine until their fingers and their sandaled feet were scraped raw and bloody. Men examined the rocks with machines that gave off strange clicking sounds, and the strangers told the children nothing beyond proclamations that they were on a glorious mission for the Emperor, followed by instructions that they should continue seeking out stones with brown or black spots.

On August 9, as Nagasaki's Urakami Valley burned in secrecy and as schoolchildren continued to be told that Japan was a sacred country destined to defeat its foes with spiritual purity alone, an officer finally explained to Kiwamu and his friends that the minerals they were mining from a fossil bacterial reef were actually flecks of radioactive uranium.

"With the stones that you are digging up," the officer said, "we can make a bomb the size of a matchbox that will destroy all of New York."

From the day the first tales of "Disease X" began filtering out of Hiroshima, the mines would become the town's secret. As fears began to spread that radiation exposure might be in some way contagious or would, in the very least, taint the children of the exposed, the uranium miners and their parents would try to protect themselves from the discrimination against marriage and employment that the survivors of the bombs were about to face.

Under this protective veil of secrecy, Kiwamu and Maeda eventually started families and settled in a quiet farming community overlooking the place where, as schoolchildren, they had been used in a "last ditch" effort to build an atomic bomb.

Living in the two-century-old farmhouse of his ancestors, Kiwamu tried to put the fears of exposure behind him, until the day he was exposed to radiation a second time.

"Once again," Kiwamu lamented, "the people were deceived by hubris-filled leaders—this time by economic planners who promoted the safety myth, that Japanese technology could never fail."

Spared the fates of Tanemori, Hattori, and other children of Hiroshima and Nagasaki, yet exposed to radiation in the mines, Kiwamu had chosen, as his family's place of refuge, the pristine-appearing fields of Fukushima. On March 11, 2011, he would suddenly come to a special unity of feeling with the Kakugawa family, whose members had departed Hiroshima ahead of the war, seeking the illusory peace of a farming community in Hawaii. To the west of Kapoho Village lay beautiful Pearl Harbor; and somewhat nearer, a sacred mountain that would one day bury the entire village beneath a lake of lava.

In the aftermath of an earthquake and tsunami that cracked ice shelves in Antarctica and tilted the Earth's axis the width of a man's fist, as Fukushima erupted into a cross between uranium power's *Hindenburg* and its Kilauea, Kiwamu bristled at government announcements that everything would be okay despite the fact that the uranium core of at least one Fukushima reactor had sunk below the water table and was erupting radioactive geysers.

"We were brainwashed during the war and we were brainwashed again after the war," Kiwamu cried out to futurity. "Maybe we will get wise the third time."[5]

A few hours after lunchtime, Dr. Hachiya's horse died. The Communications Hospital now had, instead of a constant companion, a constant supply of protein that could be cooked and dried and rationed out for at least several days.

As more patients staggered up to the hospital, more and more of them were sent to the isolation pavilion.

Hachiya, meanwhile, was pleased to discover that as his appetite and health recovered, his scientific curiosity was also reviving. He and the other surviving doctors were now dividing the contaminated (or "infected") into three groups for Disease X.

1. Those with nausea, vomiting, and diarrhea who were improving.
2. Those with the same symptoms who neither improved nor worsened.
3. Those worsening with additional symptoms, including hair loss, chills, and hemorrhagic fever.

Most of those in the third group seemed to have a frightening tendency for sudden death.

From Dr. Hachiya's perspective, neither Disease X nor anything else about the atomic bomb seemed to abide by natural laws. At least two of the newcomers to the hospital had glass in their lungs. Hachiya did not believe it until a colleague brought one of the patients to him. Sitting up in his own sickbed, the physician listened through a stethoscope and heard the tiny slivers clinking together with every labored intake of breath—scores and scores of slivers. He could not imagine what force had caused a man to inhale so much glass, or how he had managed to stay alive in this condition.

Definitely a mystery, Dr. Hachiya decided, and tried to forget about it and get some sleep. He hoped that making his bed more comfortable would help, but the doctor's bed was little more than a nest on a scorched frame, and thickening a makeshift mattress with the spread-out pages of a binderless book was simply not enough to help him lie down and shut out all he had seen these last three days. The hours wore on and Hachiya was unable to stop thinking. Every time he began to doze off, he was immediately snapped back to full wakefulness, always hearing the endless moans from below, punctuated by the occasional scream.

One of the screams came from the wife of a doctor named Hirada. The physician had died suddenly in his own isolation pavilion. Nurse Hinada, who seemed to have been in perfectly good health until the vomiting and diarrhea started, also died in the pavilion.

They gave one of the vacant beds to a little girl, newly orphaned by the bomb. The child's cries for her mother, all by themselves, would become bad enough to keep Hachiya awake well into the night, until the cries died. If any who survived in faraway Nagasaki had possessed the power to sit for a few moments on the edge of Dr. Hachiya's bed on the afternoon of August 9, and to look around, they would have realized, to their growing horror, that the physician was seeing and hearing their own future.[6]

The debris in the streets and the endless, aimless stream of alligator-skinned, ghost-walking people stopped Prefect Nishioka's car at the inner edge of the Isahaya suburb. Eight kilometers from the Urakami hypocenter, hundreds of people lay dead before his eyes. Soldiers were already piling corpses in the nearest open space, turning a primary school playground into a makeshift crematorium.

The prefect's car was equipped with one of the city's few functioning radios. A government broadcaster tried to assure the nation that Tokyo was aware of the problem in Nagasaki. The minister of war then acknowledged an attack on civilians with a new type of bomb that had caused "some damage" to the city, along with more than a hundred casualties. Later in the day, Tokyo would revise the official figure to about 500 souls.

More than three times nearer the hypocenter than Prefect Nishioka, master kite-maker Morimoto had survived with only two of his family members still alive. He would not have survived at all, if not for the cloudbanks that had shifted the target away from his house and nearly 2.5 kilometers farther north, toward Urakami Stadium. Even so, two of the kite-maker's relatives were missing in Hiroshima, and now eight more were lost in Urakami. One of these had been working near Yose Matsuo's husband at Prefect Nishioka's newest shelter. Now and forever, he would simply be among "the disappeared."

At Moment Zero, Morimoto was telling his wife about what he had witnessed in Hiroshima. "First, there came a blinding blue flash—"

A double flash cut his words short, blinking first red then blue and then flooding his kite shop in a stark yellow glare. Acting on sheer reflex, Morimoto grabbed his child and shoved his wife bodily down the steps into what until now had been merely a supply cellar, not a bomb shelter. Taking no chances, he pulled the heavy trap door down behind him and shielded his wife's and his child's bodies with his own. Once the lid was down, thunder exploded instantly overhead.

Close! Morimoto told himself. He did not understand exactly how close, until he climbed out of the cellar. The whole top of his shop had been broken off about waist-high, hauled away, and dropped on top of a house across the street. A stove was still sitting in place, with a teapot still upon it, but everything else—*everything*—appeared to have been scooped out of the building and taken up into the clouds. Envelopes with his name on them, along with shreds of singed kite paper, were presently drifting and fluttering with paper from every office building in the area, along a debris track that would spread 25 kilometers—fully 15 miles—north and east.

For all of his recent hardships, Morimoto was among the lucky ones. His shop was located in what by all appearances became a hole in both the firestorms and the radioactive downpours. Though ten in his family were now lost, Morimoto and his wife and child had suffered no burns or injuries other than the bruises sustained while tumbling into the cellar. Aside from nausea during the train ride from Hiroshima, Morimoto had escaped Disease X, and so, too, would his wife and child.

As Yamaguchi had observed, sometimes it worked out. In years to come, Shigeyoshi Morimoto would see children and even grandchildren flying his kites over a city that was fated to be symbolized by the phoenix principle.[7]

Morimoto's assistant, Doi, seemed to share his same improbable "fool's luck." Though he was still fighting against the chills and nausea of Hiroshima, Doi and his family, like Dr. Nagai's two children, happened to be located on the shadow side of a mountain when the bomb exploded 3,700 meters away, at a radius of more than two miles.

Much like Morimoto, the apprentice kite-maker was explaining Hiroshima to his wife during the minutes leading up to the critical moment. Not anticipating immediate danger, and confident that his nine-year-old had absorbed the lesson of, *Duck and cover if you hear a B-san diving*, he allowed the boy to go outside and play on the grounds of a Buddhist temple next door. Then his seven-year-old daughter, bored with the repeated warnings about a dangerous flash, asked permission to follow her brother outside, during the last seconds before the *pika*. His third child, his baby girl, was too young to be bored, and remained in her mother's arms.

"If you ever see the white flash," Doi emphasized for his wife and seven-year-old a third and a fourth time, "You must immediately prostrate yourself on the ground. And whatever you do—*whatever* you do, do not look in the direction of the flash."

Doi's seven-year-old girl stepped toward the door, expecting during this hot August morning to simply join her brother and other children on the temple grounds, and seek out a pond in which to bathe and cool down.

The flash interrupted her plans—cutting across the sky and shining through the windows as if a hundred search lamps had suddenly been aimed directly into the room.

"That's what I'm talking about!" Doi shouted. His wife jumped to her feet and began running toward the yard and the temple, but Doi tripped her to the floor and pulled their infant child down with him as the blast wave rocked the cottage, cracked windows, and punched holes through the paper sliding doors.

Like the Nagai children, Doi had no idea that on the other side of Kawabira's high ridgeline lay an 80 percent kill rate and utter devastation. Doi's seven-year-old daughter had been completely shadow-shielded from the flash. He found his son hiding inside the shrine's main building, a little bit shaken and staring wide-eyed at a toppled statue of the Mother of Mercy, but otherwise uninjured. Shock-cocooned. The only real danger appeared to be from the top half of a grandfather clock that fell out of the cloud and crashed into the shrine's yard like a meteorite. It was followed quickly by a strange, neighborhood-crossing hail of golf balls and tennis rackets . . . followed minutes later by a blizzard of paper.[8]

Only a few kilometers from Doi, traveling along the scorched faces of Mounts Kawabira and Kompira, ship designer Yamaguchi's friend Akira discovered that even at a distance, the radiative heat of the Urakami cyclone did not let him approach within 1.6 kilometers (or within a mile) of the stadium and the hypocenter. Along the river-facing side of Kawabira, the foothills were pierced by five tunnels, each housing portions of Mitsubishi's aircraft and munitions works—including two ramps for catapulting some of the country's few remaining fighter planes out against the anticipated invasion by the American fleet. The workmen outside the tunnels were carbonized and even those inside appeared to have been blast-furnaced and suffocated. All of the vegetation was gone, except for the blackened trunks of trees—blown down, each of them, in the same direction.

Akira gave up the idea of reporting to the Mitsubishi office and followed in the direction the trees were pointing. He went to the top of Kawabira, hoping, if nothing else, for a chance to assess the damage from high ground. Second assistant kite-maker Masao, who had come from Hiroshima aboard the same train as Akira, and who had walked away from the same train wreck without injury, was following this same path to the top.

When the pair of double survivors crested Kawabira Hill, the clouds streaming across the sky were so dark they reduced the sunlight to barely the strength of a full moon. Behind the hill, the far side of Kawabira's valley—the part that had been located outside Kawabira's shadow and which therefore faced the full glare of the *pika*—appeared much as Akira expected it to be: severely mauled and smoldering. But people were forming bucket brigades from the stream below and all of the houses on the nearer, shadowed side, stood as if nothing had happened to them. Nothing at all.

Akira left Masao without any parting words, and began walking down toward the still-living grass and the still-flowing stream, vowing with each painful stride and with each pause to vomit that if he somehow managed to get out of this war alive, he would never go back again to Urakami or Hiroshima, to Mitsubishi or the navy.

In time, Akira's bouts of atomic bomb disease would pass, and he would live a long life in which to evolve from a designer of warships into an advocate for peace. Along with his friend Yamaguchi and an American physicist who once designed brave new bombs, he would advocate an impossible yet simple (if only symbolic) pipe dream in which countries in possession of nuclear weapons could be governed only by mothers who were still breast-feeding babies.[9]

"In the end, all we can do is pray," one of the Jesuit brothers told Dr. Akizuki. Although he was Buddhist, Akizuki understood.

Presently, the black smoke rising from Urakami had nowhere to go. It was being contained by hills on either side of the valley the way the sides of a bathtub contain water. With gales being drawn in from the north and south, the only way out was to overflow the valley walls—so, mostly the smoke just accumulated overhead, shutting out the sun. The nearest and strongest source of light was the burning hospital complex. It blazed brightly enough to read by.

A nearby warehouse appeared to have survived reasonably undamaged. Akizuki and Nagai believed its metal roof would provide adequate shelter against the snowfall of ashes—which appeared to be irritating the lungs of Dr. Yoshioka and the other burn victims to such an extent that the open spaces of the hillside and the streets were beginning to sound like the world's largest emphysema ward.

The Jesuits helped Dr. Akizuki to spread mats on the concrete floor of the warehouse and to move Dr. Yoshioka there. Akizuki carefully removed the bandages from her face and cleaned her wounds a second time. He hoped she did not notice the pity and fear in his eyes. Splinters of glass and wood and even several twigs had been driven into Dr. Yoshioka's skin. Akizuki thanked whatever gods might be that Yoshioka's face was completely bandaged again when her mother arrived from a shadow-shielded town on the far side of the hill.

"You have done nobly," she told Dr. Akizuki, upon seeing her daughter injured and bandaged— and thankfully still alive.

Akizuki looked at the ground and shook his head, very slowly.

"You don't understand," he said softly. "I am the one responsible for her injuries."[10]

Dr. Paul Nagai would live long enough to observe that the atomic bomb not only cracked concrete and steel, it cracked human souls with equal ease and with equal indifference.

Nagai's niece Tatsue would never forgive herself for staying with Kayano and Makoto at the shock-cocooned stream on the safe side of the mountain, after she saw the fireball rising from the direction of Urakami. Tatsue wished she could have been with her mother on the other side of Kawabira to at least provide some small comfort in her final moments. And in future months, no matter how many times Paul Nagai explained to the girl that even had such magic existed—as to allow her instantly to have been transported through a strengthening cyclone of flame to her mother's side—no matter how many times he tried to tell Tatsue that the most she could ever have hoped for was to become just one more dark spot in Urakami's drifts of gray ashes, she added her own false blame for a lack of courage to the weight of her mother's death.

On the day Urakami exploded, Tatsue's brother had already escaped Saipan and managed to survive on a raft at sea with one side of his body burned and with the fingers of one hand gone. What kept him alive was the thought of returning home to see his mother and his sister alive again. For a long time, he would not ask Tatsue to explain the details of their mother's death, but between the personal bond of brother and sister, the bomb had, from Moment Zero, begun radiating invisible cracks.

Even the bond between mother and child was not immune.

Tatsue would neither forget nor forgive the way her little cousin Eiko died. Never again would she refer to Eiko's mother by any name except, "Skinny Aunt" or, "the old lady."

The aunt, like Tatsue, had been shielded behind the shadows of Kawabira hill and the 366-meter peak of Kompira. Unlike Tatsue, Skinny Aunt did run to the other side, anxious to find the Urakami school where she had last seen her eight-year-old girl.

Somewhere beyond the flattened school, beyond the tangled mass of prison bars and the dead alligator man, she heard Eiko calling to her from one of the school's shelter tunnels.

All of the other girls near the line of tunnel entrances appeared to have been simultaneously roasted and squashed like bugs. Most of them did not look human anymore, and neither did Eiko. Somehow her eyes had been shielded, but the rest of her face was a huge blister, and the whole front of her body was blackened alligator skin.

"My child was turned into a monster!" Skinny Aunt would tell Tatsue— over and over again, trying to explain it all away, thinking that Tatsue, if no one else, would somehow understand.

As Skinny Aunt told it, Eiko knew she was going to die; but she was so overjoyed to see her mother one last time that she seemed to revive. Tatsue believed that Skinny Aunt became afraid that the monster might survive.

"Mother!" Eiko said, "I couldn't walk any farther. I wanted to come to you. Please cover me up. I'm cold."

The mother stood, and said, "Wait a minute. I'll find something to make you warm. Just wait a minute—hold on to yourself."

And then she ran away, haunted from that moment and for the rest of her life by the image of little Eiko shivering alone in the dark, tormenting her forever with remembered cries of "Mother . . . Mother . . ."

"But Eiko was a *monster*," Skinny Aunt wanted to explain, and Tatsue would become all the more insulted by the woman's belief that she would understand.

"The real monsters," Tatsue would one day tell Uncle Paul Nagai, "they look just like us."

And perhaps the sainted ones, too, she would later relate. Hours after Skinny Aunt fled, another parent searching the tunnel-shelters for a missing child found Eiko still alive and kept her warm until death came to her the following morning. Eiko lived far longer than she probably should have, calling the whole time for her mother. The stranger who cared for another's child as if it were her own gave her a Catholic burial near the ruins of Urakami Cathedral and the St. Francis Hospital, making sure little Eiko's name was recorded on a stone.

Five years later, in her memorial memoir, Tatsue would record that with the passage of time, whenever her aunt spoke about that day at all, she would "fix up" the parts about how Eiko died. Each passing month, she would ask Tatsue to visit Eiko's grave for her, evidently unwilling to stand before Eiko herself.

"She kept trying to make friends with me," Tatsue would tell history. "But I [was] not to be taken in. I knew perfectly well that if such a thing ever happened again, she would desert me the way she did Eiko. So on the surface I [would] act respectfully toward her, but I really despised her. Yet

Under the mushroom cloud, within only a few minutes, a mountain of flames taller than the pyramids emerged from Urakami's "lake of flames." Just short of 1 kilometer from the detonation point and the growing cyclone of fire, on an overlook where every living creature perished during the first five seconds, the delicate arch of the Sano Tori Shrine still stood on one leg, with the other leg knocked away. [Illustration: CRP]

who [was] I to despise her when I neglected my own mother? I despise myself. I hate myself!"

In his own memorial message, Paul Nagai would record that Skinny Aunt eventually lost all rational control of herself and began running into the streets scaring little schoolgirls—trying to push them to the ground or snatch them up. He and Tatsue had no doubt that each girl reminded her of Eiko. By this time, Tatsue's brother began abusing her with curses about their mother's death, escalating eventually to slaps and bone-cracking punches—at which point Tatsue vowed to kill him where he stood if he ever tried to approach her again.

The fissures that formed in the hypocenter would still be present many years later. According to Paul Nagai: "But I am not talking about cracks

A recovery from symphonic destruction: Upper Nagasaki's Sano Tori Shrine the day after (in 1945) and in 2010. The difference between then and now is that in 21st century nuclear warfare, there is no guarantee of people coming from outside to rebuild. [Illustration: CRP]

in the ground. I am talking about the invisible chasms which appeared in the personal relationships of the survivors of that atomic wasteland. These rents in the ties of friendship and love have not closed up with the passage of time; on the contrary, they seem to be getting wider and deeper.[11] Of all the damage that the atomic bomb did, these [cracks in the human spirit] are by far the cruelest."[12]

As nightfall came to the hill of Kompira, Dr. Akizuki's father appeared unexpectedly alive, following not very far behind his mother. Their smiling faces seemed to him like an image out of a dream.

"You've not been hurt, either!" Mr. Akizuki said. As with many reunions that day, each had believed the other to be dead.

Dr. Akizuki's father began to describe a tour of terrors and odd wonders that began with a pre-*pika* detour to a law court in the business district of Central Nagasaki. The courthouse was located behind a protective hill, more than 5 kilometers south of the Urakami hypocenter. At 11:02 a.m., the elder Akizuki saw a flash outside the windows and, several seconds later, he felt the building shake. The blast was so loud that when Mr. Akizuki stepped outside, he expected to find one whole side of the courthouse caved in by a direct hit from a conventional, half-ton bomb, but locally there did not appear to be very much damage at all and even some of the windows had survived.

Walking toward the flames and smoke of Urakami, the elder Akizuki became increasingly certain that his son could no longer be alive. No fewer than twelve square kilometers of flame forced him to detour around northern Nagasaki and south Urakami, sending him eastward along the ridges of Kawabira to the saddleback of Mount Kompira. There, atop the Kompira overlook, he watched the Urakami cyclone periodically rearing up through the sea of black smoke. For a very long time, the sight held him rooted to the ground. He had never seen or heard the like of it.

He asked several people who staggered up to the overlook what had happened and if the Urakami hospital buildings were still standing.

Pleas for water and help were their only replies.

When Mr. Akizuki saw his son's hospital in flames and worked up the courage to descend toward it along the ridge, he prepared his mind for the final fatherly duty of seeking young Tatsuichiro's bones. Instead, he and his wife found their son unhurt.

"And now," the elder Akizuki said, as he looked farther down the hill and saw that his house of four generations was gone, "now I ask for nothing more."

That night, father joined wife and son in the work of providing comfort to the injured. All of the medicines and dressings had either been burned or used up, so there was very little that could actually be provided by way of comfort except words, or a kind hand, or a place to rest on the lawn. The patients, the uncounted two or three hundred of them, were sleeping or weeping and bleeding under the starless sky.

As midnight approached, the cyclone weakened and collapsed into a mere lake of flames, and down there in the bottom, black smoke began to part like the Red Sea. Noticing that the landscape was suddenly brighter at midnight than it had appeared at midday, Dr. Akizuki and his father paused and looked.

On the side of Urakami opposite the river, the ruins of several large buildings could be seen silhouetted within the flames. On this side, in the direction of the Josei Girls' School, a tall steel frame—all that remained of an engineering school—seemed to be cooling down from yellow-orange to a dull red glow when, spawning fire worms, it sagged slowly into the earth like a great ship sinking.

"Rome falls," Dr. Akizuki observed.

"What?" his father asked.

"This is how it ends," he said. "The Empire is consumed in flames."[13]

Young Inosuke Hayasaki was beyond consoling by the time he came upon a railroad station, somewhere north of Masao and Akira's wrecked train. The fires in the south painted the hills with a ruddy-red glow. Despite the comforting sound of an approaching train, Inosuke was unable to shake free of the crack that seemed to be branching through his soul, brought about by a pain unique in human history: *That, in killing all those people with drinks of water, I had become a murderer.*

Only in later years would parallel phenomena be recognized by physicians: Terminally ill cancer patients, mortally wounded crash victims and burn victims who hung on to life just long enough to see a child graduate from high school, just long enough for a loved one to return from overseas, for the first glimpse of an awaited grandchild, for reconciliation with an estranged sibling. Time and again, once that most hoped-for moment arrived, the patient let go of life, gratefully and peacefully.

Under the bombs of August, for the majority of those suffering lethal flash burns, a maddening thirst rendered water their most driving (and most final) wish.

Inosuke's observation—that the people he "killed" with his drinks of water, drank "as if it were something they had never tasted so good before in their lives"—was consistent with what medical science was yet to notice. Dozens of similar accounts were emerging from both Hiroshima and Nagasaki, soon to pass, mostly forgotten, into archives. From all accounts, "the water casualties," given the relief they so desired, were able to let go, and go in peace.

Decades would pass before the critical connection was made by medical historians; and during all those years, Inosuke would carry the undeserved burden of judging himself a "murderer."

Around the hour the first steam locomotive backed a string of boxcars into the station, the boy was already sinking into a state of no longer caring if he would ever feel quite human again. Pushing ahead of the staggering and crawling wounded, he saw this train as his chance to return home to his parents, in the village of Shimabara, nearly twenty miles downwind of where the dark, oily rain and radioactive "jellyfish goo" had fallen around the Nagai children. When he reached the train, the boy was told that the rescue cars were reserved for the injured. Being visibly uninjured, he was to be left behind with the dead, and with the still-moving dead who, usually flash-charred on one side of their bodies, walked five steps, fell, rose up, walked another five steps, and fell down again.

Inosuke was not allowed to board the next train, either—or the one after that, at which point he got the idea that if he was going to escape aboard a rescue train, he needed to make himself look like a burn victim. This was an easy task. The ground was covered with blood-soaked mud, and ashes, and even bits of burned skin. He covered himself with whatever he could scoop from the ground, imitated the stagger-and-crawl of the burn victims, snuck aboard a train that arrived with a set of passenger cars, and hid under a seat. Most of the people who followed the boy into the car were unable to sit upright and instead either lay down on the floor, or stood. To judge by what he saw from his vantage point, all of them seemed to be waiting for death to come.

For a long time, the conductor hid the train in a mountainside tunnel, only a few miles north of the Urakami suburb. An American plane had been seen outside, and no one could be sure whether it was flying reconnaissance, or whether its crew planned to drop another *pika-don*.

"What in the world is going on?" he heard a member of the Civil Defense unit say. "This person over here is dead." Another relief squad commander announced the death of another passenger, and another, and another. By the time the train started forward again, exiting the tunnel with all of its lights turned off, the clock touched 11:40 p.m.

"And the journey of death was begun," Inosuke recalled later. "And Jigoku rode with us."[14]

At approximately twenty minutes before midnight, Hirohito, the 124th Emperor of Japan, entered the conference room and sat across from Foreign Minister Togo. He was a thin, introverted, and nervous man, whose reign had begun at the age of twenty-six and had now lasted eighteen years.

The Emperor was a religious figure, said to be a direct descendent of the Sun Goddess—and now, according to Dr. Nishina and the other physicists, the Sun had touched the Earth, twice.

Togo's side of the table and Anami's side were equally deadlocked about whether to consider terms of surrender or to continue the fight. Reportedly, the debate continued for more than two hours, with each side airing the same arguments of the hour before, and the hour before that, sometimes word for word. The Emperor listened, taking it all in and quietly making notes to himself on a white pad.

Finally, about 2:20 a.m., Hirohito stood and most of the attendees heard their bespeckled, Pharaoh-like ruler speaking to them for the first time. His voice was surprisingly human, faint and high-pitched.

Foreign Minister Togo would dictate the words to his son-in-law later that morning, wanting them to be freshly and accurately burned into history. According to Togo, the century's last emperor-cum-deity announced, "I have concluded that continuing the war means destruction for the nation and a prolongation of bloodshed and cruelty in the world."

He looked past the ceiling toward the eastern sky as he spoke.

As Togo told it, Cabinet Secretary Hisatsune Sakomizu had to restrain himself from crying out loud, "We now all understand His Majesty's wishes! Please do not condescend to say another word!"

"It goes without saying that it is unbearable for me to see the brave and loyal fighting men of Japan disarmed," the Emperor said without interruption. "It is equally unbearable that others who have rendered me devoted service should now be punished as instigators of the war. Nevertheless, the time has come when we must bear the unbearable."

He looked down from the ceiling and glanced at Togo, who lowered his head; for tradition held that it was forbidden to look the Emperor in the eyes.

"I now swallow my own tears," Hirohito said, and announced his intention to give official sanction to Foreign Minister Togo's proposal to send a message to the American president, probing the enemy for its final terms of surrender.[15]

Later that morning, Charles Sweeney awoke on Tinian to the news that there was still no news from Tokyo. Apparently, the response remained *mokusatu*, meaning "to treat with silent contempt."

After breakfast, Tibbets, Sweeney, and the other members of the two missions were called to pose for group photographs in front of their planes and then to be interviewed, in order to preserve their thoughts and observations.

"We posed stiffly," Sweeney would recall. "And in proper military jargon, we recited the facts: what, when, and where."

As was often the case, the mathematics of the situation were foremost in Sweeney's mind. During the three months since Truman took office, the final advance from island to island and toward the Japanese homeland had gained momentum. During this same brief interval, the enemy had inflicted almost half of all American casualties suffered in the Pacific throughout the entire three-and-a-half years since Pearl Harbor. By Sweeney's arithmetic, the closer they came to victory, the higher the cost in American lives. By this same arithmetic, the probability of the war extending through October, and atomic bomb missions becoming routine by then, clearly seemed too high.

Sweeney dreaded the thought of another series of atomic bomb runs. Though the fire-bombing of Tokyo alone had incinerated nearly 16 square miles of the city and taken almost as many lives as Hiroshima, a crew member never knew if his own plane's incendiaries actually killed anyone. If death troubled him even remotely, there were about fifty other planes on each section of each fire-bomb raid—plenty of places to spread the blame, or hide it. Certainly, no one ever felt personally responsible for *all* the fires he saw below. With the atomic bomb there was no pretending and there was no spreading the blame. Hiroshima and Nagasaki were far more personal, because every death could be traced back to just a handful of men.

Luis Alvarez had feared that the weapons of mega-death would make war more impersonal, and perhaps even a little less distasteful as well. No one had anticipated that the opposite might turn out to be true. *Enola Gay* co-pilot Robert Lewis, for one, examined the films of "his" mushroom cloud with a mixture of wonder and revulsion. He was already beginning to miss the "good old days" of the fifty B-29 raid. The atomic bomb had changed everything. Anyone who believed he could predict what the next seventy years might bring—or even the next seven—was deluding himself. The world was not yet collectively holding its breath, though it should have been. Lewis and Sweeney understood, better than almost anyone alive, that the scientists had just given the rest of humanity something they could never take back.

Shortly before lunchtime, Sweeney received news that the White House had put out an order for a "temporary moratorium" on fire-bomb raids. Hope sprang throughout the isle of Tinian that Truman had received a response from Tokyo after all, and was giving Japan time to surrender.

Instead of being sent on fire-bombing raids, the B-29 fleet was re-assigned to drop millions more of the counterfeit bills bearing warnings to surrender in the face of total destruction. The new messages were shorter and much more to the point than any that had been dropped before—"written to deliver the news like poison darts," the crews were told. Some of the leaflets were actually written as haiku-like paragraphs. They were as close as anyone would ever come to what death threats would look like if they were written by Edgar Allan Poe.

This time, the air force had enlisted the aid of a legendary writer of love letters from the navy, along with a recently freed survivor of a Japanese POW camp who just couldn't stop writing with hatred about his captors, their ancestors, and their descendants, and who regarded the atomic bombs as "pest control." The latter was named James Clavell, and in future years he would obsess on trying to come to terms with everything he could learn about Japanese history all the way back through antiquity—then, after penning the semi-autobiographical novel *King Rat*, he would write a masterpiece called *Shogun* (though he would be more widely remembered for *The Fly*). The writer of love letters and short collections of love stories was a Quaker who, during his time in the South Pacific, had become embroiled in what was, in these days, a controversial interracial romance. Being a Quaker, James Michener was exempt from having to shoot down the Emperor's planes; so instead he offered to threaten Hirohito with nuclear annihilation. In his spare time, Michener began penning the first draft of his book about the Pacific war, which would soon evolve into the musical, *South Pacific*.[16]

While Charles Sweeney waited and hoped for war's end, a fit of intrigue, rebellion, and suicide erupted in Tokyo, and the Emperor became more cut off from the rest of the world than ever before, forced to lock himself in a hidden corner of the Palace with a handful of loyal and trusted soldiers.

As Emperor Hirohito secretly recorded two copies of his surrender on phonograph records, an admiral named Ugaki, who sided with War Minister Anami and Field Marshal Hata against surrender, ordered seven bombers to be filled with all the high-level explosives they could carry on a one-way trip. Targeting Okinawa as the presumed source of the atomic bombs, Ugaki contrived a plan for a kamikaze raid, using what he believed to be the largest non-nuclear blockbuster bombs ever designed.

The admiral hoped that by this shining example he would inspire followers to continue the fight with a glorious new fleet of airplanes turned into rocket-assisted super-bombs.

By now, at Hirohito's orders, as carried out by Foreign Minister Togo, more than half of the nation's munitions factories were shutting down. As for the rockets at Ugaki's back—which in theory would have made his plane an unstoppable target during the final dive at Okinawa—the merging of rockets with a propeller-driven bomber at such short notice had already been described by the admiral's engineers as "technologically premature." The best that Admiral Ugaki could have wished for was to come through the sound barrier on final approach. With propellers hitting supersonic air on either side of his cockpit, this could not possibly have worked out as effectively as the admiral hoped.

The last word anyone heard from Ugaki was an announcement that his target was in sight and his squadron was ready to "light the candles" and streak down upon the hangars of Okinawa.

The fireworks north of the island were faint and not particularly noisy, given their distance of at least fifteen miles. U.S. military reports recorded no kamikaze raids that day or afterward—not on Okinawa, nor anywhere else.

Admiral Ugaki's planes simply flew in formation into mystery and legend, and became one of history's ghost squadrons.[17]

The weather front that caused Charles Sweeney to relocate his target the day before had shifted, bringing perfectly clear skies and promising a typically hot and humid August day.

Dr. Paul Nagai and the rest of the St. Francis medical staff had spent the night sleeping in rows on nests of ironed-down grass and scorched paper. Nagai awoke half-believing that the events of the previous day were merely a nightmare, but when he looked down toward the gray wilderness in which his wife had most certainly perished, he accepted the reality that his whole world had been changed in a split second.

An old and previously senseless expression came quickly to mind, seeming all so clearly ironic and apt: "Under the talon of time, the blue ocean can turn into a mulberry field, and a forest can become a sea of ice."

Nagai's world was now a landscape of sudden, ungodly changes.

Though its steel and concrete skeleton still stood, the hospital had been gutted by fire. On the far side of the lawn, Dr. Akizuki and several of the nurses were cobbling together a kitchen range from piles of fallen bricks. They were already starting to prepare meals for the injured, using pots and sacks of only slightly scorched rice that someone had scavenged from the ruins downhill.

That the stream behind the hospital was bringing a steady supply of water for cleaning and cooking lulled the survivors into a sense of being doubly blessed. This day, the blessings just kept coming. Akizuki and his mother were preparing a mash of "rice milk" for several orphaned babies when the hospital's carpenter called to them excitedly, urging the doctor to follow him quickly.

The carpenter led him to an underground storehouse beneath the collapsed walls of the hospital's kitchen. The air below was unbearably hot, and Akizuki was certain that everything within the cave must already have been cooked or burned.

"Is this safe?" the doctor said, and began coughing. In one corner, a pile of coal for the kitchen's stoves was glowing bright red.

"Trust me," the carpenter replied, and led the way to a much cooler corner where two large wooden crates stood intact.

"You're a godsend!" Akizuki said, and surprised the carpenter with a powerful bear hug. When he first heard about Hiroshima, the carpenter began squirreling first-aid supplies down below, along with the kitchen's usual stores of coal and rice. The boxes of gauze and bandages near the tops of the crates, though slightly browned from the hot coals and the burning building, were still usable. More important, they had acted as an insulating buffer between the heat and the medicines deeper down. The two crates constituted less than a hundredth of the medical supplies he needed for the patients covering the lawns and the walkways—but even with a little gauze and Mercurochrome in his hands, Dr. Akizuki's spirits soared.

When he stepped outside again, a new line of the walking wounded was advancing up the hill from the direction of Urakami. A woman had gone down to the edge of the place where the cyclone had raged-and-died the night before and found her husband wandering aimlessly. She explained that he had been working in one of the factories and was sheltered behind concrete when the *pika* came down from what she believed to be almost directly overhead.

The woman had carried him leaning on her shoulder all the way uphill. "He looks fine," she said, "but the explosion injured him somehow."

The physician examined him for signs of fractures or internal bleeding. Except for minor scrapes and bruises, the man from Ground Zero did not appear to be wounded at all, and yet he had become strangely weak and feeble, and seemed to have lost interest in everything.

Akizuki stood and looked down toward the zero point. All below spread a panorama of ridges and plains on which almost nothing stood. All of the familiar buildings had been blown over, gutted, or converted to dust. Telephone poles seemed to have fared better than buildings, although most of

them were shoved over to one side. Almost none of the roads could be identified, because houses and stone fences had been lifted up and splashed across
them. Wherever electricity poles still stood, sheets of scorched clothing and
objects that resembled shreds torn from mattresses were suspended from their
wires. Near the river, where fires still burned and columns of smoke were still
rising, the iron skeletons of the Mitsubishi buildings were so twisted out of
shape that they looked like fields of reeds caught in a storm.

The valley below was dead. There was no sign of any movement, by
either human or beast.

After a while, Akizuki turned away from the scene, performed a quick
mental inventory of the supplies remaining in his satchel, and headed off toward the warehouse in which Dr. Yoshioka lay. He had reserved a portion
of his limited supply of painkillers specifically for her—still convinced, in his
heart, that by sending her upstairs to eat something and to get some sleep just
ahead of the *pika-don*, he had caused her injuries.

He found Dr. Yoshioka no better and no worse than she had been an
hour before. Working at the most gentle pace he could manage, Akizuki
added antimicrobial salves to the new dressings. As he worked, thoughts of
the strangely lethargic man from Ground Zero became increasingly intru-
sive. He began to worry that he was missing some important detail that must
not be overlooked. Dr. Nagai had mentioned to him at least two similar
cases, in which nurses who came up from the foothills with no injuries at all
were now violently ill.

And just once, Dr. Akizuki felt a cramp and a surge of nausea so strong
that if it tarried for another two or three seconds, he believed it would have
brought him to his knees.

It passed as quickly as it came and did not come again, so he explained it
away as a muscle spasm, and forgot about it.[18]

Comparative doses in tissue from prompt radiation effects for Hiroshima and Nagasaki for unshielded persons as a function of distance from the hypocenter

Distance from Hypocenter (m)	Hiroshima		Nagasaki	
	Gamma Rays (rads)	Neutrons (rads)	Gamma Rays (rads)	Neutrons (rads)
0	10,300	14,100	25,100	3,900
100	9,660	13,100	23,500	3,570
200	8,040	10,600	19,500	2,790
300	6,050	7,700	14,700	1,910
400	4,220	5,090	10,400	1,190
500	2,790	3,150	7,090	703
600	1,780	1,870	4,720	398
700	1,110	1,080	3,110	221
800 (0.5 mi.)	685	613	2,040	121
900	419	344	1,340	66.1
1,000	255	191	888	35.9
1,100	155	106	588	19.5
1,200	94.6	58.9	391	10.6
1,300	57.5	32.6	262	5.8
1,400	35.2	18.1	176	3.2
1,500	21.6	10.1	119	1.7
1,600 (1 mi.)	13.2	5.6	80.7	1.0
1,800	5.0	1.7	37.6	0.3
2,000	1.9	0.5	2.9	0.0
2,500	0.2	0.0	2.9	0.0
3,000	0.0	0.0	0.5	0.0

Note: This figure does not include secondary dosing from fallout, including black rain. A total combined dose of 600–700r from all sources is generally lethal.

In Hiroshima, the Sasaki family probably received 200r from black rain, after having initially been shielded indoors from *pika* and blast effects. At Dr. Paul Nagai's location, most people outside the Urakami hospital received lethal doses. Dr. Nagai happened to be located deep within the building at Moment Zero, terminally ill with leukemia. The hospital's bricks, steel, and concrete provided just enough shielding to spare Paul Nagai, while pushing his cancer into radiation-induced remission.

Source: Compiled by R. C. Milton and T. Shohoji in Atomic Bomb Casualty Commission TR 1968.

· 9 ·

Testament

*W*ith the survivors now accustomed to mass pyres, a curious calm settled over Hiroshima. The normal human responses to roving black fogbanks of corpse-fed flies were completely dulled. On August 10, the boy who would write the *Barefoot Gen* chronicles no longer felt able to react with excitement or fear, even when he beheld a river delta so glutted with disintegrating bodies that from that day forward, whenever low tides came to the mudflats, the earth itself would appear to be sprouting fields of twig-like rib bones.

For years to come, Keiji Nakazawa would not speak of what he had witnessed or how he responded to it. He had no choice. Soon, the MacArthur protocol would prevent anyone from speaking too loudly. And beyond official censorship, Nakazawa was governed by an old schoolyard tale about the devil, who was said to have proclaimed, "If we catch a glimpse of hell and speak of it, we are pulled back again to hell."

Only much later would Nakazawa reply to the devil's proclamation, telling all who would listen that if everyone remained silent and allowed hell to be forgotten, then hell would be all but guaranteed to come again.

Inside Ground Zero, on the fourth day after the bomb, there was simply no time for either emotion or reflection. Nakazawa spent almost all of the energy he could summon returning to the destroyed fields in search of edible stems and tubers. When thirst overcame him, he sucked the juice and the flesh of dying squash plants. Even if the food he and his brother Koji brought home was half-destroyed and rotting, their mother forced herself to eat it anyway, hoping that she would continue producing milk for the baby.

To provide better shelter for Mother and Tomoko, Keiji Nakazawa and his older brother decided to move from the street-side camp and led the family to a shed at the foot of the hill from which meteorologist Isao Kita had watched the lakes of boiling yellow dust and the streamers of black rain spreading over the city. New families migrating to the weather station hill were resented by people already living in the fringe of the blast area, especially if the newcomers arrived from the heart of the city and exhibited symptoms of Disease-X. Rumors that they carried something infectious from the bomb had spread before them.

"Rumors spread to erase the unease," Keiji Nakazawa would recall, "and people acted on them."

Along the path home from one of the fields in which Tsutomu Yamaguchi had received a brief misting of oily black rain, Nakazawa passed through an army rifle range where piles of burning corpses were so numerous that the outdoor crematoria illuminated the night, taking the place of electric lights. The boy continued homeward with one of his small bundles of vegetables, believing that he had become reasonably immune to the new realities, until he saw a woman kneeling on a slab of broken concrete, hammering a charred human skull into fine powder. He paused to watch, and the woman took no notice of him as she gathered up skull powder and sprinkled it over the wounds of a young man lying beneath a makeshift lean-to.

"What a strange thing to do," Nakazawa said with detached curiosity.

The woman gave him no reply. She lifted the young man's head, pried open his mouth, and poured in a handful of the powder. The man's nose appeared to have been bleeding for at least a day or two, and all of his hair had fallen out. Even his eyebrows and eyelashes were gone, and his entire skin surface had been bruised. The mouthful of dust made him cough up a huge clot of blood.

"Excuse me," Nakazawa said, as politely as he could, "but why are you feeding him powdered bones?"

"Putting this powder on the bruises makes them heal," she explained with an oddly flat courtesy. "And if you swallow the dust of the *pika*-man, it keeps you from dying."

"That can't be true. It sounds crazy."

"Stupid!" the woman shouted, no longer either detached or courteous. "*Hundreds* of people have been saved this way!" Then, noticing that the burn at the back of Nakazawa's head was oozing yellowish-white matter and appeared not to be healing, she offered him a handful of dust.

"No, thank you," Nakazawa said, and walked onward. Further along the path, he noticed a second woman, sprinkling dust on two burned children. Throughout the ruins, strange rumors continued to take root. *Everyone wants to help their injured [family members] so badly that they'll believe almost anything,* Nakazawa thought; and he wondered who had first come up with the idea that the bones of those touched by the *pika* could heal people.

He accepted the bone-eaters as just another strange fact of life after the *pika-don*. Meanwhile, the two Nakazawa boys continued to bring their mother and their baby sister more than repulsive scraps of vegetable matter from the fallout-swept fields. The amounts of residual radiation in the sweet potatoes and their stems were such that if Dr. Nishina or the scientists who designed the bomb's core ever passed a Geiger counter over the material, their eyes would have widened with alarm and they'd have backed up a few steps. The substances were not overtly lethal. With rubber gloves and other minor precautions they could be safely handled. Yet no one who knew their true nature wanted the soil or the food on his skin or in his body.

Keiji Nakazawa's mother still had all of her hair and seemed well, but she was already in serious trouble. In years to come, Nakazawa would wonder if there existed a point during the feeding of poison from child to mother and from mother to infant, at which one more dose of radiation was reduced to mere redundancy. He supposed he might just as well ask how many angels could dance on the head of a pin.

While the first-grader's own symptoms of atomic bomb disease were easily seen, his mother's symptoms would be hidden in progressive anemia, chronic leukemia, and bone cancer. When eventually she died and was cremated, Keiji Nakazawa would be confronted with the mystery of a body converted entirely to ashes. Already, he had seen enough cremated bodies in Hiroshima to know that the bones, though fragile and easily crushed, still retained their original shape.

"Damn you!" Nakazawa would shout to the bomb itself, to the minds that conceived it and the hands that gave birth to it. Though a coroner would give him many reasons why the skeleton disintegrated, Keiji Nakazawa never doubted that radiation consumed his mother's very bones; it had continued eating away at her even after she died.

And one evening a cry went out to the impassive stars: "Give them back! Give me back my mother's bones!"[1]

On August 10, Takashi Tanemori's father sent him away from Hiroshima to the country village of Kotachi. During the slow, nearly 100-kilometer journey, aboard what had begun as a standing-room-only train, a seat was finally made available for the boy by the increasingly apparent off-loading, at each successive stop along the sixty-mile trail, of people who had died from flash burns, radiation injury, and festering wounds.

"Daddy" continued searching for the bones of lost family members in and around the hypocenter, eating and drinking whatever he could gather along the fringes of the wasteland.

"Where could he have slept?" the Tanemori child wondered. "Did anyone give him food?" He imagined the echo of Daddy's voice calling

"Yoshiko!" over and over, across a desert where the steel ribbing of the Hiro-shima dome had somehow survived, almost directly beneath the bomb.

"While sifting through the ruins," Tanemori would record later, "my father had no idea he was being exposed to radiation, and the constant expo-sure began to destroy him. Each time he returned to me, he was more broken and despondent."[2]

On the first day of the first bomb, five-year-old Saburo Kobayashi heard his mother cry out, somewhere between the flash and the bursting apart of his grandfather's home. During the days since, he had never heard his mother's voice again. He remembered running southward toward the sea, trying to get away from Hiroshima's waterspouts and fire worms. The road had ab-sorbed the heat from the flash and its surface became like a huge frying pan freshly lifted from a flame. As he ran, Saburo realized that he had fled from the smashed house without his shoes. He alternately ran and walked on scorched feet, leaving the skin of his soles behind. He had been living ever since August 6 in a bomb shelter cave in the side of Hijiyama Hill, behind the ruins of a school.

The cave became what was informally known as "the orphans' shelter." Some children, the lucky ones, were found and taken away by relatives who heard rumors about a cave of schoolboys turning feral. One by one Saburo's companions began disappearing, either because surviving relatives had come searching for them or because, like Saburo, they were weakening and dying. Disease X carried many of them away; and then the soldiers carried their bod-ies away to the pyres.

"My hair became thinner and its color lighter," Saburo would record. About the time Tanemori's father became ill and Nakazawa learned about the bone-eaters, Saburo's skin developed the star-shaped hemorrhagic spots char-acteristic of Disease X. "The older boys caught rancids, a type of Japanese frog, and fed them to me, claiming they were tasty when grilled. I was so hungry that these frogs tasted delicious. The days passed and the number of my friends became fewer and fewer. There was not enough food for all of us and before long my body [already skinny from pre-*pika don* rationing, started to resemble] a skeleton with skin attached."

By the time the orphans began fighting one another over rancids and other diminishing sources of food, a surviving aunt heard about the cave, and found Saburo.

The boy ran into his aunt's arms and hugged her, then punched her, cry-ing, "Why couldn't you come sooner and get me?"

Only after he pushed away from his aunt's embrace did Saburo notice that one whole side of her face had been scorched by the flash. She begged him to understand that she was unable to move at all until that day, and she promised to adopt him as her own, as a son of the Fujii family.

Among the orphans of the bomb, Saburo joined a lucky minority, taken in by kindly aunts and uncles who had been related only distantly by marriage.[3] In most families, a child only distantly related was considered at best an extra mouth to feed during a time of severe food shortages; and a child who no longer had the guidance of a father was generally branded as an outcast who belonged to the streets.[4]

Nine-year-old Shoso Kawamoto was among the majority of atomic orphans who endured a cruel shunning by his aunts, his uncles, and by the long-standing bias of both Japanese society, and authority, against orphans. After his older sister succumbed to the effects of flash, blast, and radiation, he was left to wander the fringes of Ground Zero, from the Hijiyama cave to the putrid moats near the flattened ruins of Hiroshima Castle. He and the other children were desperate to live, and as the first week passed, they had begun to abandon their parents' teachings about helping the youngest and the most vulnerable.

Until the first decade of the twenty-first century, Kawamoto would refuse to speak about "how there were so many orphans that we did not have enough food to survive. We were in a constant tug-of-war over food—sometimes for only one dumpling. In the end, the strong survived and the weak died one after another. Those who [eventually] taught me how to live were the Yakuza gangsters."

The strongest of the orphans would evolve into the next and most powerful generation of the Yakuza syndicate—which would rise out of Hiroshima, driven by a fury against authority that was to be referenced with chilling clarity in Keiji Nakazawa's crime Manga, *Pelted by Black Rain*, and echoed in a Ridley Scott film's disdainful line from a Yakuza crime lord, "You turned our rain black!"

Long after the flash, the blast, and the radioactive rain, Shoso Kawamoto began locking away in his own mind what he witnessed during the rise of the Yakuza. Honor-bound to take names of people, and their actions, with him to the grave, he nonetheless believed that future historians deserved to know something of what came out of Hiroshima. From his deathbed, and referencing his own actions, only, Kawamoto provided a glimpse of how it began for him—"with the atomic orphans' bitter experiences of being unable to do anything for their dying friends, [and later,] of beating someone for our own survival, rather than out of hatred. However, we will never forget the fact that a person passed away due to the beating."[5]

Dust and smoke blew straight across Hiroshima Castle's foundations and through the Communications Hospital. The sun was almost down to touching the hills now, and even though it still had a way to go before actually reaching the horizon, the smoldering ruins and the funeral pyres and the dust were tinting it gold, almost orange. The lensing effect of the polluted atmosphere gave the ruins a ghost-image aspect, even in broad daylight.

Yoji Matsumoto, a twenty-one-year-old officer returning to the city in search of his regiment, had entered the ruins on August 10, after walking the last thirty kilometers from Saijyo Station, following the railroad tracks down from the hills. The level of devastation he found seemed unthinkable. Except for its stone foundations, Hiroshima Castle was gone. The whole castle—atom bombed. The piles of "ash flakes" and the chilling images burned into stone walls revealed to Yoji the shapes of people turning away from something, or trying to run from it. Pausing to look inside one of the trolley cars still standing on the prairie, the soldier saw a statue man whose tongue and eyelids and fingers were charcoal. After four days, the shock-cocooned corpse had stayed in place holding onto a blackened streetcar strap, and still he seemed to be glancing up at something.

The young officer continued north toward the military base that had stood between Hiroshima Castle and the Communications Hospital. There, in the land between, Yoji discovered that everyone in his regiment appeared to have died instantly.[6]

That same afternoon of August 10, as the Tanemori boy realized his father might die and leave him an orphan, and as Shoso Kawamoto resolved that he would fight and even kill to live, a woman named Shoda, much like Keiji Nakazawa, seemed to be recovering some of her strength. Her new home was the Communications Hospital's isolation ward for Disease X sufferers. She was able, at intervals, to rise from her straw mat and breathe in the relatively fresh air outside of the makeshift tent "pavilion." Dr. Hachiya, the former ant-walker, thought that any improvement among these people was a reason for raised spirits. In his worst nightmares, he had imagined a biological weapon that eventually killed everyone it infected. The report of someone actually making a dramatic recovery now made Hachiya more determined to get out of bed—even if the sutures did pull at his skin. His friend Dr. Hinoi brought a cane and helped him downstairs to the isolation pavilion where the woman lay (not yet recognized by the hospital staff as a well-known poet). On the way down, the two doctors found their eyes drawn constantly toward the hypocenter.

"Aren't you curious?" Hachiya asked.

"About what?"

"About what's in there. What does it really look like, up close?"

"I've been giving it a lot of thought," said Hinoi. "I'm not really sure I want to know. And yet . . ."

"And yet, what?"

"I have a bike that still works—and I have to make a visit tomorrow to an army supply barge docked near the gutted bank buildings. I was thinking, perhaps if you're feeling up to it—"

"Then it's a deal," Hachiya said. He would have the stitches removed early in the morning, and after their errand to the supply barge was done, they would mount, by way of detour, an expedition to the hypocenter.

When Hachiya reached the isolation pavilion, with thoughts of exploration and despair vying for first place in his mind, hope came racing toward the finish line in the form of a woman named Shoda whose pulse was strong, whose nose had stopped bleeding, and whose appetite was returning. Shoda returned a weak smile to Hachiya, and for the first time since the *pika-don*, he felt a sense of what might be called happiness.

Don't worry, he told himself a moment later, *it won't last*. As indeed it could not, once he took his first hard look at the other patients in the pavilion. On first hearing that Shoda's health had improved enormously and that there were no new deaths to report today, Dr. Hachiya had allowed himself to believe that the worst was over. But when he saw the evidence of fresh bloody urine on virtually every mat, he understood that Hinoi and the other medics were reporting only a fleeting respite.

Two women complained of having chokingly large objects stuck in their throats. Hachiya and Hinoi helped them to cough up golf-ball–sized clots of blood and phlegm. As Shoda looked on, parasitic roundworms came out of their mouths.

Hachiya jumped to his feet, pulling at least two of his stitches.

"I've seen this before!" Hinoi said. "But it happens only when people are already dead. Only when the flesh begins to decay and can no longer support them do parasites abandon their hosts."

Dr. Hachiya glanced over at Shoda and asked Hinoi to move her at once out of the pavilion and into open air. Shoda nodded in grateful agreement. As she stood, one of the dying women emitted a strangled cry and suddenly spat an amazing wad of red phlegm and tiny white worms onto the ground.

"Doctor?" Shoda whispered, trying to keep her gag reflex under control.

"Yes," Hachiya said.[7]

"I wonder if there is an operation that removes memories."[8]

Near the southern fringe of Urakami's Ground Zero, ship designer Yama-guchi, his wife, Hisako, and their child were among the few creatures still moving. Though inexplicably (and, he sometimes believed, "miraculously") alive after two atomic bomb blasts, Mr. Yamaguchi was becoming increasingly lethargic and depressed.

The engineer's side of his brain told him, logically, to be grateful that his burns from Hiroshima had sent his wife along an improbable path to shelter. Nevertheless, Yamaguchi's heart told him that his siblings were dead. His cousins were dead. A cousin's wife and their infant child lay dead in what little remained of "home."

Hisako's family had been worse than decimated. Yamaguchi and little Katsutoshi were all she had left, and she began to fear that even this would not last. A tunnel had become their only home, and as Mr. Yamaguchi's de-pression grew, his left arm and one whole side of his face had begun to swell like balloons inflating, turning purple and quite painful. The burns on his arms became gangrenous and started sprouting nests of fly larvae, at which point Yamaguchi passed out and could not be roused awake.

Hisako tried to remove the maggots but someone who seemed to know something about medicine arrived at the cave and insisted that she leave the maggots living in her husband's skin. The idea sounded to Hisako like an old wives' tale; but she put her faith in the visitor and decided that, even if it was only a myth, if it healed her husband's burns and he recovered, she would believe in it. She helped the newcomer to feed her semiconscious husband strange new concoctions made from persimmon leaves, dried rose hips, and any other sources of vitamin C that could be found, and she was instructed to cook him helpings of liver from any animal—even from rats, if they could be found. She became convinced, over time, that had she taken Mr. Yamaguchi to one of the woefully overwhelmed and undersupplied first-aid centers near Governor Nagano's side of central Nagasaki, he would surely have died.

Little by little the blisters stopped discharging blood, and the maggots, hour by hour, removed dead and gangrenous flesh until Hisako believed the bones in her husband's arms might soon be exposed.

The visitor had sprinkled a powder of crushed grape seeds and talcum on the wounds to dry them out and prevent further infection. He also suggested attaching live leeches to the still-living flesh that surrounded the worst of the burns, explaining to Hisako that leeches would keep blood circulating through her husband's wounded hands, and prevent his fingers from dying and having to be amputated.

It would all have been dismissed as witchcraft by her ship-designer husband, but he was semi-comatose and now living under the advice of the only house-calling doctor in town, so Hisako obeyed the "witch doctor" and spent uncounted hours searching for leeches and gagging on the bitter mineral water given her by the visitor. The concoction reeked of chalk and something mixed with miso that tasted how iodine smelled. In years to come, Hisako would leave physicians perplexed with assertions that, except for irritability and brief bouts of vomiting, she and the baby did not get sick at all during their stay in a tunnel on the edge of a radioactive no-man's land. And except for permanent, swelling-induced deafness in one ear, Yamaguchi would make a full and equally perplexing recovery.

The strange visitor Hisako would forever regard as her guardian angel refused her offers of thanks and devotion and, like most true heroes, simply walked away from history's stage.[9]

More than twenty-four hours had passed, and yet none of the additional doctors and medical supplies promised by Governor Nagano arrived at or near St. Francis Hospital. After the initial contact over a police radio, about lunchtime the day before, no more news appeared to be coming across the ridge from the governor's mansion.

When Prefect Nishioka arrived at Nagano's office, the governor appeared to be walking around in a state of shock. Nishioka learned that Nagano had been existing in a semi-trance state from the moment the initial estimates climbed from 50,000 presumed dead to more than 75,000—with at least another 75,000 severely wounded or near death.

The prefect had struggled for nearly a full day and night through rubble and through a second dose of radiation to cross fields of fallout and reach the governor's headquarters, only to be immediately upbraided for being late. After this, the governor paced back and forth wordlessly while his chief of foreign affairs yelled in Nishioka's face about all the staff he and the governor had lost, blaming the prefect for not warning everyone about what he had seen in Hiroshima.

"If I had done as I wished and published a pamphlet about Hiroshima," Nishioka said in his own defense, "then you fine gentlemen would have been the first to accuse me of spreading wild rumors and I could have been shot for treason."

"If it were up to me, I'd shoot you now," Chief Nakamura said, "except for the fact that your hide isn't worth the cost of the bullet."

The prefect vomited a thick yellow mouthful of bile at the foreign affairs chief's feet. Before either man could step back, a second mouthful came up, mixed with blackened speckles of blood.

"What's wrong with you?" the chief demanded.

"I think we call it atomic poisoning," the prefect said, and added, "I think I'll go to my wife, now."

"You can't leave!" the governor yelled.

"I'm probably dead already," Prefect Nishioka announced, and he thought about the black-stained leaves he had observed in the governor's garden. "Just one last thing, though. Was there a fall of black rain here, yesterday?"

"Yes. And black dust, too."

"Then I suppose we shall all be in the same boat soon," the prefect said, and left.[10]

When Dr. Nagai finally set out from the St. Francis medical outpost, downhill toward his neighborhood, two of his neighbors had already erupted into an argument over a pile of charred human remains, located midway between the foundations of their houses. All the clothing and most of the musculature had been burned away from the body, and a wedding band gave no clues to identify because it was now little more than a melted and re-solidified pool of gold. Each man was shouting that the body was that of his own wife and that he be allowed to take possession of the bones. A third neighbor joined in, pointing out that Mr. Tanaka's wife had been "kind of heavy set," and he tried to determine from the diameter of a black stain in the gray ash whether a larger than normal amount of human body fat had been cooked into the ground. He could not tell one way or the other, and for all his knowledge of human anatomy, neither would Dr. Nagai have been able to tell, had he arrived in time to stop the outburst. As he continued his journey downhill, Nagai could only pray that such an argument would not erupt over his beloved Midori.

Less than halfway home, Paul Nagai stumbled and almost passed out. He stood and stumbled a second time, and a little farther downhill he met "old Auntie Matsu," who kept him from falling a third time and told him, "You don't want to go down there."

"Why?"

"Because the people you'll meet are going crazy," Auntie Matsu warned. "They are like animals after a forest fire—dangerous and half scared to death, fighting over anything and willing to do petty little bits of evil."

Leading him back uphill, Auntie described arguments over broken bits of dinnerware turning suddenly bloody, but what seemed to bother her most was an encounter with a young woman who returned home to find her grandmother uninjured and who was singing to herself cheerfully as she washed singed, flower-patterned clothes in black well water and hung them out to dry.

"I'm so happy," the strange woman had said. "I never thought Grandma and I were such especially good people, but it's only by God's special grace that we weren't killed." Then, looking out across the center of Urakami, she announced, "Those people who were burned to death—they must have made God angry, mustn't they? They must have provoked him to wrath."

"You mean, like my baby cousin Kimiyo?" Auntie Matsu said. It seemed to her that such civilized ideas as "Judge not" and "Love thy neighbor as thyself"—in which Auntie always believed—had been lost and now belonged to an older world.

Dr. Nagai heard that by nightfall of August 10, the strange young woman collapsed and began to suffer nosebleeds. By midnight, she would die very old.[11]

At dawn of August 11, a wealthy citizen of Nagasaki arrived at St. Francis, bringing fresh white rice for his mother and for a hundred other patients, along with gleeful rumors for Dr. Akizuki—"Doctor, I hear that we have recaptured Okinawa, and dropped America's own atomic bombs on Washington and New York."

"Even if it were true," Akizuki said, "I would never rejoice over that kind of story, I swear it. Hasn't enough been lost? Is useless reciprocal killing all that we have left?"

The man went home for more supplies, and he would never speak to Dr. Akizuki again about winning a nuclear war.

In the valley below, ten-year-old Sakue Shimohira and her sister finally located their mother. She lay on the ground, carbonized and statuesque. "Together," Saku would record, "we reached out to the body and said, 'Mother.' Before our eyes, [her body] crumbled into ashes."[12]

Young Miyuki Broadwater would always remember holding onto her mother's hand and tagging along as fast as her little legs could carry her through the valley of death. In a manner similar to the strange "ground candles" through which Prefect Nishioka had walked, something near the ground seemed to be simultaneously burning Miyuki's legs and injecting poison into the skin. Below her knees, the skin would soon be thickening and turning dark brown; and it would remain this way for the rest of her life.

Terrified by what she saw in the bottom of the Urakami Valley, she eventually told historians how people and dogs, horses and cows, were completely burnt, "like charcoals." More than sixty years later, she remembered her mother holding her hand so tightly that the fingers became numb.

"Don't look to the side. Keep looking straight ahead!" Miyuki's mother warned, repeatedly. But she was just a child, and she was curious; so she could not stop herself from looking. She saw her mother pouring water from her canteen into a cup and giving it to a young man whose face appeared to have been thoroughly carbonized on one side all the way down to the skull, with the other half of his face seeming to be entirely normal.

"I have never told anyone about this," she would record for an archivist in 2010. Miyuki had feared that people would not take kindly to news of what the atomic bombs had done.[13] "A part of me wants to talk, but another part of me is afraid that people won't believe me—that this kind of thing actually happened."[14]

Much as no news except that carried by survivors was going out of the two cities, little real information was coming in. At Hiroshima's Communications Hospital, on the sunny, unusually windy morning of August 11, Dr. Hachiya heard rumors about Admiral Ugaki's victorious attack on Okinawa before he received confirmation that the earth tremor he felt two mornings before might in fact have been Nagasaki dying.

Dawn had also brought news that more people appeared to be coming down with the mysterious hemorrhagic fever, though this was the first night during which he could report that there were no new or imminent deaths in the isolation tent. Hachiya believed he was beginning to feel the first flu-like symptoms, and wondered if he might now himself be one of the infected.

"I might as well see what's happened out there before I die," Hachiya told Dr. Hinoi, and he asked to have all of the remaining stitches removed from his wounds so they could set out on the expedition they had discussed the day before.

"You mean, right now?"

Hachiya nodded.

"Well, and why not?" Hinoi said, and shrugged. "I woke up today with a bit of the gastroenteritis myself . . . if that's what we're deciding to call it this morning. We might as well go while we're still guaranteed to have the strength."

"Or before the excursion becomes two men on a bicycle with bloody diarrhea," Hachiya said, and tried to force a laugh. Hinoi stared toward the distant Dome and ignored the joke. He was all business now, mapping the route in his head, revising in accordance to the dictates of roads and debris piles. The path to the army's medical barge looked simple enough. Their starting point was already within Ground Zero, and buildings tended to be stamped more flatly into the ground here than on the landscape Dr. Nagai had tried to navigate in the hills of Urakami. In central Hiroshima, the streets were clearly visible and in most places seemed not to have been hit from the sides by avalanches of debris.

As Hinoi and Hachiya progressed, the most consistent obstacles they encountered turned out to be downed trolley wires and their supporting cables—which had to be negotiated at regular intervals, two or three times along each city block. These pauses gave Dr. Hachiya opportunities to inspect the ruins on both sides of the road. Most of the buildings had been squashed like wicker baskets stepped on by elephants. Some had burned after they were squashed. Others were simply ground down to pulp and grit. Chips from tile walls and bathtubs were localized in some of the debris piles, indicating where bathrooms had been. Fragments of crockery pointed toward kitchens, and shards distinguished by patterns of finely wrought cloisonné reminded Hachiya when they were passing through a wealthy neighborhood. The occasional burned or broken toy always brought him back to darker realities.

"Damage to the city was far worse than I had imagined," Dr. Hachiya would record, which said much about what he had seen and touched during the expedition. From atop the Communications Hospital, he had already looked across the hypocenter and had imagined quite a lot.[15]

One of the largest mansions in town must have been completely carried away by the updrafts and the fire worms; for instead of being hammered into the earth, the house appeared to have been lifted off the ground like a box and hauled away. The first-floor landing of a magnificent oak stairway was deeply charred, but otherwise it still stood perfectly in place with its handrails undisturbed—in the middle of the neighborhood of Komachi, where everything else had disappeared.

Mrs. Nagahashi, a famous musician, had lived in this most modern house in all of Japan, designed by her late husband during a kinder decade, with input from the American architect Frank Lloyd Wright. On either side of two grand pianos, built-in cabinets had stood floor to ceiling, bearing an entire library of 78-rpm records.

The westernized house was considered treasonous by most of the neighbors, and in time of war, even the mere playing of music was frowned upon—more so, playing the instruments and songs of the foreigners (or: the enemy). But even during hard times, Mrs. Nagahashi insisted on teaching the neighborhood children how to play the piano. According to her only known surviving student, Chieko Seki, who had been away with her family on the day the *pika-don* came, Mrs. Nagahashi's desire to teach music grew noticeably stronger after her son, who once had a promising musical career of his own, was killed during the battles for Saipan, Tinian, and the other outlying islands.

Like the stairway and the two charcoal pianos, everything else on the mansion's ground floor was somehow still in place, exactly where it had been at 8:15 a.m. on August 6. Behind a mound of small black drum cans that turned out to be stacks of phonograph records fused together, soldiers had found Mrs. Nagahashi in front of a Buddhist altar.[16] She looked like a praying mantis—carbonized—and no one who saw the mantis woman could escape the realization that she must have been praying at the moment of the *pika*.[17]

When he returned to the Communications Hospital, Dr. Hachiya was too tense to follow Hinoi's orders and go straight to bed. He resumed something akin to making normal visits to the patients, walking around in a filthy torn shirt, with fresh stitch holes slicked in sweat and grime. He looked and felt like a snail with a beard, and he realized he was beginning to *like* the feel and smell of his own filth.

Even when night came and exhaustion finally sent him upstairs, all Hachiya could think about were the broken toys—and as the army's funeral pyres burned under the cold stars, somewhere out there Mrs. Nagahashi still prayed. Dr. Hachiya paced the upper floor of the ruined hospital, paused from time to time to lie down on his bed frame for a few minutes, then paced again. As dawn approached, a great wind began to blow, blotting out Hachiya's view of the city behind a translucent lens of dust and pyre smoke. The gusts knocked plaster and chips of concrete from the hospital's few remaining walls.

"This I enjoyed," Hachiya would later record. "And I seemed to lose all restraint. It suited my mood."

A new day had begun.[18]

Michie Hattori, the shock-cocooned Urakami schoolgirl who returned home to discover her whole neighborhood miraculously cocooned behind a tall ridge, was drafted along with her parents and everyone else on her block into the rescue and recovery effort. By the morning of August 12, the effort was reduced mostly to the collection of bodies for a makeshift morgue on the blackened side of the ridge, where they remained beyond sight of the village while Michie and the other children gathered wood for a funeral pyre.

Almost all of the survivors who came from the blackened side were dead within a day or two. With the exception of Michie, the people who walked away from the heart of the blast zone appeared to have been exposed to something that burned them from the inside, and few of these were expected to live for very much longer.

A woman who had survived with the pattern of her kimono tattooed by the *pika* onto her skin died suddenly after coughing up what appeared to be part of her stomach. An army officer assigned Michie and several other schoolgirls to stack the bodies on the wood pile. *Maruta*, he had called the corpses—referring equally to the timbers and the dead people as "logs." And as the skin of a *maruta* woman tore off in Michie's hands, and as the flames were finally ignited and huge clouds of flies swarmed around the hot perimeter, Michie could scarcely believe that only a week before, she would have been horrified by a paper cut on her finger.

Less than an hour's walk uphill and to the northwest of Michie's town, the world seemed even more wretched to Dr. Akizuki. He glanced reproachfully at the sun; for it had risen as if nothing at all untoward were happening down here on Earth. Its serenity seemed only to intensify his gloom.

The governor's promise that an army "medical patrol" would arrive bringing supplies and relief had finally been carried out—three days late and accomplishing little more than to inoculate Drs. Akizuki and Nagai against hopefulness. Just when they began to think it was safe to suppose their situation had bottomed out and could not get much worse, something always seemed to sneak up from behind with the message that neither of them quite understood how deep the bottom could be.

Paul Nagai's aunt Matsu had warned everyone about troglodytes in the lower hills who appeared to be losing their minds. Now Akizuki and Nagai believed they were in danger of losing theirs.

The army medical patrol trucks dropped off more than a hundred additional burn victims whose gums had started bleeding, as well as their noses and bowels. Some were actually weeping blood. The patrol leader said, "They're losing blood like this because they must have breathed some poisonous gas. They are also sick to their stomachs. Find out what's causing it."

"All of our equipment is destroyed," Akizuki explained. "We do not have a single microscope still working. How are we supposed to discover what is causing the symptoms, much less to cure them?"

"You're doctors, aren't you? It's your job," the leader said, then helped himself and his crew to more than half of the medical outpost's boiled and potted drinking water, in addition to much of the remaining food supply.

If not for the fact that Dr. Yoshioka and the other patients needed him, and if not for knowing that it would have been the immediate death of him, Akizuki believed he possessed enough anger-fed strength to decapitate the army's local group leader with a single swipe of a shovel.[19]

After the patrol left, Akizuki agreed with Dr. Nagai to give himself precisely five minutes to seethe with hatred and fear, and then to dust himself off and accomplish with what few supplies remained whatever he could, until he could not.[20]

And so, with barely more than a few pounds of gauze and a bottle of iodine, he set off on his rounds, while the nurses and medical students grew progressively weaker and one by one became patients themselves. In a seemingly opposite and equal reaction, some of the patients became nurses and interns.

Mysteriously, most of the mild, pre-*pika* TB cases were feeling well enough to assist Akizuki and Nagai in their grueling schedules. Like the previously ailing Dr. Nagai, their health seemed actually to be improving, albeit by small steps. Akizuki noticed that those TB patients who had been particularly heavy smokers also seemed to be more resilient against Disease X. He chalked it up to a Darwinian natural selection effect: were their bodies not built especially well in the first place, they probably would not have survived TB long enough to see the *pika-don*.

In the afternoon, using a rice steamer as a sterilizing apparatus, using unraveled silk threads for stitches and two TB patients for assistants, Dr. Akizuki converted a burned-out library into an operating room and tried his best to repair Dr. Yoshioka's face. He found new pieces of glass coming to the skin surface between her cheek and the bridge of her nose—and another close to her eye.

The blast wave had struck the windows almost horizontally, and two or three particularly fast slivers evidently went all the way through Dr. Yoshioka's cheeks, burying themselves inside her tongue. Another shard had penetrated her blouse and her chest, embedding itself in a rib. He removed it with a dull knife and tweezers, while one of the patients held a candle and a broken mirror to provide something approximating a close-up lighting system.

In total, Dr. Akizuki managed to extract seven pieces of glass over the course of an hour, at which point Dr. Yoshioka could endure the pain and exhaustion no more. He stitched a gash through a breast and another between an eye and the bridge of her nose. The laceration through Yoshioka's upper lip yawned so wide that the assistants could not bear to watch. A large sliver of glass still remained in her lower jaw, overlooked. Glass shrapnel was particularly cruel, for even had the hospital's X-ray machine remained functional, glass would not have shown up on the films the way metal shrapnel revealed itself and would have eluded detection.

Early the next morning, those patients who were feeling able—among them the recovering TB cases—began wandering down toward the deeper, flatter ruins: first in search of their loved ones, and then in search of useful implements that might have survived. By now there were few thoughts of rescue in lower Urakami. Theirs was strictly a recovery operation.

Those who were able to find anything reminiscent of their exploded and carbonized homes turned over every fragment of roof tile—though when they reported to Dr. Akizuki what they had found, it seemed only by an act of imagination that any of them could have believed they uncovered their actual homes. All of the roof tiles in the realm of the fire mountain were broken into fragments smaller than hen's eggs. Most were heavily granulated and pitted by the *pika* and the fires. As Akizuki recorded it, once the roof fragments were pushed aside, the searchers descended into narrow strata of wall plaster and ashes, sometimes studded with fragments of bone. Though most of the radiation had by now dissipated, what fractionally remained still carried a substantial jolt, especially for people already dosed to varying degrees, and especially in the area around the hypocenter.

Those TB patients who had felt well on the third day and who did not have relatives missing near the hypocenter continued to regain their health.

By 2008, new construction at Urakami's Peace Park accidentally revealed an archaeological transect into the hypocenter. Descending through a crevice in time, researchers unearthed a flash-fossilized anthology of mid-20th-century civilization: coins and unidentified bits of metal that had glowed white hot, part of a soup bowl, a comb, two belt buckles, a wire-cutting tool, and sheathed in a residue of decayed isotopes, the carbonized fragments of a human hand. The temperatures here were comparable to the thermal shock effects seen in Pompeii's sister city of Herculaneum—where, at "only" 5 times the boiling point of water and within 1/20th second, vaporizing blood and brain matter exploded human skulls from the inside. [Illustration: CRP]

Those who descended into the foothills in search of loved ones returned with radioactive dust on their skin, and in their lungs—which began to work in concert with the usual shocks to the immune system that accompanied the inhalation of alkaline concrete dust.[21]

In his medical reports, Dr. Akizuki was eventually to call the Urakami dust "death sand." That night, however, neither Akizuki nor anyone else at or near the St. Francis Hospital campsite had any idea of a new danger that could neither be seen nor felt. Only much later would it be known to them that breezes coming up the hill brought radioactive particles as well as relief from heat and humidity. Only much later would Drs. Akizuki and Nagai understand that the returning searchers who distributed boiled rice to the patients through the nights of August 12 and 13 were already sick men. As they served dinner, their clothes shed "death sand" the way cats shed dander and hair.[22] The radioactive particles mixed impartially with diced pumpkins and apples—which the searchers stirred into everyone's miso soup.[23]

On Tinian, Charles Sweeney had seen the promising news of August 10 come and go with no word of the indicated surrender offer from Japan actually coming through. The moratorium against bombing with anything worse than leaflets with the harsh writing of Clavell and Michener had continued through the nights of August 11 and 12 and through the afternoon of Dr. Akizuki's searchers from the TB ward.

In Washington, no one knew, yet, how a deadlock in Tokyo had degenerated into a Palace revolt. On the evening of August 13, President Truman authorized General George Marshall to resume fire-bombings against Japan. During the predawn hours of August 14, Marshall ordered essentially the launch of every one of the more than 2,500 aircraft within striking range of Japan, including some 2,000 B-29 bombers. Two atomic strike bombers and their scientific instrument plane were held back, because they might be needed if further atomic bomb missions became necessary, and feasible, in September and October. Sweeney headed back aboard *Straight Flush*, flying "as though we were on a milk run," what was, in all essentials except a working core, the third atomic bomb-run on Japan.

Like *Enola Gay* and *BocksCar*, *Straight Flush* had been modified to carry a single, pumpkin-shaped bomb loaded with a multi-ton explosive charge of Torpex (with a slightly reconfigured detonation sequence, designed to produce a pre-shaped blast ring capable of cutting through anything located on ground level). On this flight, the crews were honing the skills acquired during the previous two atomic bomb runs. The *Straight Flush* pumpkin was the most powerful non-nuclear explosive ever dropped from a plane, but as Sweeney would recall, though it possessed exactly the same casing and machinery he had dropped over Urakami, "This time, it contained neither the secrets nor the horrors of the universe."

Straight Flush's target was the Toyota Motor Works at Koromo. No flak came up and no fighters—and, though *Straight Flush* was reportedly among the last of the 2,000 B-29s to release its load, this time no smoke from preceding raids obscured the target. Sweeney's bombardier reported that the "pumpkin" detonated within 200 feet of its aiming point; and the pilot concluded, much as he had concluded after eliminating the Mitsubishi factories in Hiroshima and along the Urakami River, that now Toyota could be added to Mitsubishi as a brand name that had been erased from history forever.[24]

In Hiroshima, Dr. Hachiya's morning rounds were interrupted by air-raid alarms from the river barges. In everyone's mind was the same thought: *Could the* pika *come again, after all that we have been through?* The August 6 flash had caught everyone completely by surprise. Hachiya realized that he was now shaking with fear, and as the drone of B-29 engines descended upon the wasteland, he sought the protection of a broad, steel-reinforced concrete pillar. A large squadron was approaching Hiroshima Bay from the south. At any instant, the physician expected another great flash overhead. But he cut short his own feelings of panic and made a decision that if death were to strike this hospital again, then his final moment would be with the patients, and not cringing behind a pillar.

The planes—at least two whole squadrons of them, one after another—passed noisily overhead without dropping anything. Then, suddenly, tremors began coming through the hospital's floor, and seconds later Hachiya could hear the distinctive distant detonations from stream after stream of blockbuster bombs carpeting the ground in the west. He concluded that the planes must be targeting the naval air base at Iwakuni.

At first, Hachiya felt extremely lucky to have been spared a second time, but it occurred to him that luck had nothing to do with it. There was simply nothing left in Hiroshima worth bombing. With a surge of anger, the doctor understood that his city was merely a detour along which damage wrought by the new weapon could be gloated over from on high.

In a makeshift shelter beyond the hospital, Keiji Nakazawa's baby sister had ceased crying and, strangest of all, had begun refusing her mother's milk. As Nakazawa would recall it, "Little Tomoko seemed to be quietly sleeping all the time—a baby ominously too well behaved."

Not even the squadrons clamoring overhead and the subsequent shaking of the earth roused Tomoko to cries of alarm. When he saw the B-29s, the Nakazawa boy did not think about another *pika*. He raised a clenched fist at them—realizing, like Hachiya, that the airmen came to gloat. There had been rumors from the outside about defeat, and about inevitable surrender.

"Tell me why now, this talk of surrender?" his mother had said. "Why not before?"

Less than a kilometer away, a thirty-two-year-old poet named Kurihara was asking the same questions as she carried from the foundations of her home a radioactive memento of human bone fragments stuck together like candies in melted glass. One day, she resolved, the memento should be displayed in a museum, where all humanity could come and witness its destiny, and vow to avoid it.

The bones in the glass had been flash-fossilized so quickly that some of them were still white. Kurihara was now adding frightening quantities of her own blood to the memento, from a nosebleed that seemed to be worsening each passing hour.

Somehow, her blood seemed apt. She thought of the Emperor's red and white flag—which up to now had represented the Rising Sun. But presently, the red of the Rising Sun became people's blood, and its background of white became people's bones.

"The people have spilled their blood and exposed their bones," Kurihara would say later, raising her own clenched fist against the sky—"because of the flag of blood and bones."[25]

In Tokyo, Foreign Minister Togo received reconnaissance reports that the United States fleet was gathering, lurking not very far behind the bombers. The Empire's spotter planes had evidently been allowed to observe the fleet and return without being fired upon. What they reported was not merely a fleet but an armada that seemed to put the record-breaking Normandy invasion in the minor leagues: supply ships of every size and configuration, destroyers, cruisers of indescribable variety, and several aircraft carriers.[26] The ships were grouped in formations five across and twenty deep.[27]

War Minister Anami refused to believe that the armada meant defeat and, along with Field Marshal Hata, General Shizuichi Tanaka, and a major named Hatanaka, he insisted that an all-out bombing raid on the convoy "might make the Americans rethink their actions." They amazed Togo, speaking as if none of them had attended the Imperial conference on August 9, as if even were their heads chopped off and lying upon the floor, they would somehow be able to bite the toes of their enemies and continue to fight.

A general named Mori was ordered by Hatanaka to join him in sealing the Palace grounds and preventing the broadcast of Emperor Hirohito's declaration of surrender. When Mori refused, he and his aide were shot and hacked to pieces. Major Hatanaka next conspired to seize control of the nation's radio studios, hoping to replace the Emperor's pre-recorded broadcast with an announcement of his own. Hatanaka still regarded the Emperor as a sacred figure who could not be harmed, but everyone else was fair game.

Meanwhile, General Tanaka and his staff received and compiled reports of air raids that appeared to be taking place virtually everywhere. By lunchtime, the general had confirmed to his own satisfaction that the approaching armada—which Anami insisted on dismissing as "only a phantom fleet of rumors"—did indeed exist and was slowly, surely, preparing to take aim directly at Tokyo. At this point, Tanaka withdrew his support for the military coup, and Hatanaka, joined by several other leading rebels, ended his life by suicide on the Palace lawn.

Throughout the long spasm of deadlock and a failed rebellion, any member of the Emperor's staff could be marked for summary execution and Hirohito himself was, in effect, held under house arrest.

Unable to locate and destroy either of the Emperor's two recorded declarations of the surrender, and with generals loyal to Hirohito regaining control of Tokyo's radio stations, Anami wrote, "I apologize to the Emperor for my great crime," and wandered off to write his last poems, get drunk, and slit his stomach open with a ceremonial blade. Many years would pass before the people of Japan learned what had actually transpired as the morning of August 14 dissolved into an incomparable last gasp of denial, assassination, and suicide.[28] But rumors hatched and took flight everywhere—and about everything.[29]

Kazushige was not yet born on the day Hiroshima died. As his father would tell it, Kazushige's twelve-year-old uncle Hiroshi had emerged perfectly unharmed from a school on the fringe of Ground Zero, where almost everyone else had been burned and crushed. He was rumored to be a "miracle boy," and a sign of glad tidings.

Following a set of railroad tracks homeward to the eastern hill country, the Ito boy was helped by a stranger who offered his own rice ration, and whose actions matched Prefect Nishioka's description of an encounter with a "sole survivor" schoolboy, near a railroad station. By the time the boy returned home, the rest of the Ito family was already counting him among the dead, but he had been so thoroughly shock-cocooned that there was not a scratch anywhere on his body, and even his clothes, though blackened by the rains, seemed perfectly intact.

Locally, he became symbolic of resilience against even the most impossible obstacles.

Kazushige Ito's father, Tsugio, himself only a boy during the bombs of August, would recall in future years that in the first days following the explosion, his older brother seemed well enough to take him fishing and to participate in a victorious game of baseball against a rival neighborhood team. In reality—and all too often—atomic bomb survivors were not quite as they appeared.

The burning from within started on or about August 14, at the beginning of the Buddhist Week of the Dead. One moment the two Ito brothers were playing, and in the next the older boy fell to his knees, grabbing his stomach as if stabbed. By evening, the stricken child's mother found it difficult to go near him and began to shrink away from her own son. They all shrank away, because on each exhaled breath, there came a stench that reminded family members of a corpse already lying on the ground for several days. The normal bacteria of decay were eating the Ito child's lungs and his throat, while his tongue—bloating and purple and hot—stank of rotting meat even as he still moved and tried to speak.

Finally, Tsugio's brother Hiroshi let out a bone-chilling howl. Foam and blood flecked his lips and, just as suddenly as he had sickened from the "death sand" and the rays, the miracle boy lay back and died.[30]

Meanwhile, in the blackened shell of Hiroshima's Communications Hospital, Dr. Hachiya had heard stories about people who were outside a house at the moment of the *pika* and who were shadowed from the heat ray. And yet, though escaping without any burns, they sickened and died while people who were inside the house, though severely injured by collapsing beams, were still alive. If the rumors about the bomb releasing a poison gas or of the Americans following the bomb with a biological weapon were true, then the people who crawled from inside the house should have been infected or gassed just as easily as those who were standing outside, Hachiya concluded. Whatever killed the people who were standing outside had to involve a very short-lived exposure hazard to something that had largely evaporated by the time the people trapped within pushed their way out to the surface. The more Hachiya thought about it, the more confused he became.

A visit from a navy captain who had come to Hiroshima on a medical barge brought an end to the confusion. "The *pika* itself appears to be the source of some dreadful disease," Captain Fujihara explained. "The navy has begun studying more than thirty cases, and though not a doctor myself, I can still tell you without a doubt that in each case, white blood cell counts have been crashing."

"You've *got* to get me a microscope," Hachiya said.

"I'm sorry," the captain replied. "We have only one on the barge and we're working with a cracked lens." Apologetically, he opened a briefcase and, instead of medical equipment, presented the doctor with a bottle of whiskey and several packs of cigarettes. "This isn't much," he said, "but these things may actually be harder to find than microscopes."

I'd rather have the microscopes, Hachiya thought of saying, but offered his thanks instead.

After the captain left, Hachiya lit a cigarette and began sifting through the shattered remnants of the hospital's half-dozen Bausch and Lomb scopes, hoping to cobble together at least one marginally useful piece of equipment. The effort was doomed from the start. Not a single oil emersion lens had survived as anything more than a flattened brass cylinder and glass converted once again to sand. He estimated that the blast wave must have been traveling at a speed of 200 meters—or two city blocks—per second when it struck them.

He remembered that one of the Communications Bureau's district managers had kept a microscope locked in a safe. The office holding the safe was a bunker, sheathed in reinforced concrete. It made no difference. When Hachiya found the bunker, the whole structure was bent and ruptured like a broken basket. The wind from the bomb had turned the safe completely around and smashed the steel door off its hinges.[31] The microscope was so utterly destroyed that the doctor began to appreciate more than ever before the improbability of his own survival on that first day of the *pika-don*.[32]

Dr. Hachiya's second visitor of the afternoon would remind him again of improbability and mortality—and, though bringing gifts, would accidently fill him with remorse for having lost all sense of self and joined the ant-walkers that day.

Mr. Sasaki lived across the street from Hachiya, near the Misasa Bridge. He came to the hospital bearing freshwater *ayu* fish for the patients and staff.

"How is your family?" Hachiya asked.

Mr. Sasaki explained that it had taken him several days to find them because when the *pika* flared out, he was running an errand north of the hospital, and was forced to out-race the firestorm into the hills of Ushita. Only shadow-shielding from the heat ray, and the added speed given him by an intact bicycle, had allowed him to escape without injury. Yet even from a safe distance, upriver and in the hill country, he could see that his neighborhood was "under the mushroom's stem." After the fires diminished, Sasaki navigated his bicycle through debris-strewn streets and found his home, and Dr. Hachiya's, reduced to knee-deep piles of ash. Fortunately, Shigeo Sasaki's family had traveled upriver with other survivors from the neighborhood, to a pre-arranged meeting place at which it was hoped they would all re-connect if anything terrible were to disperse them. As Sasaki traveled downriver toward the ruins, his wife and children had passed him in the opposite direction, evacuating toward the upriver, suburban hospital to which he had been assigned. He finally reunited with his wife and children, discovering them mud-soaked and looking hungry, about the same time the tremors from Nagasaki reached out toward Hiroshima.

"Little Sadako keeps talking about the bright light," Mr. Sasaki said. The child was only two, but not yet nor ever would she forget the false sunrise that preceded the great wind. Sadako's five-year-old brother Masahiro and Mrs. Sasaki were bruised and shaken but safe. They had survived the picket of fire worms that advanced into the river and became waterspouts.[33] They had even survived the rain of oil without suffering any symptoms of what Dr. Hachiya was now coming to call "atomic bomb disease."[34]

"Were they inside the house during the *pika-don*, or outside?" Dr. Hachiya asked.

"Inside," Mr. Sasaki replied, and Hachiya sighed with relief. "That's how they got bruised," Sasaki continued. "They were bounced around inside, and when they fled into the street, though the house seemed intact, it just sort of leaned slowly over to one side. And then, as the flames and the confusion grew worse, they eventually got separated from my mother and she was lost."

"*What?*"

"They never did see her again."

For all the horrors Hachiya had seen and experienced during the past week, the death of Mr. Sasaki's kindly mother felt like one punch too many in the stomach. From what Hachiya was able to learn, little Sadako's grandmother was burned to death as the firestorm developed, and like others caught in the maelstrom, once the fires seized control of the city, there was nothing that anyone could do to save her. But Hachiya had been *right there* before the fires dominated the landscape—and he remembered, vaguely, seeing the Sasaki house leaning to one side before it began to fall apart, just as Mr. Sasaki had described it.

From the moment of hearing that his friend's mother had been injured and killed only steps away from him, it did not matter to Hachiya that he had emerged from the ruins of his own house, bleeding and confused, into a world turned suddenly and violently unfamiliar. All that mattered was that instead of helping his neighbor he had joined the nearest ant trail.

Not that Mr. Sasaki, who was every bit as kindly as his mother, would ever say a word of reproach against him. Instead, he would continue to bring whatever food he could spare for his neighbor, and for those under his care. Yet from that moment, the first sting of survivor's guilt began to work its poison in Hachiya's heart, and he would never be able to meet Sadako or her father without being brought back to the picture of himself as the sort of person who walked away in a time of dire need. His only hope of avoiding the pain was to avoid *them*. It was the beginning of what Dr. Nagai of Urakami was already coming to recognize as one of those invisible cracks made by the atomic bomb—a crack between neighbors and friends, although Hachiya and Sasaki would never talk about it.

"I have one more thing for you," Mr. Sasaki said. "News from the prefect's office. This is not rumor. It comes directly through Foreign Minister Togo. An important radio broadcast is announced for tomorrow."

"What can it be?"

Neither man wanted to speculate, but both supposed that War Minister Anami was about to announce the advance of enemy fleets toward the homeland's shores. He would presumably order every man, woman, and child to fight against the Americans to Japan's own extinction—using cleavers, knives, and sharpened bamboo sticks.

For a while, Hachiya could put thoughts of ant-walker's guilt aside in favor of thankfulness for being without electricity. *We have no radio*, he told himself, and realized that living empty-handed in the Stone Age actually gave him a freedom of spirit and action he had not known since the war began.[35]

Tanemori, the boy half-blinded by the bomb during a game of hide-and-seek, greeted the morning of August 15 as the day of *Obon*, the beginning of the period during which the spirits of the ancestors returned to visit places they had wished to see during life, or decided simply to stay near, watching over their descendants and loved ones.

As the reality of his father's suffering began to send chills down his spine, Tanemori learned from the same unwelcoming relatives who had by now arrived at a decision to send father, and son, and a dying daughter outside to sleep on beds of hay in whatever shelter they could make for themselves, that on this day they would be welcomed briefly indoors. The occasion was an important announcement, scheduled to be broadcast on the radio, from the Imperial Palace.

Young Tanemori did not care what the announcement might be. With a trembling hand, Daddy held out to him a memento from his last visit to the ruined city: a fragment of bone from the chest of a child.

"This, I think," Daddy said softly, "is—"

"No! No! *No*, Daddy! Tell me this is *not* Sayoko! Tell me!"

But only the dogs replied, with a frightful howling that came from many directions at once. The howls echoed, near and far; and Tanemori felt sick.[36]

In the Hiroshima suburb near Isao Kita's weather station, Keiji Nakazawa awoke in a shed where he and his mother were no more welcomed by relatives than were the Tanemoris in Kotachi Village. Nakazawa felt strong enough this day to begin scouting for a better place to live, in addition to his usual search for food. On a patch of land near Paul Tibbets's original aiming point, the "T" Bridge, a handful of survivors were already expanding lean-to shelters into the first corrugated zinc houses, in what was to become the Hiroshima prairie's first shantytown. Nakazawa would eventually choose for himself a piece of ground barely more than a hundred paces northwest of the Rationing Hall in which Eizo Nomura had been shock-cocooned. The frame of the shock-cocooned building would one day be remodeled into a tourist center; and the shelter that Keiji Nakazawa planned to build for his mother was to occupy the same little parcel of land on which, decades later, would rise a tall pedestal, atop which a girl, sculpted in bronze, could be seen holding a paper crane up to the sky.

Along the spit of land where Nakazawa conducted his scouting operation for a new home, word spread that a radio was being set up for public broadcast near the weather station. A second public radio had been delivered by truck from the Communications Bureau to Dr. Hachiya's hospital. Something important was about to happen to Japan, but Nakazawa could *not* have cared less what happened to the country or its leaders. What he did care about was sheltering and feeding his mother and saving his baby sister.[37]

At the appointed hour, someone on the hospital steps hooked an all but completely dead car battery to the radio, and the prairie was suddenly humming and crackling with fading static. A distant voice said, "We have resolved to pave the way for a grand peace for all generations to come, by enduring the unendurable and suffering the insufferable."

Only a few people were able to hear this. All that came through clearly, before the battery failed, were the words "enduring the unendurable."

The hospital's electrician, who had been standing with his ear close to the speaker, announced that what everyone had just heard was the Emperor's own voice, and that he had just said the war was over.

"Who won?" someone asked.

"He said we must bear the unbearable," the electrician replied; and then, looking around, he added, "Who do you *think* won?"[38]

Keiji Nakazawa's baby sister, whom he had named Tomoko because the word meant "friend," was clearly dying.

Presently, some of the isotopes absorbed in his mother's bones were being stealthily removed and rerouted to her milk glands, but they had already done their work and stem cells in her bone marrow, ravaged by chromosomal dislocations, were beginning to divide wrongly in a march toward eventual chaos and death.

Nakazawa's father was dead.

Nakazawa's older sister was dead.

Nakazawa's little brother Susumu was dead.

By the night of the surrender, one of Keiji Nakazawa's neighbors had joined the feral atomic orphans. Tanaka was the child of a high-ranking officer who used to live in a mansion across the street from the Nakazawa home. During the worst of the rationing leading up to August 6, when even potato vines were in short supply for meals, the army delivered canned meats and even sweets to Tanaka's family.

Tanaka was the same age as Keiji Nakazawa and had befriended him; and although Tanaka occasionally shared food as well as toys, Nakazawa could not avoid a certain amount of jealousy and even anger. "They lived a truly luxurious life," Nakazawa would write later, "and the difference between them and us was heaven and hell."

Keiji ("Barefoot Gen") Nakazawa barely escaped becoming an atomic orphan, and lived to tell what he saw through his Manga art. [Illustration: CRP]

In his chronicles of *Barefoot Gen*, Nakazawa did not mention how his older brother Koji began wandering away, where he found new friends and became increasingly involved in the trafficking and consumption of alcohol. Koji's activities in the emerging black markets brought home rations of rice; but they also created a rift within the family. What the chronicler of *Gen* did write about was the night Tanaka, drawn by the scent of food, snuck under one of the sheet-metal slats on the side of the makeshift shack Nakazawa was building for his mother and sister. The former neighbor from across the street tried to flee with a jar of rice.

In his chronicles, Nakazawa disguised Tanaka and called him "Ryuta." During the sixty-fifth anniversary of the atomic bombings, following a controversy in which Ryuta would be wrongly declared to be a fictional character, invented to manipulate the emotions of readers, Nakazawa decided to reveal the details of a subject that had been very painful for him, and about which he routinely avoided speaking directly. In the world of *Barefoot Gen*, the strained, on-again off-again friendship between Gen and Ryuta simply faded mysteriously, leaving behind a lasting impression that leukemia or some other manifestation of atomic bomb disease must have intervened. But "Ryuta's" actual fate seemed to Nakazawa to be somewhat worse than the after-effects of radiation exposure because it might have been preventable.

"His name was Tanaka," Keiji Nakazawa would finally cry out to history, wanting the generations to remember. "He *was* Ryuta."

In Nakazawa's *Barefoot Gen* chronicles, the truth about Tanaka was located somewhere between what he wished would have happened (Ryuta as a new brother, replacing two siblings lost) and what really happened.

As Keiji Nakazawa would grow up to tell it, in his Manga and in a film, a gentle, shadowy movement under the slat where rice was stored called him to action one night, and moments later he was wrestling on broken concrete outside the shack. Finally, Nakazawa wrapped his legs around the boy's waist; and as his mother emerged from the shack commanding him to stop and as the light from her lantern struck the boy's face, Keiji Nakazawa drew back his fist to strike the thief, then drew his breath in astonishment.

The boy looked like Tanaka, yet at the same time he no longer looked at all like Tanaka. On some level of Nakazawa's thinking, the boy looked just like the little brother he was still mourning. Whether the resemblance arose from a change in Tanaka's features, brought about by near-starvation, or whether hopeful thinking made any young waif transform into a twin of Susumu, would never be clear.

"*Susumu?*" Nakazawa asked, as recalled for his late-20th-century screenplay of *Barefoot Gen*.

"I'm *not* him," the boy said, squirming away and getting ready to jump to his feet again.

"Of course you're not Susumu," Kimiyo Nakazawa said, as calmly and gently as she could. *I saw him die*, she left un-emphasized, for Keiji's benefit.

"I'm sorry I stole your food," Tanaka said, letting his friend's mother help him to his feet. He tried to explain the hunger that had been gnawing at him until at last he believed he had lost his appetite. And then he smelled cooked rice, and he could not control himself. "But God says it's not a sin to steal food if you're really, really hungry."

"Tanaka, where is your family?" Kimiyo asked.

Clenching his jaw, he answered, "They were all killed in the explosion." Tanaka alone crawled out from beneath the wreckage of the mansion. In his yard, family members had been hoisted into the air just like Keiji Nakazawa's mother, except that in this case they landed in trees and were hung from seared branches, impaled. People no longer identifiable to Tanaka as either strangers or relatives crawled silently away from the flattened home. Their abdominal muscles were sliced open and they had seemed unaware that their knees were snagging on their own dangling internal organs, drawing out ropes of intestine, yard by yard, as they crawled.

Keiji Nakazawa listened to Tanaka's story impassively, as if all horrors could now be ignored as background noise—which, in fact, they could. He was preoccupied with other thoughts.

"You look exactly like my little brother," Keiji said again, as told through his alter ego, Gen.

"I'm not him!" the boy yelled, taking a resentful step backward. "I'm Tanaka!"

"Barefoot Gen" said nothing. He simply looked at "Ryuta" apologetically, then ran into the shack and returned with a half-eaten rice ball. "Here," he said. "You can have the rest of my dinner, if you want it."

"You mean, you'd give it to me?"

"Sure."

And before he could quite hand it over, the orphan had taken a huge gulp out of the rice ball. He then tried to swallow the rest of it in a second gulp that almost choked him.

"What are you doing?" Keiji asked. "You'll get sick."

The orphan swallowed hard and said, "I didn't want you to take it back."

"I wouldn't do that," Keiji Nakazawa assured.

"Why should I believe you?"

Kimiyo Nakazawa knelt down, until her head was level with the orphan's. "Where have you been living since the explosion, Tanaka?"

"Out here, mostly."

"Well, if you're still hungry, you're welcome to finish my rice, too."

"You really mean that?"

"Of course I do."

Kimiyo watched the boy gulp down the second rice ball as fast as the first. It shocked and amazed her. Little Susumu had also been in the habit of gulping his food, as if he actually feared that someone might snatch it away from him before he had a chance to swallow.

As told through the wishful perspective of Gen, Keiji Nakazawa brought out a dented copper cooking pot and offered to "Ryuta" a spoon to scrape out any last remnants of crisped rice. He dropped the spoon, put his head right inside the pot, and began licking and gnawing the sides. "Just like Susumu used to do," Keiji whispered.

Kimiyo tried to explain to her son, and perhaps to herself, that for a child of the wilderness—a former neighbor—to have taken on Susumu's mannerisms, and for the child to have found them by accident seemed remarkable. "Somehow," she said, "it's as if he were sent here."

Keiji Nakazawa watched the orphan he wished to be his little brother licking all the way to the bottom of the upturned pot, seeking out every last trace of flavor. "Mother," Keiji said, "are you thinking what I'm thinking?"

"I am. But we're having such a difficult time feeding ourselves—" and she watched the copper pot become a large helmet over Tanaka's head. "But still, if Susumu were alive, it's what he would want us to do."

"So, it's all right, then?"

The orphan did not hear the question. His entire head and now one of his shoulders had disappeared into the pot. When at last he rolled it onto the ground and announced that he almost didn't feel hungry anymore— "almost"—he noticed that the kid from across the street and his mother were staring at him with very strange expressions on their faces. At first, he interpreted the expressions as meaning he had offended them somehow and was about to be wrestled to the ground again. Then he remembered his manners.

"Thank you!" Tanaka said quickly. "I'm so sorry. I should have said *thank you*."

He received the same stare, from both of them.

"What did I do?"

"Nothing," Kimiyo said. "Tanaka, we've been wondering. Would you like to have a home again?"

"You mean, stay here?" he asked hopefully.

"Yeah," Keiji Nakazawa said.

The boy looked scared, as if in the next moment Keiji and his mother might say, "Only kidding," and send him away again into the wilderness. As

Nakazawa's *Gen* chronicles would record it, the orphan began talking about his shortcomings and tried to explain why these were really not so bad: "I know I'm little and can't work very hard and be much help, but I can give you back rubs. Father always said I was a good back-rubber." And he went straight to Kimiyo Nakazawa's shoulders, pinching all the right nerves in all the wrong places.

"That's very kind of you," Kimiyo said, "but you don't have to work hard. We're not asking anything from you in return, Tanaka. You'll just be one of the family."

"Really?"

Kimiyo nodded, and gently stroked his head. A tiny clump of hair came out in her fingers. It did not matter. Tanaka, who had not believed he would ever feel happy about anything again, was crying with joy.[39]

Each time Takashi Tanemori's father returned from Hiroshima to their shed, his eyes and his cheeks had receded deeper into his skull. Until he unearthed a child's bone, near what he believed to be the foundation of the family home, Daddy had held out some small hope that the rest of his family were only missing, and were still alive out there, somewhere.

"Now I know where your mother is," Daddy announced. "She is not in Hiroshima. And I know that I shall see her soon." He handed his son a pair of scissors and asked, "Can you cut my hair, and make me look handsome for her?"

Takashi Tanemori held the scissors in his left hand, and began combing Daddy's hair with the fingers of his right hand, preparing to make the first cut. With barely the slightest resistance, the hair uprooted and combed out into his fingers, in great clumps.

The boy cried, "Daddy, I'm sorry. I'm *so* sorry!" He tried to push the hair back onto his father's head, pressing and patting with both hands.

"Son, it's all right," Daddy said. "Your father is very tired now. I need to rest for a few minutes." Takashi helped him to lie down, placed a soft pillow under his head, and stayed very close, listening to his breath catching on every intake, often between long pauses. Time itself seemed to have become elastic to the boy, with days becoming indistinguishable from hours. Daddy was speaking deliriously to someone who was not there in the lamplight, "as if some spirit had arrived with its secret only for him."

"Takashi, come and sit here," he said, with sudden, commanding clarity. "These are my last words for you."

"No. Make this not be."

"I want you to understand with your heart," Daddy said, taking both of the boy's hands forcefully into his own. "You will face many hardships. But to survive, you must believe in yourself and do not ever forget who you are." And the boy wondered, as he looked into Daddy's eyes and felt the vise-grip of his hands, how the fire of life could have suddenly been rekindled in him, with such great force. What had caused this newfound energy? What had empowered him to speak such words from his soul? The words were now far from delirious; they were strong, clear, and deliberate: "Follow the light of your heart, honoring your heart with truth regardless of consequences or outcome. And live for the benefit of others; then all will benefit. This is the simplest way to make the world a safer and peaceful place, so that a war like this will never happen again . . . and . . . that is enough for now."

Takashi Tanemori watched tears come to Daddy's eyes.

"This is my last teaching. I believe you do understand. You are heir to the Tanemori name."

"I understand," the boy answered, and his father fell into a deep slumber, into a seemingly painless dream-state from which he would only momentarily return. Outside their hay-filled shelter, the stars themselves were being obscured by the smoke that hovered over the burning bodies of others who had traveled into the heart of Hiroshima during the first days after the bomb.

The second-grader told his father to sleep and regain his strength, but he understood that sooner or later he was bound to face the hardships of the atomic orphans. "Even in this tiny, outlying village beyond Hiroshima," he would record, "the Death Angels were busy visiting many families."[40]

At dawn, Dr. Hachiya awoke to learn that three more of his staff were incapacitated by the new disease. The wife of the late Communications Bureau chief, who had come to the hospital volunteering her services as a nurse, now barely had a pulse. The entire inside of her mouth was a mass of hemorrhaging tissue. Her tongue and tonsils were decaying meat.

In another bed lay Mrs. Hamada. She had been exposed in a single-story wooden house about one kilometer from the hypocenter. Within minutes she had begun vomiting and felt unbelievably thirsty, as if suddenly burned deep inside. Yet by the day of the surrender she felt completely recovered and was able to volunteer at the hospital. And now, only a day later, she had awakened to the discovery that a lot of hair was lying on her pillow. As soon as she put a hand to her head, the rest of her hair began falling out in great quantities with no resistance whatsoever. Then she noticed that the skin on her arms had become extraordinarily dry and fragile, overnight. When Dr. Hachiya examined her, he found signs of extensive hemorrhaging under the skin. In a matter of hours, Mrs. Hamada had gone from being completely recovered to "condition critical."

Another patient, Mr. Hirohata, had also been feeling better lately, following some initial post-*pika* discomfort. At a radius of just under 400 meters (1,312 feet) he was much nearer the hypocenter than Mrs. Hamada, but he explained to Dr. Hachiya that he was located in one of the thicker, concrete reinforced portions of the Telephone Bureau Building when the flash came, and thus did he manage to walk away when everyone else was instantly blown apart or carbonized.

"Doctor?" Mr. Hirohata asked. "Is there any reason why my hair should be falling out and why I should feel so weak?"

"I don't believe you need to worry," Hachiya said. "You have been through unprecedented stress—and, on top of that, you have tried to work night and day here, keeping the rest of us alive."

A gentle rain began to fall, and Hachiya knew that soon the ceilings would be dripping and every bed would be damp tonight.

"Stop worrying so much," Hachiya emphasized for his patient.

Mr. Hirohata decided to follow the doctor's orders—to stay absolutely quiet in bed and to drink all of the nourishing fluids that the nurses gave him. He smiled, confident that his health would return; and he, along with Mrs. Hamada and the bureau chief's wife—would be dead by the time the first microscope arrived.

About August 20, Hachiya's team confirmed that radiation, and not a biological weapon or some unknown gas, had been the cause of Disease X. Days later than had (grudgingly) been promised by the navy, Hachiya's much-desired microscope was delivered. Many in the hospital were found to have white blood cell counts of about 2,000—far below the normal range of 6,000 to 8,000. Only Dr. Hachiya's range seemed to be hovering above 3,000. Some patients had counts of only 500; and one, with a count of 200, appeared to be dying from a full-body onslaught of the bacteria that normally broke decaying matter into soil and fertilizer.

Hachiya quickly realized that the isolation pavilion had been folly. Though strange new infections were appearing—including putrefaction while still alive—the diseases came from within, not without. According to a memo dispatched from the Omura Naval Hospital, autopsies began to reveal bone marrow so thoroughly irradiated that occasionally it had been reduced to a yellow, bile-like fluid. With immune systems rendered essentially nonexistent, bacteria that did not normally attack human flesh until after death started to take root. In many cases, bone marrow death manifested as a hemorrhagic fever that spread to all the internal organs; and in such cases the blood did not coagulate even several hours after death. The blood platelets, along with their clotting agents, were simply gone.

Other patients fell prey to signs and symptoms never seen before. Two men examined at Omura died from something that liquefied their brains and spinal cords. An infectious amoeba appeared to have been involved, a species that usually restricted itself to causing amoeboid dysentery, and against which human immune systems had long ago developed natural defenses. Yet when bone marrow ran liquid, those same organisms were able to drill through the blood-brain barrier and infiltrate the entire nervous system, where they became fruitful and multiplied. The simultaneous occurrence of so many opportunistic infections was so rare an event that it would not be seen again until the AIDS outbreak of the 1980s.

At the Omura Naval Hospital, Dr. Hachiya's colleague Shiotsuki had been examining patients from Nagasaki and Urakami since the night of August 9. The first of them were sent by train to his 800-bed facility, located 19 kilometers from the Urakami hypocenter. Even at this distance, all the windows on the side of the naval hospital opposite the direction of the blast were broken. Just as the suction effect at Clarence Graham's prison camp was more powerful than the initial blast, the rush of air backward toward Nagasaki became the part of the explosion that, in a manner opposite of what would be expected, broke windows on what appeared to be the "wrong" side of the building. Everything about the new weapon seemed to render it the most inexplicable thing the heavens had allowed human beings to create—or allowed the devil to create. All the trees on the mountainsides facing the *pika* had been so desiccated by the heat ray that their leaves were now brown, as if touched by an early autumn. Dr. Shiotsuki reported that the browning effect on the leaves extended 80 kilometers (almost 50 miles) in every direction from Urakami Stadium. Had all the leaves been dry to begin with, the resulting firestorm would have reached typhoon dimensions, at a diameter of 160 kilometers. Near St. Francis Hospital, if the eye wall became truly cyclonic and self-sustaining, the horizontal flames could easily have roared supersonic, drawing a long and narrow "hypercane" all the way into and perhaps to the very top of the stratosphere.

By August 20, Dr. Shiotsuki's medical dispatches were becoming filled with peculiar and often perplexing observations. He noticed that patients who were carrying lunch pails or wearing wristwatches and gold wedding bands, or who were in any other way in direct skin contact with metallic objects at Moment Zero, were literally branded where the metal touched skin and were almost certain to show symptoms of radiation sickness. The brandings were consistent with a hazard from the far end of the spectrum, opposite the very short wavelength gamma rays: a flash of microwaves. Metal will intercept microwaves and heat up to skin–searing temperatures. Under the *pika*, parts of Nagasaki appeared to have become an instant microwave oven. Dr. Shiotsuki also noted that although patients wearing white clothing often escaped *pika* burns, and one patient wearing a black-and-white striped shirt had actually received "burn tattoos" patterned in vertical stripes, these phenomena seemed to apply only at a radius of about two kilometers or more. Nearer the hypocenter and the stadium, wearing white or black became a moot point, for anyone caught outdoors and unshielded.

By now, at Omura, many of the young women who had volunteered to come with the train from Nagasaki to nurse the injured were beginning to show the first signs of disease. As had occurred at St. Francis and in the Communications Hospital, overwhelmed by sudden fatigue, fever, and chills, they collapsed and became patients in the very same wards they had tended as nurses.

"There was no need to explain to them what was happening," Dr. Shiotsuki would record in 1975, shortly before his death from leukemia at age fifty-eight. "We already had reports of widespread sickness in Hiroshima. We knew what was to come."

They died. Every one of them.

"Dressed in baggy mompe trousers and overalls made out of shabby material," Shiotsuki said in a belated epitaph, "the volunteer girls were far removed from beauty in any ordinary sense of the word. And yet to my mind they were incomparably more beautiful physically and spiritually than the girls who strut down the street today in blue jeans and fashionable dresses. They were the girls who, as soon as they realized they were going to die, left their beds and used their remaining strength to nurse others. I wish that just once I could have seen those girls dressed up in today's elegant high fashions; but they were given a sentence of death with the end of the war just moments away, never to know that such prosperity would ever come to Japan."

Dr. Shiotsuki's own battle against atomic bomb disease began about the time Dr. Hachiya lifted the isolation protocol at the Communications Hospital, fourteen days after the Hiroshima explosion, eleven days after Nagasaki, and about five days after Keiji Nakazawa and his mother invited Tanaka to live in their shack. Shiotsuki's white blood cell count had diminished dangerously, by about half its normal value—despite his apparently safe location, nineteen kilometers from the hypocenter. The only explanation was high-level exposure to radioactivity from an oily mist that had fallen, and from the patients themselves, whose clothing and skin and even their breath must have been emitting particles of freshly irradiated dust when they arrived on the night of August 9. During the first forty-eight hours, the radioactivity they were shedding had doubtless invaded Dr. Shiotsuki's lungs, blood, and bone marrow.

As the days passed, Shiotsuki's white blood cell count climbed back again toward normal, then continued to climb upward. Two weeks after the train arrived from Nagasaki, Shiotsuki's concern was not about too few white cells, but about far too many of them. This was the beginning of his progression toward chronic bone marrow disease. The date was August 24.

That evening, in Tokyo, General Shizuichi Tanaka surveyed the American fleet in the harbor. The general had received reports of British planes flying over Hiroshima and Nagasaki, as if on a gruesome sightseeing tour. The surrender was scheduled to be officially signed on September 2. General Tanaka, who on August 14 had withdrawn his support for the rebellion that would have prevented the Emperor's broadcast, did not wish to see this play's final act. After drinking tea with his aide, the general laid his sword down beside his cap, gloves, and six pre-addressed letters. Then, wrapping a cloth around the top of his head to reduce blood spatter, and aligning his chair in a direction that would prevent exit wound matter from smearing the six envelopes, he shot himself.[41]

Despite War Minister Korechika Anami's and General Shizuichi Tanaka's passing, government bureaucratic snafus continued to function as usual. On August 25, a truck bearing gifts from the Imperial Army's Engineering Corps arrived at Hiroshima's Communications Hospital. The soldiers delivered four broken chairs, three battered desks, two cooking pots, one potbelly stove, but no food or coal. A second truck had brought five large crates, each stuffed almost to overflowing with runway signal flags and life preservers. Dr. Hachiya's patients distributed the life preservers among themselves for use as pillows, while the children seemed to enjoy waving the flags.

Mr. Sasaki, being well connected, was able to obtain high-quality food without anyone asking too many questions. He made repeated trips downriver to help his neighbor, Hachiya, and anyone the doctor happened to be helping. On at least one occasion, he brought fish and cartons of cigarettes—the latter now being worth more than money. Indeed, cigarettes had quickly taken over as the new medium of currency. Dr. Hachiya cherished the flavor of tobacco, but he decided to hold on to the currency for as long as possible by taking only a few puffs at a time from a cigarette and then putting it away to smoke just a little more, just a little later.

During one of his cigarette breaks, Hachiya stepped outside for a breath of fresh air and encountered the first dog he had seen in nearly twenty days. Immediately nicknamed Woebegone, Hachiya noticed that the poor mongrel was carrying a bit of rotting potato in its mouth. *What a pitiful sight*, he thought, *to see a dog, by nature a meat eater, reduced to scavenging vegetable scraps.*

Most of the animal's hair was gone, so Hachiya made a diagnosis that Woebegone was suffering from radiation injury.

Somehow, this emaciated figure, trudging along with his hips bent, tail down, and hair gone, seemed symbolic.

"Let loose the dogs of war indeed!" the doctor said, startling the animal.

Above and behind him, someone shouted with excitement at the sighting of yellow electrical wires being strung in a direction generally headed toward the hospital. An army engineer arrived and announced that in a few days, Hachiya would have a telephone, and a few days after that, an electric light.

As evening approached, rainwater glistened on the walls for the third day in a row. Throughout the building and in the former isolation pavilion, clothing and bedding were sprouting black mold. And so, inevitably, pneumonia began making its opportunistic rounds from one radiation-weakened immune system to another. By the morning of August 26, four more patients lay dead.[42]

"When we reached Fukuya's, we stopped," wrote Dr. Hachiya. During one of his excursions into the depths of Ground Zero with Dr. Hinoi, it became impossible for Hachiya to believe that the skeleton-strewn department store had been converted into a functioning field hospital: "One peek into the basement was enough. It was so dark and forbidding that we changed our minds about going in."

Despite the hardships endured in the ruins of the Communications Hospital, Hachiya assured his patients that they inhabited the most functional medical facility in Hiroshima. His brief glimpse and smell of the Fukuya Department Store-turned-army-field-hospital had taught him everything he needed to know about the overall state of the rescue operation elsewhere in the city. When he ran into the widow of a friend during one of his searches for supplies, Hachiya noticed that poor Mrs. Yanagihari had become as thin as a stork.

"Where are you staying?" Dr. Hachiya had asked.

With misery in her eyes and her voice, she replied, "At Fukuya."

Fumbling for words of comfort, he said, "Well, at least I'm glad to see you weren't hurt badly."

"Yes," she said, and sobbed, "but I'm still at Fukuya."

The eight-story department store (one of Hiroshima's tallest and newest steel-and-concrete structures) stood barely more than seven city blocks from the hypocenter. The building was even more of a burned shell than the Communications Hospital; but it seemed a marvel that it had stood at all, with two people actually shadow-shielded and safely shock-cocooned inside.

Yasunori Funasaka and a friend, Hachisuka, were assigned to the Munitions Command Office, located on the second floor, on a side of the department store opposite the hypocenter, when the bomb ignited. Both men appeared to have been working in just the right spot, opposite the prevailing angle of the rays through the northwest side of the building, with the intervening six floors of concrete and steel not only shadow-shielding them from the heat ray, but also significantly attenuating a combined dose of gamma rays and neutron spray that even without the added danger of microwaves was almost twice the lethal limit. Relative to Dr. Hachiya's house, the store was so close to the detonation point that the flash and the blast seemed to have converged on Yasunori at the same instant, and he felt as if a massive force had suddenly lashed out at his body from all directions, flinging him to the floor before he could even begin to duck.

He thought about the two massive fire-bombings he had survived in Tokyo. He thought about his mother's concerns that Hiroshima would be the next city bombed and about her warning that his sudden transfer there was dangerous. "An air raid won't kill me," he had tried to joke, "so don't worry." He thought about the leaflets dropped by a lone airplane on August 5: "We deliver a personal message from President Truman of the United States. . . . At midnight tonight we will attack Hiroshima City with . . . a new fire-bomb model. Citizens, leave the city at once." At 8:15 a.m., during a split second crowded with thoughts, Yasunori realized that the promised time of the attack was a lie, while during that same split second, a vacuum-like backblast pulled up part of the floor and caved in the ceiling and instantly killed a young woman who had been standing next to him at Moment Zero.

When he stood, Yasunori realized how silly he and his neighbors had been, crowding into a backyard shelter during midnight air raid warnings. *Who could have seriously believed that the Americans would have announced a midnight raid, and then put their planes in danger by flying into a picket of flak-gunners already prepared for the appointed hour?*

Yasunori, an aviator transferred to a desk job because the empire was running out of planes, found his friend Hachisuka alive and apparently well, but with one ear badly torn and his shirt spattered with blood. The few other people who appeared to be alive remained "stupefied" in their seats. Their legs seemed simply to have failed them. In the Fukuya Building, the dividing line between shielding by several floors of overlying steel and concrete and being targeted with the majority of the gamma rays angling directly into a room was often a matter of only a few paces. Almost everyone located more than five steps northwest of Yasunori's position, or seated on the floors above, was exposed to nearly 1,300r of nerve-stopping gamma-shine and neutron spray. They moved, for a while—the scores or hundreds of them throughout the building—but their DNA was scrambled eggs, protein synthesis had abruptly ceased, and they were already dead, though some of them seemed to keep moving by sheer force of will, with what little energy still remained in their nerves and muscles until the wholesale die-off of cells unfailingly stopped their hearts.

Looking out through a wall that had fallen away, the two friends tried to comprehend the incomparable: "Heaven and Earth and the entire surface of the water had become a sea of fire." They witnessed people fleeing to one of the bridges nearby and being overtaken by a tornado of fire that piled their bodies together like packs of roasted sardines.

"If we don't get out soon, the fire is going to spread here!" Yasunori yelled, and his friend agreed. As they bolted down the stairs and toward the streets, Yasunori became aware that the staircase of an eight-story building in the path of fiery whirlwinds should have been crowded with evacuees; but it was not. They fled the fires, like thousands of others throughout the city, into the illusory safety of the nearest river. Unlike most of those thousands, the two friends had sustained no burns and no broken bones. The developing rapids—strengthened each passing second by the torrents of rain and black ice falling upstream—almost drowned them, yet at the same time carried them southward to a point at which, when they emerged exhausted on the opposite shore, they were placed far from the worst of the fires and the radioactive rain.

A day later, Yasunori Funasaka returned to the ruins of the Fukuya Department Store. One perplexing sight he encountered as he walked toward the hypocenter was the discovery of fish swimming in the river with their backs flash-burned white. Then, "by coincidence or perhaps by divine will," Yasunori would write later, "[I] happened to come across the parents of the female co-worker who, as I had seen, met an instantaneous death after being exposed to the A-bomb the previous day. The parents had come out looking for their daughter. Although I had not met them before, I was asked if I knew anything about her."

Momentarily bewildered by either coincidence disguised as fate—or by something more the other way around—he realized that he was the only person who saw what happened to her, and he led the parents to the building. The fire worms had, as Yasunori had feared, stormed through the department store, turning the girl into a skeleton. The parents recognized a delicate metal band around their daughter's wrist bones.

"Her work site was right here in the downtown area," her father said, "so I had readied myself to face up to her not making it through." He seemed grateful to know from Yasunori that death had come to her instantly and painlessly.

Near the piece of land on which Keiji Nakazawa decided to build a new home for his mother, Yasunori had found his boarding house reduced to a low mound of gray ash. There were fragments of human bone in the ash, and the bones of a cat. He concluded that the lodging and its inhabitants must have spontaneously combusted and then—pressed into the ground with tremendous force—turned into ash in a very short period of time.

And strangest of all, amid such total and seemingly instantaneous destruction, he found the contents of the backyard air raid shelter where he had spent the last midnight before the bomb, with all of its canned food and survival gear perfectly cocooned from both the fire and the blast—as if, after a moment of initial disintegration at up to forty times the boiling point of water, flames erupting near the hypocenter had been snuffed out. Yasunori found his officer's-wicker-trunk with family photographs and his winter coat inside, completely unscathed. Sixty-five years later, the trunk and its contents, still impregnated with a few atoms of half-lifing isotopes, would remain in the outdoor storage shed of his next home.

As the young officer carried the trunk away from Ground Zero, the first suburban medical teams arrived behind him, and attempted to convert the skeleton-filled Fukuya Department Store into a field hospital.

Seven-year-old Yoshiko Hidaka was among the first to arrive at the new rescue station. The child had been completely shadow-shielded on a neighbor's porch from everything except a gale of flying glass. She recorded: "A lot of people were waiting in front of the hospital, but my mother stubbornly insisted that [my] eye injury demanded immediate attention. So, I got to see a doctor right away. It took eleven stitches to sew up the cuts left by the glass shards embedded around my right eye. I did not lose my sight because the cut just missed my eye by one millimeter (by just the diameter of a pencil point's graphite base). Since my father was away fighting the war, it was the sheer vitality of my mother that saved us." But Mother soon sickened, while searching the fringes of Ground Zero for food. Stricken by "gastroenteritis" and "dysentery," and by the usual constellation of radiation poisoning's symptoms, she entered the Fukuya hospital. Like Dr. Hachiya, she was further sickened, emotionally, by the conditions she found inside—which compelled her retreat to the fresh air of the department store's roof where, on the day American ships arrived in Tokyo Harbor, she was surviving on tea and pickled plums.[43]

Emiko Nakasako and her mother had been blasted through a wall and outside of their house, nearly twenty-five city blocks east of the hypocenter. The ten-year-old still could not figure out how the same blast that crushed the house like a ripened plum had stripped off her clothes as it squirted her outdoors with no injuries at all. In the back yard, Emiko's two brothers were shaded from the flash by rows of fruit trees reduced suddenly to sticks. Each was burned where the flash came down through spaces between the leaves, before the leaves themselves roasted and curled up under the rays, then flew apart during the blast.

Nakasako would never have believed it possible that a thin umbrella of leaves could be all that was necessary to protect one from the heat ray, until she wandered onto the military training ground next door and discovered horses and soldiers flash-broiled where they had stood. The flesh on their skulls had rippled and flowed like a liquid.

Emiko Nakasako's sister Mieko had been nearer the hypocenter. She was one of the children on the other side of Keiji Nakazawa's protective wall. By the time Yasunori Funasaka led a co-worker's parents to a skeleton in the Fukuya Department store, Mrs. Nakasako had begun to develop blisters and infections from her trek through the hot zone in search of Mieko. She found the river near the school stagnating behind dams of bloating corpses, the water rising crimson with blood that still appeared to be fresh.

"Nothing was ever recovered of my sister," Emiko told a scientist, later. "But at night I saw balls of blue flames, moving back and forth over the area. These [apparitions] continued into December—like blue fire, just above the ground. They continued to appear everywhere, during the weeks in which my mother pulled bones from the fields, ground them up, and put the ash on my brother's badly burned arm (where a break in the leaf-shade had left his skin exposed to the flash).

"At the time, I thought the blue lights could be the ghosts of Hiroshima; but Buddhists know that during cremation, sometimes blue flames come out of the bones. They might have been something like that: ball lightning or St. Elmo's fire colored blue, appearing every evening and especially when it rained. They seemed to be more wispy than actually shaped like balls—and in fact it could not be said that they actually had shapes at all, in the way that even a flame has a distinctive shape. They were the only things with color in central Hiroshima. Everything was black or gray, except for the blue lights."[44]

Like Yasunori Funasaka and Kenshi Hirata, young Kenji Kitagawa had found the land in the direction of the hypocenter relatively free of the firestorms that raged everywhere else on August 6. The ten-year-old was indoors, playing an organ on the second floor of a school that flew apart around him, only 1.3 kilometers (or 13 city blocks) from the detonation point. Even deep within the shadows of the building, the blue-white flash was "amazingly strong—you can't understand, unless you were there, how indoors [in the center of the school] the blue light itself was strong enough to burn the skin."

Kitagawa had remained conscious through the flash, through a series of bangs from the compression wave and from the expanding shock bubble's lower hemisphere striking the ground, then through an implosion effect that floated Kitagawa gently into the air as the school was peeled apart around him and simultaneously pounded into the earth. He stood upon a field of debris, wondering what had happened and how he had survived. Twenty days later, he still wondered.

During the first minute after the blast, the wood in the ruins seemed simply to start burning, self-igniting; and from that moment, the guilt about his friends—all trapped or dead beneath the debris—had begun to work at him. Survivor's guilt would continue to be a dark companion, even after he reached the age of seventy-five. There was no hope of saving anyone. The fire worms reared up and multiplied too quickly along the fringes of Ground Zero, chasing Kitagawa toward the ashes of the hypocenter and toward home, and toward his mother.

The deeper he moved toward the hypocenter, the more severely burned the people appeared to be, until at last they seemed "not of this Earth," and until, near Kenshi Hirata's house, the Moramoto shock cocoon, and Yasunori Funasaka's boarding house with its cave of cocooned artifacts, the people had disappeared altogether.

The river, during those first ten or fifteen minutes, was not yet filled with bodies; but instead, in the midst of a fall of ashes next of kin to the ash-fall of floating pumice granules that buried Pompeii, the river was completely covered under a strange carpet of floating dust.

Kitagawa's mother and younger brother had been incinerated at home—instantly, just like Setsuko Hirata. One week later, his father positively identified the foundations of their home. The house itself was a knee-high hill of gray ash, from which Kitagawa's father excavated the carbonized remains of mother and child. Years later, Kitagawa would write, "I vividly remember with grief that their ashes were still too hot to touch."[45]

Twenty days after the bomb, fourteen-year-old Masahiro Kunishige wished his father would listen to his pleas to be left alone and perhaps even be allowed to die, rather than face his excruciating, five times daily treatments for the flash-burns.

Kunishige was exposed on a farm behind the Communications Hospital, where student conscripts had been assigned to grow crops for soldiers at the army training ground nearby. He and his friends had somehow been knocked instantly conscious, before reflexes allowed any of them to turn their eyes toward the flash. Kunishige came back to consciousness amazed to discover that each of the plants was burned on one side; and then, looking around, he saw that all of his friends had also been burned on one side. Their skin had turned gray, like dust.

Waves of very hot air were rushing from flash-roasted ground toward a huge cloud that had risen out of nowhere in the southwest, on a perfectly cloudless day. The head of the monster drifted slowly westward, and as the sun emerged from behind the cloud's eastern edge, Kunishige felt as if his arms, and one side of his face, and his entire back were suddenly afire.

"I hid from the sun," he recorded sixty-five years later. "The sun felt like fire."

The boy realized, then, that like his friends, he had been burned by the flash from the place where the cloud was born, some two kilometers away.

People from nearer the hypocenter came staggering toward the farm. They seemed not to feel the sun. Their flash-burns were worse than dusty gray. Their skin was the color of carbonized wood. Kunishige recognized some of the blackened people as friends from a school in the city only because they identified themselves by calling him and saying their names.

"It's so much cooler here," one of the children said. Kunishige did not know how to reply. He helped a first-grader to a place in the shade, and watched him die.

Another friend, another of the blackened children, had cried out for water, saying, "I'm so thirsty that I can't stand it anymore."

"He was the first one to drink," Kunishige recalled. "The minute he drank, he died. Those of us who were burned only gray—we drank a lot of water. A warning had quickly developed: If flash-burned people drank water, we would die. But we 'grays' survived. After we drank, the gray skin developed blisters; they bulged, and then they burst."

Kunishige's home had survived reasonably intact, behind a hill a mile beyond the farm. His father was trained in military medicine, and by day 20, Kunishige had come to regard the man as more torturer than father. As a treatment, he had started, bit by bit, to remove the flash-burned skin, in much the same manner that the Nagasaki eye doctor had treated Tsutomu Yamaguchi, who was exposed at approximately the same radius as Kunishige.

"Help me! Help me!" the boy had cried out to his mother, as each section of skin was cut and peeled away, revealing the red "whale meat" beneath. His mother pushed him down into the bed and insisted that he learn to endure the pain.

After twenty days, the flesh beneath the skin that had been cut away from Kunishige's face and arms—"It slowly replaced the removed skin," he recalled. "But the pain was severe: Imagine what it would feel like if your skin was the lid of a tin can being opened. That's what I felt. In places, I could see my own bones exposed. Five times each day, the wounds were scraped, cleaned, and dressed with a mixture of talcum powder and cooking oil. Then, on the day my father reached the upper part of my arm, I pleaded with Mother to make him stop there, and let my upper arm heal on its own. I think he saw it: Anymore cutting and I think I would have gone insane. And as it turned out, the place where he stopped never properly healed, and my upper arm developed an ugly scar. Every place where I endured the treatment, often with Mother putting her full weight on me to keep me from moving, healed well. My father knew, physically, exactly how to heal my wounds."

During the many days of cutting, peeling, and scraping, the parent of a friend from the first grade arrived for a visit. She was distraught over her child's failure to return home, and wanted to know if Kunishige had seen him.

Kunishige remembered placing the dying first-grader in the shade, but he denied ever seeing him. He could not bring himself to say, "Your son is dead."

The parents of the missing boy journeyed to the military farm where Kunishige had been working. One by one they examined the decaying bodies of three hundred children from Ground Zero whose faces had been seared black. Eventually, they identified their son by the belt buckle he had been wearing on the morning of August 6.

"So, I had seen the child die, and couldn't tell," Kunishige recorded for history. "Later, the parents figured it out—that I had lied. And I apologized. And my parents apologized. And because of the nature of the little kid, I was crying. Even though the family had a separate religious service, [afterward], every year, I would go to the kid's shrine, an anonymous figure, keeping inside of me a pain from which there was no healing."[46]

The death rate was accelerating in the Urakami hills. Drs. Akizuki and Nagai attended regularly scheduled bonfires of corpses in the hospital complex's yards. Nagai's health appeared to be steadily improving to such an extent that he and three nurses had been making wide-ranging house calls along the valley. But Akizuki's hair was thinning and he was having difficulty keeping food down. He wondered if he, himself, might be found on a pyre in a few more days. Living and dying in Ground Zero, Akizuki realized, was a matter of fate—in which the dividing line between the man being cremated and the doctor cremating him was misty and vague and entirely up to chance.

He was coming to regard radiation sickness as an insidious and omnipotent spirit that plucked out the survivors' hair and sucked out their blood.

From the hospital down to the ruins of the Josei Girls' School and the now-vanished Urakami Stadium, a pattern of death was beginning to emerge. The latest influx of patients had seemed well when they descended into the ruins and started erecting shantytowns. They had invented a new term—"the mines of the city"—which referred to articles of value buried under the piles of debris. The miners living lower down the hill, near the stadium and the hypocenter, were the first to suffer and die during the second, late-August, outbreak of radiation sickness. Dr. Akizuki was able to chart "the shadow of death," as it moved like a slowly rising tide, steadily uphill. Miners homesteading in the valley and the foothills began to be carried up to the hospital on the backs of family members who were dwelling higher along the path. Then a family of miners a hundred meters farther uphill sickened and were carried up; then a family forty meters higher; and so on, and so on.

Dr. Akizuki named the widening advance of the disease his "concentric circles of death." He imagined that it was only a matter of time before the invisible death clouds ascended to St. Francis. The incoming tide was only about fifty meters below the hospital's front yard when the rains came, building slowly from the first of September into a tropical downpour by the second, bringing the sound of rolling thunder above and the roar of newly formed waterfalls below.

By midnight of September 2, the rain descended in such torrents that when Akizuki stepped outside, it drove into his face, blinding him with the sting of rushing water. It soaked him instantly, and tore his shirtsleeves. He held on to a broken concrete pillar to steady himself—while behind, in a shattered building whose ground floor was now a rising creek, the injured and their caregivers gathered in bunches of ten and fifteen, huddling together like small birds in a nest.

"Haven't they suffered enough?" Dr. Akizuki shouted at the sky. Lightning blazed out like scores of flashbulbs . . . or baby *pikas*. It was a new kind of hell: flayed by fire, they were now to be tormented by water.

"Don't punish them this way!" Akizuki cried. "What do you want? Who are you? Haven't you done enough?"

Akizuki was thinking of the Catholic sisters and brothers who had come to help, only to become sick themselves, and now were shivering like half-drowned animals. As a Buddhist, it was difficult for him to believe with the Jesuits or with Dr. Nagai that tragedy and senseless evil were part of a divine plan.

"Why is it that you have to suffer like this?" he had asked Sister Mizoguchi, only a day before she vomited up a long strip of her own flesh and died. "Why this, for someone like you, who has done nothing but good? It isn't right!"

"I believe in providence," she had replied weakly—and then said, with a smile: "It's the will of God."

"Then God damn your providence!" the doctor now cried out to the storm, and against the universe itself.

He stayed up through the night, trying to calm the patients and cursing the storm. And in the morning, a double rainbow appeared in the sky. The higher of the two was of a brightness rarely seen in Nagasaki; and the lower apparition was of a kind never seen. It lay within a deep layer of mist, an unusual pearly color but clearly bow-shaped—a *white* rainbow.

"Something's happened," Akizuki said to a nurse named Murai. "I feel there's a change in the air—I'm sure of it." He took a deep breath and for the first time in nearly a month Akizuki felt refreshed. The constant feeling of weakness and nausea had begun to disappear in spite of a stressful night without sleep. *The world has changed*, he thought.

Though Akizuki did not have access to a Geiger counter, he was certain that if he checked he would find something different about the ground as well as the air. The rain had washed the lingering, dusty fallout deep into the ground or out to sea. The very deluge he had cursed through the night was now proving to be a merciful act of . . . *Providence*, Dr. Akizuki half believed.

From that very morning, it seemed, goose grass had begun sprouting in the wasteland. A similar storm struck Hiroshima, followed by the same multiple rainbow phenomenon, followed by wildflowers blooming out of season—so many that it appeared to some witnesses that two thousand B-29s had flown over the city dropping flower seeds instead of bombs.

Shinoe Shoda, the poet who had asked the doctors if an operation existed that could remove memories, seemed to have recovered her full strength after the rains. When she located the ruins of a school, she found evening primroses growing out of every cracked brick and every fissure in the concrete. Wild blue chrysanthemums were everywhere else. In the playground, flower stalks had erupted between ribs and through the eyeless sockets of skulls—dozens and scores and hundreds of skulls. The majority of them were little; and Shoda guessed that all of the larger bones must have belonged to the teachers.[47]

In the Hiroshima suburb of Kaitaichi, Hiroko Nakamoto, the schoolgirl who had tried in vain to keep her two pet mice alive during a period of intense rationing, was recovering from her *pika* wounds. Even the burns and a continuing scarcity of food seemed trivial, however, compared to news that an American army occupation force was advancing toward the village. Prior to the destruction of Hiroshima, all students had been shown films of what they could expect from the Americans if Japan lost the war. In the best of scenarios, they would become a caste of slave workers. Worse scenarios had caused Kaitaichi's officials to advise all women and girls to literally run for the hills and hide; but Hiroko was still held immobile by her injuries, and her aunt would not leave her.

When at last the enemy's gum-chewing soldiers arrived, they turned out to be astonishingly polite. They brought with them candies bearing strange names—*Life Savers* and *Milky Ways*.

Hiroko realized, now, that the terrifying forecasts of slavery and torture, rape and even cannibalism had been pure military propaganda, designed to enforce a nationwide fight to the death.[48]

As the two cities began to sprout grasses and wildflowers, an American navy surgeon and a Chinese interpreter arrived at St. Francis. Dr. Akizuki emerged from the far side of a brick pile and startled them.

The interpreter reached for his pistol but quickly relaxed, once he looked the doctor up and down and summed him up as looking no more dangerous than "the mayor of Hobo Village."

By contrast to Akizuki, who except for the storm had lived unshowered for nearly a month, the American's clothes were starched and clean, and he appeared to resemble a much taller version of the young and dashing romantic comedy star Vincent Price. Akizuki had been expecting Boris Karloff or Bela Lugosi.

The navy surgeon seemed appalled at the primitive conditions that prevailed on the hillside. He pointed across the hypocenter toward first-aid tents that were being erected five kilometers away, in north central Nagasaki. "You should take your people there," he advised.

Considering the conditions of his patients, it seemed to Akizuki that three miles—which was a little more than the distance across Manhattan Island—might just as well be a march to Tokyo.

"If you would be so kind as to provide us with adequate medicines," Akizuki pleaded, "my colleagues and I would like to stay here and continue with our treatment of these people."

The American looked around the burned-out ruin and sighed, then began to examine the patients. At first, they cringed, but when reassured by Akizuki that he would do them no harm, they began to relax. The newcomer quickly discovered a type of bomb injury that had not been apparent before.

"Most of them have had the optic nerves of their retinas damaged by the A-bomb's flash," the American said. "Their corneas have also been damaged, and they're infected." Even those who did not gaze into the *pika* and were not burned by the light—and who were touched by it only indirectly, were losing their eyesight. The American pressed again, "You should send them to the first-aid station in the city-center."

The patients weren't healthy enough to make the journey even if they weren't going blind, Akizuki explained.

"Well," the Vincent Price look-alike said, "the roads are all out and we have no large trucks to spare for an evacuation. But we do have penicillin and other vital supplies at the station. You should go there tomorrow and see what you can acquire."

All things considered, Akizuki was both surprised and impressed by the man who had climbed through the rubble and up the hill to examine the injured. He was much relieved that High Command's warnings about a world of rape and doom awaiting a defeated Japan seemed not to be materializing.

This was not to say, however, that everything was suddenly golden splendor. The pharmacist at the first-aid station looked at Dr. Akizuki's clothes and almost dismissed him outright as a vagrant in search of black-market drugs. When the doctor explained that an American navy officer had advised him to obtain antibiotics for the Urakami hospital, the pharmacist said, "Send your patients here."

After further explanation of the conditions at St. Francis, the pharmacist released a small amount of medicine, along with vitamin B and strong doses of vitamin C, in accordance with a radiation treatment protocol proposed by Dr. Nagai that—until such supplies had begun running out at the hospital— appeared to have brought some improvement to borderline cases, including Nagai and Akizuki themselves. The penicillin, however, was withheld, and the release of each subsequent package of vitamins seemed to require two or three treks across the hypocenter.

As Dr. Akizuki recorded it, "After the American officer's visit, our wrecked hospital, standing on the fringe of the devastated area, slipped from the minds of those who came to investigate the damage done by the atomic bomb. It went unprovided with the new drugs and the help that they could bring. Those who came to see what had become of Nagasaki after the A-bomb explosion visited the intact buildings of Nagasaki proper and stopped near the vanished stadium, and they never found out what was happening to people on the hill that overlooked the hypocenter."[49]

And so it came to pass that the most visible of the city's radiation cases became all but invisible. A committee of American and British scientific investigators met in Japan on September 11, and immediately proposed a detailed zoological survey, meter-square by meter-square, of excavation points at various distances from the hypocenter, to determine whether radiation effects produced harmful mutations in multiple generations of insects. Officially, the September 11 committee was under General MacArthur's jurisdiction, and he did not want much about the atomic bombings to become known. The zoological survey was cut short almost as soon as it began. Instead, earthworms were sampled from the ground beneath Urakami's St. Maria Cathedral and the demolished hospitals nearby. Radiation effects were determined by amputating the tenth segments from the caudal ends of several Ground Zero worms and observing the regeneration of their heads. The regeneration process appeared to occur without evident abnormalities—which absence of evidence was interpreted as evidence of absence, in terms of lingering radiation effects in human populations exposed to the bomb. A proposal from committee scientists to extend the worm study to an examination of actual human subjects being treated nearby, in Dr. Akizuki's hospital, languished indefinitely in MacArthur-esque limbo.[50]

About this time, Charles Sweeney returned to the city and led his team members to the place where a tennis court had stood, in what he calculated to be the location of the exact hypocenter. Very few people were on the prairie and in the foothills. Looking straight up into the blue sky, where at 1,890 feet the plutonium fist struck forth, Sweeney tried to form an image of what it must have been like to be standing on this spot at that moment. And he offered to his friends a simple prayer—"that ours shall be the last such mission ever flown."

As he looked outward from the hypocenter, Sweeney's gaze paused for a moment at a distant hillside, on which stood the scorched, red-brick walls of St. Francis Hospital.

Another who visited the site was Father George Zabelka, Tinian's Catholic priest. Charles Sweeney had sought out the advice of a priest on the evening he learned that he would have to fly a second atomic mission. That night, he needed to understand his church's position on the war, and to receive some religion-based confirmation that, under certain circumstances, missions such as this were righteous, or at least justified.

Sweeney had asked, "Is it a sin to wage war, Father?"

The priest said that he could not help but to have been thinking about this question at considerable length, lately—"For here I am, a cleric, in uniform, in a war."

"But you're not a combatant," Sweeney pointed out. "You simply attend to the spiritual needs of those called to fight."

"That is true. But I bless the men and their airplanes [as the crews] fly off to kill and be killed. I condone their actions by my blessings. So it's not that simple. Fortunately, our faith recognizes that man is a thinking being endowed with intellect. God wants us to think, to reason about the consequences of our actions and our inactions."

The priest spoke mostly as he was instructed to speak, and he helped the young officer to remove from his mind any doubts about his mission.

"Are these weapons of mass destruction justified?" Sweeney asked.

"War as we know it today *is* mass destruction," the priest replied. "The weapons may become more fearsome, but the moral issues are the same. Will greater weapons bring a quicker end to the war? I don't know. But you must be certain of your cause and your intentions, because the nature of modern weapons makes the stakes much higher."

He blessed Charles Sweeney; and Sweeney had prayed that he would be able to target the military complex at Kokura, and leave the civilian populations of Urakami and Nagasaki untouched. Sweeney's prayer went ungranted, and Paul Tibbets was all but calling for his court marshal for risking the bomb's loss during three attempts on Kokura, through heavy flak, until finally fighter planes were coming up at him. Tibbets had branded Sweeney a failure.

"*Some failure*," Sweeney said, and looked around.

"Father George" climbed the hill toward the seemingly abandoned Urakami medical complex, but he never ascended any higher than the ruins of the cathedral. There, the head had been torn from the statue of Maria and lay among the bricks, burned in such a manner that the melt-and-singe marks under her hollowed-out eyes made it appear that she was something skeletal, weeping. The priest excavated the cathedral's censer with his bare hands, astonished to discover that the delicate frankincense container had survived.

"I blessed the crew and the plane," he cried to a friend, decades later. "[They went] with my blessing—with the blessing of Jesus Christ and the church. I did that. The pilot of the plane was a Catholic. And we [almost instantly] obliterated the lives of forty thousand fellow Catholics, seventy-three thousand people in all."

"George, you didn't drop the bomb," his friend said. "You were there to minister to the needs of these young men."

"No, it's not that easy. I was part of it. My role was to condone it in the name of Christ."

"But," the friend said hesitantly, "did you even know what that bomb was?"

"On August 6," he explained—"No, we didn't. All we knew was that it was *special*. We said it was *tricked-up*."

"Then, you didn't know. You're not responsible."

"You can say I didn't know anything before Hiroshima about what that bomb would do. But what about three days later? I knew, then. I knew what would happen to the next city—which turned out to be Nagasaki. And yet I blessed the bomb. I blessed the crew. I blessed the instantaneous slaughter of seventy-three thousand people. God have mercy on me."[51]

By the time Shinoe Shoda found the teachers and Father George Zabelka found Urakami Cathedral's censer, Mrs. Matsuda had discovered the foundations of her home. It lay within several blocks of the Morimotos' Hiroshima mansion, and almost within sniper's range of the Fukuya Department Store. Her boy Toshihiko had come wandering out of the region with a leafy pattern of black burns along one side of his body. The boy was located at a range in which the white shirt he was wearing became barely more relevant (in terms of protection from flash burns) than the garden walls that shielded him from the blast. The white cotton had browned instantly, and Toshihiko's shadow—along with the shadows of vanished pumpkin vines and rows of hanging bean plants—left their ghostly imprints on the wall. The boy appeared to be reaching down for something when the flash came.

Historians would wrongly presume that all of the Hiroshima and Nagasaki shadow people were vaporized by the *pika* and met instant, painless death. This was rarely the case. In both cities, shadows were imprinted out to a radius of at least 2 kilometers, and in Hiroshima, under the weaker of the two bombs, only those people located outdoors in the vicinity of the Dome and the "T" Bridge, and whose entire bodies were exposed in direct line-of-sight to the bomb's rays, experienced split-second vaporization down to the bone. Farther out from the hypocenter, people were seared. The same *pika* that flash-broiled human skin also charred paint and wood. Against overwhelming odds, during the first night of the bomb, young Toshihiko was able to walk away from Ground Zero toward the wrecked school where Minami saw the blue fireflies. She and the rest of Dr. Fujii's rescue team had come to the conclusion that since the boy's face and more than 70 percent of his body had been shadowed from the flash by a hat and by the distinctive leaf patterns that left most of his skin completely unharmed, he might survive—and that was the hell of it. Toshihiko Matsuda should have survived, but upon him had fallen the gamma rays—upon him and through him. His bones soaked up gamma radiation and neutrons, and the DNA within his marrow writhed and snapped so violently that the body's ever-vigilant DNA repair systems would have been unable to cope with the scale of the damage even if the repair systems were not themselves damaged. After the first three seconds, his immune system had essentially ceased to be.

Though Toshihiko's aunts and anyone else who had been inside the house were killed when the blast crushed the two-story building to the height of a man's chest, Toshihiko appeared to Dr. Fujii to be another of Hiroshima's "miracle boys," having narrowly escaped while everyone around him died. But the rays had done their work, and the miracle boy had only a little while left to live.

Triaged as likely to survive with medical attention, he and several others among the moderately injured were sent with Minami and four nurses on the back of a flatbed truck to the veterans' hospital in the suburbs.

The discovery that Toshihiko's mother—who had been conscripted to do military work outside the city—also survived, brought new life to his eyes, but after a week his wounds refused to heal, and without any warning at all, he fell into a deep slumber and died.

Now his mother returned to the place where the horror began. Here, the circularity of the "total destruction zone" could be seen clearly. Except for the Dome, the frames of the Geibi Bank and the occasional telephone building or a department store skeleton sticking out of the earth, the landscape swept away flat in every direction to a ring of concrete ruins, approximately equidistant from Mrs. Matsuda's home. The grayish-brown debris field was interrupted by newly emerged sprawls of goose grass and wildflowers.

In the vanished and now reawakening garden, the rain-washed image of 8:15 a.m., August 6, was still telling its story. Like Nakazawa glancing down at something near a schoolyard wall at Moment Zero, Mrs. Matsuda's son appeared to have had his attention drawn suddenly to the ground. He was kneeling and handling something when the *pika* blazed forth. The part of him caught in the flash and projected onto a garden wall said so. Only the lower half of the wall still remained to tell the tale, but it was enough. Leaves and vines all but surrounded him, as he bent down to lay a hand upon a pumpkin or to pull out a weed. When the bomb flashed above Toshihiko, the leaves on the vines must surely have been shifting in the morning breeze—but the points of each of them were so sharply defined that the image had, without a doubt, been created faster than a leaf could respond to wind.

Throughout both Hiroshima and Urakami, for miles around, asphalt and paint bleached under the light; wood charred—and, on every wall still standing, shadowed window frames, telephone poles, trees, clotheslines, and even people indicated the directions of the flashes and pointed unerringly toward each city's hypocenter.

The phenomenon was exactly analogous to what happens when a wristwatch protects a tiny patch of skin from sunburn and leaves behind a shadow image of the watch and its band. The difference was a matter of degree. The Hiroshima and Nagasaki shadows were formed much more quickly, and with greater ferocity.

Though more than 70 percent of Toshihiko's body had been shielded from the flash—and mercifully, his face was kept in shadow by his hat—in the end it made no difference. Near the Geibi and Sumitomo Banks and the outer fringe of the hypocenter, the gamma rays had recolored fragments of clear glass in beautiful hues of violet. Certain diamonds, were they present, would have turned blue, green, or red.

Toshihiko Matsuda, "the marble boy of Hiroshima," was located barely more than 600 meters (about 7 city blocks) from the hypocenter, when exposed to the nuclear flash. [Illustration: CRP]

Digging below the strewn-field of roof tiles and the ashes of her home, Toshihiko's mother came across six misshapen beads of glass—her son's toy marbles. Either the *pika*, or the fire worms that came afterward, or some combination of both, had melted them into greenish, semi-transparent blobs.

Sixty-three years later, Nenkai Aoyama would feel the weight of time and improbability in the heft of two melted marbles that once belonged to "a kid down the block." Nenkai's home had been even nearer to the hypocenter than Toshihiko's. At age seventeen, Nenkai was a conscript assigned to a construction project, almost two kilometers downriver from home. It was important work, he was told—"in preparation for the final defense of Japan."

At 7:00 a.m. on August 6, he had not quite finished breakfast when his mother told him that he must hurry, even though he could easily cover the distance between home and his work detail with time to spare.

"Go, hurry!" his mother said, all but pushing him out the door.

"Bye," he said, perplexed.

This was the last conversation Nenkai had with his mother. His house was part of a Buddhist temple, located immediately next door to the Hiroshima Dome. The hemisphere of compressed air that shot down the sides of the Dome's tower appeared to have struck the stone and wood temple from above and from the sides. After the fires had died away and Nenkai returned to the hypocenter as its nearest surviving resident, he was unable to find even a trace of his home's foundations. Everything was gone. He could not imagine how to begin looking for his mother.

Across the river, under the very spot over which Hiroshima's Memorial Museum would one day stand, Mrs. Shigeko Orimen was luckier than Nenkai, after a fashion. Returning from the countryside to a hypocenter radius of five city blocks, she found her son Shigeru.

She was all alone now. One son had been taken into the navy from junior high school, and her husband was drafted into the army at age fifty. On the day of the *pika-don*, thirteen-year-old Shigeru was all Mrs. Orimen had left.

In Hiroshima—as throughout the rest of Japan—junior high school wasn't exactly school anymore, and in preparation for the final battle, the spring semester was extended through July and August. After the fire-bombings of Kobe, Osaka, and Tokyo, the army had confiscated homes along rows of whole city blocks throughout Hiroshima, and had conscripted junior high school students to assist in knocking down houses along makeshift firebreaks and hauling away the wood for military recycling.

On the last morning she saw him, Shigeru's mother had prepared for him a lunch of soy paste and barley, mixed with two spoonfuls of rice, sealed in a little tin lunch box with his name inscribed.

"Shigeru, if the fire-bombers come," she said, giving a last bit of motherly advice, "crouch down on the ground as fast as you can."

"Got it," he had replied, and then rode happily away on his bicycle.

At the place where he died, just a short walk across one of the wrecked bridges on either side of the Dome, and downriver along the shore road, the bones of Shigeru and his classmates lay where they fell—or, more precisely, where their little bodies had been pressed into the ground.

Shigeru's lunch box, with his name still etched upon it, was blackened and crushed flat. One corner jutted out through a broken cage of ribs . . . tiny ribs. His mother pried open the cover and found the food inside converted to black carbon, like her son's flesh. Yet, like every fossil, the carbonized meal told a story.

"Oh, Shigeru," his mother cried out to history. "You died before you could even eat your lunch."[52]

Damage by Thermal Rays

Degree of Damage	Distance from Hypocenter (km)		Thermal Energy (cal/cm2)
	Hiroshima	Nagasaki	
Almost everything catches fire; fatal burns	1.3	1.6	15.0
Conflagration occurs; third-degree burns	2.0	2.5	7.3
Fires occur; second-degree burns	2.5	3.0–3.5	4.5
Wood and black clothing scorch	3.0	3.5–7.0	3.0
First-degree burns	3.5	4.0–9.0	2.3

Comparative flash effects for Hiroshima and Nagasaki are gauged as minimum calories of thermal energy received at increasing distance from the atomic bombs. (Note: first-degree burns are equivalent to severe sunburn; second-degree burns produce white blistering and instant peeling with spotted coagulation; third-degree burns kill all layers of skin and include the "alligator skin" effect.) Under the Nagasaki hypocenter, thermal rays reached 160 calories per square centimeter, producing a ground temperature up to 50 times the boiling point of water (up to 4,000 deg. C). The melting point of iron is only 15.5 times the boiling point of water (or 1,550 deg. C). For further comparison, the thermal energy of the sun's rays reaching the ground in August at midday in Japan over a 3-second interval is 0.06 calories per square centimeter. 3.0 cal/cm² over this same period created shadow people out to the first-degree burn zone.

· 10 ·

Legacy: To Fold a Thousand Paper Cranes

$\mathcal{W}$ithin minutes, if not seconds, people were changed. As the skies darkened beneath the spreading Urakami cloud, fires became Dr. Paul Nagai's sole light source. He saw a colleague dancing and singing wildly atop the hospital's dormitory building. Half of the dorm's roof was already being swallowed by flames, and as the wall of the fire gathered strength and crept toward the man, his singing turned to loud laughter.

The man clearly needed saving, but the heat was intensifying so quickly that anyone running into the dorm and trying to find the stairs would never find a way out. Neither Paul Nagai nor anyone else who saw the dancer dared advance toward the blaze. Instead, they backed away from it. They could not advance even as the young colleague—out of his mind with fear, or with denial, or both—danced directly into the flames. His singing and laughter became a long scream that lasted nearly fifteen seconds, and Nagai backed up several more steps, quickening the pace of his retreat.

"Doctor . . . Doctor, what shall I do?"

Dr. Nagai all but backed into the woman, nearly knocking her over as she pleaded from extremis for him to treat her little boy's wounds. When Nagai turned to face the young mother, he backed away in another direction, without any words at all.

"Help me!" the woman cried.

She did not seem to understand that her child no longer had a head.

Dr. Nagai recalled later that those who survived the atomic bomb were, in general, the people who ignored others crying out in extremis or who stayed away from the flames, even when patients and colleagues shrieked from within them: "Those of us who stayed where we were, those of us who took refuge in the hills behind the hospital when the fires began to spread and close in, happened to escape alive. In short, those who survived the bomb, were, if

285

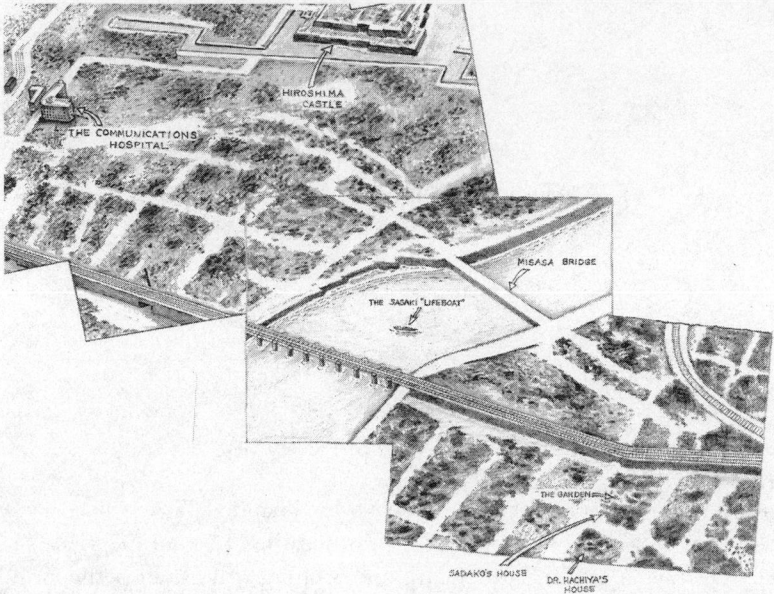

*The landscape between Dr. Hachiya's hospital and his house, after the detona-
tion, based on U.S. Bombing Survey photos. [Illustration: Patricia Wynne]*

not merely lucky, in a greater or lesser degree selfish, self-centered—guided by instinct and not by civilization. And we know it, we who have survived."

Buildings could be repaired, Nagai observed. Hypocenters could be covered up with gardens and memorial sculptures, but visitors to the rebuilt cities would never understand or even be aware that there existed a spiritual wreckage. From that first summer of the bombs, Dr. Paul Nagai suspected that this worst wreckage of all would pass like an invisible virus through multiple generations, and that none who remembered could ever fully recover.

"We who have seen and survived know what the atomic bomb can do," Nagai called out to futurity. "We carry deep in our hearts, every one of us, stubborn, unhealing wounds. When we are alone, we brood upon them; and when we see our neighbors we are again reminded of the wounds, theirs as well as ours."[1]

North in Hiroshima, Dr. Hachiya and Mr. Sasaki understood Nagai's lament. Before the bomb, they were neighbors and best friends. The family histories of

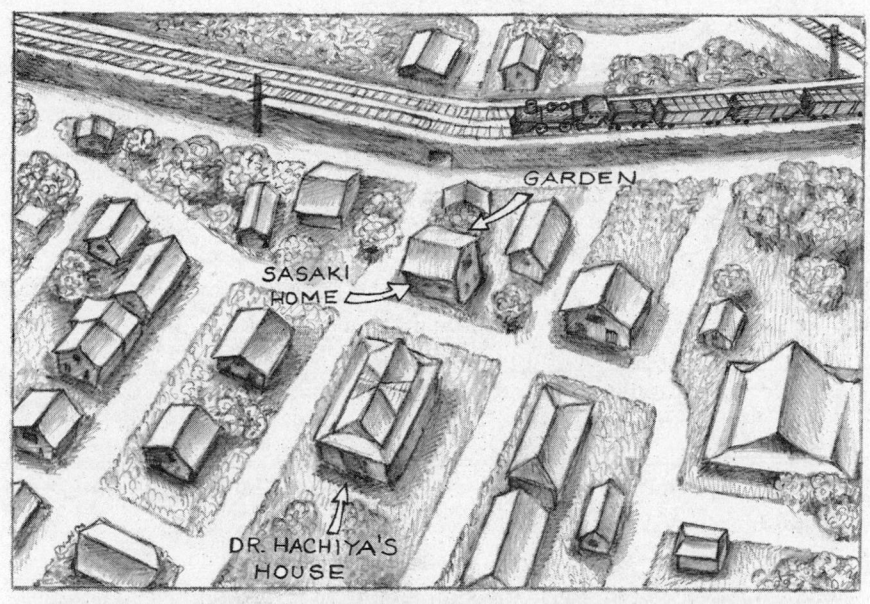

Sadako Sasaki and Dr. Hachiya's neighborhood, before and after 8:15 a.m., August 6, 1945. [Illustration: Patricia Wynne]

both men would record that Mr. Sasaki made multiple trips between the hill country and Hiroshima's Ground Zero, bringing food down to Dr. Hachiya and his patients at the Communications Hospital. And yet Mr. Sasaki's son, Masahiro, would note that after the age of six or seven, though his family would remain within walking distance of Hachiya, he did not recall ever seeing the doctor again.

In his diary, Dr. Hachiya wrote, "When [Shigeo Sasaki's] house collapsed . . . I had just reached the street in flight from [the wreckage of my own] home. Mr. Sasaki's mother was killed but [the rest of his family] escaped. If I had not been injured, I might have saved his mother because their house collapsed at my feet. . . . [This is] a sorrow without surcease."

In Hachiya's mind, it did not seem to matter that when he climbed out through the battered walls of his house, his wounds were near lethal and he emerged so completely disoriented that he briefly became one of the city's ant-walkers. By any standard of common sense if not by emotion, he should henceforth have held himself blameless. No one who knew even this small fraction of Hachiya's story would have censured him. Nonetheless, whenever he met Mr. Sasaki or his wife and their children on the street, he was reminded of little Sadako's grandmother. His only escape from remembrance lay in silent retreat and avoidance.

This was precisely what Dr. Nagai of Urakami meant when he said the bomb had created "cracks," or "fissures," between families and neighbors. History would record that not only did Mr. Sasaki never utter a word of complaint or reproach against his friend, he never gave reproach a thought. And yet a gulf yawned open between two neighbors. And the saddest cut of all was that there had never existed a basis for reproach in the first place; but the wound seemed beyond healing, and Dr. Hachiya would carry an undeserved guilt, quietly, to his grave. The physician never learned the truth. Avoidance kept him from learning.

On that day, during the minutes leading up to 8:15 a.m. and Moment Zero, Masahiro Sasaki had left his mother and his little sister Sadako at the breakfast table—running off to the backyard garden, where he commenced to play. That's where he saw two of the three airplanes. Decades later, when more was known about how events unfolded during the bombing, and in what sequence, Masahiro would come to realize that the reason he survived was that he did not see Luis Alvarez's instrument packages falling from *Great Artiste* and sprouting parachutes. He saw only the planes before his mother called him inside. Others who had watched the parachutes from this same radius, between the Misasa Bridge and the main rail line, at a distance of 1.9 kilometers, received approximately 7r from the gamma surge and neutron spray. At this 1.2-mile radius, 7r amounted to not quite 2 percent of a lethal radiation dose, but in household gardens and on the Sasaki neighborhood's streets, people were simultaneously blinded and seared by the heat ray.

As it turned out, and as random chance would have it, Sadako saved her brother from direct exposure. The two-year-old had not finished the last two or three spoonfuls of rice and fish gruel. Not wanting to leave anything to waste, Mrs. Sasaki called Masahiro inside to finish his sister's breakfast. For Masahiro, the margin separating his mother's call away from the *pika* was frighteningly small. He believed he escaped searing and death by less than ten seconds: "That's how fast it came—only the *pika* [the flash], with no *don* [no bang]."

Masahiro did not remember any sounds, either from the blast or from the planes that preceded it. It seemed impossible to him, but the *pika* and the cracking of thick wooden beams happened in utter silence. One side of the house burst open and something like a tornado suctioned Sadako out onto the street with most of the furniture. Mrs. Sasaki watched her daughter land completely uninjured on a wooden crate. The child simply sat atop the crate, looking around herself, smiling and a little bewildered, as she tried to find a more comfortable position on the cracked wood.

Little Sadako would remember only the flash, and Masahiro remembered stepping out into a world in which all the other houses had burst open or were flattened. Already, the first fire worms were hatching out. The worms grew with astonishing rapidity, and the family fled three blocks east to the waterfront, all four of them—five-year-old Masahiro, Mrs. Sasaki with Sadako in her arms, and Grandmother leading the way.

About the time the Sasakis reached the river, Dr. Hachiya had just burrowed into fresh air through the fragmenting splinters of his home, just in time to see the Sasaki house leaning and creaking toward him and falling literally at his feet. This was the beginning of the silent gulf between friends, of questions unasked, and of an unspoken guilt. Dr. Hachiya could never erase from his mind the image of Shigeo Sasaki's mother trapped inside the collapsed house. Nor could he free himself from the possibility that, as a doctor, he might have been able to help. What Hachiya never learned was that his friend's mother was not even in the vicinity. At the moment the house fell, she happened to be alive and perfectly unharmed, more than 200 meters away at the river's edge. She had remained at the waterfront for at least several minutes after the physician staggered away and joined the ant-walkers.

Masahiro Sasaki remembered that, even at a distance, the spreading tornadoes and multistoried waves of fire made his face feel sunburned. A group of men were trying to launch a half-destroyed boat, loading it with women and children as fast as they could, while they bailed and pushed.

"Anyone else?" one of the men called, motioning for people to climb into the boat immediately. Those gathered nearest the gunwales should not

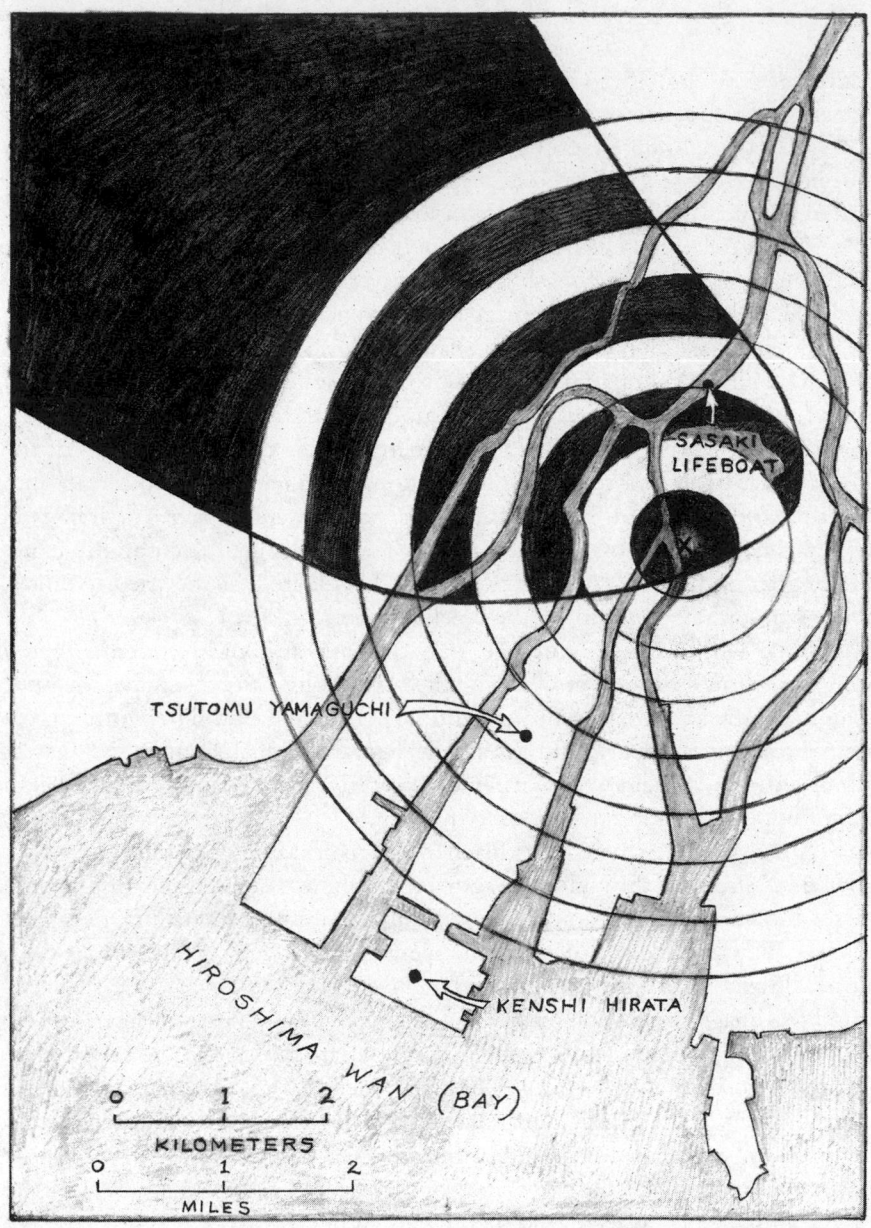

SASAKI
LIFEBOAT

TSUTOMU YAMAGUCHI

KENSHI HIRATA

HIROSHIMA WAN (BAY)

0   1   2
KILOMETERS

0   1   2
MILES

Although brief "sprinklings" of black rain were reported as far south as Yamaguchi's position in lower Hiroshima, the highest concentration of fallout was toward the northwest and the Sasaki lifeboat. Each concentric band on the map represents 1/2 km (up to 6 city blocks). Radioactive isotopes with half-lives of only a few minutes reached the lifeboat while still quite harmful. Masahiro Sasaki recalled that heat from the firestorms on both sides of the river made him and his little sister Sadako thirsty, and the children drank the black rain as it fell upon them. [Illustration: Patricia Wynne, based on U.S. Bombing Survey data] have needed more encouragement to jump in and row away, but the manifestations of the bomb confused them. Not more than fifty meters away, a waterspout came ashore and flung whole families to the ground. Tearing away their clothes, it strode inland and, shedding dozens of tons of water, it metamorphosed into an ordinary whirlwind, then into a fire worm.

Grandmother assisted her daughter-in-law Fujiko into the boat and passed the two children to her, then looked around and hesitated.

"You go," she commanded. "I must return to the house."

"You can't!" Fujiko cried.

"Look around you!" Grandmother said. On both sides of the river, and as far as Fujiko Sasaki could see upriver and downriver, a full-scale firestorm was trying to be born.

"All the food in the city is about to be burned," Grandmother continued. "We have tins of rice in the house. You'll need them to survive."

"No. It's too dangerous to go back."

"Go out to the center of the river and wait for me," Grandmother told the men in charge of the boat. "Row back and pick me up when I return with food."

"No!" Fujiko yelled, but the men pushed the boat through the mud and sand into deeper water and jumped aboard. Then, about three minutes after Grandmother ran under a train trestle and followed the nearest street westward toward home, whirlwinds of sparks and flames bunched together and stalked after her.

Masahiro remembered seeing monstrous walls of fire roaring to life along both shores. From the direction of home, he saw people burned. Many ran into the water, still in flames. Oddly, once the flames were doused and it seemed to the boy that the people were finally safe, most of them stopped moving.

Grandmother never returned from the fire, and Masahiro knew for a certainty that he would never see her again. Throughout the city, aboveground cisterns had been constructed specifically for the use of neighborhood fire brigades. Days later, when survivors returned to the Ground Zero fringe zone, they found every one of the concrete cisterns with at least two or three roasted bodies inside. Grandmother was one of the people in the cisterns. In the end, during their final seconds of life, men had ushered women and children into the hoped-for safety of the water tubs and stayed outside as the approaching firestorm threatened to submerge everyone in a lake of flames. Those inside the cisterns—usually children clinging to each other, or women embracing children—were given perhaps a precious minute more of life. None of them lived longer than they could hold their heads under the water. When they surfaced, their eyes were seared from their skulls and they inhaled pure fire into their lungs.

In the boat, little Masahiro tried to help the men to bail water. All around, the river began to fill with bodies, more than ten thousand of them in the region of the Misasa Bridge, southward toward the "T" Bridge and the Dome. Soon a score of survivors were clinging to the sides of the boat. Masahiro reached out to help a man over the gunwale and into the already half-sunk refuge, but someone in command ordered him to stop—"You'll swamp us if we bring anymore people aboard. This is not a time for compassion; it will only get us killed."

Masahiro obeyed, and resumed bailing, while half-carbonized people continued to run or stagger into the river and die. The water's surface became a logjam of corpses. The river flowed red with the blood of the dead and the dying, until the rain came—thick and black.

The very center of the black rain's path ran near the Misasa Bridge and the railway trestle—right where the Sasaki family struggled in open air in a Hiroshima lifeboat. The heat from the firestorm made Masahiro and little Sadako thirsty, and they eagerly licked the rainwater from their lips.

By the time the rains fell upon farms thirty kilometers downwind, more than an hour had passed and the worst of the bomb-generated isotopes were decayed almost out of existence. Yet even at such safe distances, cows that ate grass where the black rain had fallen experienced varying degrees of hair loss and developed a severe, sometimes fatal bovine diarrhea. Its impact appeared to be magnified in young calves.

The dose received by Sadako and Masahiro and by everyone else in their lifeboat was unknown orders of magnitude worse.[2]

The history of civilization is written in humanity's perversion of nature. In 1945, the two hypocenters were merely the latest examples. Uranium-235 was, in all essentials, the still-active remnant of the supernovae that gave the solar system life. Thinking creatures sought it out, coaxed it to beget plutonium, named the newly born element after a Roman god of death, and taught a dead star how to scream out against humanity—twice.

The atomic bomb left Keiji Nakazawa with the mystery of an unusual process that led to the disappearance of his mother's bones from the cremation pyre. It left another child, whose father was felled by "disease-X," forever perplexed about why, following the cremation of his father's body, he found "numerous shards of glass among his bones." It left a soldier who walked into the region of Nishina and Sagane's radioactive bone samples unable to quite explain the positions into which people inside a bank near the Hiroshima Dome had been frozen. It became possible to imagine that a demon from Dante's hell had waltzed through the building, overlooking Akiko Takakura and her friend Asami while touching everyone else with instant death, and posing them.

Being among the first soldiers into the hypocenter, Junichi Kaneshige was already absorbing dangerous levels of radiation by the time he entered what he believed had once been the Geibi Bank. Afterward, he would write about finding people thoroughly carbonized on the upper floors and near the windows. They fell apart at the slightest touch. Moving deeper into the ruin, he discovered a particularly horrible shock cocoon—a space in the building that had been left disconcertingly intact, preserving a moment that was more or less fossilized in the midst of symphonic devastation: "Descending the staircase to the basement," he recorded, "we found a certain female. She sat squarely upright, clad in a yukata dress amidst [what must have been] plenty of shower water coming down from the water supply tap installed above. Her face was pale, with her long hair hung over her shoulder down to her breasts. Although the surroundings had been burned down, the woman died in a dignified posture under the shower water. This scene was rather more emotion-stirring and provocative than the charred human bodies."

Junichi would eventually recover from the ravages of radiation poisoning, but never from the image of the woman within the incinerated bank.[3]

At first, Dr. Nagai had fallen into despair over the incineration of his university, his wife, his hospital, his students, and all of his research.

"However," he wrote in his memoirs, "the feeling of despair did not last, because I found a new purpose and a new hope—in a disease that had never existed before: atomic bomb disease. I had to research this new mystery. When this was decided, my dark depressed heart was filled with hope and courage. My spirit as a doctor surged. My body regained energy and I stood up."

Dr. Nagai and his nurses began traveling up to twenty kilometers a day, beyond the fringes of the fire and the blast zones, bringing cans of peaches and the strange-sounding advice not to wash away the maggots that were living in gangrenous wounds. Nagai's team became known for a distinctive theory that shoring up the immune systems of irradiated survivors by extracting vitamins from liver (even from rat liver), and by seeking out all known sources of vitamin C and vitamin B, gave the injured an increased likelihood of survival.

Throughout the suburbs, wherever the oily rains had fallen, Nagai became famous as "the maggots, liver, and peaches doctor."

Nagai's little girl Kayano recalled that when her father first arrived from Urakami, he brought a can of peaches recovered from a reasonably intact supply shelter. To Kayano, he looked very severe and worn out in spite of his curiously recovered strength. Her father's head was wrapped in bandages—each stained black and red with varying stages of drying blood. His face looked pale and filthy, and yet his eyes were shining.

Kayano and her brother Makoto excitedly showed him places in the valley where the ground and the plants were stained with dark residue from a rain of jelly and oil that had fallen on the day of the *pika-don*.

"Do not touch those places where the dark rain has fallen and dried!" he warned the children. Paul Nagai sensed, already, that the rain from the *pika-don* was bad.

"Yes, my father *did* look rather severe," Kayano remembered. "Then he brought the can of peaches from his pocket. He did not eat them himself. He saved them only for us."

In a shelter on the southwestern fringe of Urakami's Ground Zero, Mr. Yamaguchi had remained, at best, only semiconscious after reuniting with his wife and child. Twigs were still embedded in his skin from the Hiroshima blast, and a pebble had gone into his arm like a bullet. In Mitsubishi's Nagasaki office, he experienced partial de-gloving of an arm and the exposed muscle surface collected a sampling of all the debris that had whirlwinded through the room.

Yamaguchi's flesh was badly infected by the time the unknown "witch doctor" arrived and told Hisako not to remove the maggots. He also left a can of peaches and spoke about vitamin sources in the weed-covered hills nearby. The members of his team did not leave their names or accept thanks—and, though Hisako was never able to confirm it for him, Mr. Yamaguchi would always believe that his mysterious rescuer was his old basketball buddy Dr. Nagai, or the people who worked for him. There were not many other candidates. Most of the doctors in the area were killed, and Nagai's remedies were, if nothing else, distinctive.

About the time Dr. Nagai and the hospital's carpenter unearthed the last crate of canned peaches, rumors and theories began circulating about the death of the land itself. People were starting to believe that no creature would grow and survive in Urakami for seventy-five years.

"I'm already a short-timer," Nagai told his friend Akizuki, declaring that the cancer alone (though it had ceased troubling him and his hair was growing long while other people's hair continued to fall out) must already have shortened his life. "I've decided," he announced, "to build a scientific research station down in the ruins, and to place myself there as a laboratory rat."

By then, in the aftermath of the September storms, poor Dr. Akizuki's white blood cell count had dropped to half the normal level and he was beginning to hemorrhage under the skin. Even in the midst of post-deluge improvements, the vicious cycles persisted. The people who nursed Akizuki on a diet of liver and canned peaches collapsed with high fevers as he recovered his strength and began feeling well enough to visit patients again. The cared for Dr. Akizuki became the caregiver of his caregivers. Finally, Nagai collapsed— from "extreme exhaustion," according to Nagai's self-diagnosis, but Akizuki reminded him that any physician who practiced self-diagnosis had a fool as a patient and a fool for a doctor.

Akizuki suspected that persistent radiation had caused Nagai's eventual collapse and concluded that everyone who lived in or near the hills was doomed. Though the scorched limbs on the trees were sending forth new leaves, Akizuki recorded in his notes that the "abnormally bright" splashes of green under the setting sun and against the clouds seemed to him to be harbingers of death rather than signs of life.

Dr. Paul (Takashi) Nagai did not see it the same way. The ever-thickening growths of grass that had followed the September floods and the appearance of tiger beetles and cabbage butterflies among the grasses and the leaves hinted to Nagai that the seventy-five-year theory was wrong; the hills would come alive again, quickly. He began to believe that if humanity somehow managed to destroy itself utterly, nature would cover up all of civilization's mistakes in only a decade or two, spreading whole forests up the avenues and through the ruins.

From sheet-metal debris and pieces of scrap wood hauled down from the demolished medical center, Nagai built himself a hut, 600 meters from the hypocenter, in the footprint of his home's foundations. The single-room structure was located only steps away from the very patch of earth on which he found his wife's rosary with its glass beads melted.

Moving downhill into the zone of Dr. Akizuki's "concentric circles of death" and becoming the first permanent settler of Urakami was not merely a scientific exploration for Nagai but an exploration of faith as well.

As a young student, he once rented a room in the house of a family whose members had been active in Nagasaki's underground Christian movement from the time of Shogun Tokugawa's 1614 purge through the execution of the Christian leader Kichizo in 1856. Nagai married the landlord's daughter Midori—who was a direct descendant of Kichizo. His post-holocaust hut was erected over the ancestral home of Urakami's Christian underground and overlooked the site where Shogun Tokugawa had ordered the crucifixion of the Jesuits.

Mrs. Nagai's influence, and the influence of her multigenerational creed of "Love your neighbor as yourself," had once brought the doctor close to court-martial, just as, presently, it brought him closer to hypocenter radiation. As a medical army lieutenant stationed in occupied China for nearly three

NORMAL   MALFORMED   MALFORMED

NORMAL   MALFORMED   MALFORMED

NORMAL   MALFORMED

Dr. Nagai observed and recorded unusual mutations of plants growing near the Urakami hypocenter, including flowers of the Persian speedwell (top: Shimotomai, in Ishikawa and Swain, Committee Report, p 85), along with seven-and-eight-leaved clovers (middle, Nyokodo), and strange varieties of the crown chrysanthemum (bottom, Nyokodo). [Illustration: Patricia Wynne] years, he had provided treatment to Imperial shock troops, then to Chinese civilians, and finally to a wounded Chinese soldier. "When making a diagnosis," he said in his defense, "I would not take nationality into consideration."

If not for the unlikely circumstance that one of his commanders had ancestors in the Urakami underground, Nagai's story would have ended in death and obscurity in China. Instead, he was sent back to Urakami, where he discovered that deteriorating wartime conditions had left many residents impoverished, ill-fed, and in declining health. What Nagai learned in China came back with him: "When making a diagnosis and offering aid," he told his staff, "we should not take an ability to pay into consideration."

Thus it came as no surprise to Akizuki or to anyone else who knew Nagai that during the first autumn after the bomb he christened himself a laboratory rat, moved downhill into the forbidden zone, and grew his hair as long as Einstein's.

He named his hut *Nyokodo*—the "As Yourself" hermitage, in honor of the gospel passage, "Love thy neighbor as yourself."[4]

When he raised his roof and sealed it against the rain, ants were already at work, excavating tiny pebbles and carbonized chips of bone. Fifty meters in every direction, the ants flourished.

In the land between Nyokodo and the hypocenter, and for an equal distance opposite the zero point, everyone had been killed except three children and two women. All five of them happened to be shielded within Prefect Nishioka's tunnels.

By October 1945, even the "miners of the town" had fled the forbidden inner circles of Ground Zero. Nagai recorded that the plant growth continued to thicken, while thriving populations of insects were joined by mice, and finally by birds. His notebooks also memorialized flash burns on tree trunks out to a distance of 10 kilometers (about 6.4 miles), adding that, beyond Ground Zero, whatever grass and trees grew within two-to-seven kilometers—"all were irradiated at the time of the explosion and were scorched red or crisped brown." Even the shadow-shielded sides of distant hills were not spared. In the little valley where Kayano and Makoto now lived, many unscorched leaves that had been stained by the black rain withered and died.

Dr. Nagai examined two farmers who, at a distance of nearly 17 kilometers (10 miles), had cut down some wood stained with black rain and carried it on their shoulders, a day after the explosion. The next day, their arms and shoulders broke out in an itching red rash. Mosquito bites oozed pus and were very slow to heal. Their white blood cell counts were still abnormal two months later, but their overall health appeared to be slowly improving.

It seemed clear to Nagai that the effect of radiation on the human body was more violent at the beginning. As autumn gave way to winter, he wrote,

"I myself sleep in a small hut with icicles hanging on the walls and roof and with snow filtering in. I have only a thin blanket to protect me. And yet I have not contracted pneumonia, or even so much as a cold. Even if I get an injury or a scratch (as when bitten by a spider), I myself have no fear of infection or pus developing in the wounds."

Soon, even the swelling of Nagai's face, and the painful abdominal bloating effects brought about by his cancer, appeared to have gone into complete remission. The Japanese and American "bombing survey" scientists who visited him one morning were quick to report to their supervisors that the radiological effects had dissipated and that, in at least one case, might even have enhanced a survivor's health. As jokes about the health benefits of being bitten by radioactive spiders flourished, General MacArthur's Commission, assigned to investigate the effects of the bomb, chose to ignore Nagai's loudly voiced conclusion that had this been Tucson, Arizona, instead of the Urakami River valley, the radioactive dust would have lingered for a decade or more on every breeze, instead of being washed down the hills and out to sea by a typhoon.[5]

("Don't eat clams till late next year," Nagai had advised everyone.)[6]

No one in authority seemed to be listening to anything except what they specifically wanted to hear. Everything else became irrelevant. And so, inevitably, when combined with a bombing survey laboratory study that revealed Urakami earthworms to be developing normally, Nagai's results were misused to achieve a preconceived conclusion poorly disguised as science: "A city cannot be obliterated wholly by the atomic bomb. It is not so fearful. It is just another weapon, with greater physical effects than those which preceded it."

"Greater physical effects!" Dr. Akizuki raged (in a letter from the time of the commission's conclusion). "Do they really wish to make all of us who have been injured or killed by the fallout simply nonexistent?"

For Nagai's part, he was still quite frightened by the radiation effects of these new bombs. But he alone seemed equally concerned that the American, British, and Japanese scientists who visited the ruins neither understood nor attempted to investigate "what this weapon does to the heart and conscience and mind of someone who survives."

Nagai's friend Akizuki was an example of this—a thoroughly decent man plunged instantly into a cycle of remorse and rage. Akizuki could no longer face Dr. Yoshioka because he felt responsible for her exposure to the blast; and as the first winter approached its midpoint, he spoke often of wanting to cave in the back of a "stingy" American pharmacist's head with a shovel.

"They are ignoring us out here!" Akizuki said during a visit to Nyokodo. "They supply us with no medicines. They ask us nothing and they send us nothing—and we heal nothing!"

"We should not hate the people who seem bent upon ignoring us or hurting us," Nagai responded. "I have named this place *Nyokodo* because the ancient prophets—Buddha and Jesus, Hillel and Mohammad—each, near the ends of their human journeys, said essentially the same thing: 'Love others as you love yourself.'"

"That does not help at this kind of time."

"But it *does*," Nagai insisted. "This blame reflex of yours is quite natural. Yet we, more than perhaps any other people on Earth, must come to understand and to teach that the need to strike back at someone is wrong thinking and can lead to nothing good. Do you not understand that the power of the atom was a *gift*, planted in the universe at the very beginning?"

If the gift is handled properly, Nagai tried to explain, each man is given the key to the universe—"a key that may one day throw open the doors to the planets, and the stars beyond." And yet, somehow this same key had been fashioned in such a manner that it could also unlock the gates of hell.

Motioning toward the hypocenter, Akizuki asked, "You call *this* a gift from God?"

"I do not mean that this destruction is a gift. What happened here is a message of hope, and a warning. It was, in a manner of speaking, a Pentecostal apocalypse."

"I think your brain is going soft from living down here," Akizuki said.

Nagai returned his friend a laugh, and emphasized, "What happened here . . . is simply what happened. It becomes what it is. And now we must go forth and overcome the instinct for finger-pointing. We must learn to be guided by civilization and not by instinct, by mercy and not by the old tribal, territorial drumbeats. Why else do you think we have survived—we of Nagasaki?"

"I don't know. Just lucky, I guess. Or maybe just unlucky."

"Exactly the latter, I think. Does it not occur to you that those who were taken instantly or who died during those first days were perhaps the lucky ones? Even if what comes after death is merely infinite dreamless sleep, aren't they less tormented than those of us who live to grieve and to carry a survivor's scars? Perhaps those who disappeared were simply taken, and those of us who were supposedly 'saved' failed our entrance exam into heaven and were left behind because we are *meant* to stay."

"To what purpose?"

"To learn, and to teach."

Dr. Akizuki looked to the place where a melted rosary and Midori Nagai's bones had been found. Mrs. Nagai was evidently among the instantly taken. Akizuki shook his head. "I'm sorry, friend. But God had nothing to do with this. *People* did this."

"Indeed we did. We all let the words, 'Who takes a knife will die by a knife,' go through one ear and out the other. We took the greatest knowledge that science could provide and, lacking wisdom, we human beings busily made warships, torpedoes, and now atomic bombs. God did not twist and pervert nature's gifts. We did."

Akizuki shook his head again, drew Nagai's door shut, and left, angry and confused. He wanted to punch his friend for suggesting that the bombing of his city was somehow ordained by a compassionate God.

That night, Dr. Nagai wrote a wish, which he hoped would prophesy the longest strategic peace the world had ever known:

"Nuclear war ended in Nagasaki."

"Nagasaki is the period."

"Peace starts from Nagasaki."[7]

Had the chain of *BocksCar* misfortunes not placed the Nagasaki gamma-ray burst at precisely the right distance from Dr. Nagai, the remission of his cancer might not have occurred, and his voice would soon have disappeared from history. Had the uranium bomb not detonated with less than half its intended yield, the outer fringe of Hiroshima's Ground Zero would have extended far beyond Tsutomu Yamaguchi, and instead of being grievously injured, he would have ceased to exist. Located at Yamaguchi's same radius from the Hiroshima hypocenter, the Sasakis and Dr. Hachiya would also have become silenced voices, lost to history.

Yamaguchi's curious distinction of being twice bombed and having twice survived was improbable by a figure that needed to be squared or cubed, and not merely doubled. If three fuel-exhausting bomb-runs by Sweeney over Kokura had not combined with the sort of cloud cover that caused him to drop the Nagasaki bomb more than a mile off target, Yamaguchi would not have survived the first three seconds of his encounter with the second atomic bomb.

An improbable swerving of history had dictated that Sadako Sasaki and her neighbor would bear witness. Another apparently reset Dr. Nagai's life clock. *Two* unlikely swerves, one after another, had made Yamaguchi the bomb's most spectacular survivor. No one else, not even the other double survivors, had been so directly exposed to the effects of a nuclear explosion—twice.

"On August 9," Yamaguchi recalled, "the devil's column of fire stood even taller than before, as if mocking me with laughter because I thought I had escaped with my life from Hiroshima to Nagasaki. I felt as though it were a sentient beast that had literally chased me down."

Mr. Yamaguchi's wife tended to his wounds for nearly three days without sleeping, struggling to keep him alive. In Hiroshima, his skin and even the muscles in one arm had been penetrated by glassy buckshot, air-blasted across a potato field from office windows more than a city block away. In Nagasaki three days later, bits of mahogany flew away from office furnishings and pierced the same wounded arm, like poison darts. There was no medicine in the shelter, except for miso and the skin cream Hisako had brought with her on the morning of the 9th. Nonetheless, Dr. Nagai's odd ideas about maggots, fruit, and lightly cooked liver seemed to be working, though it was difficult for Hisako to keep the chickens under control. They were continually seeking out her semiconscious husband, and from time to time he remembered being awakened by the hungry birds.

"Behave yourself," Hisako warned, "or my husband will have your liver."

And it seemed that every time Hisako turned her back on the chickens, one or two of them managed to sneak past her. They went to Mr. Yamaguchi directly and began pecking and plucking the maggots out of his wounds. One of them apparently bit too deep, and a half-conscious hand reached out, still with enough strength to crush its neck. Hisako made the bird's liver into a very strong, iron-rich porridge.

The Yamaguchis were living with four or five other families, inside the very same tunnel Hisako had been building for the Mitsubishi offices, under the governor and the prefect's "Emergency Preparedness Protocol."

Aside from feeding the chickens, the next thing Mr. Yamaguchi clearly remembered was awakening in a dark cave one afternoon to the sound of two dozen people weeping. They were listening to a radio on August 15, and the Emperor's voice had just announced the surrender.

The tunnel itself was all the evidence anyone really needed to know that the war had been clearly perceived, by those in charge, to be drawing toward its final battle. Even before Hiroshima, Yamaguchi had begun anticipating the fall of Japan; so he went back to sleep, and continued to bleed from his nose and his bowels.

During the next week, soldiers were sent, under orders from the deputy governor, to assist survivors from the Mitsubishi offices. By then, all surviving engineers who knew anything about ships or steam-catapulted planes, about submarines or bomb-shelter construction, were of keen interest to the American occupation's scientists and engineers. The soldiers, under the advice of Professor Shirabe and Dr. Nagai's house-calling nurses, brought a rich supply of tangerines and cans of peaches.

As Nagai had predicted, once Hisako began feeding her husband substantial quantities of fruit, Yamaguchi's health improved to such an extent that by the first week of September he was able to return with Hisako and little Katsutoshito to their half-destroyed house, and to begin thinking about reconstruction. Nonetheless, he was still a long way from being able to make effective repairs. Even if the house had not been cracked and scorched by the *pika* ("Oh, that's bad," Hisako said), he was not up to the task. Even the saving grace of having the flames blown out by a great wind ("Oh, that's good," Hisako said), this, too, left Mr. Yamaguchi overwhelmed; for even had the same fire-snuffing wind not blown the house in two and bounced it off its foundations ("Oh, that's awful . . ."), he did not feel like working, even though repairing the roof was a straightforward engineering problem.

"I was quite able physically, and in terms of basic knowledge," he recalled. "But now, spiritually, I wasn't really quite human anymore. I moved around, day by day, like a machine, and not like a husband or a father at all."

When the September storms came, he and Hisako hid under umbrellas in the house. Hisako laughed. Yamaguchi did not—*could* not. He began to think that his soul, if not his life, had been ended by the two bombs. And then he began to think about the fate of Father Simcho of Urakami. Simcho had left before the bomb, to a place called Auschwitz.*

Simcho was a devotee to Maria who arrived with Jesuits from France and gave aid to widows and orphaned children—and, wherever possible, arranged adoptions. By 1941, Simcho and the non-German European missionaries began to draw suspicion from the military (partly based on accusations about French "secret society" chevrons, circles, and pentagram stars evolving from church decorations into city-wide symbols). The suspects were "ejected" as spies.

"Not merely ejected," Yamaguchi learned. He inquired into what happened to Simcho in Auschwitz and heard that a man in the concentration camp had been accused of stealing and hoarding food. The man was going to be either hanged with piano wire as an example to others or "sent to the gas."

"Father Simcho made a remarkable decision," Yamaguchi later taught all who were willing to listen. "He actually took the position of a man accused by the Germans of stealing loaves of bread from them. The accused man had a family out there, somewhere beyond the prison walls. Simcho had no family; so he confessed to a theft he did not commit, so that children might have their father."

---

*Tsutomu Yamaguchi's personal name for the priest who became the model for his second life was clearly "Father Simcho." This might have been either a local or personal nickname. Though associated with the French Jesuits, he appears to have been of Polish origin: A Franciscan whose official priestly name was Fr. Maximilian Kolbe, he served as a missionary in Nagasaki from 1930–1936 and became a revered friend of Dr. Nagai. Father Maximilian ("Simcho") Kolbe was murdered in Auschwitz in the place of a family man, in August 1941. The Catholic Church honored him as a saint in 1982.

With Simcho on his mind, Yamaguchi told his wife of the decision he was finally coming to: "If my life ended on August 6 and August 9, then whatever might come afterward, I should perhaps consider to be my second life?"

The white rainbow that manifested over Nagasaki in September seemed to firm Yamaguchi's resolve. What meaning was there in Simcho's example, he wondered, if someone did not remember the missionary and carry on after him, and send forth acts of human kindness in his memory, hoping that they might spread like ripples in a pond—anti-ripples, perhaps, against Dr. Akizuki's concentric circles of death?

Mr. Yamaguchi eventually walked away from engineering, especially anything connected to machines of war. As he saw it, his second life gave him only one choice: to regard himself a victim and nurture hate or to regard himself a survivor, walk in Father Simcho's path, and treat others with humanity.

And so Yamaguchi decided that his second life would be devoted to the children of Nagasaki. He became a carpenter, and then, after helping to rebuild schools along the Urakami River, he went inside the buildings and became a junior high school teacher.[8]

Misako Katani, the schoolgirl who witnessed the fire horses of Hiroshima and who would forever remember that horses could scream, also remembered her father telling her that they must flee the city. "Thank God we have relatives in Nagasaki," he said. "We will be safe there."

"Obviously, some obscure meaning of the word *safe* not found in any dictionary of the Japanese language," Katani would tell historians, "or in any other language."

She and her father had left Hiroshima aboard the same train as Tsutomu Yamaguchi, and in fact Katani's relatives lived in the same Mitsubishi housing district as Mr. Yamaguchi, at the same distance from the Urakami hypocenter.

The house was knocked on its side, yet remained curiously intact. After this, Father decided that because the bomb had apparently missed central Nagasaki and fallen farther upriver, someone might come back to finish the job, and therefore Hiroshima—which had been mostly erased—was probably a safer place after all.

Slowly making their way north, they arrived just ahead of the September 17 typhoon and narrowly escaped death a third time. A fellow traveler, Professor Mashita of Nagasaki, was not as lucky. After surviving Urakami, he had been recruited by Drs. Nishina and Sagane to monitor radiation in Hiroshima's hypocenter. His tent was blown down and his equipment destroyed by the typhoon.

When Mashita tried to shield himself from horizontal rain behind the walls of the Hiroshima Dome, loose bricks tumbled down and killed him.

"Life seems to be worth nothing more than a leaf or a straw at the mercy of the wind," wrote Dr. Akizuki, after hearing of his friend Mashita's death. "Now we have surely suffered enough. No more!"

But history was not through with the survivors. Katani's hometown house was located between the Misasa Bridge and the Dome. Even after her father saw that the fires had reduced their neighborhood mostly to dust and charcoal, he was able to convince himself that Katani's mother and little sister were only "missing." There was something astonishingly contagious about the "missing" mind-set. Though any parts of the houses left unburned appeared to have been stamped flat, Katani adopted the mind-set as well.

As she walked along a familiar road and recognized the location of her home, Katani yelled, "Mom! It's me!"

"But my voice wasn't reaching her," Katani recalled. "My father looked at our surroundings and said that maybe my mother was holding my little sister Tamie, and they were under the house. Even then, Father considered them to be only missing. I removed ashes and debris around an area one meter square . . . and there were the flakes [of blackened flesh]. I saw the ornate hairpin that my mother always wore. That is what at first caught my eye. I yelled, 'Mother!' And then I frantically sifted [through the flakes]. And underneath was my little sister—sheltered by Mother. Now, at last, Father accepted that his wife and child were not missing but were gone from him forever."

After that, Katani's father began to die.

And before the year was through, new beliefs emerged, about radiation exposure and atomic bomb disease—and in terms of marriage, people exposed in either of the cities (to say nothing about exposure in both) became untouchables.

Katani decided to keep her mouth shut, carrying inside of her the secret that she had experienced the atomic bomb twice. She made a further private decision to take her peculiar distinction of double survival as a symbol of improbably good luck, rather than the sign of a life somehow jinxed.

Having survived where so many others perished in every direction, Katani asked herself, "How could anything bad happen?"

Moving away from the ruins, she was taken in by relatives who lived far from Hiroshima and Nagasaki. She attended a distant school, where she could be free to eventually fall in love, marry, and continue her education. Her three children would be born dead, and dead, and dead.[9]

The wind from the north that had carried most of the "death sand" away from Inosuke Hayasaki's position and toward the center of the Urakami firestorm could not remove the guilt he carried over the twenty-five people he "killed" with drinks of water, and in any case the wind evidently brought him only a brief respite from what became the greater measure of his radiation exposure.

While Inosuke travelled north aboard the night train, fallout from the Urakami hypocenter cut a path of highest concentration eastward, directly across the valley in which Dr. Paul Nagai's children and their little cousins seemed initially to have been completely sheltered. Some of the cousins sickened within twenty-four hours and began dying only a few days later. The radioactive clouds, though gradually weakening, continued eastward beyond the Nagai children, directly across the farming village of Shimabara, the very place toward which fourteen-year-old Inosuke was fleeing, toward his parents, and toward the imagined hopes of putting the horrors of Nagasaki forever behind him.

Instead of being washed out to sea by the September storms, most of the unstable isotopes that fell upon Shimabara on August 9 and August 10 of 1945 drained into the network of canals and channels that irrigated the fertile but generally porous volcanic soils provided by Mount Unzen.

During the year that followed, Inosuke's family took up farming in the soil, without anyone suggesting to the townspeople that the ground had absorbed a new pollutant, or that it might remain harmful for a decade or more. Plants had a way of biologically concentrating certain isotopes above and beyond the new background levels in the soil. Though Inosuke had escaped from an unmeasurable but apparently low dosage in the upper Urakami Valley, with no signs of radiation sickness during the months that followed, even a relatively low dose became cumulatively dangerous, if a layer of radioactive food were added to it. And thus did the survivor from the Mitsubishi plant become an exceedingly rare case of radiation sickness that did not manifest until a year after the atomic bombings. He developed sudden nosebleeds and nausea, his hair began pulling out in clumps with the slightest touch of a comb, while his temperature rose to a life-threatening level, and stayed there. He knew that many had died from this same atomic bomb syndrome a year earlier, and his dreams were nightmares about how it had ended for them.

"During this time," he later reported, "I made up my mind that if my fever came down, then I would live. All I wanted to do was survive. I had become a skinny and sick fifteen-year-old boy. None of my dreams were coming true. But in this world, there were no air raids. I believed that even in poverty, there was joy to be had, living in peace. War itself was an enemy of mankind. [Now], we had freedom of speech, freedom of mind—and I knew that if I could survive my disease, I could have my own life.

"Then, after forty days passed my fever started to fall gradually; but then *all* of my hair fell out. I was a very sad sight—yet, thinking about all the people who had died, I could not be sad."

The label would come later: *hibakusha*. A war that had begun with racial arrogance against the Chinese and other Asians was producing a new, looked-down-upon, post-apocalypse race. Denied higher levels of education or employment, or even the right to marry, Inosuke eventually decided to defy human injustice by hiding his identity—becoming a silent dissident. Still, it would take him all the way up to the age of thirty-nine, in the year of the first moon landing, until he loved a woman enough to overcome his fear of the warned-against "monster children" of the *hibakusha*. Growing up, he had seen pictures of Hiroshima babies, in jars of formaldehyde, with faces that resembled pigs or deformed birds and lizards more than humans. What no one had ever told him was that the vast majority of these children were the still-born progeny of women exposed *during* pregnancy, and especially during the first trimester when radiation-sensitive cells were dividing most rapidly and even small radiation-induced errors, if created simultaneously in multiple tissue layers and not rapidly corrected by developmental DNA's feedback mechanisms, could resound catastrophically through entire organ systems.

"How," a friend would ask, as Inosuke's seventieth anniversary of the bomb approached—"How, after seeing those pictures, did you overcome your fear to have children, and tell the woman you loved that you were *hibakusha*?"

He could only laugh at the question, and reply, "I *didn't* tell her. I actually hid the fact that I was *hibakusha* until after we had two children. So, obviously she was quite surprised. But, as you now know, we already had two (*healthy*) kids, and she said, 'Well, as long as you and the kids are going to be healthy and not sick, everything is going to be okay.'"[10]

On the day of the second atomic bomb, in a tunnel not very far from the little hypocenter research outpost where Dr. Paul Nagai observed short-lived mutations in gardenias and clover during a gradual but labored recovery of nature, a young mother-to-be had survived in a tunnel shelter. For her, everything was going to be "far, far from okay." At Moment Zero, she was underground, double-checking a small hoard of emergency rations and clothing for her relatives, in the house above. In barely more than a lightning bolt's lifespan there was no longer a house above, nor any living thing, and the Nagasaki gamma-shine had already reached into the shelter, and into her womb.

Whether or not he was reading a cautionary tale into a merely coincidental line of ancient scripture, it was plain from what Dr. Nagai witnessed in the deformed flowers, and in what came afterward, that too much of what happened under the atomic bombs echoed a prophecy recorded in the twenty-fourth chapter of Matthew: "But woe to those who are with child and those who are nursing babies in those days."

For the woman in the shelter, the developmental pathway that led to growth of the brain's frontal lobes was cut short. Random facial features and major pathways to limb development were sped up and slowed down.

The child was born male, with scarcely more than an ancestral, reptilian framework of a brain, abandoned in mid-construction. His arms and legs were as the limbs of an amphibian, and he moved much in the manner of the overgrown salamanders that waddled on their bellies across the pre-Triassic/ Jurassic mudflats of central Japan's Gifu Prefecture.

As recorded by Nagasaki memorialist Kyoko Hayashi, "When he grew to twelve or thirteen, he developed sexual desires. Not knowing how to control himself, he threw himself on his mother as led by his instincts."

Still loving the being as a child, but perplexed, the mother harnessed him and leashed him to a pillar in the living room, where he howled unbearably like a wild beast and tried to gnaw through the leash. A doctor finally suggested that he needed to be calmed down like a gelded animal, and near the end, she consented to surgical removal of the boy's testicles.

In her warning to future generations, Hayashi would write that, after his gelding, the child of gamma rays and alpha particles "became a 'good' boy with dulled responses, a quiet boy who did no harm to healthy people. In the spring of his fifteenth year, he was overcome by intense convulsions, and died after quivering all day long. The only human-like response the boy had ever demonstrated was his unrestrained sexual desire before the operation."[11]

Once he settled in, Dr. Nagai was joined by other hypocenter pioneers—who, as the winter of 1945–46 became the spring of 1946, began erecting a shantytown in the ruins, eventually redirecting a stream through makeshift aqueducts, and reintroducing a streetlight here and there, with Nagai turning one wall of his little hermitage into the first local library.

As wild daisies and clover spread across the ground, and as the first hawks began to depopulate the returning mice, Dr. Nagai noticed stabbing pains in his lower spine and in his spleen. He did not need Dr. Akizuki to tell him that his remission had been only temporary. As the land between Nyokodo and the hypocenter came back to life, so, too, did carcinogens' angels.

Nagai's new neighbors offered to build extra rooms onto his shack, but he told them that he wished to travel lightly through life, and that one room with a wall of windows and an opposite wall that shelved his books was actually all he needed.

An American chaplain paid him a visit, offering building materials and two carpenters, but Nagai served him tea and said he needed nothing more. Days later, a bishop visited and, right behind him, a beggar. Nagai welcomed them both, equally, into his "palace." Two of Nagai's former students turned former South Pacific soldiers also arrived, speaking proudly of their dream to one day rise from the ruins of Urakami with swords in hand.

To all of them, Nagai said, "If you had been here on that day and at that hour, if you had seen the hell that opened up on Earth before our eyes, if you had even a glimpse of that, you would never, never entertain the crazy thought of another war. If there is another war, atomic bombs may explode everywhere and there will be no beautiful songs of distant Earth [from other planets]—no poems, no paintings, no music, no literature, no research. Only death."

After spring rains more thoroughly cleansed the hypocenter and wildflowers established a seemingly permanent dominion over the land and songbirds returned in great numbers, Dr. Paul Nagai brought his children down to Nyokodo.

One morning, he awoke to the sound of five-year-old Kayano chattering to herself in the yard. Stepping outside, Nagai found her playing house with her toys, acting out the same tea-serving game she used to play with her friends from this same neighborhood. Before her were the head of a doll, some glass bottles, plates, and part of a broken mirror, set on a table that was a scorched rock. Kayano served imaginary tea and talked with imaginary friends. All of her real friends were dead.[12]

In Hiroshima, the trains were running on schedule again, and electric lines now powered Dr. Hachiya's Communications Hospital. Though most of the bridges were still bent and fractured and navigable only by people with very good balance, the main roads had been cleared of debris and, with gasoline slowly becoming plentiful, the streets were filling up with the first traffic seen in more than two years.

Uncounted numbers of refugees, too, were streaming in and filling the streets. Hiroko Nakamoto and her aunt longed for a return of the once tranquil city. Although Hiroko knew that it would never again be the city between calm rivers she had loved in childhood, she was unprepared for the new Hiroshima, and for the true magnitude of childhood's end.

"Chinese and Koreans [many wanting to 'even the score'], and thousands of merchants from outside had moved in," Hiroko wrote—"to grab whatever they could. There were no controls. The lawless swarmed in to take advantage of the chaos. Records, maps, deeds had been destroyed. No rights could be established."

Hiroko knew all along that there would be nothing except ruin where the family home once stood. She expected the trees to be gone. She was not surprised to see the old rivers and canals, once serene, filled with debris, bones, and raw sewage. What she did not expect to see was how her once familiar neighborhood streets had become lined with crude shelters and populated by people with strange, often cruel faces. The quiet nights of childhood were now broken by the laughter of "street girls" and the shouts of orphans gone feral—among them, the one or two who occasionally joined Keiji Nakazawa as tormenting (and sometimes tormented) replacements for his siblings. "There was," Hiroko observed, "no more quiet, no more tranquility. The serene spirit of Hiroshima had been destroyed as completely as its buildings."[13]

The makeshift hospital where Minami saw the blue fireflies was a school again, attended by Keiji Nakazawa and sometimes by his rebellious, often feral little "brother" Tanaka. Electricity had reached the school, but most of the walls were slicked with mold, and every time the weather took a turn for the worse, the children endured rainstorms indoors. Chasing down and filling in all the cracks in the steel-and-concrete roof proved to be an intractable problem for carpenters. As compression waves passed, entire floors had moved and rippled—like swells at sea—before abruptly solidifying.[14]

The tin-roof shantytown near the Aioi Bridge (the "T" Bridge), now subsidized by government suppliers, provided little more comfort than the school; but the grounds on which Hiroshima's peace park would one day rise had the advantages of wide-open spaces in which to play, and to hunt food.

The Industrial Arts and Exhibit Hall, where Keiji Nakazawa's father's artwork had once been displayed, was simultaneously Nakazawa's link to a lost past and, as he would one day phrase it, "A great playground for us brats. With jungle gym skills, we climbed up and down the Dome's outer walls."

Summiting the metal spokes of the Dome itself, they could survey in a moment how much of the city had vanished. In a time long before the Dome became the centerpiece of a gated garden and motion sensors were placed around its base to put an end to tourists taking away bricks as souvenirs, Nakazawa, Tanaka, and scores of other children sought out the hiding places of doves and sparrows—which had built nests in most of the building's nooks and crannies. They competed in egg hunts, with the winners proudly crunching the eggs in their mouths and swallowing the contents raw in front of the losers.

"The Dome and its surroundings were our yard, our turf," Nakazawa recalled, with a strange undertone that was simultaneously melancholy and nostalgia.

The water beneath the Aioi Bridge covered a field of human bones. The long bones were aligned perfectly with the current. On warm days Nakazawa and his friends dove into the river through huge ruptures in the "T" Bridge's pavement. Holding his breath and gliding along the bottom for as long as he could, Nakazawa discovered just how many bodies had eventually deflated, sunk to the muddy bedding plain, and become skeletons. At the Aioi Bridge and downstream of it as far as Nakazawa could swim, and on both sides, his playground was a river of skulls.

The children had discovered how to net and spear the large shrimp, crayfish, and crabs that lived in and around the skulls.

"The crayfish were particularly thick where there were lots of bones," Nakazawa recalled. "They'd fattened on corpses. The crayfish I brought home, we skewered on bamboo spits, roasted, and ate as a family. They supplemented our deficiencies of protein and calcium."

In such close proximity to the hypocenter and the highest concentrations of black rain fallout, the supplements included traces of calcium-mimicking plutonium and strontium isotopes. Nakazawa did not know this; Nishina, Urey, and Alvarez were just beginning to suspect it. What Nakazawa did know was on which meat the crayfish had feasted, that they had grown so great. Such knowledge clearly gave his mother a creepy feeling, but the Nakazawas and Tanaka did not have the luxury of being repulsed—"And we ate them, though it did not feel quite right, though we might even have felt like cannibals."

Yet even in the midst of a mutual struggle to live, whenever a brotherly bond began to develop between Keiji Nakazawa and Tanaka, the bomb had already laid down the foundations on which the invisible cracks described by Dr. Nagai could begin to form. Keiji Nakazawa's spirit was already flayed by the time he and his mother found Tanaka and other orphans in need of a family and made a decision to help at least one of them. And, though no one was truly to blame, Tanaka's increasingly wild and resentful nature fed into his conviction that, if he was loved at all, it was only by virtue of being a convenient counterfeit stand-in for Keiji's lost brother, Susumu.

Occasionally, Tanaka stole food and tools and ran away, joining up with the stronger, sixth-grade orphans who were claiming territory near the Dome, where they sold fused roof tiles and river skulls to American G.I.s (Keiji Nakazawa called them "atomic tourists"), who began making pilgrimages to the hypocenter region.

Tanaka's absences became increasingly long. Often, after living among other feral children, he returned hungry and unwashed, to a lonely sorrow in which he would never trust Keiji to love him as a truly adopted brother.

In his chronicles of *Gen*, Keiji would tell the story of Tanaka—as "Ryuta"—with at least three different endings, ranging from how he would have liked it to turn out for them (as in the film, *Barefoot Gen*, with the boys sitting together as brothers by the river's edge), to barely hinting at how it actually did turn out. Each chronicle suggested a gulf between brothers that persisted until something unmentioned, yet as frightening and ultimately as lethal as atomic bomb disease, intervened.

By the time government officials began annexing central Hiroshima's shantytowns, bulldozing them, and subsidizing the construction of stores and office buildings, atomic orphans were scavenging copper and other metal scraps from the ruins, in order to buy food. Their mining efforts extended to the extraction of gold teeth from the fields of skulls. The government wanted to end this, and thus was Tanaka among the orphans "collected" from the streets of the planned commercial district and sent to an orphanage on the former quarantine island of Ninoshima. There was nothing for Tanaka on the island except the remnants of funeral pyres—more skulls, more gold.

Although atomic orphans were being removed from view, and buildings with neon lights began rising from the ashes of Hiroshima, it seemed to Keiji Nakazawa that on the surface, the city was being covered with beautiful new clothing—"But beneath the surface, the ugly struggle for survival went on."

Ninoshima Island might just as well have been the isle of Alcatraz, from Tanaka's point of view; so he escaped to one of his progressively infrequent reunions with Nakazawa.

By then, Hiroshima already led the nation in juvenile crime, and gangs were evolving rapidly from chaotic hit-and-miss thievery toward organization. Lone wolf criminals and the weak faced malnutrition. Tanaka was drawn ever deeper into the organized underworld.

Keiji Nakazawa shuddered at the thought of Tanaka's fate—a boy who had lived a life of wealth during the war years and who, orphaned, set his goals on being among the strong who would be leaders in the next generation of the Yakuza. If not for the strange eddy of air that had set Nakazawa's mother gently on the ground with a piece of her house, Keiji knew that he would very likely have followed Tanaka's path.

"My survival was a matter of sheer luck," Nakazawa concluded. "I simply could not think it otherwise. I gave thanks that Mom had survived."

The Yakuza gradually seized ownership of the emerging new city. Even the police feared them. Nakazawa feared them, too, and would not follow Tanaka into their world. He would always look back on having been kept away from it by his mother.

The Nakazawa boy did not have much firsthand information about what the syndicates were doing; but he did hear stories from Tanaka, from which he was able to piece together some of the history: "Yakuza used kids as bullets. They were sweet-talked—'Kill one of the other gang's leaders, and we'll make you one of our gang's leaders.' They were not only *used* as bullets; they were as expendable as bullets. They took fire. They died. The Yakuza collected unprotected orphans because no parents were around to [complain about] what happened to them, so they could be used safely. The girls were turned into prostitutes. Tanaka was used by the Yakuza as a mere tool and never did ascend to leadership. Eventually he went to jail, and bounced from jail to jail."[15]

Tanemori's beloved sister, Masuyo, died during their father's burial rites. From that day onward he was like Tanaka—*oyanashigo*, orphaned. The thought terrified him. In Japan, during the era of warlords, the *oyanashigo* were by tradition treated, through a perverse righteousness, as objects worthy only of contempt and social disgrace. Even in the postwar farming community of Kotachi, from the moment of his father's death, Tanemori became, "like a kite without a tail in a whirlwind—twisting and turning and tumbling."

Determined not to be torn apart like a kite, Tanemori told himself that he must be a lion instead, that he would restore his family to its former honor and live to seek revenge against those who had designed and built the atomic bomb.

"But how could I begin to think such things?" he would ask a friend, years later. "How could I think it, when almost from the day of my father's burial, I became a street urchin? As an orphan in those days, society cut you off from the dignity of your family roots and even from food.

"And, yes—many times I went into the garbage cans, looking for something to eat. And did you know, those rats—they were already there before me? I would shout, 'You rat! Get away!'

"I fought rats for food. I did that many times."

Nearly seventy years later, after he achieved a moderate level of fame in California as an artist who, though mostly blinded, was able to produce colorful and beautifully composed paintings (with a little guidance from his children), he would often invite a visitor who came to his studio for a meal: "Always, always, I enjoy sharing food. Why? Because I've known real hunger. Food is a life-gift, so I want to share it."

When he returned to the ruins of Hiroshima with another orphaned relative, Tanemori joined the black-market stands that, throughout 1946 and despite their often questionable meats, had become one of Keiji Nakazawa's favorite play areas. More people than Tanemori expected to find were living in shacks near the "T" Bridge. Some were living unsheltered on the streets, bringing Tanemori to even grimmer fears about the future. Even the discovery one day of caramelized sugar filled with ants did little to raise his hopes. He popped the ant candy into his mouth—his first taste of candy in more than two years. Savoring the sweetness of it could not remove Tanemori from the dark and lonely realities of Hiroshima. Something far less fortifying than sugar, and yet at the same time far more fortifying, was required.

"We were told nothing would grow in Hiroshima for the next seventy-five years," Tanemori recalled. "I stood in the smoke of a stand whose owner was grilling sparrows—and I noticed a defiant little blade of grass right next to me, emerging from the ruin. I scooped it up, no longer feeling quite so alone. If that blade of grass could live on, so could I."[16]

All around Nyokodo and along the path down to the hypocenter, burned and broken trees that appeared to be dead had continued to send up healthy green shoots.

"Another example," Nagai reiterated for Akizuki, "of how, at the very bottom, there is always the great earth."

An inspiring thought, Akizuki guessed, *if one is willing to ignore the monsters.* In a corner of Dr. Nagai's garden, a crown chrysanthemum had bloomed with its petals arranged in the flower's center, and with multiple central heads surrounding the petals.[17] And on a scorched wall, a vine of pale ivy flourished without chlorophyll—a vine whose seeds were already spreading as far away as Tokyo.[18]

Dr. Akizuki was no longer as concerned about the health of his natural surroundings as about Nagai's health. His white blood cell count had reached more than four times normal and was represented by "many mitotic figures"—which defined cancer.

"I've had a good run," Nagai said. "I guess this means I must quicken my studies and write faster."

At Akizuki's request, a microscope was delivered to Nyokodo, so Nagai could study the health of Ground Zero plants at home. As he became increasingly confined to bed, he did indeed begin writing faster; in addition to filling notebooks with biological observations, he wrote the first of thirteen books, *The Bells of Nagasaki*, which he penned between May and July 1946.

Revisiting an earlier confrontational discussion with Akizuki, Nagai read his friend a passage from the final chapter: "God concealed within the universe a precious sword. First the human race caught the scent of this awful treasure. Then we began to search for it. And finally we grasped it in our hands. What kind of dance will we humans perform while brandishing this two-edged sword?"

Akizuki shook his head slowly. "No God," he sniped. "No sword planted in the universe, either. I said it before and I'll say it again: God had nothing to do with this."

"You miss the point. Whether you see God in it or not, it's either the keys to the universe for us or the fall of our civilization, if not our extinction. So, which shall it be?"

"Stop thinking so much," Akizuki said. "You need to conserve your strength."

"Oh, I think God will keep me around longer than you anticipate. You and I both know that I need to write a lot more if I'm going to pass my entrance exam."

Dr. Akizuki did not believe Nagai needed to hurry with his entrance exam to heaven, any more than he believed an invisible friend in heaven would grade the papers. By the first anniversary of the bombing, Paul Nagai's leukemia cells had doubled once again in population from their July value. Statistically speaking, he would probably be dead within considerably less than a year.

Five months later, his second book was finished and his first was coming off the press. Ten months after that—more than three months after Akizuki expected Nagai to be exploring whatever happened (or did not happen) to one's conscious existence after death—admirers of his first book began paying visits, without any warning. One of them was Helen Keller.

Nagai wrote in his journal: "She came toward me, her hand searching in the air for my hand. Finally our fingers touched and we grasped each other's hands. In an instant, I felt the warmth of her love flow through my extremities like electricity through a closed circuit."

Helen Keller explained through an interpreter that she could not see what the weapon had done to Urakami—but more than a year later, she could smell it.

"I cannot smell it," Nagai said. "But sometimes late at night I *feel* it. The lesson I take from this place is that the person who wishes for peace does not hide even a needle as a weapon. Even when driven to the need for self-defense, if you have a weapon, you are qualified to fight—maybe—but you are not qualified to pray for peace."

Akizuki wished Nagai would stop talking like this and simply return as a patient to the newly resupplied and now nearly half rebuilt hospital. "Your Nyokodo is becoming more of a tourist attraction than a home or a proper sick room, and the visitors are draining too much of your energy."

His book was indeed bringing too many visitors: parents who had lost their children and wanted revenge . . . a representative from the Vatican who wanted a message of peace; and three monks from Tibet who sought the same. And then, two polite men from a new American establishment called the Internal Revenue Service.

"What have you done, in terms of paying your tax obligation from the sales of your book?" they inquired.

"Taxes?" Nagai asked. "I only need this workplace, as you see it here. Everything else—including the money from my writing—I have given to the orphans of this city."

"But you're not allowed to do that before settling your tax obligation."

Nagai served them tea and said, "Men with wiser voices than mine have always preached that charity is the cornerstone of faith. They tell us that if you adopt orphans into your heart, you will be the father of many children."

"Who said that?" one of the taxmen asked.

"Jesus, for one example."

"Really?"

Nagai nodded, gave the men a warm smile, and told them to drink the tea because it was good for their health.

The IRS did not bother him again, but other people continued arriving at his one-room home and workplace, as Nagai's face and abdomen began to swell, and as his strength declined to only one-fifth that of a healthy man's.

"I wanted to live here with you in quiet happiness," he told Kayano and Makoto. "But now it has become impossible to fulfill that wish."

The reconstruction of railways and streetcar lines brought even greater numbers of visitors each passing month. During the day, Nagai served each of them tea, and by the time the last streetcar left outer Urakami each evening, his own stomach was so full of tea that he could not sleep at night, so he stayed up writing while the children slept.

In the morning he was often too exhausted to join the children in play—Kayano and Makoto as well as orphans placed with new parents in neighboring homes. That he spent so much of his strength on others as to leave nothing for play pained Nagai far, far more than the advancing cancer, he told Makoto.

To Makoto, his father's guilt would become every bit as undeserved as the burden carried by Dr. Hachiya of Hiroshima. Makoto never once doubted his father's love, and he was truly thankful to him for the Nyokodo message: To stop a nuclear war, Dr. Nagai taught, you cannot rely only on governments. You have to empower the individual. Though even Nagai's own children had been stricken by black rain, and were to die young, Makoto would live long enough to pass the message forward into the next century through his own son, Tokusaburo Nagai.

"You start with an act of love or kindness to your neighbor," Tokusaburo would tell a new generation, more than sixty years later. By then a museum and library complex would surround the Nyokodo hut, in a thriving suburb whose tree-lined streets hid every trace of hypocenter scarring.

"I do not know for a fact that a spreading ripple of mutual human tenderness can overcome the darker half of human instinct," Tokusaburo would say. "But we need to try; because those of us who were born afterward can scarcely understand how scary it really was, and how important the peace is. Down this road, where the Sun touched the Earth, there are tall office buildings and tall trees everywhere—and if you search carefully, you will come upon a white statue of a young girl holding a paper crane—and beyond the statue, you'll find a dome of grass in a garden where a plaque reads 'HYPO-CENTER.' All the ruins are covered up by offices and gardens; so it's easy to forget the terror and that's why I am saying, *Start by loving your neighbors. Start, by loving others as you love yourself.* That's what Grandfather taught his children, and anyone else who would listen."

In February 1951, five years after Dr. Akizuki had expected Paul Nagai to be dead, his white blood cell count reached sixty-five times the normal value. While finishing *Maiden Pass* (a history of Nagasaki's Christian community from the time of the 1870 oppression through the destruction of Urakami Cathedral), internal bleeding in Nagai's right shoulder left his right hand paralyzed.

Nagai dictated the last few pages to nine-year-old Kayano. Having come to regard the disappearance of Urakami's "Maria" Cathedral and its congregation on August 9, 1945, as a prophetic sacrifice, he told Kayano, "Even if you are one of the last people on earth, you must be against war."

When Nagai died on May 1, 1951, Dr. Akizuki was unable to figure out what force of will had kept him alive so long. An autopsy revealed that his blood had probably become all but nonfunctional years before. It was as if Akizuki's often adversarial colleague had somehow managed to reanimate himself and walk around in a body that was already quite dead, but to Nagai's mind, and at his insistence, alive-seeming still.

By New Year's Day 1952, Akizuki had read everything Nagai wrote while living in Ground Zero, and he began asking his friend's two children to teach him everything they could remember that remained unwritten. Afterward he began to take part in honoring Nagai's work, and he evolved, like Nagai, into a man of peace and faith.

"Well, and why not?" Akizuki said to the children of Nyokodo.

"After all, haven't scientists and Buddhists, physicians and Christians been saying very much the same thing all along to those who had ears to listen? It's just that, sometimes, we use different language. Different words." And with such grace did Akizuki begin to live the rest of his life with one simple, *Nyokodo*-esque commandment: "Be kind."[19]

In the years during which Dr. Akizuki became a convert to *Nyokodo*, Hiroshima's crime syndicates were ascendant.

From young Emiko Nakasako's close perspective, the opportunists were worse than even Keiji Nakazawa had described. During the first weeks after the surrender, young Japanese girls had feared being raped by American occupation forces. The foretold American rape gangs never materialized. As it turned out, young Japanese girls, if orphaned, were preyed upon by Yakuza pimps who swept into the city, raped them, and forced them into prostitution.

"Even before the first soldiers arrived," Nakasako would record, "the adult criminals came into Hiroshima and were organizing the orphan boys to steal—almost like Fagan and Sykes in Charles Dickens' *Oliver Twist.*"

These lost boys, Nakasako recalled, might have been among the lucky ones. More than a third of her classmates were orphaned, and among the remainder, few survived to return to school. In their fight to stay alive, the weak were killed. What passed for a local schoolhouse was merely a round timber roof built around a single surviving pillar that had once held up the facade of an office building. Nakasako called it, "the Bento Box School." Its first graduating class of 1946 consisted of only one student. The underworld of Hiroshima flourished all around the school, very quickly, reaching out its tendrils—with promises of food and even wealth—to hungry, abandoned children.

As Nakasako watched, the surviving orphans developed a sincere hatred toward adult society—"because they were exploited by adult criminals," she recorded. "Should we have been surprised, therefore, when the strongest of these hate-filled orphans developed a code of their own, and became the next stage in the evolution of the underworld? Of course not! They were the inevitable result. Exploited and abused because they were abandoned and hungry, out of Hiroshima came the next generation of abusers."[20]

During his teenage years, Takashi Tanemori escaped the fate of other atomic orphans, more or less. His escape came as the illusory safety of an offer of employment in America. He had been told by a government interpreter that the United States was extending a merciful hand to survivors of Hiroshima.

Tanemori was assigned to field work on a California farm. Under the hot sun, several years of previously untreated blood abnormalities and ulcerations in his stomach began to take their toll. One night, he began vomiting blood, and was transported to a naval hospital in Bakersfield. When he was identified as an orphan of Hiroshima, countless doctors began visiting, one after another, wearing protective isolation garments.

"I had become a guinea pig," Tanemori recalled. "I was an experiment in the hands of doctors acting in the name of radiation research." Like Tanaka, he found himself in a dark place where those who seized control of his life knew that there were no parents or close relatives who would rescue him. Tanemori's disappearance was complete by the time he was transferred to the Modesto County Mental Hospital. There, doctors subjected the orphan to bone marrow sampling and spinal taps. Using the primitive medical tools of the 1950s, the tests were not only incomparably painful, but incompetent as well. There was simply no useful information to be gained about radiation exposure from spinal taps.

What he at first believed would be only days of torture became weeks of torture; and as the weeks became months, the boy had screamed out for revenge against the doctors and attacked them as best he could—"by which behavior," he would write later, "I probably confirmed their perception of me as a dangerous, crazed animal, to be kept in a cage. I nearly fainted when I first saw my disfigurement reflected in a mirror. My eyes had lost their power and were hollow, driven deep into their sockets. My cheekbones protruded. There was no beauty I could recognize in myself—either of who I had been or who I was supposed to be. I was a ghost, standing in darkness. Somehow, my soul was not dead. The inferno for revenge was keeping it alive. Revenge: My dark companion. My friend. My comforter!"

At night, Tanemori pulled sheets over himself and crawled under the bed, not wanting Daddy's spirit to look down through the barred windows and see him living in shame, like a criminal. He shoved the corner of a sheet into his mouth—"to silence my cries so Daddy would not hear me."

In the end, a nurse named Mary Furr diverted Tanemori from his journey of revenge and toward what he would later call "a bridge to forgiveness."

Mary had rallied the support of other nurses, then two doctors, and finally a judge against the doctor who was leading the radiation study. The judge agreed with Mary Furr: "The boy does not need all of this so-called medical treatment. All he needs is for someone to love him, like family."

One day, Mary entered Takashi Tanemori's cell, put her hand upon his, and promised, "No one is ever going to hurt you again." Mary had become his legal guardian, or what Tanemori would later call, his "guardian angel." As she drove him away from the hospital, Tanemori looked back through the rear window and she grabbed his arm, saying, "Don't you ever look back. You only look forward."

From time to time, Mary Furr's kindness confused him more than the spinal taps: "Her caring began to thaw a heart frozen by hatred and revenge. I just could not stop the thawing of my heart—and the thawing brought its own brand of torture."

"*No!*" Tanemori cried out one night, to the stars themselves and to his father's spirit. "Daddy, I have made a promise that even if it takes two hundred

Takashi Tanemori [Illustration: CRP]

years, I would achieve my revenge. But here I am, with Mary. Daddy, what can I do?"

The thaw continued, as did the confusion. After Tanemori learned that Mary was a Baptist Christian, he began studying to become a minister. He preached, he opened a restaurant, he married and started a family. And through all of this, his old friend, his comforter, held on, making him a self-described Jekyll and Hyde. By day he spoke of God's love, God's forgiveness; but at night, the promise of revenge too often slithered into his heart and gained dominion over his thoughts.

Then, one August morning, Tanemori believed he felt his father's presence. Next, and with what he would describe as an absolute certainty, he *saw* Daddy's spirit, standing directly before him, wearing the Shogun lineage family crest. Tanemori felt Daddy laying his hand upon his shoulder, and heard him say, "My son, my son. You have found the greatest way to avenge your enemy, by learning to forgive him."

Tanemori believed that his father knew he was finally finding home—a place called peace.

But it remained an uneasy peace.

On another August day, he was called upon to be a featured speaker at an anti-war rally in San Francisco—one of those increasingly self-contradictory rallies of the period that were becoming characterized by such slogans as "Fight for peace."

"This might be the day that I honor my heart," Tanemori said, as he drove toward the Bay Bridge with his little girl. He described to her how sharply he had been focusing his "pay-back" speech—a speech about revenge.

"Daddy, is there any other way?" Tamemori's daughter asked. When he stopped the car and turned to look at her, the child had tears in her eyes.

"I was struck by the reality that revenge breeds revenge," Tanemori wrote later to a friend. "I knew now that I would be followed by an eternal burden unless I did something to [forever] change my heart. I could not afford to pass down the consequences of revenge to my children. I saw unmistakably and irrevocably that my enemies were not the Americans (who built the bomb, who kidnapped an atomic orphan for their experiments) or the members of Japanese society (who thrust orphans into my position). The enemy was none other than me, the darkness of my own heart.

"I wiped my bitter tears with one motion, as my soul teetered between two options: Revenge or what I must do. Just as I reached for the car ignition, a white butterfly fluttered in through my open window and landed on the dashboard. It was like one of the spirits I had seen in my dream of Hiroshima, all those years ago."[21]

In Hiroshima and beyond, while Tanemori sought his bridge to forgiveness, and while Dr. Nagai became crippled by his own blood and taught Akizuki how to stand, the fortunes and misfortunes of other survivors and witnesses were being altered as dramatically as Urakami's increasingly green landscape.

Eizo Nomura, who had managed somehow to walk away alive from the Rationing Bureau's basement—only one hundred meters from Hiroshima's "Atomic Dome"—was dying from a full spectrum of medical complications.

Double survivor Kenshi Hirata, who had carried his wife's bones from Hiroshima to Nagasaki, did as Setsuko's parents had instructed him, and started a new family. When a local news report identified Kenshi as a man twice exposed to radiation who was now a father, the *hibakusha* (and soon enough their children) were already living under the spreading shadow of discrimination next of kin to the discrimination against lepers in prior centuries. Kenshi disappeared with his family so perfectly that despite the efforts of many researchers spanning more than a half century, no one seemed able to find him.

As a "prisoner of peace," nuclear physicist Yoshio Nishina continued to maintain close professional relationships with his prewar colleagues, including Luis Alvarez, Niels Bohr, and Albert Einstein, until he passed away suddenly in 1951.

Nishina's assistant Eizo Tajima had been one of the first scientists into the hypocenters of the two cities. Noticing that flash-shadows sometimes stretched out behind objects that survived the blast wave, and that they pointed like accusing fingers toward the origin of the flash, Tajima accurately determined the precise location of the Urakami hypocenter. He also excavated samples from beneath the flash point, inhaling dust that was still highly radioactive despite being mostly decayed, and sentencing himself, sooner or later, to slow death.

Paul Tibbets would outlast Tajima and Nishina, dying of natural causes in 2007, proud of *Enola Gay*'s role in history.

Field Marshal Shunroku Hata, whose survival in a Hiroshima shock cocoon led him to believe that atomic attack could easily be endured (which belief contributed to the delay of Japan's surrender) was arrested in 1945 and found guilty of atrocities as commander of 1941's Zhejiang-Jiangxi campaign, during which, according to Chinese sources, a quarter million Chinese civilians were killed. He would outlive Dr. Nagai by eleven years and would die unrepentant.

General Seizo Arisue, chief of Japanese Military Intelligence throughout the war, used his extensive knowledge about the Soviet Union and China as leverage with General MacArthur, to become a "prisoner of peace." He was, like Dr. Nishina, allowed to live free yet under guard, instead of being confined to a three-pace by two-pace concrete cell, like Hata. Arisue was instrumental in buying, for Drs. Kitano Masaji, Shiro Ishi, and their colleagues, immunity from prosecution for human experimentation in China's Unit 731 biological weapons facility, so that MacArthur's people could transfer bio-weapons technology to America's Cold War weaponeers, notwithstanding the the general's knowledge that some of his own men were among the prisoners killed during the Unit 731 experiments. None who came under the control of MacArthur's various protocols, or who encountered him personally, seemed to develop a middle-ground view; it was either love or hate. Most agreed that the American general was, if nothing else, decisive, and that, had *Hamlet* been about MacArthur, it would only have been a one-act play.

Three years after Dr. Paul Nagai died, and nine years after the war, Sadako Sasaki, the two-year-old who had survived Hiroshima's fire worms and black rain in an overcrowded lifeboat, was growing up to be an unusually athletic child whose teacher Nomura began to see her as an Olympic hopeful. During interschool sports day events, fleet-footed Sadako dominated all of the speed records, and helped to pull her class relay team from its previous standing in last place into second, and then into first.

As a reward, the class won a field trip to the Miyajima Shrine Island, where eleven-year-old Sadako promptly challenged her teammates with a race to the top of Mount Misen—up the very same steps Kenshi and Setsuko Hirata had climbed in 1945, at the beginning of a marriage that lasted only ten days.

At the peak, everyone laughed when Sadako called out to her exhausted friends, "Well, that was fun. But now I'm hungry, so when do we eat lunch?"

Another classmate cautioned that it was not safe to joke near the mountaintop, because a jealous goddess was rumored to dwell there. Sadako looked her friend in the eye with feigned severity, and said, "We've lived in Hiroshima too long to be afraid of ghosts. Just look around you."

Fully one-third of the children in their class were survivors, and more than half of this third had lost parents and grandparents, brothers and sisters.

Sadako continued, "We've lived through the atomic bomb, you and I. Nothing else as bad can happen."

Indeed, it did not seem possible. Sadako, her mother Fujiko, and her brother Masahiro had been shock-cocooned and shadow-shielded in a region where almost everyone else died. During the early photoreconnaissance flights over Hiroshima, planes had often followed the railroad tracks through Sadako's neighborhood. There, the low angle of the heat ray had cast long shadows. One individual walking across the Misasa Bridge at the exact moment of the *pika* left a ghost image pointing upriver, across the walkway, down the curb, and onto the road surface. The person who cast that shadow appeared to be one of the few shadow people who could actually be named. On that very same walkway, at 8:15 a.m., Shizuko Ohara, a petite nineteen-year-old from Sadako's neighborhood, had been walking to work and was wearing a light dress.[22] A soldier found her and assisted her to the Communications Hospital, where she died from flash burns (and probably from exposure to black rain) at approximately the moment Dr. Hachiya felt a tremor, and the sky boomed in the direction of Nagasaki.[23]

So how, Sadako wondered—how, after escaping Shizuko Ohara's fate herself, could anything unlucky ever happen? The first nine years after the war had been difficult, but everything seemed gradually to have improved. During the first two years, Sadako's family had lived with relatives a hundred kilometers upriver, in the town of Miyoshi, before returning to Hiroshima in 1947. They settled near a badly damaged steel-and-concrete school with ceilings that leaked and a gymnasium that had no roof at all. Their new house was smaller than the old one, but Father opened a hair salon in the midst of the Ground Zero settlement, less than four blocks from the school where nurse Minami witnessed the ghostly blue fireflies.

In 1954, the roof of the main building still leaked and multiple classes were being held in a partitioned auditorium, but at least the gymnasium had a new roof.[24] Athletic competition and practice sessions were Sadako's favorite parts of every school day.[25]

Though her parents spoke often of a languishing economy, Sadako felt that life was good, and that even her difficult beginnings—because she had survived where so many others died—must indeed have been filled with good luck signs.

Then, in December 1954, she began arriving home from after-school track practice complaining of being increasingly worn out. Over the course of only a few short weeks, Sadako's dinner table conversations became more and more dominated by murmurings of, "Tired . . . tired . . ." In late January, going to bed early no longer seemed to help. Gradually, she was becoming tired even at breakfast. The bad times really began gathering force in January 1955, when a new family photograph revealed by chance the first clear signs of swollen lymph nodes on one side of Sadako's neck.

Frightened by the photo, Father took her to a doctor for blood tests. The results were as horribly apparent as the swelling in the photograph: "an abnormally high white blood cell count . . . many mitotic figures . . . leukemia."

The doctors asked Shigeo Sasaki if his daughter had been exposed to black rain. And when he confirmed that this was indeed the case, the doctor bowed his head.

"Atomic bomb disease," he said, in a voice that cracked from having given this same diagnosis to scores of other parents: the most unnatural horror for all—for parents to outlive their children.

For a little while longer, Sadako felt well enough to attend school, play jump rope with her friends, and live at home; but on February 21, 1955, she was hospitalized. The disease seemed to strike like a lightning bolt. During a span of weeks, her blood counts deteriorated to levels that had taken the late Dr. Nagai more than two years to reach. Judging from the rate of her decline, a doctor told Mr. and Mrs. Sasaki that their daughter probably had less than a year to live, more likely only three or four months. Leukemia was not only incurable, its symptoms were all but untreatable, given even the best that 1955 medical technology could offer. The doctors told Shigeo that they could only try to reduce his daughter's fevers, administer painkillers, and provide occasional blood transfusions.

Sadako's mother was bewildered. Only seven months earlier, during an annual physical at the Atomic Bomb Casualty Commission clinic, doctors had said that both children's blood values were absolutely normal. Even now, Sadako did not look sick to Fujiko—merely a little sleepier than usual.

"No one is lovelier to a mother than her most miserable child," Fujiko Sasaki said later. When Sadako was born during the war there was rarely enough food and she had always been at least slightly underweight. Yet in spite of the hungry years, she grew to become so thoughtful and considerate an adolescent that Fujiko came to depend upon her; and in years to come, when Sadako visited Fujiko in her dreams she would always say, "Leave it to me, Mom," and Fujiko would awaken calling her daughter's name.

That first night in the hospital, Fujiko and Shigeo stayed in chairs at Sadako's bedside until sunrise. On any given night thereafter, Sadako went to sleep knowing that when she awoke in the morning, one of them would always be there. They kept back their tears for her, not wanting to make their child any more afraid than she already was—and, as Sadako slept, her mother held her hand and prayed to herself: "If a medicine that can cure this disease exists in this world, then let me borrow money for it, even if it costs ten million yen. Or, if it is possible, let me die in her place. Please, give the disease to me instead."

That same night and during many others that followed, Mr. Sasaki prayed the same prayer, while trying to form for himself a plan for something—*anything* he could do to help raise Sadako's spirits, and maybe give her a little more time. Dr. Nagai had famously reported that being close to one's family, being meditative, and receiving even the simplest "gifts of the heart" from loved ones could keep a patient's will to live intact, even when the body was saying, "It's time to give up and move on."

Shigeo and Fujiko had an idea for a gift from the heart. After the severe rationing years of the war were over, even though food became more widely available, money fell into short supply. Still, the Sasakis had dreamed of one day buying their little girl a fine, dress-up kimono. Money remained as scarce as ever, but Mr. Sasaki realized that a gift from the heart would be rendered even more powerful if, instead of buying the kimono (which was prohibitively expensive under the best circumstances), he and Fujiko made one with their own hands. They bought silk fabric decorated with a cherry blossom pattern— and at night, while Sadako slept, Mrs. Sasaki and the rest of the family took turns at cutting and fashioning the sleeves and belt, and all the other individual parts of the kimono, which Mrs. Sasaki checked and double-checked for quality before assembling them into the completed garment.

On the day she opened the box and ran her fingers over the silk, Sadako broke into smiles and tears at the same time.

"You did too much for me," she said. "You spent too much."

Fujiko said, "Please, model it for us," and she withdrew a camera from a large bag. She also withdrew a little silk pocketbook and a pair of zori sandals—and Sadako seemed to become filled with joy and to swell with life's surge, even as she wiped tears from her eyes.

"I'm not a good daughter," Sadako told her brother Masahiro. "It's a bad situation because Mom and Dad will be having to spend so much money for my sickness."

"There was very little income for anyone in those times," Masahiro would tell history. "Even the doctors were poor. They and the nurses gave my sister everything they could—including vitamin B injections and anti-inflammatory drugs that kept the swelling of Sadako's body under some kind of control. But all of the nurses and all of the doctors could not fund the blood transfusions beyond a monthly donation of their own blood—and there were many other leukemic children in the wards.

"So, my parents had to pay people for the blood transfusions. Father was making a living by cutting hair, and in order to fund each transfusion, he would have to serve five customers. My little sister knew the situation, and told me that she would accept it and deal with it somehow. She understood that if she received a transfusion of healthy blood, she would feel better only for about ten hours; and she saw also that economically and emotionally, it must have been getting bad for us. Here lay a grade-school girl who saw that her parents wanted to help her—a girl who also seemed to know that, except for a miracle, she really could not get better. She guessed she could probably live a little while longer if she received transfusions and medicine; but she knew at the same time that her parents' support was making them poorer. Emotionally, she was being torn in two directions."

"I just have to find a way to deal with it," Sadako told her brother, repeatedly. "We have to get by, somehow."

By March 1955 Sadako's white blood cell count seemed to stabilize at about six times the normal value, but her abnormal red cell structure brought her close to oxygen starvation and made walking even short distances difficult. A severe drop in platelet counts was causing bruising from even the gentlest touch, which raised constant fears that Sadako could be killed by a hug.

In early May, local schoolchildren brought a box of colorful paper cranes to the hospital's nurses, and showed them how to fold paper cranes themselves. Throughout the day, Sadako observed the staff carrying around the pieces of multicolored origami art. When her father arrived, she pointed to a paper crane someone had left at her bedside and asked, "What is it, about these paper cranes?"

"Why, someone probably sent the cranes as a wish for wellness to all the children here."

Shigeo remembered what Paul Nagai had written about the pain-relieving and potentially healing powers of concentrated, enthusiastic thought. He also knew of a legend, dating back to the 1600s and the Shogun era, about the crane, and about what it meant to fold a thousand of them; and this gave him an idea.

"Sadako-san," her father said cheerily, "there is a legend that the crane lives for a thousand years. And they say that if you fold a thousand paper cranes, putting your heart into each one, they will help you with your wish for wellness."

And so it began: Sadako's first three or four cranes were large and lop-sided, and the heads did not bow down quite right. After her first twenty, they became perfectly symmetrical, although when nurses came to take blood samples, the slightest movement sent two or three pieces of origami to the floor. So Masahiro brought a long, long string to the hospital, pushed a pin through the twenty paper cranes, and threaded them together.

The first twenty averaged ten centimeters in length (about the size of a sparrow). Among them was a large silver crane, fashioned from a piece of protective paper from an X-ray plate, which had been given to Sadako by one of the doctors.

"Now I have only nine hundred and eighty left to fold," Sadako announced. The difficulty now lay in acquiring enough paper, which was expensive in these times. She traveled to other patients' rooms asking for paper wrappings from get-well cards and candies. By mid-May, more silver X-ray cranes had joined the strand. Red cellophane from medicine wrappings followed the silver cranes, in addition to any piece of colorful paper that Sadako's family, the doctors, and the nurses could scrounge from anywhere, including squares of color cut from eye-catching magazine advertisements. It became a quiet group effort, with nearly a dozen people straightening all of the wrinkles out of paper scraps and leaving them under Sadako's bed.

Sadako soon discovered that conserving paper by folding smaller cranes required greater effort to make each fold. This suited her. By the end of May, the cranes were down to an average length of seven centimeters (almost the size of a hummingbird). Sadako's blood abnormalities were also down—from six times a normal white cell count to only twice normal.

She now felt well enough to go home for a weekend; and when she returned to the hospital on Sunday evening, Sadako told the doctors, "I think I have enough strength, these days, to be a good roommate."

The nurses nodded agreement, and moved her into a double room with a junior high school girl named Kiyo, who happened to be relatively energetic and very widely read, and who introduced Sadako to all sorts of fantastic, forward-looking novels, ranging from stories about Isaac Asimov's utopian robotic societies to Ray Bradbury's *Martian Chronicles* and Arthur C. Clarke's *Childhood End*.

The two girls began corresponding with other readers of fiction through hospital-sponsored pen-pal programs—and throughout their spring season surge of activity, Sadako still had enough reserve energy to show her father and Masahiro a continuous strand of paper cranes, and to announce, proudly, "Only five hundred and fifty to go. I'm almost halfway there!"

By this time, the cranes were shrinking to average lengths of four centimeters (still within the size range of the smallest hummingbird). "Her eyes were shining while she was folding the cranes," Sadako's mother observed, "showing that she wanted to survive by all means."

She was twelve years old now, and after May had phased into June, and as the cranes continued to shrink, Sadako's white blood cell count climbed from twice the normal value to three times normal. She began to run high fevers. The progress of leukemia was very similar to the effects of prompt radiation, and yet at the same time, quite the opposite. One disease produced a deficit of white blood cells; the other produced too great a wealth of them. In the latter case, the enormous quantity of white blood cells was essentially a mutant population of wild, amoeba-like animals that absorbed nutrients from Sadako without doing their assigned jobs. Instead of defending her body from disease-causing viral and bacterial intruders, many cells were joining the other side and becoming invasive organisms in their own right. Sadako's body was at war with itself, prone to infection and to an attack by her own blood against her internal organs.

The doctors offered painkillers, but she waved the needles away. At first Masahiro thought this was because the opium-based substance was rare and expensive. He heard Sadako reiterate to her father an earlier fear: "I'm a bad child to you, aren't I? I've used up so much money being sick."

Shigeo Sasaki recalled later, "The doctors recommended that we bring her fresh carrots and other vegetables. But juicing machines cost so much. We couldn't afford one and neither could the hospital—because it was listed as nonessential medical equipment and was not even regarded as medical equipment in any case. If we had owned the proper kind of juicer, we could have gotten more nutrition into Sadako even as the time approached when she would lose her appetite. Thinking about this makes me feel wretched."

"It was the cost of the morphine that made her turn away whatever comfort the painkillers might have brought," Masahiro told a relative. But even here, he eventually came to understand that he had underestimated his sister. By now he could not escape noticing that as her little body was slowly breaking down, the paper cranes continued to grow progressively smaller. By late July, after fevers began spiking so high that the doctors resorted to bathing Sadako in cold water, the cranes were down to the size of bumblebees. She had only enough energy to fold five or six per day.

In August, Sadako's white blood cell count improved to only four times normal, then to three times normal. Her crane project began to pick up pace again: fifty in a day, a hundred. *Finished.*

The thousandth crane was barely larger than a honeybee. No one knew, at this time, that Sadako had been spying on her doctors and copying their records onto a piece of paper, charting her own blood counts. A month earlier, a boy in the same pediatric ward for atomic bomb disease—a boy about her own age—died of leukemia. Sadako told her father, "It'll be me, next time."

During her low point in July, when Sadako's paper crane project had slowed down to only five or six per day, her blood values were almost as deadly as the boy's. No one ever mentioned to Sadako that the disease she had was leukemia, but she clearly understood. Her hand-copied record of blood values broke off after the other child died, and Sadako began a second string of paper cranes—which continued to steadily diminish in size. Soon, she could no longer fold the cranes with her fingers. No one could, as they diminished nearly half again, from the size of honeybees into the realm of the smaller varieties of houseflies.[26] The folds became so delicate that she used sewing needles to score and shape each wing—"As if it were a prayer," Masahiro would remember.[27]

Shigeo warned his daughter, "Soon they'll be smaller than grains of rice. If you keep up that pace, you'll wear yourself out."

Sadako said, "It's okay, Dad. I have a plan."

"The reason for this," she told her brother Masahiro, "is that I still have hope of getting well." Even if hope itself appeared to be diminishing, she decided, "I must put more of my heart and soul into each one. The smallest cranes are the most difficult of all to create. So, if I'm going to continue to do this thing, I'm going to put more and more of my spirit into each one."

"*All* of my spirit," she confided to Masahiro, as her father's prediction of cranes smaller than rice grains became prophetic, "*all* of me . . . because, in time, the smallest cranes may be all that's left of me."

On August 19, 1955, it began to look as if Sadako could begin to hope again for a miracle. Though still quite anemic, her white blood cell count was now only twice normal. She displayed for her roommate Kiyo and for her family more than a hundred miniature paper cranes on a bedside table.

"You intend to make another thousand of these?" her father asked.

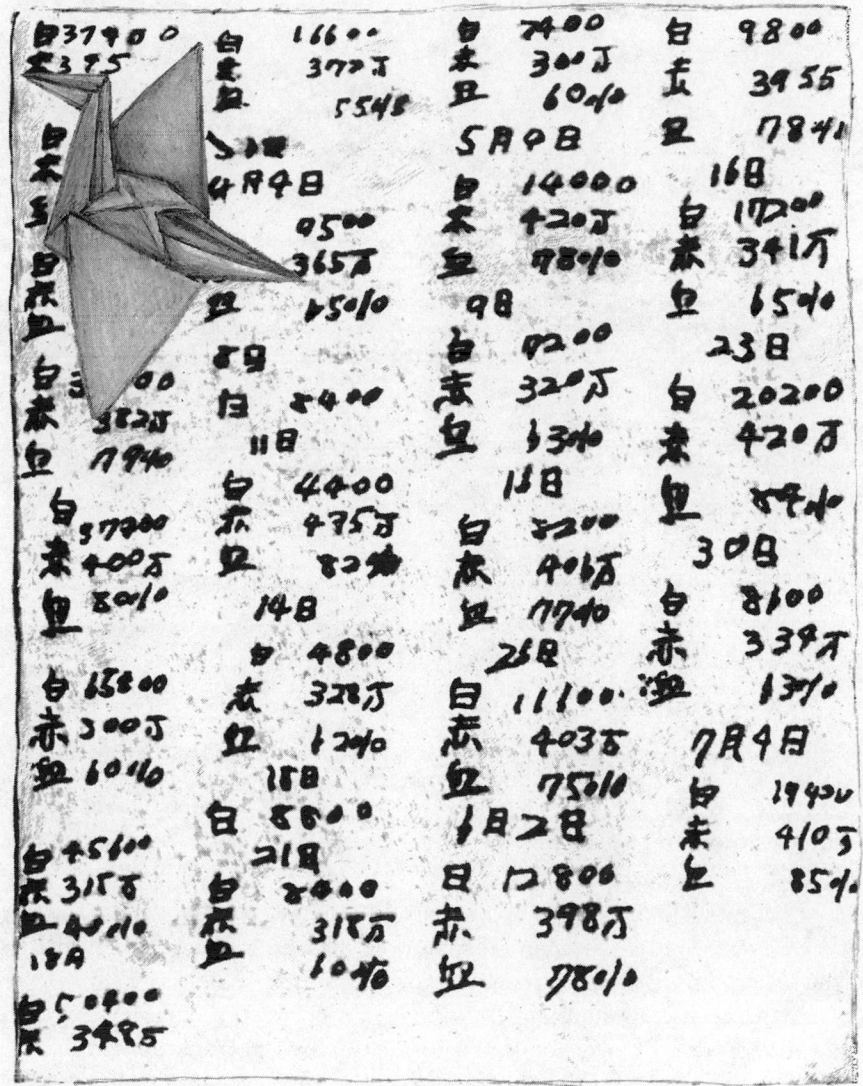

Charting atomic bomb disease: Sadako Sasaki's family and her doctors did not know at the time, but through much of 1955 Sadako was secretly spying on her doctors and copying her medical records onto a log of blood values which she kept hidden beneath her bed. [Illustration: Patricia Wynne]

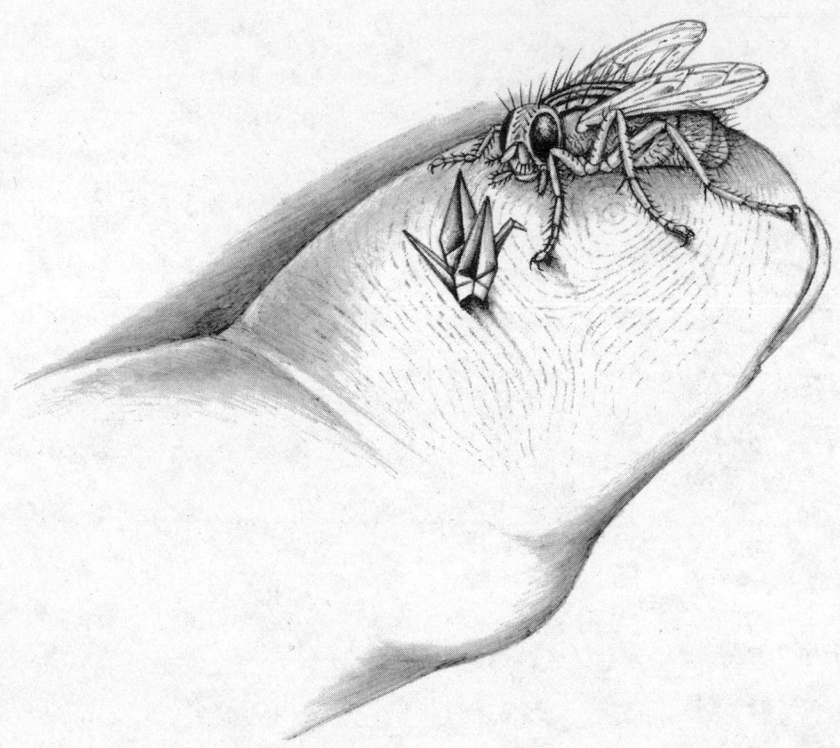

As Sadako grew progressively weaker from atomic bomb disease, the paper cranes she folded diminished below the size of houseflies, each requiring more of her concentration, more of her meditations on Omoiyari, and "never again, the A-bomb." By then, she had developed a technique for making the delicate folds using pairs of needles. The last paper crane Sadako made was smaller than most gnats. [Illustration: Patricia Wynne]

"The number isn't important anymore," Sadako replied. "What matters is the act of putting all of my concentration into each crane."

"You can't keep doing this," Shigeo said. "Save your energy. Just rest."

"Father, don't worry about me. I have my own plans. A new idea."

"But she never said exactly what that plan was," Masahiro told the children of a friend, fifty-five years later, as he placed in their hands three paper cranes, each folded with pins, down to the size of mosquitoes. "Maybe she did not have an idea consciously, of what her paper crane project might become. But maybe subconsciously, she glimpsed the future, and she knew. Maybe she saw, that day in August, the paper crane growing into a symbol of hope, carrying the message and the spirit of the word, 'Omoiyari' [or what began as a word symbolizing such empathy as to make one think always of the other person first, and which evolved into what Americans would one day come to know as 'paying it forward']. Omoiyari. Sadako had grasped this word, this principle . . . and maybe she saw it spreading outward into the world until, hopefully, it reached enough people to stop something terrible."

On that same August afternoon of 1955, a delegation of students from China arrived at the hospital. At the reception, patients heard an unfamiliar song, sung in Japanese: "*Genbaku-O-Yurusamaji*" (Never again, the A-bomb).

"Something in that song seemed to resonate with Sadako," Kiyo remembered. "She sang it to me over and over, up on the hospital rooftop, until I learned it."

In September, climbs to the rooftop decreased in number, as Sadako's white blood cell count climbed above twice the normal amount, almost to three times normal. Then, the count increased by another multiple of two . . . and another . . . and another.

Masahiro knew that his sister was now living with a great deal of pain. Something was spreading outward from her lower spine, and her left leg began to swell so large that the flesh was rupturing under the skin and turning purple.

"She never said the words, 'it hurts,'" Masahiro recalled. "Although, when a leg swells up to one-and-a-half times its normal size, the throbbing alone has to hurt. Yet she continued to refuse the painkillers. For a long time, I believed she did not want our parents to bear the expense. But later she gave us two reasons completely different from this. First, she believed that the dreamlike state that the morphine put her into might become permanent and kill her. Second, Sadako did not like a dream-state in which she could not feel the touch of her mother's hand. She wanted to be aware of our presence when we were in the room with her—wanted to be acutely aware of the people she loved most. She did not want to lose even a minute with us by floating away into a painless dream."

In mid-October, Sadako's fevers reached 40.5 degrees Centigrade (105 Fahrenheit).

About October 20, a dozen paper triangles lay under her bed, each prefolded into a starter-triangle no wider than one of Sadako's fingernails. She had, by now, folded 1,600 paper cranes. Using two pins, Sadako put the largest concentration of thought yet into a reddish-violet crane barely larger than a gnat—the last one she would ever fold.

"She was fully conscious till the very end," Masahiro would record later. "And I do not believe she had any idea, that morning of October 25, that she was about to die at any moment. I remember my father waking me and explaining that a doctor had said the time was near. I remember my mother looking at all those pieces of paper on the string and asking, 'Why didn't your thousand cranes sing? Why didn't you fly?'"

"But most of all, when I think of that morning in Hiroshima, I remember my sister just slipping away, suddenly and without suffering, as if drifting off to sleep. Only minutes before, I heard Father urging her to eat something, and she responded, 'Tea or rice, please.'"

"A nurse brought a bowl of white rice. Sadako swallowed two spoonfuls and, smiling, she said, 'It's good.' That was it. She drifted away with those two words—'It's good.'"

During the day that followed, Fujiko and Shigeo gave many of Sadako's cranes to her classmates and teachers. A few remained with the family and the rest were placed with flowers and a childhood doll in Sadako's casket, "so she could bring them to the next world," Fujiko said.

"Before she left," Masahiro explained, "my sister and I had [the] one-word saying between us, just that one, simple word: *Omoiyari*."

Masahiro did not recall that Sadako had ever read about Paul Nagai's path to *Nyokodo*. He believed that, like many people in similar situations, they probably arrived at a similar path to enlightenment through a process of tribulation. As two witnesses to the *pika-don* who returned to their separate Ground Zeros to die, each came to a place where the life remaining in them had been reduced to a matter of weeks. Then it came down to days. And finally, to precious hours and minutes that to ordinary people meant barely more than waiting time at the train station.

Masahiro had heard it said that when a person comes to a place where he or she is reduced to nothing, that's when we begin to understand the value of all things.

When Nagai "went to zero" he came back with the ancient principle of *Nyokodo*: "Love your neighbor as yourself."

For Sadako, the lesson became *Omoiyari*, which meant: "In your heart, always think about the other person before yourself."

According to Masahiro, after Sadako wore her first and last dress-up kimono, she had imagined and defined the perfect, one-and-only future marriage for herself as one in which both husband and wife lived by the principle of *Omoiyari*, and yet neither took it for granted.

More than a half-century later, Masahiro said, "That's what I want to pass down from her, to young people. I do not want the next generations to think only of paper cranes and a twelve-year-old girl dying from atomic bomb disease. I want them to think, in their hearts, always about the other person.

"You start *Omoiyari* from your family members, and from your friends. Sadako thought—and taught me—that if the principle of *Omoiyari* could spread even a little, into the right places, it might ease the world toward never seeing another *pika-don*."[28]

On a Ground Zero hillside, not very far from Nyokodo and the ruins of Urakami Cathedral, a sideways kick from the blast wave had cleanly severed one leg from a temple gate "arch." And yet the stone arch still stood intact on its remaining leg—a lone, T-shaped sentinel, seen standing guard the day after, over a neighborhood where everything else, even the tiniest insects, seemed simply to have been spirited away.

During the tenth anniversary of the bombs, as Sadako taught her brother *Omoiyari* and as China sent children with a song of peace to its former enemy, the architects of Urakami laid their blueprints for multistoried apartment buildings all around the one-legged sentinel, having decided that even as new buildings towered over it, they must leave the sentinel itself untouched.

Less than a minute's walk uphill from the sentinel, trees that had been stripped of their branches and reduced to gnarled, deeply scorched trunks were healing (and seemingly evolving) in strange ways. From the diseased tree trunks, new branches and blob-like growths of bark and green wood grew skyward, some nearly five stories tall.

In Hiroshima, camphor trees, believed to have been killed by the rays and the flames, underwent similar metamorphoses; some were transplanted from a Ground Zero cemetery to the gardens of the city's Peace Park.

As trees healed, so (sometimes after many a summer), healed the people.

In the suburbs of Nagasaki, Setsuko Hirata's parents chose to regard such changes as a tribute of their daughter's love for Kenshi and to what she would have wished for him. After their sorrowful release of Kenshi (based on their own expression of *Omoiyari*), love had come again for him. By 1955, Kenshi was remarried, and had become the father of two healthy children. After the Mitsubishi Corporation allowed its records of his survival report to be published by an American journalist in 1957, he had no choice but to disappear with his wife and their "contaminated" offspring. Setsuko's family participated in the hiding of the Hirata family's identity so well that the children themselves did not know exactly who they were.

Kenshi's daughter, Saeko, grew up to study journalism in college and was working for the Nagasaki Broadcasting Corporation when she learned, quite by accident, that she was born of what had turned out to be her father's second marriage. Though perplexed, and wanting answers, a young Japanese woman could not, in those days, simply ask her father what happened. Instead, she asked her mother, who explained for the first time about the remarriage, and about her father's first wife, who had died in a terrible fire-bombing. Saeko's mother did not mention "*double hibakusha*," or even the word, "atomic." She told a strange story about how the second true love of Kenshi Hirata's life was actually his first love, and how his first love (Setsuko) was actually his second.

At age twenty-three, about the time Japan engaged America in war, Saeko's father had been sent to the battlefield. He returned with his legs all but destroyed by malnutrition and disease, and was thereafter assigned to a desk job.

Before the war, Saeko's mother, and Setsuko, and Kenshi had grown up in the same neighborhood. Kenshi knew Saeko's mother from the time they were toddlers, and almost from the start they had become inseparable childhood sweethearts. Yet when Kenshi approached Saeko's grandfather in 1943 with a proposal for his daughter's hand in marriage, he was refused. No one knew for certain why the father had blocked the marriage; but in the militaristic atmosphere of the day, men fighting and dying in the Pacific arena gained honor, while a man at home safely behind an accountant's desk would likely have been viewed with dishonor, even if the desk job was born of Pacific injuries.

Two years after the refusal, love came to Kenshi Hirata a second time, and he married Setsuko, and brought her from Nagasaki to the city where she died.

More than a year after Kenshi lost Setsuko and Japan lost the war, Saeko's grandfather had a change of heart and allowed Kenshi to marry her mother. Saeko learned that Kenshi wept and "confessed" to her mother everything that had happened to him, including the story of Setsuko, and how he recovered some of her bones and saw them placed in a tomb that he continued to visit.

Saeko's mother had told the story—minus the part about her father sleeping on Setsuko's radioactive grave in Hiroshima, minus mention of the city's name and the part about the second atomic bomb—noting that she believed Kenshi had needed to "confess," out of some inner shame. But his first love did not hold him to any blame at all for loving Setsuko, or for losing her to a fate that seemed as much beyond all human control as it was beyond all prior human experience. Saeko's mother explained that she had long ago accepted these events. Indeed, it occurred to her mother that had Grandfather allowed her to become Kenshi's first wife, fate would have dealt them all a very different hand. She came to regard Setsuko as a sister, as the gentle kindhearted woman who traveled to a doomed city and died in her place. And so she made regular visits to Setsuko's tomb, honoring her.[29]

Meanwhile Arai, the Hiroshima schoolteacher whose student's calligraphy was flash-stenciled onto her face, was advised that a combination of plastic surgery and custom-made makeup could erase the dark letters from her skin. Arai decided that she could not erase the very last thing a little girl had written, and she chose to keep the letters that were shadow-engraved on her face until the day she died. It became her way of offering remembrance to the children who perished.[30]

In great Hiroshima—
Dawn came blazing and roaring.
In the river floating toward me—
Was a human raft.

Thus spoke Tsutomu Yamaguchi, more than six decades afterward, when describing the raft of human corpses he had used as a bridge on his way to the train that took him home to Nagasaki.

After he dried himself off and took a seat aboard the train, a stranger placed a rice ball in his hand—a ball of fine white rice wrapped in brown paper. The man must have seen that Yamaguchi was in a terrible state. His clothes and his hands were badly burned. A strange hail of burning objects that had fallen the day before, followed by at least two brief showers of oily brownish rain, had left him feverish and too nauseous to eat.

"Thank you," Yamaguchi said, motioning for the man to take the rice back. "But you'll be needing this for yourself."

"I'm getting off the train only a few stops away, and I'm told you have a long ride to Nagasaki; so please, don't be polite. Please eat it even if it feels like too much."

Mr. Yamaguchi was moved by the stranger's kindness and "humanity" in a time of emergency and overmastering uncertainty. Such examples were not particularly common in wartime Japan—or even after the war.

During the decade that followed, as the reconstruction period began to take root, the Mitsubishi Company was retooled to build cars and washing machines and phonographs. Yamaguchi was offered the opportunity to be hired back again as a ship designer, but he explained to his former employer that he would stick by an earlier decision to remain at the schools he had helped the city to rebuild, and teach the children. He learned, however, that a reason for the job offer included his total lack of long-term radiation symptoms. Discrimination had begun putting down surprisingly strong roots. In a city where officially no long-term radiation effects existed, many of those exposed to gamma rays and fallout, and who showed any signs of fatigue, shortness of breath, rashes, and frequent infections, were fired. Increasingly, people who were experiencing illness hid the symptoms as best they could (and thus did they become asymptomatic in the Atomic Bomb Casualty Commission's database).

Hiding the symptoms proved to be especially difficult for any of the thirty people who had been gathered with Yamaguchi in the Mitsubishi office when the second bomb exploded. Though they were reasonably safe from the gamma

Tsutomu Yamaguchi, one of only two double hibakusha *known to have survived within the perimeter of Ground Zero each time (kite-maker Moromoto was the other), became the only such survivor twice exposed to and injured by blast effects. In both instances, the majority of the radioactive fallout travelled in a direction opposite his position. Transformed from a designer of warships to a teacher and spiritual figure, he travelled to New York and addressed the United Nations on 2006. Yamaguchi lived to January 2010, and the age of 93. [Illustration: CRP]*

surge, most of them had relatives in Urakami. Spared from prompt radiation overdosing by an intervening stairwell of steel and concrete, they went searching for their families near the Urakami hypocenter—which, in terms of secondary exposure, was orders of magnitude hotter than Hiroshima's hypocenter.

When the Mitsubishi rehirings began, Yamaguchi alone was offered a job. He never met anyone from the August 9 shock cocoon after the war.

About the time Sadako folded her last paper crane, workers in Nagasaki began designing and building a permanent memorial museum. Like many other survivors, Mr. Yamaguchi avoided looking back over his shoulder at the past. As one of American baseball's newest fans, he took Leroy "Satchel" Paige's warning to heart: "Never look back. Something might be gaining on you."

He did, however, make occasional, very rare visits to the museum after it was completed. One day, more than a half-century after the *pika-don*, Yamaguchi saw a child from another city filming the exhibits. He walked up to the boy and asked him, "What are you going to do with this video?"

大広島山火火え
車軽さし朝焼けて
川流れ来る人召筏
二重被爆者九十三役山口彊

One of Tsutomu Yamaguchi's eyewitness Tanka accounts begins with August 6, 1945's second sunrise: "In great Hiroshima—Dawn came blazing and roaring . . ." [Illustration: T. Yamaguchi, gift to author for this book]

"When I go home, after vacation," the boy said, "I want to edit this together into a film, and show it to everyone in my school."

"I think what you are doing is very important," Yamaguchi said, and bowed with his two scarred hands held together, as if in prayer. He never did explain how his hands came to be burned, nor did the boy ever learn or suspect that the man bowing to him was a double survivor.

Were it possible, Mr. Yamaguchi would have preferred to remain anonymous forever, living peacefully in the forested countryside beyond Nagasaki with his children and his grandson, quietly sending forth little ripples of Father Simcho's teachings. But history had charted an altogether different and more conspicuous destiny—"urging me," Yamaguchi recorded, "to turn a bad thing on its head, and try to bring something good from it."

The course change began when his wife, Hisako, developed cancer. Then his son Katsutoshi developed cancer and died a week short of his sixtieth birthday in 2005. Katsutoshi appeared to be part of an emerging pattern. People who held radiation in their bodies from childhood often developed tumors by age sixty, especially if their families had fled into the paths of wind-driven fallout and black rain. Adolescents who were exposed at the age of fourteen or older and who survived were generally living full life-spans, but the cells of growing children rapidly divided and differentiated during the exposure period; thus any chromosomal dislocations (a primary pathway to cancer), if not immediately recognized and corrected by overwhelmed DNA repair systems, were not only passed onward to developing organs, but were often copied and mass-produced.

When Mr. Yamaguchi learned that the children of Dr. Nagai had also developed cancer, he started thinking: *it may be time for me to speak up.*

Little Kayano Nagai had grown up into a brilliant and graceful young woman who studied and taught art, then moved away from Urakami and Nagasaki. She was presently dying from a late-stage cancer. Her brother Makoto had graduated from the University of Tokyo and worked as a journalist until his retirement in 1995 at age sixty.[31] He then returned to Urakami and lived near his father's hermitage, where he expanded the library and teaching programs, until cancer overtook him in 2001.[32]

"And when 2006 came around, I should surely have been dead," Yamaguchi told history. "Yet there I was, in my nineties and somehow still walking around after being burned by the *pika* twice.

"It's fate," he decided. "So it can't be helped. There's no use in complaining or trying too hard to make sense of it, because it becomes what it becomes."

His friends often joked, "That guy is shameless. After experiencing two atomic bombs, dying is natural, but living is lazy."

For a long time, Yamaguchi had appreciated the jokes, and laughed along with his friends. Yet after he learned what was really happening to the children of the *pika*, it became possible for him to believe there was truth behind the old saying that one sometimes meets his destiny on the road he takes to escape it. Perhaps the time had come to shed his hard-won anonymity and to tell the story of the two cities.

"I feel that I am allowed to live for that reason," Yamaguchi told his family. "To live long enough to do what needs to be done, and say what needs to be said."

His daughter Toshiko took these words with a certain degree of trepidation. She feared that people would not understand that he had been far enough from the relatively weak Hiroshima bomb to be only minimally exposed to the gamma rays, and that in Nagasaki he had been shielded behind a steel and concrete stairwell, with the radioactive rain moving away from his location in both instances and spattering him only briefly in Hiroshima, not at all in Nagasaki. She feared that his case would be misused by someone in America or by one of the other major nuclear powers to suggest that if anyone could live a long life after surviving two atomic bombs—"then why not *three*?"—and, worse, they might suggest that the dangers of radiation exposure had been exaggerated all along.

"I have a job that needs to be finished," Tsutomu Yamaguchi said—"regardless of what others will say."

The first thing he believed he needed to say involved a reminder from the past—an old belief that if something happened two times, there would be a third. When a pair of documentary filmmakers asked him if he would speak at the United Nations, he looked to the past for signposts to the future and said the core of his message would be simply this: "We cannot let an atomic bomb be used a third time."

He remembered the story of a Catholic pope, John Paul II, who visited Hiroshima and who, while standing near a memorial draped with thousands of paper cranes, had remarked, "War is the work of man." Those were the key words for Yamaguchi, to which he added later, "What this means—if we take it as truth and even if we believe we were created by natural causes—is that it is not God who created war itself; it is humans who created war. So we can stop, if we want to."

And so, for the first time in his life, Tsutomu Yamaguchi applied for a passport and traveled to New York, at the age of ninety. And it happened that a day before he gave his speech at the UN, he took a ride on a pedal-driven cab, which snapped its chain on a steep hill near Central Park, during an afternoon of record-breaking heat.

They exited the pedicab, and Yamaguchi noticed that the driver was having a difficult time trying to repair the machine, while keeping it from rolling downhill. Yamaguchi put his weight against one end of the pedicab, and said, "I'm from Japan," then asked the driver where he came from.

"Cuba," the man said quickly, as he continued struggling with the broken chain.

"Then," Yamaguchi recalled, "I noticed he was sweating a great deal. So I pulled out my towel and wiped the sweat from his forehead. We did not speak the same language, except for a word here and there—'Japan, Cuba'—but I felt that in helping, there was something I could communicate. That simple act of giving him my towel—he looked so happy, to be helped by a stranger; and it brought me back to the man who had put a rice ball in my hand on the train from Hiroshima. And so it occurred to me then, and it stays with me still—this is something we can all do: simple acts of kindness."

At the UN, Yamaguchi struggled to hold back tears. He was looking out upon the faces of too many young people. They brought him down into recollections of the past, recollections that, in their own turn, caused him to worry about this next generation's future.

"Until there was war, nobody knew of an atomic bomb," he told an audience that included students from an American high school, about the same age as the broiled and debris-perforated boys in Hiroshima, the same age as schoolgirls he had seen flash-burned so severely that the skin of their faces appeared to have melted. He carried in his heart a Tanka poem he had written years earlier, about bodies that were burst open and heated in such manner that the fat in their tissues was converted to a waxy, rib-coating and ground-polluting soap. But presently he kept the poem to himself. Instead, Tsutomu Yamaguchi pledged to do everything he could, for as long as he could, to work for the abolition of nuclear weapons and an everlasting world peace.

"Please," he said—"everyone, study history with earnest and think about the nobility and the importance of peace. Together with you all, the good-hearted American youth, I now pray, 'God, please grant us the strength for peace.'"[33]

Later, the Franciscan scholar Mervyn Fernando arrived at the UN with students from the International Peace Boat, and introduced them to others who had grown to old age in the shadow of Hiroshima. The students discovered that, like Tsutomu Yamaguchi, the survivors seemed to worry more than most people about the future. And many seemed unhappy about the present. One man could not understand the biofuel concept of turning corn into gasoline and somehow calling the process green. "Growing food to burn it and somehow calling this environmentally friendly?" he asked. "What can be more stupid?" Others were as much concerned about the strip-mining of the oceans' fish populations and about spoiling the Earth's soils or melting the Greenland ice sheet as about present-day wars. "Train-wrecking the ecology will train-wreck the global economy," one said, "and a wrecked global economy is a noose around the neck of world peace—a guarantee of future wars."

What Yamaguchi hoped people would most remember, and carry into the future, was how he and the pedicab driver in Manhattan could not speak the same language but understood each other anyway, as simply being human beings—*one and the same, all of us.*

"So why do we fight?" Yamaguchi had asked. Whenever people gathered around him to listen—and he had many listeners, after his sixty-first anniversary of the atomic bomb (which, in his appreciation of irony and humor, he referred to as his 122nd anniversary because he had survived two of them)—Yamaguchi explained that he never ceased to ask himself this question: "Why do we fight?" And if there really was a hope for changing civilization's path, he realized, his encounter with the pedicab driver might indeed have pointed the way.

National leaders might attempt to prevent the world from knowing another hypocenter; but they need not be counted on alone. Tsutomu Yamaguchi had learned that, even in a small way, there was something he could do. "*Each of you*," he began to teach, "though you may only be a single human being—each of you can, on your own, help us to start understanding each other. That's all it takes: small steps. That's all you have to remember. Send simple acts of kindness outward, from person to person. Send forth kindness like a contagious disease."

What could be easier? Yamaguchi wondered. What could be simpler than *Nyokodo* and *Omoiyari*, or what the Americans sometimes call the "pay-it-forward" principle? He realized that his hope of change through individual acts of mutual human tenderness might sound simplistic—completely naïve, even—"but if we follow such principles, then we must emerge from the experience of war not as Japanese or American, not as Christian or Buddhist, Hindu, Muslim, or Jew; but simply as . . . human beings.[34] We have to start somewhere. *Have to.*"[35]

Masahiro Sasaki, when he was not meeting with other survivors, schoolchildren, or with the occasional representative from the Vatican, ran a hair salon with his wife in a quiet suburb far north of Nagasaki. Locally, he was famous for personally driving each of his customers back and forth with door-to-door car service, which was but one small manifestation of the *Omoiyari* principle.

During the summer of 2008, a scientist visited Mr. Sasaki in his salon. The visitor learned the word *Nyokodo* and he learned *Omoiyari*. With Masahiro's help, he was able to pinpoint—first on a 1945 bombing survey map, and later on the actual streets of Hiroshima—the exact location of Masahiro and Sadako's original childhood home. Thousands of bullet train passengers had been passing near the spot every day without knowing it. During the reconstruction years, the roof tiles and ashes were carted away and a parking lot was paved over the old foundations, evidently preserving them into the year 2008. Across the street, in the direction of Dr. Hachiya's house, a twenty-four-hour 7-Eleven store had risen from the ruins. (By 2010, an office block was built over the parking field, erasing from history the foundations of the Sasaki home.)

On the day Sadako's house was rediscovered, the scientist left flowers in a corner of the parking lot, bowed three times, and walked east toward the river. When he began filming the place between two bridges where Masahiro indicated he, Sadako, and their mother survived in a half-sunk boat, a white crane descended from the south and landed on the spot.[36]

Shigeo Sasaki's friend and neighbor, Dr. Michihiko Hachiya, died in 1980. His Hiroshima diary indicated that he burdened himself with the undeserved guilt of somehow causing the death of Shigeo's mother. Were he not a decent man in the first place, he would never have carried such guilt. A lesser man would not have felt anything. Thus did the bomb wound two families with Hachiya's own decency, with his loyalty to his neighbors, with his humanity. And so it came to pass that even after stories about Sadako and the thousand paper cranes began to spread throughout Japan, Masahiro could not recall that his father ever heard from Dr. Hachiya again—much as Dr. Nagai's "theory of invisible cracks" had said it would be.

In Urakami, Nagai's friend Akizuki's destiny was to die of natural causes in advanced old age in 2005. He supported Dr. Nagai's teachings until the very end.[37] As the decades passed, it seemed that if one followed the paths of the invisible cracks described by Dr. Nagai, through any handful of people connected to the atomic bombs, the cracks had a habit of spreading out, re-crossing, and becoming as tragically intertwined as loops and coils of radiation-scarred DNA.

Inoue Kazue, a sixteen-year-old student conscript who survived inside Urakami's Mitsubishi Arms Factory at a radius of 1.5 kilometers, never forgave

The corner on which the Sasaki house stood is seen as it appeared on the morning of August 6, 1945, two days after the firestorms died out, and during the summer of 2008. [Illustration: Patricia Wynne, CRP]

the in-laws who forced her sister to abort her baby, then forced a divorce on the girl because the couple's matchmaker had not revealed that she had been exposed to the atomic bomb.

Inoue's own husband had proceeded with the marriage in spite of warnings from his father, a scientist, that he should never marry a *"hibakusha."* Their daughter died of non-resuscitative anemia at the age of eight. The burdens the *hibakusha* carried, and the prejudices against them seemed to know no end. Though she was at the very top of her class and loved to study, Inoue was not permitted to attend college.

Wishing her husband to at least have a descendant, Inoue encouraged him to take a mistress who had been nowhere near Hiroshima or Nagasaki, and to have a child with the woman.

"When my husband became ill," Inoue recorded, "I asked [for the son] to come and visit his father at his death bed. He was very polite and a gentleman like my husband, so I thought it was fortunate for my husband to have a nice young man like him, as a son. However, it hurt me very much."[38]

By then, in Hiroshima, Shigeo Sasaki was dead at the age of eighty-seven. Fujiko Sasaki was dead.

Sadako's roommate Kiyo was dead.

Keiji Nakazawa's friend Tanaka was dying.

After a government-sponsored reclamation project drove Nakazawa and his mother from the shantytown near the "T" Bridge, he was, somewhat like Tanaka, often in trouble. He tended to get into schoolyard brawls and to run away for days and even weeks.

"Of course I fought a lot," Nakazawa recalled. *"Pika-don* people (they preferred to call us *hibakusha*) often became untouchables. We were treated like dirt by the safer and more privileged children who began moving in from the outlands. Later in life, if a young woman's family found out we had been exposed to the bomb, we were usually not allowed to marry. Even though we had survived, we weren't really allowed to live."

During his truancies, Nakazawa discovered comic books and uniquely styled animated films—which were in fact embryonic forms of the Manga artistic movement. Eventually, he became involved with the *Godzilla-and-Gamera* film teams and the creators of *Astro Boy*, while progressing toward the development of the *Barefoot Gen* books and several feature-length animated films, including one based on the diaries of Dr. Akizuki.

"The *pika* and the *hibakusha* it has created cannot happen again," Nakazawa has said. "Even before I became *hibakusha*, I was growing up ostracized because of humanity's instinct to make war. My father was arrested because he spoke against the war, and most of our neighbors were afraid of collective punishment (one bad apple and the whole neighborhood could be punished); so they hated him.

"Many, and especially a certain gung-ho uncle who had participated in Pearl Harbor, told me after the war that my father had been right all along. Nothing could be more dangerous (in terms of being led to war) than worship of the elite. In Japan, at that time, it was worship of the Emperor and his warlords. Now it is almost the same again, all over the world: worship of the powerful, and the fight to *be* powerful (sometimes with the backing of entire news organizations, telling the multitudes what to think). The powerful, then and now, use the power for themselves without regard for others. Today, if the people do not question, if they go along with the flow and are led to their doom, it will be as much their fault as the [fault of the] stupid leaders who take them there."

Fighting against the ravages of cancer, Nakazawa warned, on March 3, 2011, "My message to the future is simply this: Everyone knows that war is evil, that nuclear weapons are evil; but there are almost no people willing to really put themselves on the line to fight them. We know from Japan's experience that the military and the elite can act with Earth-shaking stupidity and that they love to fight. But if we don't stop them, we are just as stupid. We cannot have peace just by saying war is evil. We have to actively oppose every person, every organization, and every idea that is leading us to war and to the use of nuclear weapons. Across the planet, they are doing this right now—leading us to a terrible storm—and the people who don't want war must stop them."

Nakazawa knew a scientist who had discovered how only a handful of deliberately placed bombs of the "right" megatonnage could actually create a slower but very real *On the Beach* scenario. When he had fears, Nakazawa worried that Nostradamus might have been an optimist.

Keiji ("Barefoot Gen") Nakazawa became one of the longest-lived childhood *hibakusha*. His survival against exposure and cancer ended in December 2012.[39]

By the turn of the century, Dr. Kunishige's childhood friends were all dead.

Kenji Kitagawa's brother, and all of their childhood friends, were dead.

Emiko Nakasako's friends were dead.

While he was still alive, General Tibbets traveled throughout the United States, giving lectures about the bombing of Hiroshima.

When Tibbets announced that he would be giving a public presentation near the site of the Trinity bomb test, fifty-six years had passed since the Tanemori boy's blinding game of hide-and-seek. The atomic orphan had by then begun giving interviews for a BBC documentary titled *Hiroshima*, for which Tibbets was also being filmed.

Tanemori's main messages about life after the bomb ended up on the cutting room floor—including how his own people had treated him as dead, and how in America, after being used like a laboratory animal and after seething with a lust for revenge, the humanity of Mary Furr and the wisdom of his own child had saved him: "And now I want you to know that the greatest demonstration of love that I have experienced is learning to forgive."

His message seemed never to have a chance of making the final cut.

While the film was still in pre-production, Tanemori attended Paul Tibbets's Trinity lecture. He knew that Urey and Alvarez and some of the scientists who designed the bomb were horrified when they saw effects that even they had never anticipated. He wanted to ask General Tibbets a question that he did not believe anyone from the BBC had thought to bring up.

Guide-dog-assisted Takashi Tanemori sat in the third row, wearing dark glasses. The flash had burned his retinas on the left side, and what remained of his vision seemed so hyper-sensitive to light that he wore dark glasses even indoors. In daylight, he had to wear doubly-thick dark glasses, because whenever he forgot to double-up, and looked up at a beautiful blue sky, the rays of the sun shot through the holes in his retinas, struck the nerves directly, and produced flashes of pain that were impossible for him to describe.

Tanemori had crossed the bridge to forgiveness and was willing to accept that not even the scientists who lived during that first crossing of his own path with Tibbets's knew what would happen. So, certainly, Tibbets could not have known.

And yet the general, after describing the details of his training and the planning for the atomic mission, referred to the "Japs" with expletives. Each use of the expletives, connected to the word, "Jap," jolted Tanemori emotionally as every needle in his spine had jolted him physically. Tibbets's audience cheered the expletives. The majority of them were military people, and all of them stood and applauded Tibbets's description of Hiroshima under the bomb. Only Tanemori remained seated.

The fact that the man standing before him had piloted the plane that dropped the first atomic bomb did not trouble Tanemori so much as the expletives, the attitude.

Tanemori finally stood, and approached the bottom of the platform. He could hear that the entire audience had become suddenly agitated. Hostility ran through the people like a wave. *This might not have been your smartest idea*, Tanemori told himself; but he continued to advance anyway.

"*No!*" an officer shouted, blocking Tanemori's approach.

"I want to talk to the general," Tanemori said.

"No, you can't see him."

"He will see me, when he finds out that he had a hand in my life," Tanemori said, and told the officer who he was. The man, after taking a step back, walked to the front of the stage and held a brief discussion with Tibbets, then motioned to Tanemori, "*Come.*"

Tanemori explained his understanding that there was no way Tibbets could really have known what the bomb would do when he dropped it in 1945. Through the day of the Tibbets lecture, glass from the school window was still blast-embedded in Tanemori's body. The doctors came across it while making preparations to remove his cancer-ravaged stomach, along with a cancerous spleen.

He asked Tibbets, "Having discovered all the effects of radiation from the bombing—from what you know now—do you have any regrets?"

Tibbets yelled, "Heck, no! Every Japanese is thanking me, for stopping the war."

"*Every* Japanese?" Tanemori asked. He felt that he had probably mis-phrased his original question and tried to better explain himself, but for all of his efforts, the words just did not seem to come out right: "What I meant to ask is that, if a war were to happen again, and if you received a new order, today, to drop an atomic bomb on a city—*with all the facts we have now*—would you obey the order, or would you refuse?"

"I think you have said enough!" the general yelled, shaking a finger in Tanemori's face and uttering something horrible, before pushing Tanemori forcefully to one side and commanding his entourage, "Let's go!"

As Tibbets and his men walked away, Tanemori called after him, "General Tibbets, I pray for you, until you find peace in your heart!"

Tanemori continued to remember Tibbets in his prayers, and outlived him. He also outlived every one of his childhood friends from Hiroshima.[40]

All except one of Keiji Nakazawa's childhood friends—at least those who were near enough to have witnessed the bomb, as he did, were dead before the turn of the century.

Satoko Matsumoto and the rest of her family were dead.

Yoshiko Mori and her son, Hiroshi, were dead.

Masuji Ibuse, the Hiroshima poet who witnessed the "crazy iris" incident, was dead.

Firefighter Yasaku Mikami was dead.

Firefighter Mitsunori was dead.

Assistant kite-maker Doi, one of Mr. Yamaguchi's fellow double survivors, suffered no known radiation effects despite the hail of bomb-flung objects from the hypocenter into his Nagasaki neighborhood, followed quickly by a light misting over by black rain. Notwithstanding Doi's apparent escape from harm, his baby girl developed blisters, swelling lymph nodes, anemia, and frequent infections. After a few years, just as it seemed the child was about to make a complete recovery, Doi's wife became ill, developed cancer, and died.[41]

Akira Iwanaga became a clerk in the office of Nagasaki's postwar Municipal Government House, where he eventually retired in remarkably good health, then moved to the shore with his family and lived into his nineties. In December 2009, he remained, along with Tsutomu Yamaguchi, one of two double survivors still known to be alive. (He lived two more years, until January 2, 2012.)[42]

Shinoe Shoda died of cancer in 1965.

Young Dr. Yoshioka, whose blast-lacerated face filled Dr. Akizuki with a guilt that never went away, continued to live near the Urakami hospital complex until her death, about 1985. All around the complex, cherry trees seared down to their roots by the bomb came back to life, eerily turning the desert regions into restored forests and gardens.[43]

Father "Mattias" never could forget the children he had left alone on a brick tower amid the rising fire worms of Hiroshima. He descended into severe addiction and died of an alcohol-related suicide about 1985. The Jesuit philosopher John "MacQuitty" (his pen name) argued in support of and participated in a burial on hallowed ground despite his church's injunctions against such compassion for suicides. "He was a good man who tried to live by a code of kindness," MacQuitty stated. "It was Hiroshima that killed him . . . as if the bomb itself were something demonic."[44]

Masahiro Kunishige, the flash-burned schoolboy who was unable to tell the parents of a friend that he had seen their son die, continued to make offerings at the boy's grave through the year 2010 and for the rest of his life. He also continued to wear long-sleeve shirts even during the summer, for the same reasons that so many survivors hid their scars: "Prejudice against the *hibakusha* produced a long habit of covering up. A Hiroshima boy could not get married"; so Kunishige hid the "atomic tattoos."

Kunishige's wife was also exposed to the bomb. The U.S. Bombing Survey archives included a photo of Hisae, captioned as a young Hiroshima teenager whose hair fell out two months after she walked through the hypocenter in search of her mother.

"We had two children and four grandchildren," Kunishige would say, when he revealed himself after sixty-five years of silence. "Everybody is healthy, and the reason I decided to speak, was that while my father was peeling away my dead skin and trying to heal my burns, the pain was so terrible that, back then, I only wanted to seek revenge. But it was always a private joke: How could I seek revenge against the people who built and dropped the bomb? And basically, I found one philosophy: If I could put down all nuclear arms, let them be abandoned, this will be my revenge. The old Samurai warrior concept was to avenge the burning of a family member. Revenge, here, is to teach one hundred or two hundred people what the atomic bomb really does to human beings, and to send them out as hundreds of teachers. The revenge is to make the bomb itself extinct."

Kunishige understood that the Hiroshima Peace Park's Flame of Hope (which would burn until the day there was not a single functional nuclear weapon left in the world) would inevitably be put out—either because human civilization had survived its nuclear adolescence and made the bombs extinct, or because the bombs had brought civilization itself to extinction and there was no one left alive to attend the flame.[45]

Education. There was no substitute.

Double survivor Tsutomu Yamaguchi, who continued to be an avid fan of American baseball, often pointed people to Jackie Robinson's epitaph for guidance: "A life is not important except for the impact it has on other lives."

Three shock-cocooned schoolboys—Kenji Kitagawa, Keiji Nakazawa, and Kunishige—agreed, as they reminded the world that every one of their classmates had died: "Each life is important, and can bring about change. One person, one body, one drop of water to another, eventually becomes a river. One drop of water can be a great river."

Hiroko Nakamoto healed from her wounds, and eventually traveled to the United States, where she studied architectural interior design at New York's Pratt Institute. Returning to Japan, she designed the "Gateway to Peace" monument for the Hiroshima Railway Station.[46]

Misako Katani, the young double-survivor who saw the fire horses, was dead.

Masao Komatsu was dead.

Master kite-maker Morimoto was dead.

After the death of his wife, Doi fell into depression, sickened, and died.

Prefect Takejiro Nishioka continued to suffer from radiation symptoms during the months after Hiroshima and Nagasaki. Believing he would soon die, he signed his publishing organization's rights over to his wife. Mrs. Nishioka vastly expanded the family's publishing earnings, then entered politics and was elected a member of the House of Councils (Japan's equivalent of the British Parliament or the American Senate). Mr. Nishioka retreated from politics, seemed to recover his health, then sickened and died.[47]

Governor Nagano was dead.

Yose Matsuo, the closest sheltered survivor to the Urakami hypocenter, developed cancer and died.

Emiko Fukahori, one of only a handful of children to reach the Urakami shelters in time, saw her family killed near a bamboo garden six hundred meters from the hypocenter. Because death certificates were rarely written for people whose bodies were never found, she had difficulty proving to bureaucratic child-aid providers that she was a war orphan. At age sixteen, she was stricken with atomic-bomb-related anemia and was hospitalized about the same time as Sadako Sasaki. Emiko recovered, continued her schooling, and spent the remainder of her life at a Catholic retreat for meditation in Osaka.[48]

Emiko's friend Sumi-Chan was dead.

Cadet Komatsu and his friends were dead.

For Dr. Masao Shiotsuki, inhaling the fresh radioactive dust and drying black rain from the clothes of patients transported to Omura Naval Hospital marked the beginning of a long-standing fight against cancer. He lost his battle in 1978.[49]

Sumiko Kirihara, a shock-cocooned girl who lived in the same neighborhood as Sadako Sasaki, might have survived in reasonably good health if not for the black rain. Initially, all of her family escaped alive. During the three years that followed, each of them suffered sporadic episodes of bleeding under the skin and debilitating fatigue. Sumiko developed chronic liver disease, anemia, and frighteningly high fevers. Only through what she called the strength she derived from her faith in Buddhism did she pull herself out of a sickbed, after nine years, while the other seven members of the Kirihara family began to die young, one by one.[50]

Sachiko Masaki, a fellow survivor with Hajime Iwanaga at the Mitsubishi torpedo factory, died of cancer. Her mother and her sister preceded her in death.

Hajime Iwanaga was dead.

Michie Hattori, a fifteen-year-old girl who returned from a school whose surroundings had become "a graveyard with no tombstones" and discovered her own neighborhood completely shock-cocooned, moved from Nagasaki to General MacArthur's headquarters in Tokyo, where she was employed as a translator. She married an American, became Michie Hattori Bernstein, and moved to Mississippi—where she died of cancer.

Isao Kita was dead.

Ichiro Miyato, the radar man who charted the approach of Charles Sweeney's mission to Nagasaki, was still alive after the turn of the century.[51]

Charles Sweeney was promoted to general in 1956 and became commander of the 102nd Air Defense Wing (he died of natural causes in 2004).

Marcus McDilda, the captured American pilot who, under torture, invented an atomic bomb design that seemed feasible (based on vague and instantly made-up details about two spherical masses separated by a trap door made out of lead) was transferred to a more advanced interrogation facility near the Imperial Palace in Tokyo. Shortly afterward, his fifty fellow POWs at the secret police headquarters were beheaded. McDilda remained under constant guard and, he believed, in constant danger until August 30, 1945, when the Fourth Marine Regiment liberated the Omori prison camp on the Tokyo waterfront. He returned to the United States and lived to old age.[52]

Physicist Ryokichi Sagane, a leading researcher in the Germany-Japan wartime atomic bomb program (to whom Luis Alvarez's letter of warning had been addressed), was judged a nuclear asset under the MacArthur protocol. He was moved from Tokyo to Berkeley and the nearby linear accelerator facility, where he devised programs leading up to anti-proton bombardment experiments—which began to probe the first three minutes of the universe.

Dr. Luis Alvarez became an advocate for peace—first for nuclear arms reduction and eventually for the abolition of nuclear weapons. When he and his son Walter stumbled upon an iridium layer spanning New Zealand and the rest of the world, they soon discovered the nuclear winter concept, etched into rocks that appeared to be synchronous with the extinction of the dinosaurs. "If we are not very careful," Alvarez said, "then the rocks will probably write our epitaph in a global dust storm of similar proportions, and we'll be as extinct as the dinosaurs one day."

Until the day he died in 1988, Alvarez harbored a deep and seething resentment for government "white-washers" from the United States and Japan who, aided by lawyer types, attempted to officially list only a dozen people in Hiroshima—and thirty cows downwind—as having been killed by radiation poisoning. Under the MacArthur protocol, atomic bomb survivors were not allowed to publish stories about their experiences. They were not even allowed to write poems, and press censorship on this subject was total; so little more than urban legends came out of the ruins. Myths about radiation-transformed mutants began to take on the mantle of oral history, and with such grace did a MacArthur-esque joke about the health benefits of radioactive spider bites, along with the curious case of Dr. Paul Nagai's remission, reach journalist Stanley Lieber, who, like James Clavell and animated training-filmmaker Charles Addams (who created *The Addams Family* in his spare time), had been recruited during the war as a military scribe. The atomic mythology produced in Stan Lieber an inordinate fondness for flights of abstract fantasy involving radioactive transformation.[53] After the war he moved to New York City, anglicized his name to Stan Lee, and made his mark on cultural history by bringing to life *The Hulk*, *X-Men*, and, as a nod to Dr. Nagai, *Spider Man*.[54]

Dr. Harold Urey could not accept that, instead of bringing an end to war, the atomic bomb led to the Cold War–era mass production of nuclear weapons. As part of his recovery from a despair that led to severe clinical depression, Alvarez and other friends directed Urey toward solving the problems of deciphering ancient temperatures with oxygen isotopes and trying to figure out where DNA came from. With student Stanley Miller, he helped to create the famous "spark discharge" experiment in chemical evolution, suggesting that the first steps from chemistry in the direction of life were surprisingly likely. When Miller drafted their classic paper for publication in the journal *Science*, Urey crossed off his name as co-author, convinced that it would win a Nobel Prize and commenting to his student, "I already have one of those."[55] Urey died young, in the midst of writing a letter to a friend about carbonaceous meteorites and the secret of life's origins.[56]

Harold Urey's colleague Albert Einstein, whose 1939 letter to President Roosevelt triggered America's atomic bomb program, became a devoted reader of Gandhi, Nagai, and every other man of peace. Shown photographs of artifacts from Hiroshima and Nagasaki—among them a charred pocket watch with hands frozen at 8:15 and a smashed Nagasaki clock stopped at 11:02—the physicist recalled Dr. Nagai's observation that the discovery of heaven's double-edged sword, hidden in the atom, had changed everything about the human animal except its way of thinking. To this observation, Einstein added that the subsequent nuclear arms race was heartbreak, and that indeed, though Dr. Nagai's yin-and-yang "sword and gift" had changed everything except man's way of thinking, "the solution to this problem lies in the heart of mankind. But if only I had known (in my youth, about the sword), I should have become a watchmaker." Within a decade of the atomic bomb, Einstein was dead from heart failure.

During the decades after little Eiko's flash burns frightened her mother away, the unspoken shame of how the child died produced such pain that members of the Nagai family could only rarely bring themselves to visit her grave. Perhaps there was no stronger example of Dr. Nagai's cracks in the human spirit, created by the bomb; for by the first decade of the twenty-first century no one could remember any longer where Eiko was buried.[57]

Little Eiko's cousin Tatsue, the last person known to have visited her grave, was dead.

Private Shigeru Shimoyama was dead.

Nobuo Tetsutani was dead.

Tomotsu Eguchi was dead.

Dr. Hachiya's friends Hinoi, Koyama, and Kutsube were dead.

Mr. Fujii, the theological student who fled Nagasaki ahead of the *pika* and went searching for his girlfriend in Hiroshima, was dead.

Dr. Minoru Fujii continued to work in the suburbs of Hiroshima and kept in close contact with Minami until his death.[58]

Minami's friends, including Nurse Reiko Owa ("I will live remembering not to waste the lives lost in the atomic bomb attack"), nurse Fujita Misako, Hiroshi Takamoya ("Please remember Hiroshima for peace"), Saito Kaneko, and Kouno Kazuko, were still alive at the turn of the century.[59]

Akiko Takakura, the Geibi Bank survivor, remained in Hiroshima through 2008 in anomalously good health, as did Nenkai Aoyama, whose mother disappeared without a trace at the Hiroshima Dome.

Tsugio Ito, whose brother Hiroshi decayed while still alive after escaping Hiroshima, grew up in a household where both parents survived in perfect health despite overwhelming loss and despite having ventured into a radioactive hot zone near the Misasa Bridge. Tsugio eventually married, keeping secret his status as an untouchable *hibakusha* family member. Tsugio's son Kazushige, though he grew up in a family contaminated by "death sand," showed no signs whatsoever of illness. Like Akiko Takakura, Kazushige Ito went to work for one of Japan's largest banking institutions. After receiving several promotions he was transferred in 1998 to the Fuji Bank's office in the South Tower of New York's World Trade Center—where, on September 11, 2001, almost fifty-six years to the day after Tsugio sat at the deathbed of his brother Hiroshi, his son Kazushige perished at the epicenter of his family's second Ground Zero.

Hanako Ito, who braved the deserts of Hiroshima's Ground Zero in search of a son already doomed by the air he had breathed, died in September 2001, as soon as she accepted the reality that her grandson Kazushige was not merely missing in New York's Ground Zero, but had died.[60]

Mrs. Sumako Matsuyanagi remained in Hiroshima, where she lit a floating lantern and set it adrift in the river every August 6 in memory of her lost child. She continued lighting lanterns for thirty years, until she joined the boy in death.

Kuniyoshi Sato, the Mitsubishi engineer who sat across from a man matching Kenshi Hirata's description on the train from Hiroshima, and whose curiosity about what the man was carrying inside the wedding bowl was too well satisfied, had disembarked with him at Nagasaki, stepping into history as one if its most exotic survivor-types. Seeking out the most tranquil surroundings he could find, the young "double *hibakusha*" took up residence on one of Nagasaki's Amakusha Islands, where he lived a meditative existence into his nineties.[61]

The mother of Toshihiko Matsuda—"the marble boy" of Hiroshima—was dead.

Inasuke Hayasaki's parents and siblings were dead.

Nagasaki's womb-exposed gelding was dead, and also his mother.

Dean Susumu Tsunoo was dead. Mrs. Tsunoo was dead.

The Tsunoo children were dead.

Little Eiko's mother was brought one evening to a hospital, screaming obscenities. She vomited something black, shuddered and gasped for air, vomited again—and then she, too, was dead.[62]

Less than two years after Hiroshima, Minami returned to Korea and in 1950 was caught up in the invasion of South Korea from the north. "If General MacArthur had not arrived at Inchon at the last minutes of September 15," Minami recalled more than fifty years later, "I would have been burned or starved to death along with so many others. My children and I would not now know the happiness we enjoy had it not been for him."

Minami escaped with a through-and-through bullet wound—entering above her right shoulder and exiting below her collarbone. After a period of time as a refugee in her own country, with the years turning even worse for her than in wartime Japan, she made her way to Germany and finally to New York University, where, aided by a key recommendation from Dr. Fujii in Hiroshima, she was employed by the New York Infirmary, on Fourteenth Street. There, she underwent another name change: from Minami to Nancy.

She added the name Cantwell when she married Larry Cantwell.

It seemed almost inevitable that she would be stuck in traffic outside the Lincoln tunnel on the exceptionally beautiful morning of September 11, 2001. She had a firsthand view of each tower as it descended on a collapse column with a combined force of 1.6 kilotons. A favorite student was among the lost; she became part of the air that New Yorkers breathe. Eight years later, Nancy Cantwell told a gathering of young students, "We have no choice but to be born into this world. Technology is constantly making the world smaller and more interconnected, whether everyone likes this or not. My grandmother always told me, 'One hand washes the other.' Whoever leads the larger nations in the future, the large countries should help the smaller countries to develop and to live in happiness."

Her plea sounded hauntingly like *Nyokodo* and *Omoiyari*.

"This is my wish," she said. "This is my prayer."

That there shall be no more graves of the blue fireflies.

That there shall come no more black rains.

That no loved one shall ever again know what it means to fold a thousand paper cranes.[63]

On December 22, 2009, James Cameron and a small group of friends answered a call from Tsutomu Yamaguchi, to visit him at his bedside, in a Nagasaki hospital.

"Once I received your letter," Cameron said, "I had no choice but to come here and meet you." The filmmaker had grown up under the nightmare of Cold War duck-and-cover drills—producing a childhood fear of apocalypse that resonated in one way or another through all of his films. Yamaguchi was giving Cameron and his friends a deathbed challenge to devote the best of their abilities to teaching the world what had really happened.

"I would like to accept your challenge," Cameron said. "I believe you experienced both atomic bombs for a reason, making you an important link in the chain of human memory."

Yamaguchi spoke of the last scene in James Cameron's film, *Titanic*—the wonder and the spirituality of it. "I think that Mr. Cameron and I are connected somewhere—spiritually," he said, then passed on to the filmmaker a painting he had produced, depicting a dragon in twisted anguish and despair.

His daughter, Toshiko, told the director how this most special painting came to be. She explained that when her brother, who had been exposed to the bomb, died young, her father fell into a deep depression. "But I told him," Toshiko said, "that my younger sister and I were still alive and I asked him to get better." The dragon was part of the healing—Mr. Yamaguchi's first painting, executed quickly and in one sitting—dedicated to the task of continuing to protect his family. It was, according to Toshiko, "a painting to re-invigorate himself and get back on track."

"It's the only one in the world," Mr. Yamaguchi said, adding that he believed a storm was coming, and that Cameron would soon have to grab this dragon (and the approaching surge of confusion and anguish) by the horns.

Toshiko said, "There is something very spiritual about [this painting] and I think that part of my father is in it. It should give you positive energy as well."

To another, Tsutomu Yamaguchi gave a different message of healing: his recent painting of a waterfall surrounded by fireflies. Calling it "The Source," it was among the last he would ever paint, to which he had attached a letter. Yamaguchi had painted it with the motto of emerging from a terrible maelstrom to find serenity and to live a full life, for whatever length of time remained.

Cradling the dragon, Cameron had made a promise to visit the Urakami hypocenter. Toshiko turned to him and said, "My father wanted to know how you perceived the fact that he has been exposed to the radiation twice, if there is any meaning to it? What *is* the reason?"

Cameron would say later that he was moved almost beyond words by Yamaguchi's purpose to stay alive all this time after such remarkable survival— to pass on a message over one generation, two generations, to as many as he could for as long as he could. And in that room, before Yamaguchi drew them all together to hold hands in prayer, the filmmaker would recall that he could feel the waters of history closing over this experience.

After a long moment of silent thought, Cameron answered the question. "The use of nuclear weapons on human beings was unprecedented," he said.

"And because you were there to bear witness in both places (and from the unique perspective of Ground Zero, each time), you have been chosen to be a spokesperson for the need of human beings to understand never, ever to do this again for any reason."

"I think so as well," Yamaguchi said. "I think I have done my duty."

"Yes. You have done your duty."

Then, keeping his promise, Cameron visited the needle of black granite that pointed to the place of ignition, little more than a half-kilometer directly overhead. He knew that a tree near this spot, not very far from the deep tunnel in which Jose Matsuo had survived, was somehow still standing the next day, though seared almost to the core and crushed as it sank. A whole new city and whole new stands of trees had risen from the ashes, all but hiding the dark pinnacle. Cameron found something bittersweet about this; because as the people rebuilt and moved on, they were required to forget in order to live.

"But it's important not to forget," he told his friends. "So, it's up to us. Let's let the people of Nagasaki [move on and] enjoy their lives. It's the rest of the world that has to try and remember for them."

Somewhat like the visit with Tsutomu Yamaguchi, the ground beneath the hypocenter needle defied being put into words. For Cameron, there was only one other place in the world, Hiroshima's hypocenter, that had this kind of power to overwhelm his spirit, and which, at the same time, came very near to overwhelming a sense of hope.

Did it make sense to hope that enough human beings had the ability to understand each other and to find a way to avoid a type of conflict that could only be resolved by this type of weapon? Did such hope make any sense at all? It occurred to Cameron that he had lived long enough to see the human population more than double. There were at least 3 billion people who probably did not think much about what happened here; and if they did not hold it in their hearts, then they would not take the steps necessary to prevent it from happening again.

He remembered attending a very moving ceremony near Hiroshima's Atomic Dome, nearly twenty years before—a ceremony in which thousands of people lit candles and set floating lanterns adrift on the water until it became a river of light, each lantern carrying a prayer to the future, or a child's drawing, or the name of a person who was lost. One of Cameron's strongest memories of the ceremony was that he appeared to be the only non-Japanese person present in Hiroshima on that evening.

There should have been people from all over the world, he recalled.

"We ignore history at our peril," Cameron said, after placing flowers near the base of Urakami's granite needle. "So, Yamaguchi-san said something very interesting when he took [our] hands—and he said, 'My duty is done.' At ninety-three, he's done his job. He's passed the baton. So now it's up to us to do something about it, and to everyone of good conscience to do something about it."[64]

In January 2010, Tsutomu Yamaguchi succumbed to what appeared to be the fate of most *hibakusha*: a prolonged battle with cancer. He survived years with a form of stomach cancer that was often lethal within six months of discovery; and long ahead of the cancer, as far back as his daughter Toshiko could remember, his hair fell out every summer and the scars seemed to temporarily worsen, and two or three times each winter, a simple common cold progressed to pneumonia.

In a suburb of Nagasaki, Kenshi Hirata's daughter Saeko, who worked for a TV news organization, was both moved and fascinated by the story of a *double hibakusha* who had lived nearby. She did not know, yet, that another survivor of both atomic bombs lived much nearer, and that he was her own father.

About February 25, 2010, documentary filmmakers Hidetaka Inazuka and Hideo Nakamura (who had befriended Tsutomu Yamaguchi and who had attended his meeting with James Cameron) finally located Saeko, and gently revealed to her who her father had been.

"Had been," it turned out, was not the correct term. Kenshi Hirata was still alive. He was ninety-one years old; but like many of the survivors, he did not want to remember. Even those who did speak of it, as Yamaguchi had spoken, did so with great difficulty. Especially, Kenshi did not want to speak about Setsuko.

Nagasaki historian Tomoko Maekawa—who was doing all that was humanly possible to record and archive the stories of survivors before their generation vanished utterly—had volunteered for one of the world's most heart-wrenching jobs. She understood why Kenshi Hirata, like so many others, wished not to remember.

"When I listen to the stories of the survivors," the historian explained, "I can see that it is very tough for them—very saddening to remember and to tell of their experiences, almost as if they are bleeding from their hearts when they speak about it. I do not think I would be able to talk about it as they do if I experienced a similar thing."

Only slowly, between March and August of 2010, did Kenshi Hirata begin to reveal what he had hoped, for most of his life, no one would actually learn about him. He did not want to remember.

"Being a double survivor was a shameful dishonor," he said enigmatically; and for many weeks afterward it appeared that he would never say anything more about it. Hideo Nakamura and historian Tomoko Maekawa tried to comprehend what sort of survivor's guilt must have accompanied being shielded from the atomic bomb twice while his wife and more than 200,000 people died all around him.

In time, Kenshi explained that part of his shame came from the demands of Japanese society during the 1940s. Even remarriage of a widower, in those times, came under the shadow of "the district gossip committee," and was considered a dishonorable act that somehow stained the children: "So, I was not only trying to protect my children from radiation discrimination; I did not want society to carry rumors and scandals about my daughter as a second marriage daughter. And so I eliminated the secondness of the marriage."

"How can you keep it in your heart?" Saeko asked her father. "I'm amazed that you kept it secret, like a clam, for sixty-five years."

"I am relieved, to finally speak out," Kenshi said.

"I am sorry for him to now have to expose this secret after so many years," Saeko recorded for history. "In that inferno, my father was trying to find his wife. Sacrificing everything—without complaining about the pain—to find her. I am amazed. For two full days, he was searching for his wife. This is something he has been hiding for a long time. But I am delighted to see my more real father."

"I did not wish to be a *double hibakusha*," Kenshi emphasized. "This is not my wish. It just happened, because they built the bombs. So, everyone has to think about it. If we really think about each other, this should not be. Nuclear arms are not [compatible] with civilization. I think such a thing should not be existing."

And he concluded, "This is the first and last time I will speak to the world about it. These are my last words on the subject. Do with them what you may."[65]

Twenty floors high on the surviving tower of 1 Liberty Plaza, in the World Trade Center "Family Room," Masahiro Sasaki's friend Tsugio Ito, grieving for his son, had left a thousand paper cranes, carefully strung together. Attached to them was a white ribbon bearing the words, "Come back to Hiroshima." Mr. Ito drew some small consolation from knowing that his brother Hiroshi at least died surrounded by and comforted by his family. He regretted that his son died alone and disappeared without a trace when the disintegrating fuselage of Flight 175 passed directly through his South Tower office.

On the day Masahiro went to New York with his friend Tsugio and visited the Family Room, he was introduced to 9/11 survivors as a victim of Hiroshima.

Hiroshima Castle in July 1945, late August 1945, and July 2010. [Illustration: Patricia Wynne]

"I am a survivor, *not* a victim," Masahiro said sternly. And he discovered that many of the 9/11 families, years after the fall of the towers, still wanted revenge.

"More than a half century ago," Masahiro explained, "I was in much the same frame of mind you find yourselves in today. The difference is that I have had a half-century more to meditate upon this. During the first ten years or so, the feelings of families in all three ground zeros must have begun the same. But the important question is, what can be done for the future?"

Masahiro recalled that a scientist once told a theologian, "We are the sum of what we remember." And the theologian responded, "No. We are *how* we remember."

"All the suffering of the past means nothing," Masahiro said, "if we do not draw lessons from which to build a better world for tomorrow's child."

The big question, Masahiro said again, is, "What can we do for the future?"

He did not believe that the big question required big earthshaking answers delivered with all the force of wide-angle shotgun blasts. A changed way of thinking needed only to go out into the world like individual pinpricks and be given barely more than a microscopic hope of reaching some person, somewhere, who might become pivotal in history ("Do I advise my commander to attack or to talk? . . . To launch or to hold back for a while?"). Like Tsutomu Yamaguchi, he hoped that out-branching acts of kindness might, without our ever knowing it, reach into the heart of a child who has perhaps lost all hope and who thinks there is nothing good left in humanity, and change the path of someone who might otherwise grow up to create another night of black rain and blue fireflies.

"I think *Omoiyari* is the best way to start," Masahiro Sasaki said. "The worst way is to call ourselves victims. To say 'victim' requires a victimizer, and the victimizer is led to blame; and that starts the *cycle* of blame. For example, if we say 'victim of Hiroshima,' the next sentence that comes up will involve Pearl Harbor and the blaming chain gets stuck all the way in the past. Then we are completely derailed from the lesson that war itself is humanity's Pandora, and that nuclear weapons are something that came out of Pandora's Box."

If victimhood and blame become the lesson ("*Your country hurt me! You hurt me first!*") then we become imprisoned in the 1930s and 1940s, forever trapped by our past. Masahiro wanted to go forward with *Omoiyari*, in his thoughts and in his deeds.

"Think about the other person first," Masahiro told his listeners in America, where a separate genesis of a similar principle was still, albeit falteringly, trying to take root under the term "paying it forward." The essential theme went back through "as yourself" (or *Nyokodo*) to pre-biblical versions of the Golden Rule.

"Sadako understood this theme more personally and more intensely than most people ever will," Masahiro said. "And she had only enough time to begin teaching anew what most of us have so easily forgotten."

Some 9/11 survivors and their families went away from the Masahiro encounter with their way of thinking changed. Not many; for the wounds were too fresh for the majority to be moved by words. Only some were moved— just a few, in fact. But they might have been enough.

In this same year, Masahiro spoke about this same word, *Omoiyari*, in Vienna.

At the end of his talk, a boy raised his hand and asked, "Mr. Sasaki, which country dropped the atomic bomb?"

He was not expecting a question so childishly simple that it could be answered with one word. Masahiro answered, "It's been more than sixty years since the bombs were dropped. God made everyone equal. So, I forgot who dropped the bomb."

The audience, including a police officer who stood nearby, looked on in silent puzzlement. The boy, who appeared to be about eleven years old, nodded understanding and gave Masahiro a thumbs-up.

For the adults of the audience, Masahiro explained, "What I am trying to say is that it does not matter who dropped the bomb. It's not an issue. It should never be an issue for any country. It's an issue for all humanity. The important thing is that I, and Sadako, knew the feeling of *Omoiyari*—and if this principle can be taken to heart and passed down by just a few of you here in this room today, it may, in time, lessen the dangers in the world. You must overcome the sadness and come out of it by passing this simple philosophy down to the next generation. This is my wish."

Then, looking at the boy who asked the question, he said, "Children! Teach your parents."[66]

Acknowledgments

$\mathscr{F}$irst and foremost, I thank John and Jane Pellegrino, Adelle Dobie, and Barbara and Dennis Harris, Agnes Saunders, and Ed McGunnigle. This project has benefited from conversations with experts and from encounters with eyewitnesses dating back more than three decades, to my high school years, beginning with George Appoldt (then of the FBI), who first called my attention to Tsutomu Yamaguchi, Kenshi Hirata, Arai, and the existence of double survivors. He also introduced me personally to the strange cases of the doctor (personal communication) and Private Shigeru Shimoyama (also personal communication), whose poor vision had been corrected by the overpressure from the bomb.

In approximately the order in which I met or corresponded with them about the subjects covered in this book, I am indebted to Don Peterson, Amelia Sheridan, and Michie Hattori Bernstein, to Harold Clayton Urey and Luis and Walter Alvarez (the latter, on New Zealand iridium concentrations and nuclear winter; Luis Alvarez did not speak about the bomb); Father "Mattias" and Father "John MacQuitty" (whose names have been changed by request and by contractual agreements going as far back as 1986), James Michener, Norman Cousins, James Powell (Brookhaven National Laboratory, head of reactor systems [ret]), Pierre Noyes (Stanford Linear Accelerator); Francis Crick, Senator Spark Matsunaga, Rhold Sagdeev, Father Mervyn Fernando (Subhodi Institute), Ed Bishop, Sir Arthur C. Clarke, Frank Andrews (Carter National Observatory, New Zealand), Sir Charles Fleming (Geological Survey, New Zealand); Edward R. Harrison (Amherst College, Carter National Observatory, New Zealand); historian Walter Lord, philosopher/authors George Zebrowski, Pamela Sargent, Glen Marcus. Haraldur Sigurdsson and Steve Carey (volcanology, forensic archaeology, University of Rhode Island),

G. Mastrolerenzo (forensic archaeology, Vesuvius Observatory), and Charles Sheffield and Robert Genna (Suffolk Crime Lab, N.Y.) have shared in studies of comparative eruptive and explosive force, and what happens to people and objects at temperatures near and above five times the boiling point of water. I also owe Bill Schutt (American Museum of Natural History), Janet and Billy Schutt, Mary Leung—and the three "Pellegrinoids," who have proved to be perfectly consistent with Masahiro Sasaki's command of, "Children! Teach your parents!" It was the children who explained to me why thousands of paper cranes were arriving from Japan to a demolished firehouse and other landmarks within the deathscape of Ground Zero, New York, where the bundles of paper cranes became, along with the occasional flag, the only splashes of beauty and color in a gray and infinitely depressing land. The children were the first to tell the story of Sadako and the thousand paper cranes, and to bring glimmers of hope from the ashes (in the *Omoiyari* and *Nyokodo* principles).

Thanks go out to Miaka Nakao (RE: Japan WWII atomic bomb program study, University of Tokyo School of Arts and Sciences), Patricia Wynne, Charles Sweeney, Ken Goldie, Sheldon Stoff, Roy Cullimore, Lori Johnston, Jesse A. Stoff, Bill Broad (*New York Times*), the family of Nancy and Larry Cantwell, Miko Hatano (Japan Consulate, N.Y.), Hideo Nakamura, Hidetaka Inazuka, Chad Diehl, Mr. and Mrs. Hisao Maegaki, Mr. and Mrs. Masahiro Sasaki and Yuji Sasaki, Yoshinari [Tsugio] Ito, Tokusaburo Nagai, Endo Tai, Hiroshi Takayama, Tsutomu Yamaguchi, Toshiko (Yamaguchi) Yamasaki and the rest of the Yamaguchi family as well, for their remarkable hospitality and support. History is indebted to all of the people who helped, including Kenshi and Saeko Hirata and their family (and the brother of the lost Setsuko Hirata) for coming forth and providing the rest of the story, along with Akira Iwanaga and Kuniyoshi Sato. I am grateful to Hiroshi Fujii (son of Nancy Cantwell's mentor, Dr. Minoru Fujii), Kazuko Kouno, Saitou, Misako Fujita, Reiko Owa, Sigeko Wasada, Saena Magee, Kazuko Minamoto, Mr. and Mrs Tak Furumoto, Yumi Tanaka (to whom the "Burnt Maria" painting was given by Tsutomu Yamaguchi), Kae Matsumoto and her father Yoji Matsumoto, Frances Kakugawa and Victor Chan (the Dalai Lama Institute), Tomoko Maekawa (Nagasaki University), Steve Leeper (Hiroshima Peace Cultural Foundation), Keiji Nakazawa, Mark Selden (Cornell University), Hiroko Nakamoto, Akira Setoguchi, Michimasa Hirata (Tokyo Federation of A-Bomb Survivors), Setsuko Thurlow, Shigeko Sasamori, Takehisa Yamamoto, Shinpei Takada, Toshihiro Shiroishi (The Asahi Shimbun *Messages from Hibakusha* Project, along with editors Karen Godshall and Ron Andrews), Shoso Kawamoto, Takashi (Thomas) Tanemori, John Crump, Mark Baraka Strauch, Kenji Kitagawa, Masahiro Kunishige, Emiko Nakasako, Yagawa Mitsunori, Brian Taylor, M. Thompson, and Inosuke Hayasaki and Bob Kestler.

Additional special thanks also go out to Elaine Markson, Julia Kenny, Gary Johnson, Jack Macrae, James Cameron, Parks Stephenson and John Landau at Lightstorm, to Ari Beser, Eric Beser, Russell Gackensbach (via Bill Broad and Hideo Nakamura), Clifton Truman Daniel, Paule Saviano, to John Batchelor (at ABC), Ian Punnett and Lisa Lyon (at Coast to Coast AM), and Rip MacKenzie, George Greenfield (Creative Well), Susan McEachern, Audra Figgins, Alden Perkins, Sharon Kunz (Rowman & Littlefield).

Notes

Four double survivors, Tsutomu Yamaguchi, Kenshi Hirata, Kuniyoshi Sato, and Akira Iwanaga, still alive during the writing of this book, were interviewed on multiple occasions between 2008 and 2011.

CHAPTER 1. THE KILLING STAR

1. On nucleosynthesis ([p2] the stellar origins of uranium, carbon and other heavy elements): F. Hoyle, "The Synthesis of the Elements from Hydrogen," MNRAS, vol. 106, p 343 (1946); V. Trimble, "The Origin and Abundances of the Chemical Elements," *Review of Modern Physics*, vol. 198, p 877, Oct., 1977; Lyden-Bell (ed), *The Big Bang and Element Creation*, The Royal Society of London, 1982; C. Pellegrino, "Compilation of Nucleosynthesis Pathways," (in) *Time Gate: Hurtling Backward through History*, p 241, TAB, PA (1984).

2. On the purity of U-235 in the Hiroshima device (and a rush to production as a possible cause for decreased efficiency of the device) [p2]: Colin, in *Report 4.1, Elements of Fission Weapons Design* (6/16/2008), noted that the bomb was developed with the use of less than 90% enrichment: "The actual fissile load was only [approximately] 80%. . . . The explosive efficiency of Little Boy was 0.23kt/kg of fissile material (1.3%) compared to 2.8kt/kg (16%) for Fat man. Use of 93% [U-235] would at least have doubled Little Boy's yield."

3. The identification of Mrs. Aoyama as one of the people exposed outdoors and nearest the Hiroshima bomb [pp2–6], was conveyed by the nurses of Dr. Minoru Fujii's mobile rescue team, and by Mrs. Aoyama's son, Nenkai, during a July 2008 meeting (filmed) [pp2–9]. The effects of the flash on human flesh (primarily by the infrared and visible regions of the spectrum) during the first 0.3–3.0 seconds, including air temperatures at ground level, were determined from studies of "bubbled" roof tiles and other objects in the vicinity of the Aoyama home, as in E. Ishikawa et al,

The Committee for the Compilation of Materials on Damage Caused by the Atomic Bombs in Hiroshima and Nagasaki, *Hiroshima and Nagasaki: The Physical, Medical, and Social Effects of the Atomic Bombings* (Translation: N.Y., Basic Books, 1981), pp 32–36. Prompt effects of thermal shock on Mrs. Aoyama's blood and bones, at minimum five times the boiling point of water in sea-level air, were informed by on-site analysis (2001–2005) of blood-derived iron deposits on the floor of the Herculaneum Marina, resulting from 500 degrees C effects of the Vesuvius AD 79 surge cloud on more than 200 individuals (aided by personal communication with Haraldur Sigurdsson and Steve Carey, University of Rhode Island, and the staff of the Vesuvius crime lab/observatory). See Sigurdsson, et al, "The Eruption of Vesuvius in AD 79," *National Geographic Research*, 1 (1985), pp 332–387. That the Herculaneum phenomena are instructive for understanding Hiroshima was a subject discussed extensively with G. Mastroerenzo and his colleagues at the Vesuvius Observatory (2005). See "Herculaneum Victims of Vesuvius in AD 79," *Nature*, Apr. 12, 2001; C. Pellegrino, *Ghosts of Vesuvius* (Harper, N.Y., 2004), p 169–238. People in Pompeii's sister city, Herculaneum, were dead in 1/200 of a second, and were disintegrated down to tendon and bone in 1/20th of a second. This was the result of contact with hot air and dust in motion. At (and in the immediate vicinity of) the Hiroshima hypocenter, flash reflective effects on the ground heated the air to significantly higher temperatures for more than 1/3rd of a second before blast, implosion, and other disruptive effects of the atomic shock bubble pulled the hot air away. (Heated air moving over bodies while covering a distance of only 3–5 meters in 1/10th–1/20th of a second, greatly magnified the carbonization effect, in the manner of superheated air in a blast furnace.)

4. Toshihiko Matsuda, the "Marble Boy" of Hiroshima [p6]: Reiko Owa, Sigeko Wasada, and the nurses of Dr. Fujii's crew, personal communication (2008), p 2. The Matsuda case corroborates the surprisingly high measure of flash protection provided by thin materials (such as paper and leaves). This was further demonstrated during U.S. above-ground atomic tests in which animals (including piglets) were exposed (during tests *Met* and *Gamble*) to varying thicknesses of flash protection.

5. The first hundred milliseconds over Hiroshima [pp2–9]: The U.S. Strategic Bombing Survey: *The Effects of Atomic Bombs on Hiroshima and Nagasaki*, internal report, Chairman's Office, June 30, 1946, pp 1–33; E. Ishikawa, et al, pp 21–79. The next half-second, throughout Hiroshima, was reconstructed in accordance with U.S. high-speed film footage of tests near and below 15 kilotons, on structures and animals. Tests: *Hot Shot, How, Sugar, Fizeau, Fox*, and *Stokes*; at Bikini Atoll, Test *Able*; at Enewatak Atoll, Tests *Seminole* and *Sequoia*. Collectively, footage and results covered varying distances from the hypocenters.

6. The experiences of Akiko Takakura and her friend Asami, in the Geibi Bank [pp9–10, 14]: Interview in *Hiroshima*, BBC (2005); Hiroshima Memorial Museum Archive, *Hibakusha Testimonies*, Akiko Takakura. The clock tower: in John Toland, *The Rising Sun* (N.Y., Random House, 1970), p 784. Corroboration of Takakura's blast-related air-pressure effects on lungs: two nurses interviewed by Toland, p 785.

7. Shigeyoshi Morimoto, shock-cocooned in a Ground Zero mansion [pp10–11, 14]: Robert Trumbull in *Nine Who Survived Hiroshima and Nagasaki* (N.Y., Dutton, 1957), pp 38–39.

8. Private Shigeru Shimoyama's "crucifixion" and survival [pp11–12]: pp 782–788 and in a speech to Jesuits and students, about 1971 (personal communication); Norman Cousins and George Appoldt, 1972–1973 (personal communication).

9. Captain Mitsou Fuchida [pp11–12]: Walter Lord (personal communication) had interviewed Fuchida during the writing of *Day of Infamy*; Fuchida, unpublished memoir titled, *From Pearl Harbor to Golgatha* (about 1960).

10. Sumiko Kirahara's family [pp11–12, 14]: Youth Division of Soka Gakkai, *Cries for Peace* (The Japan Times, LTD, 1978), pp 178–180.

11. The Sasaki family and Sadako's recollection of the eye-stinging flash [pp12, 14, 15]: Masahiro Sasaki, personal communication, 2008, 2010.

12. Teruko Kono [p12], *Finally I Found Him, But . . . #22, Floating Lantern*.

13. Nobuo Tetsutani's account [pp12–13]: *Shin's Tricycle* (Tokyo, London, N.Y., Walker Books, 1995); also, Hiroshima Museum archive/artifact display of the tricycle itself.

14. Schoolchildren Etsuko Kuramoto's and Hiroshi Mori's premonitions (and the blue flash seen by Yoshiko Mori) [pp13–14]: Hiroshima "Floating Lantern" Archive; *Missing Children, #7; #22; Oh, Missing Etusuko, #23*.

15. Schoolteacher Arai's facial burn, shaped by the calligraphy of a child [pp13–14]: Norman Cousins (personal communication, 1987); George Appoldt (with N. Cousins, 1972–1973). Arai's paper phenomenon replicated elsewhere in Hiroshima: "Hibakusha Voices," accessible through Charlespellegrino.com/Asahi Shimbun: Disk #3, Case #116.

16. The castor bush "shadow effect" event (as actually experienced by Arai, personal communication, 1972), 1,300 meters from the Hiroshima hypocenter [pp14, 107]: American Strategic Bombing Survey photos, as in Averill A. Liebow, *A Medical Diary of Hiroshima 1945* (N.Y., W.W. Norton, from the *Yale Journal of Biology and Medicine*, 1965), p 128B.

17. See note 6.

18. See note 14.

19. See note 11.

20. See note 10.

21. The yellow flash witnessed by Hiroko Fukada [p14], and the large pieces of hail that fell with the black rain: Hiroshima Museum Archive, *Voices of Hibakusha, Testimony of Hiroko Fukada*, p 1.

22. Yosaku Mikami's interpretation of the same flash as blue [p14]: *Testimony of Yosaku Mikami*, p 1.

23. Account of the same flash perceived as red [pp14–15]: *Dr. Hiroshi Sawachika*, p 1.

24. Photographer Siezo Yamada's perception of a multi-color flash [p14]: Hiroshima Peace Media Center, Jan. 3, 2008.

25. See note 10.

26. See note 11.

27. Tsutomu Yamaguchi, the first seconds [pp15–16]: Personal communication (2008), plus unpublished memoir, *I Live to Tell My Story* (2009).

28. Military weather forecaster Isao Kita [pp16–18]: Hiroshima Museum Archive, *Hiroshima Witness #1–3*, pp 5–7; George Appoldt (F.B.I., 1973).

CHAPTER 2. GOJIRA'S EGG

1. Akiko Takakura [p19]: Hiroshima Museum Memorial Archive, *Hibakusha Testimonies*, A. Takakura, p 1; interview (in) *Hiroshima* (DVD, London, BBC, 2005); interview with G. S. Trujillo, July 30, 1990.

2. Private Shigeru Shimoyama [pp19, 31–32, 35], shock-cocoon, corrected eyesight, a "pale horse" in a landscape from the *Revelation of John*: John Toland, *The Rising Sun* (N.Y., Random House, 1970), pp 788–789, 793–794, 789, 794 (realization that the bomb was atomic, p 789); also, personal communication (courtesy of George Appoldt, FBI, and N.Y.C. Jesuits, 1970–1971); Hiroshima nurses of Dr. Minoru Fujii's rescue team (July 21, 2008, p 1). Shigeru's "Emperor's portrait incident" [p31], corroborated in Dr. Michihiko Hachiya's *Hiroshima Diary* (University of North Carolina Press, 1955), pp 183–185, and [p229], Aug. 6, 1945 description entries. Dr. Ryokichi Sagane wrote of experience, Japan's nuclear program, in unpublished memoir "Story of the Atomic Bomb," as presented by Mika Nakao, University of Tokyo (personal communication, Columbia University conference, 2009). Awareness of "secret" [p20]: physician Michihiko Hachiya (in) *Hiroshima Diary*, p 57; also Dr. Nagai of Nagasaki: Takashi (Paul) Nagai, *The Bells of Nagasaki* (Tokyo, London, N.Y., 1949, 1984), pp 56–60.

3. Kite-maker Morimoto's shock cocoon [p19], see Morimoto sources, chapter 1.

4. Tsutomu Yamaguchi, the first day [pp19, 22]: personal communication (2008–2009); Toshiko (Yamaguchi) Yamasaki, 2010, 2011; Robert Trumbull, translation of Tsutomu Yamaguchi's internal report to the Mitsubishi Corporation, in *Nine Who Survived Hiroshima and Nagasaki* (N.Y., Dutton, 1957), pp 29–33. Yamaguchi's encounter with the boys, whose skin was embedded with glass: p 13 of his memoir, *I Live to Tell My Story*.

5. The Sasaki and Kirihara neighborhood (all of them initially coughing and made thirsty by yellow and gray dust), Masahiro Sasaki, personal communication, July 2008.

6. The Sasaki and Ito families [pp20–21]: personal communication (2008–2011). Dr. Hachiya, corroboration of the Ito boy's description of the school's Olympic swimming pool, Diary, pp 2, 4, 19–20, 54–55, 189; his observation of the "ghost-walker" state of mind (pp 1, 4), and war's end with "wooden bullets and bamboo spears," p 188, and his neighbors, the Sasakis (p 185), corroborated by Masahiro Sasaki, personal communication (July 2008), as the same Sasaki family.

7. The Misasa Bridge region, Hiroshi Ito and Ryuzo, and Hanako Ito's trek toward her son near the region [pp20–22, 33, 34]: Personal communication, and memoir provided by the Ito family (written 2008); personal communication with the nurses of Dr. M. Fujii's rescue crew; Dr. Ryuso Tanaka, interviewed by students of Hiroshima University (for Museum Archive, May 16, 1995). Freezing mist and hail, descending from high altitude: Tsugio Ito, Masahiro Sasaki (personal communication, 2008, 2010), including map annotations, showing the path taken by the Ito boy: "Hiroshi— cold hail near river, icy rain . . . [and] wind-driven debris into child's mouth." Hiroko Fukada (interview with G. S. Trujillo, 1986) described cold rain and large, dangerous hail that came with it. (See also Ref 17., Chapter 1.)

8. See note 7.

9. See note 4.

10. See note 7.

11. The horror of "the tap dancer" near the Misasa Bridge [pp22–23]: personal communication, Norman Cousins (1987); oral traditions of the postwar schools told by Endo Tai, personal communication (2008); Masahiro Sasaki (2010); also on Sasaki's and Kirahara's wondering if the Earth itself had been instantly shattered. Keiji Nakazawa: people whose limbs were blast-severed: Manga, *Barefoot Gen, the Day After* (American edition, Philadelphia, New Society Publishers, 1988), pp 158–159. Nakazawa's neighbor, Tanaka (identified as "Ryuta" in *The Day After*), family "dissected" by the blast, impaled in trees: K. Nakazawa (personal communication, 2010–2011).

12. Military physician, assigned about June 1945, to teach Hiroshima's youth suicide attacks with mines, and whose vision was corrected by the blast [pp23–24]: Personal communication arranged by George Appoldt, 1974.

13. Sumako Matsuyanagi [p24]: propulsive flight into an elderly couple's house, and the fates of her two children: Hiroshima *Floating Lantern* Archive, #32, "No God, no Buddha" (includes famine food and death of her son: "[He died], saying, 'I'm sorry I got Kenji hurt.' I did not know at the time that these were his last words."); also Hiroshima nurses, Dr. Minoru Fujii's crew, via personal communication (7/21/08), p 2.

14. Yoshitaka's escape from a collapsed Ground Zero school, and shielding by bricks [pp24–25]: Hiroshima Museum Archive Testimony of Yoshitaka Kawamoto.

15. See note 13.

16. The boy whose mother wished she had let him eat the tomato [p26], related by poet Shinoe Shoda in "A Poor Student's Mother," in *Miminari* (Tokyo: Heibousha, 1962); also, nurses of Dr. Minoru Fujii's rescue crew (personal communication, July 2008).

17. Akiko Takakura [pp26–28; see also ref pp9–10 [Chapter 1]], Isao Kita [pp34–35], and Tsutomu Yamaguchi [p34], concluding all damage surrounding them wrought by a single weapon: Hiroshima Museum Archive, Hiroshima Witness #1–3, pp 5–7; also, personal communication with Tsutomu Yamaguchi (located in vicinity of Kita's weather station).

18. See note 17.

19. The witnessing of "shadow people," one of them a "charcoal person" [p28] whose corpse continued to sit in a corner, outside a Ground Zero bank building, in front of his shadow—and the carbonized corpse of a person pulling a cart with two children, found the day after: Case #11301, Case #11305, The Asahi Shimbun archive, *Messages from Hibakusha* (accessible via C. Pellegrino home page and http://www.asahi.com/hibakusha/english/).

20. See note 17.

21. See note 17.

22. The watchmaker's account (and other "ant-walkers" who survived) [p29]: Robert Jay Lifton's *Death in Life: Survivors of Hiroshima* (University of North Carolina Press, 1967, 1991), pp 25–26.

23. Dr. Hachiya among the "ant-walkers," walking in the realm of dreams: [pp2, 14, 29–30, 54–55], Michihiko Hachiya, Hiroshima Diary, U. of North Carolina Press, Chapel Hill, 1955.

24. The young military officer who obsessed, like many other people, on seemingly absurd details [pp30–31]: Robert Jay Lifton's *Death in Life*, p 28. NOTE on the nesting urge: C. Pellegrino with W. Lord, in *Her Name, Titanic*, McGraw-Hill, 1988, pp 203–215.

25. Private Shigeru Shimoyama: See chap. 1, note 8. The Emperor's portrait incident is corroborated by Dr. Hachiya's *Hiroshima Diary*, p 185 (see footnote 2.).

26. Misako Katani and her father, embarking on a journey to Nagasaki [p32]: H. Nakamura and H. Inazuka film, *Twice Bombed, Twice Survived, Part 1* (Tokyo, 2004). The "fire horse" phenomenon, captured in a series of paintings by a surviving artist (on display at the Nagasaki Museum), oral history from the children of Katani's and Sasaki's school (Endo Tai, personal communication).

27. Sumiko Kirihara's and Sadako Sasaki's families—fire worms and waterspouts [pp32–33]: Youth Division of Soka Gakki, *Cries for Peace* (The Japan Times LTD, 1978), p 179; Masahiro Sasaki, personal communication (2008, 2010). Hiroko Fukada waterspout: Hiroshima Museum Archive, Hiroshima Witness #2, pp 8–10.

28. See note 7.

29. Flash-burned bodies floating downriver to Tsutomu Yamaguchi's position [pp34–35], further detailed by witness #11305 in The Asahi Shimbun *Messages from Hibakusha* Project (accessible via the C. Pellegrino home page and http://www.asahi.com/hibakusha/english/). De-gloving and other "abstract" injuries were described by kite-maker Morimoto, in R. Trumbull (p 39), and by T. Yamaguchi in personal communication (2008), and in Yamaguchi's Tanka poems, translated by Chad Diehl, in *And the River Flowed as a Raft of Corpses* (N.Y., Excogiating Over Cups of Coffee Publishing, 2010).

30. See note 2.

CHAPTER 3. SETSUKO

1. On the Hiroshima bomb as a 10–12.5 kiloton "disappointment" (as opposed to 20 kilotons officially announced by President Truman) [p37]: Timeline #2—The 509th (Composite Group), *The Hiroshima Mission*, page 3: "8/6/45; 8:15:17–8:16AM—Little Boy exploded at an altitude of 1,890 feet above the target. Yield was equivalent to 12,500 tons of TNT." NOTE: The direction of neutrinos through Setsuko's body [p37] is determined, not by a straight-line path from the bomb's detonation point through the Earth's core, but by an angle dictated by the location of the Hirata house, relative to the bomb (location verified by the Hirata family, 2010). Robert Trumbull, *Nine Who Survived Hiroshima and Nagasaki* (N.Y., Dutton, 1957), p 24, referenced Kenshi Hirata's prior near miss of the Osaka and Kobe fire-bombings of March 13 and 17, 1945 [p38]. Mr. Hirata at Hiroshima, Aug. 6, 1945 [pp38–39, 42–43, 48–49, 54–58, 62–25]: 8/9/55, translation of K. Hirata report for Mitsubishi, Nagasaki, in Trumbull, pp 23–27, 34–35, 64–71, 76; Norman Cousins, personal communication (1987); Henshi Hirata and family, interviews via Hideo Nakamura and Hidetaka Inazuka (2010). Norman Cousins on famine food and flavorings, August

1945; also Hiroko Nakamoto in personal communication (2010) and in her book, *My Japan: 1930–1951* (N.Y., McGraw Hill, 1970), pp 50–51.

2. See note 1.

3. Father "Mattias" [pp43–44, 45] described his own, Hirata-like journey through the Hiroshima "hellscape" in personal communication (1974), corroborating people flash-carbonized at the cable cars. NOTE: Because he eventually died by an alcohol-related suicide and was a Catholic, Fr. "Mattias's" name was changed (as mentioned previously in the endnotes of *Dust* [N.Y., Avon-Morrow, 1998], p432). The name change was made at the request of his friends and family. A similar, contractual agreement to always quote a Jesuit colleague of "Mattias" accurately but to identify him only by his pen name, "Fr. John MacQuitty," as noted in the acknowledgements of *Return to Sodom and Gomorrah,* dates back to the 1980s (reaffirmed specifically for this book, 3/1/09). Such sights as were described by "Mattias" at the trolley (babies and their dead mothers) were horrifyingly common under the atomic bombs, as memorialized in the Hiroshima Museum archive, *Voice of the Hibakusha,* Testimony of Dr. Hiroshi Sawachika, p1; Japan Society Conference 5/21/10, Testimony of Takehisha Yamamoto, p2 (and personal communication, 2010).

4. Akihiro Takahashi's encounter at the wrecked trolley, ant-walkers, Tibbets [pp43–44]: Hiroshima Museum Archive, "The Turning Point," in *Hibakusha* (Tokyo, Kosei, 1986), pp 191–204; interview in *Hiroshima in Memoriam and Today,* ed. H. Takayama (Tokyo, N.Y., The Himat Group, 2000), pp 63–66; David Smith, *The Guardian,* interview with A. Takahashi, "I Don't Blame Them but I Hope They Mourn the Dead," Aug. 2005. His *Hibakusha* editor, Takayama (at Kosei), and Nenkai Aoyama reported (2008, personal communication) some of A. Takahashi's Aug. 6, 1945, encounters with nurses, soldiers, and priests (in the last group, there was no lasting specification as to whether the "priests" were Buddhist, Catholic, or other). Drawings of the rail car "charcoal people," made by children who saw them, are on display at the Hiroshima Museum (National Geographic documentary, *24 Hours After Hiroshima,* 2010).

5. See note 3.

6. Tsutomu Yamaguchi encountered the same "lantern" phenomenon as Kenshi Hirata and Prefect Nishioka [pp45, 54–55]: Trumbull, pp 29, 49–50, 53.

7. See note 1.

8. Firefighters of Hiroshima: Firefighter Yosaku Mikami [pp46–47]: Hiroshima Museum Archive, Witness #1–2, pp 4–5. NOTE: Firefighter Mitsunori and the "hibakusha piano" [pp47–50]: Arakawa Ryu in *The Japan Journal,* "Hiroshima Piano Plays Message of Peace," with additional details provided by the firefighter's son (and musician) Yagawa Mitsunori, personal communication, Sept. 11, 2010. Dr. Hiroshi Sawachika likened the pervasive smell on that first day to dried seafood (Hiroshima Museum Archive, Witness # 1–1), as did Tsutomu Yamaguchi (personal communication, 2008).

9. See note 1.

10. Morimoto, master kite-maker and double atomic bomb survivor [pp51–52]: Mitsubishi archive, translated for Robert Trumbull's *Nine Who Survived Hiroshima and Nagasaki,* pp 16, 35–36, 38–41, 73–74. NOTE: Implosive effects, heavy machinery, air-filled storm drains "vacuumed" up through the pavement, in *U.S. Strategic Bomb-*

ing Surveys, Hiroshima and Nagasaki (Washington D.C., June 30, 1946). Tsutomu
Yamaguchi, pulled by collapsing shock bubble (personal communication, 2008 and
unpublished report, "I Live to Tell My Story," translated by Hideo Nakamura, 2009).

11. On the Morimoto mansion [pp51–52], within the same approximately 750-
meter radius as the Fukuya Department Store (where people unshielded by a minimum of one layer of concrete flooring received, at up to 1.1 km, a combined potentially lethal gamma ray and neutron dose above 230r essentially instantly [see also,
RE Fukuya radius, Yoshiko Kikada, in Asahi Shimbun file # 07220, 2010; Funasaka
Yasunori, Asahi Shimbun file # 06626, 2011]): Trumbull (p 38 [possibly relying on
a statement from Kenshi Hirata]) overstated the detonation point as "almost directly
above" Moromoto (if this description is taken literally, three tiers of wood and tile
could never have prevented a lethal indoor dose above 600r); further details and
conclusions about the Morimoto house itself, consistent with Morimoto's temporary
illness, arose from discussions with Norman Cousins and George Zebrowski (1987,
1988). Their analysis of the Morimoto "mansion," filled essentially wall-to-wall and
floor-to-ceiling with books, sheds light on anomalous survival of three people in a
region where essentially no one else escaped death or severe injury: a building just
large enough to provide adequate shock-cocooning and (just barely) shielding from
prompt, cumulatively lethal radiation effects. Kenshi Hirata (in Trumbull, p 62) corroborated that the three were "very close" to the hypocenter. Substantial intervening
materials at the Morimoto and Fukuya radius (according to above-ground atomic test
results: necessitating up to a meter of wood and 8–10 cm of tiles to attenuate prompt
radiation dosage by 50%–75% [S. Glasstone, ed., *The Effects of Nuclear Weapons*, AEC,
Washington D.C., 1962, p 384]). According to Norman Cousins (in a manner consistent with being on the ground floor of a large, book-lined multi-story house no
nearer than 750 meters and with an estimated indoor dose in the range of 100r, plus
likely black rain exposure), Morimoto did, despite shielding, suffer some shock and/
or radiation-induced rapid onset vomiting.

12. The atomic cloud, as seen from Assembly Prefect Takejiro Nishioka's position [p51]: M. Hachiya, Hiroshima Diary, pp 162–164. Prefect Nishioka, completely
shadow-shielded behind a mountain [pp52–56]: R. Trumbull, pp 48–50. On page
51, Nishioka relates an encounter with a schoolboy, consistent with the Ito family's
account of Hiroshi Ito's travels in Nishioka's direction, along railroad tracks, before finally being rescued by a neighbor with a bicycle. The path was partly reconstructed on
a map by Tsugio Ito and his friend Masahiro Sasaki (personal communication, 2010).
Other information RE Nishioka (including mention of the cats that crossed a bridge
to Nishioka's position) was recorded by Nishioka's wife, as a combination of oral and
written tradition related and translated by Endo Tai and Dr. Takashi Nagai's grandson
at the Nyokodo Hermitage, and during tours of key artifact sites throughout Nagasaki,
2008 (personal communication). His encounter with cats eating a horse's intestines was
not unique (as in recordings of the hibakusha accessible through the Charlespellegrino
.com/Asahi Shimbun link: Disk #6, case # 235).

13. See note 12.

14. Key details about the Japan nuclear program during WWII [pp53–54] were
provided by a mentor (on the 1983 book, *Darwin's Universe*): Harold Urey (affirmed

during a Columbia University Conference, RE Nishina, Tajima, Nov. 6, 2009). Japanese WWII nuclear programs, additional references: Dr. Nishina, (Toland, *The Rising Sun*, N.Y., Random House, 1970, pp 794–795); Ryokichi Sagane memoir, Hiroshima Archive, IMTFE#62049 ("Termination of the War"); Eizo Tajima, Nagasaki Archive, "Testimony of Atomic Bomb Survivors #20."

15. The train that picked up speed, fanning the flames as it raced past Prefect Nishioka's location [p54] and toward a collision with a truck near Dr. Fujii's hospital: Nancy (Minami) Cantwell and the Hiroshima nurses of Dr. Fujii's crew (personal communication, 2008). Their first rescue effort was in fact at the site of this famous train wreck.

16. See note 12.

17. See note 1.

18. Residual radiation effects at the location of Kenshi Hirata's home in Hiroshima [pp56–57]: E. Ishikawa, et al, *Hiroshima and Nagasaki: The Physical, Medical, and Social Effects of the Atomic Bombings*. Originally published in Japanese, in Tokyo, by Iwanami Shoten Publishers (1979); English translation (N.Y., Basic Books, 1981), pp 73–79.

19. See note 1.

20. Sumiko Kirihara's and Sadako Sasaki's families (and the resistance of outlying communities against people escaping Hiroshima), Aug. 6–Aug. 7, 1945 [pp57–58]: Youth Division of Saka Gakkai, *Cries for Peace* (The Japan Times LTD, 1978), pp 78–80. Masahiro Sasaki on his father's ability to save them from suburban resistance: personal communication (2008).

21. See note 20.

22. Satoko Matsumoto [pp58–59], and her father, stricken by "atomic bomb disease," Youth Div. of Saka Gakki, in *Cries for Peace*, pp 157–161, and famine, p 159. Planes, and "towers of smoke," 8/6/45: also reported by Kenshi Hirata, in R. Trumbull, pp 64–65. Hiroko Nakamoto, in *My Japan*, pp 49–50, on the military worsening an oppressive famine.

23. Tsutomu Yamaguchi, on people reduced to ashes and charcoal statues [p59]: in Trumbull, pp 35, 65–66, 75. His crossing on a "raft" or bridge of floating corpses: Tanka poems and personal communication. NOTE: Kenshi Hirata (pp 65–66, of Trumbull) also described the "shadow people" and "statue people" phenomena, detailing these events further in July 2010 (interviews via Hideo Nakamura). Shadows and ash bodies: Yoji Matsumoto, in personal communication and via his daughter Kae Matsumoto (2010). Photographic examples include: Yosuke Yamahata (700 meters S-E of Urakami hypocenter), American Bombing Survey Archive, published in front matter; E. Ishikawa, et al. Tsutomu Yamaguchi, survival [pp61–62], see also chapter 1 and 2 T. Yamaguchi references.

24. See note 1.

25. Double survivor Akira Iwanaga, 8/6–7/45 [pp59–60]: Trumbull, pp 54–56, 75; personal communication via Hideo Nakamura and Hidetaka Inazuka, July 2010 (he died in 2011). NOTE: Akira was most disturbed by a screaming woman with a dead child, and another who lost a child through an abdominal wound (corroborated by Hiroshima boarding house roommate Yamaguchi, personal communication, 2008 [this horror was common: Disk #6, case #262, accessible Charlespellegrino.com/ Asahi Shimbun link, hibakusha voices]). Dr. Nagai of Nagasaki also reported this was a

frequent horror: *The Bells of Nagasaki* (Tokyo, N.Y., London, Kodansha International, 1949, 1984), p 64.

26. See note 23.

27. The canister with Luis Alvarez's monitoring equipment and the letter to Sagane, Nishina, and the other Japanese physicists can be seen on display in the Hiroshima Museum [pp62–63]; the letter is reproduced in Toland, p 800. According to Harold C. Urey (personal communication, 1979) and Charles Sweeney (personal communication 1999), a copy of the Alvarez group's letter had been placed in each of the monitoring canisters. RE Alvarez and the "nuclear winter effect," personal communication, Lewis and Walter Alvarez (1980–1981), beginning with W. Alvarez and the New Zealand signal of a global iridium anomaly apparently synchronous with the dinosaur E.L.E.

28. See note 1.

CHAPTER 4. AND THE REST WERE NEUTRINOS

1. "Little Boy's" actual yield, 10–12.5 kilotons [p67]: 509th Composite Group Historic Timelines, Timeline #2: *The Hiroshima Mission*, p 3; Eizo Tajima, Nagasaki Archive, "Testimony of Atomic Bomb Survivors #20," p 2.

2. Luis Alvarez's assessment, to Sweeney, regarding projected yield shortfall [p66]: Charles Sweeney, personal communication (1999). Assessment, 50 kiloton potential for uranium designs [pp67–68]: James Powell (Brookhaven National Laboratory), personal communication.

3. Tinian Island accident ends the debate about arming the Hiroshima bomb prior to takeoff [pp68–69]: William Parsons, BBC interview, *Hiroshima* (documentary, 2005).

4. "Dutch" van Kirk and Tibbets [pp68, 69]: BBC interview, *Hiroshima* (2005); interview in *White Light, Black Rain* (documentary, HBO, 2007). Tibbets and Parsons: *Hiroshima* (BBC, 2005); 509th Historic Timeline #2: *Hiroshima Mission*, p 2; Tibbets, in *World at War*, Part 24, "The Bomb" (London, BBC, 1973); BBC (2005) [pp70, 74–78]: Tibbets described the cyanide defense, escape maneuver from the bomb, motions of other two planes, strange effects of the detonation on fillings in teeth.

5. Russell Gackensbach's preparation for flight of *Necessary Evil* [pp69, 72–77, 79–80]: "Brevard Man Played Pivotal Role in U.S. History," *Hometown News, Brevard County*, Dec. 29, 2006; BBC interview, *Hiroshima* (2005).

6. Charles Sweeney, flight of *Great Artiste,* Hiroshima mission [pp69, 72–80, 82–83]: Personal communication (1999); Charles Sweeney, *War's End* (N.Y., Avon Books, 1977), pp 100, 154–155, 157, 163–170; the Tibbets maneuver, p 106; the inexplicable silence from Japan's leadership, pp 172-190.

7. Hiroko Nakamoto, 8/6/45 [pp70–71, 79]: Personal communication (2010); H. Nakamoto, *My Japan: 1930–1951* (N.Y. McGraw-Hill, 1970), pp 44–53, 57 (specific details, starvation diets: p 50).

8. Keiji Nakazawa, worsening food shortages [p71], personal communication (2010).

9. See note 4.

10. James R. Corliss's flight of *Necessary Evil* [pp71–78]: Tinian Island/Corliss documents revealed to the *New York Times* by Corliss's widow, Feb. 2010, quoted (personal communication and in article) by science reporter Bill Broad, in "Doubts Raised on Book's Tale of Atom Bomb," *New York Times*, Feb. 21, 2010. (Tinian/Corliss documents subsequently copied to *New York Times*, 509th Composite Group Archives, and the National Archives, along with statements from *Necessary Evil*'s navigator, Gackensbach, seated to Corliss's left.)

11. See note 4.

12. See note 5.

13. See note 4.

14. See note 4.

15. George Marquardt, the Hiroshima mission [pp71–78]: in *The Independent*, Aug. 23, 2003, and the *Los Angeles Times*, Aug. 24, 2003; Marquardt interview quoted by Richard Goldstein in, "G.W. Marquardt, War Pilot, Dies at 84," *New York Times*, Aug. 25, 2003 (like Tibbets, Marquardt personally experienced, and reported, "a taste like lead in [the] mouth").

16. See note 10.

17. See note 5.

18. See note 15.

19. See note 10.

20. See note 6.

21. Exposure of protected X-ray plates in a hospital 1 mile from the hypocenter [p76]: Kenji Kitagawa, personal communication (2010).

22. See note 15.

23. See note 10.

24. See note 5.

25. See note 15.

26. See note 4.

27. Capt. Robert Lewis, interview in *White Light, Black Rain* (HBO, 2007) [pp78–79].

28. Jacob Beser view of the mission [p78], Ari and Eric Beser, personal communication (2013, 2014).

29. See note 5.

30. See note 4.

31. See note 15.

32. See note 28.

33. See note 7.

34. See note 6.

35. Dr. Yoshio Nishina, Anami, 8/6/45 [p80]: Tatsuichiro Akizuki, *Nagasaki 1945* (London, Melbourne, N.Y., Quartet Books, 1981), p 70.

36. See note 35.

37. The Marcus McDilda incident [pp80–81]: John Toland, *The Rising Sun* (N.Y., Random House, 1970), p 795; Jerome T. Hagen, *War in the Pacific*, Vol. 1 (Hawaii Pacific University, Kenehoe Publications, 1996), p 159; Walter Lord, personal communication (1997).

38. See note 35.

39. Tsutomu Yamaguchi, aboard the second-to-last train from Hiroshima [pp81–82]: personal communication (2008). Prefect Nishioka, aboard the same train [p81], and A. Iwanaga: R. Trumbull, *Nine Who Survived Hiroshima and Nagasaki* (N.Y., Dutton, 1957) p 78. (Iwanaga, interview, Hideo Nakamura, 2010.)

40. See note 39.

41. See note 39.

42. Dr. Tsunoo arrives from Hiroshima [p81]: T. Akizuki, *Nagasaki* 1945, p 106, 115–117.

43. Events on Tinian, late 8/7/45 [pp81–83]: accounts received by Harold Urey, personal communication (1979–1980); Charles Sweeney, *War's End*, pp 172–190, and personal communication (1999).

CHAPTER 5. THE CRAZY IRIS

1. 160 kilometers from Hiroshima to Fukuyama, and the "Crazy Iris" incident [pp85–86]: Masuji Ibuse, in *The Crazy Iris* (N.Y., Grove Press, 1985), pp 17–36.

2. General Arisue and Dr. Nishina arrive in Hiroshima [pp87–88]: John Toland, *The Rising Sun* (N.Y., Random House, 1970), pp 794–795. NOTE: Arisue's and Nishina's comparison to Tunguska, and discovery that soil, teeth, bones were radioactive: personal communication, researcher George Appoldt (1972–1974). Nishina samples of hypocenter soil (in vials re-examined, 2008, 2010): Eizo Tajima, receiver of Nishina samples flown to Tokyo, Testimonies #20, p 1; "Dr. Yoshio Nishina—Japan Scientist Realized at Once that Weapon Dropped on Hiroshima was A-Bomb," *Kondo News*, Aug. 3, 2008; Juni Akechi, "Detection of Uranium [235 fission-generated isotopes, in original Nishina samples] from Atomic Bomb in Hiroshima Soil," *Hiroshima Peace Media Ctr.*, March 2010.

3. See note 2.

4. Condition of trolleys on the "T" Bridge [p88]: Hiroshi Makino, The Asahi Shimbun *Messages from Hibakusha* Project (Case # 40001, accessible via the C. Pellegrino home page and http://www.asahi.com/hibakusha/english/).

5. See note 2.

6. In Moscow, Stalin [pp88–89]: "Records of Operations Against Soviet Russia," (OCMH) *Japanese Monograph #155*; Tholand, pp 796–797; David McCullogh, *Truman* (N.Y., Simon and Schuster, 1993), pp 450–451.

7. In Tokyo, response to coded radio message from Dr. Nishina [pp89–90]: Eizo Tajima, in Nagasaki Archive Testimonies, #20; Charles Sweeney, *War's End* (N.Y., Avon Books, 1997), pp 192–193. Japan nuclear program, WWII: Maika Nakao, Columbia University Conference, personal communication (November 2009).

8. See note 7.

9. War Minister Anami on "staying the course" [p90]: IMTFE Documents #61338 (Masao Yoshizum), #61883 (Yatsuji Nagai), #61978 (Admiral Zenshiro Hoshina); Walter Lord, personal communication (1997).

10. See note 7.

11. On Tinian, Alvarez, on applying the same rule of capturing the German atomic scientists and if necessary having them killed rather than letting them become captured Russian assets [pp91–92]: Harold Urey, personal communication (1979); Charles Sweeney corroborated this, as heard by him on Tinian Island (personal communication, 1999). Even before the war in Europe ended, Walter Lord (of the OSS) related how baseball great (and OSS agent) Moe Berg was sent to assassinate German physicist Werner Heisenberg at a Switzerland lecture if Heisenberg said anything suggestive of nuclear weapons development (he did not). Lord never quite understood why Berg did not find some way of killing Heisenberg, "just to make sure," because Heisenberg was "somewhat more than suspect," in Lord's opinion (personal communication, 1997).

12. See note 11.

13. "Dutch" van Kirk's response to use of the phrase, "Nuke them" [p92]: interview, in *White Light, Black Rain*, (HBO, 2007), in reference to the emerging hatred toward the Russians, Charles Sweeney, personal communication (1999).

14. See note 11.

15. Keiji Nakazawa during the first days [pp93–95]: Interview in *White Light, Black Rain* (HBO, 2007); Victor Chan, personal communication RE the Buddhist philosophy of "giving and taking" as reflected in Nakazawa's *Barefoot Gen* Manga (2010); K. Nakazawa, personal communication (Aug. 2010); K. Nakazawa, *I Saw It* (San Francisco, Educomics, 1982). An English summary of Nakazawa's *Pelted by Black Rain* Manga can be found in Keiji Nakazawa's *Hiroshima: The Autobiography of Barefoot Gen*, translated by R. H. Minear (U.K.: Rowman & Littlefield, 2010), pp 152–153. On a fatherless and subsequently "outcast" child (Tanaka called "Ryuta"): *The Autobiography of Barefoot Gen* (2010), pp 31, 34–36, 38, 40, 48–50, 63, 90, 131; K. Nakazawa and Steve Leeper, personal communication (2011).

16. See note 15.

17. Estimated prompt radiation dosage (not counting microwaves) for Keiji Nakazawa and his mother (according to locations indicated on map by Nakazawa, Aug. 7, 2010), in accordance with table 5.1 (in) E. Ishikawa, et al, Hiroshima and Nagasaki [p95]: *The Physical, Medical, and Social Effects* (N.Y., Basic Books, 1981), p 72. NOTE: The geometric drop-off of gamma and neutron radiation is not merely diffusion over increasing spherical radii; at radius 2 km, gamma rays and neutrons have passed through equivalent two meters of water—which is 2 m of effective shielding material (personal communication, James Powell). Radiant flash penetrates this same shielding, with power to burn flesh beyond the zone of prompt radiation danger, and even to focus radiant burns, as on the shoulder of Hajime, though protected underwater.

18. See note 15.

19. Takashi (Thomas) Tanemori, the first days [pp98–100]: Personal communication, 11/13/10; T. Tanemori and J. Crump, *Hiroshima: The Bridge to Forgiveness* (CA, TVP Press, 2008), pp 41–42.

20. Eizo Nomura [pp100–101]: memoir, Hiroshima Museum Archive, including drawings by Nomura of waterspouts and the fire worms (1945).

21. Michihiko Hachiya, M.D., the Communications Hospital, 8/8/45 [pp101–104]: *Hiroshima Diary* (University of North Carolina Press, 1955), pp 8, 15, 20–29; on the number of patients and their condition (including the horse), pp 21–22, 27. Further details: Hiroshima resident (and translator) Endo Tai, personal communication

(2008), Hachiya relative Yoji Matsumoto, personal communication (2010), Hachiya neighbor Masahiro Sasaki, personal communication (2008–2012), nurses of Dr. Minoru Fujii's mobile rescue team, personal communication (2008).

22. Hanako Ito and her husband, Akio, searching for their son, Hiroshi [pp104–105]: personal communication, Ito family (2009, 2010).

23. Dr. Tsunoo's description of Hiroshima, and reactions [pp105–108]: Kohei Koyano in Nagasaki Museum Archive, *Testimonies of Atomic Bomb Survivors #12*, and Dr. Tatsuichiro Akizuki, *Nagasaki 1945* (London, Quartet Books, 1981), pp 17–19, and in the Nagai family oral history, as recited by Tokusaburo Nagai, personal communication (2008). Dr. Tsunoo's observations (including the Hiroshima castor bush and other shadow-image events) corroborated in U.S. Bombing Survey photos, as in Averill A. Liebow, *A Medical Diary of Hiroshima*, 1945 (N.Y., W.W. Norton, 1965, 1970), p 128 insert; T. Akizuki, *Nagasaki 1945*, pp 19–20, 33–35. Encounters with parents unaware that their children were missing major portions of their bodies: Akizuki, p 33. The fate of Dr. Tsunoo: Tokusaburo Nagai (2008), Tsunoo's prompt radiation exposure symptoms: Akizuki, p 146; Dr. Takashi Nagai, in *The Bells of Nagasaki*, p 36.

24. Prefect Takejiro Nishioka's actions in Nagasaki, 8/8/45, office/house/shelter (investigated archaeologically, 2008) [pp108–111, 113–114]: Robert Trumbull (N.Y., Dutton, 1957), pp 91–94; Nagano file, *Nagasaki for Peace Archive*, Wakamatsu Nagano, *Testimonies of Atomic Bomb Survivors #14*. Nagano on the Nishioka meeting: Accessible through Charlespellegrino.com/Asahi link, Hibakusha Voices (recorded in Japanese with English translations), Disk #4, Case #133. Nishioka's wife: personal communication RE the Nagano case, Tokusaburo Nagai and Endo Tai, 2008. Physical effects, nature of vomit, radiation-induced hemorrhage, how and why: Dr. Jesse A. Stoff (and anon. leukemia bone marrow transplant patients), personal communication (1992–1993).

25. Akira Iwanaga, 8/8/45 [p111]: report to Mitsubishi, translated for R. Trumbull, pp 94–95; A. Iwanaga (on self and Nishioka), interview, Hideo Nakamura and Hidetaka Inazuka, 7/2010.

26. Tsutomu Yamaguchi, 8/8/45 [pp111–113]: personal communication (2008); unpublished memoir, *I Live to Tell My Story* (translated by Hideo Nakamura, 2009). The probability against Nagasaki: Father Cieslik memoir, *Day of Destruction*, page 3. Mr. Yamaguchi was also a friend of Kuniyoshi Sato (a fellow double survivor); he affirmed (first during interview, 7/19/2008, p 9), that it was indeed Kenshi Hirata seen by Mr. Sato on the train from Hiroshima. K. Sato's story of survival in Nagasaki recorded and translated by H. Nakamura, 2010; K. Sato's description of the man on the train, bringing his recent bride's remains in a helmet-shaped bowl to her parents in Nagasaki, and Sato's double-survival [p161]: Translations [in] Richard L. Parry, *London Times* (August 6, 2005).

27. See note 24.

28. Charles Sweeney's preparations, 8/8/45 [pp114–115]: *War's End*, pp 146 (RE Admiral Purnell, photo opposite p 146), 191–193, 195–196, 200; personal communication (1999). The approach of Kenshi Hirata and the kite-makers aboard the last train from Hiroshima [p115]: Trumbull (N.Y., Dutton, 1957).

29. Dr. Minoru Fujii's arrival with food, Communications Hospital 8/8/45 [pp115–118]: *Hiroshima Diary*, pp 11, 29, 32–33, 35–36, 97, 101; Nurse Nancy (Minami) Cantwell, personal communication (2008, 2009). Dr. Hachiya identifies soldiers looting his hospital's supplies (p 33): The loss of food, distressing to donors from Dr. Fujii's and Nancy (Minami) Cantwell's team (interview, 7/21/2008, p 1, parag. 2). NOTE: Dr. Hachiya's speculation about optic nerves still working after the collapsing shock bubble's vacuum effect, also considered by Dr. Fujii's crew: personal communication (2008).

30. Setsuko Thurlow [pp118–119], personal communication (2010).

31. Shigeko Sasamori [pp119–121], personal communication (2010).

32. Takehisa Yamamoto [pp121–122], personal communication (2010).

33. The story of Nancy (Minami) Cantwell, a Korean "conscript" who became a nurse at Dr. Minoru Fujii's hospital [pp122–128]: *A Life in Three Motherlands* (N.Y., Vantage Press, 2006), pp 18–22, 25–27, and personal communication (2008–2009); Dr. Minoru Fujii's son, Dr. Hiroshi Fujii, and the nurses of Dr. Fujii's mobile rescue operation: personal communication (2008); documentary (by Hideo Nakamura and Hidetaka Inazuka), *Three Ground Zeros* (2009). On fly larvae becoming "medical devices," a possibility suspected in 1945 by doctors who survived Okinawa, RE Rita Rubin, "Maggots and Leeches: Good Medicine," *USA Today*, 7/7/2007; Bill Schutt, *Dark Banquet* (N.Y., Random House, 2008), pp 151–181.

34. Kenshi Hirata [p128], the Yawata event: Mitsubishi/Trumbull, pp 97–98.

35. Dr. Hachiya, recurring nightmare about the future (and other horrors) [pp128–129], *Hiroshima Diary*, pp 31–32, 40, 101, 114–115, 145–146; Endo Tai, personal communication (2008); the Hiroshima nurses of Dr. Fujii's crew, personal communication (2008, 2009).

CHAPTER 6. *KAITEN* AND THE FAITHFUL ELEPHANTS

1. Charles Sweeney and *BocksCar*. On history books misidentifying plane that dropped the Nagasaki bomb, and mishaps almost derailing Charles Sweeney's mission [pp131–133, 134–135, 140–141, 144–147, 154–156]: *War's End* (N.Y., Avon Books, 1997), pp 201–202, 203–205, 209–218; and weather (pp 176–178, 198, 204, 209), personal communication, 1999. Corroboration of Sweeny's deteriorating weather window: Dr. Hachiya's *Hiroshima Diary* (August 9); Nancy (Minami) Cantwell's 2008 account during her "night of the blue fireflies."

2. Dr. Paul (Takashi) Nagai, a patient in his own hospital [p133]: Tokusaburo Nagai, personal communication (2008). NOTE: Dr. Nagai's grandson was an especially enlightening source with regard to the often strained yet ultimately brotherly relationship between his grandfather and Dr. Akizuki. Nyokodo documents detail Dr. Nagai's fight against cancer, his recovery after the bomb, into and out of remission. Additional details: Endo Tai, personal communication (2008) RE the Nagasaki oral history surrounding Dr. Nagai and the origin of the Nyokodo Hermitage.

3. See note 1.

4. Fourteen-year-old Hajime Iwanaga, the *Kaiten* torpedo crews, and the children's crusade "lesson" about The Faithful Elephants [pp133–137]: Yukio Tsuchiya, *The Faithful Elephants* (Japan, Kin-no-Hoshi-Sha Co. LTD, 1951); H. Iwanaga in John Toland, *The Rising Sun* (N.Y., Random House, 1970), p 803; Endo Tai, Hideo Na-kamura, RE the Kaiten "volunteers," oral history surrounding the story of the *Kaiten* and the boy, Hajime Iwanaga. NOTE: Animal caregivers subjected to the unusual punishment of starving their elephants to death was a propagandistic example, meant to stand as a lesson to Japan's youth that they must be willing to sacrifice everything when ordered (a history sanitized for an American version of *The Faithful Elephants*, published as a children's novella in New York by Houghton Mifflin, 1988). Fred-erick Litten (p 2, http://litten.de/abstr4.htm [and in http://www.japan10cus.org/. Frederick_S_Litten/3229] in Japan Focus: "Starving the Elephants") summarizes glar-ing contradictions between the subsequent public story and actual records from the period. Litton noted that the zookeepers were also required to starve to death "doves and probably other small animals." The timing of events (summer of 1943) in actual fact precedes any true danger of air raids and the release of killer animals (including doves), by a year and a half. Litton: Governor Shigeo ordered certain of the animals to be killed in this inexplicable way (with their caregivers forced to live with them while they starved) "to use their deaths as propaganda—one especially aimed at children." Their martyrdom "fit well with the beginning of the *gyokusai* ('shattering like a jewel'), or death with honor propaganda celebrating suicidal behavior at the front."

Those toward whom the lesson was aimed, those who, like Hajime Iwanaga, were spared *gyokusai*, related later that they did not want to die and actually dreaded the day they would be the next candidates ordered into the plane or the torpedo (interviews by Hideo Nakamura, 2010). Children were told they must be ready to suffer for the Emperor: Yamaoka Michiko, *White Flash Black Rain* (U.S., Milkweed Editions, 1995), p 71; Sachiko Masaki, "A Message to the Young," in *Hibakusha* (Tokyo, Kosei Publishing, 1986), pp 146–152; Keijiro Matsushima [p136], aspired to suicide attacks, age 14, tak-ing every story of sacrifice into his heart: interviewed by David Smith, "I Don't Blame Them but I Hope They Mourn the Dead," *The Observer*, London, 7/24/2005, p 1.

5. On the encounter between the *Kaiten*-armed submarine *I-58* and the *Indianapolis* [p135] Bob Hackett and Sander Kingsepp (2008), "HIJMS Submarine *I-58*: Tabular Record of Movement," from interrogation of Commander Mochitsura Hashimoto, by J. H. Alberti (interpreter R. J. Fox): *Submarine/Undersea Warfare Div., Series III, Oper. Archive Branch, Naval History Center*. Hashimoto's *I-58* carried four manned [*Kaiten*] torpedoes. July 28, 1945, Hashimoto fires first two *Kaiten* at a tanker and the cargo ship *Wild Hunter*. A third *Kaiten* [launched] is sighted and sunk by USS *Lowry*. A last *Kaiten* suffered engine malfunctions and could not be launched. *Indianapolis* was targeted [July 29, 1945] by an array of six conventional torpedoes.

6. See note 4.

7. American witnesses to the bombs: Corporal Dale Frantz, Allied Prison Camp Number 17 [pp138–140]: George Weller, *First into Nagasaki* (N.Y., Crown, 2006), p 60 (additional details, pp 56–67, 85–113). Clarence Graham: self-published memoir, *Under the Samurai Sword* (1998), summarized by Tom Brokaw in *The Greatest Genera-tion Speaks* (N.Y., Random House, 2005), chap. 1.

8. See note 1.

9. Prefect Nishioka, 8/8/45, construction and Governor Nagano's shelter [pp141–142]: Nagasaki Museum Archive, Wakamatsu Nagano, *Testimonies of Atomic Bomb Survivors #14* (pp 1–2); Nishioka in R. Trumbull, *Nine Who Survived Hiroshima and Nagasaki* (N.Y., Dutton, 1957), pp 91–92; Endo Tai (and Hideo Nakamura), personal communication. Subterranean chambers under the charge of Prefect Nishioka's construction crews (including a partly above-ground command center near the hypocenter), excavated 2008, bring into new relevance, Ichiro Miyato.

10. T. Akizuki, Aug. 9 [pp142–144]: *Nagasaki 1945* (London, Quartet Books, 1981), pp 23–24; the precise locations of Drs. Akizuki and Nagai were hand-marked on a U.S. Bombing Survey map by Tokusaburo Nagai, with Endo Tai, 9/19/2008. At Moment Zero, both doctors were in separate but nearby buildings uphill in Urakami, at the main medical complex.

11. See note 1.

12. See note 1.

13. On Charles Sweeney's concern for larger civilian population of Nagasaki, and resolve to hit purely military target of Kokura [p145]: *War's End* (p 195). In 1999 (personal communication), Sweeney affirmed that Paul Tibbets wanted him court-martialed for flying three times over Kokura under heavy fire and risking loss of the bomb.

14. See note 1.

15. Kenshi Hirata, 8/9/45 [pp147–148]: Reaching his parents' home: Trumbull, pp 117–119; Norman Cousins, personal communication (1987); Shinji Kinoshita (on what radios were announcing at the time), Trumbull, p 105. Nancy (Minami) Cantwell, on how she and others believed they "felt and sometimes saw" the presence of the lost (personal communication, 2008).

16. Ship designer Akira Iwanaga, Masao Komatsu on same train at Moment Zero [pp148–149]: Trumbull, pp 43–46, 95, 98, 101; interview, A. Iwanaga, July 2010.

17. Tsutomu Yamaguchi, 10:30 a.m, 9/9/45 [pp149–150]: personal communication (2008); unpublished chapter from Yamaguchi, *Twice Bombed, Twice Survived* (May 2009); memoir, *I Live to Tell My Story* (2009).

18. Prefect Nishioka, witnesses the planes [pp150]: Trumbull, pp 98–99, 111.

19. Ichiro Miyato [pp150–152], a distant radar operator in direct contact with the central Urakami command center—right up to the moment of its destruction. Additional sources on Nagasaki excavations and oral histories related to radar operator Miyato: Michie Hattori Bernstein with William L. Leary, "Nagasaki Eyewitness," *World War II Magazine*, Summer 2005; George Appoldt (personal communication, 1970s) and Norman Cousins (personal communication, 1987; according to Cousins, the incident became an inspiration for the "bombing of Moscow scene" in the Cold War thriller, *Fail Safe*).

20. Michie Hattori Bernstein [p153]: how people had their humanity instantly stripped away by the bomb, and names given by children, to what they thought people had turned into, as in the case of "the alligator man" (personal communication, conference arranged by Jesuits, students, 1973).

21. Emiko Fukahori, saved by a margin of only a few paces [pp152–153]: E. Fukahori, in Nagasaki Museum Archive, *Testimonies of Atomic Bomb Survivors #29, parts 1 and 2*; Hattori and Leary, *World War II Magazine* (Summer 2005).

22. Hajime Iwanaga, underwater at Moment Zero [pp153–154]: J. Toland, p 803. At the same general radius from the hypocenter (see note 23).

23. Yukiko Kobayashi, his friends, and Yukiko's five-year-old brother are situated under varying degrees of shadow-shielding [p154]: Yukiko Kobayashi (case #11724), in The Asahi Shimbun archive, *Messages from Hibakusha* Project (accessible via C. Pellegrino home page and http://www.asahi.com/hibakusha/english/).

24. See note 1.

CHAPTER 7. A VAPOR IN THE HEAVENS

1. Dr. Hachiya, 8/9/45 [pp157–158]—friend saved by a bee sting [pp157–158]: *Hiroshima Diary* (University of North Carolina Press, 1955), pp 35–36. The tremble felt in the hospital as a possible reverberation from Nagasaki 300 km away: a distant light cutting up into the south part of the sky at approximately 11:00 a.m., Dr. Fujii's team, interview, 7/21/2008, p 1, parag. 3. Translator Endo Tai (some oral history of Nagai and Sasaki families, 7/2008): Dr. Hachiya awakened by "ground palpitations," Yoji Matsumoto, a relative of Dr. Hachiya (8/5/2010). RE visibility from Hiroshima: The flash-desiccation of tree leaves on mountainsides facing Nagasaki, to radius of 80 km (as reported by M. Shiotsuki, p 108).

2. The overloading and "blacking out" of Miyato's radar screen [p158]: in Michie Hattori Bernstein and William L. Leary's "Eyewitness to Nagasaki," *World War II Magazine* (Summer 2005).

3. Clarence Graham's story [pp158–159] was reported by Tom Brokaw, *The Greatest Generation Speaks* (N.Y., Random House, 2005), chapter 1 (see also, C. Graham, self-published memoir, *Under the Samurai Sword*, ASIN B0006E8124, 1998).

4. Prefect Nishioka's second atomic bomb [pp159–160]: translated from Mitsubishi archives for Robert Trumbull, *Nine Who Survived Hiroshima and Nagasaki* (N.Y., Dutton, 1957), pp 111–112, 114–115; additional scientific details based upon atomic tests showing what happens to air, water, vehicles, and buildings at Nishioka's distance from 22–30 kiloton air bursts. Tests include, particularly, *Able* (22kt, Bikini Atoll, 1946). Additionally, *Dog* (22kt, Nevada, 1951), *Easy* (31kt, Nevada, 1951), *Zucchini* (28kt, Nevada, 1955).

5. Kenshi Hirata's second atomic bomb [pp160–161, 193–195]: R. Trumbull, pp 119. Norman Cousins was quite familiar with the Hirata history up to the point of Hirata's disappearance about 1955 (personal communication, 1987); Eizo Tajima RE effects in the Hirata neighborhood (including the conclusion that the bomb was more than twice as powerful as the one dropped on Hiroshima), in Nagasaki Museum archive, *Testimony of Atomic Bomb Survivors #20, page 2*. Sweeney's perspective: C. Sweeney, *War's End* (N.Y., Avon Books, 1997). Interviews with Kenshi Hirata, his daughter Saeko, and Setsuko Hirata's brother, July 2010 (Hideo Nakamura, Hidetaka Inazuka).

6. Kuniyoshi Sato's journey from Hiroshima to Nagasaki [p161] aboard the second train (with Kenshi Hirata)—which in fact made him a late arrival at the ferry, for the

meeting at which Tsutomu Yamaguchi was being upbraided for having lost track of engineer K. Sato in Hiroshima: Interview, Aug 6, 2005, R.L. Parry, the *Times of London* (footnote #18, chapter 5). Tsutomu Yamaguchi, personal communication, July 2008, RE the co-worker who, on the train, sat across from a man carrying skull parts of his young bride from Hiroshima to her parents in Nagasaki, said it was K. Sato and K. Hirata who sat briefly together aboard the train. On Sato's survival at the pier, on the opposite side of the river from Yamaguchi: interview with Hideo Nakamura, 2010. (Sato recalled removing all of the glass from his home but whether this was before or after the second detonation is unclear; many in the suburbs removed all of their windows after the Urakami detonation because almost everyone was expecting a third atomic bomb.)

7. Events at the location of Dr. Nagai's children [pp162–164]: Takashi (Paul) Nagai, *We of Nagasaki* (a family memoir, N.Y., Duel, Sloan, and Pearce, 1951), pp 10–12, 31, 42. NOTE: Descriptions of animals and wooden objects exposed to the flash: Nyokodo Hermitage Museum (Tokusaburo Nagai, translated by Endo Tai, including *Genshi-un no Shhita ni Ikite*, "Survivors under the Atomic Clouds," edited by Paul Nagai: compositions of the children of the Yamazato Elementary and Junior High schools). The vertical column of smoke effect, first three seconds, corroborated in Nevada tests (*Dog, Easy, Zucchini*) and in test *Able* (air burst over Bikini Atoll fleet), including piglets, goats, filmed during exposure to heat and blast, out to 9 km radius, Nagasaki-class detonations.

Some details on the path of heavy debris field materials falling from the atomic cloud, out to a distance of more than 9 km., across the location of the Nagai children: Tokusaburo Nagai, personal communication/video interview over map and on location (2008).

8. Takami's cow bursting into flames before his eyes, and wounds caused by fireballs at radius greater than 8 km [pp164–165]: Takashi (Paul) Nagai, in *The Bells of Nagasaki* (Tokyo, N.Y., London, Kodanshu International, 1949, 1984), pp 9–10. Mount Kawabira and precise locations of the Nagai family members (including the two Nagai children) were marked on a map annotated by Tokusaburo Nagai (on location and on video, 2008). The protective mountain is named several times in Dr. Nagai's book, *We of Nagasaki* (beginning in the front matter, on p xiii). In *The Bells of Nagasaki* (p 6–8), Nagai's account of Chimoto-san records severe flash effects along unshielded areas (in direct unshaded line-of-sight to the bomb) near Mt. Kawabira, including the far side of the Nagai children's stream.

9. Akira Iwanaga and his friend Masao, on an in-bound train during the Nagasaki detonation [pp165–166]: Trumbull, pp 101–102. The stopping of the train near Michinoo Station [pp165–166]: Link to Asahi Shimbun (Charlespellegrino.com), "Hibakusha Voices" (audio in Japanese, transcripts in English), Disk #5, Case # 198. Effects [pp165–166]: Nyokodo Hermitage Museum reports (Drs. Nagai and Akizuki) about the deadly reflex of people (including gardeners at the medical complex) to glance in the direction of the flash, directly exposing their faces and eyes (also, Endo Tai translating for Tokusaburo Nagai, 2008). Tsutomu Yamaguchi, on Akira Iwanaga and others exposed on the train (personal communication, 2008). Akira Iwanaga (interview, Hideo Nakamura, 2010) provided location of his and Masao Komatsu's train,

indicating Michinoo Station as last stopping point through which train had passed, when the flash occurred, corroborated by Dr Akizuki in *Nagasaki, 1945*, p 46. During his July 2010 interview, Akira Iwanaga re-affirmed the chronology of events *preceding* the flash (corroborating Trumbull, p 101).

10. Further notes related to the first three minutes [pp166–167]: Nagano in Nagasaki Museum Archives, *Testimony of Atomic Bomb Survivors #14*. Dr. Nagai (on the Urakami firestorm), in *The Bells of Nagasaki*, pp 28, 32, 41; Nishioka, in Trumbull, p 113. The Nagai children, Dr. Akizuki, and other eyewitnesses described a large variety of objects raining down from the cloud, some being whipped up into the air by cyclones of flame springing from an immense lake of fire, as in Tasuichiro Akizuki, *Nagasaki 1945* (London, Quartet Books, 1981), p 27. Tamotsu Eguchi, in "Nagasaki," in *Hiroshima in Memoriam and Today* (Hitoshi Takayama, editor; Peace Resource Ctr., U.S., the Hamat Group, Hiroshima, 2000), pp 58–60. Further descriptions, objects falling out of the cloud [p167]: Asahi Shimbun (Charlespellegrino.com), "Hibakusha Voices," Disk #6, Witness #256.

11. Flash effects at the radius of the Kobayashi family [pp167–168]: Yukiko Kobayashi (Case #11724) in The Asahi Shimbun *Messages from Hibakusha* Project (archive accessible via C. Pellegrino home page and http://www.asahi.com/hibakusha/english/).

12. "Skeletonizing" and "auroral" events witnessed in the tunnels by Emiko and her friend Sumi-Chan [pp168–169]: Emiko Fukahori, Nagasaki Archive, *Testimonies of Atomic Bomb Survivors #29*. A similar effect witnessed by Matsu Moruchi: in *We of Nagasaki*, p 104. Survival at and near the tunnels [pp169–171]: Michie Hattori Bernstein with William L. Leary, "Eyewitness to Nagasaki Atomic Bomb Blast," *World War II Magazine* (Summer 2005). De-gloving (as witnessed by Hattori), corroborated in *The Bells of Nagasaki*, pp 22–23. Dr. Nagai also reported "strange meteors"—all manner of large debris and "dancing junk, whirling around [in the sky] with strange noises," continuing to fall for some time (approximately ten minutes or more) after the explosion, and further on de-gloving: *We of Nagasaki*, pp 136–137.

13. Yose Matsuo's survival in a deep tunnel near the hypocenter [pp172–174]: Y. Matsuo, in the Nagasaki Museum Archive, Nagasaki for Peace: *Testimony of Atomic Bomb Survivors #24*. Some criteria for comparison to what happens to people and objects at temperatures reaching or exceeding five times the boiling point of water: G. Mastrolorenzo, et al, "Herculaneum Victims of Vesuvius in AD 79," *Nature*, April 12, 2001 (also, personal communication [G. Mastrolorenzo], notes, and video log at the Vesuvius Observatory forensics laboratory, the buried Herculaneum Marina, the buried Oplantus II plantation; and the snake heads effect heat track: Pompeii's Garden of the Fugitives, House of the Snake Heads Effect, House of Menander, 2005, 2009; J. Tabor, C. Pellegrino, S. Jacobovici: "Vesuvius and the Fear of God," Episode 2 in *Secrets of Christianity*, Associated Producers, Discovery Channel/Science, 2011).

The Matsuo account (#24) records the depth and length of the tunnel along with Matsuo's location, furthest back in this shelter, and includes such key details as the body mass of 52 intervening people, between the witness and the tunnel entrance. Additional background includes personal communication (Tokusaburo Nagai, E. Tai, RE annotations on a copy of #24, 2008) and personal visit to the site of Matsuo's survival. James Powell (Brookhaven National Laboratory), during discussion of this case, noted that in addition to tunnel depth, Matsuo needed at least two meters of water shielding from the gamma ray sky-shine effect. This protection would likely have been provided by the water that makes up the majority of human body mass, if most of the women in the tunnel were standing between Matsuo and the opening, allowing her to become the closest known survivor to the Urakami hypocenter.

14. Cadet Komatsu, flight into the Nagasaki cloud [pp174–175]: John Toland, *The Rising Sun* (N.Y., Random House, 1970), pp 805–806; George Appoldt, personal communication (1973).

15. Comparisons of Hiroshima, Nagasaki detonations from B-29s [pp176–177]: C. Sweeney, *War's End* (N.Y., Avon Books, 1997), pp 218–219; personal communication (1999); George Marquardt, *The Independent*, Aug. 23, 2003 (Tibbets's interview confirms position of Marquardt's plane at Hiroshima in *World at War*, Part 24, "The Bomb," BBC, 1973).

16. Hajime Iwanaga, the world into which he surfaced [pp177–179]: in Toland, p 803; George Appoldt, personal communication (1970–1973), including discussions about Hajime's unusual observations—among these, similar phenomena that involved rapidly heated, rapidly inflating bodies in the aftermath of the pyroclastic cloud of Mount Pelè, Martinique, in 1902. Hajime Iwanaga's roving and shooting fireball phenomena were similarly described in Dr. Nagai's *The Bells of Nagasaki*, pp 9–10, 63–65. A similar phenomenon, Nishioka's ominous "flaming ground candles," was described in Trumbull, pp 49–50.

17. Sachiko Masaki, shock-cocooned inside the torpedo factory [pp179–181], and her brother, now a double-atomic-bomb-survivor: S. Masaki, in *Hibakusha* (Tokyo, Kosei, 1986), pp 146–152.

18. Michie Hattori, the shock-cocooned student, finds her village completely co-cooned behind a tall hill [pp181–182]: M. Hattori, in *World War II Magazine* (Summer 2005) and personal communication (1973). U.S. Bombing Survey photos: example of such shielding, 6/30/1946 report to the Chairman's Office, Washington, D.C., p12. The region of destruction through which Hattori passed on her way to the shock-cocooned village was also described by Prefect Nishioka in Trumbull, p 113.

19. Inosuke Hayasaki's description of what happened at the Mitsubishi naval yard steel works, at a radius of 1,100 meters from the hypocenter [pp182–185]: Interview, August 8, 2014, recorded at the West Park Presbyterian Church, New York, pp 1–6.

20. Governor Nagano, aftermath [pp185–186]: Wakamatsu Nagano, Nagasaki Museum Archive, Nagasaki and Peace, *Testimonies of Atomic Bomb Survivors #14*. Note also, sources RE Nagano's survival and actions, as referenced for chapter 6. Some observations on travel conditions and routes taken between the governor's mansion and the medical complex in the Urakami hills, after 11:02 a.m., 8/9/1945: The head of the Urakami council reached Nagano's office about 4:00 p.m., after initially calling in radio reports from the medical complex. He traveled opposite along essentially the same approximately 4–5 hour path taken by Dr. Akizuki's father (*Nagasaki 1945*, p 45). Governor Nagano's initial shock-state had been bitterly related by Prefect Nishioka's wife (E. Tai, T. Nagai, Nyokodo conference notes, Nagasaki, 7/19/2008, p 1). Nyokodo conference (p 1) also corroborates the police chief's son (referenced in Trumbull), saved indirectly by Nishioka's warnings based on his observations of the Hiroshima effects.

21. The Nagasaki Museum has in its collections, and on display, objects that actually fell out of the cloud at the radius of lower Isahaya [pp186–187], where Prefect Nishioka encountered debris and "fallout." Artifacts also include radiation-tinted glass, bones enclosed in melted glass, bent steel, shadows cast permanently onto walls at various radii from the hypocenter.

22. See note 20.

23. See note 21.

24. Dr. Akizuki [pp187–190]: *Nagasaki 1945*, pp 18, 24–36, 40 (p 36 references "the quiet reproach" from one of Akizuki's nurses). On Dr. Nagai's thoughts about the lake of fire in the Urakami Valley as a glimpse of an apocalyptic future that he believed might be preventable if humanity turned toward the way the prophets wanted humanity to live [p189]: Nyokodo papers and Tokusaburo Nagai, personal communication (2008, with Endo Tai translating). Mrs. Nagai's family history in the Urakami-Nagasaki Christian underground and its influence on Dr. Nagai: *The Bells of Nagasaki* (1949), pp xvi–xix and Tokusaburo Nagai (conference, 2008).

25. See note 23.

26. Tsutomu Yamaguchi, 8/9/45 [pp190–193]: Trumbull, pp 109–110; personal communication, July 2008 (On p 2, conference, Tsutomu Yamaguchi noted how Has ko's detour for a cream to treat his burns had changed her normal routine for that day, and thus, as a result of his Hiroshima burns, she, their child, and the babysitter were saved); unpublished memoir (translated by Hideo Nakamura), *Twice Bombed, Twice Survived* (May 2009).

27. See note 5.

28. Dr. Takashi (Paul) Nagai at the Urakami Hospital complex, and his children [pp196–198]: *We of Nagasaki*, pp 6, 17, 35, 50, 57, 92, 181–182, 184–185; Tokusaburo Nagai, noting also how the Noyokodo Hermitage was built downhill of the hospital, over the place where Mrs. Nagai died; personal communication (2008). Radiation doses at this radius from the hypocenter are based on gamma and neutron emissions (minus microwaves and black rain effects), U.S. Strategic Bombing Survey, as in summary of results (Alvarez canisters), E. Ishikawa, et al (Tokyo, Iwanami Solen, 1979, N.Y., 1981), p 72. Dr. Nagai's memoir (*We of Nagasaki*) is uniquely important, historically, because of its often intensely honest self-reflection. On pages 182 and 183, addressing his own vanity, he wrote: "That is why I kept at it. I was after recognition . . . I wanted to be called a hero. . . . The young students and nurses [many of whom would soon die] knew no such vanity."

CHAPTER 8. THREADS

1. Charles Sweeney's flight from Nagasaki to Okinawa [pp199–202]: C. Sweeney, *War's End* (N.Y., Avon Books, 1997), pp 220, 222–229; his findings and concerns afterward (personal communication, 1999).

2. On the post-Nagasaki conference at the Imperial Palace [pp202–203]: J. Toland, *The Rising Sun* (N.Y., Random House, 1970), pp 810–812; Tatsuichio Akizuki, *Na-*

gasaki 1945 (London, Quartet Books, 1981), pp 73–74; Charles Sweeney, *War's End* (1997), pp 236–237; Walter Lord, personal communication (1997), on post-WWII interviews, Dr. Nishina, Dr. Sagane. Before writing his final, traditional death poems, Anami had expressed (as in Toland, p 826) conflicting loyalties in a military coup.

3. Keiji Nakazawa, on Hiroshima, 8/9–19/45 [pp203–206]: K. Nakazawa, *I Saw It: A Survivor's True Story* (San Francisco, Educomics [Manga], 1982); K. Nakazawa, *Hiroshima: The Autobiography of Barefoot Gen*, translated by R. Minear (U.K., Rowman and Littlefield, 2010), p 42, 44, 46, 50; K. Nakazawa, personal communication (2010–2011). NOTE: Concentration of radioactive elements in living systems, involving the approximately 200 varieties of radioactive isotopes (most with very short half-lives) produced by the atomic bombs: as in, *The Committee for the Compilation of Materials on Damage Caused by the Atomic Bombs in Hiroshima and Nagasaki*, E. Ishikawa, et al (Tokyo, Iwanami Shoten, 1979; N.Y., Basic Books, 1981), pp 77–86. A soldier who participated in triage, in terms of food delivery: Case 02159, in The Asahi Shimbun *Messages from Hibakusha* Project (accessible via C. Pellegrino home page and http://www.asahi.com/hibakusha/english/).

4. Takashi Tanemori's dream [pp206–207]: T. Tanemori and J. Crump, *Hiroshima: The Bridge to Forgiveness* (CA, TVP Press, 2008), pp 27–30, 46–47; *Hiroshima Nagasaki Download* (DVD, Shinpei Tadeka, Autopus Studio, 2010); interview, personal communication, 11/13/2010.

5. Children, 1945, Fukushima uranium mines [pp207–208]: Kiwamu Ariga, interview with Martin Fackler, "Fukushima's Long Link to Dark Nuclear Past," *Ishikawa Journal*, 9/6/2011, courtesy of Mark Baraka Strauch and Takashi (Thomas) Tanemori; Frances Kakugawa (also on childhood's false escape from war), *Kapoho: Memoir of a Modern Pompeii* (Hawaii, Watermark Publishing, 2011).

6. Conditions at the Communications Hospital, on the day Dr. Hachiya's horse died [pp208–210]: M. Hachiya, *Hiroshima Diary* (University of North Carolina Press, 1955), pp 36, 39–40, 42. Bomb-related medical effects: Glass in the lungs and other organs also noted by Dr. Akizuki (p 91 of *Nagasaki 1945*) and Dr. Masao Shiotsuki at the Omura Naval Hospital, *Doctor at Nagasaki*, Kosei Publishers, Tokyo (1987), p 72. Other objects embedded in survivors' bodies: "Hibakusha Voices" (accessible through Charlespellegrino.com, Asahi Shimbun link, Disk 5, Witness 203). Omura autopsies recorded (as in Shiotsuki, p 89) the results of bone marrow death. People reported to have blood emerging through pores in skin and even to have tears of blood: Witness 342 (Disk 8). Omura Naval Hospital and (personal communication), Dr. Fujii's team: In addition to rapid bone marrow breakdown, lungs and kidneys bled out and bacteria had penetrated even the most minor skull fractures. Protists (relatives of the amoeba) that normally caused dysentery moved from the intestinal tract and dissolved spinal cord and brain tissue.

7. Tsutomu Yamaguchi, kite-maker Morimoto, and Prefect Nishioka in the Nagasaki aftermath [pp210–211]: Robert Trumbull, *Nine Who Survived Hiroshima and Nagasaki* (N.Y, Dutton, 1957), pp 108–109, 112, 121. Tsutomu Yamaguchi: personal communication (2008); written memoir, *Twice Bombed, Twice Survived* (2009, translated by Hideo Nakamura, who earlier made a film under the same title). Additional information on Morimoto: Toland, pp 802–803. Morimoto's family losses, and his

survival, recorded in personal communication by Toland with Mr. and Mrs. Morimoto (Toland, p 888). Distribution of envelopes hoisted from Morimoto's kite shop is recorded in a brief entry for the Nagasaki Museum, translated by Endo Tai (2008).

8. Morimoto's assistant, Doi: Trumbull, p 106 [pp211–212]: detailed the survival of Doi's son on the temple grounds. Some oral history on the Doi case, shadow-shielding and shock-cocooning behind a ridge, related by Endo Tai (2008); some additional material on Doi's family related by double-survivor researcher George Appoldt (personal communication 1972–1974), RE: the "strange hail" of objects that fell behind the ridge (Doi and Nagai children locations), corroborated at Nyokodo conference (with Tokusaburo Nagai), 7/19/2008, p 1.

9. Akira Iwanaga and Masao Komatsu [pp212–213]: Urakami fire cyclones seen from a ridge: Trumbull, pp 102–104, 125. T. Yamaguchi on his friend Akira (including sudden inclination to abandon path toward Mitsubishi offices and walk away from the war, paths taken after train wreck [mapped by A. Iwanaga, 7/2010]): personal communication, Yamaguchi (2008). The tunnels in the hillside were being excavated and filmed in 2008.

10. Although he was a Buddhist, Akizuki thought he could understand the Jesuit's call for prayer, before Dr. Yoshioka's mother arrived [pp213–214]: Tatsuichiro Akizuki, *Nagasaki, 1945*, pp 26–27, 45–48. Dr. Takashi (Paul) Nagai, and the "cracks in human souls" created by the bomb: Takashi (Paul) Nagai, *We of Nagasaki* (N.Y., Duel, Sloan, and Pearce, 1951), pp 94–99, 165–166, 176–177; Tokusaburo Nagai, personal communication (2008). On the locations of Drs. Akizuki and Nagai and their participation in the medical complex evacuation and long-term rescue effort: Akizuki (*Nagasaki, 1945*), p 28; Tokusaburo Nagai, personal communication (2008). Nagai cousin Tatsue Urata on Dr. Akizuki at the medical complex and St. Francis Hospital burning: *We of Nagasaki*, p 86–87; Akizuki (p 111–112) credited Nagai's nutritional methods at the rescue center with saving his life and the lives of many others.

11. See note 10.

12. On Nagai cousin Tatsue at Moment Zero [pp214–218]: The Tatsue chapter in *We of Nagasaki*. Tatsue reproaches herself for being saved in shadow-shield/shock cocoon while her mother died on other side of hill, p 84. Tatsue records how she started out with the Nagai children (p 72), how family separated into two groups (p 80); one group subsequently dying while other group, on the shadow-side, is saved; flash effects on farmhouses across a ravine, outside the edges of Mt. Kompira's shadow, in the full "sunlight" of the bomb (p 81). Little Eiko as the adopted daughter of the aunt, variously referred to as "the old lady" (p 95) and as an unnamed "skinny aunt" (Nyokodo conference, July 2008): This aunt who abandoned her child (as in *We of Nagasaki*) was never to be mentioned by name. The story told at Nyokodo (2008) was that someone else's parent cared for Eiko until she died on 8/10/45, still awaiting the return of her mother (as in *We of Nagasaki*, pp 95–96).

13. Dr. Akizuki's father at Moment Zero [pp218–219]: *Nagasaki 1945* (p 45), and what he saw of the firestorm (p 45, parag. 2). Dr. Nagai's grandson and Endo Tai (and regarding the later life of Dr. Akizuki, Chad Diehl) provided background on how Drs. Nagai and Akizuki, Akizuki's parents, and other survivors worked together at the ruined hospital complex (July 2008, p 1).

14. The nightmarish scenes at the location of the "death trains" and the guilt Inosuke Hayasaki carried after the dying of the people to whom he gave water [pp219–220]: Interview, August 8, 2014, recorded at N.Y. West Park Presbyterian Church, pp 7–13. (Conclusion on the "water deaths," derived from personal communication and theorizing with BNL physicist J. Powell, WTC medical and FDNY recovery team members, 9–11 family experiences, 2001–2015.)

15. Emperor Hirohito calls for a final conference [p221]: IMTFEE Doc. 62049, Japanese General Staff, "Record on Termination of the War"; Toland, pp 810–814; T. Akizuki, *Nagasaki 1945,* pp 73–74: C. Sweeney, pp 236, 238–239. Dr. Akizuki recorded in his memoir what became known, via IMTFEE and other in-Japan sources, of events that began at the Palace between 11:40 and 11:50 p.m., 8/9/1945 (as also in Toland, p 811); description of Hirohito's voice, preserved in recordings of the Emperor's surrender "rescript," composed, in part, from Hirohito's 8/9–10/45 meeting notes, after "discussions with Togo" (as also in H. P. Bix, *Hirohito and the Making of Modern Japan*, Harper, N.Y., 2000, p 526, parag. 2; 527; 517–518. RE also Togo to investigators from GHO Historical Section, 5/17/1949, 8/17/1950, *U.S. Army Statements of Japanese Army Officials on WWII*, Vol. 4, digitalized archive from microfilm [Shelf 51256]): In Toland (p 814), it is Togo who had the Emperor's words to him (them) "burned into his mind," and who then dictated the words to his brother-in-law. H. P. Bix (p 502) made specific reference to Hirohito, at war's end, ordering the keeper of his Privy Seal to defend at all costs, and to bring the Empire's descendant of the Sun the sacred objects, including the "curved jewel," much in the manner that ancient Rome's living-god Augustales and Egypt's ancient rulers carried such jeweled symbols.

16. 8/10/45, Tinian Island [pp222–223]: C. Sweeney, *War's End*, pp 143, 233–235, 241–243, 276. Additional sources on threatening messages dropped from planes on the reverse sides of counterfeit monetary bills, some translated by Hideo Nakamura: James Michener (who with James Clavell, wrote some of the threats), lecture in New York City, personal communication (1975). Joshua Stoff, Cradle of Aviation Museum: RE failures in the Japanese rocket program; also (RE Ugaki's final attack), Toland, pp 853–854; Akizuki, *Nagasaki 1945*, p 103.

17. Togo (RE Toland, pp 836–837) was party to the Aug. 14 shutting down of arms factories and party to actually writing the Emperor's rescript [pp223–224]: "His Majesty . . . to issue his commands to all the military . . . authorities of Japan . . . wherever located to cease active operations." Togo and Anami discussed this as the Palace rebellion loomed and the Emperor became isolated (imprisoned, in fact). This was a point at which Akizuki (p 95) reported that 40% of factory workers (arms were then the only things being manufactured) had already left their jobs. The shut-down orders had been sent out by the Emperor's allies, including Togo and Kido (the latter interviewed by Toland), in accepting the Emperor's "war's end" decision of four days before.

18. Further notes on the medical rescue efforts in the ruins of the Urakami Hospital complex [pp224–226]: Takashi (Paul) Nagai, *The Bells of Nagasaki*, pp 45, 49; T. Akizuki, *Nagasaki 1945*, pp 55–58, 61–62; T. Akizuki in Nagasaki Museum Archive, *Nagasaki and Peace, Testimonies of Atomic Bomb Survivors 11, Part 2*. Akizuki's friend Noguchi (pp 55–56) was a theology student in Nagasaki, and also a medical

complex carpenter/plumber—in fact, he was fixing a water pump in one of the hospital buildings when the bomb exploded (as noted by J. Wintz, "Nagasaki: A Peace Church Rises from the Ashes," *American Catholic*, Aug. 2005). A case of prompt dosing (absorbed by Akizuki and deeper indoors by Nagai): Nyokodo Conference, 7/19/2008, Tokusaburo Nagai, p 1.

CHAPTER 9. TESTAMENT

1. Keiji Nakazawa, on Hiroshima, 8/10/1945 [pp229–231], in *I Saw It: A Survivor's True Story* (San Francisco, Educomics, 1982); personal communication, 2010–2012: Manga, *Barefoot Gen: The Day After* (Philadelphia, New Society Publishers, 1988), pp iv, 130–137; personal communication on Tanaka/"Ryuta" portions of film, *Barefoot Gen* (Japan, Arisa Films, DVD, 2006); interview in *White Light, Black Rain*, HBO documentary, 2007; in *Hiroshima: The Autobiography of Barefoot Gen*, translated by R. H. Minear (U.K. Rowman and Littlefield, 2010), p49, 51, 60; on the atomic orphans, K. Nakazawa and Steve Leeper, personal communication (2010, 2011).

2. 8/10/1945, atomic orphan Takashi (Thomas) Tanemori [pp231–232]: *Hiroshima: The Bridge to Forgiveness* (CA, TVP Press, 2008), pp 51–52, 56, 63.

3. See note 2.

4. The "cave boy," Saburo Kobayashi, Hiroshima orphan [pp232–233]: Case 11187, The Asahi Shimbun *Messages from Hibakusha* Project (accessible via C. Pellegrino home page and http://www.asahi.com/hibakusha/english/).

5. Shoso Kawamoto, a Hiroshima orphan drawn to the Yakuza [p233]: Deathbed testimony via Steve Leeper, Hiroshima Peace Foundation, 12/20/2010.

6. 8/10/1945, Communications Hospital, ruins of the military training ground, Hiroshima Castle [pp233–234]: Michihiko Hachiya, *Hiroshima Diary*, pp 36, 38, 40, 46, 49, 120–125; Shinoe Shoda, in *White Flash, Black Rain* (U.S.A., Milkweed Editions, 1995), p 28; Kae Matsumoto, Yoji Matsumoto, personal communication (2010). NOTE: Yoji Matsumoto entered Hiroshima's military training ground near the castle ruins, four days after the bombing, leaving after maximum of two hours. A month afterward, he suffered mild to moderate symptoms of radiation exposure, including nausea and temporary loss of hair. Dr. Hachiya, on similar cases: *Hiroshima Diary*, p 120.

7. See note 6.

8. The poet, Shinoe Shoda [pp234–235]: apparently the same "girl poet Shinoe" identified in oral and written traditions of Dr. Minoru Fujii's mobile medical team, and by Dr. Hachiya's wife's relatives (including Yoji Matsumoto, 8/5/2010, p 1). Also: AtomicBombMuseum.org—RE, Shoda's poems, 1947 (in defiance of occupation censorship laws), by Tsdao Nakamura, at Hiroshima's prison print shop: *The Meaning of Survival;* See "Reiko," trans. by K. and M. Selden, *The Atomic Bomb: Voices from Hiroshima and Nagasaki* (M. E. Sharpe, N.Y., 1989), p 233, 234, 241. Shinoe Shoda describes her own ill health during the first week after the bomb, and a friend who became an atomic orphan in late August 1945. Oral history (via Y. Matsumoto and Dr.

Fujii's nurses) places the poet briefly at a field hospital—the "Comm. Hosp.," during the week after Aug. 6.

9. 8/10/45, Tsutomu Yamaguchi and his family [pp236–237]: personal communication (2008); Yamaguchi unpublished memoir, *Twice Bombed, Twice Survived* (translated by Hideo Nakamura, 2009); Yamaguchi memoir, *I Live to Tell My Story* (2009).

10. Prefect Nishioka's arrival at Nagano's office [pp237–238]: Robert Trumbull, *Nine Who Survived Hiroshima and Nagasaki* (N.Y., Dutton, 1957), p 115; Nagasaki Museum Archive, Wakamatsu Nagano, *Testimonies of Atomic Bomb Survivors 14;* Nyokodo conference, 2008.

11. Dr. Nagai's expedition down from the St. Francis medical outpost [pp238–239]: Nagai, *We of Nagasaki* (N.Y., Duel, Sloan, and Pearce, 1951), pp 100–109, 118–120, 122; Tokusaburo Nagai, personal communication (2008). Dr. Akizuki, RE the Shimohira family: T. Akizuki, *Nagasaki 1945* (London, Quartet Books, 1981), pp 66–67; S. Shimohira interview with HBO, *White Light, Black Rain* (2007).Tsutomu Yamaguchi, on Dr. Nagai team remedies that saved his life [pp235–236]: Personal communication, 7/19/2008; in *The Bells of Nagasaki* (starting p 71–83, 8/13/1945); Dr. Nagai's (and Prof. Kageura's, and Shirabe's) "strange" prescriptions recorded by Akizuki (*Nagasaki 1945*, p 111); Nagai's concept of immune support remedies, and Nagai as basketball team friend of Yamaguchi in school: Nyokodo Hermitage conference, Tokusaburo Nagai (2008), personal communication, T. and Y. Yamaguchi, 2008. Other Dr. Nagai relationships [pp236–237]: Matsu Moriuchi was aunt of Hatsue, *We of Nagasaki* (pp 65, 66). Fujie Urata (p 66) referred to Matsu as "old Auntie Matsu"; and (at the top of p 100) she was identified as "Auntie Matsu." The strange self-righteous "God-loved" girl and her death: Auntie Matsu, pp 119–120; Dr. Nagai's grandson, Tokusaburo Nagai, RE the strange girl's death: Nyokodo Hermitage conference, July 2008, p 2.

12. See note 11.

13. See note 11.

14. 8/11/1945, Miyuki Broadwater, Nagasaki [pp239–240]: in *Hiroshima Nagasaki Download* (DVD, Shinpei Tadeka, Autopus Studios, 2010). RE Sakue on the crumbling of her mother's carbonized remains: HBO interview for *White Light, Black Rain* (2007).

15. 8/11/1945, Dr. Hachiya's journey to Ground Zero [pp240–241]: *Hiroshima Diary*, p 47–55. 8/13/45 expedition (p 64–65). Exploring regions he had viewed from "atop" the hospital's ruins (p 30–32, 47, 53–54). The military supply barge and Chief Kitajima (p 44, 50). Aug. 20, the microscopes and medical supplies from Tokyo (p 99). Observations RE secrecy about Hiroshima after surrender (p 67, 87).

16. See note 15.

17. A child's description of the music teacher's mansion [pp241–242]: Seki Chieko, in *White Flash, Black Rain* (U.S.A., Milkweed Editions, 1995); Hiroshima nurses of Dr. Fujii's rescue crew, personal communication (2008).

18. See note 15.

19. Conditions under increasing exposure to radiation from the Urakami valley [pp242–243]: M. Hattori and W. Leary, "Eyewitness to Nagasaki Atomic Bomb Blast," *World War II Magazine* (Summer 2005); Matsu Matsumoto, in Nagai, *We of*

Nagasaki, pp 30–70, 166, 173, 188–189; Tokusaburo Nagai, personal communication (July 2008); Akizuki, *Nagasaki 1945*, p 66, 75–79, 80, 83, 86, 88–90.

20. Of the unwelcome soldiers who arrived at the Urakami medical complex [p244], Dr. Akizuki (p 67, 78–80). Dr. Akizuki's long-term working relationship with Dr. Nagai (p 110).

21. See note 19.

22. See note 19.

23. Food at the ruined Urakami complex [pp244–246]: "Apples" (ripe or not; apples proper or a wild fruit merely called "apples") and bits of pumpkin in miso soup were mentioned at Nyokodo (July 2008), among the ingredients added by nurses and students, as materials scavenged for soups after the bombing. On nontraditional ingredients during severe food shortages: Akizuki (p 42), "the pieces of pumpkin in miso soup," in addition to rice and pickled plums, and Dr. Nagai's sap from persimmon leaves (Akizuki, p 111). In *We of Nagasaki* (p 73), Tatsue Urata wrote, "With food scarce, we were all using wild plants and pine needles and things like that in our cooking—we had learned how from Midori [Nagai]."

24. 8/13/1945, Tinian Island [pp246–247]: C. Sweeney, *War's End* (N.Y., Avon Books, 1997), p 239–241; Sweeney, personal communication (1999).

25. 8/14/45, Hiroshima [pp247–248]: M. Hachiya, *Hiroshima Diary*, pp 71–72; Keiji Nakazawa, personal communication (8/7/2010); Sadako Kurihara, "The Flag of Blood and Bones," in *White Flash, Black Rain* (U.S.A., Milkweed Editions, 1995), p 77.

26. 8/14–15/1945, Tokyo [p248]: J. Toland, *The Rising Sun* (Random House, N.Y., 1970), pp 829–849; T. Akizuki, *Nagasaki 1945*, pp 96–97. Charles Sweeney reported having actually over-flown and observed the approaching fleet, in *War's End*, pp 241–243.

27. The Palace revolt [p248]: War Minister Anami was called to participate in the revolt as early as Aug. 12; he vacillated, and all the way through his death on the night of Aug. 14–15, Anami kept the secret of the developing military coup until after Hatanaka's actions failed (as in Akizuki, p 74, 96; Toland, p 808, 810, 826, 830–32; D. McCullough, *Truman* (Simon and Schuster, N.Y., 1992), p 459; H. P. Bix, *Hirohito* (Harper, N.Y., 2000), p 516–19. On the killing of Mori and his aide: Toland (p 841); and the deaths of Hatanaka and Lt. Colonel Jiro Shizaki on the Palace lawn (Toland, p 850) along with at least one other conspirator (Akizuki, p 97), and General Tanaka withdrawing his support from the rebellion at this time. Death of Anami (Akizuki, pp 96–97). Tanaka then moves unilaterally to end rebellion—which finally "petered out at dawn." In one of his death poems (Toland, p 847), Anami wrote, "With my death I apologize to the Emperor for my great crime."

28. See note 26.

29. See note 27.

30. Kazushige Ito and his family's Hiroshima history [pp249–250]: Ito family, personal communication (including unpublished family memoir translated by Hideo Nakamura, 2009).

31. Dr. Hachiya (medical barge, microscopes, pp 250–251, see footnote 11); his neighbor, Mr. Sasaki (Sadako and Masahiro's father) [pp250–251]: M. Hachiya, *Hiroshima Diary*, pp 56–58, 63, 72–73; Masahiro Sasaki, personal communication (2008,

2010, 2011). Dr Hachiya vividly described the collapse of the Sasaki house, and the firestorm developing, on pp 2–3, 6–7, and 72 of his *Hiroshima Diary*. Masahiro Sasaki commented on the sadness of Dr. Hachiya never understanding that nothing could have been done to save his (Sasaki's) grandmother (interview, 7/18/2008, pp 4–5). Masahiro also noted that his father had very good government connections and was able to bring food south to Dr. Hachiya's hospital, just as Hachiya had written in his diary, of his friend and neighbor, Mr. Sasaki (p 72).

32. See note 15.

33. See note 29.

34. On Dr. Hachiya's knowledge of Japan's nuclear science [pp251–252]: p 57, Hachiya's Aug. 12 diary entry.

35. See note 15.

36. Takashi (Thomas) Tanemori, on the deaths of family members [pp253, 259–260]: Personal communication and *Hiroshima: The Bridge to Forgiveness* (CA TVP Press, 2008), pp 63, 67, 69; Tanemori in *Hiroshima Nagasaki Download* (2010), interview and discussion, 11/13/2010; letter, 8/9/2011.

37. Keiji Nakazawa's family, 8/15/1945 [pp253–254, 254–259]: *Hiroshima: The Autobiography of Barefoot Gen*, translated by R. H. Minear, p 63; K. Nakazawa and S. Leeper, personal communication, 2011. K. Nakazawa, interview with HBO, in *White Light, Black Rain* (2007). On the development of Koji's problems (and Tanaka, called "Ryuta" in the "Gen" Manga): K. Nakazawa, in *The Autobiography of Barefoot Gen*, pp 16, 38; Keiji Nakazawa and Steve Leeper, Letters, 3/3/2011, 9/3/2011, 10/4/2011.

38. See note 15.

39. See note 15.

40. See note 34.

41. Dr. Hachiya at the Communications Hospital and Dr. Shiotsuki at Omura Naval Hospital, addressing increasing incidence of radiation effects [pp260–264]: M. Hachiya, *Hiroshima Diary*, pp 86, 90–93, 97–100, 102, 123–124; Hiroshima nurses of Dr. Fujii's crew, personal communication (2008); Masao Shiotsuki, *Doctor at Nagasaki*, pp 79–102, 108–109; Takashi (Paul) Nagai, *The Bells of Nagasaki*, p 56. NOTE: Dr. Nagai appears to have been the first person to suspect that wavelengths longer than the infrared had caused some of the injuries, and that people were microwaved as well as flash-burned and gamma-rayed. The final act of General Tanaka: Dr. Akizuki, in *Nagasaki 1945*, p 126.

42. After 8/15/1945, Dr. Hachiya, Mr. Sasaki, and the Communications Hospital [pp264–265]: *Hiroshima Diary*, pp 118, 133, 157. On preparing his scientific report (p 170): Dr. Masao Shiotsuki (pp 79–102, 108–109 of his memoir). Dr. Nagai's scientific record-keeping (as noted in *The Bells of Nagasaki*, pp 55–56). On the name, Urakami's red-brick "St Francis Hospital," Dr. Akizuki, p 18 of his foreword to Dr. Masao Shiotsuki's book.

43. Hiroshima and the Fukuya Department Store (field hospital) events [pp265–268]: M. Hachiya, *Hiroshima Diary*, pp 51–53; Yasunori Funasaka, Case 00626, The Asahi Shimbun *Messages from Hibakusha* Project (accessible via C. Pellegrino home page and http://www.asahi.com/hibakusha/english/); Yashiko Hidaka, Case 07229, The Asahi Shimbun *Messages from Hibakusha* Project.

44. After-effects, Hiroshima [pp268–269]: Emiko Nakasako, personal communication, 8/7/2010.

45. Kenji Kitakawa [pp269–270], personal communication, 8/7/2010.

46. Masahiro Kunishige [pp270–272], personal communication, 8/7/2010.

47. How the death rate was accelerating in the Urakami hills, when the typhoon struck both Hiroshima and Nagasaki and wildflowers began blooming in its aftermath, and Shinoe Shoda finds blue chrysanthemums among a schoolyard's skulls [pp272–274]: T. Akizuki, *Nagasaki 1945*, pp 117–123, 125, 130–137, 139, 250–251. Takashi (Paul) Nagai: *The Bells of Nagasaki*, pp 61, 68, 82. In Hiroshima, Dr. Hachiya also recorded the use of the term "mines of the city" (on page 188 of his *Hiroshima Diary*); Shinoe Shoda, in *White Flash, Black Rain* (U.S., Milkweed Editions, 1995). NOTE: Tsutomu Yamaguchi spoke about the Nagasaki rainbows that followed the storm (personal communication, 2008), and Endo Tai said that (in addition to such accounts as Akizuki, RE the storm's aftermath), there were many stories about the plant life that returned after the storm had passed, personal communication (2008).

48. Hiroko Nakamoto's survival, in the Hiroshima suburb of Kaitachi [pp274–275]: in, *My Japan: 1939–1951* (N.Y., McGraw-Hill, 1970), pp 73–74, 79; personal communication (2010).

49. Americans arrive at the upper Urakami medical complex [pp275–276]: Nyokodo Hermitage oral history, as translated by Tokusaburo Nagai and E. Tai (2008). Dr. Akizuki had in fact been expecting an American resembling Dracula (or something similarly monstrous) but was surprised by a very tall figure resembling a romantic comedy movie star (as Vincent Price had been known, 1938–1940). This description is consistent with Akizuki, p 131. On the needed but denied medical supplies [p279]: Akizuki, p 133–134.

50. A committee of American and British scientific investigators met in Japan on September 11, 1945 (marking the beginning of MacArthur's censorship protocols) [p276–277]: Weller, *First into Nagasaki* (N.Y., Crown, 2006), p 45; Akizuki, *Nagasaki 1945*, pp 138–139, 234, 147–148; Nagai, *The Bells of Nagasaki*, pp 89–94, 111–113; M. Shiotsuki, *Doctor at Nagasaki*, pp 173–174; E. Ishikawa, et al, *Hiroshima and Nagasaki: The Physical, Medical, and Social Effects* (Tokyo, Iwanami Publishers, 1979; translated from Japanese, N.Y., Basic Books, 1981), pp 80–83.

51. Americans visit the Urakami hypocenter [pp277–278]: Charles Sweeney, *War's End*, pp 255–258, 285–289; personal communication, 1999; Akizuki's memoir, (p 145); Father George Zabelka (Sweeney's priest at Tinian), in M. Moore, *Here Comes Trouble* (N.Y., Grand Central Publishing, 2011), pp 339–347.

52. Hiroshima carbonization, shadow people, melted marbles, a lunch box: Mrs. Matsuda, the "marble boy" of Hiroshima, and Shigeru Orimen's lunch box [pp279–283]: The Hiroshima nurses of Dr. Minoru Fujii's mobile rescue crew, personal communication (7/21/2008), p 2; Nenkai Aoyama, personal communication (2008). Radiation-tinted glass and other atomic artifacts described here: Hiroshima Memorial and Nagasaki Museums and at the Minoru Fujii Memorial Retirement Home for nurses and physicians. The story of young Shigeru: Shigoko Orimen, Hiroshima Museum archive, *The Lunch Box*.

CHAPTER 10. LEGACY: TO FOLD A THOUSAND PAPER CRANES

1. Dr. Nagai's self-regrets, and observations on how quickly people were changed by the bomb [pp285–286]: Takashi (Paul) Nagai, *The Bells of Nagasaki* (Tokyo, 1949; N.Y., London, Kodanshu International, 1984), p 34; *We of Nagasaki* (N.Y., Duel, Sloan, and Pearce, 1951), pp 180–181, 188–189; Tokusaburo Nagai, personal communication (2008).

2. The Sasakis' "lifeboat" near the Misasa Bridge [pp286–292]: Masahiro Sasaki, personal communication (including July 2008; May, Aug. 2010 [N.Y. and Hiroshima], filmed, with annotations on U.S. bombing survey photo-mosaic, maps); M. Hachiya, *Hiroshima Diary* (University of North Carolina Press, 1955), pp, 2–3, 72, 153–155, 262–265, 173. Black rain densities and pathways, Hiroshima: E. Ishikawa, et al, "Meterological Conditions in Hiroshima," in report by The Committee for the Compilation of Materials on Damage Caused by the Atomic Bombs in Hiroshima and Nagasaki: *The Physical, Medical, and Social Effects* (Tokyo, Shoten, 1979; N.Y., Basic Books, 1981), pp 89–91, 93, 101.

3. On a cremated body full of broken glass, and the people Junichi found in a bank near the hypocenter [pp292–293]: The Asahi Shimbun *Messages from Hibakusha Project* (accessible via C. Pellegrino home page and http://www.asahi.com/hibakusha/eng lish/); Junichi Kaneshige, Case 20003, 2010.

4. Dr. Nagai, studying "Disease X," devising treatments [pp293–298]: Takashi (Paul) Nagai, *The Bells of Nagasaki*, pp 60–61, 73–83, 96–97; Takashi (Paul) Nagai essay, "From the Ashes," in *Leaving These Children Behind*, Nyokodo papers (Nagasaki, approx 1949); Endo Tai, translation and personal communication RE the Nagai history (2008); Kayano Nagai, in *We of Nagasaki*, pp 16–17; Tsutomu Yamaguchi, personal communication, 2008.

5. See note 4.

6. On plants, animals, near Nagasaki hypocenter: Tokusaburo Nagai [pp295–298]: personal communication (2008); T. (Paul) Nagai, *The Bells of Nagasaki*, pp 83–85, 91–93, 111–112; Nyokodo papers, *The Life of Dr. Nagai* (Nagasaki, 2001); Tatsuichiro Akizuki, *Nagasaki 1945* (London, Quartet Books, 1981), p 126.

7. Drs. Nagai and Akizuki, their debates at the Nyokodo shack [pp298–300]: *The Bells of Nagasaki*, pp 91–93, 116; *We of Nagasaki*, pp 188–189; Nyokodo papers, *The Life of Dr. Nagai* (Nagasaki, 2001); Tokusaburo Nagai, personal communication (2008); T. Akizuki, *Nagasaki 1945*, p 144; George Weller, with notes from his son, Anthony Weller, *First into Nagasaki* (N.Y., Crown, 2006), pp 44–45. Takashi (Paul) Nagai, "Peace Tower," Nyokodo papers; discussions with Father Mervyn Fernando (Subhodi Institute, Sri Lanka), about what Dr. Nagai was trying to teach Dr. Akizuki (2007). Dr. Nagai on "left behind" and the "entrance exam": Tokusaburo Nagai (personal communication, 2008); *The Bells of Nagasaki*, pp 109–110. On artifacts beneath Nyokodo Hermitage: T. (Paul) Nagai, "The Rosary Chain," Nyokodo papers (undated); several, including the melted rosary chain, are on display at the Nyokodo Hermitage Museum.

8. Tsutomu Yamaguchi's faith in the example of father Maximilian ("Simcho") Kolbe [pp300–303]: Personal communication (2008, 2009); two unpublished Yamaguchi memoirs—(1) *I Live to Tell My Story*, (2) *Twice Bombed, Twice Survived* (Inazuka Productions, Tokyo, 2006, 2010); clarification of Fr. "Simcho's" identity highlighted in a letter by Brian Taylor, dated 3/2/2010.

9. On the further tribulations of Masako Katani [pp303–304]: *Twice Bombed, Twice Survived, Part 1* (documentary film, Hideo Nakamura, Hidetaka Inazuka, 2006): T. Akizuki, *Nagasaki 1945*, pp 143–144; Endo Tai and the Hiroshima nurses of Dr. Minoru Fujii's rescue crew, personal communication (2008).

10. On the greater part of Inosuke Hayasaki's radiation exposure coming from consumption of crops from the fallout-contaminated soil near Mt. Unzen, and the secret he kept from his wife [pp304–306]: Interview, 8/8/2014, recorded at West Park Presbyterian Church, New York, N.Y., pp 13–16.

11. The mother whose unborn son was fiercely irradiated in the womb, and the incomparable tragedy that followed [pp306–307]: This is only one episode in Nagasaki memorialist Hayashi Kyoko's essay, "Masks of Whatchamacallit," translated by Kyoko Selden for a memorial issue of Asia Pacific's *Japan Focus* (in press, 2015, pp 32–33).

12. Dr. Nagai and the "hypocenter pioneers" [pp307–308]: *The Bells of Nagasaki*, pp 94, 99–100, 104; T. (Paul) Nagai, in Noyokodo papers, *Leaving These Children Behind*; Tokusaburo Nagai, personal communication (2008).

13. Dr. Hachiya and Hiroshima's "Ground Zero pioneers" [pp308–309]: *Hiroshima Diary*, pp 200–206; Hiroko Nakamoto, *My Japan: 1939–1951* (N.Y., McGraw-Hill, 1970), pp 117–118.

14. On the early reconstruction period of Hiroshima's schools [pp309, 322]: Keiji ("Gen") Nakazawa, *I Saw It: A Survivor's True Story* (San Francisco, Educomics, 1982). Personal communication, Endo Tai and Masahiro Sasaki. Descriptions of mutagenic effects on plants [p313]: E. Ishikawa, et al, *Hiroshima and Nagasaki: The Physical, Medical, and Social Effects*, pp 83–86; in Nagasaki, Dr. Nagai's Nyokodo outpost notes and drawings (1945–1946).

15. Keiji Nakazawa and his mother, at the "T" Bridge shantytown [pp309–312]: K. Nakazawa, *Hiroshima: The Autobiography of Barefoot Gen*, translated by R. H. Minear (U.K., Rowman & Littlefield, 2010), pp 89, 98–101, 127; personal communication, Aug. 2010, Sept. 2011, letter, 3/5/2011, pp 4–5.

16. The orphaning of Takashi (Thomas) Tanemori and how the atomic orphans became prey [pp312–313]: T. Tanemori, *Hiroshima: The Bridge to Forgiveness*, pp 70–72, 75–76, 87, 224–228, 231; discussion and interview 11/13/2010; letter, 8/9/2011, pp 5–7; K. Nakazawa (on the orphans): personal communication (interview recorded 8/7/2010).

17. See note 14.

18. Dr. Nagai at the Nyokodo Hermitage, 1946–1951 [pp313–316]: *The Bells of Nagasaki*, pp 113–114, 116; Noyokodo Hermitage essays, "Peace Tower" and "My Beloved Children" (Nagasaki, Noyokodo Publications, undated, still in print with English translations); Tokusaburu Nagai, personal communication, 2008 (RE Dr. Akizuki, IRS visit and life in Dr. Nagai's Nyokodo research outpost).

19. See note 18.

20. Emiko Nakazako, atomic orphans [pp317–320]: Personal communication (interview recorded 8/7/2010).

21. See note 16.

22. The Sasaki family, 1954–1955 [pp320–332]: Masahiro Sasaki, personal communication (2008, 2010); letters written by Masahiro's and Sadako's mother, Hiroshima Museum Archive.

23. "Shadow people," Shizuko Ohara at the Misasa Bridge [p322]: Nancy Cantwell and the Hiroshima nurses of Dr. Minoru Fujii's mobile rescue crew, personal communication (2008).

24. See note 22.

25. See note 14.

26. See note 22.

27. Sadako's handwritten copies of her own blood values [p328] are on permanent display at the Hiroshima Memorial museum, along with her medical files and copies of letters, including a letter by her roommate, Kiyo. Details of bone marrow death in the stages of leukemia: Dr. Jesse A. Stoff (and anon. leukemia patients), 1992–1993; samples illustrating the process can be seen in the biomedical display section of the Hiroshima Museum. Sadako's "plan," and the question of whether she saw what the Omoiyari principle and her paper crane project might become: Masahiro Sasaki (video log, C. Pellegrino), May 2010.

28. See note 22.

29. Kenshi Hirata, his daughter Saeko, and what happened after Kenshi disappeared (about 1955) to protect his family from anti-*hibakusha* discrimination [pp333–334]: Interviews with Kenshi Hirata, Saeko Hirata, and Setsuko's brother, by Hideo Nakamura and Hidetaka Inazuka, March, July 2010.

30. Arai, the Hiroshima schoolteacher who decided against surgery to remove a scar (which was the very last thing a little girl had written) [p334]: personal communication; George Appoldt (1971–1973), Norman Cousins (1987).

31. "In great Hiroshima," poem by Tsutomu Yamaguchi, personal communication (2008) [pp335–341]: transcript of speech to high school students and United Nations (2006). His daughter's trepidation about him telling his story: personal communication, filmed in, *The Legacy of Tsutomu Yamaguchi* (Hideo Nakamura, Inazuka Productions, 2012).

32. Kayano and Makoto Nagai and their August 9 location in radioactive fallout path [p338]: Tokusaburo Nagai and T. Yamaguchi, personal communication (2008), combined with radiation pathway conclusions, E. Ishikawa, et al, pp 89–100; Father Mervyn Fernando, personal communication (2007, 2008).

33. See note 32.

34. See note 31.

35. See note 32.

36. Shigeo Sasaki's friend and neighbor, Dr. Hachiya, burdens himself with undeserved guilt, while in Nagasaki, Dr. Nagai's friend, Akizuki, carries on for him [pp341–343]: M. Hachiya, *Hiroshima Diary*, p 72; Masahiro Sasaki, personal communication (2008); Tokusaburo Nagai and Chad Deihl on the last days of Dr. Akizuki, personal communication (2008, 2009).

37. See note 36.

38. Inoue Kazue—a case of anti-*hibakusha* discrimination and long-term radiation effects [p344]: case 5729, in The Asahi Shimbun *Messages from Hibakusha* Project (accessible via C. Pellegrino home page and http://www.asahi.com/hibakusha/english/).

39. Keiji Nakazawa, toward, and into, the 21st century [pp344–345]: *I Saw It*; Nakazawa HBO interview, *White Light, Black Rain* (2007); letter with Steve Leeper, 3/3/2011.

40. Takashi (Thomas) Tanemori, into the 21st century [pp345–347]: Video discussion, 11/13/2010; letter, 12/2/2011; personal communication, 2012–2014.

41. On the fates of Mr. Yamaguchi and fellow double survivors [pp347, 348, 353]: Tsutomu Yamaguchi, Hideo Nakamura, personal communication (2008, 2009); Toshiko (Yamaguchi) Yamasaki and family, personal communication (2010–).

42. See note 41.

43. Notes RE fates of key people: Dr. Yoshioka from Tokusaburo Nagai, Endo Tai, personal communication (2008). On the burial of "Fr. Mattias" [p348]: Fr. "MacQuitty" personal communication (both priests' names were changed by request). Hiroko Nakamoto [p349], personal communication (2010); Prefect Nishioka [p350], R. Trumbull, p 127; Emiko Fukahori [p350], Nagasaki Museum, *Testimonies of Atomic Bomb Survivors 29*; Dr. Masao Shiotsuki [p350], *Doctor at Nagasaki*, pp 84–85; Sumiko Kirihara [p350], *Cries for Peace* (The Japan Times, LTD, 1978), p 180; Michie Hattori and Ichiro Miyato [p351], as in Hattori and Leary, *World War II Magazine* (Summer 2005).

44. See note 43.

45. Masahiro Kunishige, into the 21st century [pp348–349]: personal communication (8/7/2010).

46. See note 43.

47. See note 43.

48. See note 43.

49. See note 43.

50. See note 43.

51. See note 43.

52. On Marcus McDilda [pp350–351]: Toland, *The Rising Sun*, p 795, and marine Brig. Gen. Jerome Hagen (ret.), *War in the Pacific, Vol. 1*, Hawaii Pacific University, Kenehoe Publications (1996), pp 159–162, and Walter Lord, personal communication (1997). NOTE: There are varying accounts on McDilda's design and how far his lie went, in fooling an increasingly scientifically specialized list of new interrogators as he was transferred from one prison to another. Accounts range from his story bringing about a delay of only one to as many as three days in his execution; in any case, the delay was enough and inventiveness at short notice doubtless saved his life, because fifty prisoners of war at McDilda's first holding area were beheaded almost immediately after he was transferred.

53. Information RE Harold Urey on reports to and from Tinian (and his heartbreakingly wrong belief, "When humanity sees what science has done, they will see immediately that here is the end of war.") [pp351–353], personal communication (1978–1980). RE Luis Alvarez on nuclear winter effects and the hoped-for abolition

of nuclear weapons [pp351–353], personal communication (1980–81). Astrobiologists Harold C. Urey, Luis Alvarez, Francis Crick, and Claire E. Folsome were key advisors on *Darwin's Universe* (Pellegrino and Stoff, Van Nostrand Reinhold, N.Y., 1983) and *Time Gate* (Tab, PA, 1985)—two books that became a subject of extreme contention in the author's former home, New Zealand, where, in the judgment of a small rogue element, calling itself an "ad hoc committee" (which between 1982 and 1984 included "scientific creationists"), judged the opinions of Urey, Alvarez, Crick, Folsome, Sir Charles Fleming, and other forward-looking scientists "irrelevant," notwithstanding defenders Alvarez's, Urey's, and Crick's Nobels, and Fleming's knighthood for contributions to science.

54. Masao Shiotsuki, Setsuko Thurlow, and MacArthur-esque censorship [p351]: Shiotsuki, *Doctor at Nagasaki*, pp 137–139; Thurlo, personal communication (2010).

55. See note 53.

56. See note 54.

57. On the lost grave of Eiko and the "going mad" of Eiko's mother [pp352, 353], Tokusaburo Nagai, personal communication (2008). Dr. Minoru Fujii and his rescue crew [p352]: personal communication, N. (Minami) Cantwell, Reiko Owa, Fujita Misako, Hiroshi Takamoya, Saito Kaneko, Kouno Kazuko (2008). The Ito family [pp352–353]: personal communication (2005, 2009). Kuniyoshi Sato [p353], personal communication via Hideo Nakamura.

58. See note 57.

59. See note 57.

60. See note 57.

61. See note 57.

62. See note 57.

63. Minami (Nancy) Cantwell [p353] as she faced 9/11's developing Ground Zero: personal communication (2008, 2009). Cantwell published the English edition of her 2006 memoir, *A Life in Three Motherlands (Japan, Korea, USA)*, as a print-on-demand book, available through Amazon.com. Her friends, including Nenkai Aoyama, Hitoshi Takayama, and the nurses who took care of Toshihiko Matsuda "the Marble Boy of Hiroshima," assembled essays and survivors' accounts for her book, and for *Hiroshima in Memoriam and Today: A Testament of Peace in the World* (Asheville, N.C.: Baltimore Press, 2000).

64. James Cameron's Dec. 22, 2009, visit to Tsutomu Yamaguchi in a Nagasaki hospital [pp354–357]: Audio and video log of the hospital conference, J. Cameron (and C. Pellegrino), filmed by Hideo Nakamura, Hidetaka Inazuka.

65. The last warning to futurity from double-survivor Kenshi Hirata [pp357–358]: Interview, August 2010.

66. "Come back to Hiroshima," on a 1,000 paper cranes in the 9/11 Family Room [pp358–360]: Tsugio Ito, personal communication (2002–2003, 2010); Masahiro Sasaki, personal communication (2008, 2010–).

Index

About the Author

Charles Pellegrino is the author of twenty books, including the *New York Times* bestseller *Her Name, Titanic,* and *Ghosts of the Titanic,* which James Cameron used as sources for his blockbuster movie *Titanic* and his 3D Imax film *Ghosts of the Abyss.* Pellegrino serves as a scientific consultant on James Cameron's *Avatar* films. The interstellar vehicle seen in the first film is based on Pellegrino's and Powell's brainstorming sessions at Brookhaven National Laboratory—their Valkyrie rocket design, hybridized with Robert L. Forward's StarWisp. (Valkyrie was first introduced in AAAS 1986 Symposium Proceedings, the journal *Science*). Assessing nucleosynthesis rates, he and Francis Crick developed the Genesis and Galactic Blight theory (predicting a "moment" in the history of galaxies, during which the emergence of Earth-like planets becomes probable). With Jesse Stoff, he produced the original models predicting the discovery of hydrothermal oceans in certain icy moons of the outer solar system, and with Powell designed nuclear melt-through probes to explore those hidden worlds. He and Powell also worked closely with Senator Spark Matsunaga on the U.S./Russia Space Cooperation Initiative during the 1980s as a means of helping to reduce the probability of nuclear war on Earth. Pellegrino has developed patents and contributed to many scientific journals, ranging from *Crustaceana* to Princeton Symposium Proceedings on forensic archaeology, and (in *Nature*, Futures) a thought experiment on multiverse/string theory with George Zebrowski. He is probably best known as the scientist whose "dinosaur biomorph recipe" became the scientific basis for the *Jurassic Park* series.